文体翻译教程

顾　　问：冯庆华
主　　编：范　敏　张法连
副主编：陈　刚　刘爱华　杨怀恩
编　　者：岳守国　尹衍桐　李国庆
　　　　　张璟慧　张　弛

图书在版编目(CIP)数据

文体翻译教程/范敏,张法连主编. —北京:北京大学出版社,2013.8
(21世纪英语专业系列教材)
ISBN 978-7-301-23085-5

Ⅰ.①文… Ⅱ.①范…②张… Ⅲ.①英语—文体—翻译—高等学校—教材 Ⅳ.①H315.9

中国版本图书馆CIP数据核字(2013)第199133号

书　　　名:文体翻译教程
著作责任者:范　敏　张法连　主编
责　任　编　辑:郝妮娜
标　准　书　号:ISBN 978-7-301-23085-5/H·3375
出　版　发　行:北京大学出版社
地　　　址:北京市海淀区成府路205号　100871
网　　　址:http://www.pup.cn　新浪官方微博:@北京大学出版社
电　子　邮　箱:编辑部 pupwaiwen@pup.cn　总编室 zpup@pup.cn
电　　　话:邮购部 62752015　发行部 62750672　编辑部 62759634　出版部 62754962
印　　刷　者:北京虎彩文化传播有限公司
经　　销　者:新华书店
　　　　　　787毫米×1092毫米　16开本　23.25印张　560千字
　　　　　　2013年8月第1版　2023年12月第5次印刷
定　　　价:69.00元

未经许可,不得以任何方式复制或抄袭本书之部分或全部内容。
版权所有,侵权必究
举报电话:010−62752024　电子邮箱:fd@pup.cn

该教材得到教育部人文社会科学研究项目"电脑辅助翻译教学：理论与实务（09YJA740072）"资助，并为该项目成果之一。此外，该教材还是教育部人文社会科学研究项目"法律语言学科规划研究（10YGAZH114）"、山东省社会科学规划研究项目"《论语》文化翻译功能与文化产业发展研究（10CWXJ11）"、山东省研究生教育创新计划项目"翻译教学与研究生创新能力培养研究（SDYC11114）"与"外国文学教学研究与研究生独立人格的培养（SDYC09031）"成果之一。该教材还是上海外国语大学博士后流动站在站科研成果之一。

目 录

序 ·· 1
前 言 ··· 1
第一章 文体翻译简介 ·· 1

I 实用文体翻译

第二章 新闻翻译 ·· 10
  1 新闻文体特征 ··· 10
    1.1 词汇 ·· 11
    1.2 语法 ·· 12
    1.3 篇章结构 ··· 13
  2 新闻文体翻译特点 ·· 13
  3 新闻英语翻译原则 ·· 16
  4 新闻文体翻译策略 ·· 19
    4.1 全译 ·· 19
    4.2 缩译 ·· 20
    4.3 编译 ·· 22
    4.4 阐译 ·· 24
    4.5 译写 ·· 26
  5 本章结语 ··· 28

第三章 政论翻译 ·· 29
  1 政论文体特征与翻译特点 ·· 29
  2 政论文体翻译原则 ·· 31
    2.1 质的准则 ··· 31
    2.2 量的准则 ··· 32
    2.3 方式准则 ··· 34
    2.4 关系准则 ··· 34
  3 政论文体翻译策略 ·· 35
    3.1 语义翻译 ··· 35
    3.2 传意翻译 ··· 38

  3.3 语义翻译与传意翻译并用 ………………………………………… 41
 4 本章结语 ………………………………………………………………… 45

第四章 旅游翻译

 1 旅游翻译分类与特性 …………………………………………………… 46
 2 旅游文本文体要求 ……………………………………………………… 46
  2.1 旅游文本范围特点 ………………………………………………… 46
  2.2 旅游文本文体特点 ………………………………………………… 47
  2.3 旅游文本语篇要求 ………………………………………………… 47
 3 旅游翻译原则与标准：初阶与进阶 …………………………………… 48
  3.1 旅游翻译初阶 ……………………………………………………… 48
  3.2 旅游翻译进阶 ……………………………………………………… 48
  3.3 初进阶实译举例 …………………………………………………… 48
 4 旅游翻译原则与标准：高阶(1) ………………………………………… 54
  4.1 归类 ………………………………………………………………… 54
  4.2 性质 ………………………………………………………………… 55
  4.3 翻译原则与标准 …………………………………………………… 56
 5 旅游翻译原则与标准：高阶(2) ………………………………………… 56
  5.1 旅游文本的难点 …………………………………………………… 56
  5.2 旅游文本翻译的难点 ……………………………………………… 57
  5.3 旅游文本翻译举例 ………………………………………………… 58
 6 本章结语 ………………………………………………………………… 73

第五章 广告翻译

 1 广告文体概述 …………………………………………………………… 74
 2 广告分类及其文体特征 ………………………………………………… 75
  2.1 双关广告语篇文体特征 …………………………………………… 75
  2.2 押头韵广告语篇文体特征 ………………………………………… 77
  2.3 仿拟广告语篇文体特征 …………………………………………… 78
 3 广告文体翻译特点与原则 ……………………………………………… 78
 4 广告文体翻译策略 ……………………………………………………… 80
  4.1 双关广告语篇明示翻译策略 ……………………………………… 80
  4.2 英语广告押头韵修辞的翻译策略 ………………………………… 82
  4.3 仿拟广告语篇的翻译策略 ………………………………………… 85
 5 本章结语 ………………………………………………………………… 91

第六章 商务翻译

 1 商务英语文体特征 ……………………………………………………… 92

1.1 语体特征 ··· 92
　　1.2 语法特征 ··· 97
　　1.3 词汇特征 ··· 98
　　1.4 句法特征 ·· 101
　2 商务英语翻译原则 ·· 103
　3 商务英语翻译策略 ·· 104
　　3.1 了解东西方思维与语言表达异同 ···················· 104
　　3.2 准确理解术语与商务专业知识 ······················ 106
　　3.3 据文体特点采用不同翻译原则 ······················ 107
　　3.4 把握英汉句子结构差异 ···························· 108
　　3.5 译文体现商业风格 ································ 112
　4 本章结语 ·· 113

第七章　科技翻译 ·· 114
　1 科技文体概述 ·· 114
　　1.1 科技语言的词汇特点 ······························ 114
　　1.2 科技语言的句法特点 ······························ 117
　　1.3 单调的修辞手段 ·································· 119
　2 科技语篇的翻译原则 ······································ 120
　　2.1 逐字逐句求真求实 ································ 120
　　2.2 字里行间通顺畅达 ································ 122
　　2.3 科技语言的美感 ·································· 124
　3 科技英语翻译策略 ·· 127
　　3.1 词语的翻译 ······································ 127
　　3.2 被动语态的译法 ·································· 129
　　3.2 复杂长句的译法 ·································· 132
　4 本章结语 ·· 134

第八章　法律翻译 ·· 135
　1 法律语言的特点 ·· 135
　　1.1 法律语言的用词特点 ······························ 136
　　1.2 法律语言的句式特点 ······························ 139
　　1.3 法律语言的篇章特点 ······························ 142
　2 法律语言的翻译原则 ······································ 143
　　2.1 准确严谨性原则 ·································· 143
　　2.2 简明清晰性原则 ·································· 145
　　2.3 前后一致性原则 ·································· 148
　　2.4 语体规范性原则 ·································· 149

3　法律英语翻译策略 ·· 151
　　　3.1　法律术语的翻译 ·· 151
　　　3.2　模糊表达的翻译 ·· 152
　　　3.3　复杂长句的翻译 ·· 153
　　4　本章结语 ··· 155

II　文学文体翻译

第九章　散文翻译 ·· 157
　　1　散文文体特征与翻译特点 ······································ 157
　　2　散文分类与翻译特点 ··· 158
　　　2.1　叙事散文 ·· 158
　　　2.2　抒情散文 ·· 159
　　　2.3　写景散文 ·· 160
　　　2.4　哲理散文 ·· 161
　　3　散文翻译的功能对等 ··· 166
　　　3.1　散文翻译的内容传达 ······································ 166
　　　3.2　散文翻译的风格再现 ······································ 168
　　　3.3　散文翻译的韵律再造 ······································ 170
　　　3.4　散文翻译的意境重构 ······································ 174
　　4　本章结语 ··· 175

第十章　小说翻译 ·· 177
　　1　小说文体特征 ·· 177
　　　1.1　宏观文体特征 ·· 177
　　　1.2　微观语言特征 ·· 178
　　2　小说翻译原则与方法 ··· 179
　　　2.1　人物个性化语言的翻译 ···································· 179
　　　2.2　修辞格的翻译 ·· 181
　　　2.3　文化负载成分的翻译 ······································ 186
　　　2.4　作者风格与小说翻译 ······································ 191
　　3　文化语境与小说翻译策略 ····································· 192
　　　3.1　文本选择 ·· 192
　　　3.2　翻译策略的选择 ·· 193
　　　3.3　翻译变体的选择 ·· 193
　　　3.4　文化语境与译本多样性 ···································· 194
　　4　本章结语 ··· 194

第十一章　诗歌翻译 ········· 195
1　诗歌概述 ········· 195
　　1.1　诗歌的分类 ········· 195
　　1.2　诗歌的文体特点 ········· 196
2　英汉诗歌比较与翻译研究 ········· 197
　　2.1　英汉诗歌比较 ········· 197
　　2.2　英汉诗歌翻译研究 ········· 198
　　2.3　诗歌翻译对译者的要求 ········· 199
3　英诗汉译实例评析 ········· 199
　　3.1　韵律美的再现 ········· 200
　　3.2　形式美的再现 ········· 203
4　汉诗英译实例评析 ········· 204
　　4.1　音象美的再现 ········· 205
　　4.2　简洁美的再现 ········· 206
　　4.3　意境美的再现 ········· 207
5　本章结语 ········· 208

第十二章　戏剧翻译 ········· 209
1　戏剧文体特征 ········· 209
2　剧本翻译特点 ········· 210
3　剧本翻译策略 ········· 211
　　3.1　个性化的人物语言 ········· 211
　　3.2　口语化的语言 ········· 216
　　3.3　富于乐感的语言 ········· 220
　　3.4　简洁化的语言 ········· 222
　　3.5　动作化的语言 ········· 225
4　本章结语 ········· 227

第十三章　典籍翻译 ········· 229
1　文言文翻译的基本问题 ········· 229
　　1.1　文言文词语层翻译问题 ········· 229
　　1.2　文言文句法层翻译问题 ········· 233
　　1.3　文言文篇章层翻译问题 ········· 234
　　1.4　文言文翻译中的文化问题 ········· 235
2　翻译原则与翻译策略 ········· 236
　　2.1　翻译原则比较 ········· 237
　　2.2　理解的分歧 ········· 237
　　2.3　表达的高低 ········· 239

2.4 文化因素的处理 ……………………………………………… 240
　3 本章结语 …………………………………………………………… 242

III 影视文体翻译

第十四章　影视翻译 ………………………………………………… 248
　1　电影翻译特征 …………………………………………………… 248
　2　电影翻译标准 …………………………………………………… 248
　3　电影翻译原则 …………………………………………………… 250
　4　电影翻译实例 …………………………………………………… 251
　　4.1 电影片名翻译 ………………………………………………… 251
　　4.2 电影对白翻译 ………………………………………………… 255
　5　本章结语 ………………………………………………………… 273

各章翻译练习 ………………………………………………………… 274
各章翻译练习参考答案 ……………………………………………… 311
参考文献 ……………………………………………………………… 351

序

篇章语言学与文体学对指导翻译工作和确定译文功能具有重大的指导意义,并为翻译理论的探讨提供了新的途径。在翻译过程中,译者必须随文体之异调整译文,必须考虑目的语环境、语篇类型与语言特征等因素,根据不同的文体特征与语言功能,采取相应的变通策略。因此,翻译与文体的密切关系越来越为翻译界所重视,同时,文体翻译在英语教学中的作用也越来越受到外语教育界的重视。

范敏、张法连等编写的《文体翻译教程》的出版,标志着中国外语教育界对文体与翻译课程及教材建设的进一步推进。该教材改变过去那种单纯以词语、句子翻译作为探讨对象的做法,从语篇的角度讨论各类文本的翻译理论与实践,从文本的文体特征、功能类型、语篇翻译原则与翻译策略等维度对翻译实践中常用文体,如新闻、政论、旅游、广告、商务、科技、法律、散文、小说、诗歌、戏剧、典籍与影视等进行了系统的论述。该教材既反映了近些年来国内相关文体翻译研究的成果,也收入了编者们近年来的研究心得。

本书在编写观念、视角、思路与方法上都进行了创新:(1)观念新:涵盖了跨文化交际中的常用文体类型,并对其他文体翻译教材中很少涉及的文本类型,如政论翻译、法律翻译、旅游翻译、商务翻译、戏剧翻译与影视翻译等进行了系统的探讨。(2)视角新:书中语篇功能思想贯穿全文,强调语篇类型与功能的指导作用,倡导翻译理论与实践的结合以及文体翻译标准的多元化。(3)思路新:从篇章的角度,采用译文对比与分析相结合的办法,将词句的翻译融入其中,结合上下文语境与社会文化语境进行分析。(4)方法新:尽量运用丰富、新鲜、生动、实用的例证进行阐释分析,强调讲练结合,以练为主,更有利于翻译教学的应用性。

全书共分为十四章,并配有各章翻译练习与参考答案。第一章为文体翻译简介,主要阐述了文体翻译的概念与研究意义、国内外研究现状、语篇翻译理论对翻译教学的指导作用与存在难点、文体翻译分类与主要翻译特点等,使学习者对文体翻译这一学科有一个较为系统、全面的认识。第二章至第八章为实用文体翻译,分别阐述了新闻、政论、旅游、广告、商务、科技、法律等文体的翻译特征、翻译原则与翻译策略,指出实用文体翻译以传达信息为目的,它区别于传达有较强情感意义和美学意义的文学翻译,也区别于强调时间限制和视听效果的影视翻译。第九章至第十三章为文学文体翻译,分别阐述了散文、小说、诗歌、戏剧、典籍等文体的翻译,探讨了文学文体翻译的特点,强调文学文体翻译的艺术性,其形式与内容的不可分割性以及译者的再创造性等。第十四章为影视翻译,主要阐述了影视翻译所具有的独特的艺术表现手法、文体特色及其翻译原则与策略等。

总之,该教材采用描写翻译方法,注重理论联系实际,既注重吸收语篇理论与文体翻译的最新研究成果,又注重把翻译理论、翻译实践与翻译教学密切结合,注重发挥学生的主体作用与教师的主导作用。因此,《文体翻译教程》教材的出版将会有效改善翻译教学模式,增强学生解决翻译问题的能力,有力推动翻译教学课程与教材建设的进一步发展。

冯庆华
2014 年 5 月
上海外国语大学

前 言

21世纪是现代化、信息化和全球化的时代,充满竞争和机遇。目前社会对高素质创新翻译人才的需求对翻译专业教育提出了很多挑战。这主要表现在以下几个方面:对教育理念的挑战(偏重语言文学),对人才培养模式的挑战(偏重研究型),对教材编写、课程设置和教学内容的挑战(就业导向不足),对教师队伍建设的挑战(复合型短缺)以及对教学管理模式的挑战(模式单一)等。因此,在全球化与信息化的今天,高校翻译专业需要进行教育创新,实施创新型、复合型翻译人才培养战略是我们面临的一个重要任务。2010年由高等学校外语专业教学指导委员会英语组制定的《高等学校英语专业英语教学大纲》指出,21世纪高校英语专业人才的培养目标是,"具有扎实的英语语言基础和广博的文化知识并能熟练地运用英语在外事、教育、经贸、文化、科技、军事等部门从事翻译、教学、管理、研究等工作的复合型英语人才……这些人才应具有扎实的基本功、宽广的知识面、一定的相关专业知识、较强的能力和较高的素质。也就是要在打好扎实的英语语言基本功和牢固掌握英语专业知识的前提下,拓宽人文学科知识和科技知识,掌握与毕业后所从事的工作有关的专业基础知识,注重培养获取知识的能力、独立思考的能力和创新的能力,提高思想道德素质、文化素质和心理素质。"

这一系列的教学改革必然会带动教材的建设。高等学校英语专业英语教学大纲对此指出,"根据21世纪对外语专业人才的要求,现有的外语专业教材亟待更新和补充,有些缺少的教材需要组织人力编写。"而且21世纪的外语专业教材应该具备以下几个基本特征:"(1)教学内容和语言能够反映快速变化的时代。(2)要处理好专业知识、语言训练和相关学科知识之间的关系。(3)教材不仅仅着眼于知识的传授,而要有助于学生的鉴赏批评能力、思维能力和创新能力的培养。(4)教学内容有较强的实用性和针对性。(5)注意充分利用计算机、多媒体、网络等现代化的技术手段。"然而,我国许多翻译教材建设相对滞后于翻译学科的发展,高校英语专业使用的翻译教材大多在不同程度上受到传统语言学的影响,过多地关注词句间的对等,缺乏具体的文本类型与功能分析,使学生只能学到简单的词句转换技巧,难以培养学生的综合翻译能力与实践应用能力,难以适应当今社会对实用型、复合型翻译人才的迫切需求。随着翻译研究的进一步发展以及为了满足市场的大量需求,翻译教学也开始逐渐重视培养多元智能人才,而且翻译教材也逐渐关注文体与翻译的相互作用。目前,有关文体与翻译的教材主要有刘宓庆(2007)的《文体与翻译》、陈新(1999)主编的《英汉文体翻译教程》、冯庆华(2001/2002)主编的《文体翻译论》与《实用翻译教程》以及申雨平和戴宁(2005)主编的《实用英汉翻译教程》等。这些教材在阐述和选择翻译理论专题时,都从翻译实践需要出发,注意翻译应用理论的系统性,因此对促进我国的实践翻译研究都起到了一定的推动作用。

本教材在吸收相关教材优点的基础上,扬长避短,并根据时代与翻译理论发展的要求,以期努力做到以下几个方面:(1)编者在叙述评价实例时尽量避免传统的增词、减词、句式变化等方法解释,而更多注重语篇分析;(2)教材中所举实例尽量采用最新资料,以能更好地引起读者的学习兴趣;(3)教材编写尽量系统典型,许多重要的文体翻译类型,如法律翻译、旅游翻译和影视翻译已列入本教材的目录中。本教材通过大量实例与文本类型理论的结合,探讨了文体翻译的功能途径,指出基于文本类型理论的翻译强调文本的交际功能,翻译单位应是文本和其在交际中的功能,而非孤立的单词或句子;就具体翻译过程而言,包括判断文本类型和决定翻译目的。由此可见,文本类型理论的实际应用就在于把确定一个文本的主要功能作为翻译过程的一部分,译者不再依赖于对原文特征的分析,而是要根据翻译的环境来判断译文是否具有特定的功能。在具体的翻译过程中,译者应考虑语境和语言的交际功能,根据不同的文体特征与译文功能采取不同的翻译策略。同时,该教材强调翻译实践过程中的译文比较分析,重视译者心理活动在翻译不同文本中的作用,以此丰富文体翻译研究。

具体说来,该教材创新点主要体现在以下几个方面:

- 以语篇翻译过程为导向,重点探讨常见翻译问题的解决方法。
- 注重文本类型在语言特征、交际重点、表现方式等方面的差异,培养学生文本意识,确定翻译策略。
- 按文本类型划分为实用文体翻译、文学文体翻译与影视文体翻译,并在内容选取上有所选择,突出重点。
- 以文本类型理论为基础,并把文本类型、功能语言学与翻译研究相结合应用到该教材的编写中,更加强调语境、语域和文本的交际功能,并试图建立一种基于评价系统的翻译评估模式。
- 强调译者在选择翻译文本类型时的心理活动,帮助学生理解分析译文或者理解分析译文翻译策略背后隐含的原因。
- 在研究方法上,注重可操作性、系统性与全面性,强调语篇研究、多种译本比较研究,并采用语料库、电脑技术等进行辅助研究。
- 在知识更新上,注重前沿性,充分吸收各领域最新研究成果,紧密跟踪学科发展前沿信息。
- 在测试练习上,注重从功能文本特征、文本类型等更为客观和宏观的角度对翻译进行全面的评估。
- 在应用层面上,注重实用性与应用性,从实践者的角度,帮助广大翻译工作者解决工作中面临的实际问题。

此外,我们在使用本教材时,需要注意在教学过程中引导启发学生,注意强调文体、语篇与功能的翻译教学模式,摆脱传统的以词句为重点的翻译教学模式,并努力做到以下几个方面:

- 运用跨学科视角,翻译文本类型教学资料广泛。
- 以多学科综合的问题解决式进行翻译教学。
- 以问题的学习为起点,强调学习过程与认知心理过程。
- 发现式学习与创新式学习。

- 按研究兴趣分组(如学生每周翻译课件展示)。
- 多样化、个性化的合作学习行为(如翻译工作坊的多样性)。
- 以能力为基础的综合性评价,而不是对分离技能或某一具体翻译知识进行评价。

最后,本教材注重权威性。该教材由国内多所重点院校的专家学者参加编写。本教材的第一章至第三章由上海外国语大学博士后科研流动站在站博士后、曲阜师范大学范敏副教授编著,第四章由浙江大学陈刚教授编著,第五章由暨南大学李国庆教授编著,第六章由北京工商大学杨怀恩教授编著,第七章至第八章由中国政法大学张法连教授编著,第九章由曲阜师范大学岳守国教授编著,第十章至第十二章由曲阜师范大学刘爱华博士编著,第十三章由中国石油大学(华东)尹衍桐博士编著,第十四章由河南大学张璟慧博士编著。此外,本教材得到了上海外国语大学博士生导师冯庆华教授的鼎力相助,冯教授提出了许多宝贵且中肯的意见。另外,感谢中国政法大学的张弛博士、曲阜师范大学的顾伟老师、研究生王乐娜、刘晓鹏、孟芸、孙婷婷等,他们在文献整理与校对等方面做了大量工作。当然,由于时间、能力有限,有些错误不可避免,恳请同行专家多批评指正。

范敏
2013 年 7 月

第一章 文体翻译简介

文体翻译研究已成为国内外翻译研究领域的一个重要课题。关于文体的界定,一般认为,文体可以看做是语言使用中的变体,包括文学的和非文学的。文体、风格不仅因情景不同而有变化,而且因传播媒介(Medium)和正式程度(degree of Formality)不同而不同,有人称之为文体变换(style-shifting)。从更广的范围来讲,文学语言中的变体可以随体裁或时期的变化而发生变化。因而,我们可以说绮丽文体或奥古斯都诗体。非文学情境下的变体,如广告语言、法律语言、体育评论等,也各具特色。由此可见,文体是以一个更大或更小的范围(Domains)或语境为背景的。无论在什么情况下,文体都被看做是具有特色的东西。本质上它是一些典型语言特征的总和,这些特征或是语域的,或是体裁的,或是时代的。据这种文体来界定,在篇章(Text)层次上尤其如此。文体特征基本属于语言特征,因此文体在某种意义上来说是语言的同义词,不过,这种语言具有某种区别特征,对作品构架或主题(Theme)具有重要的意义。就某一作家的全部作品而言,文体是指作家本人所具特征的综合,即他或她的"语言习惯",称为个人语言(Idiolect)。(胡壮麟,刘世生,2004:304)

文体与语域相关,具有丰富的表现形式,如实用文体就包括新闻、政论、旅游、广告、经贸、科技、法律等不同语篇类型。这是因为在不同的语域中,语篇的措词、造句、修辞、结构都会存在某些差异。正如 Halliday 所言,"语域这一范畴用来解释人们用语言做些什么。当我们观察各种语境中所发生的语言活动时,我们发现,针对不同情境选用的适用语言类型并不相同"(1964:87)。因此,"文贵得体"非常重要。翻译之所以要研究文体,其目的就是使译文得体,而这也是评定译品高下的一个衡量标准。从翻译的角度研究文体,中外学者有不同的研究途径,但在译文应反映原文的文体特征这一点上是大体一致的。要做到这一点,对原文语言、风格与功能的剖析是必不可少的。在翻译研究领域,很多国外文章和著作,如"Text Typology and Translation","Translation as Text",*Text Type in Translation*,*Text Typology: Register,Genre and Text Type* 都论述了文体与翻译的密切联系。并且有很多学者把语篇类型、语言功能与翻译策略结合起来进行研究,如:Katharina Reiss(1971/1989),Peter Newmark(1988),Hans J. Vermeer(1989),Chritiane Nord(1997),Anna Trosborg(1997),Mary Snell-Hornby(2001)等。

在我国,很多学者结合西方理论,对语篇类型与翻译进行了较深入探讨。如李运兴(2001)、张美芳(2005)、朱志瑜(2004)、黄国文(2006)、司显柱(2007,2008)等借助功能语言学、篇章语言学与翻译研究的一些概念,从功能途径探索了语篇翻译理论和实践的一些问题。关于文体与翻译的教学,有些学者比较注重语篇类型在翻译教学的应用。例如,台湾的胡功泽将语篇分为三个层次,以利于课堂解释文体与翻译关系。第一层次:根据语言的性质分为实用类、文学类以及宗教类三大范畴。翻译的大方向是,实用类以达到译入语的实用目的为主;文学类以达到类似艺术效果为主;宗教类则要完全忠实原文语言,乃至于连字词也不得更换。第二层次,在各范畴之下,根据布勒三模式(或沟通方式的三要素)分为:以说写者为主,内容为主,阅听人为主的三大文类。第三层次,根据目前既有个别小文类的特色,如新闻,科技等以主题为主的分类所做的细部分析,在上面两层大方向之下,做出翻译的决定。陈新(1999)、刘宓庆(2007)、冯庆华(2001)等在翻译教材中把文体与翻译策略结合。如陈新在《英汉文体翻译教程》中详述了应用文、新闻、广告、科技和文学这五大类文体的语言特点及其翻译方法;刘宓庆在《文体与翻译》中把文体分为新闻报刊文体、论述文体、公文文体、描述以及叙述文体、科技文体、应用文体,并着眼于翻译实践的需要,兼顾理论和文体学问题;冯庆华等在《文体翻译论》对作品标题、散文、小说、戏剧、诗歌、幽默作品、政治作品、古典作品、正规文体等方面汉译英和英译汉进行了研究,并对中国明清小说的英译、比较文学翻译、回译检验译文、文化问题翻译、译者风格比较等方面进行了专门的探讨。

　　语篇翻译理论对于学生掌握翻译技巧、提高翻译能力具有很强的针对性与实用性。主要观点如下:

- 语篇类型划分有利于提高学生掌握翻译知识的接受能力。帮助学生从不同层面对各类文体特征与语篇功能进行分析,加强对各类翻译体裁现象的根本认识。
- 语篇类型翻译语境的发掘有利于提高学生解决问题的能力。各类文体在翻译时既受一般翻译语境制约,又受各自体裁本身所具有的特殊语境制约。
- 语篇类型翻译策略的正确选择有利于提高学生的翻译水平。文体翻译策略需要根据翻译目的、文化语境、语篇特征与交际功能等因素进行选择。
- 语篇类型翻译评估有利于提高翻译教学质量。根据语篇类型构建不同译文评价标准和各种评估参数,提高翻译教学质量评估模式的可运作性与实用性。

　　由此可见,语篇类型划分有助于成功地实施翻译课堂教学。同时,我们也应该认识到语篇类型理论在翻译教学应用中的难度。主要难点如下:

▲ 跨学科的复杂性:把语篇类型理论作为平台,借助评价理论、翻译学、语言学、文体学、教育学等探讨文体翻译教学,因此具有一定难度。

▲ 翻译理论局限性:所有的翻译理论并非适用于所有的翻译实践,因此,基于语篇类型的翻译及相关理论的应用存在一定的合理性与局限性,因而增加了研究难度。

▲ 翻译语境复杂性:语境的多维性与动态性特点,增加了意义的不确定性、语篇的多重语言功能特征及其模糊性,因此语篇分类及其翻译具有一定难度。

▲ 语篇分类的模糊性:由于每个语篇类型并非只有一种功能,因此,如何指导学生根据语篇主要功能来准确划分语篇类型是翻译教学的一个难点。

▲ 翻译教学评价主观性:由于评价与价值的评判有关,是语篇中协商的态度类型,因此会在一定程度上影响翻译教学质量的客观评估标准。

▲ 学生认知能力差异性:学生个体认知接受能力存在差异,因此,如何尽可能同步掌握翻译学习规律是翻译教学的一个难点。

　　根据国内外语篇类型翻译理论、语篇翻译实践特点以及翻译教学特征,我们在本教材中把文体翻译大体划分为实用文体翻译、文学文体翻译与影视文体翻译三大基本类型。实用文体翻译可进一步划分为一般信息翻译(如新闻、政论、旅游、广告等语篇的翻译)与特殊用途翻译(如经贸、科技、法律、医学、公文等语篇的翻译)。由于实用文体翻译的特点主要是：(1)根据委托人的翻译要求或特定情景的翻译目的,确定翻译策略,提供符合客户所需的翻译产品；(2)语言规范、朴实、准确；(3)准确再现原文所需反映的客观现实；(4)强调翻译文本的实用性和读者可接受性。因此,在翻译实用文体时,译者应重点考虑语境和语言的交际功能,根据不同的文体与译文功能采取相应的翻译策略,并可以充分利用电脑辅助翻译工具提高翻译效率。当然,这也不排除翻译发起人的目的与原文作者目的有差异的情况,在此情况下,译文可能会不忠实于原文和原作者。文学文体翻译则可进一步划分为散文翻译、小说翻译、诗歌翻译、戏剧翻译与典籍翻译,并从语篇类型的主要功能角度对其进行研究。文学文体不同于应用文体等实用文体。文学作品用文字传达思想感情,塑造生动形象,对读者施加某种特殊感染力。文学文体翻译需要译者更多地去把握原文的感情色彩,注重原文语言的创造性理解与传达。在文学翻译中,译者既要再现原作的文体风格,又要再现原作的语言艺术。影视文体翻译重在视觉的或者听觉的意象,用来给人言说或演唱,常需要伴随语言之外的音乐、画面等媒介,如电影、有声(像)广告、歌曲等,主要涉及影视作品、舞台剧等。影视作品的翻译是一种融合了文化与现代科技的语篇翻译,因此在选择翻译策略时,有时接近于实用文体翻译,有时则接近于文学文体翻译,需要特殊情况特殊分析。

姚锦清教授(2010:8)也曾经对专业翻译和文学翻译的不同进行了详细阐述,请看下图(2010:8)：

参考标准	文学翻译	专业翻译
翻译标准	原文至上("信达雅"等)	译文目的至上(翻译服务标准)
参与者关系	原作者中心,译者附庸,目标受众模糊	译者中心,目标受众明确,且备受关注
翻译思维	形象思维为主	逻辑思维为主
操作模式	个人化再创作	集体化项目操作
作品交付时间	一般较长,弹性较大	一般很短,十分强调准时交付
术语学	一般不要求	非常重视
遵循规律	艺术创作规律	市场需求与交流目的

图 1　姚锦清的文学翻译与专业翻译示意图

显然,对于不同的文体,翻译方法和译文评估标准也应有所不同。如文中所述,实用文体翻译可进一步划分为一般信息翻译与特殊用途翻译。一般信息型语篇(或祈使型/呼唤型语篇)的语言形式显然必须从属于它们的目的或效果。例如,有些广告不断地在媒体重复,其目的就是不断加深读者或观众的印象,促使他们购买相关产品。宗教和政治宣传也是如此。政论语篇的翻译注重语篇风格的严肃性、庄重性；传媒语篇的翻译则注重语篇风格的信息性、可读性。由于衡量这类译文的主要标准是看他们是否达到了与原文相同的效果,因此翻译时主要运用交际翻译,这意味着译者可能必须抛开原文的形式甚至某些语句的具体内容,以求得相同的效果。奈达曾经指出,《圣经》中的"Lamb of God"(上帝的羔羊),如果译成爱斯基摩语,应该译成"Seal of God"(上帝的海豹),因为这样才能达到和英语原文相同的效果。

特殊用途型语篇(或信息型语篇)注重内容或信息的传达,如科技语篇的翻译注重语篇风格的专业性、术语性,法律语篇的翻译注重语篇风格的严格性、精确性等。因此,对译文质量的衡量标准主要有两条:(1)译文是否准确地传达了原文的内容或信息;(2)译文是否符合地道的译入语的习惯用法和表达方式。在翻译方法上,这类文体应该主要运用交际翻译与语义翻译相结合的方法。例如,在翻译一篇科普文章时,译者应尽可能用流畅的语言精确地表达原文的意思,而不用过于在意原文的风格。如果原文有错误的话,我们甚至还应改正这些错误,不然就会对读者产生误导。

文学文体注重用各种不同的语言形式表达作者的情感和立场。每个具体的文学语篇都有自己的语言特点和艺术风格。这种语言特点和艺术风格(包括遣词、造句甚至音韵上的考虑)往往是"变异"的。忠实的译文必须充分地反映这种变异的表达方式,用相应的手段来表达原文的这种文学和美学功能。因此,评估这类译文的主要标准主要是看他们是否用相应的手段表达了原语篇的内容。换句话说,译者应该让读者充分领略到原文中的文学和美学特点,而不仅仅是提供一篇文字优美的译文。否则,读者就分不出狄更斯和海明威了。由此可见,文学文体的翻译应该以语义翻译为主。

影视文体与其他文体翻译不同,具有特殊的翻译方法和技巧。影视翻译在某种程度上可视为文学翻译的一种,但是又有其特殊的翻译特点。影视翻译具有口语化、口型化、人物性格化、情感化、情景化、大众化等特点,具有视听、认识、审美、教育、宣传、娱乐等多项功能。一部好的译制片,译文应与剧情浑然一体,台词应当自然、逼真、生活化,使观众几乎感觉不到人工配译而成。影视翻译无论是配音还是字幕声画同步翻译时,在确保对白译文能连贯表达清楚原语意义的前提下,对原文语篇层面作适当变译,从而使译文词语通俗易懂、句子简洁流畅。根据具体的语境、语义、语篇等层面,通过转译、意译、缩译等手法,将影视作品完美地呈现出来。翻译方法多采用交际翻译、多模态等方法。

总而言之,忠实于原文不应是一句空洞的口号,而应该有其具体的内容和可供操作的客观标准。具体而言,不同的语篇应有不同的衡量标准:信息型语篇翻译注重内容和信息的传达,强调译入语的规范性;祈使型语篇翻译注重译文是否产生了和原文相同的实际效果。表达型语篇翻译注重原文的表达形式及其文学和美学功能,强调原语的"变异"表达形式在译入语中的体现。而影视型语篇则注重时空与文化的制约、字幕声画同步以及语言的口语化与个性化等因素。当然,某一具体的语篇,往往存在着互相交叉的情况,信息型语篇可能有表达型或祈使型的语句或者影视型的台词、画面等,反之亦然。因此,判断译文质量时必须具体情况具体分析。现举例说明:

【例1】应用文体
公函原文:
(Date)
Dear Senator:

Senate Bill 326 does not adequately address patient care issues. I ask you to vote against S. 326 as it stands because.

—It does not ensure that treatment decisions such as how long a patient stays in the hospital are made by the patient's doctor; ...

—It does not ensure that doctors and nurses can report quality problems without retaliation by HMOs, insurance companies, and hospitals; and

—It does not give consumers access to an independent consumer assistance program to help them choose plans and get the services they need.

I urge you to vote for amendments to add these and other essential protections. America's families need a REAL patients' bill of rights, not a sham.

Sincerely yours,
(Signature)

参考译文：

尊敬的参议员：

参议院326号法案并不能适当地解决病人保健问题,我要求您否决该法案,原因如下：

——它没有确保治疗决定,例如病人的住院期限等,都是由病人的医生决定……

——它不能确保医生和护士不会因汇报质量问题而受到保健组织、保险公司和医院的报复。

——它没有为消费者提供途径,以便在一个独立的消费者援助计划的帮助下选择自己需要的医疗计划和服务。

我敦促阁下投票支持制定修订案,增添以上及其他必要的保护条例。美国家庭需要一个真正的病人权利法案,而不是骗人的把戏。

此致

敬礼！

（签名）
（日期）

上面这个例子是一封公函,也是实用文体的一种。相对于表达功能与呼唤功能而言,公函的信息功能很强。此外,公函不同于私人信件,需要注意根据写作对象的身份和亲疏远近不同,采取相应的变通策略。因此在翻译公函时,需注意文风正式、语言庄重规范、用词准确简练、内容条理清晰、意思简单易懂、避免歧义。中英文在应用文体格式上大同小异,在写作、翻译时基本可以照搬,如果有差异,可根据对译文的不同要求酌情考虑是否保留原文。

请看一则有关参观须知的公示语：

1. 进入景点请主动出示门票,一人一票。

   （儿童身高在1.4米以上应持全票）

2. 入内请勿吸烟,请勿在景点内燃放烟花爆竹。
3. 爱护公共设施和绿化。
4. 文明参观,不随地乱扔瓜皮果壳,不随地吐痰。
5. 请保管好自身携带物品。
6. 注意安全,请勿坐在窗口和栏杆上照相。
7. 请由厢房陪弄出口。

1. Please show your tickets at the entrance, one ticket for one person.

(children above 1.4 meters at full charge)

2. Please do not smoke or play with fireworks.
3. Please take good care of public properties and vegetation.
4. Please do not litter or split.
5. Please take care of your personal belongings.
6. Please do not take photos by sitting on the windows.
7. Please take your exit by the side lane.

公示语又名揭示语、标识语、标记语、警示语,是公众在公共场合所看的文字语言及图形信息。公示语具有标准性、系统性、承继性等特点以及指示性、提示性、限制性、强制性等功能。相对于表达功能而言,其信息功能与呼唤功能比较强,因此,很多情况需采用交际翻译方法。能否准确恰当地传达公示语内容,有效地实现功能对等,是公示语翻译是否成功的检验标准。请看上图中的第四条,原文是"文明参观,不随地乱扔瓜皮果壳,不随地吐痰"翻译为"Please do not litter or spit","瓜皮果壳"在译文中已经省略,因而非常简练、地道地传达出了原文的意义与功能。其他例子如请勿践踏草坪(Keep off the grass!),小心地滑(Caution: wet floor!)小心,油漆未干(Mind the wet paint!),一卡在手,出门无忧(A card for all occasions)等等,也是译者根据译入语环境所作的各种变译。由此可见,公示语翻译作为跨文化交际活动,在翻译过程中应视译入语文化环境、翻译目的与目的语读者作出不同程度的适应选择,从而最大限度实现双方交际的需求。换句话说,公示语翻译应该充分考虑外部环境及译语读者需求的因素,考虑文本的目的和功能,根据译入语的生态文化环境做出相应的适应与选择,以信息的有效传达为最终目的,而不要完全拘泥于原文本。同时,译者应发挥自身的主观能动性,充分理解所处理文本的功能目的、文化背景与文体特征,选择适当的翻译策略。

【例2】文学文体

　　古来一切有成就的人,都很严肃地对待自己的生命,当他活着一天,总要尽量多劳动、多工作、多学习,不肯虚度年华,不让时间白白地浪费掉。我国历代的劳动人民以及大政治家、大思想家等等都莫不如此。

参考译文

　　Since ancient times, all those who achieved something took life very seriously. Every day that they lived, worked and toiled, they learned something. They never wasted time. This is true of the toiling masses, the great statesmen and the great thinkers in the history of our country.

　　原文选自邓拓的《生命的三分之一》,是一篇非常有哲理的散文。散文属于文学文体,翻译时不仅要忠实、准确、通顺,还要注意原文语言的再创造。这篇散文题目吸引人,议论精当,事例典型,读来轻松愉快,娓娓规劝人们珍惜时间,富有哲理。相对于信息功能与呼唤功能而言,这篇文章表达功能比较强,因此,采用语义翻译比较好,翻译时应注意原文语言风格与语境意义的再传递,再现原文的语言艺术。第一句中"古来一切有成就的人"在译"古来"时应把"since ancient times"置于句首,而不是句尾,从而达到舒缓语气,回顾展望的作用;

而译"一切有成就的人"时,要注意两点:一是注意"all"与"all of"的区别.一般说来,"all"与"all of"都可以放在有限定词(如冠词、物主代词等)修饰的名词之前。但是,如果名词前面没有限定词,则不能用"all of"。二是注意"achieve"与"accomplish"的区别以及"accomplish"与"accomplishment"、"accomplished"的区别。这时就需要我们使用正确的英语工具——英英词典,而英汉词典至多只是起到参考或补充的作用,因为许多近义词只有通过查阅英英词典,学生才能了解它们的细微差别,才能"精确"、"传神"地根据上下文语境传达原文词义。根据英英词典 *Random House Unabridged Dictionary*(2nd Edition),"accomplish"与"achieve"分别解释为,"to bring to its goal or conclusion; carry out; perform; finish"与"to complete(a distance or period of time)",由此可见,"accomplish"是指坚持到底而终于完成了某一具体的事件、计划、任务等,而"achieve"指排除各种困难而完成宏伟目标或伟大功业。因此,根据原文上下文语境,应选择"achieve",而不是"accomplish";另外,"accomplishment"与"accomplished"虽然都是"accomplish"的衍生词,但却存在本质的差异:"accomplishment"是指"the act of accomplishing, something that has been accomplished, a quality or ability equipping one for society",而"accomplished"主要是指"completed; done; effected; highly skilled, expert"。由此可见,"accomplishment"与"成就"相关,而"accomplished"则强调"完成的"、"熟练的",与"成就"相差较远。因此需要我们仔细辨别区分。"他活着一天,总要尽量多劳动、多工作、多学习,不肯虚度年华,不让时间白白地浪费掉",如果译为"As long as he /she is alive, he/she will always try to labor, work and study as much as possible, never letting a single day slip by without any gain",则会使人产生一种非常紧张、非常压抑的感觉,另外,"study"相对于"learn"来讲更加正式,而"learn"则是"处处皆学问",如看电影我们也可以学到很多东西,这是"learn"而不是"study",因此,在此文中应该用"learn"而不是用"study"。这一段的最后一句"我国历代的劳动人民以及大政治家、大思想家等等都莫不如此"中的"劳动人民",应该译成"toiling masses"而不是"working people",因为在此句中,"劳动人民"是特指"农民"等劳苦大众,而"working people"则是泛指,包含政客、思想家等各类型的人。另外,"我国历代的"在翻译时,译成"in the history of our country"比"in our history"要更好些,虽然后者比较简练,但是从全句的贴切与语气情况来看,前者更舒展、更轻松,更加具有散文的韵味。由此可见,在翻译文学作品时,不仅注意提高我们的语言能力与英汉语言互换技巧,还要学会用自己的眼睛去观察,用自己的心灵去体会周围的世界,从而全面提高我们的语言认知、形象思维和创造性思维等综合能力。这样在做翻译实践时就能更好地理解与传达文章的内涵与真谛,译完以后,还要学会以轻松的心情来看这些文本,要用耳听,用眼看,要读出来,透过声音,进入文本的美妙世界。

【例3】影视文体

瑜是瑜,亮是亮,你我各为其主。

译文:You and I will each serve our own sides.

由于影视台词的主要功能为视听功能,重在视觉或者听觉的意象,因此翻译时需要注重观众视觉或者听觉的感受与接受程度。"瑜是瑜,亮是亮"在汉语中表达的是强调周瑜和诸葛亮在两军对阵时,各自为主人服务,不再是朋友。由于画面有限,不能将其逐字译出,尤其是在对周瑜和诸葛亮进行详细注解。此外,前半句话和后面的"你我各为其主"语义重复,因此可将这句话压缩,只译出后半句,这样既节省了画面空间,又不妨碍观众理解其意义。再如,

原文:但他这步棋下错了。
译文:He made a mistake.

"棋",在该句话指围棋,是中国文明的象征。根据中国的哲学,人们通常将战争阵法比作下棋,但是西方的观众并不明白,所以翻译时可将"棋"这一文化阻断,传达出原文的语用意义,以便于理解,而且节省了时间与空间。

由此可见,字幕翻译有其特殊的翻译特点,受时空和文化的制约。时间制约因素是指语言和图像的同步配合,字幕应保证对话的字数合理,让译语和原语在大致相同的时间内完成信息传递。另外,每行字幕必须在屏幕上停留足够观众扫视的时间,一般以2至3秒为宜。空间指屏幕上可容纳的语言符号数目。字幕有时两行,有时一行。为了满足观众的阅读需求,通常一个画面里最多出现两行字幕,每行字幕单词数大概在15个字左右,字幕随着演员的情绪、语速的变化而变化。文化制约是指迥然不同的文化传统,造就了截然不同的文化情景。影视翻译扮演着使用两种语言,在两种文化中进行两次交流传播的双重身份。因此,影视翻译的使命,是从一种社会文化语境中走出来,然后再走入另一种社会文化语境中去,是连通文化与文化之间对话与交流的桥梁。

由此看来,在分析文体时应综合考虑各种因素,并把各种因素有机联系起来,系统条理地进行分析,从而使译文的文体特征更加贴近于原文。

Ⅰ 实用文体翻译

　　实用文体翻译以传达信息为目的,同时考虑信息的传递效果,它区别于传达有较强情感意义和美学意义的文学翻译,也区别于强调时间限制和视听效果的影视翻译。因此,在实用文体翻译时,译者应重点考虑语境和语言的交际功能,根据不同的文本与译文功能采取相应的翻译策略;此外,很多语篇类型,如科技语篇与专利文献还可以充分利用电脑辅助翻译工具提高翻译效率。其主要特点是:

(1) 根据委托人的翻译要求或特定情景的翻译目的,确定翻译策略,提供符合客户所需的翻译产品,努力再现原文所需反映的客观现实。

(2) 语言规范、朴实、地道。政论语篇的翻译注重语篇风格的严谨性、庄重性与准确性,科技语篇的翻译注重语篇风格的专业性与术语性,法律语篇的翻译注重语篇风格的严格性与精确性等等。

(3) 强调翻译文本的实用性和读者可接受性。例如译文是否准确有效地传达了原文的内容或信息,译文是否符合地道的译入语的习惯用法和表达方式,译文读者读译文是否基本类似于原文读者读原文的情况等。

第二章 新闻翻译

语言使用的领域不同,表现出来的文体特征也会不同。即使同是实用文体,其具体语篇分类也有自己鲜明的特征。新闻语篇与政论、旅游、广告、经贸、科技、法律语篇相比,在文体特征、翻译特点、翻译原则以及翻译策略上具有很大差异,有其鲜明的特征。因此,新闻翻译译者除了具备优秀译者素养之外,还应具备优秀新闻工作者素养。

1 新闻文体特征

新闻文体是用概括性的叙述方式,迅速及时地报道国内外具有新闻价值的、新近发生的事实的一种体裁。新闻文体涵盖面很广,按照不同的分类标准,有各种不同的分类方法。如,按报道方式可分为新闻报道、新闻分析、新闻特写、述评、访谈等。按传播渠道可分为报纸新闻、广播新闻、电视新闻、网络新闻等。按新闻事实发生的地域和范围,又有国际新闻、国内新闻和地方新闻之分。按报道内容可分为政治新闻、经济新闻、文化新闻、体育新闻等。按事件性质则可分为"硬新闻"(纯新闻消息报道,时效性强,题材严肃)和"软新闻"(情感浓厚的社会新闻,时效性弱,题材轻松)两大类。我们在本教材所讨论的新闻文体仅限于新闻性强的新闻报道、新闻分析与新闻特写。

现在将以一则英文房地产新闻报道为例,从词汇、句法与语篇三方面对新闻英语进行文体分析。

【例1】
Hong Kong Property Transactions to Fall 2011——Centaline
HONG KONG, Jan. 3 (Reuters) —The number of property deals in Hong Kong's secondary market will likely fall by a fifth in 2011 from last year as the government clamps down on speculation, property agency Centaline said on Monday.

The number of transactions in the private housing sector in the secondary market will likely drop to around 90,000 cases this year from last year's 110,000 cases, which itself was a rise of 25 percent from 2009, Centaline said.

In terms of dollar value, transactions in the sector in 2010 rose by 45 percent to HK $415.4 billion ($54 billion), said Centaline, whose figures are widely watched by the Hong Kong market.

"With the government eagerly clamping down on property speculation, activity in the property market will likely fall this year," Centaline analyst Wong Leung-shing said, but declined to provide a dollar figure.

In 2010, transactions in 10 of Hong Kong's major housing estates rose by 41.8

percent to hit HK＄90.44 billion (＄11.7 billion) in 2010, logging the highest level since 1997, the height of the property boom, the agency said.

The number of transactions last year in Hong Kong's key estates totalled 9,916 cases, up a quarter from 2009, also hitting a 13-year peak, Centaline said.

Hong Kong is home to some of the most expensive real estate in the world due to demand from wealthy mainland Chinese and low mortgage rates since the territory tracks U.S. monetary policy as the Hong Kong dollar is pegged to the U.S. currency.

The International Monetary has since urged the Hong Kong government to implement measures to curb speculative buying.

In November 2010, Hong Kong, home of major property firms such as Sun Hung Kai (0016. HK) and Cheung Kong (0001. HK), handed out the toughest measures in about a year by raising stamp duty on short-term transactions and tightening mortgage restrictions. [ID:nTOE6AI04Z]

For the whole of last year, Hong Kong's property sub-index. HSNP rose 6.5 percent, outperforming the broad Hang Seng index's. HSI 5.3 percent.

On Monday, the first day of trade in 2011, the property sub-index was up 2.7 percent, compared with the Hang Seng's 1.7 percent gain.

1.1 词汇

新闻报道常使用某些特定新闻色彩的词汇来表达事实和事件,具体主要体现在以下三个方面:

(1) 大量使用"新闻词语"、"缩略词"与"新闻套语"

新闻报道常使用短小精悍的词语,以节省时间、篇幅,并有利于抢发新闻,如在本新闻中所使用的 deal,fall,rise,watch,hit,log,peg,urge 等词。同样,为了节省时间和篇幅,新闻常常使用缩略词。报刊上常见的首字母缩略词既包括各类组织和机构的名称,又涉及人们熟知的事物的名称。例如,在本新闻中所使用的 HK(Hong Kong)、U.S.(United States),HSI(Hang Seng index)等词。

新闻英语还经常大量使用新闻套语,如本新闻中大量使用的"say"一词,其他新闻套语如 according to...(eyewitness,AP reports,sources concerned,etc.)(据目击者、美联社、有关方面等),informative sources or well-informed source(消息灵通人士),with guarded reserve(持谨慎态度),no comments(无可奉告),on the brink of a breakthrough(即将取得进展),quoted as saying(cited as saying)(援引……的话说),in response to allegation in the *New York Times*(就《纽约时报》的提法发表评论),preferred not to be identified(不愿透露姓名的)等。

(2) 大量使用新词与外来词语

为了表达需要和追求新奇,新闻报道常常使用一些新词(包括旧词赋新义)以使文章生动活泼,并给人以新奇之感。如本新闻中使用的"home"一词,可以理解为"总部,发源地"的意思。新闻报道常常使用外来词语,如在本新闻中所使用的"stamp duty"一词来源于荷兰。

公元1624年,荷兰政府发生经济危机,财政困难。当时执掌政权的统治者摩里斯(Maurs)为解决财政上的问题,提出要用增加税收的办法解决支出困难,但又担心人民反对,便要求政府大臣们出谋献策,印花税,也从此诞生了。后来各国效仿,并根据情况设置税收内容。

(3) 大量借用人名、地名与物名

新闻报道中还经常借用各国首都、大城市等地名、著名建筑物名称以及政府首脑姓名,以替代该国或其政府及有关机构,有时还借用某个物名来表示某个意思。例如,本新闻中所使用的Centaline一词,以地名指代中原房地产公司。其他诸如此类的例子如Beantown(豆城,美国波士顿市)、Big Apple(大苹果,美国纽约市)、Big Board(纽约证券交易所的大行情板,纽约证券所/纽约股市)、Broadway(百老汇大街,美国纽约市戏院集中的一条大街)、Motor City/Motown(汽车城,底特律市)、Pentagon/Penta(五角大楼,美国国防部)、Fleet Street(舰队街,英国新闻界)、Scotland Yard(苏格兰场;伦敦警察局,伦敦警方)、Bermuda/Bermuda Triangle(百慕大[魔鬼]三角,危险的禁区)、Zhongnanhai(中南海,中国政府)、Washington(美国首都华盛顿,美国政府等)。

1.2 语法

与其他文体相比,英语新闻报道有其独特的语法特征。整体而言,其语言风格简单明了。概括起来,新闻英语有以下一些语法特征:

(1) 时态灵活性

新闻英语中有时可不受传统语法规则的限制,时态有较大的灵活性。新闻报道中动词时态简化,也常用一般现在时代替一般过去时、一般将来时、现在进行时、现在完成时等。英语新闻现在时被广泛使用是为了造成事件正在进行中的效果,给人以真实感,因而无论是标题或是正文都常常采用现在时替代过去时,从而增强读者身临其境的感受力,如上面一则新闻标题Hong Kong property transactions to fall 2011,动词非常简化,且现实感很强烈。

(2) 语态灵活性

新闻英语多用主动语态,但为了叙事客观和便利,有时也使用一些被动结构。尤其是新闻标题使用动词主动语态的频率远远超过被动语态。因为从修辞学角度而言,主动语态比被动语态更加富有感染力,所表达的意义更直接,更具有说服力,使读者感到真实可信,读来流利自然。英语新闻标题只有在事件或动作的接受者比执行者更重要时才使用被动语态,突出强调宾语部分,以引起读者注意。如上则新闻,我们发现大量使用主动语态,使新闻表述更加直接并有说服力。

(3) 引语大量使用

新闻英语经常使用直接引语和间接引语,如本新闻中所使用的"property agency Centaline said on Monday","Centaline said","Centaline analyst Wong Leung-shing said"等句型。引语的恰当使用可以有效实现新闻的信息功能与交际功能,使新闻真实可信、富有活力。更重要的是,交际性强的引语在读者和新闻主题之间建立了一种人性化的联系,从而使新闻具有现场真实性。

(4) 句式简化

报刊新闻英语与电视新闻英语都要求句式简化,但是简化的形式不同。由于报刊篇幅有限,新闻报道讲究语言简洁,将丰富的信息压缩在有限的篇幅中。报刊新闻英语多采用扩展简单句,其方法是使用定语、状语、同位语、介词短语、分词短语等语言成分来扩展简单句,如例1的第一段:The number of property deals in Hong Kong's secondary market will likely fall by a fifth in 2011 from last year as the government clamps down on speculation.

有时还使用较为频繁的插入语代替从句。插入语是报刊新闻报道文体的另一个语法特征,它在语义上具有相对独立性,可对所叙述事件进行补充说明,为读者提供更多背景资料,从而简化句子结构。因此,英语报刊里经常出现一个句子就是一个段落的情况。如示例中的第二段,The number of transactions in the private housing sector in the secondary market will likely drop to around 90,000 cases this year from last year's 110,000 cases, which itself was a rise of 25 percent from 2009, Centaline said.

1.3 篇章结构

在篇章性质上,新闻语篇也同样具备意图性、可接受性、信息性、衔接性、连贯性、情境性与互文性七个语篇特征。在篇章结构上,英语新闻有其惯常使用的布局,即标题(headline)、导语(lead)、正文(body)与结语(conclusion)。

标题通常十分简洁,常使用省略句,像冠词、动词、介词等常在标题中省略,这既可节省版面,又可使新闻的风格显得简洁明快。动词常以一般现在时态出现,旨在制造一种现实感(immediacy),增强语言感染力。例如,在示例中的标题 Hong Kong property transactions to fall 2011—Centaline,省略了冠词(the)、系动词(are)与介词(in)等,用了几个关键词即点明了其报道内容的要旨,产生了言简意赅的修辞效果。

导语一般为新闻的第一句话,通常提纲挈领地点明该条新闻的主要内容,如示例中的第一句话,"The number of property deals in Hong Kong's secondary market will likely fall by a fifth in 2011 from last year as the government clamps down on speculation, property agency Centaline said on Monday."简明扼要地概括出了该则新闻的主要内容。

正文部分则对整个事件作进一步的详细说明,在排列的顺序上,一般是比较重要的内容在前,较次要的在后,即形成一种倒金字塔形的结构。也就是说,按新闻报道的最重要的五个 W(who, what, when, where, why)和一个 H(how)头重脚轻地安排材料,把新闻的核心和结论放在最前面的导语里,然后以事实的重要性递减的顺序来安排材料,从而帮助读者迅速了解新闻要旨并利于新闻编辑。当然,由于报道事件的性质各异,作者有时也采用顺时叙述或其他方法。结语部分则通常是对整个事件进一步发挥并得出结论。上面这则新闻也不例外采用倒金字塔结构。

2 新闻文体翻译特点

翻译新闻时需注意其自身的典型特点。因为新闻作为传播媒介,有其自身的特性:大众性、趣味性以及简练性。总的来说,新闻文体语言正式程度适中,有时还带有一些会话语体色彩,这些特点决定了译者在翻译过程中注意使译文的文体风格与原文相适应。具体说来,主要有以下几个特点:

- **强调时效与时新性**

时间和速度是决定新闻翻译的价值要素,因此新闻翻译是否快、好、准是评价新闻翻译的重要标准。这是因为随着科技的进步和现代化通讯设备的运用,新闻定义已经从"新近发生的事实的报道"变为"正在发生的事实的报道",所以国际新闻的选材和翻译都得迅速及时,否则读者和观众就不能够及时了解到事件的最新进展,跨地域、跨语言、跨文化的信息传播和交流也很难实现。因而新闻报道是一种高时效、高强度的工作,新闻翻译也必须是在时效压力下以最短的时间把新闻传递给读者。

新闻报道常常使用一些新词,如:basket(一组问题等),supercrat(高级官员),dialin(电话示威),moneywise(在金钱方面),sitcom(情景喜剧),Reaganomics(里根经济学),Jazznik(爵士乐迷),Euromart(欧洲共同市场),Masscult(大众文化),atobomb(原子弹),mortgageslave(房奴),elevated highways(高架道路),information superhighway(信息高速公路),cellular phone(移动电话),value-added tax(增值税),hulahoop(呼啦圈),surfing(冲浪运动),talk(ing) show(访谈节目;谈话类节目)等新词,无一不是通过英语新闻等传播后而为人们所熟知的。译者需要熟悉这些词汇在新闻语境的意义。

随着中华文化在世界的传播,越来越多的汉语新词通过新闻渠道被世界广泛认可。例如:爱心工程(Loving Care Project),摆渡服务(shuttle service),拳头产品(hit products; competitive products; knock-out products),退居二线(retire from the leading post),自主品牌(self-owned brand),本命年(one's year of birth considered in relation to the 12 Terrestrial Branches),唱高调(mouth high-sounding words),吃皇粮(public grainfunds, goods, etc. provided by the government; salary paid by the state),打白条(issue IOU),钉子户(person or household who refuses to move and bargains for unreasonably high compensation when the land is requisitioned for a construction project),粉领族(pink-collar tribe〔women who play a major role in certain professions such as office workers, secretaries, airline hostesses, etc.〕),关系网(network of personal connections),小皇帝(the coddled offspring of China's one-child policy),代驾(designated driver),加油(the Chinese cheer Jiayou!),两思(致富思源,富而思进)(to think of the source of getting rich and of making progress after becoming affluence),剩男(*bare branches* ; *guanggun*, the surplus of "*bare branches*"; "*guanggun*", referring to unmarried men),跳槽(job-hop),下海(risk one's fortune in business)。其他直解引用的如 chow mein(炒面),dim sum(点心),kung fu(功夫),typhoon(台风)等。这类新词的出现常常是伴随着特定的政治、社会等环境而产生的,并通常首先通过报刊得以流传和推广,易于被大部分读者所接受,因此翻译时应该体现这类词汇的新异与时效特点。

此外,新闻报道还常常使用临时生造的词(noncewords),如1958年10月4日,前苏联成功发射第一颗人造卫星,英语新闻报道将它按俄文字母拼为Sputnik Satellite.之后,sputnik一词因广为使用而被载入词典,解释为"人造卫星",于是sputnik一词在英语中应运而生,随之便出现了一系列以nik结尾的新词。另外,如"taikonaut"专指"中国宇航员"。这是根据英文中已有的"astronaut"和"cosmonaut"这两个描述美国和苏联/俄罗斯宇航员的词而创造的新词,用来纪念中国"神五"和"神六"的圆满飞天和"嫦娥奔月"工程的顺利进展。因此,译者熟悉这类新闻词汇的文化背景对提高翻译质量是非常重要的。

• **注重语言浓缩与凝练**

新闻报道的语言平易朴实,简洁精练,能用非常经济的语言表达丰富的内容。如示例中的标题 Hong Kong property transactions to fall 2011—Centaline 可译为"中原地产称香港2011年楼市交易大幅下跌"。新闻中常用一些特有专有新闻词汇。例如,story 指 newsitem 或 newsreport,probe 指 news investigation。其他如:accord(give),bar(prevent),ban(prohibition),bid(attempt),boost(rise,increase),clash(disagreement),curb(restrain,control),cut(reduction),deal(business agreement),freeze(stabilization),loom(appear),blaze(fire),comb(search),row(violent argument),move(plan,decision,suggestion),shock(astonishment,blow),shun(to keep away from),viable(workable),voice(express),operation(activities),pact(agreement),woo(to seek to win,to persuade)等。因此,我们在翻译过程中应注意译入语言的浓缩与凝练。

新闻英语还经常使用其他缩略词,如:UNESCO(United Nations Educational,Scientific and Cultural Organization[联合国教科文组织]),IMF(International Monetary Fund[国际货币基金组织]),ASEAN(Association of Southeast Asian Nations[东南亚国家联盟:"东盟"]),SALT(Strategic arms limitation talks[限制战略武器会谈]),SDI(strategic defence initiative[战略防御措施]),GMT(Greenwich Mean Time[格林尼治标准时间]),PC(personal computer[个人电脑]),PR(public relations[公共关系]),PM(prime minister[总理;首相]),GM(general manager[总经理]),VIP(very important person[贵宾;要人]),TP(traffic policeman[交通警察])等。译者在汉译英过程中需要注重语言的简洁与精练,可以使用缩略词替代全部名称。如果译者不熟悉这些缩略词的意义,会很难理解原文的意义与内容。

• **遵守叙事语体特点,符合新闻写作要求**

新闻报道具有典型的叙事语体特点,如语言流畅易读,书面词语简洁得体,句式选用流线,叙述生动有力、叙事结构完整等。新闻翻译应尽量遵循这一原则,并尽量体现新闻写作的主要特点,如"倒金字塔"结构。导语开门见山,简明扼要;正文叙述应重要事实在先,次要事实在后;行文力求简洁易懂,易于读者接受。为此,新闻翻译工作者不仅需要具备扎实的双语双文化能力,同时还须具备较多的新闻写作知识和较高的新闻编辑能力,这会有助于译者根据新闻语境调整译文。广播新闻与电视新闻的语言深入浅出,具有口语化特点,且稍纵即逝,不能回看,与报刊新闻的句型特点存在很多不同。因此,为符合广播、电视新闻"为耳写"、"口语化"的特点,其句型需要更为简单,主谓分明,将长句分成几个短句,从而达到响亮流畅、易读易诵的效果。

新闻语境制约新闻翻译。新闻语境受文化因素与新闻自身特点等因素的限制。中西方重要的英语新闻一般都比较注重提供新闻来源,以增强新闻的可靠性和可信度,以使受众容易接受,如 HONG KONG,Jan 3 (Reuters)与 Orlando,Florida,June 30(AP)这两个导语该如何翻译呢?在翻译类似导语时应该根据中文新闻表达习惯,分别翻译成"路透社香港1月3日电"与"美联社佛罗里达州奥兰多市6月30日电"。还有新闻中有许多情况引用有关人士的话,如 say,其最基本的意思是"说话"、"发表意见",但也可根据情况译为 admit(承认),add(又说),agree(同意),announce(宣布),argue(主张,争辩说),ask(问,要求),claim(声称),complain(抱怨),concede(承认),confess(公认,承认),contradict(反驳,否认),suggest(建议说)。

此外,东西方文化差异也是影响新闻翻译的一个重要因素。如上则新闻中提到的mainland Chinese 一词,由于东西文化差异,有些人会误认为世界不止一个中国,除了"mainland Chinese",还会有别的"...Chinese"。其实"mainland Chinese"一词是港澳台地区居民常用词,常作"地理地貌描述"使用,或港澳新闻报道,应该译为"中国大陆人",而不是"大陆中国人"。同样,香港一般要译为"Hong Kong, S. A. R",澳门译为"Macau, S. A. R.",更正规的还要在它们之后跟 China 一词,特别适用于法律文件,软件进口(软件本地化)、演讲稿等重要场合。这是因为地理词汇的翻译融合了政治因素在内,常常体现一国的国格和主权尊严,因此翻译时一定慎重考虑。再如,A Tsar Is Born(《时代周刊》2007.12—2008.1)翻译为"王者诞生",比"沙皇诞生"要好很多。这是《时代周刊》介绍其 2007 年度人物普京总统的文章。Tsar 一词在英文中既指沙皇(emperor; the ruler of Russia until the 1917 Revolution),又有"铁腕人物"的意思(one having great power or authority)。原标题既点出普京总统来自俄国,又显示出对他领袖风范的赞赏。若直译成"沙皇诞生",容易让汉语受众产生"统治、压迫、暴政"等负面联想,所以译文将"沙皇"译成意义更宽泛、带褒义的"王者",既传达了信息,又符合中国读者的接受美学。当然,随着全球化的推广,中外文化与语言表达的容纳性会彼此增强,这可能会使原来所不能接受的词语被广泛接受。因此,翻译新闻时需要根据译文受众作出相应调整,既遵守在新闻语境中用事实说话的传播目的,又采用符合目的语受众的表达方式对内容作出适当变通。

3 新闻英语翻译原则

新闻英语翻译应该遵循德国翻译目的论所提出的"功能加忠诚"(Function plus Loyalty)的指导原则。诺德(2001:126)认为,功能是指译文在译语环境中按预定方式运作,忠诚是指译者、原文作者、译文接受者及翻译发起者之间的人际关系。由于忠诚是个人际范畴概念,是指人与人之间的社会关系,而忠信/忠实(fidelity/faithfulness)仅仅指向原文与译文的关系,因此不能把忠诚与忠信和忠实的概念混为一谈。

第一,新闻翻译的责任重大。如果翻译错误,校对、编辑和发稿人都没有发现而被国内外新闻媒体所采用,其后果将不堪设想,除了会降低本国新闻媒体的信任度,同时也会使国外和本国受众遭受不必要的信息误导。

第二,新闻受众珍视新闻报道的真实性,而真实性又是新闻传播的根本前提。一般说来,新闻翻译不同于文学翻译,其最终目标是简洁明了地提供事件信息,因而译者可以无需对原文始终心存敬意和忠实,而是根据受众需要对原文信息进行重塑、编辑、合成和转型,包括变更标题和导语,删除多语信息,增加重要背景知识,重排段落顺序等,以方便读者理解和接受。因而改变了传统意义上译者和作者以及原作品的关系,建构了一种新型的社会人际关系。但需注意,这是建立在不能歪曲原文信息的前提下进行的。

第三,新闻翻译是跨文化翻译,不能仅仅局限于字面对等,而应传达出原文内涵,尽量实现功能上的对等。因为各国的国情千差万别，从行政区划到军衔，从选举法到货币，从风俗习惯到社会生活，新闻翻译工作者都要熟悉。如同一个词"foreign minister"，由于各国政体不同，翻译时需要按照译语文化的标准调整文体风格，并选择不同的措辞。如美国的要翻译成"国务卿"，英国的要翻译成"外交大臣"，德国的要翻译成"外交部长"，日本的要翻译成"外相"。

第四，报道者报道事件的角度、立场、出发点、对事件的理解及评论等不可避免地受到其所在文化意识形态根深蒂固的影响，因而新闻传达的内容除了事实之外还有政治文化内涵。这就要求新闻译者应是具备翻译能力的新闻工作者，熟悉事件所在国的政治、经济、文化，正确识别和体味原稿的政治文化含义，准确把握这些词语在特定语境中的含义与本民族文化含义的共性和差异，把它们准确又恰当地反映出来。

第五，国际新闻中的信息内容多种多样，它们的社会功能也各不相同。因此，国际新闻翻译人员在选择翻译信息时必须是多层次的，不仅要满足所在媒体的编辑方针和意识形态立场，而且还要认识到原语和译语在文化期待上的不同，这样才能确保新闻译文的真实性和可信度，并在信息内容和功能上尽量获得不同层次受众的认可。

在该理论指导下，新闻英语翻译过程应该从语用的层面开始。首先确定翻译的目标功能，其次将原文中需要保留重现的内容和那些须根据受众的背景知识、心理期待、交际需要、媒介条件以及指示需求等因素进行调整的内容进行区分。然后根据不同的情况采取不同的翻译方法，注意始终把语篇功能作为翻译过程的焦点。此外，由于新闻文体的主要功能是传递信息，信息的准确性应放在首位。因此，新闻翻译应当给目的语读者提供准确、清晰、易懂的信息，对重要信息力求真实、完整、突出，对次要信息则淡化或省略，并力求完成原文新闻语篇的人际功能意义的传递。现以 2010 年 8 月 9 日 Global Times（《环球时报》）上的一则新闻为例。

【例 2】

Analects of Confucius Reduce Crime Rate

According to the New Strait Times of August 8, Tan Sri Muhyiddin Yassin, Deputy Prime Minister of Malaysia hosted the opening ceremony of the nation's Good Values to Prevent Crimes programme, in which Muhyiddin appealed the young people to read *Analects of Confucius*, China's classical masterpiece.

The report said that Muhyiddin had always thought highly of Confucian thoughts and moral values. When evaluating *Analects of Confucius*, he said, "In ancient China, Confucius praised highly moral education and thought it as a core idea. And Confucius's book written down the values pertaining to politics, history, ethics, education and arts, which I believe will serve to reduce crime rate."

In recent years, the Malaysian economy has developed rapidly, but also led to many social problems. Muhyiddin said, "The economic development must balance with cultural quality. Thus, the government should vigorously promote the lofty values to reduce the number of young people involved in drugs, illegal racing, baby-abandoning, gambling and excessive drinking, whose bad influences will affect the whole society."

译文：

马来西亚副首相：读《论语》能降低犯罪率

据《新海峡时报》8月8日报道，马来西亚副首相丹斯里·慕希丁·雅辛近日为全国"崇高价值观预防犯罪嘉年华"主持开幕仪式。在开幕致辞中，慕希丁呼吁青少年多读中国经典著作《论语》。

报道称，慕希丁一直以来都非常重视孔子的儒家思想及其道德价值观。在评价《论语》时，慕希丁这样说："在中国古代，孔子推崇道德教育为思想核心，其作品《论语》详尽记载了政治、历史、道德、教育、艺术等方面的价值观。我深信，这些思想将有助降低犯罪率。"

近年来，马来西亚经济发展迅猛，但也衍生出很多社会问题。慕希丁说，"经济的发展必须与人文素质平衡。因此，政府应该大力推行崇高价值观，以减少青少年涉嫌毒品、非法飙车、弃婴、赌博、酗酒等罪行，以免这些不良风气影响整个社会。"

由原文分析可以得出，该篇新闻的目的功能主要体现在以下几个方面：信息功能主要是马来西亚首相对《论语》社会价值对其社会问题影响认识的介绍；呼唤功能是呼吁社会关注《论语》，减少社会罪恶；表达功能是多用简单朴实的语言、句式以及引语等传达原文信息。因此，在翻译时应该注意原文目标功能的体现。如标题的翻译，原文的标题为 *Analects of Confucius* reduce crime rate，如果直译为"《论语》降低犯罪率"，则不能把原新闻的主要思想及目标功能传达出来，因此增加逻辑主语，译为"马来西亚副首相：读《论语》能降低犯罪率"使译文不仅忠实于原文内容，而且明确清晰，浅显易懂，能够很好地体现原文标题的社会功能。由此可见，在标题翻译时可酌情加上逻辑主语，如新闻人物的国籍、消息的事发地点等，并兼顾中英文新闻的异同，适当增补有关介绍性、注释性词语，可有利于读者理解，并避免产生误会。

此外，新闻翻译时如果仅仅拘泥于原文死译，生搬硬套，而不顾及文体和语言特点，就很难使读者产生共鸣，因此翻译时应该注意根据译入语的特点进行调整。如原文导语"According to the *New Strait Times* of August 8, Tan Sri Muhyiddin Yassin, Deputy Prime Minister of Malaysia hosted the opening ceremony of the nation's Good Values to Prevent Crimes programme, in which Muhyiddin appealed the young people to read *Analects of Confucius*, China's classical masterpiece."非常典型，用一句（一段）话就把时间、地点、人物、事件和原因等重要信息作了简要的概括，使读者一目了然。所以，导语是全文的精华和浓缩，译者必须仔细阅读，并能准确翻译出原文的含义。而汉语译文是两句话，把英文中的非限制性定语从句"in which Muhyiddin appealed the young people to read *Analects of Confucius*, China's classical masterpiece"在译文中根据汉语语言文化习惯增加了"在开幕致辞中"一词，译成独立的一句话"在开幕致辞中，慕希丁呼吁青少年多读中国经典著作《论语》"，使译文流畅易懂，避免歧义。

再如，在原文最后一句"Thus, the government should vigorously promote the lofty values to reduce the number of young people involved in drugs, illegal racing, baby-abandoning, gambling and excessive drinking, whose bad influences will affect the whole society."中，非限制定语"whose bad influences will affect the whole society"如果字字直译过来，则会引起歧义。因此，译文增加连词"以免"使语句通顺明了。如"（政府应该大力推行

崇高价值观,以减少青少年涉及毒品、非法飙车、弃婴、赌博、酗酒等罪行)以免这些不良风气影响整个社会"。

由上面分析可以看出,在翻译新闻文体时,如果我们遵循目的论的"功能加忠诚原则",不仅能真实传达新闻的本身意思,顾及文体特点,增强其可读性,而且翻译时能做到简洁精练,生动传神,准确并贴切地传达原文的意图、信息与风格。

4 新闻文体翻译策略

功能学派强调,翻译作为一种有目的的行为,应该根据其翻译目的和译文功能采取相应对策。新闻报道作为一种特殊的文体,具有独特的结构和行文语言,因此译者应尽可能发挥主体性,根据读者需求采取相应的变通翻译策略。在新闻翻译过程中,潜在的价值体系被融入到译文中去;同时所要实现的功能起着决定性的作用,即译文对于译文读者来说依然是新闻;此外,新闻翻译还受到目的文化中的意识形态的操控。基于上述原因,新闻翻译可根据新闻价值与读者需求采取全译和变译等策略。变译是指为了满足读者需求,译文可以采取增、减、编、述、缩、并、改等方法。大约有十一种变译方法,如摘译、编译、译述、缩译、综述、述评、译评、改译、阐译、译写和参译(黄忠廉,1999,2002)。在新闻报道翻译过程中,我们可以该理论为指导,在新闻语篇各层面(词汇、句子、段落、篇章)对原文进行合理变译,从而提高翻译时效性和翻译工作性价比,并满足国外读者的阅读需求。为了利于阐述,我们根据新闻翻译的特点与原则,把新闻翻译方法主要分为五种:全译、缩译、编译、阐译和译写。

4.1 全译

全译是将译出语的新闻稿全部转化为译入语新闻稿的翻译方法。该类新闻一般都十分重要,二次传播的价值比较高,且篇幅又相对适中。翻译此类新闻时必须注意逐段甚至逐句进行,既要译出原语新闻的深层内容,又要保留它的基本结构和风格。对其内容,译者不能随意增删。当然,为使译文符合译语表达习惯而进行的必要的语句调整不在此列。下面以一则2010年7月《环球时报》的新闻(节选)为例。

【例3】
CHINA'S LITTLE EMPERORS DEMAND THEIR DUE

China's youth can get a bad press. In most accounts, they are the "Little Emperors" or the "Me Generation", the spoilt and apolitical offspring of one-child families who are interested in fast cars, video games and designer goods but little else. At the main Shanghai store of Louis Vuitton there is a queue to get in at weekends — young women wait patiently in the rope line, as if they were trying to get into the hottest new LA club.

Yet the Me Generation is beginning to show its teeth. Simmering discontent about soaring house prices and the recent wave of strikes at car plants and other factories both speak of the rising and sometimes frustrated expectations of younger Chinese, who want more from their lives than their parents could dream of. It is a phenomenon that could have all sorts of consequences for China's future.

There are lots of good explanations for the strikes of the past two months, including low pay and a demographic shift that is reducing the number of young people entering the workforce. But there is also a generational shift at play. Chinese often talk about their capacity to *chi ku*, or "eat bitterness", which helps explain their resilience amid the chaos and privations of the past century. But the generation born in the 1980s and 1990s has grown up among much wider prosperity, even in poor parts of the countryside.

译文：

当"小皇帝"们长大之后

中国的年轻人是媒体苛责的对象。在多数报道中，他们被称作"小皇帝"或者是"自我的一代"，因为他们出生在独生子女家庭，娇生惯养，不关心政治，只对跑车、视频游戏和设计师设计的商品感兴趣。在路易·威登的上海旗舰店，每到周末，等待进店消费的顾客排成长龙，年轻女性耐心等候在绳子圈起来的队伍里，仿佛她们要进的是最红火的、新开张的夜总会。

然而，"自我的一代"开始逐渐抗争。对房价不断上涨的不满正在升温，加上近期汽车制造厂及其他工厂发生的罢工，均折射出中国年轻人的期望越来越高，却又不时落空。他们想要从生活中得到的东西，比父辈所梦想的还要多。这种现象可能给中国的未来造成各种各样的后果。

关于近两个月发生的罢工，有许多很好的解释，包括工人工资过低，以及人口结构变化导致加入劳动大军的年轻人减少。但是，世代的变化也在产生影响。中国人常常谈到他们"吃苦"的能力，这有助于解释他们为何能够挺过上世纪混乱而贫穷的境况。然而，上世纪八九十年代出生的这代人，包括生活在贫穷的农村地区的他们，也是在较为富裕的环境中成长起来的。

原发新闻是关于国外对于中国独生子女的一些评论看法，这也是国内人们所普遍重视的问题。因此，新闻的价值较高，译文采取了全译的方法，内容完整，风格贴切，能从内容与形式两方面完整地传达原文的意义与风格。

4.2 缩译

缩译，就是选取原作之精华加以翻译。新闻报刊文章常常因受版面限制，截长取短，以质取胜。缩译文基本上保全了原作的骨架，是原作的缩微复制品。在缩译时需要注意以下原则：原作的浓缩性、内容的简要性、浓缩的客观性、内容的报道性和译文的逻辑性等。下面是选自2011年2月14日BBC的一则新闻。

【例4】

Canada Immigration 'Reaches 50-Year High'

Canada welcomed its highest number of legal immigrants in more than 50 years in 2010, the government has said. [1]

Preliminary data show 280,636 permanent residents entered Canada last year. [2]

The number is 60% higher than the average annual number of immigrants admitted in the 1990s. [3]

"While other Western countries cut back on immigration during the recession, our government kept legal immigration levels high," said Immigration Minister Jason Kenney on Sunday. [4]

Canada's immigration policy has historically been viewed as liberal, and the current government has been keen to boost the levels of legal entrants. [5]

"Canada's post-recession economy demands a high level of economic immigration to keep our economy strong," Mr Kenney added. [6]

About two-thirds of those admitted to the country last year were permanent residents, who under this status are granted the same privileges as citizens except for a passport and voting rights. [7]

The majority of these were economic migrants and their dependents, Mr Kenney said. [8]

In addition to permanent residents, 182,322 temporary workers entered Canada in the past year, as well as 96,147 foreign students and 12,098 refugees. [9]

But while welcoming immigrants, the country has also sought to crack down on the number of illegal immigrants reaching its shores. [10]

Last year, a number of ships carrying Tamil migrants from Sri Lanka arrived in the country. [11]

At the time, Prime Minister Stephen Harper described the arrival of hundreds of illegal immigrants on the vessels as "unacceptable", and pledged to "deter this kind of behaviour". [12]

译文：

2010年加拿大移民人数创50年新高

加拿大政府日前宣布，2010年加拿大接收的合法移民人数创下50多年来的最高纪录，其中移民为永久居民的就超过28万，另外还有近40万临时工作人员、留学生以及避难人员在去年进入加拿大。加拿大的移民政策向来比较宽松，而现任政府也一直致力于促进合法移民数量。加拿大移民部长表示，在经济衰退时期，其他西方国家都先后削减移民数量，而加拿大仍保持一贯的移民水平，因为加拿大需要大量经济移民来保持本国经济的发展水平。

通过对比原文和译文，我们发现译文只是摄取了原文最主要的信息，却把原文的主要内容简洁、流畅地表达了出来，基本真实地传递了原文所主要想传达的内容，实现了原文的预期功能。

首先来看一下标题的翻译，原文为Canada Immigration 'Reaches 50-Year High'，译文为"2010年加拿大移民人数创50年新高"。通过对比发现，原文简洁明了，符合英语新闻报道习惯，而译文增加了"2010年"，使标题内容一目了然，非常明确，符合汉语新闻报道习惯。

从文章的整体结构来看，译文没有完全遵循原文逐段翻译，而是对原文的段落进行了压缩。原文一共十二段，也是十二句话，而译文只有三句话，原文中的第三、四、七、八、十、十一和最后一段在译文中没有翻译。

从文章的整篇内容来看,除了原文的第一段,第五段的译文基本实现了与原文的"对等"外,其他段落有的删去不译,有的作了调整。具体说来,原文的第一段"Canada welcomed its highest number of legal immigrants in more than 50 years in 2010, the government has said." 译为"加拿大政府日前宣布,2010年加拿大接收的合法移民人数创下50多年来的最高纪录";原文的第五段,"Canada's immigration policy has historically been viewed as liberal, and the current government has been keen to boost the levels of legal entrants." 译为"加拿大的移民政策向来比较宽松,而现任政府也一直致力于促进合法移民数量"都基本属于语义翻译,是在考虑语境下对原文的忠实翻译。原文第二段"Preliminary data show 280,636 permanent residents entered Canada last year." 译为"其中移民为永久居民的就超过28万";原文中的第九段"In addition to permanent residents, 182,322 temporary workers entered Canada in the past year, as well as 96,147 foreign students and 12,098 refugees."译为"另外还有近40万临时工作人员、留学生以及避难人员在去年进入加拿大",原文中的具体数字都省略不译,而把大概的数字准确地翻译给读者,符合汉语读者的阅读期待与阅读习惯,基本都属于交际翻译。而且原文的第九段提至译文的第一句,在译文中根据汉语阅读习惯进行了重组。原文的第四段"While other Western countries cut back on immigration during the recession, our government kept legal immigration levels high," said Immigration Minister Jason Kenney on Sunday." 在译文中为最后一句话,译为"加拿大移民部长表示,在经济衰退时期,其他西方国家都先后削减移民数量,而加拿大仍保持一贯的移民水平,因为加拿大需要大量经济移民来保持本国经济的发展水平。"除省略不译原文中的人物和时间外,其他都基本忠实地传达了出来。

这则译文可以用目的论进行解释。翻译目的论是将翻译看做一种基于原文的文本处理过程,原文对于译者来说只是信息的提供者,译者可以根据翻译的目的运作原文,并决定原文的哪些内容可以保留,哪些需要调整或改写(Nord,2001)。从以上这则新闻的原文和译文对比分析可以看出,译者根据新闻翻译语境、中英新闻文体差异以及西方读者阅读习惯,在摄取原文主要"事实性"信息的基础上,对原文内容进行了压缩与调整,包括标题的改写、段落的重组、删除等,以求达到新闻报道翻译的最终目的。

4.3 编译

新闻编译是通过翻译和编辑的手段,将以原语语言写成的新闻进行翻译、加工、综合,使之成为用译语语言表达出来的新闻的翻译方法。之所以需要编译国际新闻,原因主要有以下两个方面:首先,有些具有二次传播价值的新闻需要翻译,但对"本媒体"来说原语语言新闻存在着某种缺陷,因而在翻译过程中需要进行删减和编辑。其次,新闻媒体的版面、节目时间、制作过程等都十分有限,而为了在有限的版面和播出时间内传播更多的新闻信息,新闻编译就成了一种理想的解决方法。由此看来,与原新闻相比,编译新闻更利于二次传播,也更适合于译语语言读者的阅读。请看2003年6月27日的一则报道。

【例5】
印总理瓦杰帕伊结束访华,并与中国多位领导人会晤

新华网上海6月27日电(记者周解蓉)印度总理阿塔尔·比哈里·瓦杰帕伊结束了对中国为期6天的正式访问,于27日下午乘专机离沪回国。

这是印度总理10年来首次访问中国。中国多位领导人与瓦杰帕伊在北京举行会晤、会谈,就双边关系和共同关心的地区及国际问题广泛交换意见。双方签署了《中华人民共和国和印度共和国关系原则和全面合作的宣言》等11个合作文件,加强了两国在各个领域的交流与合作。瓦杰帕伊于22日抵达北京。在京期间,他到北京大学和两国企业界人士举办的经济合作与发展研讨会上发表了演讲。

在"九朝古都"洛阳期间,他参观了与古代印度高僧有着深厚渊源的佛教圣地龙门石窟和白马寺。在上海期间,他出席了"中印信息产业论坛"。

中印双方高度评价此次访问取得的成果。双方一致认为,访问增进了两国政府、两国领导人和两国人民之间的相互理解和信任,标志着中印双方为在新世纪加强全面合作迈出了新的步伐。

译文:

Indian PM Vajpayee Concludes China Tour

Indian Prime Minister Atal Bihari Vajpayee left Shanghai for home Friday afternoon, concluding his six-day official visit to China.

Vajpayee arrived in the Chinese capital Sunday evening as guest of Chinese Premier Wen Jiabao. It is the first visit to China by an Indian prime minister in 10 years.

Besides Beijing and Shanghai, he also visited Luoyang, an ancient capital city in central China's Henan Province.

During his stay in Beijing, Vajpayee met with top Chinese leaders, given two speeches and visited the Forbidden City.

Chinese Premier Wen Jiabao and Vajpayee Monday signed a declaration on principles for bilateral relationship and comprehensive cooperation. The declaration, together with a series of other documents signed between China and India, set out the goals and guiding principles for bilateral relations and outlined cooperation of the two countries in various fields.

During his stay in Luoyang, the Indian prime minister visited the Longmen Grottoes, one of China's three largest grotto complexes, and the White Horse Temple, a renowned Buddhist temple.

Vajpayee also attended a seminar on IT development on Thursday in Shanghai.

Vajpayee visited China in 1979 as Indian foreign minister.

通过仔细对照原文和译文,我们发现译文是在基本遵循功能加忠诚原则指导下的编译结果。

首先来看一下标题的翻译。"印总理瓦杰帕伊结束访华,并与中国多位领导人会晤"是

典型的中文新闻报道标题,采用了对称的语言结构来传达这则报道的主要内容;而译文标题 Indian PM Vajpayee Concludes China Tour 则简明扼要,只译出了印度总理瓦杰帕伊结束对华访问这件事,符合英文的表达习惯。

从文章的整体结构来看,英译文没有完全遵循原文的叙事顺序,而是对原文的段落进行了重新编排,即由原来的四个段落编译为译文的八个段落,以符合英语新闻报道中以一到两个句子为一段的行文风格。

从文章的整篇内容来看,译文除第一段导语中的翻译与原文实现"对等"外,其他段落的翻译都作了相当程度的增、删、改和调整。具体来说,译文第二段增加了瓦杰帕伊应中方总理温家宝的邀请抵京这一句;第三段概括了分布在中文原文中不同段落的瓦杰帕伊在华访问的行程;第四段增加了印度总理对故宫的访问这一句;第五段与原文第二段大致对应,没有保留原文的"(中国多位领导人与瓦杰帕伊)在北京举行会晤、会谈,就双边关系和共同关心的地区及国际问题广泛交换意见"以及他两场演讲的会议和地点,但却增加了与其签署协议的中方领导人"温家宝总理"。第六段对瓦杰帕伊访问洛阳的两处景点作了补充性介绍,但同时又省略了这两处景点与印度的关系。中文新闻报道结语部分对访问意义的总结在译文中被删除,但同时却又增加了瓦杰帕伊1979年担任外长时曾访华这一细节内容。

这则译文也可以在目的论中得到合理的解释。因为译者没有对原文一句一句的翻译,而是根据汉语语境在摄取原文主要"事实性"信息的基础上,对原文进行了编译与调整,包括标题的改写、段落的重组、背景知识的添加等,并根据英语新闻的特点对原新闻进行了编译,以求达到新闻报道翻译的最终目的。

4.4 阐译

阐译是指对新闻报道中的"行话"、"历史典故"等采用解释性的翻译方法,便于读者接受。具体说来,有关历史事件、地理名称、各国独有的机构、节日、习俗、行话、套话、历史典故等都需要用阐译法。比如"兔爷"译作"Lord Rabbit, a mythical bunny sent down from the moon to bring good health to Beijing",又如"生肖兔年"译作"the year of the Rabit, according to traditional Chinese reckoning",以便让外国读者了解这些特色文化词汇。

【例6】

① Nixon's Odyssey to China(*Time Magazine*, March 6, 1972)

译文"尼克松艰辛的中国之旅"好于直译"尼克松的中国奥德赛之行"。这是因为,相传 Odyssey 是古希腊诗人荷马(Homer)的一部英雄史诗,描述了古城特洛伊(Troy)沦陷后,希腊神话中的英雄、"木马计"(the Wooden Horse of Troy)的献策者奥德修斯(Odysseus),在海上漂流十年之久,战胜独眼巨神,制服女巫,历经磨难,最终回到祖国、合家团圆的漫长历程。这样一个特定的文化语境与由 Nixon 和 China 等微观语境交织在一起,共同限定了 Odyssey 在该语境中的喻义为:"中美关系正常化所经历的一段艰难而又漫长的历程",借古喻今,意味深长。

② The newspaper reported that the army was very discontent and that this was a sword of Damocles hanging over the government. (*New York Times*, June 30, 2005)

译文：

报刊报道说,军方十分不满,这局势像一把达摩克利斯剑悬在政府头上,情况非常危急。

在译文添加的"情况非常危急"可以把原文的文化内涵准确清晰地传达出来。在这则报道中,就运用了一则希腊典故。"a sword of Damocles"出自古代希腊的一则历史故事。公元前四世纪在西西里岛上叙拉古的统治者狄奥尼修斯一世(406—373BC)有个宠臣叫达摩克利斯,他非常羡慕帝王的豪华生活,常说:"君王是人世间最幸福的人。"狄奥尼修斯为了教训这个觊觎王位的宠臣,在一次宴会上让他坐在国王的宝座上,但当他猛然抬头,只见头顶上有一把用头发悬着的宝剑,随时都有刺到头顶的危险,他感到惶惶不安,提心吊胆。由此,便产生了"达摩克利斯的宝剑"这个典故,用来喻指临头的危险或迫在眉睫的危急情况,类似于汉语的"大祸临头"。在这篇新闻报道的汉译中,运用了阐译的翻译方法,即把某种文化及语言中的信息以增加文内注释的方式传递给另一种文化及语言,这有利于两种不同的文化和语言之间进行相互交流和渗透,对我们了解西方的文化大有裨益。

③ While giant conglomerates are crumbling in South Korea, an undaunted China is moving at full speed to construct its own industrial behemoths (Reuter, Dec, 7)

译文：

当韩国的巨型综合性企业正在瓦解时,无畏的中国却正在全力构建自己的大型工业企业。

其中的"industrial behemoths"意译为"大型工业企业",而没有译为"工业巨兽"。原文中 behemoth 源于基督教的《圣经》,是一种巨兽,据说是河马。中国读者对于这一形象并不熟悉,因此可以灵活地用其引申义来翻译,这里的"industrial behemoths"可译为"大型工业企业"。

④ The nation stood in shock and terror yesterday after three apparently hijacked jetliners, in less than an hour's time, made kamikaze-like crashes into both towers of the World Trade Center and the Pentagon, killing hundreds, maybe thousands of people and leaving countless others maimed and burned. (*The Wall Street Journal*, Sept.12, 2001).

译文：

昨日国家陷入了震惊与恐慌。三架显然被劫持的飞机,在不到一小时的时间,使其带有自杀性质的同归于尽式的撞击撞向了双塔——世界金融中心和五角大楼,导致成百甚至上千人死亡,多人致残与烧伤。

这则报道描写了美国9·11事件发生后的情况,需注意文中 kamikaze-like 所承载的文化信息。Kamikaze 由日语发音转变过来,指第二次世界大战期间日本空军敢死队"神风特攻队(神风特别攻击队)"队员、此种战术的飞机或驾驶员。神风特攻队是在第二次世界大战末期日本在中途岛失败后,为了抵御美国空军强大的优势,挽救其战败的局面,利用日本人的武士道精神,按照"一人、一机、一弹换一舰"的要求,对美国舰艇编队、登陆部队及固定的集群目标实施的带有自杀式袭击的特别攻击队。他们驾驶满载炸弹的飞机撞击轰炸目标,企图与之同归于尽。在翻译的时候,需把该词的文化内涵翻译出来,可意译为"带有自杀性质的同归于尽式的撞击"。

4.5 译写

译写中的"写"是根据特定读者,按照所译内容来写,而非自由杜撰。它必须与所译内容相关。写的方法大致有三:第一,添加相关背景信息;第二,对所译内容发表看法,加以评论;第三,对所译内容的阐释发挥,以解释读者所不清楚的内涵信息等。虽然阐译也是增加字数,揭示内涵,但不增加内容;而译写的增补性和拓展性是使原作的内容和内涵都丰富起来,使整个译作丰富起来。下面是2008年8月的一则新闻报道。

【例7】

牙买加选手包揽女子百米赛奖牌

8月16日,牙买加选手博尔特在"鸟巢"以9秒69的成绩创世界纪录摘金,成为了奥运历史上第10位非美国籍的百米冠军。继他成为首位荣膺奥运百米飞人称号的牙买加人之后,8月17日在国家体育场进行的女子100米决赛中,牙买加选手包揽所有奖牌。谢莉·安·弗雷泽以10秒78获得冠军,而谢伦·辛普森和克伦·斯图尔特以10秒98并列第二,而美国选手穆娜·李和劳琳·威廉斯表现一般,无缘奖牌。

译文1:

Jamaican Fraser Wins Women's 100m Gold Medal

Shelly-Ann Fraser led an unprecedented women's 100m Olympic medal sweep for Jamaica Sunday, devastating American rivals in a head-to-head showdown to decide the world's fastest woman. [1]

Three Jamaicans and three Americans featured in the finals but only disappointment awaited US women. [2]

One night after Usain Bolt thrilled Jamaicans by winning the men's 100m in a world-record 9.69 seconds, Fraser powered to victory in 10.78, with Sherone Simpson and Kerron Stewart sharing second in 10.98. [3]

For the Americans, Athens Olympic runner-up and 2005 World champion Lauryn Williams was fourth in 11.03; US champion Muna Lee fifth in 11.07; and 2003 World champion Torri Edwards eighth and last in 11.20. [4]

"I was inspired by last night," Fraser said. "This is a crazy Bolt effect. I am just so happy to put Jamaica on the map. No one expected me to win so there was no pressure."[5]

Fraser, whose prior claim to fame came during the runner-up finish in the 4×100 relay in last year's World Championships, surged ahead at the start and pulled away from

Simpson midway into the race. Stewart caught up with Simpson at the line for the first 1—2—3 sweep in the event. [6]

Her time moved Fraser level as the eighth-best all-time performer, alongside Americans Torri Edwards and Dawn Sowell. "We made history, just like Bolt," Simpson said. "We're all great athletes and I'm very excited about the tremendous achievement. We're very good athletes and this says a lot for our country." [7]

American Edwards, whose 2008 world-best time was equaled by Fraser, said she thought she had falsely started and expected to be called back. "I thought I had moved before the gun," Edwards said. "I had to go but I was off step. That threw me off a lot. I'm pretty sure it was a false start." [8]

Defending Olympic champion Yuliya Nesterenko of Belarus was eliminated in the semi-finals earlier. [9]

译文2：

Shelly-Ann Fraser led the other two Jamaicans to win all the women's 100 meters medals on Sunday evening at the Beijing Olympic Games. [1]

Fraser clocked her personal best in 10.78 seconds before Sherone Simpson and Kerron Stewart finished, both in 10.98, and shared the silver. [2]

Simpson said, "We made history. Just like yesterday Bolt set a new world record. We are all great athletes and I'm very excited about the tremendous achievement we've made for our country." [3]

"Today's victory boosts my confidence to win the 200m. We will also do well in the 4×100m. I believe we can beat the Americans," she said. [4]

Commenting on Jamaica's medals sweep, Stewart said, "I don't know if I should cry, smile, jump. I think this is a fabulous thing for the three of us to win the medals and for Jamaica to get one, two, three. What else can you say?" [5]

The Jamaican squad smashed the American fleet joined by Lauryn Williams, Muna Lee and Torri Edwards, who were hot candidates for the title before the Games. [6]

The Jamaican women replayed the legend created by their countryman Usain Bolt on Saturday night on the same track in the Olympic main venue. Bolt sliced the men's 100m world record by three hundredths of a second to a stunning 9.69 seconds. [7]

原文共有三句话，表达了以下三层意思：(1)8月16日，牙买加选手博尔特以9秒69的成绩成为奥运百米冠军。(2)8月17日，牙买加选手谢莉·安·弗雷泽以10秒78的成绩获女子奥运百米决赛冠军，谢伦·辛普森和克伦·斯图尔特以10秒98的成绩并列第二。(3)美国选手穆娜·李和劳琳·威廉斯与奖牌无缘。

在译文1中，前四段共有四句话，传达了原文的意思。译文1第一段，"周日，牙买加选手谢莉·安·弗雷泽击败美国选手获女子奥运百米决赛冠军"；第二段，"三位牙买加选手和三位美国选手都在决赛中出现，但美国选手令人失望。"；第三段，"在牙买加选手博尔特以9

秒 69 的成绩成为奥运百米冠军后次日,谢莉·安·弗雷泽以 10 秒 78 的成绩获女子百米决赛冠军,谢伦·辛普森和克伦·斯图尔特以 10 秒 98 的成绩并列第二。"第四段,"美国选手劳琳·威廉斯以 11 秒 03 成绩名列第四,穆娜·李以 11 秒 07 成绩名列第五,托里·爱德华兹以 11 秒 20 成绩名列第八(最后)",点出了美国选手无缘奖牌的局面。第五段至最后一段是描述牙买加和美国参加决赛选手的参赛感想与背景信息。

在译文 2 中,原文的信息内容在译文的第一段、第二段、第六段与最后一段传达出来,译文的第一段为"在周日的奥运比赛中,谢莉·安·弗雷泽携其他两位牙买加选手获女子百米决赛冠军";第二段为,"谢莉·安·弗雷泽以 10 秒 78 的成绩创个人最好纪录获金牌,谢伦·辛普森和克伦·斯图尔特以 10 秒 98 的成绩并列获得银牌";第六段为"牙买加团队击败美国由劳琳·威廉斯、穆娜·李和托里·爱德华兹组成的强势选手舰队";最后一段为,"牙买加女选手重塑了其同伴博尔特于周六晚在奥林匹克赛场的神话。博尔特以 9 秒 69 的成绩获得了男子 100 米冠军,刷新了世界纪录"。其他段落(三、四、五)描述了辛普森和斯图尔特赛后为国争光的喜悦心情。

由此可见,译文 1 和译文 2 很多内容都有创作的成分,虽然与主题完全相关,但毕竟是原文中所没有的内容。因此,译文 1 和 2 都通过译写的方法,增加了读者所想知道的信息,满足了读者的期待需要。

5　本章结语

新闻翻译属于跨文化信息传播,绝非仅仅是语言的转换,需要将信息重塑、编辑、合成和转型,以方便读者的理解和感受。由于不同语言和文化之间在话语权力和地位方面是不平等的,因此新闻翻译者需要注意新闻词语在特定语境中的文化内涵与政治含义,有意识地选择和创造文本,在翻译过程中,译者需要把握"功能加忠诚原则",根据目的语语境进行重新阐释、编译、重组和创作,如标题的变更、段落的重排,背景知识的增删等,以确保译文能够客观、简明、通顺、流畅地将信息传递给受众。因此在某种意义上来说,新闻译者已经不是普通意义上的译者,而是具备了翻译能力的新闻译者。新闻译者所关心的也不再是译文是否忠实于原文,而更多地关注译文是否客观真实地传达出原文的信息。但是,由于新闻报道的过程太多、太杂,受到的制约因素太多,包括时间与空间制约、所在媒体的编撰方针等,因此受众所得到的新闻往往是经过多重加工处理过的文本。考虑到多种制约因素,新闻翻译和编辑的过程应该是多维度的,不仅要满足所在媒体的编辑方针和意识形态立场,而且还要认识到原语和译语在文化期待上的不同,才能确保新闻译文的真实性与可信度,获得目的语读者的认可与赞同。

第三章 政论翻译

1 政论文体特征与翻译特点

政论文体包括新闻媒体政论,党政机关、政治团体的宣言、声明,报纸期刊的政治性社论、思想评论、国际时事评论,以及自然、社会科学学术论文等文章体裁。翻译界所称的政论翻译,从文体角度而言,应为议论文的翻译,包括政论文、社科论著、评论、政治性演说等的翻译。作为翻译理论与实践学科一个重要组成部分的政论翻译,历来是世界各国政治、外交、军事、经济、文化以及国际政治生活中一个不可或缺的工具,在社会发展中发挥着重要的意识形态作用,是使国际人士了解本国政治和经济发展的第一窗口。由于政论文在内容上是系统阐述自己的看法以赢得读者的认同,因此作者都力图使自己的文章具有说服力,这就必然决定了政论文具有丰富的思想内涵、构思严谨且逻辑性强的特点。政论性文章与科技文章、新闻报道、文学作品等不同。在政论文中,由于政论文使用的场合比较严肃,语气强烈,口吻郑重,有时涉及的话题比较敏感,因此政论文翻译必须考虑它本身的语体特点且要多加推敲,力求文章简洁,同时政论文的翻译要准确,与原文内容一致,不能有任何偏差和异议,否则不利于两国的文化交流,更有甚者,有可能导致国家之间的摩擦,甚至损害国家的利益。

政论文的文体特征主要如下:(1)一定的政治倾向;(2)用词庄重、典雅、规范、严谨;(3)句子结构比较复杂,句型变化多样;(4)重视修辞,兼有科技语体和文艺语体的某些特点,把科学的论证和形象的描绘交织在一起,形成自己独特的风格;(5)语篇逻辑严密,说理性强。现以 Abraham Lincoln 的"The Gettysburg Address"(《葛底斯堡演讲词》)为例说明。

【例1】

Four score and seven years ago our fathers brought forth, upon this continent, a new nation, conceived in Liberty, and dedicated to the proposition that all men are created equal. Now we are engaged in a great civil war, testing whether that nation, or any nation so conceived, and so dedicated, can long endure. We are met here on a great battlefield of that war. We have come to dedicate a portion of it as a final resting place for those who here gave their lives that that nation might live. It is altogether fitting and proper that we should do this.

But in a larger sense we can not dedicate—we can not consecrate—we can not hallow this ground. The brave men, living and dead, who struggled, here, have consecrated it far above our poor power to add or detract. The world will little note, nor long remember, what we say here, but it can never forget what they did here.

It is for us, the living, rather to be dedicated here to the unfinished work which they have, thus far, so nobly carried on. It is rather for us to be here dedicated to the great task remaining before us—that from these honored dead we take increased devotion to that cause for which they here gave the last full measure of devotion—that we here highly resolve that these dead shall not have died in vain; that this nation shall have a new birth of freedom; and that this government of the people, by the people, for the people, shall not perish from the earth.

本篇《葛底斯堡演讲词》是林肯在公墓落成典礼上的致词，虽不足三分钟，却被认为是政论文演讲词精品中的精品。林肯总统使用了许多比较正式的词语，大词、富有强烈文学色彩的词语以及排比句、强调句等，使全文措辞端庄，语体庄重，层次分明，颇有气势，表达出演讲者深厚的情感与神圣庄严的语气。因此，在翻译时，应从以下四个方面来把握：(1)句式上，长句与短句的结合、掉尾句与松散句的结合、简单句与复合句的结合，使得语篇充满哀婉动人情绪，具有强烈的感染力和宏大的气势，翻译时要注意保持这种风格。(2)要注意保持原文的各种修辞手法，如排比、对偶等，以更好地体现原文的风貌，基本的翻译策略应该是在顺译或直译的基础上讲究变通。(3)语篇措辞典雅端庄，风格洗练有力，翻译时要注重政论文的特点、文体、语境等各种因素，注重词语的锤炼。(4)内容上具有深刻的历史背景和丰富的思想内涵，旁征博引，所涉及的思想内容既有纵向的历史深度，又有横向的时代广度。因此，翻译时要求译者必须弄清原文中涉及的历史文化和社会背景知识，从句子的表层含义深入到句子的深层含义，并将其意译或以注释等其他方式表达出来。

下面是节选自此演讲词的三个译文版本，前两个译文分别由著名的翻译家张培基和许渊冲教授翻译，最后一个译文来自《英语世界》杂志。现以其中的第一句为例。

Four score and seven years ago our fathers brought forth, upon this continent, a new nation, conceived in Liberty, and dedicated to the proposition that all men are created equal.

译文1：

八十七年前，我们的先辈们在这个大陆上创立了一个新国家，它孕育于自由之中，奉行一切人生来平等的原则。(张培基译)

译文2：

八十七年前，我们的先辈在这个大陆上建立了一个以自由为思想、以人人平等为宗旨的新国家。(许渊冲译)

译文3：

八十七年前我们的先辈在这块大陆上建立了一个新的国家，这个国家在争取自由中诞生，忠于人人生来平等这一信念。(选自《英语世界》)

由以上译文可以看出，Four score and seven years ago的用法远远正式于eighty-seven years ago，因此"八十七年前"的译文远远好于"87年前"。此外，原文是排比句式，而且使用了brought forth, conceived, dedicated和proposition这类非常庄重正式的词语，因此译文应注意传达出原文的风格,由此看来,张先生的译文更好一些。

此外,政论文还有很多政治新词的应用,如:WMD(weapon of mass destruction 大规模杀伤性武器)、科学发展观(scientific outlook on development)、三个"代表"(three represents)、八荣八耻(eight honors & eight disgraces)等。在翻译这类新词时,译者需要注意捕捉到这类词语的内涵以及相关的政治内容及其意识形态,否则就会歪曲原文的含义。这一部分将在以下相关内容中进行阐释。

2 政论文体翻译原则

我们可以用合作原则来指导政论文体的翻译。合作原则是由格莱斯(1975)提出的语用原则,主要包括四个准则:质的准则(Maxim of Quality),量的准则(Maxim of Quantity),方式准则(Maxim of Manner)和关系准则(Maxim of Relevance)。下面将探讨合作原则及其在翻译中的应用。

2.1 质的准则

(1) 不要说自知是虚假的话语(Do not say what you believe to be false)。
(2) 不要说缺乏足够证据的话(Do not say that for which you lack adequate evidence)。

【例2】
联合王国政府声明:联合王国政府于1997年7月1日将香港交还给"中华人民共和国"。

译文:
The Government of U. K, declares that it will restore Hong Kong to the People's Republic of China with effect from 1 July 1997.

该段原文选自1986年中华人民共和国政府和大不列颠及北爱尔兰联合王国政府关于香港问题的联合声明。原文中的"交还"译作 restore 十分贴切。该译文一开始拟使用 return 一词隐含着英国政府拒绝承认历史上曾存在的不平等条约,因为 return 意为"to go or come back, as to an earlier condition or place(返回,如回到一个早先的状态或位置)",而 "restore" 在英语词典中的解释是:"bring back to original state by rebuilding, repairing, amending etc.",意为"通过修复、重建而恢复到原来的状态、位置或所属",因此译文应将"交还"译作 restore,而不是 return。由此可见,政论文中的用语往往体现着国家的时事政策方针,关系到国家的政治、民主、外交等政策。因此,政论文要求译者首先必须具有高度的政治敏感并站稳政治立场,对于重要的有政治含义的词语,务必审慎选择。

【例3】
• 台湾问题
译文1:
Taiwan issue(误)

译文 2：

Taiwan question（正）

• 台湾前途系于祖国统一

译文 1：

The future of Taiwan lies in its reunification with the mainland.（误）

译文 2：

The future of Taiwan lies in the reunification of the motherland.（正）

2.2 量的准则

(1) 所说的话应该满足交际所需的量（Make your contribution to the conversation as informative as necessary）。

【例 4】

深入贯彻落实科学发展观，要求我们始终坚持"一个中心、两个基本点"的基本路线。党的基本路线是党和国家的生命线，是实现科学发展的政治保证。以经济建设为中心是兴国之要，是我们党、我们国家兴旺发达和长治久安的根本要求；四项基本原则是立国之本，是我们党、我们国家生存发展的政治基石；改革开放是强国之路，是我们党、我们国家发展进步的活力源泉。要坚持把以经济建设为中心同四项基本原则、改革开放这两个基本点统一于发展中国特色社会主义的伟大实践，任何时候都决不能动摇。

译文：

To thoroughly apply the Scientific Outlook on Development, we must always adhere to the Party's basic line of taking economic development as the central task and upholding the Four Cardinal Principles and the reform and opening-up policy, known as "one central task and two basic points". As the lifeblood of the Party and the country, this basic line provides the political guarantee for scientific development. Taking economic development as the central task is vital to invigorating our nation and is the fundamental requirement for the robust growth and lasting stability of the Party and the nation. The Four Cardinal Principles are the very foundation for building our country and the political cornerstone for the survival and development of the Party and the nation. Reform and opening up are the path to a stronger China and the source of vitality for the Party and the nation in development and progress. We will continue to apply the line of "one central task and two basic points" in its entirety in our great endeavor to develop socialism with Chinese characteristics; we will never deviate from this line.

原文选自 2007 年胡锦涛主席在党的十七大上的报告。其中"一个中心、两个基本点"是中国共产党第十三次全国代表大会提出的党在社会主义初级阶段的基本路线的核心，是指以经济建设为中心，坚持四项基本原则，坚持改革开放。由于东西方文化差异，如果把汉语的"一个中心、两个基本点"直接简单翻译成"one central task and two basic points"而不作阐释，那就会使英文读者不知所云，因此译者应该在此基础上进一步补充信息，在传达原政论文宣传功能的前提下,努力把中国文化介绍给西方读者。我们看译文:"taking economic development as the central task and upholding the Four Cardinal Principles and the reform and opening up policy, known as "one central task and two basic points"对该术语做了简单阐释,意思清晰明了,因此可以说是一个成功的译文。当然这需要译者不仅要准确地把握党和国家的方针政策,紧密关注国内外的政治、社会、经济及其他方面的重大事件,而且也要更深入了解中国的传统文化和意识形态。

(2)所说的话不应超出交际所需的量

【例 5】

新时期最突出的标志是与时俱进。我们党坚持马克思主义的思想路线,不断探索和回答什么是社会主义、怎样建设社会主义,建设什么样的党、怎样建设党,实现什么样的发展、怎样发展等重大理论和实际问题,不断推进马克思主义中国化,坚持并丰富党的基本理论、基本路线、基本纲领、基本经验。社会主义和马克思主义在中国大地上焕发出勃勃生机,给人民带来更多福祉,使中华民族大踏步赶上时代前进潮流,迎来伟大复兴的光明前景。

译文:

Keeping up with the times is the most prominent hallmark of the new period. Adhering to the Marxist ideological line, the Party has been constantly seeking answers to major theoretical and practical questions such as what socialism is and how to build it, what kind of party we must build and how to build it, and what kind of development China should achieve and how to achieve it. The Party has been constantly adapting Marxism to conditions in China, and adhering to and enriching its own basic theory, line, program and experience. Socialism and Marxism have shown great vitality on Chinese soil, brought more benefits to the people, and enabled the Chinese nation to catch up with the trend of the times in great strides and see the bright future of national rejuvenation.

原文同样选自十七大报告。政论翻译要忠实于原文的内容与严肃的风格,特别是官方政论文,更应如此。由于中英文文体惯例不同,为符合译文惯例,使译语地道规范,可对汉语政论文中出现的重复词进行删减或用代词替代,但却不能对原文内容进行删减。原文有很多重复词,如"社会主义"、"党"、"基本"等,而译文则应尽量避免重复,如用代称"it"或省略"basic"等以符合英文的表达习惯。如果译文拘泥于原文形式,把原文的"社会主义","党","基本"等词一字不漏地译出来,就会破坏英语的行文习惯,违反英汉语言的差异。举一反三,"经济大起或大落,都不利于经济发展,不利于改革开放,不利于社会稳定"一句则可以只译一个"不利于",即"Both drastic upturns and downturns in economic growth are bad for economic development, reform and opening up, and social stability"。

此外,汉语中常用很多概念词、抽象词以及概括词等来表达,而英语则相反。如"邓小平是中国改革开放和现代化建设的总工程师"中"建设"一词的应用,在译成英语时完全可以省略,即"Deng Xiaoping is the chief architect of China's reform, opening up and modernization",而不需添加"construction"一词。

2.3 方式准则

(1) 避免晦涩(Avoid obscurity of expression)。
(2) 避免歧义(Avoid ambiguity)。
(3) 简练(Be brief; avoid unnecessary wordiness)。
(4) 井井有条(Be orderly)。

【例6】
几年来,我们坚持"两手抓、两手都要硬"的方针,大力加强社会主义精神文明建设,不断提高全民族的思想道德和科学文化素质,为现代化建设提供强有力的精神动力和智力支持,也有力地促进了经济和社会协调发展。

译文:
Over the past few years, we have adhered to the principle of "doing two types of work at the same time and attaching equal importance to both", worked hard to strengthen socialist spiritual civilization, continued to raise the ideological and ethical standards and scientific and cultural levels of the whole nation, provided great spiritual motivation and intellectual support to the modernization drive and promoted coordinated economic and social development.

该段原文选自2003年朱镕基的政府工作报告。原文中的"两手抓、两手都要硬"属于中国现当代独有的政治习语表达,是邓小平同志提出的关于我国社会主义现代化建设的一个重要战略思想,也是我们党和国家的战略方针。邓小平同志在不同的场合,针对不同的问题,提出过不同的"两手抓"。例如,一手抓改革开放,一手抓打击犯罪;一手抓建设,一手抓法制;一手抓物质文明,一手抓精神文明等。"两手抓"是一系列相互配套方针的统称,包含着极其丰富的内涵,其内容不尽相同,针对性各有侧重,但归结到一点,"两手抓"主要还是指同时抓物质文明和精神文明。因此,在翻译此类习语时,不能简单之直译为"grasp with both hands and do things in a strong way",否则会引起歧义。根据方式准则,为避免歧义与晦涩,译者可采用意译的办法,如此例中的译文:"doing two types of work at the same time and attaching equal importance to both",或者其他译法,如"grasping both links at the same time and attaching sufficient importance to both"。其他还有几种译法可供参考,如"giving equal importance to economic development on one hand and to the development of socialist culture and ideology on the other hand";"placing equal emphasis on material progress and ethical and cultural progress, with neither aspects neglected"。

2.4 关系准则

关系准则即说话要有关联。由于英汉语言差异,如在汉语中的某些固定习语,如果直译成英语,就会令读者不明其意,感觉前后所说内容并不相关,解决的办法是采取意译,把原文的核心含义传递出去,如"豆腐渣工程"可以翻译成"bean-curd projects, so named because they fall apart easily","砸三铁"可以翻译成"break iron rice bowl, guaranteed wages and permanent position"；"白条"可以翻译成"IOU（I owe you）note"。

【例 7】

President-elect Barack Obama said Sunday the economy will get worse before it gets better, pledged a recovery plan "equal to the task" and warned lawmakers that the days of pork barrel spending are over.

译文 1：

上周美国总统当选人巴拉克·奥巴马声称，美国经济在改善之前还会继续恶化，他表示上任后将推出一套有效的经济复苏方案，并警告立法者"花费猪肉桶"的日子已经结束。

译文 2：

美国总统当选人巴拉克·奥巴马于上周日称，美国经济尚未探底，在改善之前还会继续恶化，他保证上任后将推出一套有效的经济复苏计划，并警告国会议员别再打联邦经费的主意。

原文节选自奥巴马的发言"Obama warns economy will get even worse（奥巴马警告，美国经济将会再恶化）"。将译文比较可以看出，译文 1 把原文中 pork barrel 按照字面意义翻译为"猪肉桶"，这使得译文读者在读译文时莫名其妙。而 pork barrel 的引申意义指"议员向联邦政府为其所在选区争取用于造桥修路、筑水坝等的建设经费"。不过有时议员为了选票，会与利益团体挂钩，用申请联邦经费"奖赏"那些在竞选中给自己出过力的当地企业和群体。"猪肉桶"现在专指国会议员"为本州选民和利益集团的项目争取联邦经费"的现象，其中部分项目纯粹是浪费公共资源。因此，译文 2 更胜一筹。

3　政论文体翻译策略

就翻译策略而言，奈达(1993)认为能直译就直译，不能直译就采取迂回的办法以达到译文与原文的功能对等。纽马克(1988)认为，语义翻译与传意翻译的结合使用可以使译文更地道、更确切。根据这两位翻译家的观点，结合政论翻译的特点，我们可以采用语义翻译与传意翻译相结合的策略。

3.1 语义翻译

语义翻译是"在目的语语言结构和语义许可的范围内，把原作者在原文中表达的意思准确地再现出来"（Newmark, 1981/1988：22）。语义翻译重视的是原文的形式和原作者的原意，而不是目的语语境及其表达方式，更不是要把译文变为目的语文化情境中之物。然而，需要指出的是，由于语义翻译把原文的一词一句视为神圣，有时会产生前后矛盾、语义含糊甚至是错误的译文，因此在翻译时应特别注意。纽马克本人也认为，语义翻译并非一种完美的翻译模式，而是与交际翻译模式一样，在翻译实践措施中处于编译与逐行译之间的中庸之道（Newmark, 1988：45）。

汉语中的某些政治术语，如"科学发展观（scientific outlook on development）"、"一个中国原则（one-China principle）"、"保证人民的知情权、参与权、表达权和监督权（ensure people's right to know, to participate, to express and to supervise)"、"科教兴国战略(strategy of invigorating China through science and education)"、"生态补偿机制(ecological compensation mechanism)"等可采用字面直译法,而另一些术语则需要进行调整,需要根据语境传达出原术语的真正意义,而不是字面意义,如"不搞一刀切(without imposing a single solution)"、"'走出去'战略(go global strategy)"、"达到小康(reach the better-off level)"、"超常规发展战略(foresight development strategies)"。

【例8】

中日两国是一衣带水的邻邦。中国有一句古话:"召远在修近,闭祸在除怨。"这是管子的话。在中日两国政府的共同努力下,我们就消除影响两国关系的政治障碍问题达成了共识,这就促成了安倍首相去年10月访问中国。中日两国发展合作关系,世代友好,符合历史潮流,符合人民愿望。虽然现在两国间还存在许多问题,但是已有一个基石,就是三个政治文件。

译文:

China and Japan are close neighbors facing each other across a narrow strip of water. As the ancient Chinese philosopher Kuan-tzu observed: "To win distant friends, one needs, first of all, to have good relations with his neighbors. To avoid adversity, one needs to ease animosity." Thanks to the joint efforts of the Chinese and Japanese governments, agreement was reached on removing the political obstacle to the growth of China-Japan relations. This led to Japanese Prime Minister Shinzo Abe's visit to China last October. To promote cooperation between China and Japan and friendship between the two countries from generation to generation is the trend of history and meets the aspiration of our two peoples. It is true that there are still many problems between China and Japan, but there are three political documents between the two countries, and they form the foundation of China-Japan relations.

原文节选自2007年3月温家宝总理会见两会记者的发言。当提到中日关系这个敏感的话题时,温总理引用了典故"一衣带水"和"召远在修近,闭祸在除怨"。"一衣带水"是指一条衣带那样狭窄的水,出自《南史·陈后主纪》:"我为百姓父母,岂可一衣带水不拯之乎?",引申含义是指"虽有江河湖海相隔,但距离不远,不足以成为交往的阻碍"。"召远在修近,闭祸在除怨"这一典故出自《管子·版法》,其含意是,"要招纳远方的人们,就要先处理好近邻的关系;要避免祸端,必须先消除怨气"。中日关系的基石是两国曾经签署的三个政治文件,从政治上、法律上和事实上总结两国关系的过去,也从长远和战略上,规划了两国的未来。既然日本至今还承认这三个政治文件,则说明中日关系的基础还在。如何解决彼此之间的矛盾?既然中日两国是一衣带水的邻邦,所以,要解决中日之间现存的矛盾,必须从历史入手,让日本现领导人想起过去的师谊关系。译文基本属于语义翻译。其中的典故"一衣带水"与"召远在修近,闭祸在除怨"分别译为"close neighbors facing each other across a narrow strip of water"与"To win distant friends, one needs, first of all, to have good relations with his neighbors. To avoid adversity, one needs to ease animosity",无论从形式还是内容都非常成功、贴切地传达了原文的意思。

【例 9】

If there is anyone out there who still doubts that America is a place where all things are possible; who still wonders if the dream of our founders is alive in our time; who still questions the power of our democracy, tonight is your answer. It's the answer told by lines that stretched around schools and churches in numbers this nation has never seen; by people who waited three hours and four hours, many for the first time in their lives, because they believed that this time must be different; that their voices could be that difference.

译文 1：

假如还有人不相信美国是一个不存在不可能的地方，还有人怀疑开国之父们的梦想依然在影响着我们这个时代，还有人质疑美利坚民主的力量，那么，他们的疑惑在今夜得到了解答。在学校和教堂外面，人们排起了长长的队伍，人数之多在美国历史上前所未有。为了投上自己的一票，他们可以等待三个小时、四个小时。许多人是一生中第一次参加投票，因为他们坚信这一次必须有所变革，而他们的声音将举足轻重。

译文 2：

美国是否暗藏一切皆有可能的巨大潜力？美国是否已经实现开国者锻造的美国梦？民主信仰是否具有强大力量？如果还有人对此报以怀疑，那么今晚这里发生的一切就是答案。学校旁、教堂边，无数人都在排队投票，这一情景我们已经多年未见；3 个小时、4 个小时，他们为此而等候良久，这是很多同胞有生以来的第一次。因为他们相信，这一次，将不同以往；这一次，因为他们的呼声而有所不同。

译文 3：

假如还有人怀疑美国是否是一切皆有可能的地方，困惑于我们的建国先辈们所持有的梦想在今天是否鲜活，质疑于我们民主的力量是否强大，那么今晚这些疑问都有了答案。这是由那些在学校、教堂门外排着长长队伍的人们给出的答案，这种情形在美国历史上前所未有。为了投票，他们排队长达三、四个小时。其中许多人是一生中第一次投票，因为他们相信，这次一定与以往不同，而自己的声音肯定会使一切与过去不同。

原文是美利坚合众国民主党人巴拉克·胡赛因·奥巴马（Barack Hussein Obama）于 2008 年 11 月 5 日的竞选演讲词。这位首位美国历史上的黑人总统，同时作为白宫的新一任主人，他在胜选后随即在其芝加哥的竞选总部进行了一场充满激情的"胜选演说"。原文的前三分句最好翻译成陈述句，其中第一分句译文 1 翻译成"不相信……不存在不可能的"，故意把英语简单的原话复杂化，因此需要改进；译文 2 采用问句的方式，语气稍显强烈。关于 alive 的翻译，译文 1 译成"影响"，译文 2 译成"实现"，属于错译，因为 alive 是"活着"、"梦想没有死掉"、"还很鲜活"的意思。"must be different"译文 1 译成"必须有所变革"，命令语气非常强烈，译文 2 译成"将"，肯定语气也比较强烈，根据语境，其实应该把该词的"估计，猜测"的含义翻译出来。由此，我们尝试翻译为译文 3。

【例10】

It's the answer spoken by young and old, rich and poor, Democrat and Republican, black, white, Latino, Asian, Native American, gay, straight, disabled and not disabled — Americans who sent a message to the world that we have never been a collection of red states and blue states; we are, and always will be, the United States of America.

译文 1：

无论年龄，无论贫富，无论民主党人或共和党人，无论黑人、白人，无论拉美裔、亚裔、印第安人，无论同性恋、异性恋，无论残障人、健康人，所有的人，他们向全世界喊出了同一个声音：我们并不隶属"红州"与"蓝州"的对立阵营，我们属于美利坚合众国，现在如此，永远如此！

译文 2：

这是所有美国人民共同给出的答案——无论老少贫富，无论是民主党还是共和党，无论是黑人、白人、拉美裔、亚裔、原住民，是同性恋者还是异性恋者、残疾人还是健康人——我们从来不是"红州"和"蓝州"的对立阵营，我们是美利坚合众国，永远都是。

译文 3：

这个答案是由下列人士给出的：年轻人和老人、富人和穷人、民主党人和共和党人、黑人、白人、拉美裔人、亚裔人、美国本土人、同性恋、异性恋、残疾人和健全人。所有这些美国人，都在向世界发出一个信息，那就是，我们从来不是红州（代表共和党）和蓝州（代表民主党）的混合体；我们是，也将永远是，美利坚合众国这个整体。

该段原文同样选自奥巴马的竞选演讲词。以上三个译文基本上都采用语义翻译的策略，但是将译文比较，可以看出译文3相对来说稍微好些。原因有三：第一，"not disabled"如果译为"健康人"，则属于错译，因为"残疾"的反面是"健全"，而残疾人的身体也可以是健康的，"健康"只与"有病"相反，残疾人不是病人，而前两个译文都译成"健康人"，显然不合适。第二，sent a message是指"发出一条信息"，而不是发出同一个信息，如果译成后者，则属于增译，由此可见，前两个译文都不妥帖。第三，在"we have never been a collection of red states and blue states; we are, and always will be, the United States of America"一句中，奥巴马巧妙地使用了"state"一词，强调大家要团结，也就是说不是"红州"，也不是"蓝州"，而是美洲"合众州"，也正好是"美国"的意思，因为他接下来还要就两党支持者等问题进一步表述自己的立场。此外，译者在括号中给出注解使意思更加明确。因此，译文3从形式到内容都和原文很贴切。

3.2 传意翻译

传意翻译是"努力使译文对目的语读者所产生的效果与原文对原语读者所产生的效果相同"（Newmark,1981/1988:22）。也就是说，传意翻译的重点是根据目的语的语言、文化和语用方式传递信息，而不是尽量忠实地复制原文的文字。译者在交际翻译中有较大的自由度去解释原文、调整文体、排除歧义，甚至是修正原作者的错误。由于译者要达到某一交际目的，有了特定的目的读者群，因此他所翻译的译文必然会打破原文的局限。值得注意的是,传意翻译并不是一种极端的翻译策略,它和语义翻译一样是翻译中的"中庸之道"(Hatim & Mason,1990:7),既不像编译那么自由,也没有逐行译那么拘谨。

比较而言,语义翻译强调的是保持原文的内容,在语义翻译中,译者仍然以原文为基础,坚守在原语文化的阵地之中,只是解释原文的涵义,帮助目的语读者理解文本的意思。传意翻译强调的是译文的效果,其关注点是目的语读者,尽量为这些读者排除阅读或交际上的困难与障碍,使交际顺利进行。一般说来,如果语义翻译可能导致读者对其所指意义产生误解,或者译文毫无意义,或者译文难以理解,以致使译文的一般读者不得不将其放弃时,译者必须采用传意翻译,除非原文有意为之。此外,如果语义翻译会使读者对原语的联想意义发生严重误解,或造成原语文体价值的损失,译者也必须采用传意翻译,以便能反映出原语的联想意义。

政论文体中一些特有的汉语文化词汇在翻译成英语时,需要采用传意翻译的策略。例如,

【例 11】
- 安居工程:housing project for low-income families
- 半拉子工程:an unfinished project
- 豆腐渣工程:jerry-built project
- 畅通工程:smooth traffic project
- 长线产品:product in excessive supply
- 带薪分流:assign redundant civil servants to other jobs while allowing them to retain their rank and benefits
- 包干到户:work contracted to households
- 人才流动:brain drain
- 红头文件:official document
- 装红白脸:with some wearing the white make-up of the stage villain and others the red make-up of the hero
- 肝胆相照:treat each other with all sincerity
- 妄自菲薄:belittle oneself

【例 12】
我说中印两国友好的时间有 2000 多年,可以说占 99.9%,两国的冲突的时间很短,不到 0.1%。即使这个冲突,也已化干戈为玉帛。

译文:

I told him that the duration of time when China and India enjoy friendly relations stretched 2,000 years, or 99.9 percent of our total interactions. In terms of conflict, the conflict between our countries only lasted two years, or less than 0.1 percent of the conflict, we could always turn swords into ploughs.

原文是温家宝 2004 年在记者招待会上的发言。其中,温总理引用了汉语习语"化干戈为玉帛"。"化干戈为玉帛"语出《淮南子·原道训》。干戈指古代兵器,借指战争;玉帛指玉

器和丝织品。该习语常用以比喻争战者能舍弃纷争，追求和平。英语习语"beat your swords into plowshares"可表达相同的意思，该英语习语源于《圣经·旧约·以赛亚书》第二章第四节："And they shall beat their swords into plowshares, and their spears into pruning hooks; nation shall not lift sword against nation, neither shall they learn war any more."意思是"大家要将刀剑打成犁头，把长矛制成镰刀，各国从此和平相处，不再打仗"。因此，根据上下文，"化干戈为玉帛"译为"turn swords into ploughs"非常贴切。

【例 13】

只要我们不动摇、不懈怠、不折腾，坚定不移地推进改革开放，坚定不移地走中国特色社会主义道路，就一定能够胜利实现这一宏伟蓝图和奋斗目标。

译文 1：

The goal would surely come true if "we don't sway back and forth, don't relax our efforts, and don't get side-tracked on our way to constructing a socialist society with Chinese characteristics".

译文 2：

As long as we firmly take the China-specific route of socialism by promoting reforms and opening up with no wavering, no sluggishness and no trying our luck back and forth, the great blueprint of our aims will be (triumphantly) realized definitely.

译文 3：

So long as we steadfastly push forward the reform and opening-up policy and adhere to the socialist road with Chinese characteristics with no faith-wavering, no effort-relaxation, and no self-defeating campaigns, the grand blueprint and the goal we strive for will be definitely realized.

原文选自胡锦涛在 2008 年纪念中共十一届三中全会召开三十周年大会上的重要讲话。那么什么是"不折腾"呢？《现代汉语词典》对折腾一词作了解释：(1)翻过来，倒过去；(2)反复做某事；(3)折磨。《新时代汉英大词典》等汉英词典解释为：(1)turn from side to side, toss and turn; (2) do something again; fool around with; mess with; (3) cause physical or mental suffering; torment。应该说这两种解释大体相当。

由于在汉语政治文献中所使用的"不折腾"大多具有特定政治含义，因此翻译时需要酌情考虑词语背后所隐含的文化背景特征。例如，新中国成立以来，历次的政治运动和反复都给国家发展造成不少损伤，如今，将过去的曲折、错误一律以"折腾"称之，表明中国不再做与经济发展无关的、内耗的路线辩论或政治斗争，防止和避免各级政府官员做劳民伤财的各种行为，以保证前进方向的正确性。通过译文比较发现：译文 1 "don't get side-tracked"与译文 2 "no trying our luck back and forth"只是强调了两种可供选择的行为之间不犹豫的态度，但是没有体现出胡总书记所强调的中国共产党人继续把改革开放伟大事业推进的坚定决心和必胜信念这一内涵，即没有反映出原词语的政治色彩。其他类似不同版本的译法还有：

- don't flip flop（不要翻来倒去，朝三暮四）
- don't make much ado about nothing（不要无事生非）
- don't sway back and forth（不要反复）
- don't act recklessly（不要采取不计后果的行动）
- stop making trouble and wasting time（不要制造麻烦，浪费时间）
- avoid futile actions（不做无用功）
- avoid policy volatility（避免政策多变）

如果译为"avoid self-inflicted setbacks（避免自己造成的挫折）"也不合适，原因是setback是一个静态的概念，而"折腾"一词在原文语境中是一个动态的概念。再看译文3，"no self-defeating campaigns"相对可取，因为campaign意为"an organized course of action for a particular purpose, esp. to arouse public interest"，体现出"有特定目的性的、有组织性的政治或意识形态运动"，因此较好地体现出"折腾"的外延特征；而self-defeating意为"自我挫败的"、"弄巧成拙的"、"不利于自己的企图的"、"费力不讨好的"、"自我拆台的"等含义。因此，将"不折腾"译为"no self-defeating campaigns"能从内涵和外延上很好地解释其概念的社会语境意义，也符合执政党领导人的身份、语气特征和特定场合所传达言外语用含意特征如警示和反省等。

3.3 语义翻译与传意翻译并用

当然，在实际翻译时，不可能只采用一种方法，很多情况是两种方法结合使用。

【例 14】
- 菜篮子工程：vegetable basket project, or Non-Staple Food Project—a project for establishing production bases and increasing non-staple food supply
- 希望工程：Hope Project, a project to enlist popular support to help children of poor families receive schooling
- 863 计划：the March 1986 High-tech Program or the March 1986 program to stimulate the development of high technologies
- 两条腿走路：walking on two legs, i.e., to do two related things simultaneously
- 两个确保：guarantee for the pensions on time and in full of the living allowances for retirees and the basic payment for workers laid off from state-owned enterprises
- 三个"代表"：three represents: the Communist Party of China represents the requirement to develop advanced productive forces, and orientation towards advanced culture, and the fundamental interests of the overwhelming majority of the people in China
- 干部四化：the four standards set for leading cadres: the ranks of cadres should be more revolutionary, younger in average age, better educated and more professionally competent
- 五个统筹：five balanced aspects: balancing urban and rural development, balancing

development among regions, balancing economic and social development, balancing development of man and nature, and balancing domestic development and opening wider to the outside world

- 白色农业：white agriculture (also called "white engineering agriculture")：It refers to microbiological agriculture and biological cell agriculture
- 草根工业：grass root industry：it refers to village and township enterprises which take root among farmers and grow like wild grass
- 胡子工程：long-drawn-out project：a project which takes so long that young workers become bearded

【例15】

我们理解、信赖、关心台湾同胞,将继续实施和充实惠及广大台湾同胞的政策措施,依法保护台湾同胞的正当权益,支持海峡西岸和其他台商投资相对集中地区经济发展。两岸同胞要加强交往,加强经济文化交流,继续拓展领域、提高层次,推动直接"三通",使彼此感情更融洽、合作更深化,为实现中华民族伟大复兴而共同努力。

译文：

We understand, trust and care about our compatriots in Taiwan, and we will, therefore, continue to implement and enrich the policies and measures that benefit them, protect their legitimate rights and interests in accordance with the law, and support economic development on the west shore of the Straits in Fujian Province and in other areas where Taiwan investment is concentrated. The compatriots on both sides of the Straits need to increase contacts, strengthen economic and cultural exchanges in more areas and at higher levels and push for the resumption of direct links of mail, transport and trade, so that they will develop greater empathy and closer cooperation and work together for the great rejuvenation of the Chinese nation.

原文选自胡锦涛在党的十七大上的报告。将译文与原文对照分析,我们可以看出译文除个别词汇以外基本上采取了语义翻译的方法,忠实、准确地传达出了原文的内容。其中,需要指出的是,原文中的"三通"是指实现台海两岸直接"通邮"、"通商"、"通航"的简称。"三通"的核心是实现两岸之间的直航,即海峡两岸的飞机、船舶可以由双方机场或港口,载运旅客、货物和邮件,不经由第三地而直接航行至对岸,以便为两岸人员各项交流提供便利的交通运输条件。因此如果把此短语如果直译为"three links",就会词不达意,因此译者采取传意翻译的方法,解释为"direct links of mail, transport and trade",使读者准确地理解原短语的意思。

【例16】

建立与我国国情相适应、与我国经济发展水平相适应的社会保障体系,是一项重要而艰巨的任务。要继续做好"两个确保"工作,搞好"三条保障线"的衔接。稳步推进国有企业下岗职工基本生活保障向失业保险并轨。

译文:

We need to build a social security network suited to China's conditions and the level of our economic development. This is an important yet demanding task. We should continue improving the work of guarantee for the payment on time and in full of the living allowances for workers laid off from state-owned enterprises and for the basic pensions for retirees, known as "two guarantees", and better integrate the "three-stage guarantee" program①. We will steadily integrate the subsistence allowances for these workers into the unemployment insurance system.

① the programs for ensuring the basic cost of living allowance for laid-off workers, the unemployment insurance program and the program of subsistence allowance for needy urban residents.

原文选自2004年的政府工作报告。其译文也是基本采用语义翻译与传意翻译并重的方法。原文中的"两个确保"是指确保国有企业下岗职工的基本生活,确保企业离退休人员基本养老金的按时足额发放。"三条保障线"是指职工基本生活保障、失业保障和城镇最低生活保障。如果对这些具有中国文化特色的词直译而不作任何解释,则会令读者不知所云,不能理解原文的含义。因此,译文对"两个确保"采取了文中解释的办法,对"三条保障线"采取了文外注释的办法,这样译文读者就能够更深刻地理解汉语特有政治词汇的内涵。

【例17】

A century ago, President Theodore Roosevelt's invitation of Booker T. Washington to dine at the White House was taken as an outrage in many quarters. America today is a world away from the cruel and frightful bigotry of that time. There is no better evidence of this than the election of an African-American to the presidency of the United States.

译文1:

一个世纪前,西奥多·罗斯福总统邀请布克·华盛顿(注:黑人教育家)到白宫共进晚餐。全国各地有许多人认为这是一个骇人听闻的事件。今天的美国已经是一个完全不同的世界了,骇人的残忍和可怕的偏执一去不复返了。最好的证据就是,今晚一个非洲裔美国人当选为美利坚合众国的总统。

译文2:

一个世纪以前,西奥多·罗斯福总统邀请布克·华盛顿在白宫共同进餐,这曾引起了许多人的愤怒。但今天的美国已经远离了那个时代的残忍以及可怕的顽固。再也没有比一位非洲裔美国人当选为美国总统更能证明这一点了。

原文选自2008年约翰·麦凯恩(John McCain)的落选演讲词。美国大选后,奥巴马当选,麦凯恩落选。在演说中他对奥巴马的能力和责任表达了自己的敬意,并说到这次大选是历史性的选举,美国历史上第一位非洲裔美国总统今日产生。通过译文比较发现,两个译文大体都采用语义翻译方法。相对而言,译文1更加符合汉语习惯,更加地道,更加贴近原文,而且译文1对Booker T. Washington作了简单的文内注释,有利于读者更好地理解上下文。布克·华盛顿(Booker Taliaferro Washington,1856—1915)是美国政治家、教育家、作家和自助的倡导者,他努力引领黑人摆脱奴役,是1890年到1915年之间美国黑人历史上的重要人物之一。但是很多中国读者并不熟悉这一背景,因此需要对人名进行文内注释。

由于政论文体与新闻报刊紧密相连,因此,有时也会出现因为版面篇幅等原因而对原文进行摘译或译述的现象。

【例18】

Mr. Speaker, Mr. President Pro Tempore, members of Congress, and fellow Americans , in the normal course of events , presidents come to this chamber to report on the state of the union. Tonight, no such report is needed; it has already been delivered by the American people.

We have seen it in the courage of passengers who rushed terrorists to save others on the ground. Passengers like an exceptional man named Todd Beamer. And would you please help me welcome his wife Lisa Beamer here tonight?

We have seen the state of our union in the endurance of rescuers working past exhaustion. We've seen the unfurling of flags, the lighting of candles, the giving of blood, the saying of prayers in English, Hebrew and Arabic. We have seen the decency of a loving and giving people who have made the grief of strangers their own. My fellow citizens, for the last nine days, the entire world has seen for itself the state of union, and it is strong.

Tonight, we are a country awakened to danger and called to defend freedom. Our grief has turned to anger and anger to resolution. Whether we bring our enemies to justice or bring justice to our enemies, justice will be done.

译文1：

在正常程序下,美国总统来到这个会场作国情咨文报告,交代国家的状况。今晚,这一报告已无必要,因为国家的面貌已由美国人民表达了出来。

我们看到那些与恐怖分子搏斗的乘客所展现出来的勇气,我们也在搜救人员的努力中,看到了我们的国情。

今晚,我们是一个受危险而惊醒的国家,受召唤而保卫自由。我们的悲伤已化为愤怒,愤怒已化为决心。不论是我们将敌人绳之以法或是我们对敌人伸张正义,正义都将实现。

译文2：

(众院)议长先生、(参院)临时主席、国会议员们及美国同胞们：在正常程序下,美国总统来到国会是发表国情咨文。今晚,我们不需要这份咨文了,美国人民已经发表了。

我们看到那些乘客阻挡恐怖分子以保护陆地上的无辜平民所展现出来的勇气。这些乘客就像一位名叫托德·毕默的人一样了不起。今晚,请大家和我一起欢迎他的妻子莉萨·毕默。

我们也在搜救人员任劳任怨、筋疲力尽的工作中,看到了我们的国情。我们看到了国旗飘扬、烛火点燃、挽袖捐血以及众人的祈祷,用英语、犹太语和阿拉伯语祈祷。我们更看到了充满爱与奉献的人们,将陌生人的悲痛化为自己的悲痛。我的同胞们,过去九天来,整个世界都已经看到这份由人民谱写的国情咨文,那是笔力千钧的国情咨文。

今晚,我们是一个临危惊醒的国家,接受召唤保卫自由的国家。我们的悲伤化为愤怒,愤怒化为决心。不论是我们将敌人绳之以法或者我们对敌人伸张正义,正义都将实现。

原文是美国总统小布什在纽约"9.11"恐怖袭击事件之后,于2001年9月20日在美国国会联席会议上的演讲。译文1摘自香港《东方日报》,译文2摘自香港《明报》。显然,译文1不是"全译",而是"摘译"。但该译文与原文的基调保持了一致,且语篇满足了"衔接"与"连贯"等基本"谋篇"要素,因此是可以接受的译文。译文2则是"全译",是语义翻译的结果,也同样实现了"衔接"与"连贯"等基本的"谋篇"要素。例如,原文第四段最后一句:"My fellow citizens, for the last nine days, the entire world has seen for itself the state of union, and it is strong",译文为"我的同胞们,过去九天来,整个世界都已经看到这份由人民谱写的国情咨文,那是笔力千钧的国情咨文"。其中,"the state of union"之所以译为"(这份)由人民谱写的国情咨文",而非照字直译为"团结一致的状况",以及"it is strong"之所以译为"那是笔力千钧的国情咨文",而非译为"这是坚不可摧的(团结一致)",皆因译者考虑到了它们必须与演讲词前面的"...to report on the state of the union(……发表国情咨文)"保持结构上的"衔接"与语义、语境上的彼此呼应和连贯。

4 本章结语

政论文是作者针对当时现实生活中各种重大的政治问题和社会问题,从一定的立场出发,阐明自己的见解和主张,由于这类文章都有一定的政治倾向并涉及国家利益,因此语句措辞及其翻译都十分重要。因此,在翻译过程中,译者需要考虑政论文的文化背景和文体特点,把握政论文的翻译原则及其翻译策略,既要保留政论文文体本身所具有的严肃性和准确性,保持原作的修辞特征,同时也要根据译入语文化环境的特点,对译文作出某些调整,使之既符合译入语的习惯,同时又能够反映译出语的文化特点,这一点在汉英政论翻译中体现得尤为明显。这就需要译者既要精通东西方语言文化知识,深谙政论文体的语体特征,又要熟练运用翻译理论、翻译技巧及其翻译原则。本章所探讨的政论文的语义翻译与交际翻译策略是从整体上对政论文语篇翻译进行把握运用,具体翻译方法应该是具体情况具体分析,如可以采用增减法与重组法等翻译技巧进行翻译。

第四章 旅游翻译

1 旅游翻译分类与特性

旅游翻译可以分为笔译(如各类文本翻译,包括学术文本)、口译和导译(变数最大的一种特殊专业翻译)三大类。随着翻译学科的发展和细分,导译或导译学可以成为翻译学的一个新的分支。

作为一个大类,旅游翻译可谓内容丰富多彩、包罗万象,涉及几乎各种翻译方式和手段,是一门特别强调行业实践的翻译,强调交流有效性的翻译。

与其他文体翻译不同的是,旅游翻译(含导译)具有趣味性、理论性、客观描述性,更因其跨文化交际之特色,它还包括综合性、特殊性、灵活性、多变性及应变性。

旅游翻译的这些特性决定了旅游翻译的实践性,而在实践过程中,主要应该采用"案例分析(case study)法"和"任务型翻译法(task-based translation)",做到具体情况具体分析,不能一刀切。之所以采用这些特殊的翻译训练方法,是因为旅游翻译看似简单,实则"陷阱"(linguistic pitfall 和 translation pitfall)颇多,栽进去的学界、业界名人学者不在少数。

换言之,这个要求是通过对实际实践的描述而总结出来的一种"要求",不是事先的一种"规定性"之要求。

2 旅游文本文体要求

旅游翻译工作者应事先对旅游文本的范围特点和文体特点做必要的了解。

2.1 旅游文本范围特点

旅游文本涉及面很广。就大类而言,旅游文本包括涉及旅游资源、旅游产品、旅游会展、旅游统计、旅游文娱、旅游科研、旅游交通、旅行社、旅游饭店、旅游教育、旅游文学等的原语文本(source text,ST),与其对应的目的语(如英语)文本(target text,TT)。

若将上述范围缩小一些,ST 是指译者在工作中经常碰到的、约定俗成的那些应用型文本,包括旅游指南、旅游行程、旅游委托书、旅游意向书、旅游合同、旅游广告、旅游表格、导游解说词、景点介绍、参观点介绍、博物馆解说词、旅游推销手册、旅游宣传册、旅游地图、旅游宣传标语、文艺演出节目单、餐厅菜单、宾馆指示牌/标志、公园指示牌、参观点标语、各类通知、路标、地名、各种(旅游)会展/文本、各种(旅游)会议文本等。它们使用面广、应用频率高、实用性强、文体活泼,是旅游翻译应重点掌握的。

值得一提的是,即使是旅游文学文本,即山水诗歌、散文、楹联、古代碑文等,其 ST 又可分成静态文本(written text,WT)和动态文本(dynamic text,DT)。

正如我们之前指出的,旅游翻译并非易事。考虑到本书的定位,我们再把旅游文本范围缩小,于是主要涉及 ST 和 TT 的是旅游指南、旅游行程、景点介绍、参观点介绍、博物馆解说词、旅游宣传册、文艺演出节目单、餐厅菜单等。其他的文本的讨论则难以在此展开。

首先应掌握的旅游文本翻译,我们认为应重点掌握两类文本:导游指南和导译文本。前者涉及英汉互译,后者强调汉译英。这两类文本翻译最难教,也最难教会。

2.2 旅游文本文体特点

旅游文本,不论是英语还是汉语,都是一种应用文。英语的旅游 TT 主要分为两大类文体:分别以书面体和口语体为主。这两种语体具有不同的词汇要求和句法要求。

根据纽马克的文本分类理论,本章要特别讨论的文本可分为以下三种类型及其功能:

1. 信息型(informative text,IT),具有信息功能(informative function,IF);
2. 表达/描写型(expressive text,ET),具有表达功能(expressive function,EF);
3. 召唤型(vocative text,VT),具有召唤功能(vocative function,VF)。

具体而言,旅游指南,属 ET+EF,IT+IF,VT+VF 或三种类型及其功能兼而有之(以排在前边的类型为主),用词需生动形象、明白畅晓,句式需自然流畅、直截了当。

参观点介绍,属 IT+IF,ET+EF,VT+VF 或三种类型及其功能兼而有之(以排在前边的类型为主),用词需客观准确、通俗易懂,句式需简单句与复杂句相结合。

旅游推销手册,属 VT+VF,IT+IF 或两种类型兼而有之(以排在前边的类型为主),用词需简明生动、富有创意,句式应活泼简洁,具有整体的吸引力。

旅游合同,属 IT+IF(语体、用词等非常正式的契约型),用词与句式均须正式、规范、准确、程式化,等。后者如旅游行程(特指贴在宾馆布告栏或旅游大巴上的那种),属 IT(简单易懂的 IT)+ IF,用词和句型需简略、明了、准确,具有提示性。

旅游广告,属 VT(选词特别讲究、极富创意的 VT)+ VF,用词需短小精悍、诗情画意、独具创意,句式应活泼多样,呈现很强的整体魅力。

现编导游词,属 IT+IF,VT+VF 或两者兼而有之。但根据导游词创作过程和结果来看,它又可以分为即兴型(impromptu type)导游词、预制(pre-translated type)导游词和现编＋预制导译词,后两类还分别属于复合型(complex type)和即兴精制型(combined type)。

2.3 旅游文本语篇要求

由于我们讨论的旅游文本的范围已经缩小到"旅游指南"和"导译文本"两大类,这里的语篇要求特指这两类旅游文本的语篇要求。

通常,因中英思维模式和写作习惯不同,汉语语篇较多地使用归纳法,先旁征博引,罗列具体事实,最后得出结论。英语语篇则倾向于演绎法,主题句在文章或段落开始。本书涉及的多为单一型文本,复杂点不多,都是一种文本谈及一个主题,语篇模式和结构也不很复杂,所以语篇上的差异很少。从篇章结构上来看,"旅游[指南]文本同样体现出英语语篇多层次、立体式结构的特点;而汉语语篇则呈平面状,都是结构短小的句子串联在一起。但两者也有共同之处,那就是语句之间或段落之间虽然有一定的逻辑关系,如时间顺序、空间排列顺序(从左到右,从大到小等),但这些逻辑关系并不明显。也就是说,句子或段落之间使用的关联词不多,英语语篇大多采用代词来表示衔接,而汉语语篇则是需要从意思上体会文章的连贯"(陈刚,2008:325)。

3 旅游翻译原则与标准:初阶与进阶

"由于旅游翻译是典型的跨文化翻译,我们对这种翻译的具体要求会更有针对性。就译者而言,除具备基础的先决条件外(如较宽的知识面、较广的兴趣、一般外语'四会'的熟练程度等),他/她还应该达到以下要求。"(陈刚,2009:156)

3.1 旅游翻译初阶

由于旅游翻译(尤指汉译英)面对的受众主要是讲英语/读英语的海外旅游者,所以对译者的要求实则是相当高的,或者是最高的,因为这类翻译要求当场见效。不过,根据笔者的经验,native speakers对导译还是比较宽容的。以下是几项基本要求:

(1) 双语功底:英汉转换要做到自如、地道,特别强调语言的可接受性和交际的有效性,主要包括语法正确、文体适切、文字搭配自然等。

(2) 中外文化:熟悉中国的传统文化(如古代的、近代的)与现代、当代文化和历史,对对象国的文化、历史知之较多,对世界各国文化比较了解,具有起码的意识、感觉、概念等。

(3) 主题知识:具备足够的相关主题知识,比如行程安排知识、公示语知识、旅行指南知识、风景名胜知识、参观单位知识、导游知识等。

(4) 写作能力:较好地运用目标语进行写作的能力。这一写作能力起码涉及旅游指南文本和导译文本的写作能力,特别是创造性写作(creative writing)能力。

3.2 旅游翻译进阶

(1) 相关专/职业的素质和能力;
(2) 相关专/职业翻译的学养和能力;
(3) 相关的实践研究潜力和能力。

由于旅游翻译是一个很注重专业/职业实践的翻译,所以即使译者达到了"初阶"的要求,乃至了解了不少的理论、策略、方法、技巧等,但最终决定译文质量的关键,仍是译者的相关专业/职业的素质和能力、相关专业/职业翻译的学养和能力(包含用目标语言写作的能力)。而具备了"进阶"的(1)和(2)者,就具备了基于实践的研究(practice-based research)的潜力与能力,进而具备了旅游翻译的创新潜力与能力。

"这两个阶段的要求是对旅游翻译的一个整体要求,不仅是一个基本要求,而且也是一个相当高的要求,甚至需要终身努力。"(陈刚,2009:157—158)

3.3 初进阶实译举例

以下通过10个个案(初进阶重叠)分析,让读者有一个感性和理性的认识。这10个实例涉及旅游翻译专业/职业要求的众多主题中的10个常见主题,也是翻译的10个常见侧面:(1)专业术语;(2)行业用语;(3)典型表达;(4)固定说法;(5)广告词;(6)地名差异;(7)文化敏感性;(8)主动还是被动;(9)俗名与专名;(10)译文与市场。出于循序渐进的考虑,这10个实例比较简短,但所涉及的宏观语境(指 linguistic context, cultural context 及 situational context)实则构成了一个无形的"大文本"。要攻克旅游大文本的文体翻译难关,我们必须首先通过旅游翻译的"初阶"与"进阶"这两个必由之路。

(1) 专业术语

专业术语(ST)	TT1	TT2
外联部(旅行社)	Foreign/External Liaison Dept.	Sales & Marketing Dept.
说明:① TT1 只是字面对等,有悖于 ST 的信息功能,属于"计划经济"文体风格,主要受中央部门"中国对外联络部"译文的影响。② TT2 属于内涵对等,属于"市场经济"及"全球化"文体风格,完全再现了 ST 的真正的信息功能。		

(2) 行业用语

行业用语(ST)	TT1	TT2
餐桌转盘(饭店业)	revolving plate of the table 等	Lazy Susan
说明:① TT1 还有 plate-spinning of the table, disc-spinning of the table, turntable 等,这些译文均是张冠李戴,把杂技的"转碟"、"转盘"和留声机的"转盘"用于宾馆餐桌上的转盘,令人啼笑皆非,有违 ST 的信息功能。② TT2 属于地道译文,亦可说 rotating tray 或 dumbwaiter。有关该词的来源有几种说法,Lazy Susan 可追溯到 18 世纪。据说,当时佣人当中叫 Susan 的居多,而这种转盘不必 go anywhere,所以说佣人是比较 lazy 的。而如今,dumbwaiter 则指楼层间运送食品、餐具、垃圾等的(小型)升降机。另一种说法是,Lazy Susan 实乃一家公司所想出来的商品名称与广告手段。		

图 2　Lazy Susan

(3) 典型表达

典型表达(ST)	TT1	TT2
Early-bird announcement is a good tool to get your potential attendees interested in the meeting and convention and hopefully they will register early.(会展业/旅游宾馆)	像早起的鸟那样发出通知是得到有潜力的出席者对会议感兴趣,并希望他们将来早注册。	发出提前报到/注册通知是吸引潜在参会者及参展商的一种好方法,这些潜在的客户将有望提前报到/注册。

续表

说明：① TT1 译者将英语谚语"The early bird gets the worm（早起的鸟有虫吃）"的直译译文照搬，以为这里可用比喻修辞来翻译，造成理解错误，搭配不当，意义模糊，这跟 ST 的表达意义及功能背道而驰。此外，TT1 还存在其他不少翻译问题/错误。② TT2 译者懂得 early-bird announcement 在此的典型表达及其内涵意义，即强调"提前"、"捷足先登"，故很好地完成了再现 ST 功能的任务。TT2 的整体理解与表达要强于 TT1，望读者自行分析、比较，并思考如果不用 early-bird，还可以用其他哪些典型的表达法。		

（4）固定说法

典型表达(ST)	TT1	TT2
我们这儿的出租车是打表计价。车费由两部分组成：起步价，包括开始的两公里，最高是 x￥；接下来的公里数，最高是 x￥/每公里（自由行/散客接待）	Our taxi here is paid according to the meter. The taxi fees are made up of two parts: the start price, including the first 2 km, at the maximum rate of x￥, and the kilometer rate, at the maximum rate of x￥.	Local taxis are metered. The total fares consist of two parts: the flag-down/flag-fall fare, including the first 2 kilometers, maximum price x￥, and the meter rate, maximum x￥ per kilometer.
说明：① TT1 译者将出租车的"起步价"译成 start price，没有错，TT 的其他地方暂不评论。我们还经常把"起步价"说成 the starting price，这些都是可接受的，起码西方旅游者不会听不懂，应该是起到了信息功能的作用。② TT2 译者将"起步价"译成 the flag-down fare/flag-fall fare，这些是地道的说法，或者是 initial fare/charges。之所以举这个特例，因为对大部分中国人来说，TT1 中的"起步价"易说易懂，而 TT2 中的固定说法，知道的人就相当地少。如果国人在国外遇到相同的情况，可能会听不懂。同理，我们在回答自由行或散客的问题时，用外国人熟悉的语言介绍，效果自然就好，信息沟通自然顺畅，文本功能自然圆满完成。		

以下图示是说明这一用法的实例。

Cab/Taxi ride is cheaper in New York than in the Gold Coast, Australia.

It is cheaper to catch a cab in New York, Hong Kong and Dubai than it is on the Gold Coast—and that gap is about to widen from today.

A Newspaper—The Bulletin investigation shows southeast Queensland cab users are paying more for each kilometre travelled than the three tourism meccas, leading to concerns that increased taxi fares will directly affect the Gold Coast's already struggling tourism industry.

Taxi industry figures warned against comparing cab rates between countries, saying differing work conditions and pay rates made the task nearly impossible. However, they admitted fewer people were using taxis and lack of competition would bring further increases.

From today, taxi fares across southeast Queensland will rise by 2.39 per cent. It follows a 4.2 per cent rise last July.

Gold Coast taxi users will pay ＄2.06 per kilometre travelled and 76c for every minute spent idling, making prices comparable to Sydney and among the highest in Australia.

The booking fee on the Gold Coast is ＄1.50, while the flagfall ranges from ＄2.90 for a cab booked between 7am and 7pm weekdays to as much as ＄6.20 for a cab booked between midnight and 5am.

The Department of Transport and Main Roads sets the maximum fares for taxis in Queensland and reviews them every six months.

图 3　flagfall 的用法实例

图 4　flagdown 的用法实例

(5) 广告词(旅游宣传册)

典型表达(ST)	TT1	TT2
中国热点城市游(旅游宣传册)	China Hot Spots Tour	China Popular
说明:ST 是向海外推销中国旅游产品宣传册中的一条线路。① TT1 译者采取的是直接翻译法,用一般的标准来评价似乎不错,但在过去,hot spot 不是如此随便使用的,因为美国朗文词典(供中国读者使用的 linguistic dictionary)就只给了一个定义:a place where there is likely to be much trouble and perhaps war or unsettled government(《朗文当代高级英语辞典》,商务印书馆,1998)。② 当然语言是在不断发展的,新词新意,旧词新意,更是层出不穷。这里我们关心的重点主要还是还有更为简洁、更富魅力的译文吗? TT2 显然是首选。要更好、更有效地完成 ST 的召唤功能,通常采用 creative rewriting(创造性重写)将更为奏效。旅游翻译在这方面的要求是高于其他应用翻译的。		

(6) 地名差异

典型表达(ST)	TT1	TT2
Montreal	满地可	蒙特利尔

说明:地名等专有名词的翻译不仅是一般翻译的难点,也是旅游翻译需要特别注意的地方,因为存在着地方/区域差异。① TT1 几乎难以为中国大陆所认知,学习英语/法语翻译的大学生可能对"满地可"闻所未闻,但海外华人、跟北美关系密切的其他华人、港澳台同胞一般都知道,甚至平时就是这样使用的,比如当地的华文报纸、广播、电视等。② 虽然专名翻译有"三大原则和二小原则"可遵循,比如"名从主人"、"约定俗成"等,但对全球化语境下的翻译知之甚少,也是会导致交流障碍的。TT2 适合大陆语境,TT1 是常识,理应了解。这两者之间没有对错、高下之分,它们的信息功能、表达功能异曲同工。

(7) 文化敏感性

典型表达(导游词)	TT1	TT2
We are proud of being Orientals since we are the descendents of Oriental dragon. We have Oriental Venice in Shaoxing and Suzhou, and such Little Oriental Venice as Xitang, Zhouzhuang and Tongli. We are really proud of all these.	(完全)认可英文导游词,包括其中有关 Oriental 的用法。	We are proud of being Chinese since we are the descendents of Chinese dragon. We have Oriental Venice in Shaoxing and Suzhou, and such Little Oriental Venice as Xitang, Zhouzhuang and Tongli. We are really proud of all these.

说明:旅游翻译(含导译)是典型的跨文化翻译或交际。译者/导译员的(跨)文化敏感性(cross-cultural awareness and sensitivity)以及与此密切相关的双语能力(bilingual competence)非常重要。内地很少有外语翻译等方面的专家学者会就导游词中的典型表达提出问题乃至质疑。因此,译者 1(完全)认可用英文译写的有关导游词。然而,译者 2 对导游词中的一个关键措辞作出了决定性的修改。理由如下:其一,我们几乎很难发现"东方的/人"用英文来表达时容易产生的文化"异常"现象,故 TT 功能未能达到我们的预期效果;尽管我们对"古老的东方有一条龙,它的名字就叫中国。古老的东方有一群人,他们全都是龙的传人"了如指掌,并自豪地称自己为"龙的传人",但汉语中"东方(人)"和"东方[的](威尼斯)"的概念译成英文时,在意义和功能上均会产生语用问题和文化问题。这些"语言+文化"问题 native speakers 极易发现,而我们自己却蒙在鼓里。其二,Oriental(n./adj.)≠(在上述语境中的)东方人(的)或中国人(的)。其三,美语和英语对 Oriental 的用法是有所不同的,但两者都认为该词通常指东亚人,特指中国人或日本人;当用于描绘亚洲人时(有时)是(相当)冒犯人的、很不礼貌的用词,起码是过时用法。其四,美语认为,要想表达亚洲人(的),可接受的现代标准用法是 Asian,英语中 Asian 则倾向于指来自印度次大陆的人,而要具体描绘"中国人"或"日本人"时,应直接使用 Chinese 或 Japanese。以上有关依据来自权威的大牛津词典和大韦氏词典。无怪乎,现任美国驻华大使骆家辉(Gary F. Locke)在任华盛顿州州长时,签署一项法案,规定华盛顿州各级政府的官方文件将自 2002 年 7 月起禁止使用 Oriental(东方人)字眼,全面改用 Asian(亚裔)。华盛顿州议会认为,Oriental 字眼已经过时,且含种族歧视意味,须以较现代且不含轻蔑意味的 Asian 取代。

(8) 主动还是被动

主动还是被动	中国专家	Dr. Marco Piovaz
[TE1]The tour guide will show you all the major sights of the city.	[TE1]The tour guide will show you all the major sights of the city.	[TE2]You will be shown all the major sights of the city.

说明：① 在作为特殊语篇专业话语（professional discourse）的旅游英语文本中，被动形式还是不少见的，并非偶尔才使用。比如，作为典型举例，[TE1]得到中国专家的认可，但西方旅游学者 Dr. Piovaz 将其改为[TE2]。对此，我们也许既不了解，也不习惯。② 为突出旅游吸引物中有生命的人或动物，需要将该吸引物作为主语，此时选用的动词及短语比较多的是"be seen to do/doing"（主动语态：to see sb. / sth. do/doing）。选用 to do 和 doing 有差别吗？根据英国英语教学专家 L. G. Alexander，"We can use a bare infinitive or the -ing form after the verb of perception see. The bare infinitive refers to the complete action."并给出了很有说服力的例子。①英国语言学大家 A. S. Hornby 和国内惯用法权威葛传椝先生均给出了相同的富有特色的解答。然而，用错这类"句套子"的学生乃至学者还是不少见的，曾有针对上述短语的研究生入学试题，结果却给错了答案②。③ 限于篇幅，以下仅举 3 例。[例 1] In the dense groves on either side wild monkeys <u>are</u> <u>often</u> <u>seen</u> <u>to appear and disappear</u>. The wild mountain flowers in full bloom look like rosy clouds. [例 2] He <u>is</u> <u>often</u> <u>seen</u> <u>to walk up / walking up</u> the hill. [例 3] If the man who <u>was seen</u> <u>to take an umbrella from</u> the City Church last Sunday evening does not wish to get into trouble, he will return the umbrella to No. 10 Broad Street. ④ 可见，熟悉旅游英语的语料对学好旅游翻译帮助很大，进而对译者实现 ST/TT 文本功能起至关重要的作用。

(9) 俗名与专名

俗名与专名(ST)	TT1	TT2
佛教主要派别有大乘教和小乘教。	Buddhism falls into two major schools: <u>the Great Vehicle and the Small/Little Vehicle</u>.	Buddhism falls into two major schools: <u>Mahayana</u> and <u>Hinayana</u> or <u>Theravada</u>.

说明：① TT1 使用的是"大乘教"和"小乘教"的俗名（画线部分），通俗易懂，初、中级翻译应该首先掌握，也是旅游翻译的基本功之一。② TT2 使用的是"大乘教"和"小乘教"的专名（画线部分），高级翻译应该起码掌握两套词汇。这样碰到专业文本和学术文本，相关功能(IF＋EF)便能如愿实现。

---

① 见《亚历山大英语学习丛书·朗文高级英语语法》和《亚历山大英语学习丛书·朗文英语语法》，外语教学与研究出版社，1999/1991。

② 赵振才编著，《英语常见问题解答大词典》，哈尔滨：黑龙江人民出版社，1998。

(10) 译文与市场

译文与市场(ST)	TT1	TT2
飞水潭 飞水潭是鼎湖山空气含负离子最高的地方之一,飞瀑、绿树、幽潭组成了一个清凉世界。<u>这里常有女子弹古筝,端正的面庞、悠扬的乐曲与溪流声相互辉映,就是一幅绝美的图画。</u>	(1) ST 中的"飞水潭"译成 Flying Water Pond 是中式英文。 (2) ST 中的双下划线部分应该删去,因为弹古筝是偶尔为之,是非常量信息,意义不大。 (3) 如果要把这一信息译出,是欺骗游客,是商业道德问题。	(1) "飞水潭"中的"水"实为"瀑布",故"飞水潭"可译成 Flying Waterfall Pond 或 Flying Water Pond。用 flying 会产生一种气势,符合 ST 的表达功能。就搭配而言,苏州狮子林的"飞瀑亭"的英文正是 Flying Waterfall Pavilion,有一纯种马系谱查询网站就叫 Flying Water。 (2) ST 中的双下划线部分属于表情、美学和召唤功能的内容,实乃景点一大亮点,且是旅游营销的卖点。ST 已经写得很清楚了。更为重要的是:不管它属于历史还是眼前,理应保留。更何况即使今天停演,或许明天可以恢复,恢复后又可以停演。 (3) 如果翻译时"飞瀑抚琴"表演停演,是否还应把这个"亮/卖点"译出来呢? 答案是肯定的。译出来会违背商业伦理吗? 答案是否定的。道理很简单:<u>在英文中提供"过去信息"必须使用过去式</u>。我们在中文中不是也说:"这是飞人博尔特打破世界纪录的第 x 跑道";"这是飞鱼菲尔普斯打破世界纪录的第 x 泳道"。这些都是吸引参观者的语言,尽管这些事实都发生在过去。
说明:① 如果按照 TT1 译者的观点或理论,ST 的意义和功能则完全没有在目标语中实现,而且还是有意"去功能"。② TT2 译者不仅可以很好地完成实现 ST 功能的任务,而且特具市场营销意识,特具处理问题的策略与能力。		

综上所述,我们不难明白:旅游翻译很简单。"事实上,它是相当难的,只是多年来不少专家学者在这方面的低端与高端错误没有被披露,并加以公开讨论而已……只是人们对旅游翻译的标准、质量、要求等缺乏必要的了解而已。"(陈刚,2011:272)

4 旅游翻译原则与标准:高阶(1)

本节主要集中讨论旅游文本翻译应重点掌握的两类文本:导游指南和导译文本。经过"初阶"的学习,我们可以进入"高阶"的学习阶段。在进行实践型的讨论之前,有必要对旅游翻译的一些关键概念(key concepts)作一准确的了解。

4.1 归类

总体来说,旅游翻译属于应用翻译。但旅游文本(含笔头和口头)中包含了文学文本翻译,如山水诗歌翻译、景点楹联翻译,更有比较独立的旅游文学翻译,包括游记、小品、散文、诗词、话剧、电影等不同体裁的翻译。有关旅游主题的文本翻译中,还应包括旅游学术文本的翻译。

而归属应用翻译的旅游翻译,跟其他应用翻译一样则应归属于职业翻译暨专业翻译。

"职业翻译(professional translation)指为了建立起两种或多种语言之间的沟通而进行的将一种语言文本内容转换成另一种语言的职业。职业译者应事先受过专门的训练,并需通过实习。职业翻译主要涉及实用文本(pragmatic texts),使用的翻译策略取决于文本类型和被译文本的目的性,也取决于假设的目的语受众。译文质量根据交际规范加以评估。"(Delisle,引自陈刚,2011:226)

应用翻译属于职业翻译,也属于专业翻译(specialized translation)。后者指涉及不同专业主题和专业领域的翻译,是一种讲究高质量、规范化、准确度的翻译,它特别要求译者具备不同专业的学科背景或行业知识,甚至职业经历。

4.2 性质

旅游翻译跟其他任何翻译(translating)一样,都属于一种 skill、craft 和 art,所以旅游翻译同样表现为技能和艺术的性质和特点。"随着社会、经济、商贸、政治、教育等的不断发展,随着全球化的日益扩大,应用翻译往往跟职业翻译相提并论,或者实际上就是如此认知、如此看待、如此对待、如此操作、如此市场化、如此全球化、如此习以为常,如今如此学术化了。"(陈刚,2011:226)

由于从静态的角度描述、标准、定义及分析旅游翻译暨专业翻译未必适用,因此我们将按照 Gouadec 和 Nord 的理论对翻译性质重新定义。

定义一:翻译通过克服在语言、符号或身体方面可能不可克服之障碍,使有效的沟通成为可能——使交易得以发生。这些障碍包括语言障碍、代码障碍(对代码系统一无所知)、身体障碍(失明、失聪)等。翻译对物品、产品、服务、概念、思想、价值观等的传输极为重要。(Gouadec,引自陈刚,2011:229)

定义二:翻译即生成一种与特定源语文本保持关系的功能型目的语文本,这种关系是根据目的语文本之原有功能或所需功能(翻译目的)而加以说明的。翻译使交际行为得以发生,因为由于语言和文化障碍之存在,没有翻译,这种行为是不可能发生的。(Nord,2006:32)

根据定义一,这类翻译应是职业化、专业化的(professional)。对从业译者的职业要求,首先应是 professionalism,即具备职业特性、职业作风、职业精神、职业水准。例如在具体的实践中,旅游翻译(大量地)涉及语言翻译和非语言翻译,而其根本目的在于有效的沟通。即使源语是难以理解的(如旅游研究论文),当转换成目标语时,非但没有必要保持源语的"难懂特色"(如像文学翻译那样,注意其风格等),反而应使译文明白畅晓。这一点不仅体现于旅游语境下的诗歌等文学文本之翻译,尤其体现于旅游导译[①]。简言之,旅游翻译就是为了排除障碍,实现沟通。

根据定义二,旅游笔译是一种文本翻译。因其典型的功能性或目的性特色(为吸引旅游者,为宣传、推广旅游吸引物、旅游饭店、旅游商品、运输公司、餐饮服务、娱乐设施等),这种翻译完全可以称之为功能型/目的性文本翻译。在具体操作中,应尽可能采取以目的语文本为导向的策略和方法,有效保存源语文本中的功能,克服 ST 中存在的各种障碍,体现 TT 之

[①] 陈刚,《旅游英语导译教程》,上海:上海外语教育出版社,2010。

各项(预期)功能,最大限度地实现翻译之目的。

即使我们清楚了"什么是应用翻译或职业翻译"这个基本概念,但在具体的操作过程中应该通过理论联系实际译好这些语用文本(pragmatic texts),将"静态"的理论用来指导"动态"的实践。

4.3 翻译原则与标准

概括而言,应用翻译或者职业/专业翻译的原则与标准应该是动态的、多元的、功能的、与时俱进的。全球化的今天,静态的翻译标准,已经难以准确、客观、实际地描写并规范出翻译作为产品(translation as a product)的规格与要求。作为一名旅游翻译者,他/她应该明白(以下观点及文字参考:陈刚,2011:227—233):

(1) 职业翻译不仅仅是一种语言转换。称职的旅游界的职业译者扮演的起码是双重角色:既是双/多语高手,又是所译专业内容方面的行家或专家,还能熟练使用各种复杂的IT工具和软件。职业译者熟练掌握源语和目标语是非常基本的,然而却是远远不够的,还须掌握跟所涉文本和主题相关的背景知识等。一个职业译者未必是"全才",什么文本都会译(即具备相关资质和能力),但应努力使自己成为一名(多重)复合型译者或者"通才"译者。

(2) 职业翻译不是娱乐而是公务。原则上,职业翻译的宗旨不是娱乐,而是公务(it means business)。职业翻译涉及责任问题和经济问题,译者(作为接受者)需要处理与翻译委托人/发起者(initiator)或客户(client)之间的关系。因此,我们不能让年轻幼稚、没有职业经验的学生或"翻译"来正式承担职业/专业翻译。

(3) 职业翻译要遵守职业道德。职业翻译既然是一种职业,职业译者就必须遵守职业道德(professional ethics)和职业规范/标准。学生在校期间,之所以难以成为一名旅游方面的职业译者,正是因为 —— 也起码是因为 —— 任何人要进入这个行业(profession),是需要获得经过正式认可的翻译证书(如官方直接认可的或正式授权机构认可的)或者翻译专业学位的。而且,职业译者必须经过"学徒期"的训练,没有经过若干年的锤炼,难以成材。而译者的职业规范和职业道德等,是需要经过长期的职业生涯才能逐步认识、培养出来的。

5 旅游翻译原则与标准:高阶(2)

5.1 旅游文本的难点

(1) 原语文本(ST)的难点。涉及词汇、知识、文化、措辞、风格、感觉、功能等。这些特点既可能是书面语语体的,也可能是口语语体的。

(2) 目标语文本(TT)的难点。涉及跨文化、跨心理、思维方式差异大、语言表达差异大、常用的转换方法(文化异化、文化归化、语言直译、语言意译、文化替换、文化杂合、交际翻译、词义翻译、文化强化、文化淡化、文化增益、语言增益、文化删节、语言删节、功能改写、约定俗成等)。这些特点原则上是口语语体的,而少量的是书面语语体的。

综上所述,不管旅游文本(主要指旅游指南和导译两类)如何分类,不管它是ST还是TT,我们平时经常使用的文本往往是复杂的类型,属于一种复合文本 —— 包含一种以上功能,因此包含一种以上文本。而不同的文本类型(text type)也常常具有一些共同的语言和语篇策略,于是形成了导译文本的混杂性特征,其实旅游文本也具有混杂性特征,这些文本很难说是属于哪一特定的文本或体裁。

5.2 旅游文本翻译的难点

这里的"旅游文本翻译的难点",主要指"不容易解决的问题"[①]——即诸多旅游文本中的两种文本——导游指南和"预制型"导译文本,两者是学习旅游翻译首当其冲的难点,前者类型的文本(TT)应为 text-based translation。后者是一种比较特殊的文本,它是通过导译员之口直接说给外国旅游者(以下称旅游者)听的。它大量产生于中国改革开放,入境旅游(inbound tourism)蓬勃兴起之际。

比较而言,旅游指南(或景点指南)类文本相对比较"稳定",而(预制型)导译文本则"活泼"得多。旅游/景点指南的译写法可以比较固定,导译文本的译写法就灵活得多。这两类文本的翻译具有以下三个主要特点或原则(这些特点尤其体现于导译文本的翻译),但都是围绕一个整体功能——召唤功能(以下部分参考:陈刚,2010)。

(1) 游客反映原则(tourist-response principle)

这一原则即是文本译写原则。两类文本(尤其预制型导译词)是为海外游客服务的,翻译实践遵循"游客反映"原则实乃天经地义。换言之,you should try to impress your tourists with your narration。以下是这类导译词的主要特色:

① 整体特色。预制型导译词,其形式应不拘一格,内容应丰富多彩,描述手段应朴素生动,在很大程度上不同于一般的旅游资料或见闻。译成英语的 TT,通常是供导译员在途中、景点、娱乐场所、商店或餐厅时进行口头讲解服务用的,故又不同于即兴发挥的"现场导游"和"途中导游"。

② 具体特色。好的预制型导译词应包括 informative(内容充实),intriguing(生动有趣),realistic(真实可信),practical(实用性强),cultural(文化性强),educational(启迪受益),humorous(幽默风趣)等要素。此外,这类导译词还常常是 poetic,即恰当引用中国山水诗、诙谐生动的民间习语,具有较强的文学性,或是一篇诗情画意的散文片段,或是一个娓娓动听的故事。它是靠具有情感性、灵活性的人通过口头传播(oral presentation)的。当然,这些特色要在语言文化差异较大的英语 TT 中再现,是颇具挑战性的。

③ 异同特色。跟旅游/景点指南(如旅游资料、介绍等)的文字翻译比较,预制型导译文本要灵活得多;而预制型导译文本与即席型导译词比较,则一般不具有随感性、随机性、灵活性和鼓动性,缺乏较强的主观性。但预制型 narration 撰写者和译者可以模仿即席型文本的风格,所以预制型 narration 未必就是死板的,一成不变的。由此可见,导译词可以是一般的 narration,也可以是特殊种类的文学体裁文本。有西方学者将 a travel guide 归类于文学翻译。

[①] 释义取自《现代汉语规范词典》(李行健,2004:939),外语教学与研究出版社、语文出版社。

(2) 游客第一原则(tourist-oriented principle/tourist-first principle)

这一原则旅游翻译行为规范,是一个总体原则。换言之,旅游翻译(含导译)的服务对象十分明确:旅游业是为旅游者服务的,导译员按照合同提供的服务(包括导译服务)一定是"顾客第一,用户至上"。

(3) 文化传递原则

文化旅游早已成为国际旅游的重头戏。旅游指南及导译员介绍本国文化必不可少,国际游客了解目的地国文化又是旅游休闲的主要目的。然而,导译中跨文化难点可谓司空见惯,而且中英文化属于全世界各国文化之间差异最大的两种文化,因此在译写/处理预制型 ST 时遇到最大的几只"拦路虎"便是"一少三多",即文化对应词少和四字结构多、古诗词多、楹联多。

① 文化对应词少。具体而言,中文里的 culture-specific words/expressions(或 CSI: culture-specific items)很难在英语中简单找到对等词/对应词,但 target-language(TL)narration 中还可以"归化"表达为主。

② 四字结构多。汉语 ST 中往往使用较多的四字结构,这是汉语导游词的特色。与此相反,英语 TT 中根本就没有这种结构。

③ 古诗词多。祖国河山,诗情画意,尤其在不少江南水乡,适时引用翻译得比较成功的古诗,会富有情趣、别具一格,而且在实践中反复得到"档次高"的(well-educated)native speakers 的肯定和赞赏。如何选诗、如何译诗是处理导译词的难题之一。

④ 楹联多。楹联多是中国风景名胜的一大特色,导译员应主动向海外游客译介这种特有的文化,这不仅使普通游客受益,尤其使特殊游客受益。同翻译古诗词一样,如何选择楹联,如何翻译楹联,是处理导译词的又一难题。另请参看《旅游英汉互译教程》(陈刚,2009)第 16 章、《旅游翻译与涉外导游》(陈刚,2010)第 6 章、《西湖诗赞》(陈刚,1996)等。

当然,这里重点介绍并讨论的两种文本比较有限,难以全面再现上述有关描绘。感兴趣的读者可以自行去求证、研究。

5.3 旅游文本翻译举例

旅游翻译能力的提高,主要不是通过单句/单项翻译练习提高的,而是通过文本/语篇的整体把握和翻译才能提高的,后者涉及成为一名称职的旅游翻译者的一个前提条件——专业化/职业化(being professional)。

(1) 旅游指南英译汉。

沙漠山海,气势磅礴。可惜,此处的沙漠不是世界上最大的撒哈拉,也不是中国最大的沙漠塔克拉玛干,却是全球最大的骇人听闻的"死亡谷"沙漠。别致的景观本身就独一无二,而这类描写文本(ST),似乎也用得不多。此处作为译例"入选",也不仅仅因为它是美国的国家公园,而是有关文本语言的独特性。

【ST1】

[1]Death Valley is one of the most famous deserts in the United States, covering a wide area with its alkali sand. Almost 20 percent of this territory is situated [2]well below sea level, and [3]Badwater, a salt water pool, is about [4]280 feet below sea level and the lowest point in the United States.

Long ago the[5] Panamint Indians called this place "Tomesha"—the land of fire. [6]Death Valley's present name dates back to 1849, where a group of [7]miners coming across from Nevada became lost in its [8]inhospitable vastness and their adventure turned to tragedy. Today Death Valley [9]has been declared a National Monument and is crossed by several well-marked roads where refreshments and accommodations can be found easily. [10]Luckily the change created by human settlement has not spoiled the special beauty of this place.

Here nature[11]created a series of amazing, almost lunar landscapes, everchanging as the constant wind moves the sand about, revealing the most incredible colors. One of [12]the most extraordinary and variable parts of Death Valley is [13]the Devil's Golf Course, where [14]the border between reality and nightmare seems confused. [15]Sand sculptures stand on a ghostly ground, as evening shadows move and lengthen.

The desert is a place where man[16]feels his own impotence and inferiority, where [17]it is most difficult to make nature submit to his will...

In fact, the desert[18]reminds one again and again that [19]nature is superior to man, [20]asking the passerby eternally to respect what has been created by nature and inviting him to consider the future in the light of his past mistakes.

(选自 *California*,笔者有删节;编号与底线由笔者所加)

【TT1】

[1]死谷是美国最著名的沙漠之一,大片面积为碱性沙所覆盖。几乎20%的谷地[2]远低于海平面。被称为[3]"坏水"的盐水湖,约为[4]负海拔85米(280英尺),是全美的最低点。

很久以前,[5]帕纳明特部落的印第安人把此地叫做"托密夏",即"火之地"。[6]"死谷"的现名源自1849年,当时一群[7]淘金者从内华达州横越此地,却迷失于[8]这片荒凉的无垠黄沙,他们的历险之旅成了一场悲剧。今天,死谷[9]早已被设为"国家保护区",开通了数条标志清晰的公路穿越其间,沿途各类点心店和膳宿可以轻松找到。[10]幸运的是,人类在此安营扎寨所带来的变化,却没有破坏死谷那种特殊的美。

大自然在此[11]创造了类似月球上的系列景观,令人惊讶,变幻莫测,如同永不停歇的风将谷地黄沙吹得四处飞扬,展示出最为难以置信的各种色彩。死谷[12]最令人称奇、变化多端的景观之一是[13]"魔鬼的高尔夫球场",这里的[14]场景似乎难以分清哪些是现实,哪些是噩梦。[15]座座沙雕矗立在此,鬼影幢幢,仿佛暮色降临后的阴影在移动、在变长。

在这个死亡之谷,[16]人类感到了自己的无能为力与自惭形秽,[17]并无法让自然服从人类的意愿……

事实上,这片沙漠一再[18]提醒我们:[19]天尊人卑。[20]任何造访此地之人,请永远尊重大自然在此创造的一切,人类应惩前毖后,思考未来。

(陈刚译;编号与底线由笔者所加)

【ST1 与 TT1 对比、分析、简评】

① 【ST1】选自大型画册 *California*,介绍文本由 V. M. De Fabianis 撰写,反映了作者对人与自然的观点,富有个性。文本翻译涉及文化解读、时空转换、历史民族、文学描写、人文观念等,具有相当的难度,是综合性 rewriting 的一次很好的训练。

② 原文[1]有两种可以采纳的译文。1 是"死谷",参考《简明不列颠百科全书》;2 是"死亡谷",流行译名,甚至用于美国影片《死亡谷》。这里选择第一种。

③ 原文[2]中的 well 意指 to a great extent/degree,见译文[2]。

④ 原文[3]也有两种可接受的译文:据《美国地名译名手册》,为"巴德沃特";根据流行译法,为"坏水"。这里译为"坏水",似乎更为可取。

⑤ 原文[4]不难译,但应考虑译文对象是讲汉语的中国(大陆)读者等,要注意计量单位的转换。见译文[4]。

⑥ 翻译原文[5]有两点解释:其一,Panamint 是部落名,另外英文中有"The Death Valley Indians are called Panamint",故可以译成"帕纳明特部落的印第安人",也可以译为"帕纳明特人";其二,"... called this place 'Tomesha' —the land of fire" 中的印第安语可不译,"把此地叫做'火(焰)之地'"。之所以又可译成"火焰之地",因为英文中也用 the flaming land 解释 Tomesha。

⑦ 原文[6]可以译成"'死谷'现在这个名字可追溯至……",或者参考译文[6]。

⑧ 原文[7]常被误译为"矿工",实为"淘金者"。他们被称为 forty-niner(1849 年涌往加利福尼亚州淘金的人)或 49er。

⑨ 翻译原文[8]应注意文学色彩,运用 amplification,其中 inhospitable 在此意为 "difficult to stay or live in, especially because there is no shelter from the weather",如 inhospitable terrain(荒凉的地带)。见译文[8]。

⑩ 原文[9]中的 monument,不是指"纪念碑"。根据《简明不列颠百科全书》,national monument 是指"国家保护区"。在美国,指联邦政府为保护具有历史和科学价值的文物和地点而划出的地区,有时设为国家公园。1933 年起,各保护区由内政部国家公园管理局统一管辖。阅读英文 ST1 时,要理解不同语境中的词义,文中的 National Monument 应作为一个整体来解读,即 "any of numerous areas reserved by the federal government for the protection of objects or places of historical, scientific, or prehistoric interest. They include natural physical features, remains of Indian cultures, and places of historical importance"（见 *Merriam-Webster's Collegiate Encyclopedia*, 2000）。其中"早已……"也是对上下文的解读后译出的。参见译文[9]。

⑪ 原文[10]中的 luckily 也可以译为"令人欣慰的是"，其余部分暗含一个转折关系，参考译[10]。

⑫ 原文[11]不好译，涉及翻译技巧的综合、灵活运用。其一，"amazing"可以后置（inversion）；其二，everchanging 需注意措辞（diction）；其三，"revealing the most incredible colors"中的动宾搭配（collocation）在汉语中不好处理，暂译为"展示/现出最为难以置信/从未见过的各种色彩"，但也不妨处理得比较"异化"些："揭示出……色彩"。详见译文[11]。

⑬ 翻译原文[12]，思路、用词可以往风景名胜方向靠，如"最令人称奇/意想不到、变化多端的景观"。参看译文[12]。

⑭ 原文[13]的翻译见译文[13]，也可以译成"魔鬼高尔夫球场"。

⑮ 原文[14]直译是"现实与噩梦之间似乎没有了界限/现实与噩梦之间的界限似乎是混淆的"，但这样的译法在 TT 中意思不够清晰明了。参见译文[14]。

⑯ 翻译原文[15]颇费思考。不仅要明白如何处理复数形式的"sand sculptures"（建议技巧 amplification）。形容词 ghostly（建议技巧 inversion 和 compensation，与后一句衔接），还要创造性处理 as 从句。见译文[15]。

⑰ 原文[16]＋[17]最好协调，统一译出。用两个四字成语翻译 impotence 和 inferiority，显得较有力度。见译文[16]＋[17]。

⑱ 根据上下文，原文[18]不宜逐字翻译，见译文[18]。

⑲ 原文[19]可以直译成"自然高/优于人类"，笔者这里参考"男尊女卑"（men are superior to women）的翻译。见译文[19]。

⑳ 翻译原文[20]，宜采用创造性 rewriting，见译文[20]。

（2）旅游指南汉译英。

单个的自然景观/景点介绍有其难译之处。翻译线条须细腻，细节一旦错译、乱译、硬译，那 TT 就会误导了旅游者，或者被旅游者所"抛弃"。因此，单项景观介绍的翻译要引起译者的高度重视，尤其要做到细致入微。笔者特选中国四大淡水湖之一的洞庭湖及岳阳楼。有关介绍偏重自然与人文景观的结合。有关文本的翻译难点跟前面的不同，属于旅游翻译的另一特点，应该熟悉、掌握。

【ST2】

洞庭湖面积约[1]3 900平方公里①,为我国第二大淡水湖。[2]烟波浩渺,水天一色,辽阔壮观。[3]湖中秀丽的君山,原名洞庭山,是神仙洞府的意思。[4]此处传说很多,其中一个是关于斑竹和山名的故事。[5]传说四千多年前舜帝南巡,来到九疑山,勤民而死。他的两个[6]妃子,思念心切,寻着舜帝足迹,不远万里赶来。当听说舜帝已死,便[7]止步于岛上,[8]攀竹痛哭,眼泪滴在竹上,形成"斑竹"。二妃悲痛致死,葬于此岛。二妃当时名"君妃"和"湘妃",为了纪念她们,就[9]把洞庭山改为"君山"和"湘山"了。君山的竹子很有名,有[10]斑竹、罗汉竹、方竹、实心竹、紫竹、毛竹等。这里每年都举办盛大的龙舟节、荷花节和水上运动。

[11]滨湖的风光极为秀丽,许多景点都是国家级的风景区。最为有名的当数全国重点文物保护单位、首批国家AAAA级旅游景区的岳阳楼。

岳阳楼耸立在湖南省[12]岳阳市西门城楼上,西临洞庭湖,北通[13]巫峡,[14]与南昌的滕王阁、武汉的黄鹤楼合称江南三大名楼,而且是三大名楼中唯一的一座[15]保持原貌的古建筑,可谓古代中国[16]建筑奇迹。

[17]在建筑风格上,岳阳楼的特色是木制、三层、四柱、飞檐、斗拱、盔顶。[18]三檐三层纯木结构,高15米;全楼由中间4根[19]楠木大柱承负,[20]再用12根廊柱支撑2楼,外以12根檐柱,顶起一楼飞檐。三楼楼顶,外形酷似古代武士的头盔,故称[21]"盔顶"。[22]楼顶檐则[23]由联锁斗拱加固,[24]全楼闩缝对榫,没有用铆钉。三层楼[25]叠加的飞檐远远望去,[26]恰似鲲鹏凌空欲飞。

岳阳楼的[27]前身是东汉建安20年(215年)[28]东吴大将鲁肃在洞庭湖训练水兵时构筑的一个阅兵台。唐开元4年(716年)在阅兵台旧址建一楼阁,因位于[29]天岳山之阳,故名"岳阳楼"。宋1045年重建后,又[30]屡毁屡建。古代最后一次重建是1867年。

现存的岳阳楼,[31]两侧是三醉亭和仙梅亭。三醉亭源于神话传说[32]吕洞宾"三醉岳阳楼"而得名;仙梅亭,传说是明崇祯12年(1639年)维修岳阳楼,[33]清基时,挖掘出一块[34]无叶、却有24萼的枯梅样的石板,[35]人们以为是仙迹,特建亭纪念。

其实,岳阳楼在历史上不仅是[36]旅游者所向往的地方,而且自唐朝始,便逐步成为众多诗人、作家、画家[37]创作中的主题和游览胜地。岳阳楼保存的历代文物,[38]当推挂在三楼的[39]诗仙李白的对联[40]"水天一色,风月无边"最为著名。[41]岳阳楼下,洞庭湖边的怀甫亭,是1962年纪念唐代[42]诗圣杜甫诞生1,250周年建立的。亭中竖有石碑一方,[43]正面刻着[44]诗圣杜甫的画像和[45]《登岳阳楼》诗,[46]背面刻着他的[47]生平事迹。

---

① 史上洞庭湖面积变化很大,目前选择一个相对准确、易记的数字,仅作为笔译素材。望读者不断查证。

最为著名的散文是^[48]北宋范仲淹1046年所作的^[49]《岳阳楼记》，陈放于岳阳楼二层由12块^[50]檀木板组成的木雕屏篆刻着《岳阳楼记》全文，共368个汉字，^[51]由清书法家张照书写。特引文中^[52]脍炙人口的话语，^[53]以飨读者："^[54]衔远山，吞长江，浩浩汤汤，横无际涯；朝晖夕阴，气象万千。此则岳阳楼之大观也……^[55]登斯楼也，则有心旷神怡，宠辱偕忘，把酒临风，其喜洋洋者矣。"

（笔者根据多种官方资料重新编写，编号与底线另加）

【TT2】

[1] Lake Dongting covers an area of about 3,900 square kilometers. It is China's second largest freshwater lake. [2] Its misty, rolling waters reach so far and wide as to blend into the blue sky. [3] Across the lake to the west of Yueyang is Jun Shan (Jun Hill), a picturesque island, originally known as Dongting, which means a cave of celestial beings. [4] Many legends attach themselves to the island and one tells of a mottled bamboo and the name of the island. [5] Emperor Shun who, known as one of the five virtuous emperors of China at the dawn of human civilization, is said to have lived in 2500 BC died while on a southern inspection tour of Jiuyi Mountain on the southern bank of the lake. [6] His two wives, Princess Jun and Princess Xiang missed the emperor so much that they followed his way thousands of miles down to the lake and [7] were stranded on the island though they learned of his death. [8] Then they both clung to some bamboo and wept their hearts out. The bitters tears mottled the bamboo and there became "tear-mottled bamboos". Both died of grief and were buried on the island. As the two princesses were called Jun and Xiang respectively, the former Dongting Hill [9] was specially re-named Jun Hill or Xiang Hill in their memory. The hill has been noted for its variety of bamboo, such as [10] mottled bamboo, fish pole bamboo, square bamboo, solid bamboo, black bamboo and moso bamboo. The grand Dragon Boat Festival, lotus show and other aquatic sports are held here annually.

[11] Lakeside scenes are very attractive and many rank among the national-level scenic areas. The best-known is Yueyang Tower, both one of the national monuments and one among the first group of national 4A-grade scenic spots.

Yueyang Tower [12] stands on the west gate of [13] the city named after the tower in Hunan province. The tower faces Lake Dongting to the west and leads to [14] Wuxia Gorge, one of the Yangtze's Three Gorges, to the north. [15] It is known as one of the "three famous towers south of the Yangtze", the other two being Tengwang Tower in Nanchang and Yellow Crane Tower in Wuhan. In addition, it is the only one of the three that [16] keeps the original appearance as it is, and it is indeed an [17] architectural wonder of ancient China.

[18] Architecturally, the tower is characterized by wood, three stories, four columns, brackets (or *dougong*), and a helmet-shaped roof. [19] It is a 15-meter-high three-storied structure with three eaves, made entirely of wood. The whole building is supported by 4

[20]gigantic columns of *nanmu* wood in the center. [21]In addition, 12 corridor pillars hold up the second story and 12 peripheral columns, the first-storied upturned eaves. The tower's roof looks like the helmet of an ancient warrior, hence a "helmet roof". [22]The top eaves are braced by interlocking brackets, and the entire structure is [23]mortised together without the benefit of a single nail. The [24]multiple upturned eaves of the three-storied tower, viewed from a distance, [25]present a soaring grace.

Yueyang Tower used to be [26]the site of a navy reviewing stand erected for General Lu Su of the State of Wu in 215. A tower was constructed in 716 in the Tang dynasty on the said site. As it was situated [27]on the sunny or southern side of Mount Tianyue, it was named Yueyang Tower (Tower on the Sunny Side of the Mount). Restored in 1045 during the Song dynasty, the tower was, in later years, [28]ruined and rebuilt many times. It was finally rebuilt in 1867.

The present tower is [29]flanked by Drunk Three Times Pavilion and Fairy Mume Pavilion. According to legend, the former pavilion was put up in memory of Lv Dongbin, a wandering Tang Taoist priest who was said to get drunk there on three occasions. For the latter pavilion, another legend says that [30]before Yueyang Tower was rebuilt in 1639 during the Ming dynasty, preparations were under way, and [31]a stone slab was unearthed from under the foundation. Imprinted on the slab were sprigs of withered mume blossoms, each bearing 24 calyxes. [32]Believing this to be the work of fairies, the local people erect the pavilion specially to commemorate the discovery.

As a matter of fact, Yueyang Tower has historically been a tourist attraction, and since the Tang dynasty gradually become [33]the creative theme and the sightseeing resort for numerous poets, writers, and artists. Of all historical relics preserved in the tower, [34]perhaps the most recommendable piece is the couplet by [35]poet-immortal Li Bai in the Tang dynasty. Hung at the third floor, it reads:

[36]"*The waters and the skies merge into one color;*
The wind and the moon sail in boundless space."

[37]Near Yueyang Tower and Lake Dongting stands [38]Remember-Du-Fu (Huaifu) Pavilion, which was built in 1962 to commemorate the 1250th birthday of [39]poet-sage Du Fu (712—770) in the Tang. Inside the pavilion is erected a stone tablet. Its [40]front side is carved with the portrait of Du Fu and his poem [41]"Ascending Yueyang Tower", while its [42]reverse side with his [43]life story.

On top of that, the most celebrated essay about the tower was written in 1046 by the [44]Northern Song dynasty writer Fan Zhongyan, entitled "Yueyang Tower". Displayed on the second floor of the tower, this 368-character work is carved on the 12 sandalwood panels in the personal handwriting of the Qing dynasty calligrapher Zhang Zhao. [45]To provide enjoyment for readers, [46]the oft-quoted part of the essay is specially cited as follows:

"[47]Lake Dongting embraces distant mountains and swallows the water of the Yangtze. [48]Its mighty waves keep rolling endlessly. [49]From morning sunlight to evening glow, it presents myriads of scenes. All this is [50]the magnificent view from Yueyang Tower... Ascending the tower, one will feel delighted broad-minded, while forgetting all [51]personal ups and downs. Holding a cup of wine in the breeze, one will be [52]beaming with joy."

(陈刚译;编号与底线另加)

【ST2 与 TT2 对比、分析、简评】

① 【ST2】是一篇翻译难度颇大的景点介绍,集自然风景、文化古迹、名诗散文、对联传说、文学描述、专业描写、建筑词汇、植物词汇、百科词汇、文化负载词等于一体,而原则上须通过全译才能再现原文;如何译,为什么这样译,这对译者和读者着实是一大挑战。

② 原文[1]的翻译涉及数字的正确性,译者的职责不仅仅是单纯地翻译原文,更要对一些客观事实加以论证。解释见相关脚注。

③ "洞庭湖"可以译为如译文[1],也可以是(the) Dongting Lake。

④ 翻译原文[2]很难再现汉语的四字结构与语言魅力及力度。译文[2]则通过 hypotaxis 和 combination 加以处理。

⑤ 原文[3]中的"湖中"很容易译成"in the lake"。作为有职业素养的译者,最好了解清楚有关景点比较准确的地理位置。见译文[3]。也能译为 "Across the lake to Yueyang..."。"君山"可以处理成 Junshan, Jun Shan, Junshan Island, Junshan Hill, Jun Hill, Mound Jun 等,但从篇章角度考虑,下文会涉"君山"的 TL 表达,需将 SL 中"君"与"山"跟 TL 中 Jun 与 Hill 相呼应,因此选择 Jun Shan (Jun Hill)这样的译法和表现形式,全句翻译见译文[3]。

⑥ 原文[4]的翻译特采纳这样的结构:Many legends attach themselves to... and one tells of....但也可以是:... and some tell of...."斑竹"可以译成 mottled bamboo 或者 speckled bamboo。

⑦ 原文[5]中的"勤民"可以略译,因为舜帝南巡已经(可以)包含其意了。

⑧ 译文[5]中特为 TL 读者补充舜帝的有关背景知识,同时增加九疑山的地理位置,为下文做铺垫。

⑨ 原文[6]很容易译错。这里"妃子"不是指皇帝的妾,而是妻。由于二妃原是尧帝的女儿,所以译成如译文[6]。

⑩ 原文[7]中的"止步"没有采用主动语态,而是被处理成"be stranded on",其依据是传说当年二妃寻找舜帝未着,被大风阻于洞庭湖的君山。见译文[7]。

⑪ 原文[8]被译成两句,分别注意"攀竹"、"痛哭"、"眼泪滴在"、"形成"和"斑竹"在译文[8]中的处理。这里"斑竹"处理成 tear-mottled bamboo,比较通常的译法是 mottled / speckled bamboo。

⑫ 原文[9]没有直译,见译文[9],即"特重新命名为……"。

⑬ 特别注意原文[10]中各种竹子的译名。万不得已,不要采用学名,即拉丁名,或者一

些大词,而要选用通俗易懂的英文。见译文[10]。其中"罗汉竹",又名"人面竹"或"雷公竹",英文名还可以是 golden bamboo。

⑭ 翻译原文[11]选择了"Lakeside scenes are... and many rank among..."的并列结构。这样的译法如同处理原文[4]一样。见译文[11]。

⑮ 对原文[12]不采取音译加词义翻译法,见译文[13]。

⑯ 译文[12]可以与"耸立"相当,而且主语还是 tower。

⑰ 处理原文[13]时,特在译文[14]对"巫峡"作一个 amplification。

⑱ 译文[15]与原文[14]虽并非字字对应,但表达的是同一个意思,这主要是从语句衔接(cohesion)的角度考虑。读者不妨自己试译一下。顺便提一下,"岳阳楼"和"滕王阁"也可以分别处理为 Yueyang Pavilion 和 Tengwang Pavilion。

⑲ 原文[15]可以处理成"to keep.... as it is"的结构,意为"保持……的原貌",见译文[16]。

⑳ 原文[16] 可以按照译文[17]处理,也可以是 architectual miracle。

㉑ 原文[17] 的翻译焦点在一组建筑词汇上,请跟译文[18]一一对照、理解,并注意以下的 TT。

㉒ 注意原文[18]译成 TL 后的词序调整:高度→层数→中心词→檐数→材料。整句处理见译文[19]。

㉓ 原文[19] 中的"楠木",其产地是中国,主要地区有四川、重庆、云南、贵州、湖南等,翻译时用汉语拼音即可。"大"可以用 TL 中的 huge 或 big,另详见译文[20]。

㉔ 比较译文[21],充分注意原文[20] 中画线部分的翻译:"再用 12 根廊柱支撑 2 楼,外以 12 根檐柱"可以在 TL 中如此对应:"In addition, 12 corridor pillars hold up the second story and 12 peripheral columns..."。

㉕ 注意原文[21]的另一种译法。

㉖ 原文[22]—[25] 都涉及建筑专业词汇,比较难译,见译文[22]—[24]。其中,用 braced (to make sth. stronger or more solid by supporting it with sth.)就是为了避免重复使用 supported;介词短语 "without the benefit of a single nail"也可以是"without benefit of a single nail"或者"without the use of a single nail"。

㉗ 原文[26] 不能直译,否则 TL 读者难以按照 SL 读者的文化背景去思考、想象,而译文[25]则比较好地从功能上再现了原意。

㉘ 原文[27]不应用 predecessor 来表达。这里很简单的"used to be"便可以解决。

㉙ 翻译原文[28]时,不要遗漏 the site,见译文[26]。

㉚ 注意原文[29]—[30] 的译文[27]—[28]。

㉛ 原文[31] 的译文[29]中,使用动词 flank 能使句子显得活泼;最容易译"糊涂"的就是"梅花"。不少词典和译者都用 plum 来译梅花。须知,中国传统文化中"松竹梅"之"梅"属于观赏性植物,不是那种结果的植物,所以用 mume 比较准确。

㉜ 处理原文[32],应对吕洞宾作一简洁的概括性解释。

㉝ 原文[33]的含义模糊,甚至无法从上下文判断基本含义;原文[34]也不太好处理。笔者通过了解术语"清基"的行业意义,然后根据语境,给出译文[30]—[31]。

㉞ 原文[35]要译得好，须对ST的内涵有一个比较透彻的理解，译成TL时，思路要比较符合TL读者的思路。具体来说，要将原文paraphrase为"以为这是仙人所为的杰作，本地人特建亭纪念这一发现"。由于原文仅仅是"(以建亭)纪念"，TL读者会关心或追问"纪念什么"。在SL中似乎意会的，在TL中未必合理，往往是稍长或稍"啰唆"的中文解读，译成相应的TL反而是好的英文。详见译文[32]。

㉟ 在此，原文[36]可以换一种角度处理，用英文"tourist attraction"表达即可。

㊱ 原文[37]应尽可能处理成TL中的并列结构，见译文[33]。

㊲ 原文[38]（即"当推"）接近"首推"，故译文是"perhaps the most recommendable piece..."（见译文[34]）。

㊳ "诗仙"/"诗圣"（即原文[39]/[42]）有专门的译法，见译文[35]/[39]。

㊴ 原文[40]是一副李白的对联，很难译。笔者是杭州本地人，对西湖湖心亭上有关乾隆皇帝题写"虫二"两字的故事记忆犹新，由"風月"去边成"虫二"，寓意"风月无边"，形容"景致无限"。另据湖南美术出版社1985年出版的《巴陵胜状》，说岳阳楼三楼的木壁上，本来曾有三个隐约可见的字迹：一、虫、二，人们一直不解其意，后来李白游岳阳楼，看出这是一副字谜对联，即"水天一色，风月无边"，并当即写下了这副对联。此事仍是传说，穿凿附会的痕迹明显。总而言之，原文只有尽可能直译，至于TL读者如何透过英文读懂其中之寓意，只能是let it be so。比较译文[36]：

The waters and the skies merge into one color;
The wind and the moon sail in boundless space.

㊵ 原文[41]的翻译难度有两点：一是怀甫亭正确的地理位置；二是怀甫亭如何译更能达到跨文化交流效果。按原文直译容易confuse/mislead英文读者。经查证，怀甫亭坐落在岳阳楼院内临湖五坪台，所以出现译文[37]。译文[38]是处理"怀甫亭"的最为简易、有效的方法。

㊶ 原文[43]—[46]是常见的旅游词汇，但译成英文也有一番讲究。"正面"可以是"the front side/obverse side"，"反面"可以是"the back side/reverse side"。在某些语境下，也可以是"one side/the sunny side"（正面/阳面）和"the other side/the shady side"（反面/阴面）。请分别见译文[40]—[42]。

㊷ 原文[45]可参见译文[41]，也可以译成"On (the) Yueyang Tower"。

㊸ 原文[47]不要参照汉英词典，见译文[43]。

㊹ 原文[48]需要对作者的身份信息作一简单补充。见译文[44]。

㊺ 原文[49]中的"记"可以略译。若译成Notes on.../Record on...也行，但未必合适、地道。汉语中"记"指"记载事物的书或文章"，如游记、日记等，因此，硬把"记"译出，总嫌不准确，不是ST本来那层意思。由于ST本身带来的矛盾，难以在TL中得到合理的解决，译家们往往省略不译。如《黄州安国寺记》（苏轼），其译文是"Ankuo Temple"（林语堂译）；又如，《醉翁亭记》（欧阳修），其英文是"The Pavilion of the Drunken Old Man"（罗经国译）。

㊻ 原文[50]＋[51]在TL中的再现，实则是一个如何用英语进行地道、合理转换的问题，或曰rewriting。请尽量避免机械对译，比照译文[44]和其他相关译文。

㊼ 根据语境，原文[52]和原文[53]需进行位置调整(inversion)，其中"话语"在TL中不

太好找对应词,可以巧妙回避。请参见译文[45]—[46]。

㊽《岳阳楼记》中的引文——即原文[54]—[55]——是 ST2 中最难翻译的一处。从语法角度看,需分别补"衔远山,吞长江"、"浩浩汤汤,横无际涯"和"朝晖夕阴,气象万千"的 TL 主语,和分别补"登斯楼也,则有心旷神怡,宠辱偕忘"和"把酒临风,其喜洋洋者矣"的 TL 主语。从句法角度看,"衔远山……气象万千"需用三个 TL 短句,与其旗鼓相当;在 TL 中用两个"-ing 短语 + 主语"来翻译原文[55]中的内在关系。从词义和语用角度看,既要尽可能译出原文的气势(如"衔……"、"吞……"),又要对词语的自然、地道搭配进行严格把关。从风格(其实上述几个角度都是跟风格密切相关的)角度看,整体要符合 ST 流利畅达、简洁凝练的风格。需要特别指出的是,翻译"宠辱(偕忘)"时,这里特地不按照传统的一般译法(如 glory or shame, honor or disgrace 等),而是根据史实(范仲淹因提出政治改革主张,触动了朝廷中保守派的利益,被罢官贬放邓州),翻出内涵,即"(forgetting) all personal ups and downs"。此外,原文"壮观"意为壮阔的景象。整个引文的翻译,见译文[47]—[52]。

(3) 导译文本汉译英。

这里要讨论的文本是预制式文本,说得更为精准的话,应是(预制式)导译文本的创译。

旅游团或散客的"接送转移"服务主要指导译员接站、送站及转移途中的讲解服务。"接站"后转移途中的讲解涉及到"欢迎词"和"途中导"。以下实例是"华东黄金旅游线导游词"的文本创译。

【ST3】

[1]各位游客:你们好!首先请允许我代表旅游公司的全体员工对大家前来华东黄金旅游线观光旅游表示热忱的欢迎!

此次华东之旅,行程十二天,将游览南京、扬州、镇江、无锡、苏州、上海、杭州、千岛湖和黄山,[2]共七个城市和名山名湖各一。[3]线路较长,旅途比较辛苦,[4]我们司陪将本着"宾客至上,服务第一"的宗旨,尽心尽力地做好服务工作,同时也希望我们的工作能够得到各位游客的支持和配合,促进我们提高服务质量,从而使大家吃得满意,住得舒适,玩得愉快,走得顺利,乘兴而来,满意而归。

游客们:[5]华东地区旅游资源丰富,人文景观独特。这里是"江南鱼米之乡、山清水秀之处、历史文物之都、名人荟萃之地"。[6]从区域来讲,包括六省一[7]市,[8]从线路来说,江浙沪连同千岛湖、黄山,[9]这条将都市风光线与名山名水线融为一体的景观,[10]是国内旅游的最佳线路。

[11]华东之旅,除传统的风景名胜游、文物古迹游、佛教文化游、都市观光游、休闲度假游之外,还有许多各具特色的旅游项目可供选择。

[12]如"江南水乡及都市观光游"。[13]江南水乡以苏州和杭州为胜,[14]历来有"上有天堂,下有苏杭"之誉;[15]都市观光以上海大都市为主。[16]三地相连、交通便捷,也叫"小华东之旅"。[17]这一带,太湖风光烟波浩渺,西湖秀色清波涟漪,数百园林争奇斗艳,亭台楼阁瑰丽多姿,更有浦东新区拔地而起,金茂大厦傲视江滨,东方明珠直上云霄……[18]这些都是华东旅游的精华。

还有[19]"江南园林及山水风情游"。[20]江南园林是中国园林的一大流派,[21]它"不出城郭而获山水之怡,身居闹市而有泉林之致",[22]巧用借景,将真山真水融入其中,[23]南京的瞻园、扬州的个园、无锡的蠡园、苏州的留园和拙政园、吴江同里的退思园、上海的豫园、杭州的郭庄等,[24]无不景中有景,妙趣天成。[25]"山外青山楼外楼",点出了江南的群山有层次、园林有格局的特色。

[26]最后还要推荐一下"江南美食游"。[27]江南佳肴,色香味形驰名中外。美食种类繁多,异彩纷呈,处处飘香,[28]南京板鸭、无锡酱排骨、苏州松鼠鳜鱼、上海浦东鸡、杭州东坡肉、阳澄湖大闸蟹等,[29]无不让您一尝为快,大饱口福!

各位游客,[30]今天大家来到华东,其悠久的历史、璀璨的文化等待着您去领略;秀丽的风光、美好的山水期盼着您去欣赏,[31]但愿华东黄金旅游线之旅能够成为您的度假天堂。[32]最后预祝各位旅行期间身体健康,万事如意。谢谢!

【TT3】

[1]Ladies and gentlemen, good day! Please allow me, on behalf of our tourist company, to extend a warm welcome to you!

Our East China tour will last 12 days, [2]covering 7 cities and 1 famous mountain and 1 famous lake, that is, Nanjing, Yangzhou, Zhenjiang, Wuxi, Suzhou, Shanghai, Hangzhou, and 1000-Islet Lake and Mt. Huangshan or the Yellow Mountain. [3]This is a quite long tour and it calls for a good balance between sightseeing and relaxation. [4]The driver and I are both here to work closely and serve you in the best possible way. We look forward to your support and cooperation. And we do hope you will enjoy your trip all the way here and back home.

Ladies and gentlemen,[5] let me give you a short description of East China and highlights of some of the cities we are going to visit. [6]East China enjoys rich tourist resources and unusual tourist attractions. [7]It is known as the "home of fish and rice, a resort with natural landscape, an area of historical and cultural heritage, and a place for gathering famous people." [8]Geographically, East China includes 6 provinces and 1 [9]municipality directly under the Central Government. [10]In terms of the tourist route, [11]it is perhaps the best tour route for domestic sightseeing. For [12]it integrates modern cities and water towns with scenic lakes and noted mountains in Jiangsu, Zhejiang, Shanghai as well as 1000-Islet Lake and the Yellow Mountain.

[13]For East China tour, we offer traditional programs such as a landscape tour, cultural heritage tour, Buddhist culture tour, metropolitan tour, leisure and holiday tour, and many more SITs.

[14]Take the "Jiangnan water town and metropolitan tour" for example. [15]One finds the best Jiangnan water towns in Suzhou and Hangzhou, which represent typical features of the Jiangnan region noted for its fertile land and crisscross canals, lakes and rivers. [16]It's always been known by the time-honored saying, "Above is paradise, below are Suzhou and Hangzhou." [17]The metropolitan tour refers chiefly to the city tour of Shanghai. [18]These three cities are close and accessible to each other. [19]The tour of the

cities is locally known as the "Lesser East China tour". [20]The real highlights are [21]the visit to the vast Taihu Lake in Suzhou, the rippling West Lake in Hangzhou, garden cities decorated with a rich variety of pavilion, terrace, and tower, the skyline of Pudong New Area, the 88-storied Jinmao Tower overlooking the river, and the Oriental Pearl Tower piercing the clouds.

Another example is[22] the "Jiangnan garden and landscape tour." [23]Jiangnan gardening is one major school of Chinese landscape gardening. [24]One can appreciate (the beauty of) hills and water without going outside the city walls and enjoy (the serenity of) springs and woods while living within the downtown city. [25]One of the gardening techniques is to make clever use of borrowed views. [26]It integrates outside views of natural landscape with those inside the garden. [27]This art of gardening can be found in Zhan Garden in Nanjing, Ge Garden (Bamboo Garden) in Yangzhou, Li Garden in Wuxi, Lingering Garden and Humble Administrator's Garden in Suzhou, Tuisi Garden in Tongli (Wujiang), Yu Garden in Shanghai, and Guo's Villa in Hangzhou. [28]All these gardens feature a scene within a scene as if created by nature. [29]The poetic line "hill beyond hill and tower beyond tower" shows natural hills range after range and the artistic layout of landscaped gardens.

[30]Last but not least, I'd like to recommend the "Jiangnan Gourmet Tour". [31]Special food in Jiangnan is famous for its color, fragrance, taste, shape, and variety. [32]There are the pressed salted duck of Nanjing, Wuxi-style spare ribs braised in brown sauce, the squirrel-like mandarin fish of Suzhou, the Pudong chicken of Shanghai, the Dongpo Pork of Hangzhou (after the poet), the hairy crab of Yangcheng Lake, to name but a few. [33]I'm sure you will eat to your delight.

Ladies and gentlemen,[34] East China and its history, culture and scenic beauty are beckoning you. [35]I hope the golden tour of East China will be your paradise for travel, leisure and holiday.

[36]Finally, enjoy your trip. Thank you!

(陈刚译,并提供编号、底线)

【ST3 与 TT3 对比、分析、简评】

① 华东黄金旅游线欢迎辞(ST)是另一种情形、风格和写法,翻译难度不小,不能机械式地字字全译。但如何灵活地把握好翻译过程,保留有价值的又独具中国特色的文化和语言内涵,最后呈现得体的译文(TT),是颇有讲究的。不少汉语看似简单,但在英语中则是另一副"面相"。

② ST 画线部分[1],有比较得体的译文,参看 TT 画线部分[1]。

③ ST[2]应注意在 TT 中的位置调整,见 TT[2]。

④ ST [3] 比较中国式,TT[3]基本上是另一种思路。后半句应避免直译,换言之,不要消极地强调旅途很辛苦、很劳累(中文思路),要正面建议"劳逸结合"(西方游客乐于接

受)。

⑤ ST[4]完全是适合并针对说中文游客的,学生会发觉翻译无从"下手"。显然,完全译成英文,文字一定啰唆。参见 TT[4],读者自己揣摩、比较,不难发现:TT 言简意赅,内涵全包。

⑥ ST[5]比较书面语,注意尽可能用 TL 的口语体来转化,见 TT[5]—[7]:上下文衔接(contextual amplification),ST 中没有;"人文景观独特",应加以"泛化",不要用 unique,因为该词指"独一无二",不符合实际情况(起码"华东线"的项目安排还是自然景观多余人文景观);"江南鱼米之乡,山清水秀之处,历史文物之都,名人荟萃之地"是相当难译的,中文有一种平衡美和对称美,而且"处"、"都"和"地"(在汉语中能接受,但不够准确,如"华东"≠"都")在英文中很难处理,不能照字面译。建议译文是:(It is known as) the "<u>home</u> of fish and rice, a <u>resort</u> with natural landscape, an <u>area</u> of historical and cultural heritage, and a <u>place</u> for gathering famous people."

⑦ 西方游客对我们的行政划分知之甚少,处理 ST[6]—[8]要简单明了。"区域"的内涵不仅仅指地理位置,但译成英文,还不如单纯点,用 geographically 代之。"市"要译成"直辖市",以示区别。"线路"应指"旅游线路/路线"。参见 TT[8]—[10]。

⑧ ST[9]—[10] 在 TL 中需调整位置,以符合英文表达思路,见 TT[11]—[12]。

⑨ ST[11]涉及诸多业内常用特殊名词和表达法,注意 TT[13]。其中,"各具特色的旅游项目"用 SIT(special interest tour)来表达,"可供选择"可以省略,不必硬译成"...for you to choose from"等。

⑩ ST[12]—[13]相当难译,大家会对"江南"、"水乡"、"都市观光游"、"尽在……"等一些常见语言现象感到"左右为难",甚至"束手无策"。国内权威的汉英词典对"江南"的译文不是(很)不够准确,就是过于宽泛,起码不是用来(特别)描绘江浙一带——苏南浙北地区的。我们仅提供部分有关"江南"的具体英文表达法:the Jiangnan, the Jiangnan region, the Jiangnan area, the reticulated canal region of the Jiangnan, the canal region of Jiangsu and Zhejiang Provinces, Jiangnan..., the Jiangnan region, the canal-laced lower reaches of the Yangtze River 等①。"水乡"除 water town 外,还可以是 water village、waterside village 等。详见 TT[14]—[15]。

⑪ ST[14]中的俗语有若干种比较好的英译文,这里笔者选用乔治·布什在杭州祝酒词中的说法。见 TT[16]。

⑫ ST[12]和 ST[15]中的"(大)都市"在 TT 中应保持一致,见 TT[17]。

⑬ ST[16]中"三地相连、交通便捷"可以合并成一句,"小华东之旅"应考虑"小"的译法。详见 TT[18]+[19],注意"be close and accessible to..."和"be locally known as..."这样的结构和表达。

⑭ ST[17]—[18]的转换成 TT[20]—[21]时,结构作了头尾调整。翻译 ST 的要点是使文字简约、口语化,但事先要很清楚地认识到:"烟波浩渺"、"秀色"、"清波涟漪"、"数百园

---

① 这些表达法均引自 Knapp 的 Chinese Bridges。陈刚还有另外十几种有关"江南"的英文表达法,用于不同的文本和语境。

林争奇斗艳"、"瑰丽多姿"、"拔地而起"、"傲视江滨"、"直上云霄"等写景状物的表达法,不必机械的做翻译;"亭台楼阁"中的"楼"与"阁"在英文中只需用一个词;"浦东新区"中的"区"实为 district,即上海市中一个行政区,但过去一直用"(New) Area",故沿用。此外,"(浦东新区)拔地而起"被灵活处理成"the skyline of (Pudong New Area)";"金茂大厦(傲视江滨)"经增益成"the 88-storied Jinmao Tower (overlooking the river)";"东方明珠"应为"东方明珠塔",而"直上云霄"解读为"高耸入/插云"。

⑮ ST[19]中的"(江南园林及)山水风情游"只需处理成"山水游"即可,"风情"为"虚词";而"山水(游)"不必直译(因为前边还有"江南园林及"),可以简洁地译成"landscape (tour)"或"natural landscape (tour)"。同理,"山水画"可以译为"a painting of mountain and water/mountain-and-water painting/a landscape painting"。

⑯ ST[20]—[24]属于难句。详见 TT[23]—[28]。其一,这里的"园林"指古代中国人基于"天人合一"哲学观之"山水园林",所以"园林"可以译成(landscape) gardening。其二,"不出城郭而获山水之怡,身居闹市而有泉林之致"只要意译即可。其三,"借景"可根据语境处理成"borrowing a view/scene 或 borrowed views/scenes",然后作一补偿(compensation),见 TT[26],或者"use the scene outside or inside a garden to harmonize with other scenes in the garden"。其四,ST[22]+[23]应该合并处理(combination),并注意 ST[23]中双底线园林名称的译法,园林名称的翻译很有讲究,建议平时多多总结。其五,翻译 ST[24]时,特别注意跟上句的衔接;"妙趣天成"实则应解读为"似乎天成",译成". . . as if created by nature","妙趣"已包含在整句中,不必直接译出。

⑰ ST[25]亦属于难句。首先,"山外青山楼外楼"是南宋林升的《题临安邸》的首句,可以处理为"mountain beyond mountain and tower beyond tower",但这里宜调整为"hill beyond hill and tower beyond tower",因江南的山多为 hill。其次,"(点出了)江南的群山有层次、园林有格局的特色"只能在充分理解的基础上"巧译"。详见 TT[29]。

⑱ ST[26]的翻译要有结构上的整体观念。这篇欢迎词后半部分的举例结构,处理成英文后是:Take. . . for example. Another example is. . . Last but not least. . ."美食游"比较好的译文是"gourmet tour"。

⑲ ST[27]中对江南佳肴特色的描述应合并、简约成"色、香、味、形、多"。"佳肴"的译法不少,最为通俗易懂的英文是"special food"。详见 TT[31]。

⑳ ST[28]涉及菜名翻译,需要开一个主题课系统地讲。其中,"东坡肉"较为简洁、有效的处理方法是 Dongpo Pork (after the poet),千万不要误解并处理成"唐僧肉"。"大闸蟹"的译文有"Chinese mitten crab, hairy crab, big sluice crab, Dazha crab"等,而"阳澄湖大闸蟹"则简单地处理成"the hairy crab of Yangcheng Lake"。值得一提的是,英文中比较地道的举例法是 —— there are A, B, C, D. . . to name but a few,以免挂一漏万。有关译文,见 TT[32]。

㉑ ST[29]的简洁处理,见 TT[33]。

㉒ ST[30]—[32]的处理原则及技巧是概括化(generalization)、简化(simplification)和创译(creative translation)。详见 TT[34]—[36]。

切记,创译之理念和方法应是贯穿于始终的。

6 本章结语

总体来说,旅游翻译原则属于应用翻译。但旅游文本(含笔头和口头)中包含了文学文本翻译,如山水诗歌翻译、景点楹联翻译,更有比较独立的旅游文学翻译。有关旅游主题的文本翻译中,还应包括旅游学术文本的翻译。而归属应用翻译的旅游翻译,跟其他应用翻译一样则应归属于职业翻译暨专业翻译。

旅游文本,不论是英语还是汉语,主要是一种应用语文。旅游文本(ST+TT)主要分为两大类文体:书面体和口语体。本章讨论了诸多旅游文本中比较常用、比较重要的两类:旅游指南和导译文本。前者涉及英汉互译,后者强调汉译英。这两类文本比较难教、难学。

旅游指南,分别属于 expressive 文本、informative 文本和 vocative 文本,并分别具有 expressive 功能、informative 功能和 vocative 功能;但更多的情况是,旅游指南兼有上述三种类型及其功能,用词需生动形象、明白畅晓,句式需自然流畅、直截了当。

导译文本,或导游词,属 informative 文本并具 informative 功能或 vocative 文本并具 vocative 功能,或者两者兼而有之。但根据导游词创作过程和结果来看,它又可以分为即兴型导游词、预制导游词和"现编+预制导译词",后两类还分别属于复合型和即兴精制型。

旅游翻译的原则与标准,在初阶、进阶、高阶三个阶段分别论述。对初阶的要求涉及双语功底、中外文化、主题知识和写作能力;对进阶的要求涉及相关专/职业的素质和能力、相关专/职业翻译的学养和能力和相关的实践研究潜力和能力;对高阶的要求涉及(作为应用翻译或者职业/专业翻译的)旅游翻译的原则与标准——即是动态的、多元的、功能的、与时俱进的。

高阶的要求还涉及旅游文本翻译的难点,主要指导游指南和"预制型"导译文本。这类翻译要遵循以下三项原则:游客反映原则这一原则(即文本译写原则)、游客第一原则(即旅游翻译行为规范,是一总体原则)、文化传递原则(即"以我为主"原则)。

此外,旅游翻译能力的提高,除了熟悉、了解本章所讨论的旅游翻译分类及特性,旅游翻译文本文体要求,旅游文本语篇要求,旅游翻译初阶、进阶与高阶,旅游文本的翻译原则及标准,两种常见的旅游文本(亦是旅游文本翻译之难点)等之外,除了认真、细致地研读、实践本章提供的各项有代表性的旅游翻译案例之外,读者务必做到:

(1) 广泛阅读旅游翻译的各类文本(具体见本书的"参考文献");

(2) 在完成有关教科书要求的基础上,继续寻找没有指导、答案的原语文本,自行多翻译练习;

(3) 多多了解旅游界的有关行业、工种乃至岗位;

(4) 通过在旅游公司兼职(前提是有国家颁发的英语导游证),进行有针对性的笔译实践及导译实践。

第五章 广告翻译

1 广告文体概述

广告是人们日常生活中经常运用的一种言语活动形式。从文化语境角度看,广告的社会目的和功能一般遵循 E.S. Lewis 提出的 AIDA 原则(A/attention/引起注意,I/interest/产生兴趣,D/desire/具有欲望,A/action/付诸行动)(黄国文,2001:299)。译文广告语篇和源广告语篇一样,具有很强的功利性,因此同样要注意其语篇宏观结构设计的艺术性和语言表达的得体性。

广告是一种特殊的语篇类型。对广告语篇可以从文化语境层面和语篇语言层面进行分析。Malinowski 把语境分为两个层次:文化语境和情景语境。文化语境是更高层次、更抽象的语境。系统功能学家们认为语篇体裁是有阶段、有目的的社会活动,不同的语篇体裁有着不同的社会目的,不同的社会目的可由不同的语篇体裁来实现。Ventola 认为,在讨论体裁时,应该考虑到"体裁的参与者所要达到的社会目的"。Martin 和 Eggins 也把体裁和社会目的以及功能作用连在了一起;他们认为从人际功能的角度看,人们使用语言的目的决定了语篇的体裁地位。在日常生活中,人们总是用语言做事。"在询问语言在一个具体语篇中所起的作用,在分析我们怎样用语言来做这一切,我们就是在描述体裁了。"由此可见,系统功能语言学家把社会活动的目的和体裁定位紧密地连在一起。当讲述发生在某人身上的事情,我们就用叙述体语篇体裁,当描述某人或某物,我们就用描述体语篇体裁。一个语篇的广告体裁地位很大程度上取决于该语篇的社会目的。只要该语篇的社会目的是为了吸引受众以达到推销某种产品或服务的目的,就应该将它列入广告体裁。

广告从广义上可分为商业广告和非商业广告。相对于以非盈利为目的的非商业广告而言,美国市场协会(AMA)把商业广告定义为"由可认定的广告主出资通过各种媒体,本意是劝导人们购买他们的产品或服务,或是接受他们的观念"。可见,广告语篇体裁的主要社会目的是"传递情报,改变人们对广告商品的态度,诱发其行动而使广告主获得利益"。英国语言学家 Torben 则将广告的社会功能概括为:传播信息、树立形象和劝说与刺激消费的功能。

从功能语法的角度看,吸引消费者注意、强化消费者记忆和打动消费者是文化语境层面的目的(purpose of cultural context),也是任何商业广告的最终社会目的。传播信息、树立形象和劝说与刺激消费的功能,属于文化语境层面的社会功能,为语篇的体裁目的和社会目的服务。不同于其他体裁,广告是一种复杂而又具有独特性质的语篇体裁,具体表现在广告具有非常复杂且多面性的多种语篇功能,如信息功能、表情功能、美感功能等。这些语篇功能可能会在语篇的某一阶段同时存在。Reiss 称具有这种语言现象的语篇为复合类型语篇

(compound type)。这些语篇功能在文化语境层面发挥其独特的社会功能,为语篇体裁的最终社会目的服务。广告语篇社会交流活动的参与者是广告主和广告读者。就广告主而言,由于对广告受众的合作成功与否没有肯定的把握,为了获得成功和达到目的,广告主常会利用图文并茂的各种文字形式和修辞手段来为自己服务。

Jakobson 在《语言学与诗学》(1960)一书中说,诗学必须解决语言信息怎样成为艺术品这一难题。广告语篇也面临同样的问题,即语言信息怎样才能成为艺术品,以达到吸引读者眼球的目的。在广告语篇中恰当使用修辞手法是提升广告语言吸引力的一个重要手段。研究表明,各种修辞手法在广告这个体裁平台上发挥着极大的体裁魅力,表现出极强的语用功能。做好广告修辞语篇的翻译工作,使译文广告既能传达原广告语篇的信息内容,又能成为艺术品,是我们应该钻研的课题。笔者认为,广告修辞语篇的翻译应该从宏观和微观两个层面入手。前者主要从语篇的体裁目的和功能入手研究翻译策略的制订;后者主要从语言层面入手,探讨具体翻译方法的选择。广告修辞语篇的翻译研究如果只停留于局部或微观层面,往往会就事论事,产生不可译或不知怎样译的困惑。因此,本章尝试从宏观和微观两个层面入手,探讨以人际功能为主要倾向的广告语篇的翻译问题。

2 广告分类及其文体特征

2.1 双关广告语篇文体特征

广告双关语是广告语篇体裁中常见的修辞手法之一。广告双关语涉及双重或多重语义场,产生双重或多重文化语境和语篇语境含义。广告双关语的修辞效果具有含蓄与幽默的语篇特点。从广告语篇接收者角度看,它可产生语义模糊和多向语义联想,更能引起消费者注意。

英语修辞学对双关的定义包括两个方面:一是从语音出发,二是从语义出发。前者构成谐音双关,后者构成语义双关。根据牛津字典,双关解释为"用一个词去暗示两种或两种以上的意义或引起两种或两种以上的不同联想,或用两个发音相同或相近而意义不同的词去暗示两种或两种以上的意义或引起两种或两种以上的不同联想,以产生一种幽默效果"。依照《辞海》的定义,"双关语"为修辞学的辞格之一,即利用语言文字上同音或多义的关系,使一个词或一句话关涉两层或多层意思。从功能语法角度看,"层"的内涵应该是指"语域",即一个词或一句话可以从两个或多个不同的语域或语义场构建和解释。"语义场"是功能语法的一个重要理论概念,它指发生的事情、讲述的语篇内容等。双关修辞格主要是利用音或义的巧合,进行同音异义转换,有意使语句同时兼有双层或多层语义场含义,即表层语义场含义和内容层语义场含义。表层语义场含义是掩饰义,深层语义场含义是所指义。

广告双关主要以两种类型出现:第一种是一个词本身可能具有两层含义,第二种是广告语篇宣传的公司或产品品牌名称含有某种其他意义,构成双关,称为品牌双关。双关广告通常具有表层语境意义自足和完整的特点,其暗含的深层语义场含义对广告受众来说有时难以捕捉。双关修辞格具有的双重或多重语义场的特点使语言显得含蓄幽默、活泼有趣,具有吸引广告受众的巨大魅力,因此成为了广告设计者们热衷选择的修辞手法之一。因为广告受众对广告语篇产生的兴趣越浓厚,记忆力就越强,最终采取购买行动的可能性就越大。当广告受众面临两种或多种语义场意义的选择时,为了克服双关带来的语义模糊性,他们要透过语言的表层,主动从各种途径选择一个能加工广告双关语篇真正含义的语境,领会广告主所要表达的深层语义场内涵。寻找最佳关联所付出的努力能帮助广告受众对产品发生兴趣,增强对产品的记忆,从而采取购买行动,这样,广告双关语的社会功能得以完成,广告语篇的体裁目的和社会目的得以实现。

广告双关语的语篇主要有以下几点:

① 含蓄委婉,耐人寻味。应该指出的是,我们是在语言层面探讨广告双关的语篇特点,在文化语境层面探讨其社会功能。如上所述,虽然广告主可根据不同受众、不同产品而设置不同内容的广告,但广告的基本社会功能是吸引受众采取购买行动。广告双关语能以它含蓄委婉、寓意深刻的语篇特点吸引受众,实现其语篇的社会功能,其原因是从潜在顾客的角度讲,广告双关语含蓄委婉的语篇特点使广告受众在弄清广告双关语所要表达的真正内涵过程中,必须花费额外的精力和代价。这个探索和挖掘的过程可帮助广告受众记住商品名称,激发购买欲望,同时诱发潜在的购买行动。这样,广告双关语的社会功能得以实现,广告语篇体裁的社会目的得以完成。例如:

【例1】

牵挂你一生,爱戴你一生。(黄金首饰广告)(《光明日报》1997年6月18日)

这则广告通过"爱戴"这个词创造了双关语义场。"爱戴"表层语境语义场指喜欢佩戴该品牌的黄金首饰,深层语境语义场是把"爱戴"看作是一个具有表达固定意义的词组,意为是"深爱并珍重"。广告受众在仔细捉摸之后,方可知道其还有另一层隐秘的深层语境语义场含义。这则广告通过"爱戴"这个具有双重语义场的双关词组,营造了一个让人心领神会、情意浓浓的气氛。广告受众在弄清其另一个隐藏的含义后,领悟到了双关修辞语含而不露的语言特点所产生的一种特殊美感,会有一种物有所值、劳有所报的成功快感。

【例2】

成功之路,从头开始。(飘柔洗发水)

"从头开始",一语多义。"头"有两层语义场含义:1) 指人的器官;2) 指开始。在这则双关广告语篇中,将其意义理解为成功要从基础开始,也是很自然的。但当广告受众得知这是洗发水广告时,就会对"头"有不同的新想法和新认识。不论在中国文化和西方文化里,美人都是和美发连在一起的。美丽的头发可塑造美丽的外表,更富于魅力、更有自信,因而更能把握机遇,获得成功,这才是这则广告深层语义场的内在含义。

由此可见,广告双关语在信息传递时关涉两层或多层语义场,第一层是显性的,第二层是隐性的,而隐性义才是作者或说话者要表达的本意。"双关话语有两层意义(其实也包括两层以上的意义在内),但说话人真正意义不在表面那层意思,而在骨子里的那层意思"。双关作为一种修辞方法,可使受众产生一种神秘感和好奇心,促使他们关注和思考下去。亚里士多德说:"人们喜欢被不平常的东西打动。"这两则双关广告就创造了一种不平常的东西,打动了广告受众的心,吸引了他们的注意力。

② 幽默风趣,智慧闪现。广告双关语多以褒义的内容形式出现,可帮助产生整体语篇

的幽默效果。从位于文化语境层面的语旨的角度看,由于广告语篇体裁的参与者广告主和广告受众之间的合作关系的功利性质和合作成功的把握性不确定,广告双关语所产生的幽默效果可帮助广告受众减少对广告所持的一种不信任态度,排除一开始对广告就抱有的一种逆反心理。幽默效果给受众带来了轻松愉悦的心情,使受众在和谐的交际氛围中心悦诚服地去读广告,因而更容易接受广告语篇所传递的商业信息,增大了交际活动成功的几率。例如:

【例3】

谁能惩治腐败?(新飞电冰箱广告)

一看到这则广告,读者的注意力马上都会被吸引住,因为腐败现象是民众十分关注的问题。他们会情不自禁地问,是否国家又出台了对付和惩治腐败的新政策。但仔细一看,这是一则电冰箱广告,就会马上联想到"腐败"在此指的并不是政治腐败,而是食品腐败。一个是具有政治方面的语义场,一个是属食品方面的语义场,两个内涵完全不同的语义场整合在一起,构成了创意巧妙的双关。在今天反腐倡廉的大背景中,自然会产生极大的幽默效果,让人留下深刻的印象。类似广告双关语所产生的幽默效果在广告语篇中比比皆是。可见,通过对多义词、同音词或谐音词、异义词的巧妙运用,广告双关语把语言文字的双重语义场连在一起,在特定的语境中表达出一明一暗的双重含义,这种由此及彼的语用效果帮助构建了语言本身的幽默与活泼,给广告受众以回味和想象的余地,增加了对广告的兴趣,激发了人们的购买欲,以实现广告双关语的社会功能和完成广告语篇的体裁目的。

③ 简明扼要,经济高效。广告双关语备受广告主青睐的另一个主要原因还在于,广告双关语具有简明扼要的语篇特点和经济高效的社会功能。从广告主角度讲,简洁十分重要,因为广告版面非常昂贵。"双关就很经济,因为两种意思融到一个词或短语中。事实上,双关是一种广告商推销产品时所用的一种十分省力的手段。"对受众来讲,面对铺天盖地的广告,受众的接受力是有限的。广告双关语所具有的简明扼要的语言特点不仅发挥了经济高效的社会功能,并在广告这个特殊的语境中起到能够引起消费者注意的社会效果,为语篇体裁目的的实现发挥了独特的作用。例如:

【例4】

真正的谋杀者。(杀虫剂广告)

我的名声是吹出来的。(电风扇广告)

2.2 押头韵广告语篇文体特征

从功能语法的角度看,广告主要是吸引消费者注意,打动消费者心弦,促使消费者购买。为了达到这个功利性很强的社会目的,广告主常常会利用图文并茂和各种修辞手段来为自己服务。图文并茂的广告,不仅应使广告受众感到视觉美,同时还应使他们感受到语言的音乐美。押韵是构建语言音乐艺术美的主要手段之一。从文化语境的层面看,由于它的社会功能和广告语篇体裁的社会目的相一致,无标记地实现了广告的体裁目的,因此成为广告制作者十分青睐的修辞手段之一。

英语广告常采用的韵类有头韵(alliteration)、元韵(assonance)、押韵(rhyme)、假韵

(consonance)等,如"Never late on Father's Day"中两个元音 /ei /帮助产生了元韵。在英语广告语篇中,最为常见的是头韵。alliteration 一词源于拉丁语的 lettere,意为"repeating and playing upon the same letter"。《韦氏新大学辞典》把头韵定义为两个或两个以上邻近的词或音节中起首辅音的重复。头韵在古英语的诗歌中独领风骚,如英国史诗"Beowulf"(《贝奥武夫》),"King Arthur"(《亚瑟王》)等。随着诗歌中脚韵和其他韵律的发展,头韵才降到了较为次要的地位。但头韵仍旧作为一种语音修辞格,频频出现在各类语篇,特别是在英语广告语篇中,它不仅赋予语言音韵美和节奏美,同时还渲染和烘托了语篇气氛和感情,加强了语篇主题的表现力。

2.3 仿拟广告语篇文体特征

陈望道在《修辞学发凡》中说:"为了滑稽嘲弄而故意仿拟特种即成形式的,名叫仿拟格。"英语称仿拟为 parody。parody 一词源于古希腊词 paroidia,原意为"beside, subsidiary or mock song"(离题的、辅助的或嘲弄性的歌曲),后来泛指通过类似卡通漫画家式的技巧,对某一作者所使用的词语、风格、态度、语气和思想的模仿。广告之所以成为仿拟修辞大显身手的平台,其根本原因是仿拟修辞格可产生幽默睿智的语篇功能,可起到吸引受众,延长其记忆,促使其产生购买行为的社会功能。同时,仿拟可使广告受众有一种似曾相识的感觉,容易被广告受众所接受,因而无标记地实现了广告的体裁目的和社会目的,成为广告体裁中最为常见的修辞手法之一。

3 广告文体翻译特点与原则

传统上,广告分为名目繁多的亚语篇体裁,如修辞类广告,包括比喻广告、拟人广告、双关语广告、排比广告等;营销创意广告,如承诺、定位、诱惑、服务、产地、公关等。过多的广告亚语篇体裁分类会对宏观层面翻译策略选择的理论性探讨带来种种困难。因此,我们可尝试采用功能语言观,从文化语境层面的语篇社会体裁目的和功能入手,从三大元功能角度把商业广告语篇分为:(1)以概念功能为主要倾向的商业广告,(2)以人际功能为主要倾向的商业广告。前者的语篇功能是传递信息,后者旨在感染读者。广告是一种目的性很强的文本,任何形式的商业广告都要通过吸引广告受众来达到敦促对方完成购买行动的社会目的。以概念功能为主要倾向的商业广告吸引广告受众的手段是提供产品和服务的具体客观信息,因此译文应该"直接、完整地传递源语文本内容",直译是这类亚广告语篇的主要策略;比较而言,以人际功能为主要倾向的商业广告语篇,吸引广告受众的主要手段是运用各种语言表现形式,为了感染目的语受众,译文可以再造"文本形式,以直接实现预期的接受者反映"(Reiss,1989:109)。因此,可以采用灵活多变的翻译策略,只要能达到和源语篇在文化语境层面上的对等就是好译文。

首先我们分析一下双关广告语篇。我们可以从情景语境和三大元功能的角度理解双关广告语篇。情景语境是由语义场、语旨和语式三大成分构成。"语义场"是功能语法的一个重要概念,它指社会活动中所发生的事情、所讲述的语篇内容等。双关辞格主要是利用音或义的巧合,进行同音异义的暗换,有意使语句同时兼有双重或双层含义;表层含义和深层含义,表层含义是掩饰义,深层含义是所指义。所谓"两层"意思,从功能语法的角度看,指两个"情景语境"或两层"语义场",即一个词或一句话可从两个不同的"情景语境"或"语义场"层面进行构建和解释。由于每一句双关话语客观上都存在着两个不同的语义场,因此需要话语创建者的进一步明示和话语接受者的进一步推理,究竟哪个语义场才可表现广告主的真实意图。广告双关语通常出现在广告标题中,其表层语义场意义常常是自足和完整的,因此,其深层语义场含义对广告受众来说有时难以捕捉,要求话语接受者付出额外努力,排除表层语境含义,寻找最佳关联,以领悟广告主的真正意图。广告双关语主要以两种类型出现,第一种是一个词本身可从两层语义场含义进行解释。例如:

【例 5】

The driver is safer when the road is dry; The road is safer when the driver is dry.

这则广告由两个整齐对称的句子构成。dry 可以从两个层面解释,一是"干燥",即路面不滑,二是"没有沾酒"。dry 在两个分句中各取一义,帮助构成了双关广告语篇。这则双关广告语篇以巧妙的构思和睿智的用词吸引了司机和行人,给司机以警示,不要喝酒开车,如若不然,就会导致危险。

广告双关语第二种类型是以广告语篇所宣传的公司或品牌名称含有某种其他意义而构成双关,也可称之为品牌双关修辞格。例如:

【例 6】

"美的"牌家电,美的全面,美的彻底。

该广告借助品牌名称"美的"与形容词"美的"字形相同、语音相近为条件构成了广告品牌双关修辞格(当然,有人认为这不是双关)。"美的"涉及两个语义场,既指产品的品牌,又指产品所具有的外表美丽和质量过关的特点。品牌双关修辞格这种独具匠心的用法必然会导致重复修辞格(repetition)的出现。这则广告除"美的"连续重复外,还涉及了语篇句型结构的多次重复:"美的全面,美的彻底"。既突出和强调品牌名称,又实现了吸引广告受众的社会功能。

【例 7】

Money doesn't grow on trees. But it blossoms at our branches.

译文 1:

树上是长不出钱的,但却能在我们劳依得银行的各"枝"行里开花结果。

译文 2:

劳依得银行帮你理财,使财增值。(劳依得银行广告)

我们首先从主位推进角度分析这则广告。按照 Danes 的观点,每个小句都有自己的主位。在一个由两个或两个以上小句组成的语篇中,整个语篇随着小句主位的推进而展开。在语篇展开过程中,前后句子的主位和述位、述位和述位、主位和主位之间会产生某种联系和变化,称为主位推进。Danes 提出三种主要的主位推进模式(patterns of thematic progression)(Danes,1974:118—119)。这则广告语篇属于其中的主位同一型或平行型模式,即主位相同,述位不同。主位是小句的出发点,构成这个语篇的两个小句的主位都是"钱",因此"钱"是该语篇讨论的主题。

从概念功能看,这则广告由 5 个实词构成:money,trees,grow,blossoms 和 branch,其中 trees,grow,blossoms 和 branch(如当树枝讲)属同一个语义场范畴,但它们与语篇小句的主位和语篇的中心词 money 不属同一个语义场,因此无法构成整体语篇连贯。Guy Cook 说,读者在阅读时如感到语篇不连贯,应该而且总是要往上一层寻找连贯,直到找到为止(Cook,1994)。branch 既可指树枝,又可指银行的分行,联系语篇语境,这则广告宣传的是劳依得银行的理"钱"优势,如从另一个语义场角度把 branch 看作银行的支行,语篇的连贯即可形成。因此,语篇的深层语义场含义是:只要顾客把钱存到劳依得银行的任何支行里,他们的钱就会开花结果。branch 帮助构成语义双关和双关广告语篇。

此外,这则广告使用比喻修辞格,把"银行"比作"大树",把"支行"比作"树枝",使银行具有生命的绿色;把"钱"比作"花",使之脱俗高雅,以此吸引广告受众。译文 1 采用基本直译＋保留双关明示法,译文中"各枝行"中的"枝"与"各支行"中的"支"读音相同,构成谐音双关。通过启用保留双关明示法,译文不仅明示源语篇的深层语义场含义,而且保留源语篇的幽默与含蓄,获得和源语篇同样的语境效果。译文 2 采用广告口号形式明示源语篇的深层语义场含义,读起来朗朗上口。在广告双关语篇的交流中,译者和广告语篇受众面临的是两种或多种意义的选择。为了帮助目的语读者排除双关语义的模糊性,快而准地领会广告文本所要表达的深层语义内涵,明示翻译策略应是首选策略。

其次,我们再来简单分析一下仿拟广告语篇和押头韵广告语篇。

仿拟广告语篇通过对谚语、名言和警句的模仿,使广告读者通过对被仿拟谚语的联想,深刻感悟仿拟广告的新颖创意和深刻寓意。在目的语中能找到相同或相似的仿拟表达方式进行翻译,是仿拟广告的首选翻译策略之一。就以人际元功能为主要倾向的广告翻译而言,研究表明采用套译手法进行翻译可获得极佳的语境效果,能够圆满完成广告的体裁目的,符合奈达的心理近似学说(psychological proximity)。从文化语境层面看,商业广告及其译文都属有特定目标的体裁活动,即宣传产品,吸引顾客,使他们付诸行动,购买商品。只要译文能获得和原广告语篇在文化语境层面上的对等,完成广告的体裁目的,就是好译文。

我国历来享有"诗国"的美称,音韵是我国诗、曲中传统的艺术手法之一。但由于汉语自身的特点,辞格中没有"头韵"一说。那么对于英语广告头韵修辞应该采用怎样的翻译策略来弥补翻译过程中的美感剥损呢?我们可以从功能语法理论观入手,认为好译文需要实现目的语语篇和源语语篇达到文化语境层面的对等。广告语篇的翻译应是灵活多样、不拘一格的。

4 广告文体翻译策略

4.1 双关广告语篇明示翻译策略

(1) 保留双关明示法

由于双关的自身特点,译文无法用与原文相同的双关修辞法,这个观点已基本成为一个定论,但并不绝对。中西语言和文化之间存在许多共核与共性,某些双关语在一定语境中有直译或半直译的可能性。如在前面提到的例子"Money doesn't grow on trees. But it blossoms at our branches",原文双关 branches 译为"枝行",就是一个很好的例子。又如:前面的例子"从头开始"(飘柔),译为"Start ahead"(Rejoice)。"头"和 head 所具有的共同语义场内涵使通过直译法保留源语篇的双关修辞表现形式成为可能。"从头开始"是熟语,具有完全自足的表层含义。"飘柔"是洗发水广告,由于洗发水和"头"有着更为直接的关系,读者会领会到"头"的另外一个语义场含义:"头"或"头发"。ahead 由前缀 a 加 head 构成,虽然在表层含义中似乎和"头"没什么联系,但深层次地去思考,ahead 的英文解释"from the head, from the beginning"仍和"头"密切相关;同时 ahead 和 head 的发音也十分相似,因此 ahead 在此可引起两种不同的联想,暗示两层语义场含义,构成和中文双关广告相同的语义双关表现形式。产品商标 Rejoice 为整个语篇提供语境,帮助读者快而准地把握语篇的深层语义场含义。

(2) 体裁转换明示法

系统功能语法首先是从语篇的生成结构入手探讨语篇的体裁地位。就双关广告的翻译而言,译文可通过改变源语篇的体裁结构来明示源广告双关语篇的深层含义,以达到与源语篇在文化语境层面上的对等。例如:

【例 8】

"美的"牌家电,美的全面,美的彻底。

译文 1:

Midea home appliances are really beautiful—beautiful from head to toe, beautiful inside out.

译文 2:

Midea home appliances are really beautiful—beautiful in quality and beautiful in appearance.

这是广东顺德"美的"家电的广告。该广告借助品牌名称"美的"与形容词"美的"字形相同、语音相近构成了广告品牌双关修辞格,"美的"既可指品牌,又可指产品美丽的外表和质量。

原文广告是一个由两个偏正结构短语组成的广告口号语篇,译文改用了描述体体裁的综述—具体描述的语篇模式。许多语言学家,如 McCarthy(1990),Hoey(1983),Coulthard(1977),根据描述体语篇不同阶段之间的逻辑语义结构,提出三种常见的语篇结构,其中综述—具体语篇模式被认为是描述体语篇中最为常见的一种模式。描述体语篇体裁的社会目的是向读者提供信息,这和商业广告的社会目的一致,因此成为商业广告体裁一种常见的表现形式。

译文 1:Midea home appliances are really beautiful,(综述)(They are) beautiful from head to toe,(具体描述 1)(They are) beautiful inside out.(具体描述 2)

译文 2:Midea home appliances are really beautiful,(综述)(They are) beautiful in quality,(具体描述 1)(They are) beautiful in appearance.(具体描述 2)

译文中,"美的家电"中的"美的"采用音译的方法,但 Midea 没有译出原语语篇"美的"这个品牌的双重语义场含义。通过启用综述—具体描述的语篇模式,译文明示了原文双关的深层含义。译文1在内容上基本采用了直译。译文2明示了美的家电美的深层含义:不仅在外表,而且还在质量。两个译文都是由三个归属类型关系过程小句构成,"载体"作主语,属无标记关系过程句,帮助构成译文排比修辞格。通过对形容词 beautiful 的反复重复,强调了"美的家电"的魅力和功能,弥补原语语篇在翻译过程中因双关修辞格的缺损而造成的美感剥损。

(3) 拆分增补明示法

双关广告的翻译也采用一分为二的拆分法,来明示深层语义场含义。例如:

【例9】

牵挂你一生,爱戴你一生。(黄金首饰广告)

译文:

Love you and treasure you; wearing you, all my life.

这则广告通过"爱戴"这个词创造一个双关语境。"爱戴"既可指"喜欢佩戴"这个品牌的黄金首饰,又可指"尊重和深爱"。译文通过拆分增补法,把这个广告双关语拆分为两个短语,以明示其深层语义场含义和表层语义场含义。译文的前两个小句"Love you and treasure you"启用心理过程和一般现在时,表示"爱你"和"珍惜你"的这种情感状态;后两个小句"wearing you, all my life"启用物质过程和现在进行时。物质过程表示人在外部世界所做的事和发出的动作。"wearing you"指我已采取了购买行动,此刻我佩戴着你;"all my life"强调我的决心:我将一生一世永远佩戴你。该广告通过作者和黄金首饰之间的对话形式,拟人化地生动表达了作者对这种首饰的情感,以达到感染他人采取购买行动的目的。

【例10】

Try our sweet corn; you will smile from ear to ear.

译文:

尝尝我们的玉米吧,包您吃不停,乐不够!

这则广告中,ear 可看作是具有双重语义场含义的多义词,根据语篇语境,ear 既可指"麦穗"或"苞米",又可指"耳朵"。"smile from ear to ear"既可看成一个习语,泛指"笑容可掬",又可指两个动作,指审视着一个一个的苞米时所发出的会心微笑。此广告乍一看给人的感觉是:在品尝我们的玉米时,你会非常满意,笑得合不上口。仔细捉摸,ear 还可当"苞米"讲,这就使语篇又有了审视着一个一个的"苞米"或"麦穗"的深层意思。广告双关语所产生的幽默生动的语篇效果,强调了玉米的可口和香甜,增加了语言的表现力和感染力,给广告读者留下了深刻持久的印象。译文尝试把原文的双关词拆分为两个短语:"吃不停,乐不够",以明示其双重语义场含义。

4.2 英语广告押头韵修辞的翻译策略

(1) 四字词语策略

汉语四字格有两大特点,使之成为英语广告押头韵修辞格翻译的最佳选择策略:① 语义表达简明扼要;②能帮助语篇产生一种明快的节奏感。汉语的四字格一般是以两个字为一个节奏,即两个音节为一个音步,两个节奏多通过平仄搭配、抑扬交错构筑一个完整的四字格形式。其鲜明的节奏和优美的旋律虽无法完全对等地再现英语头韵词的音响效果,但可收到良好的补偿效果。例如:

【例11】

Sensuously smooth. Mysterious hymellow. Gloriously golden. Who can resist the magic of Camus XO Cognac?

译文:

诱发美感,光滑柔和;神秘高雅,芬芳香醇;荣耀尊贵,帝王金色;有谁能抗拒康涅克白兰地的魔力?

这是康涅克白兰地酒的广告。原语语篇由描述体语篇和一个反问句构成。描述体语篇由三个关系过程小句构成,都启用了省略形式,只保留了形容词和其修饰语,分别从口感(Camus XO is) Sensuously smooth,味觉(Camus XO is) Mysterious hymellow,和颜色(Camus XO is) Gloriously gold 入手对产品进行描述,描述体语篇整体结构和谐工整,形容词前都有其相应的副词修饰,同时启用了押头韵修辞格,分别是押头韵 /s/(Sensuously smooth),/m/(Mysterious hymellow),/g/(Gloriously golden) 和 /c/(Camus XO Cognac)。通过重复相同字母或相同语音形式的手段,给读者一种高雅、优美的听觉享受,使人诵读之下难以忘怀。汉语译文试用四字格形式进行翻译,以保留原语语篇结构整齐的特点,和弥补翻译过程中造成的押头韵美感剥损。

【例12】

The Relentless Pursuit of Perfection.(Lexus automobile)

译文:

追求完美,近乎苛求;凌志轿车,永不停歇!

这是 Lexus 牌汽车广告,其基本含义为"近乎苛求地追求完美"。这则广告一组押头韵词语是围绕 /p/ 这个辅音展开的:Pursuit 和 Perfection。Pursuit 和 Perfection 都属该语篇的核心词汇,所构成的押头韵使整个语篇显得富有韵律和节奏感。汉语译文采用了四字格形式的排比结构,由两部分构成:第一部分描述了源语语篇核心词汇所含的主要概念意义"追求完美"和原语语篇副词所含的概念意义"近乎苛求";第二部分首先写出商品品牌,在品牌"凌志轿车"后加了"永不停歇",以表示汽车制造者的决心和志向。四个并列的四字词语,使译文语言显得明快流畅,节奏优美和谐。

【例13】

Flexicare keeps you Flexible and Active Always.

译文:

富利凯使你:睿智机敏,灵活柔韧,永葆活力。

从产品名称上分析,我们可以看到 Flexicare 是由形容词 flexible 的前两个音节+care

构成,顾名思义,就是这种食品可保持和增加你的身体柔韧度,广告又通过 Flexible 和 Active 两个词明示了产品的这一特点。Flexicare 和 Flexible 都是以 Flexi 开始,构成押头韵修辞。通过品牌名称和语篇主要词汇的辅音重复所构成的押头韵强调食品的功能。人人都希望保持强健柔韧、活力无限的身体,Flexicare 正是这种食品。译文用四字词语通过增补法翻译,获得和原语语篇文化语境层面的动态对等。

(2) 对偶句策略

对偶指相邻的短语或句子通过语法、结构的对称关系实现意思上的对仗或反衬效果。对偶句具有音节整齐匀称、节律和谐优美的特点。用汉语的对偶形式来译英语中的头韵,能体现语言的均衡美和音乐美,可对英语的头韵修辞作一补偿。请看个案分析。

【例 14】

Minimize lines, maximize your savings.（Relvo 牌化妆品）

译文 1:

钱包多省钱,面部少生线。

译文 2:

美丽不需千金,美丽只需一点。

译文 3:

省钱有方,驻颜有术。

这则广告语篇集三种修辞于一身。① 排比修辞（parallelism）：两个小句都是以动词＋名词（宾语）的形式出现,构成排比；② 对比修辞格（antithesis）：minimize 和 maximize 一组具有相反意义的动词帮助构成对比修辞格；③ 两个小句的第一个动词分别都是以辅音 /m/ 开始构成押头韵修辞。该广告的目的是宣传该产品物美价廉,可减少和抹去你脸上的皱纹,又不会使你钱包羞涩。广告构思巧妙,寓意深刻。译文试用对偶句或四字词语进行翻译,用尾韵来替换头韵,以获得和原语语篇在文化语境层面的对等。

【例 15】

Slim, stylish, silver.（扫描仪广告）

译文 1:

银色线条显精简,时尚光辉在闪现。

译文 2:

外显精简之美,内藏时尚韵味。

这则广告语篇属于描述体语篇体裁,由三个关系过程小句的省略形式构成。三个用来描述这种扫描仪器特点的形容词都以辅音 /s/ 开头,构成押头韵修辞,语言简洁工整,令人倍感时尚。译文采用增补法,用对偶句进行翻译,以再造原广告语篇中音韵美的神韵。

(3) 汉译英中的译文押头韵翻译策略

汉语广告中的排比、拟人、重复等修辞格在译成英语时,可采用押头韵手法,以弥补源语广告语篇中的美感缺损。请看下面的案例分析。

【例 16】
优良的品质,优惠的价格,优质的服务。("三优"牌家具)

译文:

Unrivalled quality, unbeatable prices, unreserved service.

源语广告语篇启用了排比修辞手法。从概念元功能看,这则广告从潜在顾客最为关心的三个方面入手宣传自己的产品:品质、价格和服务;从篇章元功能看,三个排比句都是"形容词+名词"构成,形容词都以"优"开头;从人际元功能看,三个以"优"字开头的并列形容词和"三优"品牌家具名称前后呼应,帮助构成了语篇的整体连贯。译文试用押头韵修辞进行翻译,unrivalled, unbeatable, unreserved 三个形容词都以 un-开头,优美的韵律配上均恒的结构,完美地再现了源语语篇的内涵和美感,取得了很好的文化语境效果。这则广告的英语译文让我想起了牛津大学为再版的《牛津英语词典》所做的广告词:"There are only two words for it—unbeatable and unbelievable.",其中 unbeatable 和 unbelievable 通过以 un-开头,巧妙地运用了头韵修辞。

4.3 仿拟广告语篇的翻译策略

(1)"仿拟+明示"翻译策略

仿拟广告如在目的语中能找到相同或相似的仿拟表现形式进行翻译,可看作是仿拟广告翻译策略的最佳选择。请看以下案例分析。

【例 17】
East is east and west is west, but Brown's meat is best. (The Canadian Brown Meat Company)

译文:

龙肉凤肉,不如咱家的布朗肉。

原文仿拟了英语谚语"East, west, family is the best";译文仿拟了汉语谚语:"金窝窝,银窝窝,不如咱家的狗窝窝。"原文和译文都通过一定的文字改动,明示了该广告的卖点。译文仿拟手法的运用惟妙惟肖地传达了原文的信息内容和感情色彩,保留了原语篇仿拟修辞所创造的风趣幽默的语用效果。

【例 18】
桂林山水甲天下。(桂林旅游)

译文:

East, West, Guilin is the best.

原广告语篇仿拟的是一句著名唐诗,英语译文仿拟了西方妇孺皆知的一句谚语(参见例 17)。通过一定的文字改动,明示了该广告的目的。看到这则译文广告,西方游客会情不自禁地把桂林和家放在一起对比,联想到桂林和家一样,都是世界上最美、最好、最温馨的地方。

【例 19】

Two birds, one stone. （Astelin antithistanmine spray）(*Reader's Digest*, April 2007)

译文 1：

一石二鸟,一喷多效,Astelin 喷鼻水。

译文 2：

Astelin 喷鼻水——一箭双雕,一喷双效。

这是一则治疗多种过敏性鼻炎的喷鼻药广告。原语语篇仿拟修辞用得很妙,给读者留下丰富的想象空间：鼻子是由两个鼻腔构成的,在此喷鼻药水被比喻为石头,鼻腔被喻为飞鸟的跑道。药水喷入鼻孔就好像是一石打中了两只鸟,能立刻消除鼻腔疾病。汉语译文"一石二鸟"可以说在概念、人际和篇章元功能上都和原仿拟语篇取得了高度的一致。通过增补"一喷多效",译文明示了这种药的主要功能和效果,同时还帮助构建了语篇的和谐韵律和对偶结构。译文 2 和译文 1 宏观结构相同,仿拟＋明示。"一箭双雕"和"Two birds, one stone"具有相同的概念和人际意义,同时"一喷双效"中"双"和"一箭双雕"中的"双"字重复,帮助构建了重复修辞格；"雕"和"效"押尾韵,构成押韵修辞格。仿拟使之亲切,重复加强记忆,押韵朗朗上口。几种修辞集一身,共同帮助完成译文广告的体裁目的。

【例 20】

有目共赏——上海牌电视机。

译文：

Shanghai TV—seeing is believing.

电视要通过图像和观众交流,眼睛在欣赏电视节目的过程中起重要作用。"有目共赏"妙就妙在无标记地表现了这则广告的这一情景语境。"有目共赏"在此还是个具有双重语义场的广告双关：① 指看电视；② 暗示上海牌电视机上乘的质量与功能,有眼睛的人都不会否认这个毋庸置疑的事实。译文"seeing is believing"在概念、人际和篇章元功能上都和原仿拟语篇一致,属直译。译文在这则广告语境中也具有两层语义场含义,构成广告双关。第一层语义场含义是指只有亲眼看到的东西才能真正相信,说明的是一个宽泛的真理；第二层语义场含义是说当你亲眼看到在我们上海牌电视机和它播放的节目时,你就会知道我们的电视机质量的确好。

【例 21】

Eimskip Airline fresh or frozen—all the way. （Custom House Outdoors, 2007, spring）

译文：

怡之航,冷冻保鲜,一路领"鲜"。

看到这则广告,读者马上会联想到莎士比亚在 *Hamlet* 中的名句独白 To be or not to be,译文启用"明示＋仿拟"修辞翻译法。四字词语明示了原语篇所含的主要信息：该航班运输的食品可冷冻保鲜。仿拟修辞翻译法套用了"一路领先",通过把"先"更换为"鲜",不仅再一次强调了该语篇的深层语义场含义和卖点,又保留了原仿拟语篇的诙谐幽默感。

【例 22】

Not all cars are created equal. (*Mitsubishi*, 11, 2005)(《汽车杂志》2005 年 11 月)

译文：

人人生而平等,车有优劣之分:车中精品。

三菱汽车公司在打入美国市场时,广告词套用了《美国独立宣言》中"All men are created equal"的名句,目的是向美国人显示三菱汽车独特的款式和性能。译文采用"套译+明示"翻译策略,最后用四字词语"车中精品"总结了广告的卖点和目的。

【例 23】

Where there is a road, there is a Toyota.

译文：车到山前必有路,有路便有丰田车。

原文套用了英语中常见的一句谚语"Where there is a will, there is a way",汉语译文启用了"套译+明示"翻译策略,译文第一句套用了古诗"船到桥头自然直",第二句明示了广告的卖点。译文还启用了顶针修辞格,使译文富有音乐美和诗歌美的韵律。

(2) 套译法

用仿拟修辞进行翻译的方法叫做套译。也就是说,套译是指套用译入语中某些人们熟悉的谚语、成语或是名人名言进行的翻译。现举例说明。

【例 24】

Color touches the most important parts of our. (Sensient)

译文：

人靠衣装,食靠色装。(食品着色剂)

译文套用了谚语"人靠衣装,马靠鞍装",暗示这种食品着色剂不仅可使食品外表迷人,还可使食品美味可口。

【例 25】

有多少南方摩托车,就有多少动人的故事。

译文：

Where there is a South motor, there is a moving story.

该译文套用了"Where there is a will, there is a way"这个谚语。同时这则译文还启用了押头韵和双关修辞格。"动人的故事"译为"moving story"而不是"touching tale",其原因是 moving 和前一句的 motor 都是以辅音/m/开始, story 和前一句的 South 都是以辅音 /s/ 开始,构成了押头韵修辞,使译文产生一种音韵上的象征美和节奏美。同时 moving story 可构成双关,理解涉及两个语义场：一是指令人感动；二是指汽车在跑动,使读者脑海中闪现出生动形象的画面,无标记地表现了该广告的情景语境。

【例 26】

中原之行哪里去? 郑州亚细亚。(郑州亚细亚超级商场)

译文：

When in Zhengzhou, do as the Zhengzhounese do—go shopping in the Asian Supermarket.

原语语篇属对话体裁，一问一答。译文套用了谚语"When in Rome, do as the Romans do"，稍加改动，明示了广告的卖点是敦促人们去亚细亚超级商场购物。仿拟英译广告可给外国客人一种宾至如归的感觉，吸引前来郑州参观的外宾在游玩之余去"亚细亚"看看。

【例 27】

随身携带，有备无患。/随身携带，有惊无险。（速效救心丸）

译文：

A friend in need, a friend indeed!

原广告指速效救心丸要随身携带，以防患于未然。译文套用英语谚语，揭示出原广告的概念内涵和该药的功效：生命遇到危机时，它会像朋友一样帮你摆脱险境，起死回生。译文仿拟语篇中的拟人表现手法，赋予产品以生命力，让人倍感亲切。

【例 28】

Bearing Point：Management & Tecconsultants

We know at the end of the day, there is no end of the day.（*Fortune*, 5, 2007）

译文：

山重水复疑无路，柳暗花明又一村——毕博科技管理咨询公司，夜以继日竭诚为您服务！

译文仿拟了一首古诗。从概念、人际和篇章三大元功能的角度看，这首古诗都生动、形象、准确地表现了原语语篇的内容：我们知道即使白天结束，我们的工作仍未结束，将继续竭诚为您服务。古诗的仿拟使译文显得高雅、亲切，易记易诵。

【例 29】

Dr Scholl's Heel Pain? Take a hike.

译文 1：

Scholl 牌爽健鞋垫：同步同治，步步为"赢"。

译文 2：

Scholl 牌爽健鞋垫：徒步远行，走掉疼痛！

原语语篇采用了问题解决模式。问题部分：脚痛吗？解决部分：穿 Dr Scholl's 除脚痛鞋垫去徒步远行吧。译文1仿拟了和该语篇语境内容十分吻合的四字成语"稳扎稳打，步步为营"，其中"步步"和鞋垫有关，更换"营"为"赢"，暗示 Scholl 牌爽健鞋垫可帮你走掉疼痛获得健康，起到了较好的语用效果。译文2采用了四字词语翻译策略，明示了 Scholl 牌爽健鞋垫的治疗功效。

【例 30】

Small cog, big machine? Jobs that make a difference.

译文：

勿以"轮"小而不为！大机器离不开小齿轮！（Naturejob 公司）

这是一家帮助介绍工作的公司广告，启用了品牌双关修辞。这家公司的名字叫 Naturejob，因此广告中的 job 就具有了双层语义场含义：一是指公司名，二是指公司将为您提供的工作。译文仿拟了"勿以恶小而为之，勿以善小而不为"，借以说明一个深刻的人生哲理：单个的人是一颗小小的螺丝钉，但和社会这个大机器融合在一起，就可以发挥大作用。我们给您提供的工作虽平凡，但可帮助您展示才华，为社会做贡献。

【例 31】

It ain't bragging when it is true. （Jim BeamWhisky）

译文：

酒香不怕巷子深，事实无须标榜。（Jim Beam 威士忌酒）

这是一则威士忌酒的广告。原语篇中的 ain't 给语篇增添了浓浓的口语化色彩，其语用效果是让人联想到酒后人们轻松随意的话语表达形式，帮助加强了广告的感染力。原语语篇是酒广告，仿拟译文的概念内容也是卖酒；从篇章功能看，仿拟译文也十分口语化，原文与译文在语境上的吻合使仿拟译文获得了和原语语篇同样的体裁目的。

(3) 其他翻译策略

当目的语没有和原仿拟语篇相对应的谚语和名句时，可另辟蹊径，采用其他翻译策略，如直译、对偶、四字词语、反问等。请看以下案例分析。

【例 32】

Pictures speak louder than words. （Sanyo typewriter）

译文：

图片的质量胜过一切言辞的夸耀。（三洋打印机）

原广告套用了谚语"Facts speak louder than words"，译文基本采用直译策略。

【例 33】

Sometimes beauty is more than skin deep.

译文：

外表固然美，内质更为优。（沃尔沃汽车广告）

原文套用了英语谚语"Beauty is but skin deep"，通过增加 more than，强调了沃尔沃汽车不仅外表美，而且内在功能更为优的特点。汉语译文启用对偶句，"外表"对"内质"，一外，一内，构成反衬；"固然"对"更为"；"美"对"优"。从概念元功能看，译文译出了原文的主要信息内容；从人际元功能看，中文对偶句弥补了因英文仿拟修辞缺失而造成的美感缺损，保留了原仿拟语篇的魅力。

【例 34】

Ugly is only skin deep.

译文：

丑陋只是外表，真美更为重要——金龟车。

这是德国福斯汽车公司"金龟车"的广告。原广告把"Beauty is only skin deep"改为"Ugly is only skin deep"，意思是说金龟车外表虽丑，但实惠耐用。我们试用结构工整、押韵上口的两个对偶句来翻译。

【例 35】

ArthroMedix pain relief cream：No pain is your gain!

译文：

消除疼痛，一身轻松——ArthroMedix 疼痛一消灵。

原广告仿拟英语谚语"No pain, no gain"，通过一定改动，轻松幽默地说明这种药的功能。译文启用了一对四字词语，由隐形因果关系连接，短小精悍，押韵上口。

【例 36】

Don't iron while the strike is hot.

译文：

罢工运动如火如荼，岂能只在家中做家务。

这是一则 1970 年全美妇女组织（NOW）为争取平等待遇所举行的罢工口号。原语语篇套用了美国家喻户晓的名句"Strike the iron while it is hot"。iron 在广告中意思是"熨衣服"，在此引申为"做家务"和"只顾自己的小家，对罢工漠不关心的一种态度"。译文押尾韵，句式工整，读起来流畅顺口。

【例 37】

Sense and simplicity.（Philip Mobile Phone）

译文：

简约之美，智慧之选。

这是一则飞利浦手机广告，广告词仿拟的是简·奥斯丁的小说 *Sense and Sensibility*《理智与情感》。简单的语言本身就无标记地象征着这种手机简单美观的外观，译文采用同样的文体，以获得和原语语篇同等的语境效果。

【例 38】

Fit or Fat.

译文 1：

选择健康 or 选择肥胖。

译文 2：

是选择健康还是乐于肥胖。

这是一篇劝人们积极参加体育锻炼的广告,主词 Fit 和 Fat 重复了/f/辅音,构成了押头韵修辞;Fit 和 Fat 属一组反义词,帮助构成了对比(antithesis)修辞格;两个主词用 or 连接,语篇整体结构仿拟了"To be or not to be"。译文1用四字词语翻译,把 or 原封不动地移下来,从形式上看像是一座小桥,把两个内涵相反的概念连在一起,表面上是给广告受众一个选择的空间和自由,实际上是敦促大家减肥。译文2用语言明示了这个语篇含义。

【例39】
To B. A. or not to B. A., that is no question. (British Airlines)

译文:
选乘英国航空公司的飞机,这还用说?(英国航空公司)

这则广告也是仿拟仿莎士比亚的名句"To be or not to be"。译文通过改换语篇体裁,用反义问句翻译,显得亲切自信。

【例40】
All roads now lead to one hotel.

译文:
香格里拉大酒店,条条大路通向她。

译文试以工整和富有韵律的结构,来弥补原语语篇在翻译过程中因仿拟格的缺损而造成的美感剥损。

5 本章结语

本章主要就双关、押头韵以及仿拟三种广告语篇的文体特征及翻译策略作了探讨,分析了广告语篇的特点、社会功能以及以人际功能为主要倾向的广告语篇的翻译策略。

为了让目的语受众能快而准地把握好双关广告的真正卖点,明示语篇的深层语义场含义是最佳翻译策略之一。在具体翻译时可采用保留双关明示法、体裁转换明示法和拆分增补明示法三种翻译明示法。广告体裁中的英语押头韵具有帮助构成语言音韵美、节奏美、意境美和象征美的语篇功能。鉴于汉语无押头韵,通过具体案例分析,可以看到汉语的四字词语、对偶等修辞手法是弥补在翻译过程中英语押头韵广告美感剥损的最佳手段。此外,仿拟广告语篇通过对谚语、名言和警句的模仿,使广告读者通过对被仿拟谚语的联想,深刻感悟仿拟广告的新颖创意和深刻寓意。在目的语中能找到相同或相似的仿拟表达方式进行翻译,是仿拟广告的首选翻译策略之一。

总之,广告语篇翻译的评判标准有其自身的独特性。以人际功能为主要倾向的商业广告,由于其体裁目的的特殊性,翻译策略的制定和译文好坏的评判标准都不应只停留在语言的微观层面,而更应从宏观层面,即语篇的文化语境入手,以广告体裁的社会目的为视点,看译文是否取得了和原文同等的表现力和感染力,达到了同样的体裁目的,取得了同样的社会语用效果。只要能够达到文化语境层面的效应对等,就是好译文。

第六章 商务翻译

商务英语是关于国际商务及经贸领域中应用的英语。商务涉及的面非常广泛,包括金融、投资、保险、财会、经营管理、市场营销、信息处理、对外经贸、合同和法律文书等。商务英语是商务文化群体中所特有的专门用途英语,是英语的一种功能变体,与普通英语相比,其词汇运用有独特性。商务英语的语言要求严谨、准确、缜密;句法方面的一个重要特征就是经常使用结构复杂的长句,运用很多的修饰词、从句等限定和说明成分,因此句子结构显得复杂而又冗长;同时商务英语所用语言有其独特的风格和含义。翻译商务英语时必须准确理解原文的含义,熟悉相关术语,熟练掌握各种文体的特点,研究、把握英汉两种语言句子结构的差异。

1 商务英语文体特征

1.1 语体特征

(1) 语体正式,修辞方式丰富。

商务英语的语体相对而言比较正式规范,商务合同中经常使用一些很正式的词语和一些带有古体特征的词语,如 hereby(特此),herein(于此),status quo(现状)等。古语词一般已不通用,但古语词可增加严肃、正式的意味,因此使用古语词可体现商务信函、商务合同、法律文书的严肃性和正式性。虽然商务英语的语言特点总的来说是平实严谨的,但也常运用比拟、比喻等修辞手段来增加文章的可读性,使行文更加流畅。

【例1】
The Employer <u>hereby</u> covenants to pay the Contractor <u>in consideration of</u> the execution and completion of the works and the remedying of defects therein the Contract Price or such other sum as may become payable <u>under the provisions of</u> the Contract at the time and in the manner prescribed by the Contract.

译文:
业主特此立约保证在合同规定的期限内,按合同规定的方式向承包人支付合同价或合同规定的其他应支付的款项,以作为本工程施工、竣工及修补工程中缺陷的报酬。

【例2】
This Contract is <u>hereby</u> made and concluded by and between Jason Co. (hereinafter referred to as Party A) and Flying Fish Co. (hereinafter referred to as Party B) on July 10th, 2010, in New York, United States of America, <u>on the principle of</u> equality and

mutual benefit and through amicable consultation.

译文：

本合同双方，杰森公司（以下称甲方）与飞鱼公司（以下称乙方），在平等互利基础上，通过友好协商，于2010年7月10日在美国纽约签订本合同。

【例3】

Within 60 days after the arrival of the goods at the destination, should the quality, specifications or quantity be found not in conformity with the stipulations of the contract except those claims for which the insurance company or the owners of the vessel are liable. The buyers shall, have the right on the strength of the inspection certificate issued by the CCIC and the relative documents to claim for compensation to the Sellers.

译文：

在货到目的口岸60天内如发现货物品质、规格和数量与合同不符，除属保险公司或船方责任外，买方有权凭中国商检出具的检验证书或有关文件向卖方索赔换货或赔款。

上面英语合同中的画线部分是十分正式的用词，在一般的口语中或其他问题中较少使用。

【例4】

IBM has a quite handsome increase of productivity this year.

译文：

国际商用机器公司今年的生产率有了大幅度的提高。

这个句子用了"移情（empathy）"的修辞手法，即通常把表达人的感情的词转类用于物体，此句中把人对高效率的赞赏心情转移到IBM的实际报告之中。

Crest whitens white是佳洁士的牙膏广告语，可以译为：佳洁士牙膏使牙齿更白。第二个单词和第三个单词的第一个字母都是w，这是英语中押头韵的修辞格式。

【例5】

The carnage in stock funds—the biggest money-spinners for management companies—is far bloodier.

译文：

股票型基金市场内的竞争更为惨烈，而股票型基金曾经是基金市场中最赚钱的买卖。

spin的意思是"纺纱"，本文中的money-spinners喻指最赚钱的买卖或企业。

【例6】

In recent years yet another breed of financial entrepreneur has emerged. Enemies of the industrial status quo, they are takeover artists and spin-off specialists who have forced nothing less than restructuring of corporate America. They are bringing about the "creative destruction" by which capitalism regenerates itself.

译文：

近年来，又有一种类型的金融家已经崛起。他们是产业现状之大敌、兼并大师，也是分散经营的专家。他们促成了美国企业界的改组。他们带来了"创造性的破坏"，使资本主义不断更新。

这个句子中的 entrepreneur 和 status quo 都是非常正式的用法，而 creative destruction 则是一种叫做"矛盾修辞法"的修辞方式。

(2) 语言正式、精练，用词严谨，词意准确

商务英语所用语言比较正规，常有一定的格式和套话。请看下面几个例子：

【例7】

Your early reply to our specific inquiry will be highly appreciated.

译文：

如蒙早日答复我方的具体询价，将不胜感激。

这是外贸应用文中询价函电中常用的句型之一。名词短语"your early reply"要比"if you can reply early"正式精练得多，而被动语态"will be highly appreciated"也是很正式的用语。

【例8】

Upon first presentation the buyer shall pay against document draft drawn by the seller at sight. The shipping documents are to be delivered against payment only.

译文：

买方凭卖方开具的即期跟单汇票，于第一次见票时立即付款，付款后交单。

这是合同中有关即期付款交单的托收条款。upon 常用在合同、法律文书中，表示"在……后立即，在……的时候"，如：upon examination... 表示"经审查后……"。在条约、规章、法令等文件中 shall 表示义务或规定，其意思是"应，必须"，如：The new regulation shall take effect on June 1st. 译为"新章程自6月1日起实施"。

【例9】

We have received your letter of May 3, enquiring about the best terms of the goods.

译文：

贵公司5月3日来函就该商品优惠条款的询盘已经收悉。

【例10】

We make you the following offer subject to your reply reaching us not later than noon time December 23.

译文：

现报盘如下，此盘以你方12月23日中午前复到为有效。

offer 意思是"报盘"(包括货名、规格、数量、价格、船期及答复期限等)，常见的搭配有

make offer, send offer, give offer 等。subject to 以……为条件（为准）。如，subject to your immediate acceptance 以你方立即接受为条件。

【例 11】

It shall be subject to ratification or acceptance by the signatory states.

译文：本公约须经签字国批准或接受。

【例 12】

The production and business operating plans of an equity joint venture shall be submitted to the competent authorities for record and shall be implemented through economic contract.

译文：

合营企业生产经营计划，应报主管部门备案，并通过经济合同方式执行。

（3）内容缜密、周到，结构复杂，意思完整

由于涉及双方或几方面的利益，商务合同、文件或一个条约所给的定义、条款和内容必须精确。为了做到准确无误，不产生任何差异，用英语拟订、书写这些文件、合同时，除用词恰当外，还会用许多从句、短语来修饰或限定其内容，因此结构复杂，句子冗长，有时甚至显得有点臃肿。请看例句：

【例 13】

Inspection: It is mutually agreed that the certificate of quality and quantity or weight issued by the manufacturer shall be part of the documents for payment under relevant L/C. However, the inspection of quality and quantity or weight shall be made in accordance with the following: ...

译文：

商品检验：双方同意以制造厂出具的品质及数量或重量证明书作为有关信用证项目下付款的单据之一。但是，货物的品质及数量或重量检验应按下列规定办理：……

句子中"that the certificate of quality and quantity or weight issued by the manufacturer shall be part of the documents for payment under relevant L/C是主语从句，it 是形式主语，"It is mutually agreed"用的是被动语态，意思相当于"Both parties agreed..."，但前者比后者要正式。"...issued by the manufacturer"是一个过去分词短语，用来修饰"the Certificate of quality and quantity or weight"。

【例 14】

If the shipment of the contracted goods is prevented or delayed in whole or in part due to force majeure, the seller shall not be liable for non-shipment or late shipment of the goods of this contract. However, the seller shall notify the buyer by cable or telex and furnish the latter within 15 days by registered airmail with a certificate issued by the Promotion of International Trade attesting such event or events.

译文：

由于不可抗拒的原因，致使卖方不能全部或部分装运或延缓装运本合同货不负有责任。但卖方须用电报或电传通知买方并须在15天内以航空挂号信件向买方提交由国际贸促会出具的证明此类事故的证明书。

【例15】

Of course, building a modern economy carries costs too. Different countries will manage these costs in different ways. But the problems China has had to deal with in recent years are familiar to Britain and other countries undergoing major economic transition: the conundrum of unleashing enterprises while keeping inflation in check; the social consequences and complexity of reforming uncompetitive or declining industries.

译文：

当然，建立现代经济是有代价的。各国应付这种代价的方式也不尽相同。而中国近年来面临的一些问题是英国和其他处于重大经济转折时期的国家所熟悉的；即如何在控制通货膨胀的情况下使企业获得发展，如何处理由于改造缺乏竞争力或是每况愈下的工业所造成的复杂的社会后果。

第一句点明主题"建立现代经济是有代价的"，接着解释各国应付这种代价的方式，以及处于重大经济转折时期的国家所面临的那些问题。第二句是转折句，起承上启下的作用，第三句不但句子长，而且结构也比较复杂，分词短语"undergoing major economic transition"作定语修饰"Britain and other countries"，其后的两个并列短语"the conundrum of unleashing enterprises while keeping inflation in check; the social consequences and complexity of reforming uncompetitive or declining industries"是解释各国所面临的问题。为了清楚地说明主题，使内容和意思完整，作者不得不用这种结构复杂的句子来阐述，用一个简单的句子是表达不了这个意思的。

【例16】

The time has long since arrived to recognize commercial representation as a profession *per se*, the successful exercise of which is positively correlated with careful initial selection of commercial representatives, the level and content of their formal education and specialized training, the length and variety of their pertinent experience, and the quality of support they receive from the trade promotion organization (TPO) or ministry at home.

译文：

驻外商务代表的工作实际上是一种专门的业务——早就应该这样看待这个问题。要把这项工作做好，首先是要选择好驻外商务代表，要考虑他们所接受的正规教育和专门培训的程度和内容，他们过去有哪些和有多少相关的经验，以及他们能够从国内的贸易促进机构和贸易部得到什么样的支持。

本段选自一篇介绍驻外商务代表的文章。从英语的角度看，全段只有一个句号，也就是说它是一句话，里面包含两个从句"... of which is positively correlated with..."和

"... they receive from the trade promotion organization (TPO) or ministry at home",其中第一个是由"名词＋介词(of)＋关系代词（which）"引导的定语从句，从句里面的四个名词短语"careful initial selection of commercial representatives, the level and content of their formal education and specialized training, the length and variety of their pertinent experience, and the quality of support"都是并列成分，作介词 with 的宾语。*per se*，是一个拉丁语，意思是"本身；本来；本质上"，意思相当于"in itself, by itself"。不难看出用这么复杂的句子给出一个定义，其目的就是使这个定义更准确。若要把这个句子翻译成汉语，需要将其拆开，才能使译文意思清楚，文字干净利落。

【例 17】

Convinced that a system of copyright protection appropriate to all nations of the world and expressed in a universal convention, additional to, and without impairing international systems already in force, will ensure respect for the rights of the individual and encourage the development of literature, the sciences and the arts.

译文：

确信适应于世界各国并以某种世界公约确定下来的用以补充而不是损害现行国际制度的版权保护制度，将保证对个人权利的尊重及鼓励文学、科学与艺术的发展。

【例 18】

Each contracting state undertakes to provide for the adequate and effective protection of the rights of authors and other copyright proprietors in literary, scientific and artistic works, including writings, musical, dramatic and cinematographic works, and paintings, engravings and sculpture.

译文：

各成员国承担对文学、科学及艺术作品(包括文字的、音乐的、戏剧的、电影的作品，以及绘画、雕刻与雕塑)的作者及其他版权所有者的权利提供充分、有效的保护。

1.2 语法特征

为了做到语言简洁、内容表达客观公正和有关事项描述的准确无误，在商务英语的使用中常出现大量的被动语态、祈使句、非谓语动词、情态动词以及各种从句。例如：

【例 19】

All commercial papers sent for collection must be accompanied by a remittance letter giving complete and precise instructions.

译文：

寄出托收的一切商业票据，必须附上一封托收函。上面要有完整而又确切的托收指示。

【例 20】

In case the contract is concluded on CIF basis, the insurance shall be affected by the seller for 110% of invoice value covering all risks, war risk, SRCC. risks (i. e. Strike,

Riot, and Civil Commotions).

译文：

在到岸价基础上订立的合同,将由卖方按发票金额110%投保综合险、战争险、罢工险、暴乱险和民变险。

这是一份合同中有关保险的内容,句子中用了被动语态(is concluded, shall be effected)、非谓语动词(covering)、情态动词(shall),另外还用了 in case 引导的条件句。

【例 21】

All disputes arising from the execution of, or in connection with, this contract shall be settled amicably through friendly negotiation. In case no settlement can be reached through negotiation, the case shall then be submitted for arbitration. The location of arbitration shall be in the country where the defendant has his domicile.

译文：

凡因执行本合同所发生的或与本合同有关的一切争议,双方应通过友好协商解决。协商不能解决的应提交仲裁,仲裁地点为被告户籍所在地。

这是一份合同中有关仲裁的内容,句子中用了被动语态(shall be settled, shall then be submitted)、非谓语动词(arising)、和三个情态动词(shall)。

1.3 词汇特征

(1) 商务英语术语和词汇专业性强,缩略语广泛使用

商务英语术语和专业词汇十分丰富,这是由于其涉及的范围和领域比较广而且专业性也强。例如,在报刊和新闻中我们常见的 inquiry(询盘), offer(发盘), counter offer(还盘), acceptance(受盘), claim(索赔), import/export quota(进口/出口配额), trade terms(贸易条款), an export item(出口项目), repeat order(续订单), pro forma invoice(形式发票), FOB(free on board)离岸价格, GDP(gross domestic product)国内生产总值, floating exchange(浮动汇率), CIF(cost, insurance and freight)成本、保险费加运费的到岸价格, B/L(bill of lading)提货单, L/C(letter of credit)信用证, Enc(enclosure)附件, P.S(postscript)再启, bank draft(银行汇票), ASAP(as soon as possible)尽快, B2C 是英文 Business to Consumer 的缩写,中文简称为"商对客",是电子商务的一种常用模式,而像淘宝这类从商家直接面对消费者销售产品和服务的网站,也因此习惯被称为"B2C 网站", force majeure(不可抗拒之力), particular average(单独海损), customized logistics (定制物流), judicial review(司法审查)等。翻译时要首先弄懂这些术语和缩略语的含义,并对涉及的相关专业知识有一定的了解,就能比较准确地翻译出地道的中文。

(2) 广告英语用词简洁、生动、形象,语言朗朗上口,夸张幽默

商家做广告的目的主要是促销,广告词就要做到引人注意,易于记忆,读起来朗朗上口,赏心悦目;为了节约广告费的开支,广告又必须简洁明快;为了吸引消费者,广告常运用夸张幽默的语言和丰富多彩的修辞手段使其更形象、逼真。例如"Slip on her fingers and she'll know what's in your heart"是一个销售钻石的广告。通过使用人称代词,让消费者感到非常的亲切,拉近了销售者和消费者的距离。请看以下例子:

【例 22】

① Crest whitens white.

译文:

佳洁士牙膏使牙齿白上加白。

whitens white 是英语中的头韵法(alliteration),即相邻几个单词的首字母发音相同,这样读起来很上口。

② Feel good, fast food.

译文:

快餐食品,可口温馨。

此句中 good,food 运用的是英语中的尾韵法(end rhyme),即每行中的最后一个单词音素相同。

③ Tides in, dirt's out.

译文:

汰渍(洗衣粉商标名)到,污垢除。

此处运用的是英语中的对照法(contrast),通过 in 和 out 对照,夸张地说明其洗衣服的效果。

④ Take Toshiba, take the world.

译文:

东芝(日本著名电器商标,此处指手提电脑)在手,世界在握。

这里用夸张的手法说明其电脑性能的威力。

⑤ Fresh up with Seven-Up.

译文:

君饮七喜(一种饮料),提神醒脑。

⑥ Things go better with Coca-Cola.

译文:

饮用可口可乐,必定万事吉祥。

⑦ Choose once and choose well.

译文:

随意挑选,保您满意。

此处运用了头韵法和排比的修辞方法。

(3) 说明书用词准确,意思明白易懂

【例 23】

Washing: Soak the clothes in warm water below 30℃ for a while before you brush them slightly. Dry by airing after squeezing the water out. Avoid dry cleaning, machine cleaning and drying in the sun. Don't wring out. No coloring.

译文:

洗涤:将衣服投入 30℃以下温水浸透后取出,摊平后轻刷,渍水过净后挤压出水分晾干,不可拧干,不可干洗,不可机洗,不可暴晒,不准染色。

这个使用说明书中用了许多祈使句(Soak the clothes..., Dry by airing..., Avoid dry cleaning..., Don't wring out. No coloring.)、非谓语动词(airing, squeezing)来表达一系列的命令和注意事项。

【例 24】

Storage: Keep the clothes in the dry place. The clothes need airing in the rainy season.

译文:

储藏在干燥处,梅雨季节需翻晒。

下面是一篇药品说明书:

【例 25】

Indications: A kind of local anaesthetics. It is used for the patients who need a local anaesthesia while the urethra is being checked and treated.

Administration & Dosage: See the Directions for details.

Remarks: See the Directions for details.

Storage: Keep in a well-closed container.

Package: A rightly closed bottle having the wave shape of letter A and the volume of 10ml is made of plastic.

The Number of Instrument of Ratification:

Jing Wei Yao Zhun Zi (1996) 103196th.

译文:

适应症:局部麻醉药。经尿道施行的检查和治疗需要局部麻醉者。

用途用法:详见说明书。

注意事项:详见说明书。

贮藏:密闭保存。

包装:10ml 全塑 A 字形波纹管式密封保险瓶。

批准文号:京卫药准字(1996)第 103196 号。

(4) 合同、标书的条款规定翔实,语言表达方式必须准确周密,不能产生歧义

商务合同制约着双方的权利、义务和利益,任何一方都想从谈判、合同、协议及随后的交

易中获取最大的利益,而商务合同一经签订就具有法律说服力。所以英语商务合同条款规定的十分翔实,双方的职责、权利、义务都一清二楚,无论从措辞、结构及行文方式上都格外严谨和正式。否则,签约的某一方会遭受意想不到的损失。

招标(invitation for bid, call for tender)和投标(submitting tender)是一种以契约的方式确定双方的工程项目或其他项目的合作关系。与合同语言一样,其文体正式古朴,用词严谨准确,思维缜密,逻辑性强。下面是一则招标和投标的公告:

【例 26】

招标:

INDIA SARDAR SAROVAR (NARMADA) PROJECT

Credit Number 1553-IN

Canal Lining

Prequalification

Applications are invited to pre-qualify for lining the canal of the Narmada Main Canal kilometers 9 to 21. The work is to be completed within 20 months and is estimated to cost US $ 8 million.

The work comprises 681,000 cubic meters of excavation; 110,000 cubic meters of embankment; 1,435 cubic meters of lining and allied work.

Prequalification documents are available from the Executive Engineer, Narmada Project, on payment of a demand draft for rupees 600 or the equivalent in US dollars or UK pounds sterling.

Completed applications are due on 15 January 1998, local time.

译文:

印度 SARDAR SAROVAR 运河衬砌工程项目招标

信用贷款号 1553-IN

NARMADA 主运河衬砌工程 9 至 21 公里项目招标。该工程要求 20 个月内完成,估计造价为 800 万美元。

该工程包括 681000 立方米挖掘土方,110000 立方米的堤岸,1435 立方米的衬砌及相关工作。

招标文件可从 NARMADA 项目工程处购买,每份为 600 卢比,或相当于 600 卢比的美元或英镑。

完整的标书提交日期为当地时间 1998 年 1 月 15 日。

1.4 句法特征

英语是一种形合的语言,主要通过语法手段表达其句法之间的关系,所以句式完整,多用复合句,特别是在正式问题中;汉语是一种意合语言,主要利用语义来表明短语和句子之间的关系,句法结构比较松散,许多成分可以省略。

【例 27】

In 1998, America introduced so-called "business method" patents, granting patent monopolies for new ways of doing business, which not only ushered in a wave of new applications but was also probably inhibiting commercial innovation that had never received legal protection in the past.

译文：

1998年，美国引入了所谓的"经营方法"专利，授予做生意的新方法以专利权，这不仅掀起了新一轮的申请热浪，并且很可能会抑制以前从未受到法律保护的商业创新。

【例 28】

Thirty-five years after computer scientists at UCLA linked two bulky computers using a 15-foot gray cable, testing a new way for exchanging data over networks, what would ultimately become the Internet remains a work in progress.

译文：

美国加利福尼亚大学洛杉矶分校的计算机科学家们用一条15英尺长的灰色电缆将两台庞大的计算机连接在一起，试验一种通过网络交换数据信息的新方法，35年后的今天，因特网最终的发展前景仍然在不断探索中。

【例 29】

When the United States entered just such a glowing period after the Second World War, it had a market eight times larger than any competitor, giving industries unparalleled economies of scale.

译文：

二战结束后，美国恰恰进入了这样一段辉煌的岁月，其市场是任何竞争者的八倍，这为其工业经济提供了前所未有的规模。

上面这几个长句子中有状语从句，还有分词短语、动名词短语、介词短语，结构比较复杂。翻译之前首先需要弄懂英语的语法结构，才有可能看懂原文的意思。

【例 30】

Should you find interest in any of the items in our catalogue, please do not hesitate to send enquiries.

译文：

如贵公司对目录中的任何项目感兴趣，敬请径直寄来询盘。

【例 31】

Your early reply will be highly appreciated.

译文：

如蒙早日复信，不胜感激。

【例 32】

It would be appreciated if you could quote your prices of CIF New York for computer.

译文：

请报计算机的纽约到岸价，将不胜感激。

以上几个句子是商务函电中常用的几种表达方式，简洁、清楚，有利于高效的商务交流。

2 商务英语翻译原则

每个专业都有一些本专业的术语和文体特征，译者需要具备比较扎实的语言基础知识和应用能力，熟悉并了解两种文化之间存在的差异，尽量多掌握某个专业的语言表达特征和一些该专业的特殊表达法，准确完整地确定每个单词、词组的含义，然后用一般读者能理解的词语和表达法来选择对应的汉语译文。商务英语是普通英语与商务各领域专业知识的结合，商务英语除具有普通英语的语言学特征之外还有其独特性。商务英语翻译首先应该遵循基本的翻译准则，在此基础上学习相关的专门知识，熟悉该专业常用的行业术语，就能比较准确地完成翻译任务。

"忠实、通顺"是翻译的基本原则。"忠实"是指译文的意思同原文所表达的含义和传递的信息要一致，原文的内容不能随意增加或减少，要保持信息等值。翻译不是创造，译文须把原文的思想内容、信息和语言风格准确无误地表现出来。"通顺"是指译文的语言表达要符合该语言的规范，不能死板地逐词逐句翻译，也不能出现晦涩难懂的语句，即译文的语言和行文方式都要符合商务文献的语言规范和行文规范。商务英语翻译的更高标准是"功能对等"，即经过翻译，译文与原文之间在信息内容、信息承载方式、交际目的和交际效果等方面最大限度地保持不变。

【例 33】

In wealth countries, the debate about biotech is tempered by the fact that we have a rich array of foods to choose from — and a supply that far exceeds our needs.

译文：

在富裕的国家里，因为有大量丰富的食品可供选择，而且供应远远超过需求，所以关于生物技术的争论相对缓和一些。

原文中有一个同位语从句 that we have a rich array of foods to choose from，从句的广泛使用是商务英语的一个特点，中国学生要逐渐地熟悉这种句法结构。在翻译时可将同位语从句翻译为状语从句，用汉语中常见的"因为（由于）……所以……"。

【例 34】

I have the honor to notify you that we have commenced a business as commission agents for North American goods.

译文：

我们已经开始了经营代销北美货物的业务，特此通知。

如果按照原文的顺序直译的话是"我很荣幸地通知你,我们已经开始了一项业务,来作为北美货物的代理。"这样的翻译确实做到了忠实于原文,但是汉语译文不够地道、通顺,需要前后顺序和个别词语略作调整,译文就比较符合汉语的习惯了。

【例 35】

Should you desire, we would be pleased to send you catalogues together with export prices and estimated shipping costs for these items.

译文:

若贵方需要,本公司将乐意寄上商品目录和这些项目的出口价格以及预计的运输费。

译文将原文的 we 和 you 分别译为"本公司"和"贵方",不但忠于原文的意思,也体现了礼貌原则,更符合外事往来的习惯。

3 商务英语翻译策略

3.1 了解东西方思维与语言表达异同

思维习惯和语言表达方式是辩证统一的,语言是思维的载体,思维支配语言,这是人类语言行为的主要特征。无数事实表明汉民族和英语民族在思维习惯上存在着本质的差异,正是这种差异决定了英汉两种语言反映客观现实的不同表达方式。

英语思维习惯于"形合"造句法。英语民族强调"人物分立",重视形式论证,把整体分解,注重天然,尤其重视空间天然真实性。这种思维习惯反映在语言上就是英语造句主要采用"形合"法(hypotaxis),这一点在语言学界已成定论。英语常用各种发达的关系词以及连接手段造句,即注重显形接应(overt cohesion),注重句子形式,注重结构完整,注重以形显义。英语中的连接手段和形式,如关系词、连词和形态变化形式,不仅数量大、种类多,而且使用十分频繁,因而句子较长。这种长句以 S-V 结构为主干,以谓语动词为核心,经常再加上一些从句,所以从句套从句的现象俯拾即是,因此有的语言学家形象地把英语句子称为"葡萄型结构",葡萄的主干很短,上面附着丰硕的果实。

汉民族历史上讲究"天人合一",重视整体抽象,注重心理时空,特别强调时间顺序原则,注意空间移动。这种思维习惯反映在语言上就是汉语造句多使用"意合法"(parataxis),少用甚至不用形式连接手段,注重以神统形(参见杨自俭《小议几类汉语句子的英译》)。汉语词法没有形态变化,也没有非谓语动词形式,更没有关系副词和关系代词,尽管有连词和介词,但数量要比英语少得多,使用频率也较低。汉语断句不严,思维单位好像不是句子而是句组甚至是段落,词语之间的内在逻辑关系常常在不言之中,即隐含在字里行间。"这种造句法可以叫做编年史手法(chronicle style),着重动作的记录,着重时间的顺序,先者先之,后者后之,把一一发生的事件如实按次说出。"

可见汉语的特征是用分句或流水句逐层叙述思维的各个过程。这样,汉语的句式常常呈现"流散型",也就是说,汉语的语段呈流散式铺排延伸,疏放相连,挥洒自如,汉语的气势和神韵便在这些短促而形离神聚的语句中表现得淋漓尽致。汉语的这种特点同时也大大地限制了其单句的长度,所以汉语的句子不能像英语那样层层环扣,不断扩展延伸。

【例 36】

And with a key conference of rich and poor nations looming in China's Hong Kong in December, the word from negotiators is grim:Hopes for major new tariff reductions are fading, marking the fourth year that the Doha Round of trade liberalization has remained deadlocked.

译文:

12月,发达国家和发展中国家将聚集中国香港,召开一次意义重大的闭门会议。而对于这次会议,谈判代表们的话语是严峻的:认为新的一轮大幅度关税减让的可能性越来越小,意味着今年多哈自由贸易谈判又陷于僵局,这已经是多哈回合的第四个年头了。

这是一个结构复杂的长句子,主句是"the word from negotiators is grim","marking the fourth year that the Doha Round of trade liberalization has remained deadlocked"是现在分词作状语修饰主句,在这个状语中又有一个 that 引导的同位语从句。本句翻译为汉语时将原来的一个句子分成几个分子,符合汉语的表达方式。

【例 37】

If any of the joint ventures wish to assign its registered capital, it must obtain the consent of the other parties to the venture.

译文:

合营者的注册资本如果转让必须经合营各方同意。

英语的主语是 any of the joint ventures(任何合营企业),翻译成汉语时却将原文的一部分宾语变成了主语,因为英语中的主语常考虑能否作后面动词所表达的动作的执行者,汉语相对而言比较随便。

【例 38】

We hand you herewith an order for 100 tons bar iron as per the particulars on the annexed specifications, and shall be glad to hear that you are able to complete the same.

译文:

兹随函寄上100吨铁条订单一份。条件按附带规格中的具体规定。如贵公司能供货,当不胜感激。

在这个句子中,英文是一个句子,里面有一个并列谓语"and shall be glad to hear"和一个宾语从句"that you are able to complete the same"。如果我们将其翻译成一个长句子,汉语显得不伦不类,将其分成三个句子来处理就顺畅得多。

【例 39】

If the negotiations between the rich nations and the poor nations make headway, it is intended that a ministerial session in December should be arranged.

译文：

要是富国和穷国之间的谈判获得进展的话，就打算在12月份安排召开部长级会议。（翻译成表示假设的分句）

3.2 准确理解术语与商务专业知识

一些商贸英语的用法和日常英语的用法不大相同，我们平常所熟悉的一些普通名词在经贸英语中意思经常会有一些变化，如何翻译这些术语和习惯表达法，以及这些词应该和哪些词搭配都是非常重要的。近来随着经济发展的全球化趋势，新的词语层出不穷，在翻译时我们必须根据上下文去把握和理解其真正的含义。如：

marine insurance policy	海运保险	shipping order	装货单
confirmed letter of credit	保兑信用证	bill of exchange	汇票
acceptance	承兑	sight bill	即期汇票
futures	期货交易	margin	保证金
license	许可证	tender	投标
promotional mix	推销组合	barter system	易货制
reserve	储备金	outstanding	（股票、公债等）已公开发行并售出的
discount rate	贴现率	joint venture	合资企业
CIF (Cost Insurance and Freight)	成本保险费加运费		
foreign exchange dealing	外汇交易		

例如：

【例40】

We live in an era in which information, goods and capital speed around the globe, every hour of every day.

译文：

我们生活在这样一个时代，信息、货物和资金每时每刻在世界上流动。

【例41】

We are in receipt of your fax reminder dated today. The remittance from our bank to yours was made yesterday and you should be able to confirm receipt in your account today.

译文：

我们已收到贵方今日的传真催款单。汇款已于昨日由我方银行汇给贵方银行，贵公司应在今日贵方的账户上确认收到。

【例42】

Since World War II, the US has been the world's largest economy and, in most years, the world's largest exporter.

译文:

自从第二次世界大战以来,美国一直是世界上最大的经济大国。在大多数年份中,它又是世界上最大的出口国。

这个句子里 economy 的本意是"经济",根据上下文的意思,此处的意思是"从经济角度看这个国家",这里翻译成"经济大国"。

【例 43】

Any claim by the buyers regarding the goods shipped shall be filed within 15 days after arrival of the goods at the port of destination specified in the relative Bill of Lading and supported by a survey report issued by surveyor approved by the sellers.

译文:

买方对于装运货物的任何索赔,必须于货到提单规定的目的地 15 天内提出,并须提供经卖方同意的公证机构出具的检验报告。

这里 claim 的意思变为"索赔",Bill of Lading 的意思是"提单"。

3.3 据文体特点采用不同翻译原则

文体不同,其语言风格就不同,比如经贸合同的语言非常精练、正式,有很多附加成分修饰。因此,在翻译前,应熟练掌握各种文体的特点,针对不同文体采用不同的翻译原则。

【例 44】

It shall be subject to ratification or acceptance by the signatory States.

译文:

本公约须经签字国批准或接受。

英语用了 shall,汉语翻译时为了表达这种非常正式的文体用"应,可"等词。

【例 45】

Kindly tell us what steps you are going to take in the way of compensation for the damage.

译文:

敬请告诉我方将以什么方式来补偿这次损失。

Kindly tell us... 使得说话的语气显得十分客气。

【例 46】

We would appreciate receiving details regarding the commodities.

译文:

如能告诉该商品的详细情况,则不胜感激。

【例 47】

We must make claim on you for compensation with regard to this shipment, for it is not equal to the sample submitted, and contains large lumps, which will all have to be extracted before we are able to sell it.

译文:

此次所寄来的货品与样品大不相同,且混有不少大块,在销售以前不得不全部清除。为此只好向贵公司提出损失赔偿。

【例48】

We hereby add confirmation to this credit and we undertake that documents presented for payment in conformity with terms of this credit will be duly on presentation.

译文:

兹对此证加保兑并保证于提示符合此证条款的单据时履行付款。

3.4 把握英汉句子结构差异

英汉两种语言的主要句子结构大致是相同的,然而也经常有差异比较大的情况。英语句子结构比较复杂,句子成分常有各种修饰词,如定语、状语等,而且修饰成分有时又比较长,如用定语从句、状语从句、同位语从句等,因此英语句子结构比汉语的句子结构复杂得多,但是这种复杂句子条理和轮廓却都很清晰,很容易分清主句和从句。汉语常用一个个结构比较分散的短句子构成,修饰成分比较短也比较少。因此,在翻译的过程中一般使用分译法和合译法来处理两种语言结构方面的差异。

(1) 深刻理会词类转换,把握好句子、段落之间的联系

就句子内部而言,英语重形合,句子各成分联系紧密,汉语重意合,结构松散,更多依赖句内各成分的顺序。就句子之间的联系而言,汉语重视句子之间的联系,而英语不太重视句子之间的联系。

【例49】

The economic growth rate has been <u>noticeably</u> affected by the chaotic state of the market.

译文:

经济增长的速度受到市场混乱的影响,<u>这是显而易见的</u>。

noticeably 是副词,修饰谓语动词 affected,翻译时将其当做一个句子来处理反而符合汉语的习惯。

【例50】

During the half-hour talk, the two sides exchanged views on the choice of terms of payment, but they made no <u>mention</u> of the mode of transportation.

译文:

在半个小时的商谈中,双方就付款方式交换了意见,但没有提到运输方式。

mention 是名词,译成汉语时要变为动词。

【例51】

Our terms are cash within three months of date of delivery, <u>or subject to 5 percent discount if paid within one month</u>.

译文：

我公司付款条件为交货后3个月内交付现金。<u>如一个月内付清货款，可打95折</u>。

原文中"or subject to 5 per cent discount if paid within one month"只是句子中的一部分，而"if paid within one month"实际上是起到了一个从句的作用，这样安排使句子各成分的内在联系十分紧密。由于汉语的特点，当我们翻译这个句子时，须将其拆成两个句子，因为汉语讲究句子之间的联系。

【例52】

This will be particularly true since energy pinch will make it difficult to continue agriculture in the high-energy American fashion <u>that makes it possible to combine few farmers with high yield</u>.

译文：

这种困境将是确定无疑的，因为能源的匮乏使农业无法以高能量消耗、<u>投入少数农民就可能获得高产</u>的美国耕作方式继续下去了。

【例53】

The food supply will not increase nearly enough to match this, <u>which means that we are heading into a crisis in the matter of producing and marketing food</u>.

译文：

食品供应的增加将赶不上人口的增长，<u>这意味着我们将面临着生产和销售食品的危机</u>。（本句采用分译法）

【例54】

There used to be dozens of people <u>who stood a long line for hours in order to buy some pork</u>.

译文：过去常常有数十人排长队<u>在那里站几小时，为的是买一点猪肉</u>。
（采用分译法，将定语从句变为状语从句）

【例55】

Time would be needed to set up a new economic order in the world.

译文：

在世界上建立新的经济秩序是需要时间的。（被动语态结构翻译为"是……的"）

【例56】

Furthermore, it is obvious that the strength of a country's economy is directly bound up with the efficiency of its agriculture and industry, and that this in turn rests upon the efforts of scientists and technologists of all kinds.

译文：

再者，显而易见的是一个国家的经济实力与其工农业生产效率密切相关，而效率的提高则又依赖于各种科技人员的努力。

（采用顺译法）

【例 57】

Until such time as mankind has the sense to lower its population to the point where the planet can provide a comfortable support for all, people will have to accept "unnatural food".

译文：

除非人类终于认识到要把人口减少到地球能为所有人提供足够食物的程度，否则人们将不得不接受"人造食品"。

（状语从句的翻译法）

【例 58】

Plants which mine refine crude ores are often located in countries other than those in which the crude ores are mined.

译文：

提炼矿石的厂房通常不是设在采矿石的国家而是设在其他国家。

句法分析：这是一个主从复合句，主句为"Plants which refine crude ores are often located in countries other than those"，which 引导的定语从句修饰 plants，in which 引导的定语从句修饰 those。要点：those 在这里不是连接比较级，而是当"除……外"解释。none other than 意思是"除……外，不会是别的"。but 与 than 相当，在这里也当"除……外"解，都可译作"不是别人，正是"。本句型为强调判断句。

【例 59】

For example, in the early industrialized countries of Europe, the process of industrialization — with all the far-reaching changes in social patterns that followed — was spread over nearly a century, whereas nowadays a developing nation may undergo the same process in a decade or so.

译文：

在先期实现工业化的欧洲国家中，其工业化进程以及随之而来的各种深刻的社会结构变革持续了大约一个世纪，而如今一个发展中国家用 10 年左右的时间就可以完成同样的过程。

根据上下文，句中 spread 是"持续"、"花了"的意思，undergo 作"经历"讲，但在翻译时也要按上下文灵活地处理。

（2）适当增词、减词，平衡好断句与并句的关系

英汉两种语言句子结构、表达方式、修辞手段的特点不尽相同，所以在翻译的时候为了

使译文更加精练,更符合汉语的表达习惯,有时需要省略部分词语,而有时为了使译文更清楚,可按意义、修辞和句法的需要在译文中加入虽无其词而有其意的词,使译文更加通顺地表达出原文的思想内容。同时可以将原文的一句话分成几句话,也可以根据具体情况把两句话合成一句话,或将原文的顺序作适当的调整,这样做的目的是使译文的意思完整、准确。

【例 60】

We are pleased to have received your invitation to the symposium on Internet.

译文:

非常高兴收到参加互联网会议的邀请。

(省去代词"我们")

【例 61】

Perhaps you have overlooked the fact that your account for July purchases has not yet been settled.

译文:

也许您忘了 7 月份购货账还没有结算。

(名词 fact 不译出)

【例 62】

This year the export quantity of black tea increased by 20 percent, and jasmine tea by 30 percent.

译文:

今年红茶的出口量增加了 20%,花茶的出口量增加了 30%。

(增加原句的省略词)

【例 63】

All preparation must be done well before you sign a contact.

译文:

在签合同之前,所有准备工作都必须做好。

(增加名词)

【例 64】

We have handled textiles for more than 30 years.

译文:

我公司经营各种纺织品已有 30 多年。

(增补表示复数概念的词)

【例 65】

The problem whether the quality of the products is up to requirement has not been settled.

译文：
产品质量是否合乎要求这个问题尚未解决。
（把同位语从句提到 the problem 前）

【例66】
But considered realistically, we had to face the fact that our products were less than good.

译文：
但是现实地考虑一下，我们不得不正视这样的事实：我们的产品并不理想。
（补译：用冒号将同位语从句分开处理）

【例67】
The government tried <u>unsuccessfully</u> to curb inflation throughout the country.

译文：
政府试图控制全国范围内的通货膨胀，<u>但没有成功</u>。
（将原文中的一个副词翻译成一个句子）

3.5 译文体现商业风格

商务英语中大量使用专业术语，文体非常简洁，翻译成汉语时要按照等同原则力求做到译文的简洁，采用公文体，格式符合商业风格的规范。

【例68】
The above-mentioned drafts have been duly accepted.

译文：
上述汇票已获即时承兑。

【例69】
Insurance: To be effected by the sellers for 110% of invoice value covering All Risks and War Risk from warehouse to warehouse.

译文：
保险：由卖方按发票金额的110%投保一切险和战争险，仓至仓。

【例70】
Please forward the goods by rail to New York, to order of Messrs. Smith Co. there.

译文：
请将货物用铁路运至纽约，收货人为史密斯公司或其指定人。

【例71】
Some of the clauses in your L/C No. 12 are not in agreement with the stimulations of the SC.

译文：
贵方第 12 号信用证中的一些条款与销售合同的规定不符。

4　本章结语

　　商务英语以适应职场生活的语言要求为目的，内容涉及商务活动的方方面面。其语言特征独特，专业性词汇和术语较多，常使用大量套语。

　　国际商务活动要求信息传递的准确性，不能有丝毫的歧义，从事国际贸易的双方在具体的贸易活动中会使用大量的程式化的套语，而这些套语已经在国际商务交流中被广泛地接受和运用。为了避免误解和歧义，商务英语的句法表达十分严谨，各种从句、非谓语动词短语、被动语态等被广泛地运用。同时为了交易的顺利进行，商务英语在表达上需要语气客观，要体现礼貌原则。由于从事国际贸易的主体往往是不同的地区和国家，文化习俗、历史背景大不相同，某些词汇所表达的内在涵义可能会存在着一定的差别，从事国际贸易的各方须了解这些细微的区别，了解并遵守国际交往惯例，以达到沟通和交易的准确无误。

　　商务英语的译文应遵循"忠实"、"通顺"、"地道"、"统一"的标准。因此，要做好商务英语翻译，需要具备深厚的专业知识，对国际贸易的相关术语与文化知识要有较全面的了解。同时，还要掌握商务英语翻译的基本原则和技巧。只有将这几方面的技能有效结合，才能在商务英语翻译中得心应手。

第七章 科技翻译

1 科技文体概述

随着现代科学技术的发展,科技翻译已经变得越发重要。科技文体有其自身的特点与规律。本章将主要探讨科技英语的翻译。科技英语(English for Science and Technology)已发展成为一种重要的英语文体,它与新闻报刊文体、论述文体、公文文体、描述及叙述文体、应用文体一起,并称为英语的六大主要文体。在时代浪潮的推动下——尤其是加入WTO之后,我国不断融入世界科技的全球化大环境之中。随着经济的迅速发展,我国投资环境不断改善,来我国投资建厂、进行技术合作的外商和国外专家越来越多,经贸往来洽谈,科学技术交流也日益频繁。科技英语作为ESP的一个重要分支、科技交流的工具和科技信息的载体,其翻译的重要性是不言而喻的。

从广义上来说,科技英语泛指一切论及或谈及科学或技术的书面语和口头语。具体包括:①科技著述、科技论文、科技报告、实验报告等;②各类科技情报及其他文字资料;③科技实用手册,包括仪器、仪表、机械和工具等的结构描述和操作规程;④科技会议、会谈及交谈用语;⑤科技影片或录像等有声资料的解说词等。科技英语虽然不是一种独立存在的语言,但在词汇、词汇结构、语法结构等方面确有其本身的特点。它作为英语的一种语体,在翻译上也有其特殊的方法和要求。科技语言在表达上注重科学性、逻辑性、严密性和正确性,同时还有极强的专业性和实用性——这一点主要体现在准确的用词、简练的语言、客观的表达方式、清晰的条理以及确切的内容上。如何利用对这些特点的了解做好科技翻译正是这一章将要予以介绍的内容。

1.1 科技语言的词汇特点

科技词汇是在各个科学学科和专业中所应用的词汇的总称,其中既有一般常见的词汇,也有各个学科和专业中的专业词汇和行业术语。随着科学技术的不断发展,日益更新的技术所带来的词汇爆炸也使得科技语言中词汇的更新速度极快,且每门学科或专业都会有其自身的一套具有精确而又狭窄含义的名词和术语。虽然不同领域内的词汇各有其特点,但是所谓万变不离其宗,总的来说,科技词汇的特点可以归纳为以下四点:专业词汇适用面较窄;同一词汇在不同学科领域内词义不同;派生词在词汇中所占比重较大;名词的用途较广。

(1) 适用范围较窄的专业词汇

科技词汇中的专业词汇指的是那些只用于某个专业或学科的专门词汇或术语。这些词汇词义精确而狭窄,且针对性极强,一旦脱离了它所在的专业的话就几乎很难看到这类词汇的踪迹。因此,在做专业性较强的文献翻译时,对于该文献所属专业内的专门词汇和术语必须要有所了解。它较窄的应用范围也要求在翻译时务必要做到准确对应,以免出现不必要的翻译错误。当然,随着科技的进步,一些原本局限于自身领域内的专业词汇也逐渐发展成为一般常用的普通词汇,比较常见的有 radio,television 等。在这种情况下,原本的适用范围就得以扩展了。

(2) 在不同领域内对应词义不同的半专业词汇

除了适用范围较小的专业词汇外,在科技语言中还有一种半专业词汇,或者叫通用科技词汇,即在不同专业内都经常使用的词汇。这些词汇的数量较大,使用范围比纯科技词汇要广,出现频率也比较高。虽然它们的意义随着所使用的领域的不同而发生变化,但是在不同的专业内,它们各自的含义还是比较稳定的。一般来说,这类半专业词汇在基础语言中也是比较常见的词,但是它们在科技语言中的特定含义和基础语言中的含义差别极大。以 pencil 为例,在一般英语中它是"铅笔"的意思,但是在光学中它指的是"光线锥"、"射束",在热学中 color pencil 不是"彩色铅笔"而是"笔型温度计",在机械专业中 mental pencil 指的是"焊条",在气象学中 pencil rocker 指"(高空气象观测用的)小型火箭"。又如 ceiling,在一般英语中词义为"天花板"、"顶板",但它在航空领域中指的则是"绝对升限"或"最大飞行高度",在气象学中则是"云幕高度"的意思。从下表中也可以看出一些词语在基础英语和科技英语中词义的差别。

【例 1】

单词	基础英语意义	科技英语意义
couple	双,对	力偶,电偶
moment	瞬间,片刻	力矩,动量
translate	翻译,解释	变换,转移
stress	强调,重点	应力
monitor	班长	监控,控制
revolution	革命	转动,回转

(3) 派生词

派生词指的是通过合成、转化、派生等构词手段而构成的词汇。这种词汇在科技语言,尤其是科技英语中俯拾皆是。常见的前缀和后缀有 auto-(自,自动),bi-(双,重),counter-(逆,对应),extra-(额外的),hydro-(水),inter-(相互,在……之间),micro-(小,微量),multi-(多),pseudo-(伪,拟),semi-(半,部分),super-(超,过分),trans-(横过,贯通),-graph(书写物,复制的形象),-ism(主义,学说),-logy(……学,……论),-scope(范围,机会),-ship(性质,状况,职业)等。这些前缀和后缀和不同的词组合在一起,构成了科技词汇的一大部分。值得注意的是,尽管大多数前缀在普通词汇和科技词汇中的意思往往是相同的,但是元音前缀 a-却是个例外。在一般英语中,a-前缀一般用来表示状态,例如 awake,asleep 和 alive 等。但是在科技英语中,a-这个前缀代表的意思则是派生词和原词根意思相反,如 asymmetric(不对称的),astatic(不静止的),achromatic(无色的)等。

科技词汇,尤其是专业词汇中,有不少词是由希腊、拉丁语词素构成或直接借自希腊语、拉丁语的。如 chlorophyll 一词就是由希腊语词根 chlor- 和 phyll 构成的。值得注意的是,这类词的屈折变化和原语种的词形变化是基本保持一致的。常见的例子有 phenomenon 的复数 phenomena 等。

与派生词相类似的有缩写词和缩略词。在科技语言中,缩写词和缩略词是十分常见的,如 C(current 电流),max(maximum 最大),min(minimum 最小),radar(radio detecting and ranging 雷达),laser(light amplification by stimulated emission of radiation,激光),BASIC(Beginner's All-Purpose Symbolic Instruction Code,基本通用信号指令密码)等。这些词具有理解简易、简便易记、经济省时等特点,在各类科技文献和日常生活中运用广泛。

(4) 名词的多种用途

相比其他专业性语言来说,在科技语言里,出于客观性和准确性的考虑,往往大量使用名词,而不是像新闻语言或者广告语言,动词和形容词的使用频率较高。造成这种现象的一部分原因是名词比相对应的动词和形容词显得更为客观,另一方面则是因为在科技语言中,对现象和过程的描述远远高于对动作的描述。因此,科学工作者在选词上更偏向使用名词。因此,在科技语言中,名词扮演着极为重要的角色,它的用途也十分广泛,在这里我们主要讨论它的两种常见用途,即名词连用形式和用名词或名词中心词组来表示动词概念。

a. 名词连用形式

所谓名词连用,指的是在中心词前用名词来对中心词予以修饰、用名词来充当形容词的现象。在科技英语中,这种几个名词并列使用的现象是十分常见的。

【例 2】

oil pump 油泵

pressure difference 压强差

water pump valve 水泵阀

internal combustion engine 内燃机

low voltage direct current 低压直流电

b. 用名词或名词中心词组表示动词概念

在科技语言的遣词造句上,作者往往都倾向于使用抽象名词和普通名词(或词组)来取代动词的功能,特别是从动词、形容词等衍生而来的抽象名词。在日常生活中常常用动词来表达的意思或概念,在科技语言中则常用对应的名词形式进行表达。举例来说,在科技语言中,"you can rectify this fault if you insert a wedge"这句话会被 rectification of this fault is achieved by insertion of a wedge 这种说法所代替。原句中的 rectify 和 insert 两个动词都被各自对应的名词形式 rectification 和 insertion 所取代了。对科技工作者来讲,这种用表示"事实"的名词来取代动词的行为比单纯表示"事实"来得更加真实客观,更符合科技语言的要求。

除了直接用动词对应的名词形式来进行表达之外,在科技语言中还常常出现用以名词为中心的词组来表达动词概念的现象。

【例3】

keep **watch** over	密切注视
make a **claim** to	要求
give no **evidence** of	不足以说明

在这些词组中,黑体词是词组的中心词,同时,无一例外的都是名词。事实上,句子的动词概念是落在这些黑体的名词上的,而不是落在前面的 keep, make, give 等动词上。这种用名词中心词组来表示动词概念的现象是科技语言中经常出现的现象,在翻译时也是应当注意的地方。

1.2 科技语言的句法特点

总体来看,科技文本一般具有语言规范简练、文体质朴而正式、陈述客观等特点。这些特点在句法上体现为以下四个方面:被动语态、短语结构、复杂长句、条件句。本小节中将从这四个方面对科技语言的句法进行大致说明。

(1) 被动语态的广泛使用

和法律英语一样,在语态的使用上,科技英语侧重于使用被动语态,这是与科技英语自身的特点密不可分的。众所周知,科技文献所阐述的对象往往是事物、现象或过程等客观存在的事实。因此,为了强调这种客观存在性并弱化掉行为主体的存在,科技工作者常常选择被动语态作为主要的表达形式。以使用第三人称为特点的被动语态不仅强调了事物的客观存在,避免读者产生作者在进行主观臆断的印象,同时将读者的注意力集中在所阐述的事物身上,从而方便将精力集中起来投诸于对事物及其现象的分析研究上。根据英国利兹大学 John Swales 的统计,科技英语中的谓语至少 1/3 是被动语态。

【例4】

First of all, the preparation for giving the injection must be carried out. In selecting the medication, it must be triple checked to ensure that the right medication and dosage is being given. This is done by checking the order against the medication card, against the label on the drug container.

观察上例可知,在这个短短三句话的段落中,使用了三处被动语态,每一句的谓语动词都采用了被动语态的形式,突出了 "the preparation for giving the injection"、"medication"、和 "selecting" 这三个事实(动作),给读者留下了清晰明了的印象,有助于他们对文章的理解。如果换成主动语态的话,则无法达到这个目的和效果。

此外,使用被动语态将最重要的信息放在了句子开头的位置。这样不仅能引起读者的兴趣,同时达到了科技语言传递信息的本质目的,清楚地将最重要的内容最优先地表达了出来,有时还能起到避免歧义的作用。

【例5】

Electrical energy can *be stored* in two metal plates *separated* by an insulating medium. Such a device *is called* a capacitor, or a condenser, and its ability to store electrical energy is termed capacitance. It is *measured in* farads.

在这段话中,斜体标示的四处使用了被动语态,在它们之前的主语信息量比较大,将之前置不仅比较醒目,而且避免了长句子容易出现的歧义问题,使得整个句子自然流畅,叙事清晰明确。

意义的名词+of+名词+修饰语,在汉语里则表现为"的"字结构的频繁出现。这里也可以与前文谈到的用名词或以名词为中心的词组表示动词概念的内容进行比较分析。

(2) 短语结构的广泛使用

a. 名词化结构

《当代英语语法》在提到科技英语时指出,大量使用"名词化结构"是科技英语的特点之一。作为一种行文简洁、表达客观、内容确切、信息量大的文体,科技语言中大量的名词性结构一方面对文章本身所表达的"事实"进行了强调,一方面又达到了简洁明了说明信息的目的,实现了文章的简明清晰之美。常见的名词化结构形式是表示动作。

【例6】

① Archimeds first discovered the principle of displacement of water by solid bodies.

② The rotation of the earth on its own axis cause the change from day to night.

③ 抚触与高压氧联合促进中重度缺氧缺血性脑病康复临床研究

④ 圆钢管混凝土柱在轴压下局部屈曲的临界载荷

b. 非限定动词短语

科技文章要求行文简练、结构紧凑。因此,为了用最少的篇幅来表达清楚自己的意思,科技人员在写作时往往舍弃直接用主谓结构的完整句子来表达意思的做法,而是选择使用非限定动词短语来予以表述,从而达到缩短句子又不改变原有意思的目的。非限定动词短语的使用是科技语言中广泛出现复杂长句的原因之一。

【例7】

Being a good conductor, copper is generally used to conduct electricity.

Materials to be used for structural purposes are chosen so as to behave elastically in the environmental conditions.

c. 以介词短语、形容词短语为代表的后置定语

这类短语的使用通常出现在科技英语中。在科技文章中,出于对语言的简练程度和准确程度的要求,在行文中经常使用后置定语,尤其是介词短语和形容词短语。这些短语的主要作用是对主句表达的信息进行补充,实现意思的完整表达。

【例8】

① The difficulty in developing a videophone stems from having to stuff huge amounts of information through a thin copper-wire phone line; compare this task with pouring water from a gallon jug into a straw.

② The main factor in the measurement is that a noise source of known sound power, and preferably with radiation and frequency characteristics similar to those produced by the machine to be tested, is available.

(3) 复杂长句的广泛使用

科技语言在表达上注重说明事实和逻辑的严密性,因此在叙述上往往一气呵成。在这种对表达的完整性和充分性有所要求的背景下,科技文本中复杂的句子和扩张的机构俯拾皆是。这些长句结合了前文所提到的被动语态和短语结构,同时还兼有并列结构、省略、倒装语句或其他类型的从句,使得句子形成了一个难以理解的复杂整体。因此,复杂长句既是科技语言的显著特点,也是翻译的难点。

【例9】

① Oxygen is also injected upwards into the molten bath through the refractory walls providing close control of thermal and chemical conditions, superior process flexibility, high reaction rates and minimization of refractory, dust, and other problems encountered with conventional tuyers or top-blowing.

② With the advent of the space shuttle, it will be possible to put an orbiting solar power plant in stationary orbit 24,000 miles from the earth that would collect solar energy almost continuously and convert this energy either directly to electricity via photovoltaic cells or indirectly with flat plate or focused collectors that would boil a carrying medium to produce steam that would drive a turbine that then in turn would generate electricity.

③ 由于电子计算机能够从大量的分散地区中的任何一个得到消息,并在一两分钟,甚至几秒钟内进行必要的计算,作出答复或者向分散在工厂周围的一个或几个同样数字的地区发布命令,所以电子计算机用于加工工业的自动控制是最理想的。

(4) 条件句的广泛使用

在科技语言中往往需要提出假设并进行推理,因此在行文的过程里经常会使用各种各样的条件句,用以表达假设、建议、推测、怀疑等情境。这些条件句可以分为未定虚拟语气和纯粹虚拟语气。

【例10】

① In radioactive changes one would have to assume that a charged helium atom (2 protons and 2 neutrons) went off whenever an alpha particle was emitted.

② If the radius of the nucleus were one mile, what would be the radius of an atom?

③ 万一盖上有裂缝,有毒气体就会漏出而造成污染。

1.3 单调的修辞手段

首先,与文学作品、新闻报道不同的是,科技语言自身客观、质朴的特点使得文章中一般不会使用比喻、拟人、夸张、反语等修辞手段,而是直接对事实或过程进行真实完整的叙述。它的文体特点是:清晰、准确、精练、严密。

【例11】

① The range of a voltmeter may be extended by means of a series resister called multiplier as shown in Fig. 2. The full-scale reading of the meter alone may be 15 volts. With the multiplier 250 volts may be required to move the pointer to full-scale, 135 volts across the multiplier and 15 volts across the meter.

② 一般来讲，干燥一种固体指的是从固体材料中去除相对少量的水或其他液体，从而使残留液体的含量减少到可接受的低值。

其次，科技人员在撰写科技论文时，往往采取直截了当的表达方式，以达到和其他科技工作者直接准确地交流科技信息的目的。在这一大前提下，文章中就出现了许多被广泛接受的符号和公式，以避免产生误解。

【例 12】

① If $d=2$, then $d^2=4$.

② To increase the rate of reaction, a catalyst is used.

③ If a solution is found, then proceed with the next stage.

此外，在科技语言中，所运用的时态大都限于一般现在时、一般过去时、现在完成时和一般将来时这几种，其他时态运用极少，这是与科技文体自身的限制密切相关的。作为一种主要阐述客观真理和事实的文体，科技文体在时态的运用上往往并不体现出对时间性的需求，因而大部分的科技文献都采取一般现在时，偶尔在描述过去进行的研究时会使用过去时和现在完成时，在表示对将来的期望或计划时，则会使用一般将来时。除此以外其他类型的时态在科技文献中运用极少。

2　科技语篇的翻译原则

科技语篇作为科技交流的工具和科技信息的载体，其翻译的重要性不言而喻。随着科学技术的突飞猛进和经济的迅速发展，科学技术的交流也日益频繁。在这个大背景下，对于科技语言的翻译的需求也越来越大。然而，在现今的翻译市场上，科技翻译仍然呈现出良莠不齐的局面。造成这种局面的原因正是必要的翻译规范的缺乏。所谓没有规矩不能成方圆，没有一个完整的评价体系来对科技翻译的质量进行评估，对翻译好坏的界定也就很难进行了。而在这之中，对于翻译时应当遵守的原则的制定是应当最先被提出并放在首要位置上的。这是因为，只有在共同的基本原则的指导下进行的翻译，才能放在同一标准上进行对比比较。同时，基本原则的制定也有利于译者在进行翻译时利用这些原则作为翻译的参照，避免出现太多的谬误。在这里，结合国内外的研究成果和翻译实践，将科技翻译的原则简单地归纳为以下三点：逐字逐句求真求实，字里行间通顺畅达，追求科技语言的美感。

2.1　逐字逐句求真求实

无论什么类型的翻译，我们首先要注意的就是翻译对原文的忠实。好的翻译，最基本的就是要将原作品的内容和思想完整而准确地表达出来，并力求和原作品在风格上贴近。翻译作为联结相异文化的桥梁，其中的任何一点偏差都可能造成理解和表达上的谬误，对于力求真实准确的科技语言来说更是如此。在科技翻译中，任何一点小的错误，甚至是表达的模糊都可能对科学研究、学术交流产生不良影响，甚至造成重大损失。因此，在科技语言的翻译中,最重要的一点就是逐字逐句求真求实。要做到这一点,首先就要从宏观的层面对文章的大致内容和思想进行把握,比如,这篇文章主要讲的是什么、涉及哪些专业领域、文章想要传达的思想是什么、采取了怎样的方式来进行传达的等。在了解了文章的大致信息之后,就要深入到微观层面上,对文章的各个段落、每个句子,甚至是单个词语进行认真分析和反复推敲。最后要再回到宏观层面上,完成从微观层面对宏观层面的审视,对是否"求真求实"的翻译进行审视和反思。

【例13】

The screen is viewed through a window led into the column.

事实上,如果按部就班,将"a window led into the column"译成"在柱子上开了窗户",一定会让人大感不解。事实上,在这句话中,window 和 column 都是半专业术语,前者指的是显微镜的"窗洞",而后者指的是显微镜的"镜筒"。因此,恰当的译法应该是:在镜筒前部开了窗洞,通过它可以看到荧光屏。通过这个例子我们可以看出,在科技语言的翻译中,我们对每字每句都要采取严肃谨慎的态度,弄清楚它们在特定领域中的意思,避免出现指鹿为马之类的表达或是与原意南辕北辙的翻译。

【例14】

The ways in which damage may be produced by the parasites include the following: trauma or physical damage, lytic necrosis, stimulation of host-tissue reactions, toxic and allergic phenomena, and the opening of pathways for the entry of other pathogens into the tissue.

译文:

寄生虫所造成的损害包括下列几种:创伤或机械性损伤、液化性坏死、刺激宿主组织产生反应、毒性作用和变态反应现象,为其他病原体进入组织打开门户。

在本例中,physical damage 的译法是一个难点。这个词组既可以译成"身体损伤"、"肉体损伤",也可以译成"物理损伤"等,但是根据前文的 trauma(创伤)来看,译为"机械性损伤"似乎更为贴切。

作为科技语言中一个重要的组成部分,各种专业术语和半专业术语的广泛使用集中反映了科学概念和科技内容,是科技信息的主要载体,也是科学论述的必要条件。译者在对这些词语进行翻译时一定要做到准确无误,才能正确地理解和再现原文的内容。此外,除了对术语的翻译外,对原文的句式结构和逻辑关系的翻译也必须建立在透彻理解的基础上。

【例15】

① This include the rubber, elevators and ailerons, whose function is to control the aircraft in fight; and the wings which provide the lift necessary to overcome the weight of the aircraft and lift it through the air.

原译:

其中包括方向舵、升降舵和副翼,它们的功能是操纵飞行中的飞机和机翼,机翼则是提供克服飞机重量和使之升入空中所必需的举力。

改译：

其中包括方向舵、升降舵和副翼以及机翼。方向舵、升降舵和副翼的作用是操纵飞机的飞行,机翼则是提供克服飞机重量和使之升入空中所必需的举力。

② 在正常情况下地位配置的那个阀是备用的。

原译：

The valve positioned downward is not in use normally.

改译：

The valve positioned below is not normally in use.

在以上两个例子中,①句里的 and 是翻译的难点。对句子中 the wings 的并列成分的理解是翻译这句话的关键:它的并列成分是 the rubber, elevators and ailerons,还是 control 后面的 the aircraft? 而通过观察句子,发现在 the wings 前面使用的是分号,证明 the wings 是和 the rubber, elevators and ailerons 在同一等级上的,它们都是 include 的宾语。了解了这一点后,对句子的翻译就比较容易了。在②句中,把 downward 一词改译成了 below,这是因为 downward 一词作为形容词有两种解释,既可译为"向下的",也可译为"下面的",这就使得读者对译文可能产生错误的理解——"朝下放置的那个阀通常不用",而把它改为 below 之后意思就比较清楚了。

总而言之,求真求实对科技翻译具有重要意义,是科技翻译所必须遵守的第一准则,对它的强调应当始终放在科技翻译实践的首要位置。正如前文所述,对科技语言中一字一句,甚至一个标点符号的改动,都可能造成意义上的南辕北辙和理解上的错误,甚至造成严重的损失。作为一门以追求事实为基础的语言,科技语言所要强调的也正是真实和准确。为了自始至终地维持科技语言的高度准确性和严谨性,译者在翻译时要每分每秒都要毫不松懈地对译文进行严格的考据和审视,力求做到逐字逐句求真求实,不扭曲和误读原文的意思。

2.2 字里行间通顺畅达

翻译的通顺一般指的是译文必须要文理通顺,能够为读者所理解,符合现代语言规范,而不是死译硬译,使得译文生硬不通、结构混乱、逻辑不清。因此,无论是从翻译本身还是从读者的角度来讲,翻译的通顺都是翻译必须重视的问题,而科技语言自身内容的艰深使得翻译的通顺显得更为重要。试想,如果译文本身读起来就前后不通,又怎么能让读者理解文章的内容呢? 因此,通顺畅达是科技翻译的一个重要原则。

上至一个词的理解,下到对整篇文章结构的把握,都是"顺"在文章中涉及的内容。众所周知,英语和汉语从属于两种不同语系,它们在语言符号、句子结构和表达形式上都有各自的特点。它们之间巨大的差异是造成它们之间的互译尤为艰难的原因之一。要做到这两种语言互译的通顺,就必须充分考虑这两种语言各自的语言特点,力求在忠实于原文内容的前提下,用规范化的译文语言来进行翻译,使得译文符合译入语的语法结构和表达习惯,容易为读者理解。与此同时,科技翻译还必须注意科技语言的表达特点和英汉两种语言在科技表达上的不同。只有兼顾这几点,才有可能使译文通顺畅达。

【例16】

If the design problem is rather complicated, an electronic computer can solve it within sixteen hours after running through 16,000 possible designs.

译文：

这个设计问题虽然非常复杂，但是电子计算机快速审阅了16000个可供选择的设计方案后，便在16个小时之内解决了这个问题。

这个译文是较好的一种译法，它在忠于原文的前提下，对原文形式做了大胆的突破：首先，原句使用的是if引导的条件状语从句，但是译文将之改变成让步状语从句，从而显得更容易理解；同时译文和原文的语序也有所不同，原文是比较典型的英语表达，即将状语放在句子的末尾处，而译文将原文中的状语部分提前，这样更符合汉语的表达习惯。此外，根据上下文语境将design的意思扩充至"设计方案"，又将running through引申为"快速审阅"，使得译文显得精确而通俗易懂。

【例17】

① The plastic-encapsulated transistors which are more susceptible to moisture than metal cap transistors are less suitable for military use.

原译：

比金属壳晶体更易受潮的塑封晶体管不太适于军用。

改译：

塑封晶体管比金属壳晶体管更易受潮，因此，不太适于军用。

② Mild steels are not so hard as medium-carbon steels because they contain less carbon.

原译：

软钢没有中碳钢那么硬，因为含有较少的碳。

改译：

软钢不如中碳钢硬，因为其含碳量较低。

③ 结果表明，黏弹性阻尼器对悬臂张弦立体桁架结构的节点位移和杆件轴力都有很好的控制效果，并给出了实用性的工程建议。

原译：

It is shown that the viscoelastic damper is very effective to mitigate earthquake responses of long span roofs. It can give a reference to design, research and application of this structure.

改译：

It is shown that the viscoelastic damper is very effective to mitigate earthquake responses of long span roofs. Thus, it can give a reference to design, research and application of this structure.

在第一个例句中,原译和改译的差别主要体现在对句子的拆分和加上的那个"因此"上,经过改动之后,修改译文明显比原文显得生动活泼得多,也更容易理解。原译过长的定语不符合汉语的表达习惯,在表达上显得不够明确。因此,尽管两种译法所表达的意思是一样的,但是后者明显是更好的选择。在第二个例句中,原译存在的问题主要是不符合科技体裁,表达很不正式。在前文讨论科技语言的特点的时候我们提到了科技文体是一种比较正式的文体,因此,在追求译文的通俗易懂时也不能忽视其体裁本身对于语言的正式性的要求。译者在做科技翻译时要注意使用正式规范的表达,不能盲目追求通俗易懂而忽视了文体自身的特殊性所带来的隐性要求。而在第三个例子中,由于上下句间存在因果关系,因此,在翻译时加上 thus 这个连接词之后句子显得更为通顺,逻辑上也更为缜密。

"通顺"作为翻译的一个普遍性原则,在科技语言的翻译中又有其自身的特殊性。它包括横向和纵向两方面的通顺:一方面,译者要注意根据语言环境的不同来对文章细节进行处理,并在准确表达原文意思的基础上注重根据英语和汉语各自表达习惯对表达方式进行调整。英语的表达往往注重语言上的变化,不仅常常用同义词和同义结构之间的互换来表达意思,避免重复,同时在句型结构上也多有错综复杂之感;而汉语表达则呈现出词汇重复使用和语法结构较明确的特点。另一方面,除了对细节的把握之外,译者还要从整体风格上对文章进行把握。既要用通顺的语言表达原文内容,又要注重风格的一致性,使译文在符合译入语表达习惯的同时又能呈现出科技文献所应有的特点。只有在这两方面达到统一,才能使译文通顺畅达,充分传达其语言符号所承载的信息。

2.3 科技语言的美感

很多人认为对于偏重讲述事实和事理的科技语言来说,由于自身表达特点的限制,它应该是归类于缺乏美感的语言之中。这是因为科技语言既没有华丽的辞藻进行修饰,也没有各式各样的修辞手法,叙事的客观性和逻辑性又限制了其在文章结构上无法进行过多的变化和创新。和文学语言相较而言,科技语言的确显得较为单调而缺乏变化,但这并不意味着科技语言缺乏美感。事实上,科技语言的美感主要体现在逻辑美、整体美和简洁美这三个方面,而对于这三个方面的追求则集中代表了科技翻译对"美"的追求。

科技文章中最具特色的美就是逻辑美。科技文章作为一种表达科技事实、概念、原理和解释自然现象的文体,它在阐述时往往呈现出逻辑缜密、推导合理、无懈可击的特点,使得文章具有极强的说服力。这种逻辑上的美感是其他类型的文体无法与之相媲美的。在进行科技翻译时,要注意前后文逻辑上的一致,做到环节相通、连贯顺畅,不要出现逻辑上的谬误,这才能实现译文的逻辑美。

【例 18】

① Many man-made substances are replacing certain natural materials because either the quantity of the natural product cannot meet our ever-increasing requirement, or, more often, because the physical property of the synthetic substance, which is the common name for man-made materials, have been chosen, and even emphasized, so that it would be of the greatest use in the fields in which it is to be applied.

译文：

人造材料通称为合成材料，许多人造材料正在代替某些天然材料，这或者是由于天然物产的需要不能满足日益增长的需要，或者往往是由于人们选择了合成材料的一些物理性质并加以突出而造成的，因此，合成材料在其使用的领域中具有极大的用途。

② 假设核心混凝土刚性很大，通过压杆和圆柱壳两种模型，假定了位移函数的三角函数形式，用能量法求解圆钢管混凝土柱在轴压下局部屈曲的临界载荷和临界压力。

译文：

It is assumed that the rigidity of core concrete is great. Based on two kinds of models—the strut and the cylindrical shell respectively, when the displacement function is given in the form of trigonometric function, the local buckling critical load and stress of the concrete-filled circular steel tubular column subjected to axial compressing are solved by using the energy approach.

在第一个例句中，原文句子结构比较复杂，在主句下有表示原因的状语从句，状语从句中又套有非限定性定语从句，是典型的科技英语的表达方式。英美人惯用这种方式来实现对意思完整而充分的说明。但是这种说明方式和汉语的惯用表达并不太一样，比起这种复杂扩张的结构，汉语句子往往显得简单而独立，逻辑上的联系往往是通过逻辑联系词来实现的。因此，在译文中译者将非限定性定语从句抽出来单独成句，最后的结果状语从句也分开来进行翻译，这样做既符合汉语的表达习惯，又使得汉语读者读起来较容易理解。在第二个例子中，原句是用了三个短的从句来解释后文"求解"的论证方法和过程，而在译文中，就用了一个复杂结构的长句来予以说明。

科技语言的"美"的第二个方面是它的整体美。无论是科技英语中各种复杂的句型还是科技汉语中独立的句子，它们在整篇的科技文献中都是为了体现同一个概念而存在的。这种对于同一个复杂概念的完整呈现，体现了科技语言的完整美。它和前文提到的逻辑美是紧密联系在一起的：一方面，层次分明的说理使得读者感受到科技语言清晰明了的逻辑之美；另一方面，这种条理清晰的说理又是前后连接起来所共同形成的一个整体。因此，在翻译的过程中，要句句斟酌字字分析，以保持这种整体美。具体来讲，这种对整体美的追求主要包括以下四个方面：事实信息的完整、语法范畴的完整、词义内涵的完整和语句整体的统一。可以说，整体美的实现是建立在忠实和通顺的翻译的基础上的，其中也包含有对逻辑美的追求。

最后，科技语言的美还体现在其语言的精练和简洁上。精练简洁是公认的美，简洁的语言往往予人以明快直率的美感。而科技语言的一个突出特征就是精练，这是因为其适用范围限制了其在表达上必须要用最少的文字符号传递最大的信息。因此，在科技语言中往往少有赘余之语，可谓是字字珠玑。这种精练之美既体现在词汇层，也表现在句法层，因此在翻译的过程中，必须深入细致地分析词汇和句法，以使译文在语言上简短精练、一目了然，而不是显得繁琐冗赘，有许多不必要的重复。

【例 19】

① All living things must, by reason of physiological limitations, die.

原译：

由于生理上的局限性的原因，一切生物总是要死亡的。

改译：

由于生理上的局限，一切生物总是要死亡的。

② 少自由度并联机器人结构简单，便于控制，成本低，在许多领域具有广泛的应用前景，是目前机器人研究领域中的重点、热点和难点。

原译：

Imperfect-mobility parallel robots are structural simple, ease of control and cost low. They have broad application prosperity in many fields, and are currently the key, hot and difficult spot in the robot study field.

改译：

Imperfect-mobility parallel robots are the focus of much attention in the field of robotics owing to their simple structure, ease of control, low cost and promising application in many areas.

在第一个例子中，原译比起改译明显赘余得多："……的原因"和"由于"在语义上相互重叠。在不需要强调的前提下，这种重复是多余的。而将它删除之后，改译显得更加简洁明快，表意也更加清晰。在第二个例子中，相互重叠。在不需要强调的前提下，这种重复是多余的。而将它删除之后，改译显得更加简洁明快，表意也更加清晰。在第二个例子中，原译的缺点则在于它是用汉语的思维习惯来进行翻译的，导致翻译出来的句子结构松散，表达内容重点不突出，读起来也不够通顺。改译将几个汉语短句合并成了一个英语长句，这样结构就比较紧凑，也更符合英美人的思维方式

总之，从科技文章的特点来看，大多数文章都呈现出逻辑性强、结构严密、术语繁多、词汇量大、内容艰深、语言严谨精确等特点，这就对译文提出了极高的要求。因此，在科技语言的翻译过程中，在满足"求真求实"和"通顺畅达"这两条原则的前提下，译者也应适当地追求译文的美感，注重对原文逻辑美、整体美和简洁美的实现。这三项原则可以和严复所提出的"信达雅"的翻译三项准则相互进行参考。"信"指的是译文要忠实于原文，"达"指的是译文的通顺达意，而"雅"则体现了译文对于美感的追求，它们与上文所提到的三原则恰恰是相互对应的，只是在"达"和"雅"的追求上，科技翻译更注重在准确诚实地反映原文信息的前提下所进行的对译文的简洁流畅通顺的追求。译文必须和原文一样，在叙事上清晰明确、条理分明。译者在进行科技翻译的时候，应当遵循上述三项原则，尊重原文，在充分理解原文意思的基础上逐字逐句进行翻译，务求准确严谨，切忌加入自己的主观情感，始终抱着冷静挑剔的态度来面对每一篇科技文章，避免似是而非的随意心理是做好科技翻译的最基本前提。

3 科技英语翻译策略

现在主要从词语、语态、句子、语篇等几个层面进行分析。

3.1 词语的翻译

(1) 科技术语的翻译

科技术语常见的译法有四种：意译法、音译法、形译法和综合译法。从字面意思来看，意译法指的就是根据原词的实际含义译成对应的汉语或英语术语，这种译法广泛运用在科技术语的翻译中，具有概念明确、易懂易记的优点；音译法则主要根据词汇的发音来进行转化，这一方法主要适用于计量单位名称、人名、地名、公司名、首字母缩略语以及一些还未完全了解的新术语，对于最后一种情况而言，随着对新术语的了解的深入，可能出现用新的意译的术语来代替原有意译术语的情况，如 vitamin（维他命）现在译为"维生素"；形译法则是结合词语自身特点和所指物的特点进行的词语转换；综合译法则主要是音译法和意译法的结合。具体请看下表所示的例子。

【例 20】

翻译方法		英文	中文
意译法		basic automation	基础自动化
		info-highway	信息高速公路
		mathematic mod	数学模型
音译法		radar	雷达
		montage	蒙太奇
		ampere	安培
形译法	象形译法	crossbit	十字头、星型钻
		H-beam	工型钢
		T-track	锤形径迹
	原形译法	X-ray	X 射线
		V-belt	V 形皮带
		a-brass	a 黄铜
综合译法		radar-man	雷达手
		Internet	因特网
		logic circuit	逻辑电路

（2）缩略词的翻译

缩略词一般采取音译的方法。有些术语是由几个词的首字母缩写而成的，如果意译就会造成译名太长不够简洁的问题，同时太长的译名看上去也不太像术语，因此大多可以采取音译的做法，但一般在首次译出的时候加以注解，对音译的缩略词的内涵予以阐释。

【例21】

托福 TOEFL（Test of English as a Foreign Language）把英语作为外语的考试
雅思 IELTS（International English Language Testing System）国际英语语言测试系统
欧佩克 OPEC（Organization of Petroleum Exporting Countries）石油输出国组织
Sonar 声呐（sound navigation and ranging）声波导航和测距设备

（3）其他译法：词语的转译

转译在某种程度上来说和意译有许多相似甚至相同的地方，但是它比意译的范围要小。科技语言中词语的转译一般指的是以下两种情况：词义的转换和词性的转换。

a. 词义的转换

词义的转换主要是指在科技语言的翻译中根据译入语的表达习惯等需要，将源语原本的意思加以修改，转换成更适合译入语文化和表达形式的意思。

【例22】

The shortest distance between raw material and a finished part is precision casting.

译文：

把原材料加工成成品的最简便的方法是精密铸造。

从上述例子可以看出，词义的转换主要是基于表达的需要。在例句中，把 shortest distance 翻译成"最简便的方法"，使得表达更自然，更符合汉语的表达习惯。

b. 词性的转换

和词义的转换一样，科技语言翻译中词性的转换也是基于表达需要之上的。在实际翻译时可以根据自身需要，在形容词、名词、动词等词性之间进行相互转换，力求实现表达的通顺、流畅、自然。

【例23】

① Glass is more soluble that quartz.

译文：

玻璃的可溶性比石英大。（形容词转译成名词）

② Laser is one of the most sensational developments in recent years because of its applicability to many fields of science and its adaptability to practical uses.

译文：

激光是近年最惊人的科学成就之一，因为它可以应用于许多科学领域，也适合各种实际用途。

在上述两个例句中，①句在翻译时，把 soluble 这个形容词转译成了"可溶性"这个名词；

而在②句中,applicability 和 adaptability 这两个名词被转换成了动词,原句的名词性结构被转换成了动宾结构,使译文更符合习惯使用动词的汉语的表达习惯。

3.2 被动语态的译法

被动语态作为科技英语中被广泛使用的语态,是科技英语语体表现的习惯特征之一。在翻译时要特别注意对被动语态的处理,尤其是英语被动句的汉译。基本上被动语态的翻译可以采取以下两种策略:①将被动句转换成主动句;②保持原有被动结构不变。具体来看,每种大的翻译策略又包含对应的各种小的技巧和策略。

(1) 将被动句译为主动句

英语和汉语作为两个不同的语言系统,在很多地方都存在着巨大的差异,这点在被动语态的使用上也不例外。在汉语中习惯用主动语态来表达,在英语中却常使用被动语态来进行表达。例如:"We are kept strong by exercise."这句话如果直接按照英语的被动语态来进行翻译的话,就变成"我们被锻炼保持得健康",这样十分别扭。因此,将它译为主动语态的"锻炼能促使我们身体健康"就比较符合汉语的表达习惯。因此,在翻译时不应被原文的语法结构所束缚,而是要根据译入语言的特点进行合理适度的改变,从而使译文通顺流畅,便于读者理解。

a. 主语不变

这种译法是将原主语译为主语,并在之后接相应的主动态动词,事实上可以把它看做是省略了"被"字的被动句。这是因为,在汉语中,往往并不用"被"字表达主动意义,而是采取主动语态的形式,如"书放在书架上"。如果固执地要在这种汉语的习惯表达中加上"被"字,反而显得生硬突兀、不太自然。

【例 24】

Several approaches to the problem of ladle skull slag or deoxidation-scum removed was being tried.

译文:

罐内结渣、炉渣或脱氧浮渣清除问题的几项解决方案正在实验中。

b. 主语译为宾语

这种译法是将原本句子的主语译为宾语,而将句子中提到的行为主体或相当于行为主体的介词宾语译成主语。事实上,这种译法可以看做是将原句子的被动语态还原成主动语态之后再进行翻译,一般适用于行为主体比较明确的时候。

【例 25】

Friction can be reduced and the life of the machine prolonged by lubrication.

译文:

润滑能减少摩擦,延长机器寿命。

上例的翻译其实可以看做是将原句还原成"Lubrication can reduce friction and prolong the life of the machine"之后进行的直译。对于行为主体比较明确的含有被动语态的句子来说，这种译法不失为一个好的选择。

此外，当没有明确的动作主体，但有可以作为主语的介词性等短语结构时，也可以考虑这种译法。

【例 26】

Communication satellites are used for international living transmission throughout the world.

译文：

全世界都将通讯卫星用于国际间的实况转播。

在这个句子中，译者将 throughout the world 这个介词短语翻译成"全世界"，并将它作为整个句子的主语，这是符合汉语的表达习惯的。在找不到句子行为主体时不妨考虑此类可以代替行为主体功能的短语。

c. 无主句

与英语相比，汉语的无主句是自身的一大特色。相对于英语清晰的主谓结构而言，汉语的无主句要显得随意得多，因此在翻译上也就扮演着更为灵活的角色。因为英语的被动语态往往是省略动作主体的，无主句在被动语态的翻译上就具有极大的适用性。将无动作发出者的英语句子译为汉语的无主句，必要时还可以加上"人们"、"大家"等泛指性主语或"把"、"使"等字，是翻译被动语态的一个可取策略。

【例 27】

① Smoke victims should be warned to stop smoking, to exercise and control cholesterol.

译文：

应当警告吸烟受害者停止吸烟、加强锻炼和控制胆固醇。

② Potassium and sodium are seldom met in their natural state.

译文：

人们很少见到自然状态的钾和钠。

③ Temperature is changed quickly from room temperature to 125℃ and is held there for at least 15 minutes.

译文：

使温度很快地从室温升高到125℃，并至少保持15分钟。

d. 固定译法

这里所提到的固定译法主要指的是在英语中以 it 为形式主语的被动句。此类句子在英语中所占比例较大，翻译时一般按照主动结构来译出，即将原文中的主语从句放在译句的宾语的位置上，而把形式主语单译为一个独立句或分句。因为以 it 为形式主语的句子本身有很多固定的句型，此类固定句型在长期的翻译实践中也形成了比较固定的译法，下表列出了一些比较常见的 it 句型的译法。

It is believed that...	人们相信,大家相信……
It is estimated that...	据统计(推算)……
It has been found that...	已经发现,实践证明……
It must be kept that...	必须记住……
It is predicted that...	据估计,据预计……
It must be realized that...	必须了解(认识,明白)……
It is suggested that...	有人建议……
It is understood that...	人们理解,不用说……

(2) 将被动句译为被动句

当我们不想强调行为主体或需要对动作接受者进行强调的时候,我们也可以考虑将英语的被动句仍然译成汉语的被动句。

a. 汉语的"被"字句

在英语里说到被动语态就是 be done 的形式,在汉语中则突出地表现为"被"字句。一般来说,当句子中出现"被"字的时候,这个句子往往就是被动句了。因此,要实现从被动语态到被动语态的转变,最直接最简便的方式就是把它译成"被"字句。对于那些既可以译成主动句也可以译成被动句的句子需要结合文章自身特点和表达的侧重进行取舍。

【例 28】

① Solution to the problem was ultimately found.

译文：

这个问题的解决方法终于被找到了。

(编者注：这句话也可以译为"人们终于找到了这个问题的解决方法。"如果侧重点是放在解决方法上,就应优先选用被动句式的译法,但如果重点是强调找到了解决方法这个事实上,则主动句式可能更符合要求。总而言之,还是应该具体情况具体分析,重点是要符合译文的整体风格和具体要求。)

② When the electrons fly away from the hydrogen nuclei, they are attracted toward the oxygen atoms.

译文：

当氢原子的电子飞离其核时,这些电子就被吸向氧原子。

b. "把"字句、"由"字句、"受"字句等

除了被字句之外,汉语里还有许多其他表达被动语态的方式,比较常见的就是"把"字句、"由"字句、"受"字句等。我们常说的"把书包里放满书"、"水分子由氢原子和氧原子构成"等句子其实也是被动句。在翻译时灵活运用这些表示被动语态的句型可以使译文免于重复之虞,同时使文章显得自然流畅,更符合汉语的表达习惯。

【例29】

① The outside of the converter is made of steel plates.

译文：

转炉的外壳由钢板制成。

② Because of its cost, it is limited in practical use.

译文：

由于成本问题，它的实际应用受到了限制。

③ After sealing the header is cleaned and then the leads are clipped to the desired length.

译文：

封焊后把底座清洗干净，然后把引线剪到所需长度。

c. "是……的"、"为……所"、"加以……"等句型

除了单字以外，还有"是……的"、"为……所"、"加以……"这类汉语句型可以用来表达被动语态。译者在进行翻译时应当进行灵活选择，避免同一句型的反复使用，使得译文生硬死板，缺乏科技语言的流畅简洁之美。

【例30】

① The temperatures and pressures are controlled and adjusted with these switches.

译文：

温度和压力是用这些开关来调节的。

② Plastic articles are not damaged by water.

译文：

塑料制品不会为水所损坏。

3.2 复杂长句的译法

在前文中提到，科技语言着重事实和逻辑推导，因此它对于表达的完整性和逻辑性的要求比较高，在表达时也往往采取一句到底、一气呵成的形式，这就使得在科技英语中复杂长句俯拾皆是。译者往往对此类长句的翻译感到十分头疼。一方面是句子长所带来的理解上的困难，另一方面也与科技英语自身的专业性有关。因此，要做好复杂长句的翻译，译者不仅要对句子的语法结构进行深入分析，将整个复杂长句分解开来，还需要从英文、中文和知识广度和深度这三个方面加强自身能力。此外，这类复杂长句的翻译也并非毫无规律可循，具体来讲，有以下几种翻译方法：

（1）顺序而译

顺序而译指的是译文的表达顺序和原文并没有太大差别，这种译法主要使用于原文叙述层次和汉语习惯表达相近的情况之中。主要表现为按原文句子结构的排列顺序进行翻

译,而无需加以调整或拆分。

【例 31】

We try to stop an overload before it becomes a short circuit, and after a short circuit happens, we try to stop the flow of energy through it as quick as we can.

译文：

我们极力防止超负荷以免出现短路,而在出现短路之后,我们则设法尽快地切断通过电路的电流。

例句译文的表达顺序和原句基本是一致的,一般来说,当长句中的从句成分对主句的叙述顺序并没有太大影响的时候就可以考虑使用顺译法,这也是最省力的一种译法。

(2) 倒序而译

倒序而译,顾名思义,就是使用和原句的表达顺序相反的顺序进行翻译。英语往往习惯先提出结论,然后用从句来指出原因,而汉语则喜欢先说原因或条件后给出结论。这种情况可以考虑使用倒译法,以符合汉语读者的阅读习惯。

【例 32】

For use as a design formula, this equation can be rewritten because the maximum-shear-stress theory was assumed.

译文：

因为假设出了最大剪切应力原理,使用设计公式时,可重写等式。

在例句中,原本放在句尾的原因状语在翻译后被提至了句首。这种先说原因再说结果的表达方式,是倒译法的典型应用。

(3) 拆译法

拆译法的实质是把原句中较长的句子成分,或是不易安排的句子成分拆开来译成短句。一般来说,以下句子成分是可以拆开来单独译出的：非限定性定语从句、状语从句、介词短语、分词短语以及各类并列句和从句等。

【例 33】

The satellite is circulating around the earth with its storage batteries being charged by solar cells.

译文：

卫星正围绕着地球运转,其蓄电池由太阳电池供电。

在上例中,with 引导的介词短语被提出来单独成句,两者之间的联系在原句中以 its 一词体现,翻译成汉语后则变成了代词"其"。事实上,在很多场合,译者都可以考虑拆译法。这种译法既能使翻译后的句子更为简短灵活,符合汉语的表达习惯,也有助于译者分清句子结构层次,避免发生逻辑错误。

4　本章结语

　　翻译标准的问题在翻译界一直是争论不休的翻译理论问题。尽管各种关于翻译标准的观点和主张层出不穷，其核心是要达到对原文的忠实。科技英语有其独特的特点，其翻译一样要遵循词通意达的原则。要使译文与原文在科技内容上完全一致，尤其需要注意词义与语域等几个方面。上文所讲到的一些技巧的灵活使用都是建立在对原文内容和实质的透彻理解和准确把握的基础上的。译者在进行科技英语翻译时，要从整体出发，结合专业内容，通过对词汇和语法的分析，彻底弄清原作的内容和逻辑关系之后，再结合汉语的表达习惯，用汉语恰如其分地表达出来。出于科技英语自身的特殊性，译者在翻译时一定要慎之又慎，用科学的态度去对待每字每句，这样才会做出好的翻译。

第八章 法律翻译

随着我国对外开放程度的进一步加深和经济全球化进程的日益发展,国际合作也越来越频繁。在这一进程中出现了大量的法律文本,如合同、协议、公告、宣言、条约以及各种法律法规。对这些法律文本的翻译已经成为促进国际交流与合作的一个重要组成部分。

法律英语作为专门用途英语(ESP)的分支之一,具有极强的应用性和功能性,它所涉及的领域和人群与一般的文学翻译有着很大的不同,因此,针对法律语言进行的翻译既包括对一般翻译知识的应用,又具有其自身的特殊性。法律语言(legal language 或 statutory language)这一术语起源于西方,原义是指表述法律科学概念以及用于诉讼和非诉讼法律事务时所选用的语言或某一语种的部分用语,后来亦指某些具有特定法律意义的词语并且扩展到语言的其他层面。同其他社会方言一样,法律语言是人们根据社会文化环境和交际目的、交际对象等语用因素,在长期使用中形成的一种具有特殊用途和自身规律的语言功能变体。

法律语言的使用场合,决定其具有独特的结构和固定的行文方式。作为一种工具性语言,法律语言用词上的专业性、句法上的固有模式化特征、译文风格上的权威性和庄严性等特征都对译者提出了严格的要求。要做好法律文体翻译,除了要掌握基本的翻译知识和技能,还需要对法律语言的特点有所了解,在翻译的时候要恪守法律语言翻译的几项基本原则,做到求真务实,准确严谨。

本章将从法律语言的特点、翻译原则、翻译策略等方面对法律文体翻译进行论述。

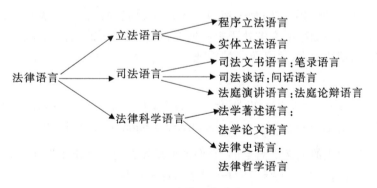

图 5　法律语言分类

1　法律语言的特点

法律本身的特殊性使得法律语言和其他专业语言相比,具有其独特的性质,对这些特征的了解和掌握是做好法律文体翻译的前提条件之一。本节将从法律英语和法律汉语两方面对法律语言的特点进行阐述分析,为读者进行法律翻译做好理论准备。在此之前,有必要对法律语言的分类进行一个了解。

本节将从法律语言的用词、句式、篇章这三个方面来对法律语言的特点进行说明。

1.1 法律语言的用词特点

无论是篇章还是段落,甚至是单个句子,都是由一个个的词所组成的,因此对某种语言的特点进行分析,首先就要分析它的词汇。法律词语的运用在法律语言中起着举足轻重的作用,可以毫不夸张地说,法律词语翻译好了,法律翻译的一大部分也就完成了。

在法律英语语言特点的研究领域,Mellinkoff 曾将法律词汇分为以下几类:

① 含有法律专业意义的普通词(common words with legal meanings)
② 古体词(Old and Middle English words)
③ 外来词(loan words: words of Latin or French origin)
④ 法律专业术语(technical terms)
⑤ 正式用语(formal words)
⑥ 并列词(juxtaposition)

除了② ③之外,其他类型也适用于法律汉语的。此外,孙懿华、周广然将法律语言概括为法律专业术语、法律工作常用术语和民族共同语中的其他基本词和非基本词等三类。在这些研究的基础之上,我们可以将法律词汇的特征主要归纳为以下几点:专业性、保守性、精确性与模糊性、正式性、近义词和对义词的使用、词汇来源的多样性等。

(1) 法律词汇的专业性

作为一种专业性语言,法律词语无疑是具有自己的专业特色的。这一点主要体现在专门法律术语、普通词汇的法律化以及法律行话这三个方面。

a. 专门法律术语

顾名思义,专门法律术语指的是一般只用于法律领域、词义单一、表达准确且不含感情色彩的法律词汇。它在法律语言中处于中心地位,是频繁使用的词汇类型,并且最能体现法律语言精密、明确、用法固定、语义单一的特征。

【例 1】

汉语词:法人,自然人,正当防卫,无行为能力人,第三人,过错责任,过失责任

英语词:defendant, mule, plaintiff, recidivism, bigamy, serial killer, homicide, affray

这些专门法律术语的词义是固定的,它们的使用场合也有一定的限制,因此在翻译的时候要注意词汇的对应,切忌出现指鹿为马、混淆术语等现象。

b. 普通词汇的法律化

普通词汇的法律化指的是有些作为日常用语中的常用词的词汇,在放到法律语境中就具有了特定的意义。这些词语看似熟悉,但其意义可能与日常生活中所使用的意义大不相同,或者是在日常使用中词义所涵盖的范围较广,但在法律语境中则是特指某些范围内的人事物。正是因这些词汇在日常生活中也会广泛使用,所以在实际使用和翻译的时候,很容易出现望文生义和误用的现象,因而成为了法律语言翻译的难点之一。

【例2】
　　同居：① 若干人一起居住；夫妻共同生活；男女双方未办理合法登记手续而共同生活在一起。（普通语境）
　　　　　② 男女双方没有办理结婚登记手续而共同生活。（法律语境）
　　Issue：① The old man died without issue.
　　　　　② Drug testing of employee is a sensitive issue.

c. 法律行话

任何建立在独特知识和技能之上的行业或职业都会发展出一种独特的话语体系，即"行话"。一方面，行话确保了行业内部交流的精确性和经济性，提高了行业内部成员之间的交流效率；另一方面，它又是外显的符号，对于外行人而言，这种符号足以激发他们对于这个行业的好奇、尊重或畏惧的感觉，如此就可能在内外之间划界，有时甚至可以强化某种行业化权力的合法性。

法律行话，即我们所说的"法言法语"，也是一套相当独特的语言。如："供认不讳"、"善意买受"、"要式合同"、"共份共有"，英文中的"aid and comfort, will and malicious act, at issue, due care, sole and unconditional owner"等。法律行话不同于法律术语，它是法律相关行业从事者之间的语言，既可适用于同行之间，也可以适用于法律专业人士和普通民众之间。

（2）法律词汇的保守性

法律词汇的保守性主要体现在词语的沿用上。这种沿用无论是在法律汉语中还是法律英语中都是十分常见的。从法律英语来说，古英语、中古英语、拉丁词汇以及法语词的使用在很长的历史时期内变化甚微，将几百年前的法律文件和今天的法律文件进行对照的话，仍然能发现许多相同的词汇，而在法律汉语中也有为数不少的延承下来的词汇。

【例3】
　　汉语词：自首、诉状、犯罪、原告、大赦等。
　　英语词：bequeath, manslaughter ·················· (old English)
　　here-(hereunder), there-(therein), where-(whereby) ·················· (Middle English)
　　ex post facto, ad hoc ·················· (Latin)
　　jury, alien, voir dire ·················· (French)

为什么法律词汇如此保守呢？Peter Tiersma 在他的著作 Legal Language 中给出了如下几点理由：

① 相较日常用语而言，这些古词汇要更为正式；
② 成文法等既成法规和法官意见作为法律的主要来源，其中旧文本的词汇和句法对当前的法律语言具有深远影响；
③ 特定术语已经有了权威的解释，对这些术语的修改和替换需要极为谨慎；
④ 对于法律从业人员而言，最安全和方便的方法往往是将既有词汇进行反复使用而不是去寻找新的；
⑤ 经历过时间考验的词汇往往看上去更具有权威性；

⑥ 传统词汇的使用也有利于保持行业的神秘性和排外性。

(3) 法律词汇的精确性和模糊性

法律语言给人的一贯印象就是表达上的清晰和准确。一般来说，法律语言的使用都是字斟句酌、精益求精的，这是为了达到表意的精确和无歧义。精确用语的使用在法律语言中是十分常见的。

【例 4】

① 禁止任何人利用任何手段扰乱社会秩序。

② The Congress shall assemble at least once every year, and such a meeting shall be on the first Monday in December unless they by law appoint a different day.

但是，精确用语的使用并不意味着法律语言将模糊用语完全排斥在外。事实上，正是精确用语和模糊用语的共同使用才实现了法律语言中意义的准确表达。

【例 5】

① 在法庭审判过程中，如果诉讼参与人或者旁听人员违反法庭秩序，审判长应当警告制止。对不听制止的，可以强行带出法庭；情节严重的，处以 1000 元以下的罚款或者 15 日以下的拘留。

② After service, the defendant is entitled to a certain period of time within which to file his pleading, or answer, to plaintiff's petition.

在上述两例中，"情节严重的"和 certain 都是模糊词语。使用模糊词汇的主要原因是法律语言的高度概括性：因为它需要涵盖的范围比较广，所以在表意上往往使用词义比较模糊的词语，以这种不确定性来实现所要求的概括性。

(4) 法律词汇的正式性

法律语言是一种严肃、严谨和庄重的语言。这种特定的语言风格使得它在词语的选用上也偏向于使用正式书面体，用词正式、规范、委婉。

【例 6】

普通用词	法律用词
夫妻	配偶
打官司	诉讼
around	approximately
obey	comply with
according to	in accordance with
before	prior to
buy	purchase

此外，情态动词（如：必须、可以、不得、禁止、shall、may、should 等）的使用也能表现法律语言的指令性、承诺性和宣告性。相较普通的谓语动词而言，情态动词的使用也更能体现法律语言的庄严和不可违抗性。

另外,法律词汇中近义词和对义词的使用也能表现法律语言的正式性。法律语言中常有配对词或三联词,即两个或三个意思相同或相近的词构成一个短语,来表达法律上本来只需要一个词就能表达的概念。这种近义词的并列使用,在语效上产生了严肃、准确、严密的效果,体现了法律的严谨性,同时确保了表意的完整和准确。

【例 7】
① 寻衅滋事最是指出于不正当目的的恣意挑衅、无事生非、起哄闹事,进行扰乱破坏,情节恶劣的行为。
② sole and exclusive
③ each and every

此外,实践中还存在强调差别的近义词的并用,其使用目的是为了保证意思表达的完整和准确。

【例 8】
① obligation and liability
② 盗窃

对义词是指意思相互对立的词语,它被广泛地应用于法律语言中,通过词语之间的对立关系来表示相互对立的法律关系。

【例 9】
① 原告和被告
② 自然人和法人
③ felony and misdemeanor
④ employer and employee

(5) 法律词汇词源的多样性

前文在讲述法律语言的专业性和保守性时已经提到,法律语言的词源是多种多样的。事实上,就法律英语而言,它现今的词汇是从凯尔特时期开始,受到盎格鲁—撒克逊人和丹麦人的语言影响,同时深受拉丁语和法语的熏陶,广采各家之长,在进入到新时期之后,又广泛借鉴了世界各国法律语言用语,现在的法律英语词汇体系才得以形成。法律汉语的发展过程也是如此。尤其是在建国后,我国的法律建设广泛借鉴了英、法、美、德、日等国的法律用语,现今法律语言中的许多词汇都是舶来品。

此外,还值得一提的是,随着科技进步和时代的发展,新兴领域内出现的新词汇也渐渐伴随着新的需要进入到法律词汇的领域中来,比较突出的就是生物科学和信息技术这方面。这些领域内新型犯罪的出现也导致了新的词汇的加入,从而进一步扩大了法律词汇的范围,为之带来了新的活力。

1.2 法律语言的句式特点

就像任何专业性语言都有其自身惯用的句式和句法结构一样,法律语言在这方面也有自己的特点。具体体现在以下几个方面:复合句、被动句和否定句的广泛使用,名词化结构的频繁出现,对特定词汇、短语甚至句子的反复强调和重复,代词使用较少。

(1) 复合句、被动句和否定句

在法律语言中简单句屡见不鲜,这点在法律汉语中表现为无主语句的使用,而在英文中则呈现出主谓齐全的场景。然而,与这种简短句式同时出现的还有许多结构复杂的长句。这一方面是为了确保法律语言的准确性和严密性,通过复合句来对内在的逻辑关系进行说明;另一方面则是因为复合句所包含的信息量较大,在描述较复杂的法律概念或规则的时候能够达到叙述详尽、逻辑严密和层次清楚的效果。

【例10】

① 期货交易所因下列情况之一解散:章程规定的营业期限届满,会员大会决定不再延续;会员大会决定解散;中国证监会决定关闭。(并列)

② 凡由该协议引起的,或与该协议有关的,或在执行该协议中发生的一切争议或分歧,应通过友好协商解决。(选择)

③ 在装货港不止一个,并且其中一个或多个港口被冻结时,船长或船舶所有人可选择在通航港装载部分货物,并按(b)项规定为船舶所有人利益在其他港口装满货物,或在承租人不同意在通航港口装满货物时宣布合同无效。(递进)

④ 为昭信守起见,管理会秘书一人及成员两人特此签字立据。(目的)

⑤ If a Party breaches any of the representations or warranties given by it in Articles 18.1 or repeated in 18.2, then in addition to any other remedies available to the other party under this contract or under applicable laws, it shall indemnify and keep indemnified the other Party and the company against any losses, damages, costs, expenses, liabilities and claims that such Party or the Company may suffer as a result of such breach. (假设)

⑥ The court may only deal with a case after the Commission has acknowledge the failure of efforts for a friendly settlement and within the period of three months provided for in Article 32. (条件)

⑦ With respect to those territories to which this Convention is not extended at the time of signature, ratification or accession, each State concerned shall consider the possibility of taking the necessary steps in order to extend the application of this Convention to such territories, subject, where necessary for constitutional reasons, to the consent of the governments of such territories. (转折)

⑧ The progress to the statute book of the necessary legal infrastructure for electronic commerce has in many countries been delayed by a difficult and politically sensitive debate created by the concerns of law enforcement authorities that the widespread use of strong encryption may facilitate crime and terrorism to a degree that will destabilize civilized governments. (解释)

被动句则主要用于规定行为人的权利义务以及相关法律后果。此类表达要求句子的重点应该在于对动作本身进行的描述而不是对行为人的强调,同时要求突出动作的承受者。

被动句的使用能够达到上述的表达效果,使得法律条文显得更为客观公正,整个文本呈现出庄严肃穆的特点。

【例11】
① 双方因本合同引起的一切争议,应首先通过友好协商予以解决。
② If price is not stated in this order, it is agreed that the goods shall be billed at the price last quoted, or billed at the prevailing market price, whichever is lower.

除了复合句和被动句以外,在法律语言中还存在着为数不少的否定句。否定句指的不仅是包含"不"或者"没有"这样明显的否定词的句子,还包括有"禁止"、"mis-"等词语的句子。在立法中此类句子的应用尤其多,立法者利用否定句来告诉人们哪些事情是他们所不能或不应该做的,从而达到命令、威慑及指导的目的。

【例12】
① 委员长、副委员长连续任职不得超过两届。
② Neither Party hereto shall assign this Agreement or any of its rights and interest hereunder without the other Party's prior written consent, which shall not be unreasonably withheld.

(2) 名词化结构

名词化(nominalization)是指从其他某个词类形成名词的过程,或指从一个底层小句得出一个名词短语的派生过程。它是有关句子和名词短语的一种语法过程,主要指广泛使用能表达动作或状态的抽象名词或其名词功用的非限定动词(卢敏,2008)。在法律文本中,尤其是英文法律文本中,名词化结构的使用是十分频繁的,大多数可以使用动词的场合都会用名词化结构来取而代之,这是为了行文的流畅及表意的客观准确。

【例13】
① 国家提倡劳动者参加社会义务劳动,开展劳动竞赛和合理化建议活动。
② Modification of a labor contract shall be implemented through consultation and agreement of the parts involved.

(3) 强调和重复

人们往往对法律文本中冗长的句子大加诟病,事实上,这是与法律文本中所出现的大量的强调和重复紧密相关的。正是文本中对同一概念的反复强调和重复使用,才造成了句子的冗长难懂;但从另一方面来说,这一点也确保了法律文本的准确和严密。因此,尽管有些时候有的词语看上去十分多余,但是出于严谨和准确的考虑,仍然要加在文书里面。举例来说,要表达"Jane Smith 的遗嘱"这个词组的意思,其实只用"Will of Jane Smith"这几个词就可以了,但是实际上按照规范的要求,它应该翻译成"Last Will and Testament of Jane Smith",其中 last 这个词是强调,will 和 testament 这两个词意思重合了,从语义上来讲,"Last Will and Testament of Jane Smith"和"Will of Jane Smith"是一样的,但是前者明显比后者来得庄重、严肃和严密。

这一点可以和前面谈到的词语中近义词的并列使用相互对照,互为参考。

(4) 代词使用

在法律文本中,代词的使用是比较少的,比起"他"、"我们"、"he"、"it"之类的代词,律师和法官等更习惯于直接指出代词所代表的人或事。这一方面能够防止歧义、指代不清等状况的出现,另一方面也体现了法律语言严谨务实的特点。

【例 13】
① 本协议构成双方关于本协议标的的完整协议,对本协议的任何修改,只有通过书面形式并经双方签字后方能生效。
② Where all the parties to a maritime dispute are aliens stateless persons, foreign enterprises or organizations and have agreed in writing to be subject to the jurisdiction of a maritime court of the People's Republic of China, notwithstanding that the place that is actually related to the dispute is not within the territory of the People's Republic of China, the said maritime court of the People's Republic of China shall have jurisdiction of the dispute.

此外,在实际操作中,律师们也常用副词短语来取代单个副词(如用 at slow speed 取代 slowly),或者用较严肃正式的连词或连词短语来取代平常使用的连词(如用 in the event that 取代 if,用 prior to 取代 before,用 subsequent 取代 after 等),这些都是出于对法律语言本身的特点的考虑而采取的手段。

1.3 法律语言的篇章特点

纵观法制定、法实践和法研究的整体语言表述,全篇语体的特征首先是具有仪式性。静态地看,法律语言有一副正襟危坐的姿态。动态地看,每一段法定程序使用的语言都是正规而严肃的。

法律为相应的社会设立行为标准模式,而标准要有示范的作用。同时,法律语篇的固定形式使得语言也趋于标准化,具有整体上的示范性。示范性不仅指达到了一个标准的境界,而且还要通过这个标准实现辐射性的调控目的。

法律语言篇章结构的程式化是法律语言的一大特色。法律文书对篇章结构的格式要求很严格。所谓"没有规矩不成方圆",法律文书的严格的篇章结构就是法律文书的"规矩"。通过法律从业者们长期的积累运用和不断修改,各类法律文本都形成了各自的格式,并通过这些格式体现了文本的功能要求和本质目的,使每一个文本都能称之为一个逻辑严密、意义完全的整体。这种固定的格式对保持法律法规的严密性和统一性和充分体现法律的规范性起到了至关重要的作用。

对法律文书类型的统一性和差异性的研究对翻译工作的顺利开展至关重要。因为这种研究能够揭示原文本的具体要求、功能以及文本的本质,能够帮助译者超越词汇、句法或文体的等值问题,养成一种文本体裁的系统意识。每一篇法律文体都是一个逻辑严密的整体,而不是相关内容的简单罗列,这种严格的特殊程式便是比较固定的语篇格式。这种格式的固定性有利于保持法律法规的严密性和统一性,能使法律的规范性得到最充分的体现。同时该格式性为法律法规的理解提供了一个较为固定的语境,可以减少对法律法规的曲解和误解。

2 法律语言的翻译原则

谈到翻译,不能避免的一个问题就是翻译的原则,或者称翻译的标准。一个界定好的标准体系不仅有助于推进翻译活动的进行,也为评价翻译活动的好坏提供了准绳。按照翻译的原则进行翻译实践、使译文质量符合翻译的标准是翻译工作者不断努力以期达到的目标。切实可行的标准对发挥翻译功效、提高翻译质量也具有重要意义。

对于法律语言的翻译来说,法律翻译是一种法律转换和语言转换同时进行的双重工作,从而与其他文体的翻译有一定的差别。由于法律文件具有高度的严肃性和严密性,法律翻译必须准确无误地译出原文,遣词造句上要仔细斟酌,切忌因一味追求"达"和"雅"而随意解释或删除原意。因此,准确严谨应当是法律翻译的第一标准。根据法律翻译实践和有关专家学者对法律翻译的研究论述,将法律翻译的基本原则归纳如下:准确严谨、清晰严明、前后一致、语体规范。

2.1 准确严谨性原则

法律是由行使立法权的国家机关按照立法程序制定并由国家政权保证执行的行为规则。语言作为法律的表现形式和法律信息的载体,必须体现法律的这种社会职能。法律的严肃性决定了法律语言必须准确和严谨。法律文件要求语言准确,法律文件的翻译亦是如此。准确性是法律文本翻译的根本,忠实于原文内容、力求准确无误是法律翻译区别于其他文体翻译的一个重要的特征。法律文本的翻译稍有差错或语义含糊不清,哪怕是微小的失误,都可能在经济上、政治上造成极大损失,招致严重的后果。比如有的译者在涉外销售合同的翻译中把 earnest money,具有担保性质的"定金",译为"订金",以致在外商违约时"订金"被解释为"预付款",使外商逃脱了双倍返还定金的责任。由此可见,法律译文的准确严谨是法律翻译的根本。请看下列例子:

【例 15】

In judicial opinions, judges will usually refer to themselves as "the Court".

原译:

在判决意见书中,法官常把自己称为"本庭"。

改译:

在判决书中,法官常把自己称为"本庭"。

原译文存在翻译欠准确严谨的问题。例句中的 judicial opinion 被译为"判决意见书"不准确。凡是法院的判决,不论其内容如何,均具有权威性,具有法律效力,不能视之为"意见"。英美法院所作出的 opinion(又称 court opinion 或 legal opinion)就是指判决书,切不可望文生义,将 opinion 轻易地译为"意见书"。

【例 16】

Damages for breach of contract by one party consist of a sum equal to the loss, including loss of profit, suffered by the other party as a consequence of the breach.

原译：

一方违约所导致的损害包括因其违约而使另一方遭受损失的金额，含利润损失。

改译：

一方违约的损害赔偿金包括因其违约而使另一方遭受损失的金额，含利润损失。

原译文存在意思表达不准确的问题，主要是因为没有很好地理解法律术语 damages 一词的准确含义，而是把它当成普通词汇来理解，结果造成译文的意思失真。根据 Merriam-Webster's Dictionary of Law 的解释，damage 的含义为 "loss of harm resulting from injury to person, property, or reputation"；而 damages 的含义为 "the money awarded to a party in a civil suit as preparation for the loss or injury for which another is liable"。因此，damages 为普通词汇时，其意思是"损害，损失"；而原文中的 damages 一词是法律名词，其意思是"损害赔偿金"。法律英语中有不少类似词汇，其单复数表达的含义完全不同，翻译时要格外小心。

【例 17】

The balance shall be settled upon the arrival of the goods at the port of destination.

原译：

货到目的港后付清余款。

改译：

货到目的港后即行付清余款。

原译文中使用"后"，对时间的限制较为模糊，不够明确，这样往往会使不法商人有机可乘，利用该词的模糊性故意拖延付款时间。因此，为保证译文的准确严谨性，应加上"即行"两字，明确限定付款期限，使译文的意思更精确。

【例 18】

所有董事会成员须有合营方委派和撤换。

原译：

All the directors shall be appointed and replaced by the parties to the venture.

改译：

All the directors shall be appointed and removed by the parties to the venture.

原译文是严重"失真"的，因为与中文的"撤换"对应的英文是 removed 或 ousted，而 replaced 只有"替换"的含义，这与"撤换"的含义是不同的。

【例 19】

外国公司在中华人民共和国境内设立的分支结构的登记，应按照国务院的有关规定办理。

原译：

The registration of a branch as subsidiary set up by a foreign company within the territory of the People's Republic of China shall be conducted in accordance with the relevant provisions of the State Council.

改译：

The registration of a branch or a subsidiary set up by a foreign company within the territory of the People's Republic of China shall be conducted in accordance with the provisions of the relevant administration regulations issued by the State Council.

公司的分支机构有两类：一是分公司 branch，二是子公司 subsidiary。本句中的"分支机构"是泛指，应理解为分公司和子公司，译成"a branch or a subsidiary"更准确。"按照国务院的有关规定办理"应解释为"按照国务院有关行政法规的规定办理"。按照我国的法律制度，法律由全国人民代表大会颁布，国务院负责制定行政法规。我们所说的国务院有关规定，实际上是指"国务院制定颁发的有关行政法规的规定"，因此译成"in accordance with the provisions of the relevant administration regulations issued by the State Council"更准确严谨。

准确和严谨对法律翻译来说有着非常重要的意义，是法律翻译的最根本原则。准确和严谨在法律翻译中的重要性无论怎样强调都不会过分，因为法律文件，无论法令、规定、合同、约定等均涉及有利害关系的各方的权利和义务，而法律文件所要阐明的就是权利和义务。为了维护法律的尊严，不至于产生语义上的分歧而发生纠纷，译文中的一词一语都应力求无懈可击。准确严谨正是指导法律文体翻译的重要原则。

2.2 简明清晰性原则

国家的法律语言通常都是这个国家最正式、最规范的语言。原则上讲，用精确的词语表达明晰的法律概念，是法律语言最重要的特点和最基本的要求。法律文本起草人往往喜欢使用那些奇特、深奥的专业词汇或词组，结果使法律文体充斥着过多难懂的行话或专业术语，非法律专业人士甚至是法律界人士想要真正理解这些法律语言也并非易事。法律如果写得不清楚就会变成陷阱。同样，如果法律条文翻译得不清晰，含糊其辞，模棱两可，这些法律条文不但会无法执行，甚至也可能成为陷阱。即使原文没有陷阱，译文也会使之成为理解的陷阱。

法律翻译的清晰简明性原则体现在使用清晰简明的词语和清晰简明的句式两方面。

（1）使用清晰简明的词语

【例 20】

The remainder of the testator's property should be divided equally between all of our nephews and nieces on my wife's side and my niece.

这是美国阿肯色州最高法院的一个真实的案例。立遗嘱人本人只有一位侄女，而太太则有 22 位侄儿、侄女。在这 23 人中是平均分配还是先"一分为二"？可见立遗嘱时行文的清晰度稍有疏忽就会惹出财产纠纷案，同时也给译者的工作带来了困惑。根据阿肯色州最高法院的判决，这份遗嘱的一半最后还是被判给了立遗嘱人的侄女。虽然原文用连词 between 而不是 among 已表明立遗嘱人要"一分为二"的意图，然而，如果把原文写得更清晰一些，恐怕这场官司根本就不会发生。本句可以改为"The remainder of the testator's property should be divided equally between all of our nephews and nieces on my wife's side as one party and my niece as the other"，可译为"立遗嘱人剩余财产应由我妻子方所有的侄儿、侄女和我的侄女双方平分"。

【例 21】

外商投资企业生产的出口产品，除国家另有规定的产品之外，免征关税。

原译：

Export products manufactured by foreign-invested enterprises, except those under other existing regulations by the State, shall be exempted form Customs duty.

改译：

Exports manufactured by foreign-invested enterprises are duty-free, unless otherwise regulated by the State.

"出口产品"完全可以用一个单词 exports 表示，其含义等同于 export products；"免税"直接用 duty-free 清晰明了，"除另有规定外"改为 unless 引导更简洁明快。

【例 22】

If any person over the age of 16 years who has the custody, charge or care of any child or young person under that age willfully assaults, ill-treats, neglects, abandons or exposes such child or young person…such person shall be guilty of an offence.

原译：

任何超过 16 岁而对不足该年岁的儿童或少年负有看管顾、照顾责任的人，如故意殴打、虐待或遗弃该儿童或少年……也属犯罪。

改译：

任何超过 16 岁而对不足该年岁的儿童或少年负有看顾、照看及照顾责任的人，如故意殴打、虐待、疏忽、抛弃或遗弃该儿童或少年……也属犯罪。

本例中 custody，charge，care 三个概念比较难翻译，其含义略有不同：custody 指"法律上的抚养权、看顾"；charge 含有"带领，负责，照看"之意；care 意为"照顾"。所以要逐一译出这几个词的含义，并且用词要尽量清晰简明。

（2）使用清晰简明的句式

法律语言在句法上应表现为结构简单、表意清晰。无论是英语还是汉语要尽量避免使用过于复杂的句式和晦涩难懂的词汇。只要能将意思说明白，绝不用一个多余的词。

【例23】

The law holds that the individual is responsible for his acts. The law also indicates what is good and right, and what may and should be done. It also indicates what is evil and wrong, and should not and may not be done. The law further holds that what is evil and wrong is a crime and may not be done, and if done, render the doer liable to punishment. The law also recognizes the principle that man has free will and that, with certain exceptions, he exercises free will in commission of any crime that he may commit.

原译：

法律认为公民应对自己的行为负责。法律还规定什么是美好和正确的，规范了什么是邪恶和错误的，法律还进一步明确规定哪些邪恶和错误的事是不能做的违法行为，如果某人做了这样的事，那么该行为人就要受到惩罚。同样，法律还承认这样一个原则，每个公民除犯罪自由外都具有自由意志，如果某人在各种违法活动中实施其自由意志那么他就可能触犯法律。

改译：

法律规定人人应对自己的行为承担责任，分清善良和正义，规范了人们的行为准则；法律还认为，作奸枉法即是犯罪，法不可恕，谁要以身试法，必将受到严惩。法律所主张的原则是人人享有自由意志的权利，但利用意志权利而犯罪者除外。

本例原文共有五句，句首简单明了，后面的句子长度逐一增加，但并没有增加得过长，并且所有句子的主干保持着相同的"名词＋动词＋直接宾语"的结构，形成了平行结构，而宾语从句所表达的内容随着附加成分的增多愈加具体，体现出推进式的逻辑思维方式。原译文虽然译出了原文的意思，但是语言松散，措辞随意，句法不严谨，呈口语化趋势，无法体现原文句式安排的匠心和威严性特征。改译运用书面语和法律术语，在句式上又根据汉语特点作了适当的调整，将原来的五句变成了两句，而两句中又分别包含了两个并列句，还适当地运用了汉语的四字结构表意法，既缩短了句子的长度，又浓缩了表达的内容，和原文一样体现了法律文本的庄严性和威严性。

英语是形合语言，造句注重形式接应，要求结构完整，主语具有显著的作用。除省略句外，每个英语句子都必须有主语。法律英语中没有省略句，所以句句都有主语，这也是造成法律英语中被动语态多的原因之一。而汉语是意合语言，造句注重意念连贯，主语的作用不显著，无主句随处可见，所以没有太多的被动语态。但是无主句并不是省略了主语的句子，而是习惯了就这么讲，其主语究竟是什么，往往不容易判断，但是在各种语言环境里它都能表达完整而明确的意思。如果法律英语原句中的被动语态强调的只是行为本身，而无需说明行为主体，则可以译成无主句，达到句式简明的效果。

【例24】

为了维护国家基本经济制度，维护社会主义市场经济秩序，明确物的归属，发挥物的效用，保护权利人的物权，根据宪法，制定本法。

译文：

In accordance with the Constitution Law, the Law is enacted with a view to maintaining the basic economic system of the state, protecting the socialist market economic order, clearly defining the attribution of the res, bringing into play the utilities of the res and safeguarding the real right of the right holder.

本例中，"制定本法"前有五个并列的目的状语，这是典型的中文法律文件的句子结构。我们在译成英语时，应按法律英语的表达习惯作结构调整，把"制定本法"放在句首，译为"This Law is enacted…"。五个并列的目的状语置于后面，将目的状语"为了"译为"with a view to"，后接五个并列的成分。这种行文方式既符合英语的表达习惯，又简洁明快。

法律文字本身就已经给人累赘繁琐的感觉，因此法律文件的翻译人员有责任把原文的意思表达得清晰明了。如果原文运用了复杂、冗长的句式，译者未必需要用同样复杂的句式来翻译原文。简明清晰是法律翻译的一个必要原则。译者可采用灵活的手段，尽量将译文的意思用简洁、精练的词语和句式表达出来，以便准确地传递相关信息。

2.3 前后一致性原则

法律翻译的前后一致性原则是指在法律翻译的过程中始终用同一法律术语表示同一法律概念的原则。在法律翻译的过程中，我们应自始至终地坚持用同一术语表示同一概念。那些看似同义或近义的词语都有可能表示不同的概念。在法律翻译的过程中如果碰到两个或两个以上看似同义或近义的法律术语，我们应该清楚地认识到它们并非同一术语，而应尽最大的努力分辨它们之间存在的语义差别，运用确切的词语将它们准确地表达出来。

【例25】

You can't serve drinks to minors. You should know that a person, such as a minor who have a right under the authority of a guardian.

译文：

你不能卖酒给儿童。你应该知道一个未成年人的权利是受监护人管辖的。

只看汉译句子，读起来也很顺畅，但对照一下原文，同一个 minor 却被翻译成"儿童"和"未成年人"两种表述方式。根据法律英语翻译前后一致原则，最后统一翻译成"未成年人"。

【例26】

保税区的减免税货物、保税货物的监管手续费，应当按照《中华人民共和国海关对进口减税、免税和保税货物征收海关监管手续费的办法》办理。

译文：

The Customs supervising fees on the import goods with duty reductions and exemption and that on the goods in bond shall be collected in accordance with the *Customs Regulations of the People's Republic of China Governing the Collection of Customs Supervising Fees on Import Goods Granted with Duty Reduction or Exemption and the Bonded Goods*.

仔细研究英译文,我们发现其中的 goods in bond 和 Bonded Goods 都是指"保税货物",这就犯了法律翻译前后不一致的错误。

【例 27】
应纳税的款项包括现金支付和汇款支付。

译文:
The taxable payments include payments in cash and disbursement by remittance.

原文的两个"支付",译文却用两个近义词 payment 和 disbursement 表示,这就违反了法律翻译前后一致的原则,要选择其一才可。

法律文体的行文中,无论是在原文的写作还是在翻译中,所用的词汇及句型的重复率是非常高的。越是正式程度较高的法律文章越是如此。法律文献的写作及法律翻译的内在规律不允许创新,也不能一味追求词汇句型的丰富变化。前后一致性是法律翻译必须遵循的准则。

2.4 语体规范性原则

这里我们所说的语体指的是语言和文体。所谓法律翻译语言规范化,就是要求翻译人员不但要具有较高的双语水准,而且要对各项法律,尤其要对普通的法律概念、基本术语的表述规则有相当的了解,否则,他的译文或许符合翻译的基本要求,但在专业人士看来可能仍然是外行话,严重的情况下甚至会造成法律概念的混淆。比如,在规范的立法语言中,不能随意删减用字。我们不能把"应当"简化成"应",把"或者"简化成"或",也不能想当然地认为"第三者"、"第三人"和"第三方"意思相同,可随便换用。当然,这里所说的"规范"还包括法律语言问题格式的规范。无论是立法语言、司法文书语言还是查证语言,其表现形式都有其自身的格式规范,译者要尽量保持原文的格式风貌。

法律翻译除了要求语言功能的对等之外,还应照顾到法律功能的对等。所谓法律功能对等就是说源语和译入语在法律上所起的作用和效果的对等。唯有如此,才能使译入语精确地表达源语的真正涵义。专业术语是法律英语中最重要的元素,准确翻译专业术语自然是达到"法律语言规范化"的必要步骤。专业术语的作用在于以最简洁的单词或词组叙述一项普遍接受的复杂的法律概念、学说或法则,使法律从业者能用较简单的语言相互沟通,因此词的内在意义通常远比其外在形式复杂。译者如单就字面意义直译,或望文生义,将无法正确而完整地传达原文词语的真正涵义。例如,几乎任何一份外贸货物进出口合同都涉及如何处理"不可抗力"的条款。根据词义,该短语可译为"force beyond human power"、"force controlled by God",或"irresistible force",然而只有把它译成"force majeure"才是最地道、专业、规范的译法。再如,英美法中的 motion 一词常被翻译为"动议",虽然 motion 在一般英语中的意思是会议中的动议,但如果作为诉讼程序上的专业术语来说这一翻译就不准确了。*Black's Law Dictionary* 对该词的定义为"a written or oral application requesting a court to make a specified ruling or order",所以"申请"比"动议"更适合。

【例 28】
When an investor, through securities trading at a stock exchange, comes to hold

individually or with any other person 5% of the shares as issued by a listed company by means of agreement or any other arrangement, the investor shall, within three days as of the date when such shareholding becomes a fact, submit a written report to the securities regulatory authority under the State Council and the stock exchange, notify the relevant listed company and announce the fact to the general public. Within the aforesaid prescribed period, the investor may not purchase or sell any more shares of the listed company.

译文：

通过证券交易所的证券交易，投资者持有或者通过协议、其他安排与他人共同持有一个上市公司已发行的股份达到5%时，应当在该事实发生之日起3日内，向国务院证券监督管理机构、证券交易所作出书面报告，通知该上市公司，并予公告；在上述期限内，不得再行买卖该上市公司的股票。

本例中涉及的术语和专有名词不少，securities trading（证券交易），a stock exchange（证券交易所），share（股份），the Securities Regulatory Authorities（证券管理机构），the State Council（国务院）等，这些词的翻译一定要符合规范，体现专业性。除了本例中的术语和专有名词以外，make known to the public 这个动词短语译为"予以公告"也体现出法律专业特征，如果译成"让公众知晓"或"通知大家"，将使译文黯然失色。

法律翻译规范化原则不仅涉及法律词汇的翻译，而且涉及法律文件中常用语法、句型等的翻译。如果译文具有很高的法律专业水准，自然有利于各方更有效地解决法律事务。例如，表示义务性规范的语言，汉语表达为"有……义务"、"必须"，英语表达则为"It is the duty of...", "have the duty to do sth", "shall"等；表示授权性规范的语言，汉语表达为"（享）有……权利"、"有权……"、"可以"，英语表达式为"have the right to...", "enjoy rights of", "be entitled to", "may"等。

【例29】

中华人民共和国公民有依照法律纳税的义务。

译文：

It is the duty of citizens of the People's Republic of China to pay taxes in accordance with the law.

【例30】

Citizens and juristic persons shall enjoy the right of honor.

译文：

公民、法人享有荣誉权。

语体规范化原则主要是指在法律翻译中使用官方认可的规范化语言或书面语，避免使用方言和俚语；译文要尽可能从格式上体现原文，保留原文的格式风貌。虽然在法律文书的起草和翻译中有许多规则，如慎用被动语态、外来语、重复语、缩略语等，但译者首先要注意的是必须采用专业规范的法律用语，尤其是现行法律中已有界定的词语，真正做到"法言法语",译文得体。

总而言之,英汉两种法律语言都有其自身的特点和规律,这些特点和规律决定了法律翻译的基本原则。片面追求"信、达、雅"而忽视法律语言的特点必然会影响到翻译效果,甚至会导致法律纠纷,造成无法挽回的损失。法律翻译四原则是相互依存,缺一不可的。法律翻译的基本原则来自于法律翻译实践,这些基本原则又会很好地指导法律翻译实践。

3 法律英语翻译策略

3.1 法律术语的翻译

法律术语的翻译是法律翻译的一个极为重要的方面。词汇作为语言的基础,对它的翻译的好坏直接决定了翻译质量的高低。一旦翻译错误,就可能造成误解甚至纠纷。在前文中我们讲到法律术语主要包括法律专门术语、表示法律意义的普通词汇、专业行话等。它的保守性、多源性和模糊性等特征使得对法律术语的翻译成为了法律翻译的一个难点。本节将对法律术语翻译的相关策略进行粗略探讨。

(1) 术语翻译必须符合法律语言的特征和词汇表达习惯

在翻译时,除了对译文的准确性有所要求,译文的风格也需要和原文保持一致,在法律翻译中的具体体现就是译文和原文一样,需要具有法律的庄严和权威性。这使得在词汇翻译上,译文的词汇选择和表达形式必须符合原文的词汇特征。比如,"但是"一词在做普通翻译时我们可能将它翻译成 but 或者 however,但是在法律英语中则要译成 provided that,这是因为后者比前者更严肃,也更具有权威性。同理,"并且"应该翻译成 in addition 而不是 also,"怀孕妇女"应该翻译成 expectant mother 而不是 pregnant woman,children 可能根据语境翻译成"未成年人",诸如此类的例子不胜枚举。

【例 31】

工资、薪金所得,是指个人因任职或者受雇而取得的工资、薪金、奖金、年终加薪、劳动分红、津贴、补贴以及与任职或者受雇有关的其他所得。

译文:

The term "income from wages and salaries" means wages, salaries, bonuses, year-end extras, profit shares, subsidies and allowances derived by individuals of their tenure of office or employment as well as any other income related to their tenure of office or employment.

在上例中,如果将黑体部分的 as well as 改成 thereof,就能更加充分地体现法律文体的保守性和权威性,符合法律英文文本常用古旧词汇的语言特征,同时文章也显得更加简洁。

(2) 原文和译文法律内涵的一致性

由于英语国家和中国在法律文化上具有很大差异,很多词汇在字面上似乎相互对应,但是实际上它们的法律内涵是不对等的。如果贸然直译的话,就不可避免地会造成误解,甚至引起纠纷。这就提醒我们,在进行法律翻译的时候,要注意分析译文和原文所表达的法律内涵是否一致。在不一致的情况下，就要舍弃直译的做法，转而选择意译的做法，力求使译文表达的法律概念和原文内涵相同。举例来说，"物证"一词往往被翻译为 material evidence，这种译法看上去是可取的，但事实上，这两者的法律内涵是不同的。"物证"在我国法律里指的是"对查明案件真实情况有证明作用的有关物品或物质痕迹"，而 material evidence 指的是"evidence having some logical connection with the consequential facts or the issues"，即"与案件的事实或结果存在逻辑关系的证据"，其中既包括实物证据又含有言词证据。因此，"物证"的准确翻译应该是 real evidence 或 physical evidence，而非直译出的 material evidence。

此外，对于那些在译入语中不存在对应法律概念的词语，可以采取释义的方法，直接对词语内涵作出解释，这种策略对于那些各自法律文化中独有的法律概念尤其适用。

3.2 模糊表达的翻译

前文在讲到法律词汇的特点的时候，说到了模糊词语在法律语言中的使用。事实上，对于模糊词语和模糊表达的翻译是法律翻译中的一个棘手的问题。一般来说，对模糊词语的处理有以下几种方法：

(1) 对等译法

对等译法从某种程度上来说也就是词对词的直译，即用译入语中表示相同概念的模糊词语来翻译原文中的模糊词语，它们在意思上和形式上都是一致的。

【例 32】

If a sentence of imprisonment is imposed, there are limits on the term of imprisonment—no more than six months or less than three years.

译文：

如对之作出徒刑判决，其刑期也有限制——或不超过六个月或少于三年。

在上例中，no more than 对应的是"不超过"，less than 对应的是"少于"，两者无论在意思上还是在形式上都是对等的，可谓是模糊对模糊。

(2) 变异译法

有时，一种语言中用一个词表达模糊概念，而另一种语言中表达同样的模糊的概念的词语与这种语言的表达在形式上并不对等，这种用非对等形式的模糊词来译模糊词的译法就叫做变异译法。

【例 33】

The state constitution provides that it is lawful for the citizens to carry guns. In recent years hundreds and hundreds of innocent people have died of this and one need not look for a lesson.

译文：

该州宪法规定，公民携带枪支是合法的。正因为如此，最近几年成千上万的无辜的人惨遭身亡，教训历历在目。

本句中将 hundreds and hundreds of 译为"成千上万"就是典型的变异译法。
(3) 具体情况具体分析
由于英汉两种语言存在着巨大的差异,很多情况下想要寻求完全的对等是不可能的,这时候就可以在不影响理解的基础上具体情况具体分析,进行灵活处理。

【例 34】
① It is two and two makes four that the corporal punishment administered by the defendant was minimal, and not excessive.

译文:
很明显,被告所施加的体罚属最低限度而并未过当。

② Conditions of probation may be imposed on the offender is the court considers them necessary for securing his good conduct or for preventing a repetition of the offences and the commission of further offences.

译文:
法院认为为了保证罪犯循规蹈矩或防止其再犯或者重新犯罪,必要时得对罪犯规定假释的条件。

在①句中,"two and two makes four"确切词语,在翻译时则灵活处理成了"很明显"这样一个比较模糊的词句;而②中 good conduct 这一模糊词语在译成中文则选择了"循规蹈矩"这样一个成语,也是具体情况具体分析的一个典型例子。由此可以看出,在翻译词语时需要结合语境进行综合考量,在一种语言中使用的是语义精确的表达并不意味着在另一种语言中就不能用模糊词语来进行表达,反之也是一样的。只有根据语境进行反复斟酌推敲,才能得到准确得体的译文。

3.3 复杂长句的翻译

复杂长句的广泛使用是法律英语的特点之一。这些句子结构复杂,逻辑性强,一直以来都是法律翻译的难点之一。翻译这些复杂长句,我们首先要从语法分析入手理解句子的完整意思,而后在理解的基础上将其意思用通顺的汉语翻译出来。翻译好长句,主要采取"切割法",即在原文句子中的主从句连接处、连词处、关系代词处切断。翻译时,首先要注重理解源语,要耐心读懂长句,分析长句中各意群的关系,然后按意群及其逻辑关系译成汉语分句,这样才能使译文结构层次分明,意思连贯,语言通顺,逻辑性强。

具体来说,复杂长句的翻译主要有以下几种方法:
(1) 顺序而译
所谓顺序而译,指的就是按照原文的顺序组织译文。当英文长句陈述的是一连串按时间顺序或逻辑顺序安排的动作时,它与汉语的表达方式是比较接近的,因此可以考虑按照原文的顺序译出。

【例 35】
If the seller, in accordance with the contract or this convention, hands the goods over

to a carrier and if the goods are not clearly identified to the contract by marking on the goods, by shipping documents or otherwise, the seller must give the buyer notice of the consignment specifying the goods.

译文：

如果卖方按照合同或本公约的规定将货物交付给承运人，但没有在货物上加标记，或以装运单据或其他方式清楚地注明有关合同，卖方必须向买方发出列明货物的发货通知。

在上述例子中，句子的结构比较清晰，两个假设一个结论，和汉语的表达方式是一致的，因此可以按照原文语序进行翻译。

(2) 逆序而译

英语长句是按照英语语法习惯和顺序进行表达，和汉语的语序有可能完全相反，为了符合汉语的表达，就必须逆向翻译。

【例 36】

The Seller shall not be responsible for the delay of shipment or non-delivery of the goods due to Force Majeure, which might occur during the process of manufacturing or in the course of loading or transit.

译文：

凡在制造或装船运输过程中，因不可抗力致使卖方不能或推迟交货时，卖方不负责任。

在上例中，原句的逻辑结构是"结论＋原因状语＋定语从句"，而翻译成汉语之后则变成了"定语＋原因＋结论"。由此可以看出，原文和译文的逻辑结构是截然相反的，这是因为先说原因后说结论更符合汉语的表达习惯。因此，译者在翻译时从汉语读者的角度出发，对句子的表达顺序进行了改动，使之更容易为读者所接受。如果还按照原句的表达顺序进行处理的话，译文就会显得生硬难懂。

(3) 重组而译

如果一个英语句子无法按照原有顺序翻译，则应当考虑按照汉语的表达习惯进行表述。译者可以考虑将原句的结构拆开，根据原义用汉语重新整合，以时间先后、因果、假设等逻辑关系相继译成一句或几句意思连贯、内容完整的句子。

【例 37】

The enduring significance of the Shanghai Communique is symbolized by the fact that two of the participants in the ceremony fifteen years ago—Ambassadors Han Xu and Winston Lord—are now charged with even greater responsibilities for promoting good relations between our two countries.

译文：

15年前，曾参加上海公报签字仪式的两位人士，韩叙大使和温斯顿·洛德大使，现在都肩负着促进我们两国友好关系的更为重要的责任，标志着上海公报具有持久的意义。

在上文中，译文和原文在时间上的安排顺序不一样。原文是从现在提及过去，而译文则刚好相反。译文从汉语的表达习惯进行考虑，对原文句子进行了拆分重组。在进行法律翻译时，译者可以根据实际情况考虑此类重组句子的译法，以求更通顺更自然的表达。

（4）断句而译

英语习惯于用长句表达比较复杂的概念，而汉语则更偏好使用若干短句进行叙述。因此，在翻译时，我们可以考虑将英语的长句拆开翻译，将英语的长的复合句翻译成短小精悍的汉语句子，这就是断句而译的译法。这种译法一方面更符合汉语读者的阅读及思考习惯，另一方面也使得译文的意思更加连贯，同时可以避免由于长句所带来的诸如歧义和逻辑错误等问题。

【例 38】

Either Party may terminate the contract in case of failure on the part of the other Party to fulfill or perform any of its obligations hereunder and in the event that such failure remains unremedied sixty (60) days after the service of a written notices described in Article X below by the non-defaulting Party to the other Party specifying the failure in question and requiring it to be remedied.

译文：

如果一方未完成或未履行其在本合同项下的任何义务，而且未按照下述第 X 条规定在另一方向其送达书面通知，指出其违约行为并要求其予以改正后六十（60）日内，其仍未予以改正，另一方则可以终止本合同。

分析上述例子可以看出，在分析原文的基础上，译文主要采取了逆序法来进行翻译，并将其中的状语进行了分解，用较为短小的汉语句子来进行表述，使得译文的逻辑比较清楚，也更容易理解。

综合来看，复杂长句的翻译并没有所谓的定则，主要还是在原句的基础上进行理解，然后用适当的汉语表达方式来进行表述。英语和汉语在句法结构上的差异主要表现为：英语注重结构形式，严谨而序列性强；汉语注重表达意思，形散而神不散。无论句子有多长多复杂，它都是按照基本的语法规则组成的。因此，只要译者弄清英语原文的句法结构，找出整个句子的中心"骨架"，分清语法层次，然后分析各层意思之间的逻辑关系，最后按照汉语的表达方式表达出来，就能够清楚明确地翻译好复杂长句了。

4　本章结语

法律翻译具有措辞严谨、逻辑性强、用词专业、句子复杂等特点。法律翻译是法律体系框架内的交际活动，做好法律翻译要遵守一系列的原则，而不同类型的翻译对译员又提出不同的要求，译者要具体问题具体分析才行。成功的翻译应该基于对法律语言特点的深入的了解，包括对语言特点、语篇特征等各个层面的充分把握以及对法律文化以及相关商务、专业的熟知，它特别要求译者具有不凡的语言驾驭能力和理解力。所以，做好法律翻译需要译者同时通晓法律知识、法律文化和中外语言，译文表述也需要符合法律专业规范。

II 文学文体翻译

文学文体与应用文等实用文体有很大不同。在文学翻译中,译者既要再现原作的文体风格,又要再现原作的语言艺术。其主要特点有:

(1) 形式和内容的统一

文学是一门艺术,文学作品的内容和形式是不可分割的有机整体。形式的重要性不亚于内容,因为形式本身就是传情达意的方式,在很大程度上,形式的艺术性也决定着内容在多大程度上能被读者接受。尽管对翻译的标准有着不同的理解,但在文学翻译中,形式至关重要,不能仅仅翻译"意思"而忽略形式。

(2) 文学翻译的风格

要使译文尽量与原文等值、实现风格的传递,译文自然要使用文学语言。确切地说,译诗歌要使用诗歌的语言,译小说要使用小说的语言,译散文要使用散文的语言,译戏剧则要使用戏剧的语言。以诗歌为例,即使是叙事诗,也不应当把它译成小说的形式。在翻译的过程中要把握文学语言的基本特征和在不同体裁中呈现出的具体特点,再现原文的语言艺术。

(3) 译者的语言修养

文学翻译也是一种文学再创作。因此,好的译者必须娴熟掌握双语转换技巧,提高对两种文化的洞察能力,对翻译所涉及的两种语言多读、多写、多译、多比较、多思考,全面提高自身的翻译批评素养。

第九章 散文翻译

1 散文文体特征与翻译特点

散文是一种常见的文学体裁,篇幅短小,语言简洁精练,结构层次简练,具有文笔流畅、意境清新、前后呼应、浑然一体的特点。散文语言的一大特色是语言凝练、优美,富于哲理、诗情、画意。杰出散文家的语言又各具不同的语言风格:鲁迅的散文精练深邃,茅盾的散文细腻深刻,郭沫若的散文气势磅礴,巴金的散文朴素优美,朱自清的散文清新隽永,冰心的散文委婉明丽,孙犁的散文质朴无华,刘白羽的散文豪爽奔放,杨朔的散文立意精巧,培根的散文隽永深远。当然,一些散文大家的语言,又常因内容而异。

散文有三个鲜明特点:一是篇幅短小,精练隽永;二是散而不乱,形式灵活;三是长于抒情,语言优美。散文有清新的、凝重的、喜悦的、悲伤的、积极的、平静的、落寞的,数不胜数。但万变不离其宗:文笔一定优美,表述一定流畅,形散而神不散。而且在结尾处,一定要有点睛之笔,突出主题,表现出散文的思想。一篇散文的成功之处在于引起读者共鸣,绵绵悠长,令人回味。好的散文,其记叙、议论都带有强烈的感情,字里行间都渗透着感情。散文的文字,在历史与现实、理性与感性之间,往往穿梭自如,有着不多见的优雅和沉实。

在逗留西方的漫长岁月里,文学巨擘林语堂先生用英文创作或翻译的一系列作品(包括散文作品),曾经轰动欧美文坛,并且影响深远。《吾国与吾民》中的章节既有林先生的创作,也有他翻译的中国经典散文和诗歌,无论从思想上、内容上还是语言上来说,都是一本难得的上品读物。《吾国与吾民》是林语堂第一部在美国引起巨大反响的英文著作,是他在西方文坛的成名作与代表作。林语堂的英文作品有的曾被美国大学选入教材,有的被政府高层倚为了解中国之必读书,被视作阐述东方文化的权威著述。下面的原文选自齐鲁书社《郑板桥全集》,译文摘录自外研社的英文版《吾国与吾民》(林语堂译)。

【例1】

吾弟所买宅,严紧密窠,处家最宜。只是天井太小,见天不大。愚兄心思旷远,不乐居耳。是宅北至鹦鹉桥不过百步,鹦鹉桥至杏花楼不过三十步,其左右颇多隙地。幼时饮酒其旁,见一片荒城,半堤衰柳,断桥流水,破屋丛花,心窃乐之。若得制钱五十千,便可买地一大陂,他日结茅有在矣。吾意欲筑一土墙院子,门内多栽竹树草花。用碎砖铺曲径一条,以达二门。(郑板桥:《郑板桥全集》)

译文:

The house you bought is well-enclosed and indeed suitable for residence, only I feel the courtyard is too small, and when you look at the sky, it is not big enough. With my unfettered nature, I do not like it. Only a hundred steps north from this house, there is the Parrot Bridge, and another thirty steps from the Bridge is the Plum Tower, with vacant spaces all around. When I was drinking in this Tower in my young days, I used to look out and see the willow banks and the little wooden bridge with decrepit huts and wild flowers against a background of old city walls, and was quite fascinated by it. If you could get fifty thousand cash, you could buy a big lot for me to build my cottage there for my later days. My intention is to build an earthen wall around it, and plant lots of bamboos and flowers and trees. I am going to have a garden path of paved pebbles leading from the gate to the house door. (Lin Yutang: *My Country and My People*)

原文语言简练,思想新颖,感情充沛,想象丰富,耐人寻味。译文再现了原文的艺术表现力和感染力,重塑了原文的意境与神韵,并且译出了字里行间的情感,显示了林语堂高超的艺术造诣和非凡的文化和英汉语言修养。由此可见,散文翻译是一门艺术而不是简单的复制。译者与作者必须心心相印,灵犀相通。翻译不仅要译出眼泪,而且译出悲哀;不仅要译出笑声,而且要译出欢乐;不仅要译出浪漫,而且要译出优雅。语言是文化的载体,而翻译是语言的转换过程,也是文化的移植过程。语言的相互转换需遵循语言的规律,文化的移植则需适应读者的需求。文化"传真"要求译语从文化意义的角度,准确地再现原语传达的意义,充分体现散文的风韵也是至关重要的。译者要准确把握散文语言的节奏美,并恰当地予以转换,很好地体现原文的种种文笔技巧,也是文学翻译的最高层次。

2 散文分类与翻译特点

散文具有记叙、议论、抒情三种功能,与此相应,散文可分为叙事散文、抒情散文和写景散文。当然,还可以从其他角度分类。

2.1 叙事散文

叙事散文是以写人记事为主的散文,通讯、特写、传记、回忆录、游记等都属于记叙文的范畴。叙事散文侧重于从叙述人物和事件的发展变化反映事物的本质,强调时间、地点、人物、事件等因素,从一个角度选取题材,表现作者的思想感情。叙事散文以叙事为主,叙事情节不求完整但求集中,叙事中的"情"渗透在字里行间。叙事散文的情节虽然只是片段,但很有条理,渗透其间的是"情",是人间的真情,或是浓烈的亲情友情。充分展开联想是叙事抒情的重要表现手法,为此,唯有翻译出叙事性形与神的结合点,才能更好地体味散文的感情,领悟情感的意境美,散文的"神美"也就无遗地展现在读者面前。

【例 2】

On the semi-dry pebble riverbed to the south of the village, there existed a country fair, antique and resourceful, with sufficient local products for fair-goers. The fair was Granny's Mecca, with thrills and zest, once every five days. The butchers had the buyers' pork cuts bundled up in the center with rice straw, or if, in season, wrapped up in big sunflower leaves. The rice straw and sunflower leaves were quite a sight in my brain, but they go totally out of use nowadays. From time to time, freshly netted river shrimps, alive and kicking, were what Granny favored purchasing so as to better our fare. The almost-transparent shrimps were reddened by sautéing, as the kids' delicacies of the season, tasty and nutritious. (Yue Shouguo: *Fragmental Impressions of Granny*)

译文：

小村南面，有一乡村集市，地处半干涸的河床，鹅卵石遍地。此集市古已有之，应有尽有，为赶集的人提供丰盈的土产。五天一次的集市是奶奶向往的地方，每次前往，她总是心情激动，兴致盎然。屠夫将猪肉切块，用稻草从中间部位为顾客捆好；或者，如果适逢季节，就用大大的向日葵叶把猪肉给包裹起来。稻草和向日葵叶是我记忆中的难忘景象，如今却已事过境迁。偶尔，奶奶喜欢买来活蹦乱跳的网捕河虾，用来为我们改善伙食。爆炒之后，原先几近透明的河虾变得红彤彤的，那是孩子们的季节美味，可口又有营养。（岳守国：《奶奶印象片段》）

既然叙事散文的灵魂是一个"情"字，那么在翻译过程中就要着力传达原文的情。作者在描述奶奶这一人物的时候，对自己童年时代的一草一木充满了留恋和热爱，反映了作者非常怀念那些已经不知何去了的岁月，进而表现对奶奶的怀念。把祖孙情融入景色的描述中，原文的情境美在译文中得以挥洒，尤其是译者密集地使用四字成语或类四字结构，使得译文增色不少。原文的优美和清新在译文中得到另一形式的复现，一幅古朴返真、令人向往的乡间风景图轴徐徐展现在读者的面前。

对于描述性情景，因其可译性较强，可采取直译法；对于较难翻译的可采取意译和注释法等。翻译与文化密切相关，译者如何处理翻译中的文化因素呢？对此，翻译界有两种完全相反的意见，即"异化"与"归化"。前者主张，译文以源语或原文作者为归宿，后者则认为译文以目的语或译文读者为归宿。译者应识别和欣赏语言独特印记，运用适当的翻译策略，进行较为周全的分析和准确的判断。然后就可以确定对原文的取舍和传译的手法，调动目的语中有关文化、语句和修辞等方面的手段，从而在目的语文本里有效地再现源语的效果。

2.2 抒情散文

抒情散文注重表现作者的思想感受，是抒发思想感情的散文。这类散文虽有具体事物的记叙和描绘，但通常没有贯穿全篇的情节，其突出的特点是强烈的抒情性。它或直抒胸臆，或触景生情，洋溢着浓烈的诗情画意，即使描写的是自然风物，也赋予了社会内容和思想感情。优秀的抒情散文感情真挚，语言生动，还常常运用象征和比拟等手法，把思想寓于形象之中，具有强烈的艺术感染力。张扬感情，抒发胸臆，散文中的景致、人物、事件均可以指向感悟。感悟写得清楚明白，如同记叙文的主题一样，明白晓畅，让人觉得可喜，引人思考。散文翻译过程中，原文的情感必须以优美的语言形式表达出来，达到情感与美感的完美结合，进而产生情感震撼的审美效果。

【例 3】

我喜欢看树枝上那淡淡的嫩绿，它是春天的使者，它是一天清晨的开始……我喜欢天空中那淡淡的云,它将天空衬的更高更蓝更宽……我喜欢淡淡的风。春风轻吻脸颊,秋风抚面温柔,夏天的风送来凉爽,冬天的风带来清凉……我喜欢喝淡淡的茶,淡淡之中才品出它余味的清香,淡淡的苦才是它原来的味道……我喜欢追求淡淡的友谊。彼此之间不需要天天在一起,偶尔一句:你好吗?思念就像发芽一样蔓延开来……我喜欢淡淡地思念一个人,静静地将自己包围在沙发之中,任思绪在回忆里飘荡……(佚名:《淡淡的思念,淡淡的爱》)

译文:

I like the subtle fresh green budding from the branches of the tree—the herald of spring, ushering in the dawn...I like the subtle flow of cloud that makes the sky seem even vaster, more azure and immense...I like the subtle wind. In spring, it steals a kiss on my cheek; in autumn, it caresses my face; in summer, it brings in cool sweet smell; in winter, it carries a crisp chilliness...I like the subtle taste of tea that lasts long after a sip. The subtle bitter is what it is meant to be...I like the subtle friendship that does not hold people together. Instead, an occasional greeting spreads our longings far beyond...I like the subtle longing for a friend, when I sink deeply in a couch, mind wandering in memories of the past...(Nameless:*Subtle Longing*,*Subtle Love*)

散文是长于抒情的文体。作者在其中尽可以敞开心扉,诉说忧乐,妙悟自然与生命,解读社会与人生,品味生活与人情,与读者进行心与心的交流、对话和碰撞。感情怎样渗透到散文中呢?我们知道,散文作者的感情贯串于通篇文章中,从构思命题到篇章结构,从语言运用到思想内容,无不表现作者的思想情绪。其中,感染更强烈的是情景合一的艺术境界。当作者用感情来描绘客观对象时,或者说外界景象触动作者的情思时,作品就有了境界。上文看似感情淡淡,但淡淡的情中透射出深沉的思念,不尽的情感。它没有喧闹,没有张扬,有的只是缕缕扯不断的情感弥漫开来。在翻译的时候,译者可采用小词,白描般地刻画人物思想的脉动。优美散文的基本要求是语言准确、通顺,而散文翻译更高层次是从美学视角予以审视。散文翻译是一种美学实践,不仅要传达原文的形式美,而且要传达原文的内容美和风格美,做到原文和译文的形式美、内容美和风格美和谐统一。

2.3 写景散文

写景散文是以描绘景物为主的散文。这类文章大多在描绘景物的同时抒发感情,或借景抒情,或寓情于景,抓住景物的特征,按照空间的变换顺序,运用移步换景的方法,把观察的变化作为全文的脉络。生动的景物描绘,不但可以交代背景,渲染气氛,而且可以烘托人物的思想感情,更好地表现主题。散文翻译应考虑译出语所体现的形式、内容和意境的完美统一,同时也应意识到译入语的语义结构和文化定势。如果原文文笔不凡,情境可人,那么译文就应当和原文一样文字优美,语言如诗。

【例4】

在家乡的日子,在如丝的四月江南,在我的房间里,每到清晨5点多钟,似梦似醒之间,窗外已是天光大亮。迷迷糊糊醒眬之时,却能够在耳聆听一阵阵鸟儿的呢喃,感受到鹁鸪鸣怒,绿杨风急妩媚那样的春天的清晨,扬花似雪,想来也是越禽声里春光晓,苍翠浓荫满院子,自己还在睡梦中,可以听见鸟儿婉转清亮的"啾——啾啾啾"的鸟鸣,鸣声像水滴一样,圆滑、透明,曲折跌宕的歌声。那声音时而低沉,时而高昂,令人沉醉。

(梅:《晨来鸟窥蝉》)

译文:

  Those days in my hometown were just as the soft willows in South River in April. At five o'clock in the morning, I used to be in the dream in the bedroom when it was at daybreak outside the window. In the indistinct or blurred mind, I would listen to a burst of twittering of birds and feel their mood. It was the early spring morning and the green poplar in breeze so charming to send the petals as flakes of snow. The spring scenes could be known by the voice of birds in the thick verdant shade of my yard. In my dream I might hear clearly the chirps of birds, which were like a song to sing like drops of water, tactful and transparent, with twists and turns. High and low at intervals, the voice would make people drunk deeply.

(Mei: *Bird Peeping at the Cicada in the Morn*)

  一切景语皆情语,译文在重现原文景物中,需注重其中蕴含的情感因素。在对其加以辨别和确认之后,译者要选择感情色彩浓厚、风格鲜明的表达方式进行情感的重铸,使译文与原文一样情景交融,震撼人心。成功的散文译作要赢得读者,除形式美之外,还应具有内容美。内容美的统一,要求译文正确地传达原文的内容,避免信息的扭曲和失真。著名美学家朱光潜曾说:"翻译好比画家作画,先抓住客观人物的形状和神态,然后用画笔把它表现在画面上。同样,译者要先掌握一种语言所表达的思想感情、风格,然后运用翻译技巧,在另一种语言中把它表现出来。"

2.4 哲理散文

  哲理是感悟的渗透,思想的火花,理念的凝聚,睿智的结晶。它纵贯古今,横亘中外,包容大千世界,穿透人生社会,寄寓于人生百态,闪现思维领域的万千景观。哲理散文以种种形象揭示生命的真理,给人一种透过现象深入本质、揭示事物底蕴的审美效果。哲理散文重在摒弃浅薄,达到一种思想情性相通、生命交感、灵气往来的境界。哲理散文拥有丰富的内涵,把自然、社会、人生从多个角度进行了融合,在本质上表达了对情感的一种依赖。哲理散文不是干巴巴的议论,而是寓含了情感和思想,是蘸满了审美情感汁液的思想。从字里行间去解读心智的深邃,理解生命的本义,这是哲理散文艺术美之所在。

  哲理散文的巅峰之作当属培根的散文了,弗兰西斯·培根(Francis Bacon, 1561—1626)是英国哲学家、作家和科学家。只要细品慢咽我们就会发现:唯物的世界观与辩证的思想在培根的哲理散文里闪现。培根哲理散文短小精悍,重点突出;人生体验,真知灼见;论理深刻,逻辑严密;语言优美,诗意盎然;活泼风趣,充满智慧;排比反衬,妙语连珠。文章引经据典,旁征博引:圣经故事、古代神话、历史名人、帝王将相、名言警句、诗句格言、比喻联想,俯拾即是,美不胜收。历史已经证明,培根的哲理散文集真、善、美于一体,是哲学、文学、艺术三结合的传世经典。两百年后，著名英国诗人雪莱这样赞美培根的散文："他的语言有优美而庄严的韵律，以美感动人心弦；他的论述有超凡的哲理，以智慧启迪理智"。不可讳言，培根的哲理散文对中国读者难免感到陌生，甚至感到有些过于雕琢，不太自然。翻译中也常常遇到困难，最大困难可能来自对原文的理解，尤其是结构复杂、逗号又多的长句，以及引用拉丁文而又不容易查到的内容。

【例 5】

　　Virtue is like a rich stone, best plain set; and surely virtue is best, in a body that is comely, though not of delicate features; and that hath rather dignity of presence, than beauty of aspect. Neither is it almost seen, that very beautiful persons are otherwise of great virtue; as if nature were rather busy, not to err, than in labor to produce excellency. And therefore they prove accomplished, but not of great spirit; and study rather behavior, than virtue. But this holds not always; for Augustus Caesar, Titus Vespasianus, Philip le Belle of France, Edward the Fourth of England, Alcibiades of Athens, Ismael the Sophy of Persia, were all high and great spirits; and yet the most beautiful men of their times. In beauty, that of favor, is more than that of color; and that of decent and gracious motion, more than that of favor. That is the best part of beauty, which a picture cannot express; no, nor the first sight of the life. There is no excellent beauty, that hath not some strangeness in the proportion. A man cannot tell whether Apelles, or Albert Durer, were the more trifler; whereof the one, would make a personage by geometrical proportions; the other, by taking the best parts out of divers faces, to make one excellent. Such personages, I think, would please nobody, but the painter that made them. Not but I think a painter may make a better face than ever was; but he must do it by a kind of felicity as a musician that maketh an excellent air in music, and not by rule. A man shall see faces, that if you examine them part by part, you shall find never a good; and yet altogether do well. If it be true that the principal part of beauty is in decent motion, certainly it is no marvel, though persons in years seem many times more amiable; pulchrorum autumnus pulcher; for no youth can be comely but by pardon, and considering the youth, as to make up the comeliness. Beauty is as summer fruits, which are easy to corrupt, and cannot last; and for the most part it makes a dissolute youth, and an age a little out of countenance; but yet certainly again, if it light well, it maketh virtue shine, and vices blush.

(Francis Bacon：Of Beauty)

译文 1：

　　德行犹如宝石，朴素最美；其于人也：则有德者但须形体悦目，不必面貌俊秀，与其貌美，不若气度恢宏。人不尽知：绝色无大德也；一如自然劳碌终日，但求无过，而无力制成上品。因此美男子有才而无壮志，重行而不重德。但亦不尽然。罗马大帝奥古斯提与泰特思，法王菲律浦，英王爱德华四世，古雅典之亚西拜提斯，波斯之伊斯迈帝，皆有宏图壮志而又为当时最美之人也。美不在颜色艳丽而在面目端正,又不尽在面目端正而在举止文雅合度。美之极致,非图画所能表,乍见所能识。举凡最美之人,其部位比例,必有异于常人之处。阿贝尔与杜勒皆画家也,其画人像也,一则按照几何学之比例,一则集众脸形之长于一身,二者谁更不智,实难断言,窃以为此等画像除画家本人外,恐无人喜爱也。余不否认画像之美可以超绝尘寰,但此美必为神笔,而非可依规矩得之者,乐师之谱成名曲亦莫不皆然。人面如逐部细察,往往一无是处,观其整体则光彩夺目。美之要素既在于举止,则年长美过年少亦无足怪。古人云:"美者秋日亦美。"年少而著美名,率由宽假,盖鉴其年事之少,而补其形体之不足也。美者犹如夏日蔬果,易腐难存;要之,年少而美者常无行,年长而美者不免面有惭色。虽然,但须托体得人,则德行因美而益彰,恶行见美而愈愧。

（王佐良译：《谈美》）

王译一共 513 字,言简意赅,惜墨如金。王佐良提出的翻译标准是"可靠"、"可读"。"可靠"就是忠实,"可读"就是流利。这一提法比较中肯和客观。英语原文古朴典雅、联想丰富,译文着力表现原文的境界。王先生说,翻译时要辩证地看——尽可能地顺译,必要时直译;任何好的译文总是顺译与直译的结合。一切照原作,雅俗如之,深浅如之,口气如之,文体如之。王先生不但是这样说的也是这样做的,他翻译的《培根论说文集》已成经典,随意一个句子都翻译得既准确贴切,又符合汉语习惯,并且在没有改变原作意思、文体和口气的情况下,用优美的汉语表达出来。

王佐良的翻译观,即文化意识、"神似"、读者至上,对读者产生了深远的影响。王先生认为译者应当胸怀两种文化,追求译文与原文的整体一致,并以读者为先。培根是四百年前英国的哲人名士,学富五车,文震朝野,其散论札记当时亦属上乘之作。在英国文学史上,培根的文论以其思想精深、艺术精湛和文学精绝而风骚独领。翻译这样的经典文论时,究竟应该采取何种风格呢?用下里巴人式的通俗时语,还是用阳春白雪般的古典雅言呢?从时下流行的几个译本来看,有精雕细琢的典雅之译,亦有平铺直白的通俗之译,更有文白夹杂的并举之作。在这些译作中,王佐良教授的古典式翻译,无疑是影响最大的、传播最广的,且最为译界和读者称道和推崇的成功力作。其译作中的一些经典句子,在学界几乎耳熟能详,为人津津乐道。

王佐良先生以保持原作的风格为要,遣词造句通俗洗练,朴素无华,最大限度地再现原文意义,成功地转述了原文的信息功能、美感功能和表情功能,传达了原文完整的意义。译文流畅地道,通俗简洁,堪称意义相符、功能相似的范例之作。王先生认为,译者需传达整个概念或整篇情感,要在音韵和节奏等因素上忠实原作的风格和意境,传达原文的新鲜和气势。王先生在理解原文的深度上,在辞章的运筹上,以及在传情达意的准确度上无不显示出过人的功夫。他的译文措辞得体,洗练精确,行文流畅,脉络清晰,文体适当、严谨一致。译文与原文在内容和风格上实现了高度的契合,堪称形神兼备的佳作。

译文 2：

善犹如宝石,以镶嵌自然为美;而善附于美者无疑最美,不过这美者倒不必相貌俊秀,只须气度端庄,仪态宜人。世人难见绝美者兼而至善,仿佛造物主宁愿专心于不出差错,也不肯努力创造出美善兼备之上品。故世间美男子多有身躯之完美而无精神之高贵,多注重其行而不注重其德。但此论并非放之四海而皆准,因古罗马皇帝奥古斯都和韦斯帕芗、法兰西国王腓力四世、英格兰国王爱德华四世、古雅典将军亚西比德以及伊朗国王伊思迈尔一世皆为志存高远者,但也都是当时的冠王美男。至于美女,天生容貌胜过粉黛胭脂,而优雅举止又胜过天生容貌。优雅之态乃美之极致,非丹青妙笔所能绘之,亦非乍眼一看所能识之。绝色者之形体比例定有异处。世人难断阿佩利斯和丢勒谁更可笑,后者画人像总是按几何比例,前者则将诸多面孔的最美之处汇于一颜。除画家本人之外,此等画像谁也不会喜欢。虽说笔者认为画家可以画出比真颜更美的容貌,但他必须得靠神来之笔,而非凭借什么规则尺度,这就像音乐家谱写妙曲得靠灵感一般。世人可见这样的面庞,若将其五官分而视之则一无是处,但合在一起却堪称花容玉颜。倘美之要素果真在于仪态之优雅,那长者比少者更美就不足为奇,须知美人之秋亦美。假如不把春青视为优雅得体之补足,年少者多半都难称俊秀。美貌如夏日鲜果易腐难存,而且它每每使年少者放荡,并给年长者几分难堪;但笔者开篇所言仍然不谬,若美貌依附于善者,便会使善举光彩夺目,使恶行无地自容。

(曹明伦译:《论美》)

曹译一共597字,语言流畅,文笔精美。译文再现原文美的含义:不只是外表的美,重要的是内在的美。培根的思想成熟,言论深邃,富含哲理,这一切都在他的随笔和散文中淋漓尽致地表现出来。在深刻理解培根哲学思想的基础上,曹先生得以充分发挥他的文学才华,使译文明白流畅,同时不违作者原意。曹译风格通俗而不失典雅,许多译文的用词造句是现代白话,但同时隐涵文言文的结构与手法。译文很好地把握了原文的思想和语言特色,语言贴近原文的风格,因此具有相当的可读性。译文渗透着浓浓的文学之气,而且读译文的感觉犹如读原文,没有斧凿的痕迹,充分释放了原文的散文境界。

一个真正的翻译家一生要接触许多作品。我们知道,即使同一个作家,甚至同一件作品,其风格也不是单一的。因此翻译家可以有自己的风格,但决不能以自己的风格去取代原作者的风格。从《论美》的翻译中,曹先生显示了领会并再现不同风格的才能。在句式吻合、语言简洁、译笔准确生动等方面都有建树。曹译除了在思想内容和语言文字上兼顾形神之外,还疏通了不少疑难之处,为读者的阅读开辟了一条坦途。可以想见,在对原文融会贯通之后,曹先生奉献出了得心应手之作。

曹明伦说,译者每每有这样一种考虑:"若令原作者用中文表达其原意,他(她)当做何语?"这是对形似与神似关系的最精彩阐释,是他十几年如一日伏案译出五百万字后吐出的一句至理名言。在吃透了原作之后,一位优秀翻译家便化身为原作者,贯通了二者之间的隔膜,淋漓尽致地再现出原作的风采。正由于译者处处从原作者的思维方式出发,曹译《论美》才会处处珠玑,朗朗上口。培根随笔文体简洁,几乎是格言式的措辞协调优美。对比原文与译文,我们有理由认为,曹译形神兼备,传达了原作的风采神韵,使读者充分领略到培根是一位文笔简练、思路缜密的散文家。

曹明伦教授近年来专门从事翻译学与比较文化研究,绘制了翻译理论定位图,辨析了翻译研究在中国的名与实,指出了翻译理论与实践结合的方式和途径,倡导"最接近、最自然"二元简单翻译标准,赢得了学界好评。

高明的作者善于抓住哲理闪光的瞬间,形诸笔墨,写就内涵丰厚、耐人寻味的美文。时常涵咏这类美文,自然能在潜移默化中受到启迪和熏陶,得到洗礼和升华,这种内化作用无疑是巨大的。哲理散文以种种形象浸润生命的真理,揭露万物之间的永恒相似,其深邃性和心灵透辟的整合,揭示事物的底蕴,具有震撼性的审美效果。哲理散文体现的思维方式,可以使读者体悟文中蕴藏的深厚的文化底蕴和文化积淀。

【例 6】

Youth is not a time of life, it is a state of mind, it is not a matter of rosy cheeks, red lips and supple knees, it is a matter of the will, a quality of the imagination, a vigor of the emotions, it is the freshness of the deep spring of life.

Youth means a temperamental predominance of courage over timidity, of the appetite for adventure over the love of ease. This often exists in a man of 60 more than a boy of 20. Nobody grows merely by a number of years; we grow old by deserting our ideas.

Years may wrinkle the skin, but to give up enthusiasm wrinkles the soul. Worry, fear, self-distrust bows the heart and turns the spirit back to dust.

Whether 60 or 16, there is in every human being's heart the lure of wonders, the unfailing childlike appetite for what's next and the joy of the game of living. In the center of your heart and my heart, there is a wireless station: so long as it receives messages of beauty, hope, cheer, courage and power from men and from the infinite, so long as you are young.

When the aerials are down, and your spirit is covered with snows of cynicism and the ice of pessimism, then you've grown old, even at 20, but as long as your aerials are up to catch waves of optimism, there's hope you may die young at 80.

(Samuel Erman: *Youth*)

译文:

青春不是年华,而是心境;青春不是桃面、丹唇、柔膝,而是深沉的意志,恢宏的想象,炙热的恋情;青春是生命的深泉在涌流。

青春气贯长虹,勇锐盖过怯弱,进取压倒苟安。如此锐气,二十后生而有之,六旬男子则更多见。年岁有加,并非垂老,理想丢弃,方堕暮年。

岁月悠悠,衰微只及肌肤;热忱抛却,颓废必致灵魂。忧烦,惶恐,丧失自信,定使心灵扭曲,意气如灰。

无论年届花甲,拟或二八芳龄,心中皆有生命之欢乐,奇迹之诱惑,孩童般天真久盛不衰。人人心中皆有一台天线,只要你从天上人间接受美好、希望、欢乐、勇气和力量的信号,你就青春永驻,风华常存。

一旦天线倒塌时,锐气便被冰雪覆盖,玩世不恭、自暴自弃油然而生,即使年方二十,实已八十。

(厄曼:《青春》)

Samuel Erman 这篇哲理散文,半个世纪来在其读者群中得到广泛欣赏,美国麦克阿瑟将军生前反复品味,深得其妙,将其视为座右铭。译文灵活运用翻译技巧对原文进行了归化处理,再现了原文行云流水般的特点。不仅在句子层面上自然流畅、准确细致、雅俗得当,而且还有语篇神韵的再创造,既完美地保持原文的信息又译出风格。不漏翻译痕迹,没有斧凿迹象,阅读译文,感觉好像是在阅读原文,这种理想译境,令人称颂,堪为典范。

翻译文学作品,光传意是远远不够的,还要注意保持原作的感情、韵味、意境和风格。翻译散文,译者必须对原作者的生活经历、创作背景、艺术观点有深刻的了解,同时还要深谙英汉两种语言的不同表达方式。也就是说,译者必须具备较高的文化素养。除此之外,不同的语言文化背景及各异的表达习惯,往往使读者误解或不理解原作的意义,因此译者要注意体现原作的文风,否则译文就没有什么可读性,像白开水一样,索然无味。

3 散文翻译的功能对等

功能对等理论由美国翻译理论家尤金·A·奈达(Eugene A. Nida)提出,所谓"功能对等",就是说翻译时不求文字表面的死板对应,而要在两种语言间达成功能上的对等。根据奈达的翻译理论,文化差异的处理与从语义到文体将源语再现于目的语是紧密相连的。只有当译文从语言形式到文化内涵都再现了源语的风格和精神时,译作才是优秀的作品。奈达指出:"翻译是用最恰当、自然和对等的语言从语义到文体再现源语的信息"。奈达有关翻译的定义指明,翻译不仅是词汇意义上的对等还包括语义、风格和文体的对等,翻译传达的信息既有表层词汇信息也有深层文化信息。

3.1 散文翻译的内容传达

一篇流利酣畅的散文,应该首先忠实于原文。但是,如果只求忠实,译得佶屈聱牙,含混晦涩,那读来就索然无味,兴趣全无。严复(1854—1921)在翻译《天演论》的例言中说:"译事三难:信、达、雅"。这三字标准高度概括了翻译的三种境界,成为一百年来公认的翻译标准。钱歌川这样引申严复的三字标准:"所谓'信',就是对原文忠实,'达'就是译文要明白晓畅,'雅'是译文的文字要优美流利。"他还引述严复的话说:"求达也就是求信,因为信而不达,译尤不译,忠于原文,而不能使读者理解,自然失去了译介的意义"。下面是现代作家许地山(1893—1941)著名散文《落花生》的汉语原文最精彩的后半部分及两种英译,是张培基先生和Poplar先生的译文,我们从内容的传达角度进行对比分析。

【例7】

爹爹说:"花生底用处固然很多;但有一样是很可贵的。这小小的豆不像那好看的苹果、桃子、石榴,把它们底果实悬在枝上,鲜红嫩绿的颜色,令人一望而发生美慕的心。它只把果子埋在地底,等到成熟,才容人把它挖出来。你们偶然看见一棵花生瑟缩地长在地上,不能立刻辨出它有没有果实,非得等到你接触它才能知道。"

张译:

"It's true that peanuts have many uses," said Father, "but they're most beloved in one respect. Unlike nice-looking apples, peaches and pomegranates, which hang their fruit on branches and win people's instant admiration with their brilliant colors, tiny little peanuts bury themselves underground and remain unearthed until they're ripe. When you come upon a peanut plant lying curled up on the ground, you can never immediately tell whether or not it bears any nuts until you touch them."

Poplar 译：

Dad said, 'No doubt, the groundnut has many uses. Yet, it has one valuable quality. This small nut is not like those good-looking apples, peaches and pomegranates, which hang their colorful fruits on the branches and invite admiration. It buries its fruit under the ground, and lets itself be dug out only when it is ripe. If you happen to see a groundnut plant crouching there, you cannot decide at only whether it has fruit or not. You can only know this by getting into touch with it.'

由原文与译文比较可看出：(1)张译"可贵的"为"beloved"欠当。(2) Poplar 将"令人一望而发生羡慕的心"译为 invite admiration (招摇)，虽意义有些出入，但因其简洁，仍愿保留。(3)"等到成熟，才容人把它挖出来"张先生的译文要好得多。张译简洁利索，仅仅 5 个英语单词就把话说清楚了，而 Poplar 却用了 10 个单词，显得有些拖沓。

【例 8】

我们都说："是的。"母亲也点点头。爹爹接下去说："所以你们要像花生，因为它是有用的，不是伟大、好看的东西。"我说："那么，人要做有用的人，不要做伟大、体面的人了。"爹爹说："这是我对于你们的希望。"

张译：

"That's true," we said in unison. Mother also nodded. "So you must take after peanuts," Father continued, "because they're useful though not great and nice-looking."

"Then you mean one should be useful rather than great and nice-looking," I said.

"That's what I expect of you," Father concluded.

Poplar 译：

We all said yes. Mother also nodded her head. Dad continued 'So, you should learn from the groundnut and be useful people instead of those grand or beautiful ones.' I followed, 'Then a person should be helpful and not just seemingly grand or decent?' Dad replied, 'That's my expectation on you.'

由原文与译文比较可看出：(1)张译"in unison"意指 in complete agreement，在程度上有些过了。(2)张译"take after"意指 resemble somebody(相似于某人)，而原文"要像花生"，意指向花生学习，故张译不当。Poplar 译为 learn from，颇为妥当。(3)翻译"伟大、体面的人"关键在于如何理解这几个字。考虑到文章写作背景，应指当时的军阀政客，无疑这两个词在这里带有贬义。因此直译为 great, decent 显然不可，需加 seemingly。Poplar 的译文中的 seemingly 处理得很好。就此而言，张译则有改进的余地。big 与 grand 是与这里的"伟大"比较接近的词；"beautiful people"指"rich fashionable people"，略带贬义，而这正是原文文化背景应该折射出的意义。经过对比分析，本段中 Poplar 的译文在把握汉语原文由时代背景所体现的微妙意义上略胜一筹，可以说细微之处见功夫。

【例9】
　　我们谈到夜阑才散,所有花生食品虽然没有了,然而父亲底话现在还印在我心版上。

张译:
　　We kept chatting until the party broke up late at night. Today, though nothing is left of the goodies made of peanuts, Father's words remain engraved in my mind.

Poplar译:
　　We talked over the table till near midnight. Though none of those groundnut dishes remains, Father's words are still imprinted on my mind.

　　由原文与译文比较可看出,张译的 broke up 似乎有些大词小用。尽管 break up 与 party 搭配,但 break up 指 disperse, go in different directions。文中的语境只是一家人,谈不上"四散离去"。而 Poplar 的译文把"夜阑才散"中的"才散"隐含在句子结构中,不再使用动词,可谓棋高一着。能不运用动词却能表达动词的意义,这可是汉译英的一步妙棋。

　　由此可见,翻译的根本任务是求忠实地传达原文的意义,力求译文与原文的对等,但事实上很难实现话语之间的绝对对等。也就是说,只能寻求译文最大限度地切近原文,使译文行文自然,不带翻译腔。奈达指出:所谓最切近的自然对等,是指意义和文体而言,而意义是第一位的,风格是第二位的。最切近的自然对等,是指意义和文体而言,功能对等一说更具说服力也更科学。语言的功能是指语言在使用中所能发挥的言语作用,不同语言的表达形式必然不同。要么是语音、语法不同,要么是表达习惯不同,但是它们的功能却是相近或相似,功能对等又比意义对等更为准确。

3.2 散文翻译的风格再现

　　风格是散文艺术生命力的重要体现,译文能否再现原文的风格是散文翻译成败的关键。散文的风格体现在韵律、意境和情感中,译者应深刻理解原文的风格特点,把握原文中独特的风格印记,以合乎译入语的结构和句法,尽可能将原文的风格再现出来。散文的风格是以恰当的语言手段,完美地体现作品主题思想的产物。译者要想把握住原作的风格,必须面对词句的微观分析和篇章结构的宏观把握。可以说,散文的风格体现在抑扬顿挫的韵律之中,体现在情景交融的意境之中,也体现在触人心弦的情感之中。而这一切,都只能通过遣词造句和句法结构的巧妙组合体现出来。

　　现以《瓦尔登湖》的翻译为例简述风格翻译。梭罗生态散文《瓦尔登湖》(*Walden*)的汉语译本之多令人眼花缭乱,徐迟译本成为林林总总的十几种译本之一。在徐迟长达60多年的文学生涯中,文学翻译是贯穿始终的。在他为数众多的译作中,《瓦尔登湖》是他最珍爱,也最有代表性的一部,也是国内第一个汉语译本。《瓦尔登湖》所投射出的人文理念,已成为人类向往自然、融入自然、渴望与自然和谐相处的象征。这是一本宁静、恬淡、充满智慧的书。它分析生活,批判世俗,句句惊人,字字闪光,见解独特,耐人寻味。许多篇页皆为形象描绘,优美细致,像湖水般纯洁透明,像山林般茂密翠绿;它说理透彻,十分精辟,给人启迪,是一本清新、健康、引人向上的书。对于天空、大地、花草、动物、森林、湖景,书中都有细致入微的、极其动人的描写。这里有大自然澄净的空气,而无失敬于大自然带来的环境污染。捧读书卷,静心回味,读者只感觉到心灵的纯净,精神的升华。

【例 10】

 I have a great deal of company in my house; especially in the morning, when nobody calls. Let me suggest a few comparisons, that some one may convey an idea of my situation. I am no more lonely than the loon in the pond that laughs so loud, or than Walden Pond itself. What company has that lonely lake, I pray? And yet it has not the blue devils, but the blue angels in it, in the azure tint of its waters. The sun is alone, except in thick weather, when there sometimes appear to be two, but one is a mock sun. God is alone—but the devil, he is far from being alone; he sees a great deal of company; he is legion. I am no more lonely than a single mullein or dandelion in a pasture, or a bean leaf, or sorrel, or a horse-fly, or a bumblebee. I am no more lonely than the Mill Brook, or a weathercock, or the north star, or the south wind, or an April shower, or a January thaw, or the first spider in a new house.

(Henry David Thoreau: Walden)

译文 1:

 我在我的房屋中有许多伴侣;特别在早上还没有人来访问我的时候。让我来举几个比喻,或能传达出我的某些状况。我并不比湖中高声大笑的潜水鸟更孤独,我并不比瓦尔登湖更寂寞。我倒要问问这孤独的湖有谁做伴?然而在它的蔚蓝的水波上,却有着不是蓝色的魔鬼,而是蓝色的天使呢。太阳是寂寞的,除非乌云满天,有时候就好像有两个太阳,但那一个是假的。上帝是孤独的,——可是魔鬼就绝不孤独;他看到许多伙伴;他是要结成帮的。我并不比一朵毛蕊花或牧场上的一朵蒲公英寂寞,我不比一张豆叶,一枝酢浆草,或一只马蝇,或一只大黄蜂更孤独。我不比密尔溪,或一只风信鸡,或北极星,或南风更寂寞,我不比四月的雨或正月的溶雪,或新屋中的第一只蜘蛛更孤独。

(徐迟译:《瓦尔登湖》)

译文 2:

 我在自己的房屋内有许多同伴,尤其是在没人造访的清晨。让我打个比方,或许能描绘出我的一些状况。我并不比高声欢叫的潜水鸟更孤单,我也不比瓦尔登湖更寂寞。我真想问问这寂寥的湖有谁为伴。在这蓝色的湖面上,没有蓝色的妖魔,却有蓝色的天使呢。太阳本是孤寂的,除非乌云密布,有时天空会出现两个太阳,而其中一个必定是虚幻的。上帝也是寂寞的——但是妖魔却不寂寞,他有许多同伴,总会拉帮结派。我不会比一朵毛蕊花或原野上的蒲公英寂寞,也不比一片豆叶、一棵酢浆草、一只马蝇、一只黄蜂更寂寞;同样,我既不会比密尔溪、一只封信标、一颗北极星、一阵南风更孤独,我也不比四月里的雨、正月里的溶雪或新房子里的第一只蜘蛛更寂寞。

(戴欢译:《瓦尔登湖》)

 徐迟的译本纵然瑕疵难免,但有一点是鲜明的:译文紧紧把握原文的那份天然、简洁、朴实的写作风格。做到了文如其人、人如其文、天人合一、人文合一,把原作的神韵再现了出来。风格是一个作家的创作标志,要将其作品翻译成另一种文字,风格总是需要考虑的要素之一。可是,由于东西方文字及文化的巨大差异,要将源语作品的风格"原汁原味"地在译入语中传达出来谈何容易!但是,文学翻译又必须再现原作风格,风格是不可回避的但却是可知的,而且在一定程度上可以再现,这在译界已成共识。梭罗的原作创造出一幅幅生态美、心境美的画卷,译文综合词、句、篇各方面的要素,将原作的风格特征从几个方面予以再现。译作中小词的频繁运用、修辞格的移植都成全了原作本应散发的魅力。

通过上面两段译文的对比,戴译与徐译同样再现了原文的那份天然、简洁和清新,小句、短句成为译文结构的主体。原文的风格被复制,意境得到忠实、传神的转述。仔细品读译文,我们仍能感觉到一些细微的差别。I am no more lonely than the loon in the pond that laughs so loud 徐译为"我并不比湖中高声大笑的潜水鸟更孤独";戴译"我并不比高声欢叫的潜水鸟更孤单",前者拘泥于原文的字面的直译,没有顾及读者的说话习惯。后者则付诸意译,更耐品读。就 pasture 一词,徐译为"牧场",戴译为"原野",显然前者更确切。就 a single mullein or dandelion in a pasture, or a bean leaf, or sorrel, or a horse-fly, or a bumblebee 一句,徐译为"一朵毛蕊花或牧场上的一朵蒲公英寂寞,一张豆叶,一枝酢浆草,或一只马蝇,或一只大黄蜂";戴译为"一朵毛蕊花或原野上的蒲公英寂寞,一片豆叶、一棵酢浆草、一只马蝇、一只黄蜂"。就量词的运用来说,戴译更可取。徐译两个量词的音重叠了:"一枝,一只,"略显单调拗口,缺乏音韵的变化美。戴译对原著过长的段落重新分段,将语意转化的文字划分小节,让文字读起来更有节奏感,重新设计的节题优美练达。

翻译是一门深不见底的学问,一段看似简单平常的原文的翻译也绝非易事。要想与原作者思维同步,译者需要走进原作的生活背景,走进原作者的心理世界。梭罗当年写作的心态是这样的:静静地卸载城市的喧嚣,用心写下孤独。他思考人生,让读者心如净水般澄澈。让我们感到敬畏和震撼,原来一个人的生活可以是这样的。他的一生是如此的简单而又芳香四溢,虽然短暂而又意蕴深远。他的精神世界绚烂多彩,而且是精妙绝伦。

若干年前,"风格是否可译"曾经在翻译界引起激烈的争论,多少年后,尘埃落定,目前"风格可译"的观点正渐渐成为共识。翻译实践证明了风格的可译性,优秀译作也都巧妙地再现了原作的风格,所达到的艺术效果与原作不相上下。当然,由于语言、文化等方面的不同,译者的文学素养、认知能力等与原作者必然存在差异,百分之百地再现原作风格是不可能的。风格的可译性只能是一个相对的概念,译者的责任在于:尽量减少翻译过程中对原作风格的扭曲和破坏,尽可能地贴近原作风格,还原一个真实的原作境界。

3.3 散文翻译的韵律再造

声响与节奏产生的内在律动使散文语言流畅,富于乐感,适合声情并茂的朗诵,这是散文风格的一个重要方面,也是散文独特魅力的源泉。英语和汉语的句法结构不同,因而声响和节奏也不同,译者必须采用灵活变通的翻译方法再现原作的神韵。如果将一篇汉语散文比作一首中国传统乐曲,那么其英译文就应该是一首西洋乐曲,演奏的乐器不同,演奏方法自然也不同。对原文句法的机械复制充其量只能得原作之"形",而不能得原文之"神"。译者必须深入感受、体会、领悟原作的旋律,再以适当的技巧再现其神韵,而这种再现同样应该是自然流畅、毫无雕饰痕迹。

散文的节奏没有诗的强,这使得译者有较大的空间来组织译文。对于不同的作品,应分析原文的节奏,随机应变。散文节奏通常通过重复、对偶、对仗、对称以及语句的构成形式等表现出来。除此之外,在翻译过程中,应充分理解那些为烘托意境服务于感情需要的节奏形式。如果原文属于激昂向上的情感,译文在形式上也应为节奏铿锵、明快的表达方式;如果原文表达悲怆、抑郁的意境,那么译文也就应采用节奏缓慢、音韵压抑的句式和词语。当然,成功的散文译作要赢得读者,除仰仗形式美之外,还应首先忠实于原文。

以下是朱自清先生的名篇《荷塘月色》(Moonlight over the Lotus Pond)的节选,也是该杰作的最精彩部分。两个对比用的译文均出自我国英语界的大家,译文 1 由朱纯深翻译;译文 2 由张培基翻译。两种译文在再现原文内容和形式方面追求"化境",读起来朗朗上口,使人感觉是在读原汁原味的写景状物的英语散文。两篇译文皆具有艺术韵律的美感,语言自然、准确、地道、活泼、鲜明、生动。在传达原文内容及形式信息方面,符合译文语言习惯,不露斧凿之痕。译文再现了《荷塘月色》的语言特色,基本保留了原文的艺术性和美学性。译文与原文辉映,词与词之间,句与句之间,结构整齐,布局紧凑,与原文相映成趣。

【例 11】
　　曲曲折折的荷塘上面,弥望的是田田的叶子。叶子出水很高,像亭亭的舞女的裙。层层的叶子中间,零星地点缀着些白花,有袅娜地开着的,有羞涩地打着朵儿的;正如一粒粒的明珠,又如碧天里的星星,又如刚出浴的美人。微风过处,送来缕缕清香,仿佛远处高楼上渺茫的歌声似的。这时候叶子与花也有一丝的颤动,像闪电般,霎时传过荷塘的那边去了。叶子本是肩并肩密密地挨着,这便宛然有了一道凝碧的波痕。叶子底下是脉脉的流水,遮住了,不能见一些颜色;而叶子却更见风致了。

译文 1:
All over this winding stretch of water, what meets the eye is a silken field of leaves, reaching rather high above the surface like the skirts of dancing girls in all their grace. Here and there, layers of leaves are dotted with white lotus blossoms, some in demure bloom, others in shy bud, like scattering pearls, or twinkling stars, our beauties just out of the bath. A breeze stirs, sending over breaths of fragrance, like faint singing drifting from a distant building. At this moment, a tiny thrill shoots through the leaves and flowers, like a streak of lightning, straight across the forest of lotuses. The leaves, which have been standing shoulder to shoulder, are caught trembling in an emerald heave of the pond. Underneath, the exquisite water is covered from view and none can tell its color; yet the leaves on top project themselves all the more attractively.

译文 2:
As far as eye could see, the pool with its winding margin was covered with trim leaves, which rose high out of the water like the flared skirts of dancing girls. And starring these tiers of leaves were white lotus flowers, alluringly open or bashfully in bud, like glimmering pearls, stars in an azure sky, or beauties fresh from the bath. The breeze carried past gusts of fragrance, like the strains of a song faintly heard from a far-off tower. And leaves and blossoms trembled slightly, while in a flash the scent was carried away. As

the closely serried leaves bent, a tide of opaque emerald could be glimpsed. That was the softly running water beneath, hidden from sight, its color invisible, though the leaves looked more graceful than ever.

原文重彩浓笔描述荷花的妩媚和迷人之处,颇有色彩。两个译文把握住了这一点,在措词与句法上复制了原文那诱人的荷塘景致。原文使用大量比喻、比拟手法,生动地描写了荷花的风姿。两种译文也基本采用了类似的方法进行翻译,译文读者能够很容易联想到原文作者笔下的动人景色。这是极细节化的描写,一串串明喻使原文生动形象,令人过目难忘。

"曲曲折折的荷塘上面,弥望的是田田的叶子。"原文句子中频频出现的迭声词和平行结构,传达出音义相映,时空延绵,形象通感。译文1采用了不同的手法力图取得相应效果,其中有头韵法:winding...water;有准押韵:meets,field,leaves。译文1以 what meets the eye 为主语;译文2以 the pool 为主语。从表意与原文的表达重心来看,译文1更传神一些。

平行结构的多次运用,也是原文的文体特色之一,非常有效地加强了文字的节奏感。译文1利用英文平行结构的类似效果,产生了相应的感染力。译文1中有:some in demure bloom, others in shy bud;还有 like scattering pearls, or twinkling stars。使用平行结构,可以让读者感觉顿挫有致,顺口悦耳,具有节奏感。而且这种结构便于表达感情,增强语气,突出所强调的内容,形式上工整匀称,语言凝练,再现了原文的对称美和均衡美。

"正如一粒粒的明珠,又如碧天里的星星,又如刚出浴的美人。"原文是几近对称的明喻结构,极具音韵美,两种译文如法炮制,因而美感依在。译文1:like scattering pearls, or twinkling stars, our beauties just out of the bath。译文2:like glimmering pearls, stars in an azure sky, or beauties fresh from the bath。译文1把"碧天里的"隐而不译,信息略有丢失;译文2的 in an azure sky 则有更多的忠实。

"叶子本是肩并肩密密地挨着,这便宛然有了一道凝碧的波痕。"译文1把"肩并肩密密地挨着"直译为 standing shoulder to shoulder,从而复制了原文的拟人手法,而且 shoulder to shoulder 还有一种对称美,但似乎"密密地"的意义没有译出来;译文2的 closely serried 虽然意义也很到位,但总觉失去了一个本应有的、生动形象的修辞格。

【例12】

月光如流水一般,静静地泻在这一片叶子和花上。薄薄的青雾浮起在荷塘里。叶子和花仿佛在牛乳中洗过一样;又像笼着轻纱的梦。虽然是满月,天上却有一层淡淡的云,所以不能朗照;但我以为这恰是到了好处——酣眠固不可少,小睡也别有风味的。月光是隔了树照过来的,高处丛生的灌木,落下参差的斑驳的黑影,峭楞楞如鬼一般;弯弯的杨柳的稀疏的倩影,却又像是画在荷叶上。塘中的月色并不均匀;但光与影有着和谐的旋律,如梵婀玲上奏着的名曲。

译文1:

The moon sheds her liquid light silently over the leaves and flowers, which, in the floating transparency of a bluish haze from the pond, look as if they had just been bathed in milk, or like a dream wrapped in a gauzy hood. Although it is a full moon, shining through a film of clouds, the light is not at its brightest; it is, however, just right for me—a profound sleep is indispensable, yet a snatched doze also has a savor of its own. The moonlight is streaming down through the foliage, casting bushy shadows on the ground from high above, dark and checkered, like an army of ghosts; whereas the benign figures of the drooping willows, here and there, look like paintings on the lotus leaves. The moonlight is not spread evenly over the pond, but rather in a harmonious rhythm of light and shade, like a famous melody played on a violin.

译文 2：

Moonlight cascaded like water over the lotus leaves and flowers, and a light blue mist floating up from the pool made them seem washed in milk or caught in a gauzy dream. Though the moon was full, a film of pale clouds in the sky would not allow its rays to shine through brightly; but I felt this was all to the good—though refreshing sleep is indispensable, short naps have a charm all their own. As the moon shone from behind them, the dense trees on the hills threw checkered shadows, dark forms loomed like devils, and the sparse, graceful shadows of willows seemed painted on the lotus leaves. The moonlight on the pool was not uniform, but light and shadow made up a harmonious rhythm like a beautiful tune played on a violin.

原文采用清新的语言、新奇的联想和别致的比喻，呈现出一幅立体的荷塘月色图。两篇译文遣词造句上力求传达原文的形象美和音乐美，从整体效果上追求原文的意境。本段的两种译文均采取了长句、复合句形式，原文中的流畅美、繁复美跃然纸上。例如，"月光如流水一般，静静地泻在这一片叶子和花上。"译文 1：The moon sheds her liquid light silently over the leaves and flowers；译文 2：Moonlight cascaded like water over the lotus leaves and flowers。译文 1 与译文 2 都运用头韵法：译文 1 有 liquid light, leaves；译文 2 有 lotus leaves。笔锋所到之处，着力再现原文那静静的、富有层次的荷塘美。此外，两相对照，译文 1 把原文的意义全部转述，而译文 2 却难以见到"静静地"这一意义的迹象，但译文 2 的 cascaded 极富优美的动感，把"泻"字转述的灵动自然。原文那看似简单的一个句子，实际上动中有静，静中有动，韵味无穷。一旦转译到位，定然如读原文，妙笔生花。

再如，"又像笼着轻纱的梦"，译文 1：like a dream wrapped in a gauzy hood，译文 2：(seem) caught in a gauzy dream。两个译文均保留了原文的修辞格：明喻。前者峰回路转，耐人寻味；后者运笔经济，言简意赅，可谓布局紧凑，与原文相映成趣。再如，"弯弯的杨柳的稀疏的倩影，却又像是画在荷叶上。"译文 1：whereas the benign figures of the drooping willows, here and there, look like paintings on the lotus leaves. 译文 2：and the sparse, graceful shadows of willows seemed painted on the lotus leaves. 译文 1 的 benign figures of the drooping willows 和译文 2 的 graceful shadows of willows 用来描写朦胧的岸边柳树都很有韵致，两种译文各有千秋，平分秋色，真可以说佳作共赏。

由此可见，两种译文在原文内容和形式方面追求"化境"，读起来朗朗上口，使人感觉是在读原汁原味的写景状物的英语散文。两篇译文皆具有艺术韵律的美感，语言自然、准确、地道、活泼、鲜明、生动。在传达原文内容及形式信息方面，符合译文语言习惯，不露斧凿之痕。译文再现了《荷塘月色》的语言特色及韵律特征,基本保留了原文的艺术性和美学性。译文与原文辉映,词与词之间,句与句之间,结构整齐,布局紧凑,与原文相映成趣。

3.4 散文翻译的意境重构

散文讲究美,这种语言美又是内容和形式统一的产物。郁达夫曾说,"所有的美文都是诗。"按这样的论述来划分作品的话,无疑,散文最接近诗,是一种在形式和意境上最接近诗的美文,因此,有的韵文本身就被冠以"散文诗"。是诗一样的美妙文字,自然就应当有诗一般美妙的意境。尽管从中国古典文论"意境"观的角度来看,散文的意境较之于诗歌的要逊色一些。散文的原文是美的,这要求在翻译成另一种文字时,也必须是美的。散文翻译应充分考虑译出语所体现的形式、内容和意境的完美统一,同时也应意识到译入语的语义结构和文化定势。译文应当和原文一样是美的文字,诗一般的语言。语言形式上的美感特征通常是直观可感的,具体表现为文字组合结构的形式美和音位组合结构的音乐美。一篇优美的散文首先让人感受到的是它的文字优美,它必然表现在作家的遣词造句上,表现在行文的音韵和节奏上,也表现在各种各样的美学修辞格上。

【例 13】

It completely hid everything beyond that distance, except a few ruddy or yellow treetops, which here and there emerged, and were glorified by the early sunshine, as was likewise the broad surface of the mist.

译文 1:

它完全地盖住一切在那个距离以外,除了几堆红的或黄的树顶,它们在这里同那里透露出来,并且被照亮给那清早的阳光,像被大雾笼罩的广阔的平面。

译文 2:

它把那个距离以外所有的东西都盖住了,只剩几堆红色或黄色的树顶,这一搭、那一搭透露出来,正像那大雾的广阔平原一样,都给清早的阳光照耀得鲜明夺目。

译文 3:

远方的一切消失得无影无踪,唯有四处的红黄色的点点树梢,就像一片浩瀚的烟雾,在晨光的照耀中依稀可见。

在原文本中,个体意象为:"雾","树梢","晨光"。将其整合为整体意象即意境为:描绘了清晨阳光透过雾霭,将点点树梢染成或红或绿的颜色,一片生机蓬勃的景象跃然纸上。其中"情"是生机盎然,清新活泼的;"境"是晨光点点洒在树梢上,透过晨雾显现出来,灵动跳跃。三种译文都反映了诗歌的"境",而后两种译文在意境的传译上优于第一种,从而贴切地传达了原文的"情"。译文 1 只是语言层面的简单对等,没有建构起心理意象,只是将个体意象机械地简单罗列,因此原文本中的意境没有在译文中得到成功的再现。译文 2 的译者首先通过品读原文,欣赏到了原文本中的"情"与"景",并从中抽离出个体意象,再在头脑中形成格式塔意象,意境在译文中得到了完整的再现,感情得到了较好的传达。

"情"和"境"传译得最为成功的是译文 3,该译文创造性地将第一句变换视角,从而与下文的"树梢"衔接更为紧密。将"glorified"一词译为"依稀可见",更贴合原文的"境",个体意象与整体的建构和谐一致,感情得到很好的传达,因而意境也完好转存。在散文翻译过程中,应回归原文,尽量传达原文包含的多层次的信息,做到译文和原文的形式、内容和风格的统一,给读者以美的享受,让读者欣赏到散文蕴含的美感和真谛。

【例14】

On one of those somber and rather melancholy days, in the latter part of Autumn. When the shadows of morning and evening almost mingle together, and throw a gloom over the decline of the year, I passed several hours in rambling about Westminster Abbey. There was something congenial to the season in the mournful magnificence of the old pile; and, as I passed its threshold seemed like stepping back into the regions of antiquity, and losing myself among the shades of former ages. (Washington Erving: *Westminster Abbey*)

译文：

时值晚秋,气象肃穆,略带忧郁。晨昏的阴影,几近混沌一体,不可分辨。衰季之际,终日昏暗,我漫步西敏寺,数小时之久。古寺巍巍,虽有哀气氛围,然季候还算宜人。跨进门槛,我似乎觉得自己置身远古,隐身于古代的幻影之中了。(岳守国重译：《西敏寺》)

上面的原文是华盛顿·欧文的《西敏寺》开头的一段。欧文被称为"美国文学之父",他的作品文笔优美,语言生动,长于运用幽默与夸张的艺术手法。欧文的语言典雅细腻,文采飞扬,把浪漫主义奇想和日常生活场景的真实描写、幽默和抒情结合在一起。情真意切,动人心魄,给人启迪。对比中英两种文字,原文峰回路转,曲径通幽。经过几十次修改润色的译文典雅古朴,气象森森。字斟句酌,两相比照,译文再现的意境可圈可点,译者复制出来的境界同样古朴幽幽,令人神往。细细品味,译者密集运用四字格结构,再现原文的意境美。四字格特有的美学价值主要表现在四个方面：音韵上的节奏美,形式上的整齐美,内容上的意象美,行上文的简洁美。因此读起来朗朗上口,给人以抑扬顿挫的节奏感。

钱钟书先生在《林纾的翻译》一文中提到："文学翻译的最高标准是'化'。把作品从一国文字翻译成另一国文字,既不能因语文习惯的差异而露出生硬牵张的痕迹,又能完全保存原有的风味,那就算得上'化境'"。若能将散文翻译达到"化境"(realm of configuration),那必是一种理想的境界。在翻译中利用词汇技巧或修辞手段可使文字更具感染力,并使译文既符合译入语的表达习惯,又保持原作的神韵和风姿,达到原作的艺术效果。译者需领悟原文的艺术特色,提炼原文精华,发挥译语优势,再现原文的语言技巧,还原美妙的艺术境界以及含蓄而炽热的情感。

4　本章结语

散文翻译应从整体上再现原文的意境和氛围,这样散文意境核心的审美情操、审美倾向等才能从深层次上得以传达。译者兼有双重身份：既是特殊身份的读者,又是特殊身份的作者。译者通过阅读原作同作者对话,通过建构译作同原作对话,并且通过发表译作与译文读者对话。散文译者既要注意原文情感的深沉真挚,又要注意抒情的度,不矫情也不滥情,使转译出来的情感与原文的审美情趣同步。散文翻译是一种艺术的再创造,译者不仅要准确把握原文的语言特色,遣词造句、布局谋篇也要合乎译入语的习惯。同时还要在译文中巧妙运用并再现原文的情感,符合原语审美传感的最佳效果,并给读者留下适度的想象空间,让他们到文字的背后去发掘情感的内涵。

  翻译过程可以说是"二度创作",然而译者并非可以随心所欲,不要背离原著的风貌,不可凭个人倾向去自由发挥。有人将文学翻译喻为"戴着镣铐跳舞",形象地揭示了译事维艰的本质。译途漫漫,译者须持之以恒地磨炼译笔,不断提高文化和语言素养,最终方可能使译作臻于化境。散文翻译重在分析原文,深入理解,提炼精华,领悟妙处,付诸笔端,一语服人,这是重铸原文并再现原作丰姿的过程。一切景语皆情语,译文在重现原文景物或人物描写过程中,需注重其中蕴含的情感因素。译者要选择感情色彩浓厚、风格鲜明的表达方式进行情感的重铸,使译文与原文一样情景交融,震撼人心。

第十章 小说翻译

小说是读者面最广的一种文学体裁,是一种借助艺术虚构来表现社会现象或现实生活的叙事性文本。小说家们意图通过环境的描述、人物的塑造和情节的编排来揭示社会矛盾、反映社会生活,由此影响审美主体的理智、情感和意志,从而引导读者去认识生活,使他们在享受美的同时,受到心灵的教化。作为一种通过语言反映生活、反映现实、表达思想、抒发情感的艺术形式,小说以表情为主要目的,通常兼具艺术性和思想性,旨在通过艺术化的语言外壳来表达作者的思想感情,并引起读者的共鸣。

1 小说文体特征

译者在翻译小说时,首先要熟悉小说的基本文体特征,只有掌握了这些特征,才能准确把握目标文本(即将要翻译的小说原作)的语言特点和艺术美,进而在翻译过程中有意识地把握和传递原文的内容与风格。概括来说,小说文本的文体特征主要包括宏观和微观两个层面。

1.1 宏观文体特征

叙事性特征是小说与其他文学体裁最重要的一个区别特征。提及小说,大家都会想到那些形形色色、丰满生动的人物和曲折动人、紧凑缜密的故事情节,还有人物演绎悲欢离合的或宏大或精致、或愉悦或凄惨的场景。这些便是叙事性的三个具体要素:环境、人物和情节,即通常所提及的"六何"——"何时、何地、何人、何物、为何、如何"。环境要素通过时间地点的具体化体现出来,交代故事发生的各种背景,如历史、社会、文化、民族背景等;人物要素通过人物外貌刻画、心理和行动描写、人物之间的关系、人物对待外部事物的态度等诸方面体现;情节要素则重在点明故事发生的原因和具体过程。叙事性特征的三个具体要素之间相互渗透、相互映衬,通常称为小说的三要素。叙事性把小说与散文、诗歌、戏剧等其他文学体裁区别开来。散文可以是纯粹的抒情或议论;诗歌(长篇叙事史诗如《木兰辞》或《荷马史诗》等除外)常常只是景物描写或几点感悟;而戏剧不但在叙事视角等表现形式上受到时空等条件的限制,戏剧中的故事叙述讲究由一个个冲突的提出、发展和解决完成。

虚拟现实性是小说文本的另一特征。小说是"来源于生活,又高于生活"的文学形式,是真实性与虚拟性相结合的艺术创造。虚拟性与真实性的比重因小说而异。神话、科幻小说的虚拟性更强,故事情节或人物形象含有超现实或超逻辑的色彩,而大多数小说则更贴近生活。但小说家们孜孜追求的故事真实性,是指如何使读者产生如见其人、如闻其声、如临其境的感觉,并非像报告文学家那样如实、精确地呈现真实生活。小说往往以对现实生活的细致观察和准确把握为创作前提,在现实的基础上进行艺术加工和艺术创造。

主题上的包容性和表现形式上的自由性是小说的又一特征。首先,小说主题,或小说内容,几乎涉及生活的方方面面,可以说是包罗万象。以主题分,有社会小说、爱情小说、教育小说、经济小说、法律小说、医学小说、哲理小说、政治小说、历史小说、侦探小说、军事小说、传奇小说(包括神话)、冒险小说、科幻小说、英雄小说、宗教小说等十多种类型。其次,小说的表现形式具有极大的自由性,具体表现在以下三方面:

① 从叙事视角来看,有全知视角、限知视角、外视角、内视角等之分,采用不同的形式展示一个叙事世界,作者可以采用无所不知的全知视角展现故事的来龙去脉、人物的对话、人物各自的优缺点或情感变化和内心活动等;也可以以某个人物的视角为基点的限知视角去展开故事,描述叙事者与人物的关系、对周围事物的感知等,作者对于世界人事的审视通过具体人物的眼光来完成;或者由一个限知视角转移到另一个限知视角,从几个不同人物的视角形成视角的流动来推移故事的发展;还可以在这全知视角和限知视角之间自由转换。

② 从文体上来看,散文、戏剧、诗歌等文学文体,甚至法律、新闻、商务等非文学文本都可以随着不同身份人物的出场轻松纳入小说的叙事框架。

③ 从故事情节展示的顺序来看,小说可以采用顺叙式、倒叙式或者插叙式的故事结构。

1.2 微观语言特征

主题上的包容性和表现形式上的自由性、虚拟现实性和叙事性等特征是小说与其他文体在宏观方面的区别。小说是以场景描述、人物刻画和情节设计为主,从语言表现层面上看,这要求小说语言首先必须细致具体、形象生动;人物是三要素的中心,每个人物必定有一个特定的身份,一个鲜明的个性,一套与自身身份、个性相匹配的话语模式,人物形象才更加丰满,才能更加真实可信。

(1) 语言的形象性

小说创作主要借助具体细致的描绘来营造真实可信的氛围,渲染某种特定的情绪,刻画独具特色的人物形象,使读者如临其境、历其情、见其人。这要求小说语言必须准确传神,生动形象,崇尚具体而力避抽象,因此通常选用最富表现性的词汇,即要求选词的精确传神。例如,如果一位英语作家意图描写一个人行走的动作,他会在 walk(步行,散步)、wander(漫步)、hover(徘徊)、linger(闲逛)、stroll(漫步)、parade(漫步,散步,尤指为让别人看到而在公开场合行走)、hobble(蹒跚)、stagger(摇摇摆摆地走)、march(大步走)、trot(小跑)、run(奔跑)、tramp(重步走,踏行)等多个表示形态各异的行走动词中斟酌取舍,选择一个最为贴切的字眼。

丰富多样的修饰词也能使描述准确和具体、鲜明而生动有力。拟人、比喻、借代、讽刺、夸张、双关、拟声、通感等修辞手法在小说中被广泛运用。在恰当的地方使用恰当的修辞格还可以达到特殊的艺术效果,能起到事半功倍的作用,这是许多作家追求的目标。如 Emily Brontë 在 *Wuthering Heights* 中对女主人公 Catherine 的描写:"So that, instead of a <u>wild, hatless savage jumping into the house and rushing to squeeze us all breathless</u>, there <u>lighted from a handsome black pony a very dignified person, with brown ringlets falling from the cover of a feathered beaver, and a long cloth habit which she was obliged to hold up with both hands that she might sail in</u>."这段细致的描述把一个曾经活泼可爱、风风火火

的 Catherine 描述得非常传神，与眼前这个端庄淑女形成鲜明对比，人物形象更加丰满、具体、生动，如果把文中这些修饰语（画线部分）去掉，这种效果是无论如何也达不到的。

（2）语言的个性化

小说语言的个性化主要表现在人物语言的个性化上。所谓人物语言个性化，就是指人物语言应符合人物所独有的身份、经历、职业、爱好、文化修养、在特定环境和特定人际关系中所表现出来的思想感情等性格特征。作家为了生动地再现形形色色的人物的个性，常常模仿他们各自的语言，使他们说出合乎自己身份、地位、教养、性格的话来。有的可能非常文雅，有的则会十分粗俗，有的则是方言俚语，极不规范，这是作家借人物语言塑造人物形象的一个重要手段。如马克·吐温在 The Adventures of Huckleberry Finn 中对吉姆的描写："Pooty soon I'll be a —shout'n for joy, en I'll say, its all on accounts o'Huck, I's a free man en I couldn't ever ben free ef it hadn't ben for Huck; Huck done it. Jim won't ever forgit you, Huck; you's de bes'fren'. Jim's ever had; en you's de only fren'ole Jim's got now."吉姆与哈克说话时，语言中充斥着讹读、省音、不合语法、用词不当之处，这是个未受过教育的黑人奴隶；"free"、"Huck"的重复出现让吉姆对获得自由的欣喜和对哈克的感激之情表露无遗。曹雪芹著《红楼梦》中的元春省亲时对她父亲说："田舍之家，虽齑盐布帛，终能聚天伦之乐，今富贵已极，骨肉各方，然终无意趣！"元春的话以富于文采又结构规整的四字格为主体，与自己的父亲谈论起深宫落寞、渴望亲情时也是如此稳重、正式，这是一个诗书望族出来的女子，深受礼教约束，虽面对的是自己的父亲，却时刻谨记自己已身为皇妃，谨守君臣之礼。

2 小说翻译原则与方法

古今中外都出现过大量的小说名著，它们以高超的艺术手法、生动的故事情节、鲜明的人物形象、广阔的社会信息和作者对社会的深邃观察等流芳于世。作为一种文学文本，小说具备信息功能、表情功能、美感功能和呼唤功能等，表情功能与美感功能是小说的主要功能。这些作者意图如何在译作中体现出来，是小说译者追求的目标。译者在承担小说翻译任务之前，除具备扎实的双语功底和跨文化能力、必要的翻译理论及翻译技巧之外，还必须熟知双文化中与小说有关的文学知识，具备一定的文学修养。小说翻译除了要遵循翻译的一般规律外，还有其独特规律和特点。译者应尽量把原作的信息以恰当的形式准确地表达出来，并能够适度移植原作的艺术美，取得与原作相似的艺术效果和艺术感染力。理想的小说翻译是译作和原作在思想内容、语言形式以及交际功能等方面实现对等。

2.1 人物个性化语言的翻译

人物语言和相互间的对话是塑造人物形象最有效的一种方式，通过人物语言，读者可以获得说话者的信息，如人物年龄、性别、教养、态度以及说话时的心理等。孩子的话语词汇句式都较为简单，女性语言则通常语气较为婉转，受过教育的人语言更加规范，生气时的语气强烈而犹豫时的语言可能会比较啰唆或带有停顿。某个人物在何时何地会说什么，该怎么说，都是作家深思熟虑、多次推敲的结果。这些语言形式和语言风格可以使人物形象惟妙惟肖、精彩传神,极具真实感和感染力,译者要想塑造出同样精彩的艺术形象,必须抓住那些突出人物个性的话语结构或词汇,挖掘这些形式和风格特点背后的创作意图,充分发挥自身的创造性,以"传神达效"为准则,在目的语中寻找恰当的语言形式。

【例1】
　　Because you don't save, Mr. Deasy said, pointing his finger. You don't know yet what money is. Money is power. When you have lived as long as I have. I know, I know. If youth but knew...

(James Joyce：*Ulysses*, Chapter II)

译文1：
　　"因为你不攒钱,"戴希先生指着他说,"你还不懂得金钱意味着什么。金钱是权。当你活到我这把岁数的时候就懂啦。我懂得,我懂得。倘若年轻人有经验。"

(萧乾、文洁若译)

译文2：
　　"这是因为你不存钱,"戴希先生伸手指着他说。"你还不懂得金钱的意义。钱就是权。将来你活到我这个年龄就明白了。我是懂的,我是懂的。少壮不晓事嘛。"

(金堤译)

　　戴希先生惯以长者身份自居,时常对年轻人谆谆教导:"pointing his finger"和"When you have lived as long as I have"两句鲜明地描画出一个自恃年长而对年轻人指手画脚的人物形象。两译文都巧妙地添加了语气助词再现人物口吻,译文2的"少壮不晓事嘛"比"倘若年轻人有经验"更具有原文人物倚老卖老的神韵,口吻更加传神。

　　许多中国小说家对人物语言同样是千锤百炼。《红楼梦》这部中国经典小说是一本鸿篇巨制,是各色人等交替出场的大舞台,有名有姓的女性形象就超过一百多位,个个都性格鲜明,相貌、谈吐、品性、嗜好等也各不相同。作者曹雪芹的语言驾驭能力让人叹服,往往三言两语便能使人物形象呼之欲出,下面是史湘云与林黛玉的一段对话:

【例2】
　　二人正说着,只见湘云走来,笑道:"爱哥哥、林姐姐,你们天天一处顽,我好容易来了,也不理我一理儿。"黛玉笑道:"偏是咬舌子爱说话,连个'二哥哥'也叫不上来,只是'爱'哥哥'爱'哥哥的。回来赶围棋儿,又该闹'幺爱三四五'了。"……湘云笑道:"这一辈子我自然比不上你。我保估着明儿得一个咬舌儿林姐夫,时时刻刻你可听'爱'呀'厄'的去,阿弥陀佛!那时才现在我眼里呢!"

(曹雪芹:《红楼梦》,第20回)

　　有些人说话时舌尖常接触牙齿,因而吐字不清,即俗称的咬舌子,很多作家也会运用这种特别的发音方式塑造人物,使作品人物形象更多样化,更贴近生活。史湘云出场的次数并不太多,但作者仅利用"二"与"爱"不分的发音特点就勾勒出了她的活泼、率真、可爱,说话咬舌的特点更是让她个性鲜明。林黛玉口齿伶俐、好挖苦人又不饶人的性格特征也刻画得入木三分。两人互相取笑、嬉闹,情趣盎然。同时,一个"爱"也触动了林黛玉的心弦。在英美等以英语为

母语的国家也有一些人发音不清,译者可以模仿这些人的说话方式来翻译,如霍克斯的翻译:

译文:

Just then Xiangyun burst in on them and reproved them smilingly for abandoning her:"Couthin Bao, Couthin Lin, you can thee each other every day. It'th not often I get a chanthe to come here; yet now I have come, you both ignore me!" Daiyu burst out laughing:"Lisping doesn't seem to make you any less talkative! Listen to you:'Couthin'! 'Couthin'! Presently, when you're playing Racing Go, you'll be all 'thicktheth' and 'theventh'!"… "I shall never be a match for you as long as I live," Xiangyun said to Daiyu with a disarming smile. "All I can thay ith that I hope you marry a lithping huthband, tho that you have 'ithee-withee' 'ithee-withee' in your earth every minute of the day. Ah, holy Name! I think I can thee that blethed day already before my eyeth!"

(David Hawkes 译)

改掉"爱"字谐音虽然是一个损失,但是这一点在原文中毕竟只是一个暗示,对于整个故事情节的描写没有太大的影响。在人物对话翻译中,我们追求的是"传神"、"化境",主要是"咬舌子"产生的幽默效果和艺术美感。David Hawkes可谓独具匠心,在译文里相应地运用了一连串的/θ/替换/s/,读来令人忍俊不禁,耳边犹如响起朗朗笑声,人物形象仿佛浮现在眼前。此处英译时若用脚注或文中注释等办法补足,就显得有些笨拙,会影响行文流畅。这样以错译错,充分利用译语的优势,无需任何特别解释就能让译文读者领略其中妙处,所取得的艺术效果毫不逊色于原文,已"能如风格以出",可谓佳译。

要想像上述译者那样再现原文形神毕肖的人物对话,必须认真体会人物的语言特点,是学究气还是口语化,心情是气愤的还是愉悦的,把握其中的气质神韵。此外,译者还要熟悉译入语中相应人物的语言习惯,唯有如此,才能译出原文的个性化语言特色,让译文像原文那样具有可读性,成为优秀的译作。

2.2 修辞格的翻译

修辞格在英汉语言中都可以见到,如拟人(personification)、明喻(simile)和暗喻(metaphor)(通称为比喻[comparison])、借代(metonymy)、讽刺(irony)、夸张(hyperbole)、双关(pun)、拟声(onomatopoeia)、通感(synaesthesia)、移就(transferred epithet)、反复(repetition)、对偶(antithesis)、仿词(parody)、排比(parallelism)、委婉(euphemism)等。它们在小说中运用广泛,中外小说家借助适合特定对象和特定场合的得体的、适度的修辞手法描述场景、刻画人物,常常可以准确生动地表达出自己的意图,便于读者接受和理解并增加语言的感染力和艺术效果。英汉语修辞格在分类和使用上有一定的相似之处,但又不尽相同。有一些修辞手法在英汉两种语言之间可以相互转换,另一些修辞手法虽然英汉语都有,但由于语言环境、美学观念等方面的原因,表现效果和使用频率却不同,还有一些修辞手法是汉语特有或英语特有的,这就要求译者根据具体情况采用不同的翻译方法。

"修辞手段是翻译过程中运用的主要语言手段之一。译品质量跟修辞形式的正确运用很有关系"(方梦之,2004:175)。修辞格翻译应力求译文能在传递原文内容的基础上有效地再现原文的修辞效果,兼顾信息功能和美学功能的传递,否则译文即使在大意上与原文差不多,也会使原文的精神和风格受损,削弱语言的表达力。修辞手法在小说翻译中可以有直译、替换、意译、直译意译结合等多种处理手段,视翻译目的和功能的表达效果而定。

(1) 直译法

为了形象、传神地表现原文特色,翻译时应尽量使用对应的修辞格,从而使源语与目的语在语言形式和意义上相对等。通常,拟人、比喻、夸张等修辞手法可译性较高,常可采用对应的修辞格,甚至相同的结构进行翻译,也就是直译。在英汉两种语言的修辞手法和表现效果无甚差异的情况下,直译既可传达原文的意义,又可保持原文的修辞风格,丰富译文的语言表达力,兼顾信息功能和美学功能的传递。如:

【例3】

When I saw my charmer thus come in accompanied by a cavalier, I seem to hear a hiss, and the green snake of jealousy, rising on undulating coils from the moonlit balcony, glided within my waistcoat, and ate its way in two minutes to my heart's core.

(Charlotte Brontë: *Jane Eyre*, Chapter XV)

译文:

当我看见那个把我弄得神魂颠倒的女人,由一个好献殷勤的男人陪着进来时,我似乎听到了一阵嘶嘶叫,绿色的嫉妒之蛇,从月光照耀下的阳台上呼地窜了出来,盘成了高低起伏的圈圈,钻进我的背心,两分钟后一直咬啮到了我的内心深处。

(黄源深译)

看到心上人和别的男人一起出现,强烈的嫉妒之情让罗切斯特难以忍受,在 Charlotte Brontë 的笔下,内心的"嫉妒"被比喻成"一条绿色的蛇",形象地刻画出男主人公对 Jane Eyre 的强烈爱情。译文不但把比喻直译过来,还根据目的语表达习惯添加了拟声词"呼地",男主人公内心的强烈感受表露无遗,表达效果得到充分移植。

钱钟书先生是一位善用修辞的小说家。《围城》这部作品能够脍炙人口的一个重要的原因就是里面的 600 多个生动形象、新颖别致的比喻,极大地满足了读者们的审美情趣。这些凝聚智慧、饱含哲理的比喻把作者内心深处的深刻感受、人生体验和对时世的态度不露痕迹地外化成文学语言,形成了独具特色的"钱钟书式的比喻"。为传译出这种颇具特色的写作风格,Jeanne Kelly 和毛国权两位译者的合译本对其中的许多比喻手法进行了直译:

【例4】

方鸿渐看唐小姐不笑的时候,脸上还依恋着笑意,像音乐停止后袅袅空中的余音。许多女人会笑得这样甜;但她们的笑容只是面部肌肉软操,仿佛有教练在喊口令:"一!"忽然满脸堆笑,"二!"忽然笑不知去向,只余个空脸,像电影开映前的布幕。

(钱钟书:《围城》,第3章)

译文:

Fang Hung-chien noticed that the trace of a smile lingered on Miss T'ang face when she was not smiling, like the last few notes that float in the air after the music has ceased.

Many women can smile just as sweetly, but their smile is only facial muscle calisthenics, as if a drillmaster were barking the order, "One!" and suddenly the whole face would be wreathed in smiles, then "Two!" and just as suddenly the smile would vanish, leaving a face as blank as the screen in a movie theater before the movie starts.

(Jeanne Kelly & Mao Guoquan 译)

上面这段文字最精彩最传神的就是三个比喻,给整段文字增添了生气,读来清新有趣:(1)唐小姐的笑容比成音乐的余音,一个满脸笑容的女孩形象呈现在眼前。(2)人们很少将"许多女人的笑"和做操联系起来,可作者抓住了两者都很快这一特点,形容一些人笑容消失之快就像听口令做操一样,风趣俏皮。笑本应活泼随意,自由自在,而现在却要像做操一样,整齐划一,令行禁止。这完全违背了笑的本质,因而就更显得滑稽可笑。(3)作者把失去笑容的脸比成电影开映前的布幕,生动而又别致。译者对这三个比喻全部采用直译法,意义未变,而修辞美也得以保留,正是兼顾文本的信息功能和美感功能的结果。

(2) 替换法

上文提到,有些修辞手法可以在译语中找到对应的修辞方式,直译法能达到意义与修辞形式兼顾、文本的信息功能和美感功能并存,这一点并非绝对。修辞与一个民族的文化传统有密切的关系。由于英、汉民族在语言环境和美学观念上的不同,修辞的具体构成会有差别。例如,以比喻为例,原文的喻体移植到译文中可能会引起不同的联想或者译出来显得拖沓或不自然,那么就会歪曲原意或者给读者带来不同的心理感受,会歪曲原文信息功能和美感功能。另有一些修辞手段虽然英汉两种语言中有类似的分类(如双关),但是因语言差异和具体语境的限制在译语中以同样形式译出相对较难;还有一些属于英语或汉语特有的修辞手法(如英语的押头韵、汉语的析字和谐音),无法在目的语中找到对应的修辞形式。在这几种情况下,译者就必须变通,替换其中的某一部分(如比喻中的喻体)或整体替换,以尽量保留原文的信息和修辞手法。例如,英语修辞 mimesis 指文学作品中对人物拼写错误或方言等说话方式进行模仿的修辞方法,就可以替换成汉语中再现人物错误用词的"飞白"这种修辞手法,虽然汉语"飞白"与英语 malapropism 在分类上更对应:

【例 5】

"Can you spell, Buck?" I says.

"Yes," he says.

"I bet you can't spell my name," says I.

"I bet you what you dare I can," says he.

"All right," says I, "go ahead."

"G-o-r-g-e J-a-x-o-n there now," he says.

(Mark Twain: *The Adventures of Huckleberry Finn*)

译文:

"你认识字吗,叭克?"我就说。

"我认识,"他说。

"我敢说,你不会写我的名字,"我说。

"我敢说,你会的事情我都会,"他说。
"好了,"我说,"你说吧。"
"你的名字是左右的左,志气的志,节省的杰,客人的克,牲口的生——怎么样?"他说。

(张万里译)

通过语法、拼写等错误形式,两个顽劣、无知、好胜的顽童形象已夺纸而出,充满童趣,声形并作。译文利用"叭"、"杰"、"克"、"生"四个别字巧妙地暗示出孩童的无知。此译文既从意义上符合原文本意,又传译出原文的音韵节奏,巧臻声态,人物形象栩栩如生。

【例6】
宝钗道:"你又禁不得风吹,怎么又站在那风口里?"黛玉笑道:"何曾不是在房里的,只因听见天上一声叫唤,出来瞧了瞧,原来是个<u>呆雁</u>。"宝钗道:"呆雁在哪里呢?我也瞧一瞧。"黛玉道:"我才出来,他就'<u>嗤儿</u>'的一声飞了。"

(曹雪芹:《红楼梦》,第 28 回)

译文:
"Why are you standing there in a draught?" asked Paochai. "You know how easily you catch cold."
"I was indoors until I heard a strange bird-cry. When I came out to look it was only <u>a silly goose</u>."
"Where is this silly goose? I'd like to see it."
"As soon as I came out it <u>flapped</u> away."

(杨宪益、戴乃迭译)

此处黛玉把宝玉比成一只呆雁来讥笑宝玉因宝钗的美而一时痴呆和失魂落魄。而英文"wild goose"在英语读者的心目中很容易和莎士比亚的"wild goose chase"(像追逐大雁一样追逐不可能得到的东西)相联系起来,不能与汉语意象对应,因此,译者换成英语读者熟悉的"goose",为此,原文"天上"被省译。汉语的拟声手法非常灵活,几乎能够描摹出生活中的任何一种声响,但是"嗤儿"的儿化韵音响效果在英语中很难表示,因此变通为另一个拟声效果的"flap"。

(3) 意译法
即使是同一修辞格,中西方在一些修辞手段的运用频率上存在差别,如,受汉民族文化传统的影响,汉语中大量使用比喻,用得既多且广。汉语修辞以整齐、对称为主,以参差错落为辅,并且汉语非常容易组合成音节数目相同而结构上平行的对偶。汉字使用偏旁部首的造字特点还产生了若干特殊的修辞手法,如回文、顶针、谐音双关等。oxymoron(矛盾法)、zeugma(轭式搭配法)和 alliteration(押头韵)是英语中常用而汉语中少用或没有的修辞手法。对于以上情况,在无法变通的情况下,可采用意译、加注等方法。

英语中的 zeugma 是用一个词(动词、形容词或介词)与两个以上的名词搭配,两个名词在意义上不相干或第二个名词与动词或形容词等不能构成自然搭配,但却因借助前一个词的正常搭配而被读者接受。汉语没有这种修辞格,因此英汉翻译时大多进行意译,如苏格兰小说家萨基(Saki,原名 Hector Hugh Munro)的著名讽刺幽默短篇小说 *Mrs. Packletide's*

Tiger (《帕克莱泰德夫人的老虎》),其中有这样一段描写:

【例 7】

Mrs. Packletide had already arranged in her mind the lunch she would give at her house in Curzon Street, in Loona Bimberto's honour, with <u>a tiger-skin occupying most of the foreground and all conversation.</u>

(Saki: *Mrs. Packletide's Tiger*)

译文:

帕克莱泰德夫人心中已经把欢迎鲁娜·宾伯顿太太的午宴安排好了,宴会在她克瑞大街的家中举行,<u>把一张虎皮放在最显眼的地方,为的是使人们的话题总是以虎皮为中心。</u>

(张国荣译)

原文中的"occupy"一词与"foreground"和"conversation"两个名词搭配,采用的是轭式搭配法这一修辞手段。其中,"occupy"与前一个名词形成自然搭配,而与"conversation"则是超常规的搭配。这种新颖别致的词语组合使文辞生动活泼、风趣幽默。作者用这一修辞格把帕克莱泰德夫人想用虎皮来炫耀自己"勇敢"的这种虚荣心刻画得淋漓尽致。译成"(虎皮)占据在最醒目的地方"显然不够通顺,因此译者进行了意译。

下面例 8 中的原文出自《红楼梦》。黛玉午歇,与宝玉对脸闲聊,一股幽香自黛玉袖中发出,宝玉便拉住她的衣袖,闻个不住。黛玉讥他,宝玉便绘声绘色地给黛玉讲了一个林子洞耗子精的故事,最后说:

【例 8】

"我说你们没见过世面,只认得这果子是<u>香芋</u>,却不知盐课林老爷的小姐才是真正的'<u>香玉</u>'呢!"

(曹雪芹:《红楼梦》,第 19 回)

译文 1:

"It is you who are mistaken. You have seen too little of the world to understand. The vegetable tuber is not the only kind of <u>sweet potato</u>. The daughter of our respected Salt Commissioner Lin is also a <u>sweet potato</u>. She is the sweetest sweet potato of them all."

(David Hawkes 译)

译文 2:

"You ignorant lot!"…"You only know what <u>sweet taros</u> are but don't know that the daughter of Salt Commissioner Lin is <u>sweeter than any taro</u>."

(*Note: This is an untranslatable pun. The Yu in Daiyu's name has the same sound as Yu meaning "taro" in Chinese.*)

(杨宪益、戴乃迭译)

利用小耗子偷的"香芋"与"香玉"(袖中散发香味的黛玉)的谐音双关,宝玉编排故事调侃黛玉的情趣展现无遗。而汉字一字一音,且音、形、义兼备的特性,在英译文中则只好以传递意义为重,以意译或意译加注的方式译出。

汉语修辞以整齐、对称为主,以参差错落为辅,并且汉语非常容易组合成音节数目相同而结构上平行的对偶,积累了数量可观的四字格、四字成语,这些形式在翻译时往往进行意译,如《红楼梦》中的元春省亲时对她父亲说:

【例9】

"田舍之家,虽齑盐布帛,终能聚天伦之乐,今富贵已极,骨肉各方,然终无意趣!"

(曹雪芹:《红楼梦》,第18回)

译文1:

"Simple farmers who live on pickles and dress in homespun at least know they joys of family life together. What pleasure can I take in high rank and luxury when we are separated like this?"

(杨宪益、戴乃迭译)

译文2:

"What is the use of all this luxury and splendour,"… "if I am to be always separated from those I love—denied the tenderness which even the poorest peasant who seasons his bread with salt and pickles and dresses in hempen homespun is free to enjoy?"

(David Hawkes 译)

四字格极富文采又结构规整,音律紧凑,元春的话显得严肃正式、稳重得体。两译文都是意译,但是译文1不仅在选词和词义搭配上,还在句式上注意到四字格的结构简练这一点,使用了较为简短的句式,与译文2相比,无论原文的信息还是形式均较贴近原文。

修辞手法的翻译并不限于以上几种,一种修辞手法也不仅限于一种翻译方法。意义与修辞效果历经翻译过程而能并存是译者追求的目标,但是如果一味追求修辞形式的对等或为修辞而修辞,若造成以修辞害意、译文晦涩难懂,就得不偿失了。因此,修辞手段的翻译原则应该是意义第一,修辞第二;信息功能与美感功能兼顾为上策,只顾信息功能而放弃美感功能只能算是退而求其次的选择,译者要根据具体情况进行灵活处理。

2.3 文化负载成分的翻译

由于地理环境、历史发展、社会结构等诸多因素,各民族在长期的生活和实践中形成了各自不同的生活方式、意识形态、宗教信仰、风俗习惯和文学艺术等,形成了不同的文化。"不同的文化使用不同的语义范畴分解和描述世界。因此,一种文化里有的语义在另一种语言里可能就不存在"(Lado,1957:78),这种现象被称为词义空缺,这些在另一种语言里找不到对应或相近表达方式的词汇,就是文化负载词。换言之,文化负载词指那些反映某个民族独特文化事物或概念、承载本民族文化信息、在译语中没有对应语的词汇。

中英文化的巨大差异,使英汉语之间存在大量的文化负载词。文化负载词是民族文化智慧的结晶,蕴含着深厚的民族文化底蕴。除词汇外,小说中还出现了大量的人名、地名、典故、成语等语言形式,也蕴含着丰富的文化信息,却无法在英汉互译中找到完全对等的成分,因此,此处使用"文化负载成分"一词把它们涵盖在内。小说翻译作为一种跨文化交际形式,文化负载成分的翻译决定着译本的文化负载量和跨文化交际目的的实现程度。既然在两种语言中找不到完全对应的形式,小说译者只有尽最大可能重现文化负载成分的信息,根据具体的结构和语义特点、不同的翻译目的,灵活选用音译、直译、意译、加注等翻译方法。

1. 音译法

为完整保留原文所承载的文化信息、进行跨文化交流,一些文化负载成分,如人名、地名、某些文化特有的事或物可以进行音译。

	原文	译文
人名	Hindley Earnshaw	亨得利·恩肖
	Catherine Linton	凯瑟琳·林顿
	Heathcliff	西斯克里夫
	林黛玉	Lin Daiyu
	贾宝玉	Jia Baoyu
	薛宝钗	Xue Baochai
	史湘云	Shi Xiangyun
	秦可卿	Qin Keqing
地名	Liverpool	利物浦
	Gimmerton	吉默吞
	圆明园	Yuanmingyuan
其他专名	logic	逻辑
	coffee	咖啡
	阴阳	yinyang
	磕头	kowtow
	太极	taichi

还有一些专名翻译时用补足通名的方法进行信息补偿,以便于理解;对于一些由专名和通名组成的专名,翻译时一般音译/意译专名而直译通名。如:

	原文	译文
专名	十里街	Ten-li Street
	仁清巷	Renqing Lane

此外,"London"(伦敦)、"Liverpool"(利物浦)、"England"(英格兰)、"Oscar Wilde"(奥斯卡·王尔德)、"Shylock Holmes"(夏洛克·福尔摩斯)等这些译名已经是约定俗成的译法,一般不再另译。

2. 直译法

一些文化负载成分的翻译可以采用直译,既可以使译文简洁明了,又能保留原语文化信息,例如,别名、人名、地名、一些文化特有事与物等的翻译:

	原文	译文
别名	凤辣子	Peppercorn Feng
文化特有项	号脉	feel the pulse
	龙舟	dragon boat
	春卷	spring roll
地名	Wuthering Heights	呼啸山庄
	Thrushcross Grange	画眉山庄
	赤瑕宫	Palace of Red Jade
	葫芦庙	Gourd Temple/Bottle-gourd Temple
	大观园	The Grand View Garden
	怡红院	Happy Red Court

3. 意译法

一些文化负载成分的翻译若采用音译或直译可能会引起误解或表述不清，因此为译文的流畅和文化交流的目的，需要舍弃原文形式，着重传递原文的信息，进行意译。

【例 10】

...Where Mattie, encircled by facetious youths, and bright as a blackberry under her spreading hat, was brewing coffee over a gipsy fire.

（Edith Wharton：*Ethan Frome*）

译文：

玛蒂的身边围着一圈嘻嘻哈哈的年轻人，她头上戴着一顶阔边的帽子，漂亮得像一颗乌莓，正在一堆野火上煮咖啡。

（吕叔湘译）

原文中的"gipsy fire"原指像吉普赛人那样在野外点火烧饭，在这里意译成"野火"。

【例 11】

人都满了，连立足也难，我只得挤在远处人丛中看一个老旦在台上唱。

（鲁迅：《呐喊·社戏》）

译文：

There was hardly any standing-room and I had to squeeze into the crowd at the rear to watch an actor singing an old woman's part.

（杨宪益、戴乃迭译）

京剧是我国国粹，角色有生、旦、净、末、丑之分。"老旦"是旦角的一种，代表着老年妇女，音译、直译都很难让译语读者理解。以上这些文化信息若要加注，又要牵出生、净、末、丑其他四类角色的解释，较为冗长，因此，如果翻译目的不是为了严格的文化交流，为行文流畅，就可以尽量简练地意译出其基本内容。

4. 加注法

为了能尽量译出源语承载的文化信息,考虑到译文读者的接受情况,为方便读者理解,一些历史/神话人名或地名、历史事件、典故、成语等的翻译,可适当运用解释性文字作为补偿手段,用加注的方式添加文化背景知识。加注法与音译、直译、意译结合,可以采取文内注释或文外注释的形式。

(1) 文内注释(Notation within text)

如果解释性文字非常简短,加入到文内不影响译文的流畅性,可以进行文内注释,相当于音译/直译加意译兼用的翻译方法。

【例12】

原来女娲氏炼石补天之时,于大荒山无稽崖练成高经十二丈,方经二十四丈顽石三万六千五百零一块。

(曹雪芹:《红楼梦》,第1回)

译文:

Long ago, when the goddess Nü-wa was repairing the sky, she melted down a great quantity of rock and, on the Incredible Crags of the Great Fable Mountains, moulded the amalgam into thirty-six thousand, five hundred and one large building blocks, each measuring seventy-two feet by a hundred and forty-four feet square.

(杨宪益、戴乃迭译)

"女娲"是中国神话中的人物,"女娲补天"的故事在中国几乎人尽皆知,而音译成 Nü-wa 对英美读者来说仅仅是个人名,因此译者在译文内补足了 goddess 这一信息。

(2) 文外注释(Notation outside text)

文内注释要求增补的解释性文字非常简短,如果解释性文字较长,加入到文内影响到译文的流畅性,就会使译文拖沓冗长,此时就要使用文外注释。

【例13】

He peered sideways up and gave a long low whistle of call, then paused a while in rapt attention, his even white teeth glistening here and there with gold points. Chrysostomos. Two strong shrill whistles answered through the calm.

(Joyce: *Ulysses*, Chapter I)

译文:

他侧目向上斜视,打了个悠长而低沉的口哨,向下招呼,然后停下来凝神静听,露出了一口闪烁着金色斑点的白牙。克里索斯托莫斯。两声尖利的口哨声穿破宁静回答了他。

(注释:莫里根满口金牙并一直模仿神父的举止和口吻使斯蒂芬想到了基督教早期的创始人之一圣约翰·克里索斯托莫斯[345—407]。克里索斯托莫斯曾任君士坦丁堡大主教,善于传教和解经,故有"金口约翰"之称,其名 Chrysostomos 在希腊语中即"金口"的意思。)

(刘若愚译)

中国读者对基督教创始人之一 Chrysostomos 其人其事很陌生,译者通过注释增补基督教背景知识,帮助读者了解为何斯蒂芬会看到莫里根"闪烁着金色斑点的白牙"而想到 Chrysostomos。要解释清楚这一典故,所需篇幅较长,为使语义连贯又能传递英美文化方面的信息,译者采用了文外注释的方法。

【例 14】
贾珍一时来回:"在神前拈了戏,头一本《白蛇记》。"贾母问:"《白蛇记》是什么故事?"贾珍道:"是汉高祖斩蛇方起首的故事。第二本是《满床笏》。"贾母笑道:"这倒是第二本上?也罢了,神佛要这样,也只得罢了。"又问第三本,贾珍道:"第三本是《南柯梦》。"贾母听了便不言语。

(曹雪芹:《红楼梦》,第 29 回)

译文:

Presently Jia Zhen came to report that lots had been drawn before the shrine for the operas, and the first was to be *The White Serpent*. "What's the story?" asked the old lady. "It's about the First Emperor of Han who killed a serpent, then founded the dynasty. The second is *Every Son a High Minister*." "So that's the second?" The Lady Dowager nodded, smiling. "Well, if this is the wish of the gods, what must be must be. And what's the third?" "*The Dream of the Southern Tributary State*." At this she made no comment.

(Note: *Every Son a High Minister*: A story about Guo Ziyi of the Tang Dynasty. *The Dream of the Southern Tributary State*: Based on a Tang story in which a scholar had a dream of great wealth and splendour; then he woke up and found it was just an empty dream.)

(杨宪益、戴乃迭译)

《白蛇记》、《满床笏》、《南柯梦》同为戏曲剧名,《白蛇记》借贾珍之口说出其意义,而《满床笏》与《南柯梦》译者意译后分别作了文后注解。在理解了曲目的同时对于戏曲中蕴含的文化内涵也有所了解,可以获取与源语读者同样的文化信息。

此外,一种文化负载成分的翻译并非只局限于一种译法,看下例:

【例 15】
案上设着武则天当日镜室中设的宝镜,一边摆着赵飞燕立着舞的金盘,……

(曹雪芹:《红楼梦》,第 5 回)

译文:

On a table stood an antique mirror that had once graced the tiring-room of the lascivious empress Wu Ze-tian. Besides it stood the golden platter on which Flying Swallow once danced for the emperor's delight.

(David Hawkes 译)

对武则天这个在中国家喻户晓的历史人物,音译其名的同时添加了"the lascivious

empress",弥补了英美读者中国历史知识的空缺;而"飞燕"是因其身轻若燕而得名,具有别号的性质,因此译者进行了直译,后面添加"for the emperor's delight"点明这是一位皇帝近前的舞女。前面译例中的"女娲"进行音译和文内加注,而"大荒山无稽崖"却进行了直译,其后的中国特有长度单位"丈"则意译成英语的"feet"。总体说来,文化负载成分的翻译大多以传递原文文化信息、促进文化交流为主要着眼点,译者要看到翻译目的、读者的语言与文化具有的制约作用,根据具体情况来采用恰当的翻译方法。

2.4 作者风格与小说翻译

小说风格除在整体上与其他类型的文本有差别外,一个作家的小说与其他作家的小说之间通常在风格上也有所不同。小说家有各自的生活和教育背景,遣词造句有自己的特点。无论海明威的简洁朴素还是乔伊斯的艰深晦涩,鲁迅的辛辣还是钱钟书的幽默,文学作品的艺术风格说到底应该是作家思想气质、文化修养、语言功底和生活积累等基本素质的体现。很多作品仅看语言就能知道是出自哪位作家之手,就是因为作家往往在创作过程中逐步形成了自己独特的语言风格。这些在作品中表现思想内容的艺术手段的总的特点与内容是有机结合的。取消一部作品的风格,也就取消了这部作品。翻译一部文学作品,只忠实地译出其内容,而不顾其风格,不能算是真正的翻译,因为所产生的译本没有把原著真实的面貌传达给读者。换言之,小说翻译必须关住原作风格的传递。

哈代常使用长句和短句交叉的语言风格在《苔丝》中体现得非常充分,作家常用省略句达到一定的艺术效果,如对苔丝美貌的描述:

【例 16】
One day she was pink and flawless; another pale and tragical. When she was pink she was feeling less than when pale; her more perfect beauty accorded with her less elevated mood; her more intense mood with her less perfect beauty.

(Thomas Hardy: *Tess of the d'UrbervilleShylock*, Chapter 3)

译文 1:
有的时候,她就娇妍、完美;另有的时候,她就灰白、凄楚。她脸上娇妍的时候,就不像她脸上灰白的时候那样多愁善感;她更完美的美丽,和她较为轻松的心情相互协调;她更紧张的心情,和她比较稍差的美丽互相融洽。

(张谷若译)

译文 2:
今天光艳照人,白玉无瑕;明天却又沮丧苍白,满面苍凉。鲜艳,往往是出于无忧;而苍白,却总是由于多愁。胸中没了思虑她便美丽无瑕,一旦烦愁涌起,便又容色憔悴。

(孙法里译)

原文中省略句的出现使叙事节奏简洁轻快,给句子增加了韵律感。译文 1 把句式补充完整,但有损原文的简洁轻快,译文 2 保留了平行结构和省略句式,与原文风格相当,高下立显。

中国作家钱钟书的作品贯通中西、古今互见、幽默讽刺,其语言风格带有明显的个人色彩。Jeanne Kelly 和毛国权两位译者对各种诙谐幽默的比喻、夸张都进行了再现,原文风格得到了很好的保留,往往能让读者忍俊不禁。如:

【例 17】

沈太太生得怪样,打扮得妖气。她眼睛下两个黑袋,像圆壳行军热水瓶,想是储蓄着多情的热泪,嘴唇涂的浓胭脂给唾沫进了嘴,把黯黄崎岖的牙齿染道红痕,血淋淋的像侦探小说里谋杀案的线索,说话常有'Tien!''Ola, la!'那些法文慨叹,把自己身躯扭摆出媚态柔姿。她身体动一下,那气味又添了新的一阵。鸿渐恨不能告诉她,话用嘴说就够了,小心别把身体一扭两段。

(钱钟书:《围城》,第 3 章)

译文:

Mrs. Shen was rather odd-looking and very heavily made up; the two black bags under her eyes were like round canteen bottles, filled probably with hot, passionate tears; the thick lipstick had been washed into her mouth and colored the yellowish, rough ridges of her teeth red, making her teeth look like hemorrhoids dripping with blood or the clues to a bloody murder in a detective yarn. Her speech was full of French exclamations such as "Tien!" and "O la la!" as she squirmed her body around into various seductive poses. Each twist of the body let off a fresh wave of the smell. Hung-chien wished he could have told her that it was quite enough if she'd just talk with her mouth and be careful not two twist herself in two.

(Jeanne Kelly & Mao Guoquan 译)

文学翻译理论家们认为,凡真正的翻译文学,贵不在译作是文学味很浓的文学作品,而在于译作是贴近原著风格的文学作品。换言之,译者翻译一部作品,最高目标是要忠实地再现原著的艺术风格,原作是雅是俗、是简是繁、是直白是含蓄、是严肃是幽默,译者都应该细细体会,并尽量在译文中体现出来。

3 文化语境与小说翻译策略

任何翻译活动都是在一定的社会文化语境下进行的,以源于社会文化生活、反映社会文化生活的小说为对象的小说翻译更是如此。

3.1 文本选择

纵观中国近现代翻译文学史,我们便可以清楚地看到社会现实、社会思潮等社会文化因素对文本选择的影响。无论是小说翻译的主题选择还是输入来源都离不开一定社会文化因素的推动和制约。

我国 20 世纪初的小说翻译以社会、教育和爱情主题的文本数量较多,社会小说的翻译数量居于首位(姜秋霞,2009:45)。这主要是因为,自晚清时期的"小说界革命"到"五四"运动后出现的新文化运动,都意图通过文学革命改造社会、重铸民魂。小说易于在人民大众中普及,因此一些学者就想利用西方小说中的先进思想开化中国国民。他们翻译了大量反映普通人生活的社会小说,尤其是许多批判现实主义作家的作品,意在引起深受帝国主义侵略和压迫的中国人民对国家命运和自身处境的关注。例如,林纾翻译《巴黎茶花女遗事》(今译《茶花女》)、《黑奴吁天录》(今译《汤姆叔叔的小屋》)等众多小说作品的初衷即是为向国人灌输爱国主义思想;周氏兄弟合译《域外小说集》也是他们"改良思想,补助文明"的翻译思想的产物,希望通过翻译媒介寻求与中国社会模式相同或相似的东西,以引起读者的共鸣,激发人民的革命热情。

从输入来源上看,"20 世纪以前,渴望变革的中国社会将注意的焦点放在英、法等欧洲先进的资本主义国家"(姜秋霞,2009:54)。20 世纪初,俄国文学在世界文学中的强势地位已逐步确立起来,十月革命的胜利又让中国知识分子看到了近代中国摆脱受压迫受奴役状况的希望。他们对俄苏的革命道路和模式产生了认同感,进而大量译介俄苏文学,如鲁迅翻译的《毁灭》、《死魂灵》等。

3.2 翻译策略的选择

小说翻译的目的可以是教化的、研究的、传道的、审美的、消遣的及维持生计的,不同的翻译目的会影响翻译的策略选择。译者对文本的处理有两种策略——归化和异化。归化指让作者靠近读者、遵从译入语文化的翻译策略,译者往往使用直译法使译文尽量忠实于原文;异化则是让读者靠近作者、遵从原语文化的翻译策略,为保证译文能被译语读者接受,译者往往根据译语文化需求对文本进行改动。

译者采用归化还是异化策略,是受社会文化语境制约的。例如,林纾等人的翻译倾向于"归化",因为当时的"西风"浸入仍属初始阶段,当时的中国读者对西方文化仍需要适应,引进西方的新思想新知识要以符合译语读者的接受心理为重。因此,林纾翻译西方小说时,在文体上借助于文言小说以及笔记的传统文体和当时流行的报章杂志文体,语言上使用文言文,在内容上则对与当时的价值观及审美观相符的部分进行增补、相悖的进行删减,例如,为使译文符合中国传统的"孝、悌、忠、信"等道德伦理观念和大众的欣赏习惯,林纾把很多原文的标题改写成带有"记、传、传奇、录、史"等典型的中国古代小说叙事标题,在译《块肉余生述》(今译《大卫·科波菲尔》)时大段删减原文的人物性格或衣着描写等使情节更加紧凑,以便符合中国小说以情节连贯的故事性见长的写作传统。而鲁迅更倾向于异化策略主要是因为中国读者文化心理开放程度深,强调译文应有"异国情调"且意图"不但在输入新的内容,也在输入新的表现手法",既借鉴西方先进思想,又丰富早期白话文的表达方式。

3.3 翻译变体的选择

任何作品总要考虑到效果,考虑到读者。翻译活动的成果——译作,最终是要呈现给译语读者阅读的,因此翻译活动还要关注接受者,即译语读者的反应。当译者的翻译目的由忠实于原文转向博取译语读者的接受、以为译语读者服务为中心时,翻译活动自然就把译语读者列入翻译体系之中,译者会根据不同读者的需要对译文作出相应调整。

除通常所见的对原文信息总体上不增不减的翻译,即尽量完整保留原作的内容与形式的"全译"之外,"据特定条件下特定读者的特殊需求",译者可以"采用增、减、并、缩、改等变通手段摄取原作有关内容的活动"(黄忠廉,2000:96)。进行"变译",即选用不同的翻译变体。变译大致包括摘译、编译、译述、缩译、综述、述评、评议、改译、阐译、译写、参译等11种方式(黄忠廉,2000:6)。如阿瑟·韦利英译《西游记》时,考虑到本国读者的读书方式与口味以及艺术效果,将书名改译为《猴王》,并省略了许多情节,略去了穿插在故事叙述中的许多诗词,译本删减至原书篇幅的三分之一,是摘译和缩译的结合;儿童读本摘译和缩译的程度更高,而且还对其中的一些部分进行阐译和改写,以吸引小读者或者便于他们理解。

3.4 文化语境与译本多样性

翻译应该充分体现作者的创作意图,但是,不论译者在译文中反映得多么全面细致,由于译者世界观不同、生活经历不同、文化素养不同、所处时代、鉴赏水平不同,他们会对同一作品的思想内容作出不同理解,从不同的角度去感受,产生不同的联想与共鸣,从而会产生不同的译本。

用艺术的语言叙事的语言特点和艺术美,进而在翻译过程中有意识地再现,译本是译给整个文化演进过程中某一个阶段的读者的,而每一代读者在审美趣味、接受水平、直觉能力上都有所不同。这样,一个译本可能在一代人中受欢迎,而到了另一代人中则受到冷落。再者,由于语言随社会的发展而发展,随社会的变化而变化,同一词语在不同的历史时期往往具有不尽相同的含义。例如,林纾翻译的《英孝子火山报仇录》、《孝女耐儿传》所用文体是他心目中认为比较通俗、较随便、富于弹性的文言文,符合当时人们的语言接受心理,但随着时代的变迁,许多林纾翻译小说由于白话文的普及、人们思想的变迁而被重译。

4 本章结语

文学创作是用艺术的语言叙事、画物、言情,使读者受到感染或教诲。由于英汉语之间的差异较大,在词汇、句法和语篇、语用、风格特色等方面存在诸多不同之处,因此英汉互译不可能达到信息的完全对等,信息的损失或增加、变形时常发生。尽管如此,译者应该在对原文充分理解,对信息的量和表达形式准确把握的基础上,尽自己所能从各个层面进行适当的选择和调整,寻找最佳翻译方法,最大限度地贴近原作,首先是语义信息,然后是文化信息和作者风格信息,并且兼顾信息量和信息传递方式这两个方面。译者不仅要考虑篇章和词句的需求,还要关注社会、民族、时代的需要去再现原作的中心思想、风格、创作意图和艺术手法等。

第十一章 诗歌翻译

中国古代将不合乐的称为诗,合乐的称为歌,现代一般统称为诗歌。诗歌是人类文学作品的最早形式,也是最完美和最简洁的语言表达方式。早在文字产生之前,诗歌就一直伴随着人类的精神生活和物质生活,成为人们不可或缺的伙伴。诗歌是心灵的窗口,透过它可以看到人类的情感和智慧;诗歌是艺术的结晶,可以使读者感受到语言的魅力;诗歌又是历史文化的明鉴,能够折射出人类社会发展的轨迹。它运用精练的、富有节奏和韵律的语言,以强烈的感情和丰富的想象,高度集中地反映社会生活,传达人们对于世界的感受和经验。

1 诗歌概述

诗歌起源于上古的社会生活,来源于古代人们的劳动号子和民歌,因人们生活中的劳动生产、两性相恋、原始宗教等而产生的一种有韵律、富有感情色彩的语言形式。中英诗歌均有悠久的历史和丰富的遗产。

英语诗歌起源于盎格鲁—撒克逊时期(410—1066),当时著名的诗歌是 Beowolf(《贝奥武夫》),用头韵体写成,共有 3000 多行,讲述一位日耳曼部落传奇英雄的故事。英语诗的发展分为古代→中世纪→文艺复兴时期→启蒙运动时期→浪漫派→现代派→后现代派几个阶段。

我国现存最早的诗歌集《诗经》(又称《诗三百》)共收入自西周初年至春秋中叶大约五百多年的诗歌一共三百余篇(11BC—6BC)。汉语诗歌发展脉络清晰,从《诗经》开始,汉语诗歌历经《楚辞》→汉赋→汉乐府诗→建安诗歌→魏晋南北朝民歌→唐诗→宋词→元曲→明清诗歌→现代诗的发展历程。

1.1 诗歌的分类

在漫长的发展历程中,英汉语诗歌均产生出不同的风格和流派,产生了多种多样的表现形式。根据不同的原则和标准,诗歌可以划分为不同的种类。

(1)以作品内容的表达方式划分,有叙事诗和抒情诗两类。

有比较完整的故事情节和人物形象的称为叙事诗,包括史诗、叙事诗、诗体小说等;抒情诗则主要通过抒发诗人的思想感情来反映社会生活,根据作者对客观事物的态度和诗歌内容,抒情诗又可分为情歌、颂歌、哀歌、田园诗、山水诗、讽刺诗、史诗等,不要求描述完整的故事情节和人物形象。

(2)以作品语言的音韵格律和结构形式划分,有格律诗、自由诗和散文诗。

格律诗是对诗的行数、诗句的字数(或音节)、声调音韵、词语对仗、句式排列等有严格要求的诗歌,如我国古代诗歌中的律诗、绝句和词、曲、英语的十四行诗;自由诗不受格律限制,无固定格式,注重自然的、内在的节奏,押大致相近的韵或不押韵,字数、行数、句式、音调都比较自由,语言比较通俗,是近代发展起来的一种诗体,如惠特曼的《草叶集》;散文诗兼有散文和诗的特点,通常篇幅短小而富有哲理,有诗的意境和激情,像散文一样不分行、不押韵,注重自然的节奏感和音乐美,如鲁迅的《野草》。

1.2 诗歌的文体特点

诗歌是高度集中地概括反映社会生活的一种文学体裁,它饱含着作者的思想感情与丰富的想象,在表达人类创作精神、情感和愿望的同时,以它特殊的语言方式和深邃的思想内涵来感染读者、启发读者。诗歌是最古老也是最具有文学特质的文学样式,是纯文学,是语言艺术的最高表现形式。无论是汉语诗歌还是英语诗歌,都能以最少的字数表达出其内心的强烈情感,都强调其语言的工整性,都重视音调的韵味。概括来说,除散文诗外,诗歌语句一般分行排列,注重结构形式的美,同时语言最精练,音韵最和谐,表达手法最精致,情感最丰富。

(1) 简练的语言

诗歌的语言可以说是高度凝练,诗歌是最讲究语言简洁性的文学体裁。诗人的选词造句通常干净利落、言简意赅。中国古典诗歌是语言简洁的代表,历代诗歌作者都非常注意炼字、炼句,如柳宗元的《江雪》仅用"千山鸟飞绝,万径人踪灭"十个字即点明了环境的清冷,勾勒出空旷寥廓、幽寂冷漠的背景。

(2) 和谐的韵律

和谐的音韵、鲜明的节奏、整齐的诗行是诗歌的基本特征。中西方诗人在写诗的时候既要用语言所包涵的意义去影响读者的感知又要调动语言的声音去打动读者的心灵,使诗歌产生音乐的效果。诗歌节奏是音组和停顿的有规律的安排,汉英诗歌都讲究节奏和谐、抑扬顿挫。此外,汉英诗歌都讲求诗句的尾韵,尾韵使诗歌朗朗上口,给诗歌增添音乐性,让读者获得美的感受。凡优秀的诗篇,多是通过音节的均匀、语言的对称达到节奏的和谐,通过押韵或平仄的交替使用,使音调和谐动听。

(3) 丰富的修辞

诗歌的表现手法很多,而且历代以来不断地发展创造,运用也灵活多变。我国最早流行而至今仍常使用的传统表现手法有"赋、比、兴":"赋"是直接陈述事物的表现手法;"比"是用比喻的方法描绘事物,表达思想感情;"兴"是托物起兴,即借某一事物开头来引起正题要描述的事物和表现思想感情的写法。此外,比喻、比拟、夸张、借代、设问、反问、反语、双关、叠字、谐音等修辞手法也在英汉诗歌中经常出现。这些表现手法常常综合运用,互相补充,使诗歌语言极富形象性。

(4) 充沛的情感

情感是一切文学创作的原动力,诗歌也不例外。情感不仅作为一种动力存在于诗歌的孕育和创造过程,它还是诗歌的直接表现对象。可以说,诗歌的主要任务就是抒情,因此诗歌语言总是极具抒情性,诗歌即是将情感纳入一种优美节奏中的语言艺术。抑扬顿挫的音韵节奏、灵活多样的修辞形式都是为了更贴切地表达作者深刻的思想和强烈的感情。触景生情,感物言志,沉思冥想等切入手法把他们的爱恨情仇,或悲壮或欣喜、或激昂或沉稳、或咏唱或哀婉的心境,表达得淋漓尽致。

诗歌是语言的艺术,对作品的语言表现力做具体的、深入的挖掘有助于准确把握作品的立意和思想感情倾向,进入作品深层次的意境。

2 英汉诗歌比较与翻译研究

诗歌是语言的精华,更是文化的结晶。诗歌的写作不可能独立于民族的语言、地理、历史、风俗等文化语境而存在,因此诗歌烙上了深深的语言和文化印记,特定的语言和文化成就了诗歌独特的韵律节奏和审美情趣。中西方在语言、文化方面存在着明显差异,熟悉这些差异对于英诗汉译或者汉诗英译都非常重要。

2.1 英汉诗歌比较

中国的诗歌可以分成古体诗、近体诗和现代诗。古体诗和近体诗主要以唐朝为分界线:唐以前的《诗经》、楚辞、乐府诗和唐代的古风等通常称为古体诗,较为自由,没有严格的对仗要求,也没有押韵的限制;唐以后的诗歌称为近体诗,对字数、句数、平仄、押韵等都有严格的规定的诗歌,也称为韵律诗。汉语现代诗歌源于西方现代诗体,"实际上是上世纪初中国现代文学草创时期的舶来品,各方面都承袭了西方现代诗歌的特点"(邵志洪,2005:395),大多是不受格律限制的自由诗,因此中西诗歌的差异主要在韵律诗方面。整体上看,"同英语相比,汉语古典诗歌在音韵、节奏、押韵、语言形式等方面有着更为严格的要求"(同上)。

(1) 形式

汉语格律诗非常讲究形式,我们熟知的五律、七律和五绝、七绝、词等可谓是篇有定句,句有定字,字有定声,韵有定位,极其严格。有些英语古体诗也讲求韵律,如莎士比亚十四行诗通常由三个四行诗体组成,韵脚交替进行,最后是押韵的双行诗体,整个韵脚是ababcdcdefefgg。总体来说,虽然英语格律诗也有严格的押韵和节律要求,但并未像汉语格律诗那样对每个字/音节都"斤斤计较"。

(2) 韵律

英语诗歌的押韵在形式上要比古汉语格律诗复杂。但是,汉语韵律诗必须押韵,押在诗行末尾,行与行之间通常形成 aaba 式韵法(rhyming scheme),还常常借助双声、叠韵、叠音来求得音调的和谐;英语诗歌行末押韵或不押韵,押韵方式也更加多样,行与行之间两行转韵(aabb)、隔行押韵(abab)、隔行交互押韵(abab)和交错押韵(abba)等韵法,还有根据单词内音素重复的部位不同而形成的头韵(alliteration)、谐元韵(assonance)、尾韵(rhyme)等。

节奏方面,汉语诗歌突出平仄关系,而英语诗歌则表现其音节关系:一个汉字就是一个音节,因此汉语诗歌以平仄音调来形成节奏,以"顿"为停顿或声音延长,通常四言二顿("二/二")、五言三顿("二/二/一"或"二/一/二")、七言四顿("二/二/二/一"或"二/二/一/二");而英语语音轻重差别明显,诗歌遂以轻重音的有规律的交替形成节奏,基本节奏形式为轻重音构成的音步(foot),各行都要讲究一定的音步数量,常见的音步形式有抑扬格(Iambus)、扬抑格(trochee)、抑抑扬格(anapaest)、扬抑抑格(dactyl)、抑扬抑格(amphibrach)和扬抑扬格(dactyl)六种。

（3）抒情方式

概括来说，英语诗歌通常开门见山、直抒胸臆，而汉语诗歌则以含蓄为美。"西诗多直率，汉诗多含蓄；西诗多铺陈，汉诗多简约；西诗文辞朴实，汉诗辞藻华丽；西诗擅长条分缕析，汉诗崇尚韵外之致"（张传彪，2005：73）。"'言不尽意''成文'以'尽意'，这是汉语古典诗学形式理论的基本思路之一"（刘方喜，2005：83）。基于这种思路，汉语诗词倾向寓情于景、赋情于物，推崇恬淡含蓄、似言未言的独特表达方式，留给读者充分的想象空间。汉语诗歌重在含蓄，其特点是意在言外，常常不是直接叙述，而是曲曲折折地倾诉，言此而意他，或引而不发，或欲说还休，让读者去体味。

2.2 英汉诗歌翻译研究

中西诗歌虽历史悠久，但中西诗歌交流却是 19 世纪才开始。钱钟书认为最早翻译成汉语的英语诗歌或许是美国浪漫主义诗人朗费罗（Henry Wadsworth Longfellow，1807—1882）的代表诗作"A Psalm of life"（《人生颂》）（钱钟书，2002：134），具体翻译年代不详；另一更加普遍的观点认为，英国桂冠诗人弥尔顿（John Milton，1608—1674）的一首十四行诗"On His Blindness"（《自咏目盲》）译介到中国的时间更早，这首诗的汉语译文发表在 1854 年香港传教士主办的中文期刊《遐尔贯珍》第九号上（孙翀，2009）。今存我国翻译史上第一本外国诗歌翻译集是 1914 年日本东京三秀舍印梁绮庄出版的苏曼殊译《拜伦诗选》。

汉语诗歌翻译成英语也是在近代才发展起来。19 世纪下半叶英国汉学家理雅各（James Legge，1814—1897）把《诗经》译本收入他 1861—1872 年陆续出版的五卷本 The Chinese Classics（《中国经典》），当作儒家经典来译介（马祖毅、任荣珍，2003：232）；美国翻译中国古典诗词的第一部结集应是诗人庞德（Ezra Pound，1885—1972）1915 年出版的 Cathay（《华夏集》），共收入中国古诗 14 首，其中《诗经》一首，其余为屈原、李白、王维的诗（马祖毅、任荣珍，2003：348）。

近年来，诗歌翻译实践及理论研究日渐蓬勃，一些学者开始对诗歌翻译史进行系统梳理，如海岸 2007 年出版的《中西诗歌翻译百年论集》。此外，译界讨论最多的诗歌翻译问题主要集中在可译不可译、形式与内容的关系以及由此衍生出来的诗歌翻译批评等几个方面。

（1）可译不可译的问题

中西审美习惯不同、民族心理有别、哲学传统迥异以及语言文字方面的差异等种种因素使得中西诗歌差别显著，具有各自的特点。"含蓄"、"简约"和"崇尚韵外之致"的诗风和汉语本身具有的诗性特质推动了汉诗"象"、"意"关联的诗性表达，而"直率"、"朴实"和"擅长条分缕析"的英诗却强调形与意关联的明晰化。诗歌的文学特性、中西语言及文化殊隔良多及译者自身差异等因素的存在使诗歌翻译深处迷雾，"诗歌是否可译"，尤其是汉语诗歌"意象"的可译不可译译界曾争论不休。

美国著名诗人弗罗斯特给诗下定义为"诗就是在翻译中丧失掉的东西（Poetry is what gets lost in translation）"。这说明译诗之艰难，许多学者援引这句话论证诗歌的不可译。今天，纯粹的不可译论者已经不多见，而且争论归争论，诗歌翻译实践虽然踯躅而行，却是无可辩驳地前进着。其实，说"诗不可译"，主要是指诗味难译，诗的音韵美难译，并不是说诗歌不能翻译。

宏观上相似的生活环境和大体相近的生活经历、情感体验以及对于某些相同事物的相同感受,反映到储存社会生活经验、反映文化的特征的语言上,就产生了东西方对于某些意象有着相同或相似的描写。这些语言间的共性虽然有限,却使翻译成为可能。再者,诗有不同的诗:有的明白畅晓,有的艰深晦涩,有的韵律严整,有的不受律法所限,情感丰富而又风格多样,诗与诗之间也存在翻译难度的差别。事实证明,翻译本身是可能的,诗歌翻译也是可能的,只是翻译的难度更大,对译者的要求更高。

(2) 形式与内容之争

诗歌无论在形式还是内容上都颇为复杂,许多译者受诸多条件的限制往往保留其形式,却不能反映其内容,或是体现了其内容,却又失去其形式,"形"、"神"难以兼得,因此,在内容与形式之间,诗歌译者常常左右为难,形成了许多论题:① 诗歌直译论;② 诗歌意译论;③ 诗歌翻译格律论;④ 诗歌翻译散体论;⑤ 形似论;⑥ 神似论;⑦ 诗歌翻译音美、形美、意美论;⑧ 诗歌翻译多元标准论等。这些论题有不同程度的重合之处,况且,无论主张直译者还是主张意译者,都允许变通(辜正坤,2007)。

我们必须清楚的是,诗歌翻译是艺术欣赏与艺术创造的统一。虽然在结构完全不同的英汉两种语言之间转换,单纯追求语言形式的移植或许会歪曲诗歌整体神韵,但是"以诗译诗"几乎已成为翻译界的共识。像翁显良译《天净沙·秋思》时采用的散文释义法,以散文体翻译格律诗歌毕竟在情感表达方式方面差别甚大,改变了诗歌的建行模式,诗也就不成为诗了。通常情况下,诗歌首先要翻译成诗歌的形式,只是"诗歌翻译的'再创造'空间大于其他文学形式"(李谧,2004:84)。

2.3 诗歌翻译对译者的要求

诗难译,要将其译得传神则更难,"因形害义"和"因义弃形"都不是理想的翻译结果。一方面要尽量保留诗之所以为诗的形式特征,另一方面又要再造原诗的艺术意境,这就要求译者充分发挥翻译主体的创造性进行艺术再创造。诗歌翻译无疑成了整个文学翻译领域中最具挑战性的领域,对译者的要求也是最苛刻的。进入诗歌翻译及诗歌批评领域之前,译者必须具有:

(1) 扎实的双语基本功,对词汇间的细微差别具有极高的敏感度;
(2) 古诗的翻译更是一项艰巨的工作,要求译者具有深厚的双语古文功底;
(3) 高超的双语、双文化转换能力,熟知中英社会、文化、历史、地理等相关知识;
(4) 深厚的文学素养,对中英诗歌传统及诗歌知识的全面把握;
(5) 对诗歌翻译理论及策略的准确理解与熟练掌握等。

3 英诗汉译实例评析

英语诗歌创作有着1500多年的历史,从古至今产生了很多名篇佳作。这些作品不仅是英语民族的优秀文化遗产,也是全世界文学宝库中的灿烂明珠,是全人类共有的精神财富。中西语言隶属不同的语系,在长期发展和演变的进程中,逐步在文法、句式、修辞、格律、表现手法等诸方面形成了自己的特点。英语诗歌有其自身的诸多文体特点,如诗体的形式美、格律和音韵表现出的音乐美以及传情达意的语意美等。相比之下,英语诗歌"直率"、"朴实"和"擅长条分缕析"的明晰化表情达意手段不难移植,而英诗汉译的难处和重点,主要体现在韵律和风格形式的再现上。

3.1 韵律美的再现

英国诗歌之中保存下来的最古老的长诗《贝奥武夫》已经具有比较严格的韵律形式:每行一般有四个重音,其中三个重音押头韵。英语诗歌无论古典的还是现代的,都有自己的特殊韵律形式。英语诗歌的韵律形式主要通过重音、节奏、押韵等表现出来。下例即是美国浪漫主义诗人朗费罗的代表诗作"A Psalm of life":

【例1】

A Psalm of Life

Tell me not in mournful numbers,
Life is but an empty dream!
For the soul is dead that slumbers,
And things are not what they seem.

Life is real! Life is earnest!
And the grave is not its goal;
Dust thou art, to dust returnest,
Was not spoken of the soul.

Not enjoyment, and not sorrow,
Is our destined end or way;
But to act, that each tomorrow
Find us farther than today.

Art is long, and Time is fleeting,
And our hearts, though stout and brave,
Still, like muffled drums, are beating
Funeral marches to the grave.

In the world's broad field of battle,
In the bivouac of Life,
Be not like dumb, driven cattle!
Be a hero in the strife!

Thrust no future, howe'er pleasant!
Let the dead Past bury its dead!
Act-act in the living Present!
Heart within, and God o'er head!

Lives of great men all remind us
We can make our lives sublime,
And, departing, leave behind us
Footprints on the sands of time;

Footprints that perhaps another,
Sailing o'er life's solemn main,
A forlorn and shipwrecked brother,
Seeing, shall take heart again.

Let us, then, be up and doing,
With a heart for any face;
Still achieving, still pursuing,
Learn to labour and to wait.

(Henry Wadsworth Longfellow)

朗费罗以浓郁的激情咏唱出对人生的热爱和对美好生活的追求，激昂奋进的词句使这首诗在发表之初就引起轰动。不仅如此，诗人娴熟完美的表现技巧也受到许多读者青睐。整首诗语言简朴流畅，句式上反复咏叹，内容上层层深入，节奏整齐明快，音韵和谐自然。每个四行组都采用了abab隔行押韵的韵式，每节一三诗行由四个抑扬格音步组成，二四行由三个半音步，最后半个为一个重读音节，整齐之中稍有变化，严谨而不失活泼，读起来起伏有致、铿锵有力，与诗歌内容相得益彰。

生之赞歌

莫唱伤感调：
梦幻是人生！
须知灵魂睡，
所见本非真。

生命真而诚！
坟墓非止境；
生死皆垢尘，
岂是指灵魂。

逸乐与忧伤，
均非天行健；
君子当自强，
翌日胜今天。

光阴似白驹，
学艺垂千秋；
雄心如闷鼓，

葬曲伴荒丘。

世界一战场,
人生一军营;
莫效牛马走,
奋发斯英雄!

莫信未来好,
过去任埋葬。
努力有生时,
心诚祈上苍!

伟人洵不朽,
我亦能自强,
鸿爪留身后,
遗泽印时光。

或有飘零人,
苦海中浮沉,
睹我足印时,
衷心又振奋。

众生齐奋发,
顺逆不介意;
勤勉而戒躁,
探索又进取。

——苏仲翔译

译文 2:

人生颂

别用悲切的诗句对我唱:
"人生只是虚幻的梦一场!"
因为昏睡的灵魂已死亡,
而事物不是看来那模样。

人生多真切!它决非虚度!
一抔黄土哪里会是它归宿;
"你来自泥尘,得重归泥尘。"
这话所指的并不是灵魂。

我们命定的终点和道路,
既不是享乐,也不是悲苦;
行动吧;要让每一个明天

发现我们比今天走得远。

学艺费光阴,时日去匆忙,
任我们的心勇敢又坚强,
却依然像那蒙住的鼙鼓——
敲打着哀乐走向那坟墓。

在风云世界的广阔战场,
在人生征途的野宿营帐,
别像默默的牛羊任驱赶!
要争做英雄,能征惯战!

将来再美好也别空指望!
让死的过去把死的埋葬!
干!在活生生的现在就干!
胸中是赤心,头顶有上苍!

伟人的生平向我们指出:
我们能使此生超群脱俗——
一朝逝去,时间的沙滩上
将留下我们的脚印行行。

在庄严的生活之海航行,
也许有兄弟会遭遇不幸,
会因为航船沉没而绝望——
但见那脚印,又变得顽强。

就让我们挺起身,行动起来,
凭对付任何命运的胸怀;
不断去收获,不断去追求,
永远在学着苦干和等候。

(黄杲炘译)

译文 1 的每个诗行的音节数和顿数整齐划一,与原诗相比谨严有余而活泼不足;况且,为此而牺牲掉了行与行间的押韵,几乎未形成任何形式的韵式更是一大缺憾。译文 2 采用 aabb 韵式,朗朗上口,韵脚以声音响亮的 an、ang、ai 等为主,铿锵之声可与原诗媲美;同时,每个诗行十个音节,分为四顿,每顿二至三个音节,整齐严谨中略有变化。两个译文相比较,译文 2 在韵律美的再现方面优势尽显,可谓与原诗异曲同工。

3.2 形式美的再现

诗歌的形式是诗歌赖以生成的不可或缺的一部分,简短、整齐的诗行在视觉上就区别于其他任何文体。人类在创作诗歌之初,就自发地赋予诗歌某种形式,诗歌内部的诗行排列与缩进、诗行的行数与长短、参差错落、句式等往往都有特殊安排。诗歌的形式并非只是一种花瓶式的摆设,而是因其极大地有助于诗情诗理的表达而构成诗歌内容的一部分,具有表意功能。在某些情况下,有些诗专门以形式美取胜,诗歌的形式还与诗人的风格密切相关,若离开了诗人匠心独创的形式美,诗歌本身的美也就流失殆尽了。独特的诗歌形式是诗人匠心独运的结果,并有助于诗歌情韵义理的表达。请看下例:

【例2】

A Christmas Tree

Star

If you are

A love compassionate

You will walk with us this year

We face a glacial distance, who are here

Huddld

At your feet.

(William Burford)

诗歌的形式美是诗美的重要组成部分,诗歌的意义也体现在其形式之中,像上例这类拟形诗的内容与形式更是有机的统一体:诗歌名为"圣诞树",诗行也排列成一棵圣诞树的形状——一颗闪耀的"星"高悬至顶,伞形的"树冠",诗人还特意把"Huddled"一词略去了一个"e"以描画出细细的"树干"。

译文:

圣诞树

星啊

你那爱中

如果含有怜悯

来年就和我们同行。

这里我们面对冰河距离

拥挤

在你脚底。

(黄杲炘译)

翻译以拟形诗为代表的这些以形式取胜的诗歌时,就必须把形式因素考虑在内,甚至把原诗的形式美作为翻译重点。译文可以说是用汉语把原诗的"圣诞树"进行了整体复制——"星"高高在上、"树冠"的形状、加粗"拥挤"二字造成的坚实"树干"之感(译者还说用"拥挤"一词的繁体效果也是一样的,甚至更为自然)均保留了原诗的面貌,堪称佳译。

4 汉诗英译实例评析

我国是一个诗歌的王国,诗赋词曲都曾在文学史上独领风骚,大放异彩。中国古典诗歌用词不多,却运用比喻性意象或典故等修辞形式,蕴含着大量信息和深刻含义,理解起来还需费一番工夫,更不用说翻译起来该有多难。况且,汉语本身就是"一种心灵的语言、诗的语言",具有饱含"诗意和韵味"的"艺术气质"。这种重感悟、体验的诗性特质更是开放了多向度的解释空间,与西方语言重逻辑、精确性强的特点大相径庭,这极大地提高了汉语诗词英译的难度。要译好一首中国古诗,不仅要把握简洁工整的韵律特征及形式,传递音象美和形式美,还要捕捉其含蓄隽永的精神实质,传递意象美。

4.1 音象美的再现

音象美即诗歌的听觉形象,主要包括诗的韵式和节奏。诗歌是一种极具音象美的艺术形式,译诗必须追求音象美,才能保持原诗的风格和情趣。相对于英诗音韵的灵活多变,汉诗音韵则显得严谨工整。中国古典诗歌音节固定,平仄交替,又有顿的划分,再借助行与行之间的押韵形成优美而强烈的节奏,赋予诗歌独特的韵律美。李白、杜甫、王维、辛弃疾等古代大家的诗词,字字珠玑,其音韵、节奏美不胜收。下例是杜甫《登高》的前两句:

【例 3】

登高

风急天高猿啸哀,渚清沙白鸟飞回[huái]。
无边落木萧萧下,不尽长江滚滚来。

(杜甫)

译文 1:

Gazing Away from on High

Under the lofty sky, the wind sweeps and gibbons sadly cry;
Over the white sand ford in clear water, birds hover and fly.
In the boundless forest, falling leaves swirl and twirl around;
On the endless Yangtze, rolling waves crash and splash along.

(丁衡祁 译)

译文 2:

On Climbing the Heights of the Ninth Day of the Ninth Moon

The wind keen, the sky high, the gibbons wailing.
Blue islands, white sand, and sea birds flying,
And everywhere the leaves falling,
Then the immeasurable great river in torrent.

(Nee Wen-yei 译)

译文 3:

On the Height

The wind so swift, the sky so steep, sad gibbons cry;
Water so clear and sand so white, backwards birds fly.
The boundless forest sheds its leaves shower by shower;
The endless river rolls its waves hour after hour.

（许渊冲译）

杜甫这首诗被誉为"古今七律第一首"，是中国古典诗歌中音象美的扛鼎之作。整首诗对仗工整，音韵和谐，是七言四顿的"二/二/二/一"式，平仄相间，句间呈 aaba 式押韵，颔联又含有双声叠韵，体现着诗人"沉郁顿挫"的诗歌风格。译文 1 通过选择某些音节重复词汇，如 swirl and twirl 和 crash and splash 等，也保留了一部分韵律方面的听觉意象；译文 2 无论是句与句之间还是句子内部皆未能成韵，音象美几乎消磨殆尽，甚是遗憾；译文 3 韵律优美，头韵、尾韵、行内停顿交替使用，极富审美效果，"shower by shower, hour after hour"的运用既铿锵悦耳又和谐对称，听觉美与视觉美并蓄，而且意义并无损失，是译者追求"音美、意美、形美"的典型译例。

4.2 简洁美的再现

中国古典诗歌非常讲究炼字。古诗语言意味深远，但语言极度简练，往往几十个字即包含着极其丰富的内涵。柳宗元是著名的唐宋散文八大家之一，他的诗多作于贬谪之后，抒发抑郁不平的感慨，诗风简练淡雅，语言峻洁流畅，感情诚挚，韵味含蓄隽永。下例是柳宗元的那首传世五绝——《江雪》：

【例 4】

江雪

千山鸟飞绝，
万径人踪灭。
孤舟蓑笠翁，
独钓寒江雪。

（柳宗元）

译文 1：

Fishing in snow

From hill to hill no bird in flight;
From path to path no man in sight.
A lonely fisherman afloat
Is fishing in lonely boat.

（许渊冲译）

译文 2：

River Snow

From a thousand hills, bird flights have vanished;
On ten thousand paths, human traces wiped out;
Lone boat, an old man in straw cape and hat,
Fishing alone in the cold river snow.

（Burton Watson 译）

诗人通过景物的渲染刻画出一幅清冷肃静的雪景,以突显"蓑笠翁"不畏严寒的身姿,折射出诗人自身的孤独之情和傲岸之态。原诗仅 20 个字就创造出了夸张和对偶等修辞手法、押 ue 韵的工整韵式以及幽远的意境,诗人利用高超的艺术技艺创造出令人折服的简洁之美。两译文在篇幅长度上的差别一目了然:译文 1 非常简短,共 25 个单词而能兼顾韵律美(aabb 韵式)、形式美(前两句的形式对称)和意境美(孤独、傲岸),可以说是三美并蓄;译文 2 不仅韵律美受损(尾韵呈 abbc 形式),形式上也不如译文 1 工整,而且 33 个单词排列起来篇幅较长,缺少简洁之美。

4.3 意境美的再现

意境美是中国古典诗歌的突出特点之一,译者历来都非常重视汉语古典诗歌英译时的意境美再现。意境是诗人通过对具体形象的渲染和刻画创造出的一个情景交融的艺术空间,包括生活形象的客观反映和作家情感理想的主观创造这两个方面。意境创造的基本单位是现实的物质载体——意象。中国古典诗歌中的意象看似互相独立,但却貌离实合,而超乎意象之外的却是一个完整的意境,给人一种悠长的回味和不尽的遐思。中国古典诗歌的最独特之处即在于意象叠加的意合特征,这也是中国古典诗歌翻译的重点。历代诗人都重视意境美的营造,马致远的《天净沙·秋思》是其中的佼佼者:

【例 5】

天净沙·秋思

枯藤老树昏鸦,
小桥流水人家,
古道西风瘦马。
夕阳西下,
断肠人在天涯。

(马致远)

译文 1:

Tune to "Sand-pure Sky"

Autumn Thoughts
Dry vine, old tree, crows at dusk,
Low bridge, stream running, cottages,
Ancient road, west wind, lean nag,
The sun westering,
And one with breaking heart at the world's edge.

(Wayne Schlepp 译)

译文 2:

Tune:Tian Jing Sha

Withering vines hanging on old branches,
Returning crows croaking at dusk.

A few houses hidden past a narrow bridge,
And below the bridge quiet creek running.
Down a worn path, in the west wind,
A lean horse comes plodding.
The sun dips down in the west,
And the lovesick traveler is still at the end of the world.

(丁祖馨、Burton Raffel 译)

　　这首曲凝练简洁,28 个字包含了 12 个独立意象——"枯藤"、"老树"、"昏鸦"、"小桥"、"流水"、"人家"、"古道"、"西风"、"瘦马"、"夕阳"、"断肠人"、"天涯",前 9 个意象连续铺排烘托最后一句"夕阳西下,断肠人在天涯",表达了漂泊天涯的游子的思乡之情。每个意象都透射出诗人心中"情"尽染眼中"景",勾画出一幅凄美的秋景图,是情与景的自然统一。"枯藤"、"老树"、"昏鸦"、"小桥"、"流水"、"西风"、"瘦马"、"夕阳"、"天涯"这 9 个意象在两译文中的措辞及所选修饰语基本相似,而原曲中的"人家",两译文分别用"cottage"和"houses",相较而言,"cottage"透射着原文的宁静祥和,也正是这种温暖和谐的氛围勾起旅人对家的思念和渴望。"古道"在译文 2 中译为"worn path"太具体。决定全曲情感内涵的"断肠人"译文 1 译为"one with breaking heart",处理得非常地道,是英语中表示伤心的惯用语,比较贴切且保留原文中"断肠"的模糊性,仍旧留有想象的余地;译文 2 译为"the lovesick traveler",把"断肠"的原因归结到"lovesick"上,整首诗的意味发生了彻底的变化,一首千古传唱的思乡曲成了溢满相思的爱情咏叹,把满眼的悲伤归结到一个"情"字上,情感内涵在传译过程中出现了接近于"质"的变化,如果这样说言过其实,至少这么处理也太具体明晰。原曲的 12 个景物意象在两译文中全部得以保留,只是修饰语的差异赋予译诗不同的情感内涵,有"思念家乡"和"思念恋人"之别,景相似而情不同。整体看来,译文 1 更加忠实地传译了深邃、朦胧和动感的意境美。

5　本章结语

　　尽管诗歌翻译难度大,但一个成功和负责的译者是不会仅尽力译出诗歌的准确意思,放弃对诗歌形式的诠释。所谓的"因形害义"和"因义弃形"都不是理想的翻译结果。将诗歌的形式和思想原汁原味地翻译过来,让读者能确实地感受、领略到异国诗歌的美感,是每位诗歌译者追求的目标。译诗的最高标准应是内容和形式的高度统一,意美、形美、音美浑然一体,注意原诗格律、形象,特别是意境、气氛的再现,力求保留原诗的意义、情感及神韵风格,是每位诗歌译者孜孜以求的目标。要在充分理解原诗的情况下,根据原诗的具体特点进行翻译,原诗是以形式取胜的翻译时就以形式为重,原诗以韵律特征突出的翻译时就要尽量再现其韵律美,原诗以意境美为生命力的必要时可以牺牲一定的语言形式。

第十二章　戏剧翻译

戏剧与小说、诗歌、散文常被认为是文学的四种基本体裁,是世界文学非常重要的组成部分。戏剧是一门古老的舞台艺术,早在人类文字形成之前就已初具雏形,到现代发展成为内涵丰富的文学艺术形式,运用文学、导演、表演、音乐、美术等艺术手段来塑造人物和反映社会生活。

1　戏剧文体特征

戏剧,指以语言、动作、舞蹈、音乐、木偶等形式达到叙事目的的舞台表演艺术的总称。

我国戏剧理论家王国维在《宋元戏曲考》(1912)中写道:"必合言语、动作、歌唱、以演故事,而后戏剧之意义始全"(夏写时,1982:1),这句话常被看作我国最早的"戏剧"定义。广义上的戏剧内容丰富多样,按照艺术形式和表现手法不同可以划分为话剧、歌剧、舞剧、诗剧、歌舞剧、相声剧等;按照内容的性质,可以分为悲剧、喜剧和正剧;还可以按照题材所涉及的方面,分为现代剧、历史剧、神话剧、儿童剧、科学幻想剧等,或者按照主题、情节分为情节剧、社会问题剧、心理剧等;或者按照篇幅规模分为多幕(或多场)剧和独幕剧、大戏和小戏等。本书仅探讨狭义上的"戏剧"翻译,即话剧的翻译。话剧是从"20世纪初传到中国,综合文学、表演、导演、美术、音乐、舞蹈等多种文艺成分,而以说话(对白、独白、旁白)为主要表现手段"(中国大百科全书出版社编辑部 1998:174)。

戏剧常常以剧本(或称脚本)形式出现,可单独作为文学作品供读者阅读、欣赏,体现出鲜明的艺术性和较强的可读性以吸引读者,具有其他文学作品的共性。与小说文本相似,剧本也是借助于场景和情节等艺术现实来塑造人物的叙事性文本,又融合了散文和诗歌文本的特点,感情色彩充沛、语言简练、富于韵律。同时,剧本又有其自身的特点。绝大多数戏剧创作与翻译的目的是将剧本搬上舞台进行表演,所以必须符合舞台艺术的要求。这使剧本具有二重性:文学性和表演性。剧本的基本特征可以概括为:

(1) 内涵丰富

戏剧的发展与社会的发展息息相关,人类生产的发展、都市社会的形成和科学技术的进步都推动了戏剧的发展,同时它们也为话剧创作提供了丰富的素材。从内容上看,剧本几乎涉及文化的所有领域,内涵丰富细致,人物形象通常是特定时期某个社会阶层的典型。剧作家同样意图通过典型形象的刻画表达深刻的思想内涵,是基于生活积淀的艺术表现形式。

(2) 空间和时间上的高度集中

剧本要搬上舞台,面对观众。无论多宏大的历史场景都要浓缩到剧场小小的舞台上,无论多长的时间跨度都要浓缩为短短几个小时的剧场演出。同样,丰富的社会文化及思想内涵必须高度浓缩,空间和时间上则尽可能集中,要用最有限的空间和最短的时间传递尽可能多的信息。

(3) 矛盾冲突要尖锐集中

戏剧的最大特点就是通过尖锐而集中的矛盾冲突来刻画人物形象,揭示人物性格,并通过人物的命运表达自己的观点和思想。剧作家需要通过尖锐的矛盾冲突表达自己的观点和思想;另一方面,剧本必须有集中尖锐的矛盾冲突,才能吸引观众,给他们留下深刻的印象或者引发他们的思考。

(4) 语言个性化、简练、口语化、动作性和音律感

为了保证剧本能够成功上演,剧作家在创作时除了体现个人风格以外,还需要遵守戏剧语言的一些普遍特征。戏剧语言主要以对白(dialogue)、独白(soliloquy)或旁白(aside)的形式出现;对白是人物间的对话,是戏剧刻画人物性格、表现人物关系、叙述故事情节的主要手段,是剧本的主要组成部分;独白是人物的自言自语,是戏剧角色背着台上其他剧中人向观众表达自己的思想和情感的一种舞台艺术手段;旁白是剧作家对故事情节、人物心理加以叙述、抒情或议论的另一种舞台艺术手段,借以传递更丰富的信息,表达特定的情感,启发观众思考,通常在剧本中所占比例极少,许多剧本甚至没有旁白。

在剧本(话剧)创作过程中,它往往凭借对白来叙述故事的情节,刻画人物的性格,烘托故事的气氛,因此剧本语言有其他艺术种类不具备的特点。受演出时间和空间的限制,人物头一次开口时就凸现出他的性格来,做到开口就响,且讲究简练,最忌讳沉闷、啰唆;观众社会层次多样,舞台表演的即时性和无注性等特点要求戏剧语言尽量口语化,让观众一听即懂,还能暗示行为意图、心情、心理状态、感情、感觉等,具有显著的动作性。作为一种视听艺术,好的戏剧语言读起来应当富有节奏感、朗朗上口。概括来说,戏剧人物的语言具有个性化、口语化、简洁化、韵律性和动作性的特点。

2 剧本翻译特点

东西方戏剧都有着悠久的历史和古老的传统,然而东西方戏剧交流在一个多世纪之前才真正开始,戏剧翻译研究更是如西方著名的翻译理论家苏珊·巴斯奈特所说:"... an apt one for this most problematic and neglected area of translation studies research"(是一未经解决但却受到忽视的翻译研究领域)(Bassnett & Lefevere, 2001:90)。戏剧翻译的主体是剧本,即为戏剧表演所创作的脚本。

某一体裁翻译的特点与标准总是与这种体裁的特点密切相关。戏剧作品与其他文学体裁有诸多不同之处,因此,戏剧本身的特点——文学性与表演性的双重特征就决定了剧本翻译与其他文学体裁的翻译也有所区别。莱斯曾根据原文本功能将文本分为"信息型"(informative)、"表达型"(expressive)及"感染型"(appellative)三种文本(Munday 2001:74)。信息型文本旨在向读者描述事物或事件、提供信息;表达型文本注重文学性,主要目的在于传达文本的美学效果;感染型文本目的在于引起读者产生某种特定的反应。各种文本类型之间并非界限分明,文本功能也并非非此即彼,大多数文本会同时兼有以上三种功能,但在程度上存在差别。就原剧本与译本功能来看,一个剧本在本国上演给本族语观众看,丝毫没有语言与文化的障碍,因此"信息"功能并不突出,主要的文本功能是"表达"与"感染",重在

给观众以美的享受,引起他们的共鸣。但是剧本一经翻译,搬上国外舞台展现在非本族语观众的面前,首先应增强"信息"功能,让译入语观众理解故事的内容,同时保证"表达"与"感染"功能的传达,通过翻译剧本的表演使观众产生共鸣,获得美的享受。具体说来,剧本的翻译特点主要有以下三点:

(1) 剧本翻译目的的特殊性

一般来说,剧本翻译以把译入语剧本搬上译入语国家的舞台为目的。当然剧本也有为阅读而创作的,这叫做案头剧,把外国剧本作为文学作品介绍给本国读者是剧本翻译的目的之一,但纯粹为阅读而翻译毕竟是少数,恐怕也是有违作者初衷的。这种特殊的翻译目的要求译本要像原剧本一样注意舞台演出的即时性,舞台演出不可能像其他文学作品那样增加帮助理解的注释,只能尽量以简洁易懂的语言去再现原剧本的各种信息。

(2) 剧本翻译受众的特殊性

创作剧本主要是为舞台演出,因此剧本翻译的服务对象是剧院观众,而诗歌、散文和小说翻译的服务对象是读者。影视翻译的服务对象同样是观众,与戏剧翻译有很多共性,但影视翻译受到的制约比戏剧翻译更大,受演员说话时口形、停顿、示意动作、说话时间的制约,配音要尽量配合原有画面。

(3) 剧本翻译要求的特殊性

剧本同时兼顾文学性和表演性,这种二重性对剧本翻译提出了特殊的要求。应该说,把剧本作为文学作品来翻译和将其搬上舞台所要考虑的因素不尽相同。前者所涉及的因素要比后者单纯得多。有人说以舞台演出为目的的剧本翻译是用笔译的方式寻求口译的效果,以说明剧本翻译的特殊要求,这样说的确很有道理。因为,戏剧是一种视听艺术,演员的话转瞬即逝,在剧本翻译过程中,译者除了忠实于原剧本的内容以外,还应特别注意戏剧翻译的特殊规律:既要保证剧本的文学性,让对白个性化又富于音律感,讲究音韵和谐、抑扬顿挫;又要兼顾译本的即时接受性,要简洁清晰,让观众一听就懂;同时还要关注译本的可表演性,使译文的对白富于动作性,便于演员在台上表演。

3 剧本翻译策略

翻译目的论认为,"整个翻译行为的目的是决定翻译过程的首要原则"(Nord 2001:27),强调翻译目的与翻译过程、翻译策略之间的密切相连,译文的"充分性"是评价标准,只要译文能达到目的语交际环境中的目的,就是好的翻译。剧本的"感染"功能与"表达"功能,主要通过剧作家为人物设计的语言——对白和独白来实现。对白和独白是戏剧人物性情的符号和标志,具有个性化、口语化、韵律感、简洁化、动作性的特点。剧本的文学性要求人物语言个性化,以塑造独特、丰满的舞台艺术形象,实现"表达"功能与"操作"功能;剧本对可表演性的要求则对应着剧本语言的口语化、简洁化、动作性并富于韵律感,使剧本更易于搬上舞台,台词朗朗上口,富节奏感,适合演员在剧场演出,便于观众的即时接受,以实现剧本的"感染"功能与"表达"功能。剧本翻译就是以剧本的这些人物语言特征为重点进行的翻译活动。

3.1 个性化的人物语言

人物语言的个性化指人物语言应符合人物特有的身份、经历、性格、爱好、文化修养及其在特定环境和特定人际关系中所表现出来的思想感情等性格特征。小说作者在刻画人物时可以通过叙述和描写来为人物对话补充信息,但剧本作者却必须要隐身,除简单的旁白外,不能有任何插话的地方。戏剧作品主要通过演员的动作、台词等方式把故事情节、人物性格及人物关系表现出来,所以剧本语言必须个性化。

一部戏往往涉及数个甚至几十个人物,优秀的剧作家善于运用与该人物的性格相吻合的各种"性格语言",通过人物语言就能塑造出个性突出的人物形象,可谓"千人千面,千面千腔"。在翻译剧本时译者也应充分考虑人物的性格特征,抓住人物语言的突出特点,设计出富有个性、生动活泼的人物台词,努力使译文也能像原文那样做到"闻其声,知其人"。

威廉·莎士比亚(William Shakespeare,1564—1616)这位戏剧大师笔下的每一个人物都颇具艺术特色。《无事生非》(*Much Ado about Nothing*)是莎士比亚的四大喜剧之一,写于剧作家的创作成熟期,内容热闹欢乐,富有哲思,意图探寻男女关系中的自我意识以及真诚与尊重。剧中的男女主角——Benedick 和 Beatrice 是一对欢喜冤家:他们两人均伶牙俐齿、自恃较高,总是一见面就互相抨击,后来在朋友设计下坠入爱河,两人都改变很多,能够勇于承认自身的缺点并诚恳大方地接受批评,最终成为一对互相信任、互相尊重的情侣。下例是两人在故事开始一次会面时的场景,Messina(梅辛那)总督 Leonato 带着女儿 Hero 和侄女 Beatrice 等人迎接凯旋的 Don Pedro 亲王和他的部下 Claudio、Benedick:

【例 1】

Don Pedro	Good Signior Leonato, you are come to meet your trouble: the fashion of the world is to avoid cost, and you encounter it.
Leonato	Never came trouble to my house in the likeness of your grace: for trouble being gone, comfort should remain; but when you depart from me, sorrow abides, and happiness takes his leave.
Don Pedro	You embrace your charge too willingly. — I think this is your daughter.
Leonato	Her mother hath many times told me so.
Benedick	Were you in doubt, sir, that you askt her?
Leonato	Signior Benedick, no; for then were you a child.
Don Pedro	You have it full, Benedick: we may guess by this what you are, being a man. — Truly, the lady fathers herself. — Be happy, lady; for you are like an honourable father.
Benedick	If Signior Leonato be her father, she would not have his head on her shoulders for all Messina, as like him as she is.
Beatrice	I wonder that you will still be talking, Signior Benedick: nobody marks you.
Benedick	What, my dear Lady Disdain! Are you yet living?
Beatrice	Is it possible disdain should die while she hath such meet food to feed it as Signior Benedick? Courtesy itself must convert to disdain, if you come in her presence.
Benedick	Then is courtesy a turncoat. — But it is certain I am loved of all ladies, only you excepted: and I would I could find it in my heart that I had not

	a hard heart; for, truly, I love none.
Beatrice	A dear happiness to women: they would else have been troubled with a pernicious suitor. I thank God and my could blood, I am of your humour for that: I had rather hear my dog bark at a crow than a man swear he loves me.
Benedick	God keep your ladyship still in that mind! So some gentleman or other shall escape a predestinate scratcht face.
Beatrice	Scratching could not make it worse, an 'twere such a face as yours were.
Benedick	Well, you are a rare parrot-teacher.
Beatrice	A bird of my tongue is better than a beast of yours.
Benedick	I would my horse had the speed of your tongue, and so good a continuer. But keep your way, i' God's name; I have done.
Beatrice	You always end with a jade's trick: I know you of old.

(William Shakespeare: *Much Ado about Nothing*, Act I, Scene I)

Leonato 与 Don Pedro 热情寒暄，两人提到 Hero 时，她却未发一言，即使 Benedick 和 Leonato 以她为话题开玩笑，莎士比亚也未给 Hero 安排任何台词，但一位端庄文雅的淑女形象却建立了起来；Beatrice 为 Hero 打抱不平，出言反击 Benedick，两人皆语言犀利而富于修辞，各自使用了许多比喻性的语言讽刺挖苦对方。这些信息在朱生豪先生的译文当中都准确再现：

译文：

彼 特 罗	里昂那托大人，您是来迎接麻烦来了；一般人都只想避免耗费，您却偏偏自己愿意多事。
里昂那托	多蒙殿下枉驾，已经是莫大的荣幸，怎么说是麻烦呢？麻烦去了，可以使人如释重负；可是当您离开我的时候，我只觉得怅怅然若有所失。
彼 特 罗	您真是太喜欢自讨麻烦啦。这位便是令爱吧？
里昂那托	她的母亲好几次对我说她是我的女儿。
裴尼狄克	大人，您在问她的时候，是不是心里有点疑惑？
里昂那托	不，裴尼狄克先生，因为那时候您还是个孩子哩。
彼 特 罗	裴尼狄克，你也被人家挖苦了；我们可以猜想到你现在长大了，是个怎么样的人。真的，这位小姐很像她的父亲，小姐，您真幸福。因为您是像这样一位高贵的父亲。
裴尼狄克	要是里昂那托大人果然是她的父亲，就是把梅辛那全城的财富给她，她也不愿意生得像他那样一副容貌的。
琵特丽丝	裴尼狄克先生，你怎么还在那儿讲话呀？没有人听着您哩。
裴尼狄克	哎哟，我的傲慢的小姐！您还活着吗？
琵特丽丝	世上有裴尼狄克先生那样的人，傲慢是不会死去的；顶有礼貌的人，只要一看见您，也就会傲慢起来。

裴尼狄克	那么礼貌也是一个反复无常的小人了。可是除了您以外,无论哪个女人都爱我,这一点是毫无疑问的;我希望我的心肠不是那么硬,因为说句老实话,我实在一个也不爱她们。
琵特丽丝	那真是女人们好大的运气。因为否则她们就要给一个讨厌的求婚者麻烦死了。我感谢上帝和我自己冷酷的心,我在这一点上完全跟您一致;与其叫我听一个男人发誓说他爱我,我宁愿听我的狗向着一只乌鸦叫。
裴尼狄克	上帝保佑您小姐永远抱着这样的心理吧!这样某一位先生就可以逃过他命中注定的抓破脸皮的厄运了。
琵特丽丝	要是像您这样一副尊容,抓破了也不会使它变得比原来更难看的。
裴尼狄克	好,您真是一位好鹦鹉教师。
琵特丽丝	像我一样会说话的鸟儿,比起像尊驾一样的畜生来,总要好得多啦。
裴尼狄克	我希望我的马儿能够跑得像您说起话来一样快,也像您的舌头一样不知道疲倦。请您尽管说下去吧,我可要恕不奉陪啦。
琵特丽丝	您在说不过人家的时候,总是像一匹不听话的马儿一样,往岔路里溜了过去,我知道您的老脾气。

(朱生豪译)

译文通过精心选词和保留原作的修辞手段等向译入语观众准确传递出各出场人物的身份及性格信息,还原人物的艺术形象,给观众以美的享受。总督以"多蒙殿下枉驾,已经是莫大的荣幸"这样正式的措辞欢迎亲王,亲王以"令爱"称呼总督的女儿,非常符合各自的贵族身份和当时的情形。Benedick 出场的两句话——"您在问她(是否是您的女儿)的时候,是不是心里有点疑惑?"以及"要是里昂那托大人果然是她的父亲,就是把梅辛那全城的财富给她,她也不愿意生得像他那样一副容貌的"就显示出他尖牙利嘴、好挖苦人这一性格特点,后面与 Beatrice 的对白中暗示 Beatrice 是个会"抓破脸皮"的泼妇,说她是话多的"鹦鹉教师"、舌头跑得像"马儿"一样快且"不知道疲倦"等更是加深了人们对他的印象;"可是除了您以外,无论哪个女人都爱我,这一点是毫无疑问的"又显示了他的傲慢自负,人物形象更加丰满清晰。Beatrice 声称,"与其叫我听一个男人发誓说他爱我,我宁愿听我的狗向着一只乌鸦叫"以及"要是像您这样一副尊容,抓破了也不会使它变得比原来更难看的"来讽刺 Benedick 的自负,又说 Benedick 是"畜生","像一匹不听话的马儿一样,往岔路里溜了过去"可谓针锋相对。欢迎仪式最终演变成了 Benedick 和 Beatrice 的一场唇枪舌战,两人的性格特点表露无遗。朱生豪的译文不仅保留了原文的修辞性语言,对人物台词中蕴含的言外之意和语气都拿捏得非常到位,人物形象信息传递非常准确。

中国戏剧家老舍的代表剧作《茶馆》以 19 世纪末、20 世纪初的北京为背景展开,场景是一个叫"裕泰"的大茶馆,剧中几十个人物来自社会各个阶层。这部话剧在戏剧界是有口皆碑的"一句台词勾画一个人物"的优秀剧作,很多次要人物虽出场不多,但仍旧形象鲜明,这都归功于老舍先生为每个人物量身定做的一套个性化语言。人贩子刘麻子把人家女儿卖给太监当老婆却自觉是帮人解困,他的儿子小刘麻子只出现两次就让人印象深刻:他和他爸爸一样,是个不知廉耻、没有道德的无赖,甚至把他爸爸被当街砍头的事拿来炫耀:

【例2】

小刘麻子　小丁宝,你来啦?
丁　　宝　有你的话,谁敢不来呀!
小刘麻子　王掌柜,看我给你找来的小宝贝怎么样?人材、岁数、打扮、经验,样样出色!
王 利 发　就怕我用不起吧?
小刘麻子　没的事!她不要工钱!是吧,小丁宝?
王 利 发　不要工钱?
小刘麻子　老头儿,你都甭管,全听我的,我跟小丁宝有我们一套办法!是吧,小丁宝?
丁　　宝　要是没你那一套办法,怎会缺德呢!
小刘麻子　缺德?你算说对了!当初,我爸爸就是由这儿绑出去的;不信,你问王掌柜。是吧,王掌柜?
王 利 发　我亲眼得见!
小刘麻子　你看,小丁宝,我不乱吹吧?绑出去,就在马路中间,咔嚓一刀!是吧,老掌柜?
王 利 发　听得真真的!
小刘麻子　我不说假话吧?小丁宝,可是,我爸爸到底差点事。一辈子混的并不怎样。轮到我自己出头露面了,我必得干得特别出色。……

(老舍:《茶馆》,第三幕)

小刘麻子声称"必得干得特别出色"竟是要联合沈处长霸占王利发的茶馆,与他爸爸如出一辙的无赖嘴脸。中国表演艺术家和戏剧翻译家英若诚先生结合自己的演出经验,把人物语言翻译得非常传神:

译文:

Pock-mark Liu Jr　　Hi, Little Ding Bao, so you're here!
Ding Bao　　On your orders! How could I refuse?
Pock-mark Liu Jr　　Manager Wang, what do you think of this little baby I've found for you? Looks, age, fashion, experience — she's a real smasher!
Wang Lifa　　Only snag is I can't afford her.
Pock-mark Liu Jr　　No problem. She doesn't want any wages. Rig, baby?
Wang Lifa　　No wages?
Pock-mark Liu Jr　　Leave it all to me, old man. Me and baby have got a way all worked out. Haven't we, baby?
Ding Bao　　Sure, without your crooked ways, where would you be?
Pock-mark Liu Jr　　Crooked? You've said it! So was my old man. He was nabbed rig here! If you don't believe me, ask Manager Wang. Wasn't that so?
Wang Lifa　　Saw it with my own eyes.
Pock-mark Liu Jr　　See, baby, I'm not just shooting my mouth off about something that never happened. He was dragged rig to the middle of the street, and with one big whack of the sword, his nob was chopped off. Rig, old

	manager?
Wang Lifa	I heard that whack.
Pock-mark Liu Jr	So I wasn't just telling you stories, baby, was I? But my old man didn't have what it takes. All that work, but he still didn't get far. Now it's my turn, and I'm going to hit the big time! ...

（英若诚译）

英若诚先生的词汇选择、语气拿捏都非常准确，人物形象的再现非常成功。小刘麻子夸奖自己擅做主张为茶馆找来的女招待丁宝说"— she's a real smasher!"，破折号和感叹号使人物语气显得洋洋自得。其父因做缺德事被砍头，不以为耻，反以为荣，还说"he still didn't get far"，自己要更"出色"，把当时混乱的时局看成是能有渔利的"the big time"，投机钻营的流氓无赖形象清晰可见。简短的场景中小刘麻子多次使用"rig, baby?""Haven't we, baby?""Wasn't that so?""Rig, old manager?"等与丁宝和王利发攀谈，看对方并不买账时，小刘麻子却自说自话，刻画出一个陶醉于自己、以不光彩手段经营茶馆这一"宏伟"计划的人物形象。

3.2 口语化的语言

个性化的人物语言使剧本具有了文学魅力，作为舞台视听艺术，人物台词还应该尽量口语化（文学性较强的诗剧除外）。总体来说，剧本语言比其他文学体裁的语言更倾向于口语化，这首先是因为舞台表演的即时性——舞台演出不可重复。一方面，作为舞台表演艺术，流畅、自然、简洁、口语化的台词更便于演员的舞台演出；另一方面，观众对于台词的理解需要一次完成，非常依赖口语的直接效果。其次是因为剧本故事的真实性要求：虽然因为教育背景或性格特征等因素，剧作家会为某些人物设计较为书面化的语言，但剧本中的大多数人物来自日常生活，剧本创作要想给观众以更多的真实感、引起他们的共鸣，必然要让人物的语言更加通俗化、口语化，更加贴近观众的生活现实。口语化随即成为戏剧语言最突出的特征之一。

为保留译本的可表演性，翻译时译者要使译本对白通俗易懂，更口语化。苏珊·巴斯内特（Susan Bassnett）提出的"动态表演性"原则（Principle of Performability）即是要在剧本翻译中保留原剧本的这一特征——翻译戏剧要考虑到剧本潜在的"动态表演性"，要求语言翻译须像原剧本一样容易上口，演员读来顺畅，观众听来不觉吃力。

阿瑟·米勒（Arthur Miller，1915—2005）是美国半个世纪以来最杰出的剧作家。他的作品针砭时弊、直言不讳，其中《推销员之死》是其最有影响的代表作。剧本以20世纪40年代的美国纽约中下层社会为背景，围绕着推销员Willy的生活展开。下面是Willy与妻子Linda的对话，通俗易懂、句式简洁，是典型的口语化对白：

【例3】

Willy How can he find himself on a farm? Is that a life? A farmhand? In the beginning, when he was young, I thought, well, a young man, it's good for him to tramp around, take a lot of different jobs. But it's more than ten years

now and he has yet to make thirty-five dollars a week!
Linda　He's finding himself, Willy.
Willy　Not finding yourself at the age of thirty-four is a disgrace!
Linda　Shh!
Willy　The trouble is he's lazy, god dammit!
Linda　<u>Willy, please!</u>
Willy　Biff is a lazy bum!
Linda　They're sleeping. Get something to eat. Go on down.
Willy　Why did he come home? <u>I would like to know what brought him home.</u>
Linda　I don't know. I think he's still lost, Willy. I think he's very lost.
Willy　Biff Loman is lost. In the greatest country in the world a young man with such—personal attractiveness, gets lost. <u>And such a hard worker.</u> There's one thing about Biff—he's not lazy.
Linda　<u>Never.</u>

(Arthur Miller: Death of Salesman, Act I)

Willy 与 Linda 的对白词汇和句式都偏向口语体——词汇简单、句式简短而且随意，带有插入成分，如"I thought"、"well"，还有几个省略句，如：

A farmhand?　　　　　(Is being a farmland a life?)
Willy, please.　　　　(Willy, please stop saying these words!)
And such a hard worker. (And he is such a hard worker.)
Never.　　　　　　　　(He is never lazy.)

译文1：

威利　他在牧场里怎能找到胜任的工作？这算生活吗？当个牧场工人？开头，他年轻的时候，<u>我寻思着，好吧，一个年轻人，到处流浪，各种各样的活都干，对他有好处。</u>可是如今过了十多年，他还是一星期挣三十五块钱！
林达　他在找自己胜任的工作，威利。
威利　三十四岁还找不到自己胜任的工作，真丢人。
林达　嘘！
威利　毛病就在于他懒惰，<u>他妈的</u>！
林达　威利，请别说了！
威利　比夫是个懒汉！
林达　他们在睡觉。找点东西吃吃。下去吧。
威利　他回来干什么？<u>我倒想知道是什么风把他吹到家里来的。</u>
林达　我不知道。我想他还在彷徨，威利。我想他很彷徨。
威利　比夫·洛曼在彷徨。在这个世界上最大的国家里，一个如此颠倒众生的年轻人居然会彷徨。而且是这么一个卖力干活的人。<u>比夫这个人不管怎么说吧，倒是不懒。</u>

林达　一点不懒。

(陈良廷译)

译文2：

威利　他呆在农场上怎么发挥长处？那也叫生活吗？当个农业工人？<u>一开头，他还年轻，我想嘛，年轻人，到处闯炼闯炼也好，各种行当都试试。</u>可是已经过去不止十年了，他一个礼拜还挣不了三十五块钱！

林达　<u>他还没得发挥呢</u>，威利。

威利　三十四岁了还不得发挥，就是丢人！

林达　嘘——！

威利　毛病就在他懒，<u>他妈的</u>！

林达　威利，我求求你！

威利　比夫就是个懒汉！

林达　他们都睡了，你去吃点东西，下楼去吧。

威利　他回家来干什么？<u>我想知道他为什么回家来。</u>

林达　我不知道。我看他还是没找到方向，威利。我看他很空虚。

威利　比夫·洛曼居然找不到方向。在全世界最伟大的国家，这样一个年轻人——<u>这么招人喜欢的年轻人</u>，居然找不到方向。而且他多么勤奋。别的不说，比夫有一条特点——他不懒。

林达　从来不懒。

(英若诚译)

两译文都使用了较为口语化的译入语（下划线部分）翻译原作，保留了原作词汇和句式方面的简短和随意，尤其是"我寻思着/我想嘛"、"他妈的"、"是什么风把他吹到家里来的"、"不管怎么说吧"和"这么招人喜欢的年轻人"等这样生活化、口语化的语言拉近了剧中人物与中国观众之间的距离。但也有一些词汇相对较为正式，尤其是译文1中的"胜任"、"懒惰"、"彷徨"、"如此颠倒众生"等词汇偏向书面化，整体来说正式程度高于译文2。整个《推销员之死》剧本中，英若诚采用了北京方言翻译原剧本40年代纽约中下层社会的语言，包括某些土语，使中国观众通过戏剧了解了那个时代和背景下美国下层劳动人民的生活状态，取得了很好的艺术效果和接受效果，使得译本的各项功能得以实现。

再看一段汉语剧作英译的例子。老舍先生著《茶馆》中的裕泰大茶馆是当时许多人喝茶、聊天、聚会的地方，人物语言非常贴近日常生活，从前面的例子就可以看出这一点，我们看下面的片断：

【例4】

报　童　掌柜的，长辛店大战的新闻，<u>来一张瞧瞧</u>？

王利发　<u>有不打仗的新闻没有</u>？

报　童　也许有，您自己找！

王利发　<u>走！不瞧</u>！

报　童　掌柜的，你不瞧也照样打仗！（对唐铁嘴）先生，您照顾照顾？

唐铁嘴　我不像他,(指王利发)我最关心国事!(拿了一张报,没给钱即走)

[报童追唐铁嘴下。]

王利发　(自言自语)长辛店!长辛店!离这里不远啦!(喊)三爷,三爷!你倒是抓早儿买点菜去呀,待一会儿准关城门,就什么也买不到啦!嘿!(听后面没人应声,含怒往后跑)

[常四爷提着一串腌萝卜,两只鸡,走进来。]

常四爷　王掌柜!

王利发　谁?吆,四爷!您干什么哪?

常四爷　我卖菜呢!自食其力,不含糊!今儿个城外头乱哄哄,买不到菜;东抓西抓,抓到这么两只鸡,几斤老腌萝卜;听说你明天开张,也许用得着,特意给你送来了!

王利发　我谢谢您!我这儿正没有辙呢!

常四爷　(四下里看)好啊!好啊!收拾得好啊!大茶馆全关了,就是你有心路,能随机应变地改良!

王利发　别夸奖我啦!我尽力而为,可就怕天下老这么乱七八糟!

常四爷　像我这样的人算是坐不起这样的茶馆喽!

(老舍:《茶馆》,第二幕)

译文:

Paper boy	Hey, manager! Latest news about the figing at Changxindian. Won't you buy a copy?
Wang Lifa	Any news about people not figing?
Paper boy	Maybe. Look for yourself!
Wang Lifa	Go away! I'm not interested!
Paper boy	Won't make no difference, manager! The figing'll go on just the same. [To Tang the Oracle] Sir, you interested?
Tang the oracle	I'm not like him. [Points at Wang Lifa] I'm always concerned about affairs of state. [Takes a copy and sneaks off without paying.]

[The Paper Boy runs off after him.]

Wang Lifa　[To himself] Changxindian! Changxindian! That's near here. [Shouts] Master Li! Master Li! You'd better go for the food rig away. The city gates are sure to close soon. We won't be able to get anything. You heard me? [When no answer comes from the back, he goes towards there angrily.]

[Master Chang enters with a string of pickled turnips and two chickens.]

Chang	Manager Wang!
Wang Lifa	Who's that? Why, Master Chang! What are you doing these days?

Chang	<u>Selling vegetables. Earning my own living.</u> I'm not going to knuckle under. Today there was such a pandemonium outside the city. I couldn't pick up any vegetables. All I could get were these two chickens and some pickled turnips. I heard you're opening tomorrow. <u>Thoug these mig come in hand</u>, so I broug them along.
Wang Lifa	Thanks a lot! I didn't see how I was going to manage.
Chang	[Taking a look around] Nice! Very nice! <u>You've done it up well</u>! All the large teahouses have closed down. You were the only one sharp enough to make the most of the changes and reforms.
Wang Lifa	Thanks for the compliment! I do my best, but if the country carries on in this mess, it'll all be wasted.
Chang	Well, the likes of me won't be able to afford a seat in such a posh teahouse, <u>that's for sure</u>!

（英若诚译）

老舍先生的台词设计以生活语言为基础进行了细致的加工，日常生活的北京方言从剧中人物的口中自然而出，贴切而生动，如台词中穿插着"来一张（报纸）瞧瞧"、"有……没有"、"抓早点儿"、"待一会儿"、"不含糊"、"今儿个"、"没辙"这些充满生活气息的词汇，使人物形象更加真实可信、丰满生动。译文也使用了一些生动真实的口语语言结构，例如以"rig/fig/thoug/mig/broug"这些简写形式分别代替"right/fight/thought/might/brought"的完整拼读，"(Here is the) Latest news about the figing at Changxindian"、"(It) Won't make no difference"、"you（are you）interested"、"You（have you）heard me"、"(I'm) Selling vegetables. (I'm) Earning my own living"和"(I) Thoug these mig come in hand"等简化句式，"done it up"、"that's for sure"等也是欧美日常常用结构，这些均使台词更加简洁且口语化，人物形象得以完整再现，正是译者考虑到目的语观众的接受习惯而做的精心安排。

3.3 富于乐感的语言

上面所讲的剧本语言口语化主要指人物语言的词汇和句法层面，许多优秀的剧本还要在人物语言的语音层面进行加工和锤炼，即使是没有音乐伴奏的话剧台词也要给观众带来听觉上的冲击。出于舞台演出效果的需求，话剧人物的台词也要开口即响，具有一定的音乐性，这可以看做是剧本语言口语化的一个特殊表现。具体来讲，就是语言的节奏、语音、语调等要便于演员在舞台上说出来，不会结巴拗口，也没有不必要的停顿，富有节奏感，朗朗上口。

莎士比亚戏剧创作于16世纪下半叶到17世纪初，以现代英语语法的标准判断稍偏于正式，人物语言富于乐感，如在《威尼斯商人》(*The Merchant of Venice*)这部喜剧中：

【例5】

Launcelot　　I will go before, sir. Mistress, look out at window, for all this; There

	will come a Christian by, Will be worth a Jewess' eye. (*Exit Launcelot*)
Shylock	What says that fool of Hagar's offspring, ha?
Jessica	His words were, 'Farewell, mistress'; nothing else.
Shylock	The patch is kind enough, but a huge feeder; Snail-slow in profit, and he sleeps by day More than the wild cat: drones hive not with me; Therefore I part with him, and part with him To one that I would have him help to waste His borrow'd purse. Well, Jessica, go in; Perhaps I will return immediately; Do as I bid you; shut doors after you: 'Fast bind, fast find.' A proverb never stale in thrifty mind. (*Exit*)
Jessica	Farewell; and if my fortune be not crost, I have a father, you a daughter, lost. (*Exit*)

(William Shakespeare: *The Merchant of Venice*, Act II, Scene V)

译文 1：

朗西洛特	我先走了,小姐不用听这话。要在窗口探望;有一基督徒来到窗前,值得犹太女郎看一眼。(下)
夏 洛 克	那个夏甲的后裔胡说什么,啊?
杰 西 卡	他说,"再会了小姐";没有说别的。
夏 洛 克	这傢小子倒还忠厚,可是真能吃;该效力的时候像蜗牛一般慢,白昼睡觉赛过野猫!懒虫是和我合不来的;所以我辞退他,让他帮一个人,帮那个人浪费他的借贷来的金钱。好,杰西卡,进去吧;也许我立刻就回来;照我吩咐的去做;就把门关好;"门关得严,多剩钱。"是俭省人永不嫌陈腐的好格言。(下)
杰 西 卡	再见;如其我的命运好,我丢了父亲,你也丢了女儿了。(下)

（梁实秋译）

译文 2：

朗西洛脱	那么我先去了,老爷。小姐,留心看好窗外;跑来一个基督徒,不要错过好姻缘。(下)
夏 洛 克	嘿,那个夏甲的傻瓜后裔说些什么?
杰 西 卡	没有说什么,他只是说,"再会,小姐。"
夏 洛 克	这蠢才人倒还好,就是食量太大;做起事来,慢腾腾的像条蜗牛一般;白天睡觉的本领,比野猫还胜过几分;我家里可容不得懒惰的黄蜂,所以才打发他走了,让他去跟着那个靠借债过日子的败家精,正好帮他消费。好,杰西卡,进去吧;也许我一会儿就回来。记住我的话,把门随手关了。"缚得牢,跑不了",这是一句千古不磨的至理名言。(下)
杰 西 卡	再会;要是我的命运不跟我作梗,那么我将要失去一个父亲,你也要失去一个女儿了。(下)

（朱生豪译）

英语本身就轻重音间隔,富于韵律,莎士比亚戏剧的语言更是凝练优美,铿锵有力,许多台词都富于乐感,如上例中:(a)"There will come a Christian by, Will be worth a Jewess' eye";(b)"'Fast bind, fast find.' A proverb never stale in thrifty mind."以及(c)"Farewell; and if my fortune be not crost, I have a father, you a daughter, lost."这三处中,(a)这两句台词音节数量相等,轻重间隔相似并以/ai/音押尾韵,韵律规整如两行诗歌;汉语一字一个音节,译文1"有一基督徒来到窗前,值得犹太女郎看一眼"押/ n/尾韵,比译文2的处理方法更具乐感。(b)句中的谚语内部句式工整且押尾韵/aind/,听上去节奏明快、整齐悦耳,后句中的 mind 一词继续以/aind/结尾与前面相呼应。这一音韵特点在译文1"'门关得严,多剩钱。'是俭省人永不嫌陈腐的好格言。"中得以再现,而译文2"'缚得牢,跑不了',这是一句千古不磨的至理名言。"却只译出了格言内部的押韵,与后句没有音韵方面的回应。(c)句中/ost/的押韵效果在两译文中均未再现,无论是译文1还是译文2,尾韵的缺失使台词的乐感大打折扣。当然,整体来讲,梁实秋译文比朱生豪的译文更具乐感,能给观众带来更多听觉上的艺术享受。

3.4 简洁化的语言

戏剧是简洁的艺术形式。受剧场演出的时间限制,戏剧的情节发展较快,戏剧中的伏笔、悬念很快就得以解开,这要求剧作者将大量信息压缩在简短的人物语言中,在较短的时间内向观众完整地展现故事情节和丰富的戏剧冲突。因此,戏剧语言不能像散文语言那样含蓄唯美,也不能像小说语言那样有很多的描述或铺垫,戏剧中人物的语言格外简洁、清楚明了,最忌含混不清。剧本译者在翻译时除忠实传达对话内容之外,还要尽量再现原作简洁清晰的语言特征,以保留原文对话的节奏和速度,否则将影响故事进展和表演效果。

《茶馆》是老舍先生在语言艺术上成就最高的话剧作品,他设计的台词以生活语言为基础进行锤炼和加工,每个人物的语言都简短而自然:

【例6】

康　六　刘爷!十五岁的大姑娘,就值十两银子吗?

刘麻子　卖到窑子去,也许多拿一两八钱的,可是你又不肯!

康　六　那是我的亲女儿!我能够……

刘麻子　有女儿,你可养活不起,这怪谁呢?

康　六　那不是因为乡下种地的都没法子混了吗?一家大小要是一天能吃上一顿粥,我要还想卖女儿,我就不是人!

刘麻子　那是你们乡下的事,我管不着。我受你之托,教你不吃亏,又教你女儿有个吃饱饭的地方,这还不好吗?

康　六　到底给谁呢?

刘麻子　我一说,你必定从心眼里乐意!一位在宫里当差的!

(老舍:《茶馆》,第一幕)

译文1:

Sixth-born Kang　Elder Liu! Is a fifteen-year-old girl only worth ten taels?

Pockface Liu	If you sold her into a whorehouse you'd perhaps get a few taels more. But you're not willing to do that.
Sixth-born Kang	She's my own flesh and blood. How can I…
Pockface Liu	She's your own, but you can't afford to feed her. Whose fault is that?
Sixth-born Kang	It's because it's impossible for us peasants to get by these days. If we could manage even a bowl of gruel a day for each of us, and I still wanted to sell my daughter—then, could I call myself a man?
Pockface Liu	That's you peasants' problem, not mine. You asked me for help, and I got you a good deal. I also found your daughter a place where she can fill her belly. Isn't that enough?
Sixth-born Kang	Just who's she being sold to?
Pockface Liu	You'll be delighted when I tell you — he's a palace official.

（霍华译）

译文 2：

Kang Liu	Master Liu! A fifteen-year-old girl only worth ten taels?
Pock-mark Liu	A brothel mig give you a few taels more, but you don't want that.
Kang Liu	My flesh and blood, how could I…?
Pock-mark Liu	But you can't feed her. Who's to blame?
Kang Liu	We peasants can't live any more. If we had a bowl of gruel each every day… and I still wanted to sell my daughter, then I'd be a beast!
Pock-mark Liu	That's your problem, not mine! You asked me to help you, so I'll see to it you're not cheated and your daughter fills her belly. What more do you want?
Kang Liu	Who's she being sold to?
Pock-mark Liu	This should please you. A palace official!

（英若诚译）

英若诚先生曾提出，"口语化和简练"是剧本翻译中"必须首先考虑的原则"（1999：4）。他自己曾当过话剧演员，翻译剧本总是反复推敲译本中的台词是否适合舞台演出。比较霍华和英若诚的译文，可以看出两译文在画线部分的繁简之分更加明显，后者的译文语言更加地道、简洁流畅。

剧本语言要求简洁化，译者在处理剧本中的文化内容时更要注意这一要求。文学文本涉及许多文化内容，如与原语文字密切相关的文字游戏、双关语等特殊语言现象，小说文体可以根据具体的结构和语义特点、不同的翻译目的，灵活选用音译、直译、意译、加注等翻译方法（见小说翻译"文化负载词的翻译"部分）。剧本翻译也有加注的情况，这是为阅读进行的翻译，而演出文本没有加注的可能，舞台演出的视听性和即时性不允许剧本翻译添加各种帮助理解的注释,剧本翻译的无注性要求译本的语言不仅要自然、简洁,台词口语化,使演员读起来顺畅,观众听起来不觉得吃力,而且还要充分考虑到观众的接受心理和文化习惯,既不能对原文中的双关语、歧义句以及有关文化现象进行注释,也不能为了保留原文的地方语言特色而音译某些词语。

《威尼斯商人》是莎士比亚的一部代表剧作,在这部古典戏剧精品中,典故、双关比比皆是:

【例 7】

  Shylock These be the Christian husbands!
      I have a daughter;
      Would any of the stock of <u>Barrabas</u>
      Had been her husband rather than a Christian.
      We trifle time. I pray thee pursue sentence.
        (William Shakespeare:*The Merchant of Venice*:Act Ⅳ, Scene Ⅰ)

译文 1:

  夏洛克 这些便是相信基督教的丈夫!我有一个女儿,我宁愿她嫁给<u>强盗</u>的子孙,不愿她嫁给一个基督徒。别再浪费光阴了,请快些儿宣判吧。

                   (朱生豪译)

译文 2:

  夏洛克 ……我有一个女儿,我宁愿她嫁给巴拉巴的后裔中的任何男子,也比嫁给基督徒强。……

  注:巴拉巴,即让出十字架给耶稣的那个强盗。

                    (梁实秋译)

上例原剧本中的 Barrabas 出自《圣经》,是耶稣受难时与耶稣一同受审的强盗,犹太群众选择释放强盗而将耶稣处死。对熟谙基督教教义的西方观众来说,Barrabas 能激发较强的联想意义,与"强盗"一词迅速联系起来,而中国观众对《圣经》较为陌生。朱生豪将这一人名意译成"强盗"既能体现语用意义,充分地表达出犹太人夏洛克对基督徒的仇恨——视他们连强盗都不如,又能保证原文的简洁性,可谓一举两得,遗憾之处在于原剧本中的文化内涵无法传递。而梁实秋将 Barrabas 按人名翻译惯例音译成"巴拉巴"后,添加注释来揭示典故信息,可以帮助中国观众了解剧本的文化内涵。两种处理方法各有长处,适用于不同的翻译目的:朱生豪翻译的剧本更适合舞台演出,而梁实秋翻译的剧本更适用于以阅读为目的的剧本翻译。

英若诚在把老舍先生的代表剧作《茶馆》翻译成英文时,对文化内容一般采取文内处理的方式,以不影响舞台演出和观众的即时接受。如:

【例 8】

  康 六 谁呢?
  刘麻子 庞总管!你也听说过庞总管吧?伺候着太后,红的不得了,<u>连家里打醋的瓶子</u>

都是玛瑙作的！

康　六　　刘大爷,把女儿给太监做老婆,我怎么对得起人呢?

刘麻子　　卖女儿,无论怎么卖,也对不起女儿!你糊涂!你看,姑娘一过门,吃的是珍馐美味,穿的是绫罗绸缎,这不是造化吗?怎样?摇头不算点头算,来个干脆的!

(老舍:《茶馆》,第一幕)

译文:

Pock-mark Liu　　The Grand Eunuch Pang! Even you must have heard of him. A personal attendant of the Empress Dowager, her great favourite! Even the vinegar bottle in his house is made of agate!

Kang Liu　　But Master Liu, please, how could I ever face my daughter again if I sold her to be the wife of a eunuch?

Pock-mark Liu　　But you are selling her, aren't you? How can you face her any way? Don't be a fool! Think about it. Once she's married, she'll eat delicacies and wear brocades! I call that a lucky fate! Well, make up your mind, yes or no. Let's get it over with!

(英若诚译)

原剧本中几处涉及文化的部分译文都视具体情况进行了恰当的处理:"太监"对许多西方观众已不陌生,译者直译成"eunuch"未加任何解释;"连家里打醋的瓶子都是玛瑙作的"直译成"Even the vinegar bottle in his house is made of agate",也不难猜出这是一种夸耀财富的表达手法;"吃的是珍馐美味,穿的是绫罗绸缎"的两个四字格意译为"eat delicacies and wear brocades",结构对称而意义表达充分;"摇头不算点头算"这个熟语也进行了意译,以"yes or no"来表达出询问的意思,简单明了。

3.5 动作化的语言

日常生活中,人们说话时总是带有一定的语音语调、面部表情、肢体动作等辅助手段。在戏剧中,演员的舞台表演不仅通过台词表现人物特征和人物关系,同样也使用适当的身体语言来表现人物的行为意图、心情、心理状态、感情、感觉等内心活动。生动的台词需要与之相协调的动作才能体现得更加充分,在剧本创作中,剧作家总是力图把这些动作压缩到剧本语言中,以帮助演员通过阅读剧本就能选择出恰当的身体语言来表现人物心理。换言之,戏剧语言应具有丰富的动作性,或者叫"动作潜台词",即决定演员动作表演的"动作文本"(gestic text)/"潜在文本"(subtext)(Bassnett & Lefevere,2001:90)。

动作化的人物语言饱含人物丰富而复杂的思想活动,是推动故事发展和突出性格特征的有力保证。译者在翻译剧本时也应选用动作化的语言,使人物的内心活动能够通过语言活灵活现地展现在观众眼前,力争在译本中保留原剧本的"动作文本",帮助译入语观众充分理解剧本的"潜台词"。如阿瑟·米勒著《推销员之死》中的主人公 Willy 与妻子 Linda 的那段对话中,Willy 抱怨大儿子 Biff 说"The trouble is he's lazy, god dammit!(毛病就在他懒,他妈的!)"和"Biff is a lazy bum!(比夫就是个懒汉!)",英若诚均进行直译,保留原文的詈骂,以表达出 Willy 对儿子不成材的极度失望。然而最后一句"There's one thing about Biff—he's not lazy.(别的不说,比夫有一条特点——他不懒。)"又显示出 Willy 在生活的重压下已难堪重负,开始有些话语前后矛盾、思维错乱了,译文同样予以直译,把这一潜台词进行完整移植。对 Linda 的台词,译文进行了一定的改动:英若诚把简短的"Shh!"添加了破折号译成"嘘——!",声音的延长使嘘音更加柔和,非常符合 Linda 贤妻良母的形象;后面的"Willy, please!"则处理为"威利,我求求你!"言辞更加恳切,慈母对儿子的维护、对丈夫坏脾气的无奈表现得更加充分。这些都对演员揣摩人物说话时的语气及内心活动有极大的帮助,也能够帮助观众更加贴切地理解人物形象和故事情节。

中国剧作家曹禺著《雷雨》是中国话剧的典范之作,被称为"中国现代话剧成熟的标志性作品",在艺术上具有很高的成就,剧中人物的语言饱含着动作,非常符合舞台演出的要求。下面是鲁大海代表工人去周公馆谈判却被告知其他三个代表已离开时的片段:

【例9】

周朴园　不许多说话。(回头向大海)鲁大海,你现在没有资格跟我说话——矿上已经把你开除了。

鲁大海　开除了!?

周　冲　爸爸,这是不公平的。

周朴园　(向周冲)你少多嘴,出去!

(周冲愤然由中门下。)

鲁大海　好,好。(切齿)你的手段我早明白,只要你能弄钱,你什么都做得出来。你叫警察杀了许多工人,你还——

周朴园　你胡说!

鲁侍萍　(至大海前)走吧,别说了。

鲁大海　哼,你的来历我都知道,你从前在哈尔滨包修江桥,故意叫江堤出险,——

周朴园　(厉声)下去!

仆人们　(拉大海)走!走!

鲁大海　你故意淹死了两千二百个小工,每一个小工的性命你扣三百块钱!姓周的,你发的是绝子绝孙的昧心财!你现在还——

周　萍　(冲向大海,打了他两个嘴巴)你这种混账东西!

(大海还手,被仆人们拉住。)

(曹禺:《雷雨》,第二幕)

译文:

ZHOU　　　Hold your tongue. (*turning back to Lu Dahai*.) You're no longer in a position to speak to me, Lu Dahai—firm's already sacked you.

HAI　　　Sacked me!

CHONG　　That's not playing the game, Father.

ZHOU　　　(*Turning to Zhou Chong*) You shut up and get out!

(*Zhou Chong departs in high dudgeon through the centre door.*)

HAI	All right, then. (*Grinding his teeth*) Your dirty tricks are nothing new to me. You'd stoop to anything so long as there was money in it. You get the police to mow down your men, and then you—
ZHOU	How dare you!
MA	(*Going to Lu Dahai*) Come on, let's go. That's enough.
HAI	Yes, and I know all about your record too! When you contracted to repair that bridge over the river at Harbin, you deliberately breached the dyke —
ZHOU	(*Harshly*) Get out of here!
SERVENTS	(*Tugging at Lu Dahai*) Come on! Outside! Out!
HAI	You drowned two thousand two hundred coolies in cold blood, and for each life lost you raked in three hundred dollars! I tell you, creature, you've made your money by killing people, and you and your sons stand accursed for ever! And now on top of that you —
PING	(*Turling himself on Lu Dahai and striking him twice in the face*) Take that, you lying swine!

(*Lu Dahai returns a blow, but is seized and held by the servants.*)

（王佐良译）

鲁大海的台词中,"开除了!?"一句的感叹号和疑问号显示出他听到工友的背叛和自己被开除后的震惊与疑问,译文"Sacked me!"只有惊讶而失掉了疑问,动作性有所削弱;"哼"表现出他对鱼肉工友血汗的资本家周朴园的鄙视,翻译成"Yes"使他的语气更加自信。"你胡说!"一句显示出了周朴园见到自己的丑恶发家史被揭露时的震惊与气急败坏,译文"How dare you!"使一个表面宽容大度的伪善资本家鄙视劳动者的语气表现得非常充分。侍萍说"走吧,别说了。"明显带有无法解决父子争端的无奈,译文"Come on, let's go. That's enough."表达出她想要带走儿子以阻止争执的急切语气,再现贴切。仆人们赶鲁大海"走!走!（Come on! Outside! Out!）"的动作性较强,译文语气急切,突现出一群资本家走狗的形象。周萍听到鲁大海揭露父亲——自己佩服和景仰的"模范市民"、"模范家长"的阴暗和罪恶时,极力维护,冲口而出的"你这种混账东西!"翻译成"Take that, you lying swine!"不仅以添加"take that"加强与前面动作的衔接,而且把"混账东西"变通为"lying swine"表示出他对鲁大海所揭露内容的不可置信和愤怒。整体来讲,原剧本台词的动作性在译本中得到了很好的移植,译本的"动作潜台词"同样丰富,有助于演员的舞台演出。

4 本章结语

戏剧丰富的语言表现形式和深厚的文化底蕴使其成为受众人数较多的艺术门类,随即成为跨文化交流的一个有力途径。剧本翻译不仅将国外优秀的剧目引入国内,同时,也向全世界打开我们璀璨的戏剧艺术宝库。从目的翻译论的角度来看,剧本翻译必须为特定的翻译目的服务。如果把剧本作为以阅读为目的的文学作品来翻译,那么我们就可以从剧本中的语言和文化角度入手进行翻译;如果把剧本作为演出蓝本来翻译,那么译文必须考虑台词的动作性,还要考虑观众的接受能力和审美需求,尤其是他们对异域文化的接受程度,适当采纳归化式翻译策略。对普通的译者来说,兼顾剧本翻译的文学性和表演性,充分再现原剧本语言的个性化、口语化、韵律感、简洁化和动作性等特点确非易事,必须在具有广博的知识、熟知剧本翻译相关理论的基础上进行大量的实践练习。

第十三章 典籍翻译

在中西文化交流中,中国古典作品的翻译把中国经典思想介绍给外国读者,在世界思想史上产生了重大影响。在被称为"东方的世纪"、"中国的世纪"的 21 世纪,中国古典作品的翻译日益引起重视。在这样的背景下,在翻译教学中加强中国古典作品的翻译教学及研究显得尤为必要。本章我们将选取几篇有代表性的文言文,在比较分析不同译本的基础上,总结古典作品英译的基本问题和规律。

1 文言文翻译的基本问题

文言文无论在用词、句式等方面都不同于现代汉语,与英语语言相比差异更大,翻译中不仅存在理解的问题,也存在表达的问题。以下以《战国策》中的《邹忌讽齐王纳谏》为例,分析两个译本,谈谈文言文在词语层、句法层、篇章层以及文化层等的特点及翻译中应该注意的问题。

1.1 文言文词语层翻译问题

在文言文翻译中首先要正确理解词语的含义。文言文中存在古今异义、一词多义、词性活用等现象。在理解词语时必须结合文言文的具体时代和上下文,准确把握词语的用法和含义。概括起来,词语的理解存在以下几种情况:

(1) 古今异义词:

由于时代的演变,文言文中的很多词语与其在现代汉语中的用法和含义差别很大,例如《邹忌讽齐王纳谏》一文中"讽"在文中是"规劝"的意思,而今意为"讽刺"。"窥镜"的"窥"古意为"照",而今意为"偷看"。"明日,徐公来"一句中的"明日",意思是"第二天",而今意为"明天"。"宫妇左右莫不私王"一句中,"左右"的意思是"身边的大臣",而今是方位名词,"私"意为"偏爱",而今意为"自私"。在翻译这类词语时必须弄清其原意,不要与现代汉语中的用法相混淆。例如下面几个例子:

【例 1】

朝服衣冠,窥镜。

译文 1:

One morning, after putting on his clothes, he stole a glance of himself in the mirror.

译文 2:

After putting on his robe and hat one morning, he examined himself in the mirror.

如上所述,这里"窥"古意为:照,看。译文 1 "stole a glance of himself"虽然很形象,但是与原意不符。译文2则准确把握了该词在文中的意思。

【例2】

明日,徐公来。

译文1:

The following day, Mr Shu himself came to see Chi.

译文2:

The next day, Lord Xu himself called ...

这里"明日"意为"第二天",不是"明天",因此不能译为"tomorrow",只能如这两个译文,翻译为"the following day, the second day"。

【例3】

今齐地方千里

译文1:

Now Tsi is a kingdom of a thousand square li

译文2:

Now Qi has a thousand square li of land

"地方"在现代汉语里是一个词,意为"地点",而这里指"土地方圆"。两个译文都准确地把握了它的用法。

(2) 一词多义:

一词多义是文言文中的普遍现象。例如下列句子中的"之"含义不同:

齐国之美丽者也(的)

问之(代词,代这件事)

吾妻之美我者(取消句子独立性)

徐公不若君之美也(取消句子主谓之间独立性)

孰视之(代词,指徐公)

暮寝而思之(代指这件事)

朝廷之臣莫不畏王(的)

由此观之(代词,指这件事)

臣之妻私臣(的)

王之蔽甚矣(取消主谓之间独立性)

群臣吏民能面刺寡人之过者(的)

数月之后(连词,无意义)

燕,赵,韩,魏闻之(代词,指上文所说的事)

当"之"作为虚词使用,无实际意义时,翻译中要立足于全句,使之符合译文的习惯和规范。当它相当于现代汉语的"的"字使用时,有时需要根据具体情况,表达出它所表示的所有格关系。

【例4】

臣之妻私臣

译文1：

My wife is partial to me

译文2：

My wife through partiality

【例5】

群臣吏民能面刺寡人之过者

译文1：

All ministers, officials and common people who can point out my mistakes.

译文2：

All those of my ministers, officers and subjects who dare to rebuke me to my face...

值得注意的是，当"之"作代词使用时，译文中可以还原为所指代的人或者事物，也可以根据上下文使用译文语言中相应的代词。例如：

【例6】

暮寝而思之

译文1：

So he lay in his bed and thought...

译文2：

In bed that night he thought the matter over and reflected

【例7】

孰视之

译文1：

studied him carefully

译文2：

examining him carefully

再比如，下列句子中的"于"含义也不同，也要根据具体的上下文选择合适的表达方式来翻译。

【例8】

欲有求于我也（向……）

译文1：

He had something he wanted to ask of me.

译文 2:

My visitor was governed by the fact that he wanted something from me.

【例 9】

能谤讥于市朝(在)

译文 1:

criticize me and my government at the market place

译文 2:

censure me in public

【例 10】

皆以美于徐公(比)

译文 1:

They all said I am handsomer than Mr. Shu.

译文 2:

All assured me that I was the finer man of the two.

该文中还有很多其他的一词多义的词语,必须根据上下文判断其词义,选择适当的表达方式和翻译策略。

(3) 词性活用:

理解和翻译文言文还要特别注意词性活用现象。例如"朝服衣冠"一句中,"朝"本是名词,是"早上"的意思,但这里用作状语,相当于"在早晨";而"服"一般是"名词",这里活用为动词,意为"穿戴"。再比如下面一句中的"美"和"私"。

【例 11】

吾妻之美我者,私我也。

译文 1:

My wife praised me because she is partial to me.

译文 2:

Partiality made my wife call me the more handsome.

"美"和"私"都是形容词,用作动词,前者意为:"以……为美"、"认为……美",后者意为"偏爱"。两个译文虽然选用了不同的句式,但根据这一用法进行了处理。

(4) 虚词的使用:

虚词的使用是文言文词汇的一大特色,常用的有"之"、"乎"、"者"、"也"、"矣"、"哉"等。这一类词语的翻译需要根据不同情况区别对待。例如上面所讲到的"之"字,要根据不同的用法和含义选择适当的表达和翻译策略。对于"也"等语气助词,无需找到对应的语气词。

【例 12】

欲有求于我也。

译文 1：

He had something to ask of me.

译文 2：

He wanted something from me.

有些语气词表示较强的语气,要立足于句子层面,有时需要选择适当的句式把句子的语气表达出来。例如：

【例 13】

由此观之,王之蔽甚矣。

译文 1：

So it seems to me that it is hard for you to hear the truth.

译文 2：

Judging by this, Your Majesty is very likely to be misinformed.

1.2 文言文句法层翻译问题

文言文中有一些常用的特殊句式,例如选择句、判断句、倒装句、省略句等,这些句式在翻译中需要予以特别重视。例如：

【例 14】

我孰与城北徐公美？

吾与城北徐公孰美？

这两个句子是文言文中常用的选择句,句(1)是句(2)的倒装句。这类句子要选择相应的英语句式来表达。

译文 1：

Who do you think is handsomer, Mr. Shu of the north city or me?

译文 2：

Which of us is the better looking, Lord Xu of the north city or I?

此外还有其他形式的句式,例如宾语前置:"忌不自信"→"忌不信自"。状语后置:"欲有求(于我)也;此所谓战胜(于朝廷)(此所谓[于朝廷]战胜)。这些句式的翻译需要根据英语的习惯进行调整。

文言文中的省略句可以根据上下文的具体情况同样译为省略句,也可以把省略的内容补出。例如,"与座谈"一句,完整的形式应为"邹忌与之座谈"。

文言文中还有判断句,常见的形式是"……者,……也"。例如：

【例 15】

城北徐公,齐国之美丽者也。

译文 1:

Mr. Shu of North city was a gentleman noted for his handsomeness.

译文 2:

(Since) Lord Xu of the north city was one of the most handsome men in the State of Qi.

【例 16】

吾妻之美我者,私我也。

译文 1:

My wife praised me because she is partial to me.

译文 2:

Partiality made my wife call me the more handsome.

例 15 中,"者"意为"……人",例 16 中意思是"……原因",翻译中以相应的英文来表达。

1.3 文言文篇章层翻译问题

文言文翻译的问题不仅表现在字、词、句的层面。近年来,在话语分析和篇章语言学理论的启发下,翻译研究的视角也从词句层面上升到篇章层,因为翻译不仅仅是词句的转换,它是一个从原文语篇到译文语篇的转换过程,是一个动态的跨文化交际的过程。文言文翻译中也应该关注篇章层面的问题。

文言文翻译要特别注意整体性。例如,由于汉语相对重意合,英语相对重形合,两种语言的语篇在衔接和连贯手段上存在一些差异。英语语言重视形式的衔接和连贯手段,相对来说,汉语形式上的手段则弱一些。这一差别在文言文与英语的比较中表现更加突出,例如代词的省略,连词的省略等等,翻译时要根据英语语篇的特点来处理。例如:

【例 17】

明日,徐公来,孰视之,自以为不如;窥镜而自视,又弗如远甚。

译文 1:

The following day, Mr Shu himself came to see Chi. Chi studied him carefully and thought him much handsomer than himself. He examined himself in the mirror and was convinced that he was far less handsome than Mr. Shu.

译文 2:

The next day, Lord Xu himself called and Zou Ji, examining him carefully, suspected that he was outmatched. Another look in the mirror convinced him that he fell far short of the other.

原文中多处省略了主语人称代词,而在英语语篇中需要根据衔接和连贯的要求补出。"窥镜而自视,又弗如远甚"与"熟视之,自以为不如"相比呈语义增强之势,两个译文使用同样的处理方法,增添了"(was) convinced",使译文非常连贯。再比如:

【例 18】

宫妇左右莫不私王,朝廷之臣莫不畏王,四境之内莫不有求于王;由此观之,王之蔽甚矣。

译文 1:

All the palace ladies and attendants are partial to you. All the courtiers are afraid of your power. And all the people have something to ask of you. So it seems to me that it is hard for you to hear the truth.

译文 2:

All your court ladies and attendants are partial to you, all your ministers are afraid of you, and all your subjects hope for favours from you. Judging by this, Your Majesty is very likely to be misinformed.

原文前三个小句句式相同,结构整齐,与句子后半部分形成因果关系。译文 1 添加了"and"、"so"等连接词,译文 2 除添加"and"之外,使用"this"来译"之",与上文形成照应关系,两个译文的处理都保证了译文的衔接和连贯。

除了衔接和连贯手段之外,有时可以立足于上下文,选择相应的翻译策略和表达方式,以保证语篇的整体性。例如:

【例 19】

城北徐公,齐国之美丽者也。忌不自信,而复问其妾曰:"吾孰与徐公美?"妾曰:"徐公何能及君也?"

译文 1:

Chi dared not take her word for it and asked his concubine the same question. His concubine said, "Mr. Shu cannot compare with you."

译文 2:

Zou Ji still had his doubts and posed the same question to his concubine, who gave him the same answer.

原文中的直接引语"吾孰与徐公美?"与上文重复,这两个译文都没有直译,而是根据上下文使用了替代,避免了行文的重复,但不影响行文的整体性。

1.4 文言文翻译中的文化问题

文言文中有一些特殊的文化词,例如,有关朝代、地方、人物的专门词汇,历史典故等等。如果缺乏相应的文化背景知识,就不能正确地理解文言文。而在翻译中如果不作特殊的处理,就会因为缺乏相应的背景信息给译文读者造成理解上的困难。在处理这些文化词语时可以采用不同的策略,从具体的翻译技巧来讲,可以采用解释性翻译、加注、增译等等。《邹忌讽齐王纳谏》的两个译文采用的是不同的策略和技巧。例如:

【例20】
于是入朝见威王

译文1：

Chi then went to the Court and said to King Wei of Tsi

译文2：

Then he sought an audience with King Wei

从人物关系来看，邹忌与齐王是臣和君的关系，体现了中国文化中的等级关系，译文1并没有刻意体现这一关系，而译文2使用"sought an audience"，含有"拜见，下级觐见上级"的含义。再比如：

【例21】
由此观之，王之蔽甚矣

译文1：

So it seems to me that it is hard for you to hear the truth.

译文2：

Judging by this, Your Majesty is very likely to be misinformed.

译文1直接使用第二人称代词来翻译"王"，而译文2则使用了相应的称呼"Your Majesty"，点明了人物的身份和关系。

【例22】
燕、赵、韩、魏闻之，皆朝于齐。

译文1：

The neighboring countries Yen, Chao, and Han, and Wei heard of what the king had done and came to acknowledge the state of Tsi as their leaders.

译文2：

When the states of Yan, Zhao, Han and Wei knew this, they all paid homage to the king of Qi.

译文1增加了"the neighbouring countries"，交代了这些国与齐国的关系，而译文2则采用了直译。

以上探讨了文言文翻译中在词汇层面、句法层面、篇章层面以及文化方面的翻译问题，文言文翻译的问题并不仅仅限于此，在处理具体的篇章时还会遇到其他各种各样的问题。从两个译文的比较可以看出，不同的译文会表现出不同的倾向，采用不同的策略和技巧。但是，能否正确地理解原文，并选用适当的译文准确地传达是文言文翻译的根本前提。

2 翻译原则与翻译策略

现以《桃花源记》的三译文为例进行比较分析。陶渊明的《桃花源记》以武陵渔人进出桃花源的行踪为线索,以发现桃源、做客桃源、离开桃源、再寻桃源的情节,描绘了一个理想的桃源世界,深受人们喜爱。这篇文章也被多次译成英文。本节将比较 Herbert A. Giles、林语堂、黄俊雄所译的三种译文,从理解、表达以及文化三个方面进一步探讨文言文翻译中的翻译原则、翻译策略等问题。

2.1 翻译原则比较

在分析译文之前,首先考察一下这些译者的翻译思想。这些思想部分体现在编选这些译文的序言中,如 Giles 和黄俊雄的译文。Herbert Giles 的翻译目的在于向外国读者介绍中国历朝历代的经典文学作品。他在其前言中指出,翻译过程中坚持文字上的准确性,以方便学中文的学生。但在不影响主要思想的前提下,删除一些大众读者不易拼读的名字和典故(Giles,1923:i—ii)。黄俊雄的译文选自《英译中国小小说选集》,目的是把中国的小小说介绍给英语读者,且假设对象为具有中等文化水平的英语读者。译者指出,要记住读者的要求,"代表中文作者,竭力把原作翻译成英语读者爱看的译文",把古代文学翻译成朗朗上口的英语。他同时也表示,"译文必须忠实于原文,而且在目的语中应该像原文中一样优美"(黄俊雄,2008:i—iv)。

由这些序言体现出来的翻译思想可以看出,这些译者都基本坚持忠实和可读性的原则,既考虑到要忠实于原文,又考虑读者的要求。在林语堂的翻译思想中体现着同样的原则,他的翻译思想主要体现在著名的《论翻译》一文。该文提出了翻译的三条标准:"第一条是忠实标准,第二是通顺标准,第三条是美的标准。"三条标准分别对应着译者对原著者的责任、对中国读者的责任以及对艺术的责任。他认为翻译是艺术,"不可不注意于文字之美的问题"(罗新璋,1984:417—432)。

2.2 理解的分歧

上文我们指出,各位译者的翻译思想中都体现着忠实于原文的原则。理解准确无疑是实现这一原则的首要前提。通过比较我们会发现,各位译者对原文的理解存在很多不同之处。

首先,译文的题目有同有异。《桃花源记》中的"源"字,本意是"水源",古代还有"水中平原"之意。按照文中所写,渔人忽逢桃花林,欲穷其林,在林尽水源的山里发现了一个与世隔绝的地方、一个和乐祥和的社会。"桃花源"所指的就是这个地方,喻指避世隐居或理想中的美好地方。三个译文的题目:

【例 23】

桃花源记

译文 1:

The Peach-Blossom Fountain (Giles 译)

译文 2:

The Peach Colony (林语堂译)

译文 3：

Peach Woods（黄俊雄译）

译者选择的侧重点显然不同。Giles 用"The Peach-Blossom Fountain"，突出"泉"。林语堂使用"The Peach Colony"，colony 意为"a group of settlers, a separate or separated group"，显然以"桃花源人"为中心。而黄俊雄译"Peach Woods"明显侧重于"桃花林"。题目的侧重点不同，译文语篇的中心因而也是不同的，说明三位译者对《桃花源记》的故事有着不同的认识。

《桃花源记》原文中某些地方本身存在歧义，不同译者往往有不同的理解。例如：

【例 24】

男女衣着，悉如外人。

译文 1：

The dress of the people who passed along or were at work in the fields was of a strange cut.（Giles 译）

译文 2：

The dresses of the men and women were like those of the outside world.（林语堂译）.

译文 3：

The farmers..., dressed in clothes the fisherman has never seen, all looked like aliens.（黄俊雄译）

这里的"外人"一词，本身存在语义上的含混，因此这句话就有截然相反的理解，一种理解是"男男女女的穿着完全像桃花源外的人"，另一种理解是"男男女女的穿着跟桃花源外面的人都不一样"。林语堂按前者处理，而 Giles、黄俊雄则理解为后者。

原文中还有某些"空白"和不确定的地方，需要读者根据自己的经验和理解去填充。例如，在渔人穿过山之小口之后，进入桃花源人所住的地方，原文只是描写渔人眼里看到的图景，并没有明确说明这个地方的地貌特征，不同读者心目中自然会有不同的图景。Giles 将此理解为"a new world of level country"，林语堂理解为"a wide, level valley"，黄俊雄则是"a vast plain"。

【例 25】

见渔人，乃大惊，问所从来。

译文 1：

One of the inhabitants, catching sight of the fisherman, was greatly astonished.（Giles 译）

译文 2：

They were greatly astonished to see the fisherman and asked him where he had come from.（林语堂译）.

译文 3：

The villagers were greatly surprised to see the fisherman, asking where he had come from. （黄俊雄译）

这里需要译者根据自己的理解添加"主语"。三位译者的填充也表现出两种倾向：林语堂和黄俊雄都选择复数主语，按"（村人们）见渔人"来理解，而 Giles 则选择了单数主语，按"（有一个村人）见渔人"来理解。

2.3 表达的高低

除了对原文理解有些不同之外，三个译文在篇章表达方面也存在一些差别。在形式方面，如断句、句式和语态的选择以及段落组织方面，各译文间的异同一目了然。例如，"鸡犬相闻"一句，Giles、黄俊雄都使用了被动语态。"不足为外人道也"一句，在原文是直接引语，而林语堂则采用了间接引语。再比如：

【例 26】

林尽水源，便得一山，山有小口，仿佛若有光。

译文 1：

He found that the peach trees ended where the water began, at the foot of a hill; and there he espied what seemed to be a cave with light issuing from it. （Giles 译）

译文 2：

And when he came to the end of the grove, he saw a spring which came from a cave in the hill. Having noticed that there seemed to be a weak light in the cave. （林语堂译）

译文 3：

Leaving behind the peaches, he reached the end of the river. A mountain with a dim little cave came into sight. （黄俊雄译）

三个译文无论是对原文的断句和译文的组句都不相同，Giles 和林语堂完全以"渔人发现"为中心，偏重于叙事，都使用了多个同义动词。黄俊雄虽然也以"渔人发现"为中心来叙事，但并不忽视"山有小口，仿佛若有光"一句的描写。

三个译文对原文中的一些描写片断的处理显示出它们之间的不同。《桃花源记》中的描写语言生动简练，景物历历在目。没有这些生动的描写，"桃花源"不会成为人们心目中向往的世外之境，理想之乡。例如：

【例 27】

芳草鲜美，落英缤纷

译文 1：

The beauty of the scene and the exquisite perfume of the flowers （Giles 译）

译文 2：

The beautifully grassy ground was covered with its rose petals. （林语堂译）

译文 3：

The fragrant wild grass, exceptionally fresh and lovely, was dotted by the dazzling beauty of the fallen peach petals. （黄俊雄译）

这 8 个字出自原文第一部分，写渔人发现桃花源的时间、经过和沿途所见的奇丽景色，这 8 个字勾勒出一幅富有诗意的画面。Giles 把该句转译成一个名词结构，和"渔人甚异之"合句，这种"模糊化"处理偏重于叙事，淡化了描写，失去了原文描写的生动性，缺乏诗意。其他两个译文都注意到该描写的重要性，林语堂的译文和黄俊雄的译文描写的都是静态之景，即"草上覆盖着落花"的景色，但各自所呈现的景色又是不同的；与 Giles 和林语堂的译文不同，黄俊雄的译文的文学性更强，精心选择了形容词"fragrant"、"wild"、"fresh"、"lovely"、"dazzling"，着力于景色描写，动词"dotted"的使用，增加了译文的生动性。再比如：

【例 28】

土地平旷，屋舍俨然，有良田美池桑竹之属。

译文 1：

...a new world of level country, of fine houses, of rich fields, of fine pools, and of luxuriance of mulberry and bamboo. （Giles 译）

译文 2：

He saw before his eyes a wide, level valley, with houses and fields and farms. There were bamboos and mulberries. （林语堂译）

译文 3：

Then came a vast plain with neat houses, lovely ponds, mulberries and bamboos dotting fertile land. （黄俊雄译）

此处描写渔人进入桃花源中看到的景象，原文这一句描写的语言简朴畅洁。相比较而言，其中 Giles 和黄俊雄的译文虽具体句式不同，但都较切近于原文简洁的风格。

三个译文对这些描写片段的处理，不仅显示了译文表达上的不同选择和风格，也显示了兼顾忠实和可读性的困难。

2.4 文化因素的处理

文化因素的处理是文言文翻译中的一个重点，特别是原文中一些涉及历史背景方面的知识往往会使译文读者感到陌生，影响阅读和理解，需要译者采取相应的策略。上文中我们已经指出，Giles 的策略是在不影响主要思想的前提下，删除一些大众读者不易拼读的名字和典故。《桃花源记》中涉及文化方面的因素主要是朝代、年号。例如，开头一句"晋太元中，武陵人捕鱼为业"中的"晋太元"，Giles 译为"Towards the close of the fourth century A. D."，直接隐去了中国的朝代和年号，代之以具体的时期。黄俊雄的译文前言中也解释了相关的翻译原则，但与 Giles 不同，他采取超常规的先释义、加词添字后翻译的做法，所以黄俊雄没有使用年号，而是使用皇帝号和朝代，并在括号里加入具体的时期予以补充，译为"In Emperor Xiaowudi's years in Eastern Jin Dynasty (376—396)"。林语堂使用了音译法，译为"During the reign of Taiyuan of Chin"。

原文中还涉及秦、汉、魏、晋等朝代，对不了解中国历史的英语读者来说，这无疑会成为理解的障碍。原文如下：

【例 29】
自云先世避秦时乱，率妻子邑人来自绝境，……问今是何世，乃不知有汉，无论魏晋。

译文 1：

... they informed him that their ancestors had sought refuge here, with their wives and families, from the troublous times of the house of Ch'in, ... they then inquired about the politics of the day, ignorant of the establishment of the Han dynasty, and of course of the later dynasties which had succeeded it. （Giles 译）

译文 2：

They said their ancestors had come here as refugees to escape from the tyranny of Tsin Shih-huang (builder of Great Wall) some six hundred years ago, and they had never left it.... They has not even heard of the Han Dynasty (two centuries before to two centuries after Christ), not to speak of the Wei (third century A. D.) and the Chin (third and fourth centuries). （林语堂 译）

译文 3：

... telling him that in order to escape the persecution of the cruel dictator Emperor Qinshihuang (259—210 BC), their forefathers, together with their wives and other people from the country, came to this place nobody had set foot in. ... Then they asked him what dynasty it was. They didn't even know there was the Han Dynasty, let alone the Wei and Jin Dynasties. （黄俊雄 译）

由此处译文可以看出，Giles 和黄俊雄都坚持了与上文"晋太元中"一贯的翻译原则。Giles 此处处理得较为简单，直接音译"秦"和"汉"，而对于"魏晋"还是采用模糊处理，使用"later dynasties which had succeeded it"来替代。黄俊雄在处理"避秦时乱"时加词"the cruel dictator Emperor Qinshihuang"，并补上具体的年代，有利于读者直接了解"秦时乱"的实际情况。与黄俊雄相同，林语堂也充分考虑了读者的接受，将"秦时乱"具体化为"秦始皇的暴政"，并借助世人皆知的"the Great Wall"，消除读者的陌生感。

原文中涉及文化的地方还有"黄发垂髫，并怡然自乐"。"黄发"，旧象征长寿，这里指老人，而"垂髫"，意思是"垂下来的头发"，这里指小孩子。"黄发垂髫"指的是"老人和小孩"。此处林语堂、Giles、黄俊雄都直接取其所指义。

《桃花源记》的这 3 个译文前后间隔 100 多年，译者背景各不相同，但在其翻译思想中都体现了追求忠实和可读性的原则。然而，三个译文不仅对原文的理解存在分歧，在译文表达和文化因素的处理方面也各自选择了不同的策略和技巧，体现了译者对原文的不同认识和独特的风格。

3 本章结语

本章我们以《邹忌讽齐王纳谏》的两个译文和《桃花源记》的三个译文为例分析了文言文翻译的基本问题、原则和策略。通过不同译文的比较显示,在文言文翻译中,不仅存在字词的意义理解问题,比如古今异义词、一词多义、词性活用、虚词的使用等,也存在理解的歧义和文学的空白等问题。这要求译者不仅要注意字词使用的上下文,还要借助相应的辞书工具,弄清原文本意,以免发生理解上的错误。在译文表达方面,既要根据英汉语在用词和句式方面的差异选择符合译文表达习惯的表达方式,还要特别注意文言文中的一些特殊字词和句式,例如省略句、倒装句、选择句以及一些特殊语气词的使用,如"也、矣"等等。此外,文言文翻译中涉及一些特殊的地名、人名、文化典故等文化因素,根据具体的翻译要求,可以适当采用解释性翻译、加注、增译等,补充相应的背景信息,以消除译文读者理解上的障碍。

附录1:

邹忌讽齐王纳谏
《战国策》

邹忌修八尺有余[1],而形貌昳丽[2]。朝[3]服衣冠,窥镜[4],谓其妻曰:"我孰[5]与城北徐公美?"其妻曰:"君美甚,徐公何能及君也?"城北徐公,齐国之美丽者也。忌不自信,而复问其妾曰:"吾孰与徐公美?"妾曰:"徐公何能及君也?"旦日[6],客从外来,与坐谈,问之客曰:"吾与徐公孰美?"客曰:"徐公不若君之美也。"明日,徐公来,孰视之,自以为不如;窥镜而自视,又弗如远甚。暮寝而思之,曰:"吾妻之美[7]我者,私我也;妾之美我者,畏我也;客之美我者,欲有求于我也。"

于是入朝见威王[8],曰:"臣诚[9]知不如徐公美。臣之妻私臣,臣之妾畏臣,臣之客欲有求于臣,皆以美于徐公[10]。今齐地方[11]千里,百二十城,宫妇左右莫不私王,朝廷之臣莫不畏王,四境之内莫不有求于王;由此观之,王之蔽[12]甚矣。"

王曰:"善。"乃下令:"群臣吏民能面刺[13]寡人之过者,受上赏;上书谏[14]寡人者,受中赏;能谤讥于市朝[15],闻寡人之耳者[16],受下赏。"令初下,群臣进谏,门庭若市。数月之后,时时而间进[17]。期年[18]之后,虽欲言,无可进者。燕、赵、韩、魏闻之,皆朝于齐[19]。此所谓战胜于朝廷[20]。

注释:
1. 修八尺有余:身长八尺。古代的尺比现在短。
2. 形貌昳丽:容貌很漂亮。昳丽:光艳。
3. 朝:早晨。
4. 窥镜:照镜子。窥:看。
5. 孰:谁。
6. 旦日:明日。
7. 美:(动词)称美,赞美。
8. 威王:齐威王。
9. 诚:确实。
10. 以美于徐公:以为我比徐公美。
11. 方:方圆。
12. 蔽:(受)蒙蔽。

13. 面刺：当面指责。
14. 谏：规劝。
15. 谤讥于市朝：在公共场所议论。
16. 闻寡人之耳者：闻于寡人之耳。
17. 间进：偶然进谏。间：间或，偶然。
18. 期年：满一年。
19. 朝于齐：到齐国去进见齐王。
20. 此所谓战胜于朝廷：这就是所谓在朝廷上战胜敌人。

译文 1：

Against Yes-men

Translated by Lin Yutang

Tsou Chi was over eight feet tall and of decent appearance. One morning, after putting on his clothes, he stole a glance of himself in the mirror and asked his wife: "Who do you think is handsomer, Mr. Shu of the north city or me?" His wife said, "You are very handsome, how can Mr. Shu compare with you!"

Mr. Shu of North city was a gentleman noted for his handsomeness. Chi dared not take her word for it and asked his concubine the same question. His concubine said, "Mr. Shu cannot compare with you." Next morning a guest came and after chatting for a while, Chi asked him, "Who do you think is handsomer, Mr. Shu or me?" And the guest replied, "Mr. Shu is not as handsome as you."

The following day, Mr Shu himself came to see Chi. Chi studied him carefully and thought him much handsomer than himself. He examined himself in the mirror and was convinced that he was far less handsome than Mr. Shu. So he lay in his bed and thought, "My wife praised me because she is partial to me. My concubine praised me because she is afraid of me. My friend praised me because he had something he wanted to ask of me."

Chi then went to the Court and said to King Wei of Tsi, "I am definitely not as handsome as Mr. Shu, but because my wife is partial to me, my concubine is afraid of me and my friend had something to ask of me, they all said I am handsomer than Mr. Shu. Now Tsi is a kingdom of a thousand square li with one hundred twenty cities. All the palace ladies and attendants are partial to you. All the courtiers are afraid of your power. And all the people have something to ask of you. So it seems to me that it is hard for you to hear the truth."

"Well said," replied the king. He then issued an order: "All ministers, officials and common people who can point out my mistakes shall receive the highest class of rewards. Those who write letters to advise me shall receive the second-class rewards. And those who can criticize me and my government at the market place so that it reaches my ears shall receive the third-class reward."

When the order was issued, the king was deluged with a torrent of advice, and the court was crowded with people. After a few months, people would only come intermittently with advice. And a year later, there was no mistake of the government which had not already been thought of and pointed out by somebody. The neighboring countries Yen, Chao, and Han, and Wei heard of what the king had done and came to acknowledge the state of Tsi as their leaders. This is called winning the war at home.

译文 2：

Frankness Rewarded

Translated by Huang Junxiong

Zou Ji was over six feet tall and strikingly handsome. After putting on his robe and hat one morning, he examined himself in the mirror and asked his wife, "Which of us is the better looking, Lord Xu of the north city or I?"

"Your looks are perfect," replied his wife. "How can Lord Xu compare with you?"

Since Lord Xu of the north city was one of the most handsome men in the State of Qi, Zou Ji still had his doubts and posed the same question to his concubine, who gave him the same answer.

The following day a visitor called, and as they sat chatting Zou Ji asked him, "How do I compare in appearance with Lord Xu?"

"Lord Xu is not nearly as handsome as you, sir," his visitor assured him.

The next day, Lord Xu himself called and Zou Ji, examining him carefully, suspected that he was outmatched. Another look in the mirror convinced him that he fell far short of the other. In bed that night he thought the matter over and reflected, "Partiality made my wife call me the more handsome, fear made my concubine do the same, while my visitor was governed by the fact that he wanted something from me."

Then he sought an audience with King Wei and said, "I am well aware that I am not as handsome as Lord Xu, yet my wife through partiality, my concubine out of fear, and a visitor in hope of a favour, all assured me that I was the finer man of the two. Now Qi has a thousand square li of land and one hundred and twenty cities. All your court ladies and attendants are partial to you, all your ministers are afraid of you, and all your subjects hope for favours from you. Judging by this, Your Majesty is very likely to be misinformed."

The king saw the truth of this and issued the order: "All those of my ministers, officers and subjects who dare to rebuke me to my face will receive high rewards. Those who offer written remonstrance will receive lesser rewards. Those who censure me in public, if their words reach my ears, will receive a lower reward."

After the proclamation of this order the palace gate at once became as thronged as a marketplace with men coming to remonstrate. A few months later some still came from time to time; but after a lapse of a year, eager as men were to speak, they had no charges to bring. When the states of Yan, Zhao, Han and Wei knew this, they all paid homage to the king of Qi. This is what is known as a victory won at court.

译文 1 选自林语堂. 林语堂中英对照丛书. 天津:百花文艺出版社,2002.
译文 2 选自 中国文学出版社编. 中国文学(古代散文卷). 北京:外语教学与研究出版社,1998.14—17 页。

附录 2:

桃花源记
陶渊明

晋太元[1]中,武陵[2]人捕鱼为业。缘[3]溪行,忘路之远近。忽逢桃花林,夹岸数百步,中无杂树,芳草鲜美,落英缤纷[4]。渔人甚异[5]之。复前行,欲穷其林[6]。

林尽水源[7],便得一山,山有小口,仿佛[8]若有光。便舍船,从口入。初极狭,才[9]通人。复行数十步,豁然开朗[10]。土地平旷[11],屋舍俨然[12],有良田美池桑竹之属[13]。阡陌交通[14],鸡犬相闻[15]。其中往来种作,男女衣着[16],悉[17]如外人。黄发垂髫[18],并怡然自乐。

见渔人,乃大惊,问所从来[19]。具答之。便要[20]还家,设酒杀鸡作食。村中闻有此人,咸[21]来问讯[22]。自云先世避秦时乱,率妻子邑人[23]来此绝境[24],不复出焉,遂与外人间隔[25]。问今是何世,乃[26]不知有汉,无论[27]魏晋。此人一一为具言[28]所闻,皆叹惋。余人各复延[29]至其家,皆出酒食。停数日,辞去。此中人语云[30]:"不足为外人道也。"

既[31]出,得其船,便扶向路[32],处处志[33]之。及郡下[34],诣[35]太守,说如此[36]。太守即遣人随其往,寻向所志^{37},遂迷,不复得^{38}路。

南阳刘子骥^{39}高尚士也,闻之,欣然规往^{40}。未果^{41},寻^{42}病终。后遂^{43}无问津^{44}者。

注释:
1. 太元:公元376—396年,晋孝武帝年号,是东晋孝武帝司马曜的第二个年号,共计21年。
2. 武陵:晋郡名,在今湖南常德一带。
3. 缘:循,沿着。
4. 落英缤纷:落花繁多的样子。落英:落花。一说,初开的花。缤纷:繁多的样子。
5. 异:惊异,诧异。这里的意思是"对……感到诧异"。
6. 穷其林:走到那片林子的尽头。穷:尽。
7. 林尽水源:林尽于水源,意思是桃林在溪水发源的地方就到头了。
8. 仿佛:隐隐约约,形容看的不真切的样子。
9. 才:仅。才通人:仅容一人通过。
10. 豁然开朗:形容由狭窄幽暗突然变得宽阔明亮的样子。豁然:一下子。开朗:开阔而明亮。
11. 旷:空阔,宽阔。
12. 俨然:整齐的样子。
13. 属:类。
14. 阡陌交通:田间小路交错相通。南北小路叫阡,东西小路叫陌。
15. 鸡犬相闻:(村落间)能互相听见鸡鸣狗叫的声音。相闻:可以互相听到。
16. 着:穿着。
17. 悉:全都。
18. 黄发垂髫(tiáo):指老人和小孩。黄发:黄色的头发,旧时是长寿的象征。垂髫:垂下来的头发。
19. 从来:从……地方来。
20. 要:同"邀",邀请。
21. 咸:都。
22. 问讯:打听消息。讯:消息。
23. 邑人:同县的人。
24. 绝境:与世隔绝的地方。
25. 间隔:隔绝,不通音信。
26. 乃:竟然。
27. 无论:不要说,更不必说。
28. 为具言:为(桃花源中的人)详细地说出。为:对,向。具:同"俱",完全,详尽。
29. 延:邀请。
30. 语云:对(他)说。"语"后面省略了代渔人的"之"字。
31. 既:已经,以后。
32. 便扶向路:就沿着原来的路(回去)。扶:沿着,顺着。向:原先。
33. 志:(名词作动词)作标记。
34. 郡下:指武陵郡城下。
35. 诣:拜见。
36. 说如此:说明了像这种情况。
37. 寻向所志:寻找以前所作的标记。志:作的标记。
38. 得:取得,获得,文中是找到的意思。
39. 刘子骥:名骥(lín)之,《晋书·隐逸传》里说他"好游山泽"。

40. 规:计划,打算。
41. 未果:没有实现。
42. 寻:不久。
43. 遂:终于。
44. 问津:问路,访求。津:渡口。

III 影视文体翻译

影视不仅是一种文化载体,其自身也是文化的一部分。无论是作为一种艺术形式,还是作为一种文化载体,影视作品都反映了其特定的时代、国家、民族与地域的社会文化,表现了其特有的文化价值观念。因此,影视翻译必须置于整个社会文化语境中进行。影视文体翻译的主要特点有:

(1) 影视作品的翻译是一种融合了文化因素与现代科技的语篇翻译,因此在选择翻译策略时,有时接近于实用文体,有时则接近于文学文体,因此特殊情况特殊处理。

(2) 不仅重视影视剧本语言层面的因素,而且重视与语言密切相关的社会文化因素。

(3) 重视视觉或者听觉的意象,用来给人言说或演唱,常需要伴随语言之外的音乐或画面等媒介,如电影、有声(像)广告、歌曲等。

(4) 重视影视剧本所具有的独特的艺术表现手法和文体特色,如以对话为主,语言的生活化、口语化程度较高,丰富的言语活动以及身势语等。

(5) 注重考虑现时观众的客观需求、审美趣味和接受水平,最终使观众的期待视野与译作的初衷实现和谐的统一。

第十四章　影视翻译

1　电影翻译特征

当今世界,除了口传与文本之外,意义还借视觉来传播。"视觉文化"这一领域涵盖了摄影、绘画、建筑、雕塑、园艺、电视、电影、广告、舞台艺术、服装设计等内容。自19世纪,视觉借各种各样的手段得以拓展,视觉经验成为商品,重塑受众的记忆与经验。"视觉文化"是文化历史走向当代的一种新的形态,它在多元的文化环境中显现出自己的个性,多维的走向中呈露出独特的构成。

毋庸置疑,电影是信息时代的产物,是视觉文化的一种。电影自诞生至今,已逾百年。百余年中,经过一系列电影大师的不懈努力,开创了艺术电影的典范,改变了受众对电影的既定观念,电影从一种单纯的娱乐形式一跃成为可与文学、戏剧、音乐、绘画、舞蹈、雕塑、建筑等比肩而立的独立的艺术门类。如今,电影已成为"后工业化"信息社会中的一个亚文化体,即所谓"电影文化"。电影文化由电影生产(企业组织、制作、发行)、消费(放映)、社会影响、研究等多方面组成,并涉及政治、经济、法律、科技、教育、宣传、艺术、风俗、人文科学等各个领域。

在传统的文学形式(文字文本)依然存在的今天,一种以新产生的技术化媒体(电影)来创作或解读传统媒体(文字文本)的方式在不自觉中进行着。当某些思考还在坚持文字的文学先于电影而存在,甚至为年代顺序所限,以文字文学的判定模式来作为衡量后者的标准时,视觉媒体如电影所带来的冲击性力量却正在改变着整个世界的存在方式。换言之,电影对整个世界的建构与解构是无法避免的。因而,关注电影领域是必要的。本章所要探讨的,就是电影的翻译。

当面对电影时,翻译工作者所翻译的对象、所涉及的领域,是形形色色的。可以说,电影翻译涉及的是这个光怪陆离的大千世界:上至天文,下至地理;各行各业,三教九流;恋人之间最缠绵的呢喃,法庭上罪犯最猥亵的语言。凡此等,皆为翻译的对象。电影翻译主要牵涉电影片名与对白翻译。当然,由于配音的需要,还有一种要求更严格的特殊翻译,即影视配音的对白翻译。由于在现实中,大量外来影片是以原声辅以目的语字幕对白的形式出现的,配音的对白翻译并非大多数,因此,本章只将配音的对白翻译作为普通对白翻译的一种特殊形式来讲解。

2　电影翻译标准

电影翻译有其独特性,在某种意义上来说,它也是属于翻译的一种。在当代的翻译活动中,谈论较多的是奈达的"功能对等"理论与德里达对包括奈达等的理论在内的解构。在奈达的"功能对等"中,如何使目的语与始发语表达意义相同的"同一",是实现"功能"的"对等"的唯一使命。此理论界定的根本是"同一",即不论是目的语,还是始发语,都应该有能力表达出它;不仅要表达出它,还要使受众完全"自然地"理解它,领会它的意义。这样,不论是始发语还是目的语中的受众,她/他们都要能够"自然地"倾听到那唯一的可能的翻译。这意味着,任何不同的语言,都可以在表达那个唯一的方面走到一种共同性之中,并且实现最大程度上的同一与统一。追求同一与统一,实质上是种"中心"主义的表现,其根源是西方的逻各斯中心主义。

然而,在哲学家们,尤其是德里达的笔下,"意义"已成"延宕"之势,永远是"缺席"的。从索绪尔的"差异"概念出发,德里达生造出一个词 difference。它既指"差异"——能指与所指之间、所指与所指之间、能指与能指之间的不同;又指"拖延"——"意义"在解释之中,其真正面目总是被推迟到来。换言之,确定的意义是不存在的。因为意义的不确定与不存在,任何"中心"或"结构"也就不复存在,诸如体系、体制、制度乃至形式等等,既无存在的基础,也没有存在的可能性。这就是德里达对包括奈达等的理论在内的解构。那么,假若奈达等的理性(主义)真的被彻底解构,人的思想所依据的东西是否还存在?如果不存在,那便意味着,人的存在等同于"无意义",或人本身就是"无意义"。不仅如此,"未来"永远是"未来",不曾来到,因而永远没有也不会来到。这其实是一种虚无主义。

由于翻译是人的翻译,人是变动的,是"历史性"的人:作为对同一作品的翻译,不同译者的翻译是不同的,具有变动性,因而是"历史性"的;即使是同一译者对同一作品的翻译,译者也是在不停地自我变化之中,她/他可能会不断修正自己以前的翻译,因而,也是"历史性"的。由此而论,尽管德里达的解构主义有着虚无主义的倾向,但"解构"的积极意义在于,它提醒我们,要关注诸如奈达等源于西方哲学传统的理论家的那种对人的束缚及对人的历史性、变动性的漠视。

蔡新乐在其专著《翻译的本体论研究:翻译研究的第三条道路、主体间性与人的元翻译构成》中,对翻译的相关问题的论述颇具启发意义,或许可以成为电影翻译的某种标准。蔡新乐认为,翻译是人的翻译,是人的文化或跨文化活动,而人是变动的,而不是也不应该是一成不变的、"结构化了"的人。而目前对翻译活动的探讨往往只是就翻译过程本身的可操作性进行的探讨,而且在很大程度上只是停留在对经验的总结上,或者只是作为一种言语运作的翻译,即对翻译的语言能力与转化功能所做的一些的基本探索。但是,这样的探索既不能说明人在其中扮演的角色,也无助于突出人的主体的形成与作用发挥。本来是人的翻译却成了翻译的翻译,人在翻译当中被异化了。

蔡新乐指出人与她/他所置身其间的文化是一体的。因而,在探讨翻译的时候,对于人的问题有必要给予充分的关注。只有在认可了人的个体特性的情况下,才能有针对性地去探索这一由个体及其差异形成的翻译世界。书中提出了人的"元翻译构成",即翻译世界中多元格局的基础或根基——假若没有个体的对自我统一性(unity)及它的个性(identity)的保护意识,翻译便是不可想象的。也就是说,翻译的立足点在于,人维护自身完整性的本能:无论是原作者,还是译者,都本能地具有对自身完整性的保护。换言之,人不是在她/他自身之外去思考，因而才能有在她/他自身之外展示这样的思考的可能性。这种自我保护的本能，形成翻译活动中多元的格局，而多元的格局，才是翻译存在的基础：假若语言、文化、思维模式完全一样，哪里有翻译存在的可能性与必要。

鉴于对人在翻译中的关注，蔡著提出翻译的"（之）间"性，或间（隔）性中的翻译。因为翻译始终是在某两种语言、两种文化、两个主体（作者与译者）之间进行的活动，一味突出某一单一主体的作用，不但是不正视翻译的复杂性，而且也是不可能的。翻译是关系（之间）的结晶，也是关系的表现。在这个意义上，翻译的主体应该是"间主体"，即两个主体之间，而不是过去说的"单纯的主体"。这也是翻译的基本运动路线：翻译就在人与人之间发生，而正是这种"间"促成了翻译的可能性、可行性与可操作性。

蔡著强调，当面对某一对象时，一定要把它视为一个整体，这样就简化了它的复杂性、多重性以及多元格局；但在认识过程当中，则应还原它应有的多元状态。也就是说，在翻译的过程中要对翻译与人的关系给予充分重视。具体说来，就是要关注两个主体——作者与译者——之间的互动交流，正视其中的多元复杂性，承认翻译的变动性/历史性。

当然，就现实而论，采取的立场与观点不同，翻译就会呈现出不同的甚至截然相反的面貌。"绝对"并不存在，因此上述提到的所有的翻译理论或判断标准也只是相对的：它们之间有可能是对立的，也有可能是互补的。

3　电影翻译原则

根据本章上述翻译理论，结合电影翻译的特殊性，有以下原则可供读者参考：

在翻译过程中，译者不可避免要带上自己的个体性，也很难由一种文化完全跨越到另一种文化中，那么电影翻译作为两个主体及两种文化的"之间"，如何在"之间"找到一个合适的平衡点，然后去翻译，这是电影翻译中首先应考虑的问题。为了考虑这个"之间"的关系及其平衡点，各种翻译策略都是可行的，诸如直译、意译、直译与意译结合、略去不译、转译等等。也许会有读者质疑，上述翻译策略的运用在过往的译论中也是常常出现的。的确如此。然而，置"之间"性理论于上述翻译策略之上，使其为理论指导的积极意义在于，"间"性理论时刻提醒我们，在运用各种翻译策略的过程中，要关注的是两个主体、作者与译者之间的互动交流。这两个个体，各自都不可避免地带有文化、民族、审美、习俗的不同，所以，在翻译过程中，要有那种好似人与人之间友好相处时的互相照顾、换位思考的人性关怀。换言之，没有任何一方是可以独断的、以自我为中心的。

其次，要承认翻译活动中的变动性与多元性，就要抛弃"任何原文都只有唯一一种可被接受的译文典范"的观念，谨慎、认真地去翻译，同时也要以一种严肃的审美眼光去看待别人与自己一样谨慎、认真翻译出的译文。

再次，翻译过程中，一边要总结一些原则，以供后来之用，一边也要有随时打破既定原则的勇气，因为翻译是人的翻译，不是任何僵化的结构可以套牢的。

另外，本章的任何举例与点评及与之相关的归纳出的经验、得、失，都具有符合该个案的合理性，然而，举例与点评本身并不一定指向真理本身。

最后,本章提供的各种原则,也只是一种尝试。

4 电影翻译实例

4.1 电影片名翻译

【例 1】

Pearl Harbor

译文:

《珍珠港》

点评:这部美国影片讲述的是二战中著名的珍珠港事件,译名直译为《珍珠港》,不仅名实相当,而且不会让人不知所云,因为大多数中国人对珍珠港这个地方及珍珠港事件并不陌生。翻译电影片名时,如果字面直译能够完全传达原文的意思,且不会让读者产生误解,则完全可以进行字面直译。

类似的例子还有,*Roman Holiday* 直译为《罗马假日》。

【例 2】

The Man in the Iron Mask

译文:

《铁面人》

点评:*The Man in the Iron Mask* 译为《铁面人》,既保持了原片名的含义,又符合汉语的习惯,体现了汉语的美。

类似的例子还有 *The Sound of Music* 译为《音乐之声》;*I Dreamed of Africa*,省去"I",译为《梦见非洲》;*Forever Young* 译为《永远年轻》或译为《青春永驻》,都是可以接受的,前者有种期盼的动感在里面,后者更书面化。

【例 3】

Anastasia

译文:

《真假公主》

点评:由英格丽·褒曼主演的影片 *Anastasia* 讲述的是一位自称是俄国末代沙皇的小女儿 Anastasia 的妇女,为了证明自己公主的身份,而在欧洲各国奔波的故事。这部影片的片名被译成《真假公主》。之所以如此,一是中国受众不熟悉这位公主的名字,二是该部影片确实是围绕"公主"身份展开的,这样翻译过来的片名能更好地表现原片的主旨,也更吸引受众。这就是在原文化与译入文化之间找平衡。

类似的例子又如 *The Bridges of Madison County* 译为《廊桥遗梦》。影片以地名为名,如果直译成《麦迪森县桥》,就根本体现不出影片中那对中年男女主人公情意绵绵、相见恨晚的爱情故事。相比之下,《廊桥遗梦》的译名不仅突出了原片主题,而且意境深远,给人浪漫而缺憾的联想。此外,*Speed* 译为《生死时速》,将影片那扣人心弦的紧张场面表现得淋漓尽致。*I'll Got Home for Christmas* 译为《一路闯关过圣诞》,和影片中主人公为了赢得圣诞礼物——心爱的跑车而历经千辛万苦赶回家过圣诞节的故事情节相得益彰。*You've Got Email* 的译名是《网络情缘》,比起直译《我收到了你的邮件》更忠实于该片的主题。

【例 4】

Water World

译文:

《未来水世界》

点评:有些电影片名如果仅直译,表达不出整个片名的意思,或会引起目的语受众的误解,就需充分考虑译语的表达手段,结合意译,以补充原名隐含之意。影片 *Water World* 是一部科幻片,讲的是在可预见的未来,洪水淹没了几乎所有的陆地,毁灭了人类文明,久居水上的一些幸存者身上长出了鳃,主人公马纳里就是其中的一位。故事情节就是围绕马纳里和其他幸存者为了争夺一张陆地地图而展开。如果直译为《水世界》,会使人以为是科教片。在"水世界"之前加上"未来"二字,片名听起来更像一部科幻片,意义既明确又有吸引力。

类似的例子还有,如大家熟悉的动画片 *Alice in Wonderland*,译成《爱丽丝梦游奇境记》,"梦游"二字的添加名副其实,因为故事发生在爱丽丝的梦里。*Lucky Number* 译成《幸运彩票》而非直译为《幸运号码》,是因为"number"在该片中特指的是彩票的号码,《幸运彩票》——这个译名意义更清晰,更能被受众所理解。还有 *Sister* 译成《修女也疯狂》,也是充分考虑目的语的文化构成而采取直译加意译。

【例 5】

Paradise

译文:

a.《伊甸园》;b.《金童玉女》

点评:影片 *Paradise* 译为《伊甸园》或《金童玉女》,都是可以接受的。这两个译名,侧重点有所不同。看完全片,受众会明白,原作者是通过作品诠释他理想中的伊甸园——在远离尘世的喧嚣与罪恶的孤岛上,处处绿草如茵、繁花似锦、藤萝缠绕、古木参天。两个不约而同从充满罪恶、尔虞我诈的现实社会中逃亡出来的陌生的少男少女,在美好的大自然的感召下,在开创生活的共同奋斗中相识、相知,过起了纯真、自然而又充满诗情画意的生活。影片多处照搬《圣经》中有关伊甸园的情节,使男女主人公宛若亚当、夏娃转世。影片表达了作者对现实世界的失望和对理想世界的向往。由此,《伊甸园》的直译名侧重的是影片的环境,只要具备一些西方文化背景知识的人便都知道伊甸园的美好;而《金童玉女》的译名是对片中男女主人公美好关系的侧重,是具有中国文化特色的对象亚当与夏娃般美好而相配的青少年男女的称谓。

【例6】

Waterloo Bridge

译文：

a.《滑铁卢大桥》；b.《魂断蓝桥》

点评：影片 Waterloo Bridge 译为《滑铁卢大桥》或《魂断蓝桥》都可以接受，但后者对中国受众明显更具诗化的感染力。如果直译为《滑铁卢大桥》，稍稍具有一些西方历史知识的受众就应该能猜到此影片讲述的是悲剧故事，直译使片名显得凝重、大气；即使对相应的历史知识一无所知或一时没有将思绪与拿破仑的惨败相连的受众，也会期待在这滑铁卢大桥上会发生怎样的故事。译为《魂断蓝桥》，是隐含在译者本身的本民族文化的因素在不自觉地起作用：中国古代蓝桥相会的故事与西方的悲剧电影之间发生联系。于是，"魂断蓝桥"四字将浪漫、哀婉的情调扑面带给中国受众，并准确把握了整个故事的脉搏。综合看来，译为《滑铁卢大桥》，译名凝重、大气，没有任何过错；译为《魂断蓝桥》，译名哀婉、传神，适合中国受众。

【例7】

Erin Brockvich

译文：

《永不妥协》

点评：外国的电影多喜欢用人名或地名做片名，借以突出主人公的形象，或事件发生的地点。而中国受众对外国人名、地名感到陌生、拗口，如果只考虑原片名的因素进行直译，势必会降低受众的兴趣。因此，译者往往要使原名与自己的文化之间产生互动：考虑受众的接受。茱莉亚·罗伯茨 2000 年主演的影片 Erin Brockvich 中，影片主人公 Erin 有着执著的性格和永不妥协的精神，于是，将其译作《永不妥协》，就是这种考虑"之间"的关系的结晶。如果译者按字面把片名直译成《艾琳·布罗克维奇》，不但难以记忆，也缺乏艺术感染力。

再比如电影 Thelma & Louise 译为《末路狂花》，Dolores Claiborne 译为《热泪伤痕》，都是中文片名取得不错的例子。若直译为《塞尔玛与路易丝》、《桃乐若丝·克莱朋》，就很难让人有印象。

【例8】

Englishman Who Went Up a Hill but Came Down Mountain

译文：

《神圣的大山》

点评：从中国受众的欣赏角度出发，影片译名不宜过长。有些外国电影片名较长，翻译时应格外注意，比如影片 Englishman Who Went Up a Hill but Came Down Mountain，如果直译过来简直不像一部电影的名字，建议译为《神圣的大山》，既简洁明了，又高度概括主题。翻译是人的翻译，译者应敢于打破原片名的束缚，在把握好分寸的前提下，从各种关系"之间"出发考虑译名。

【例9】

Gone with the Wind

译文：

a.《飘》；b.《乱世佳人》

点评：一些由家喻户晓的文学作品改编的电影，片名既可采取与原著一样的译名，也可采取别译或另译。比如由小说 Gone with the Wind 改编的电影，既可译为与原著一样的《飘》，也可根据影片拍摄时实际的侧重，另译为《乱世佳人》。这里，不仅仅是一个直译或意译的问题，而是带有对电影是一门独立的艺术门类的承认的意味——电影，即使是由某一原著改编而来的电影，也已不再是原著的小说本身，而是电影艺术，文学艺术与电影艺术是各自独立且比肩而立的艺术门类，不能用评判小说的标准去衡量改编电影。换言之，某种意义上说，改编的电影已经与原著脱离了关系，所以，对改编电影的译名，可以与原著一致，也可根据电影的实际侧重另译新名。

类似的例子有 Hamlet，可译为《哈姆雷特》或《王子复仇记》；Rebecca 可译为《吕贝卡》或《蝴蝶梦》。

【例10】

Pride and Prejudice

译文：

《傲慢与偏见》

点评：对经典名著改编的电影翻译采取与原著相同的翻译方式，并非不承认电影作为独立艺术门类的地位，而是借受众熟悉的名字，便捷地传达影片的主要内容。如果没有更好的别译名，采取与原著相同的影名翻译是可取的。

类似的例子有很多，比如《奥塞罗》（Othello）、《李尔王》（King Lear）、《麦克白》（Macbeth）、《罗密欧与朱丽叶》（Romeo and Juliet）、《大卫·科波菲尔》（David Copperfield）、《简·爱》（Jane Eyre）、《嘉莉妹妹》（Sister Carrie）、《幸运的吉姆》（Lucky Jim）、《朱利斯·恺撒》（Julius Caesar）、《德伯家的苔丝》（Tess of the D'urbervilles）、《儿子与情人》（Sons and Lovers）、《呼啸山庄》（Wuthering Heights）、《华盛顿广场》（The Washington Square）、《威尼斯商人》（The Merchant of Venice）、《汤姆索耶历险记》（The Adventures of Tom Sawyer）、《格列佛游记》（Gulliver's Travels）、《艰难时世》（Hard Times）、《远大前程》（Great Expectations）、《卡丝特桥市长》（The Mayor of Caster Bridge）、《愤怒的葡萄》（The Grapes of Wrath）、《教父》（God Father）、《仲夏夜之梦》（A Midsummer Night's Dream）、《第十二夜》（Twelfth Night）、《野性的呼唤》（The Call of the Wild）、《海狼》（The Sea-wolf）；A Dream of Red Mansion（《红楼梦》）、Water Margin（《水浒传》）、The Song of Youth（《青春之歌》）、Red Crag（《红岩》）、Journey to the West（《西游记》）等。

【例11】

Ghost

译文：

a.《幽灵》；b.《人鬼情未了》；c.《第六感生死恋》

点评：由于种种历史原因，虽同受中华文化的熏陶，但大陆、香港、台湾三地对同一部影视片名的翻译各异，如 Ghost，大陆译为《幽灵》/《鬼魂》，香港译为《人鬼情未了》，台湾译为《第六感生死恋》。另一部影片 Pretty Woman，大陆译为《漂亮女人》，香港译为《风月俏佳人》，台湾译为《麻雀变凤凰》。又如，影片 The House of the Spirits，大陆译为《英华世家》，香港译为《第六感之恋》，台湾译为《金色豪门》。Mrs. Doubtfire 刚上市不久，一些刊物译为《道尔希特菲尔夫人》，另一些刊物译为《惹火太太》，而该片在香港被译为《窈窕奶爸》。这些译名的不同，主要是文化的差异，或不同译者自身的不同特性与原片名发生了不同的互动。上述译名均可接受，但有些译名是稍胜一筹的，比如《风月俏佳人》，"风月"二字暗示了女主人公的身份，"俏"字带有俏皮的喜剧色彩，暗示了原片的风格。而《第六感生死恋》这样的译名，因为类似的名字太频繁地被使用，反而失去了自身的特点，让人与其他影片混淆。更有甚者，由于受商业利润的驱使，片面追求上座率，有些译名常使用刺激和煽情的字眼，往往表现在"大"字滥用、"血"字飞溅、"魔鬼"出没和"情意"外露四个特点上，致使很多影片因片名雷同而失去自身特性，这也是翻译中需要避免的。只有谨慎、认真、平衡而又具有一定个性的翻译，才是较为合适的翻译。

【例 12】

《花样年华》

译文：

In the Mood for Love

点评：《花样年华》的英文片名翻译并未沿用影片中周璇演唱的歌曲《花样的年华》的英译 Full Bloom，而是译为 In the Mood for Love，是出于要体现影片主题的需要。"in the mood for"表示"有意做什么"、"想要什么"，意在渲染着一种（主人公）内心渴望的状态或气氛，表现出对爱的向往。《花样年华》是一部唯美、浪漫的爱情文艺片，从色彩、服装、场景到片名、情节、人物，从造型到叙事，所有电影元素的运用使整部影片充满了一种独特的情调，正好体现了该片唯美的主题。

4.2 电影对白翻译

【例 13】

《花样年华》In the Mood for Love

① 周慕云：你不是还在医院吗？

    阿　炳：哎，麻烦多着呢！别再说了，先借我 30 块！

    周慕云：干什么？

    阿　炳：哎呀，帮帮忙，名誉攸关。

    周慕云：怎么回事？

    阿　炳：哎……还不是那个阿海！那天他到医院来看我，说有两场稳赢的马，十拿九稳。我看他挺有把握的，连线都来不及拆，一个劲儿地跑出医院，把老婆本儿掏出来,去马场搏一搏,结果输了个精光。

周慕云:那你活该,拼死还要去赌。

阿 炳:唉,我以为负伤上阵,必有鸿运。谁知道只剩两块钱。一赌气就去关中找贵妃去了。

周慕云:病成这样你还去找女人?

阿 炳:想冲冲喜嘛!

译文:

Zhou Muyun: You've out of hospital!

Ah Bing: Don't mention hospital! Lend me HK $30!

Zhou Muyun: What for?

Ah Bing: You gotta help me save face!

Zhou Muyun: What's the big deal?

Ah Bing: It's Ah Hai's fault. He gave me a racing tip, said it was a sure thing. Before they've taken out the stitches... I bet everything I had. And I lost my shirt!

Zhou Muyun: What did you expect?

Ah Bing: I though t it was my lucky day. Anyhow, I had only HK $2 left. So I went to the whorehouse.

Zhou Muyun: You were in no shape for sex!

Ah Bing: I thought it would improve my luck.

点评:"冲冲喜"是典型的中国文化用语,一种中国旧时的迷信风俗,意指一个家庭或地方出现不祥之事时,通过办喜事来驱除所谓作祟的邪气,希望有好运转来。阿炳赌场失意,希望情场得意,驱除晦气。在这里,译者恰当地将这一典型的文化词语作了处理,采用了意译的方式,消除了异化翻译可能给目的语受众带来的陌生感。试想一下,如果"冲喜"在这里被译为"to have sex with a whore to get rid of my bad luck at the track",目的语受众能明白其中的文化内涵吗?而且,字幕翻译的时空局限性和瞬时性也不允许加注解释。"improve my luck"的译法保留了原文的意义,实现了交际的目的——简洁、达意,这是可取的。另外,像"老婆本儿"、"负伤上阵,必有鸿运"等俗语都作了意译处理,这都是灵活的、变通的翻译。

② 苏丽珍:干嘛无缘无故请我吃饭?

周慕云:今天收了稿费,你的那份又不肯要,只好请你吃饭了。

苏丽珍:其实关我什么事?我只是在旁边打打边鼓而已。

译文:

Su Lizhen: Why a special dinner tonight?

Zhou Muyun: Since you won't take your share of the writing fee...

Su Lizhen: All I did was giving you some thoughts.

点评:"打边鼓"是出自戏剧的专业术语,原意是"旁敲侧击"。这里,苏丽珍的意思是说,她只是为周慕云写作出了些点子,没做别的什么。意译为"give some thoughts",正符合原意。

③ 苏丽珍:下次吧……慢慢打(麻将)啊!

译文:

  Su Lizhen: Next time.... Enjoy your game.

点评:"慢慢打(牌等)"、"慢慢吃"、"慢慢走"、"慢慢挑(衣服或别的商品)"等都是富有中国文化特色的礼貌用语。如果把其中的"慢慢"译出来,目的语受众恐怕难解其意。这里,译者没有逐字死译为"Play slowly",而是人性化地考虑了符合目的语表达习惯的说法。

  此外,该片中诸如"慢慢走"、"你走了"等礼貌用语都作了相应的处理,按语境的需要分别译为"Bye"、"Good evening"等,给目的语受众自然的感觉。另外,其他告别用语如"我先回去了"、"我先走了",译者都根据两种文化之间的平衡作了灵活的处理,分别译为"I'll leave you in peace"、"I'll be off, then"、"I should go"、"I'll be going"等。

④ 阿　炳:说的是啊,像我这样的人,是个直肠子,哪有心事?
  周慕云:那怎么办?

译文:

  Ah Bing: I'm just an average guy, I don't have secrets like you.
  Zhou Muyun: So?

点评:译文对"是个直肠子,哪有什么心事"作了压缩性意译。"直肠子"这一中国特色的文化意象,如果直译,恐怕目的语受众也难以接受。

  其他例子及其译文,也用字极为节省,表达干净利落。有人说,王家卫的电影台词和场景精简得不多余一个标点符号,没有一句废话。如果以《花样年华》作为例证的话,此话一点不假,而其英译也恰当地再现了原片的语言风格。如:

⑤ 何先生:那好吧。如果做完事情我还没回来,你先走,我来锁门好了。

译文:

  Mr. He: Leave when you're ready. I'll lock up.

⑥ 苏丽珍:领带很好看啊!
  何先生:你看得出我换了领带?我还以为差不多呢。

译文:

  Su Lizhen: That tie looks good on you.
  Mr. He: You noticed? It's much like the old one.

⑦ 苏丽珍:麻烦你到前面停一下。
  周慕云:干什么?
  苏丽珍:我在这儿下车好了。
  周慕云:还是我先下吧。

译文：

Su Lizhen： Please pull up here!
Zhou Muyun：Why?
Su Lizhen： I'll get off first.
Zhou Muyun：No, let me.

【例 14】

《卧虎藏龙》Crouching Tiger, Hidden Dragon

① 守住真气，我一定回来。

译文：

Save your energy. I'll be back.

② 用这口气，练神还虚吧。

译文：

Use it to meditate.

③ 道元真人年初从武当山路过这里，说起你正在闭关修炼。

译文：

Monk Zheng said you were at Wudan Mountain. He said you were practicing deep meditation.

点评：这几例中的"真人"、"真气"、"闭关修炼"等都是道教术语。"道元真人"中的"真人"指道家所说修行得道的人，多用作称号。由于一般西方受众对道教了解甚少，译者在此借用了 Monk 一词，代指道教"真人"。"真气"是道家功的核心之一，也是今天中医的原理和依据，指人体内能使各器官正常地发挥功能的原动力。道家功讲究通过静坐来凝神调息，以贯通经络达到修身养性之目的。

字幕对白出现在银幕下方，是瞬时性的，在这种局限下，译者借用了英语中的"energy"、"meditation"等基本意思相近的词语来对这些源语文化词语进行一般化，使受众瞬间了解影片的基本信息。

④ 娘说鲁老太爷是朝内的大官，又是三代翰林。

译文：

The Gous are a very powerful family.

⑤ 三教九流，往来人等。

译文：

Here, you'll find all sorts of characters.

点评：有些文化语言，难以找到替代词，完全删除又不利于影片理解，此时译者使用了缩减翻译方法，即简要译出原文化词的精髓要旨。

"三代翰林"是对朝中大官的进一步补充，意味着这是个名门望族。译者此处没有直接翻译"三代翰林",而是将全句意义压缩为"是个有权势的家族",简单明了。

"三教九流"本来指儒、佛、道教和儒家、道家、阴阳家、法家等,中国文化色彩浓重。此处译者抛弃了该词的文化色彩,压缩译成 all sorts of characters(各种各样的人)。

⑥ 跟着我惹来不少的江湖恩怨。

译文:

Too many men have died at its edge.

⑦ 在江湖上走来走去的,是不是很好玩?

译文:

It must be exciting to be a fighter, to be totally free!

⑧ 江湖上也要有所联络,九门提督才坐得稳。

译文:

Contacts in the Jiang Hu underworld can ensure your position.

⑨ 李慕白突然交出青冥剑,又退出了江湖。

译文:

Li Mubai gave up his sword and his warrior days.

⑩ 化装成江湖卖艺的,一路跟上北京城里来的。

译文:

He went undercover and followed her here.

点评:有些文化词语含义抽象,必须结合上下语境理解,于是译者使用了改写式意译。以"江湖"一词为例,该词含义抽象,语境不同,含义不同。为此,译者较多地使用了改写法,以寻求两种语言之间的平衡。

"江湖恩怨"被译者直接改译为"仇杀"。在"江湖上走来走去",反映了说话人玉娇龙对传统礼教的反感和对自由生活的向往,译者对人物内心准确把握,将之理解为"作一个自由自在的斗士"。而"江湖上也要有所联络"中的"江湖"却是指与朝廷和官方相对的势力,译者处理为 underworld(黑社会)。"退出了江湖"被译者改译成"放弃当武士的生活"。"化妆成江湖卖艺的"实际是指"隐藏身份、秘密跟踪"之意。这些例子反映了译者对语境的准确理解和充分考虑"之间"的关系。

⑪ 我乃是潇洒人间一剑仙。

译文:

I am the invincible sword goddess.

⑫ 我宁愿游荡在你身边做七天的野鬼,跟随你,就算落进最黑暗的地方。

译文:

I would rather be a ghost drifting by your side, as a condemned soul, than enter heaven without you.

点评:"仙"即"神仙",就是长生不老的人(immortal),是道教用语。"成仙永恒"是道教追求的终极目标。而"god and goddess"是西方宗教中具有超自然力量、能控制自然或现实世界某一部分的神,与由人修炼而成的"仙"有本质区别。

依据中国传统迷信的说法,人死后会有7天的过渡期,即灵魂在这世上逗留7天,然后去冥界见阎王。而西方的基督教信奉的是,人死时要接受耶稣基督的赦免,被洁净罪过后上天堂。译文基于对两种信仰的了解,对源语文化作了处理,使英译文本更容易为信奉上帝的西方人理解。

【例 15】

《越狱》Prison Break

① **Veronica Donovan**: I deserve to know, I loved him as much as you did.
   Michael Scofield: Past tense for you, maybe. Not me.

译文:

维罗妮卡·多诺万: 我应该知道,因为和你一样,我曾经爱过他。

迈克尔·斯科菲尔德:你的爱是过去时,而我不是。

点评:《越狱》*Prison Break*,由布莱特·莱特纳导演,温特沃什·米勒主演,是美国FOX电视台2005—06年的热播剧。《越狱》的剧情惊心动魄:天赋极高的建筑师迈克尔·斯科菲尔德(Michael Scofield)的哥哥林肯·巴罗斯(Lincoln Burrows)被控杀人入狱,被判死刑。迈克尔坚信哥哥清白无辜,自己设计"抢银行"入狱,与哥哥关进同一座监狱,以实施越狱计划,力图营救哥哥。他事先把监狱地图纹在自己身上,查阅监狱关键犯人的资料,周密部署越狱计划。与此同时,陷害林肯入狱的副总统派出特工加紧行动,对他们进行再次迫害。最后,在同样想越狱的犯人的配合下,几经周折,兄弟俩成功逃出监狱。

这句对白中,迈克尔说维罗妮卡对他哥哥林肯的爱只是过去的事情了,根据对白中实际话语的表达意向,"过去式"被改写成了"过去时",它们两个一个是说句子的时态问题,一个是说动词的状态,有区别,也有联系。译者没有对其进行解释,给出的字幕"你的爱是过去时",只要有基本英语常识的受众都会理解和明白。

影视作品的翻译有必要让受众了解一些异国文化,而非处处需要完全考虑目的语中是否有对应的词汇,这也是在翻译中让目的语受众学习、了解外国文化的一种很好的方式。

② **Paul Kellerman**: In this case, we're hoping you'll suspend that position, at least temporarily.
   Bishop: If the inmate appeals to me for intervention, how can I turn my back on him?

译文:

保罗·凯勒曼:这个案子我们希望您能保留您的立场,至少是暂时的。

主教: 如果囚犯需要我的干预,我怎么能袖手旁观呢?

点评:当然,有些翻译若采用目的语中完全没有的词汇或方式去翻译,目的语受众根本无法看懂。这种情况下,就又需要在"之间"寻求平衡点。"turn one's back on sb."是英语里常见的一个习惯用语,译者没有把它按字面意思直译成"掉转脸去不理睬或拒绝帮助"等,而选取了出自宋代大文豪苏轼《朝辞赴定州论事状》"弈棋者,胜负之形,虽国工有所不尽,而袖手旁观者常见之,何则?"中的"袖手旁观",可谓贴切兼雅俗共赏。

③ **Sara Tancredi**： I believe in being part of the solution, not the problem.
Michael Scofield：Mmm. Be the change you want to see in the world. What?
Sara Tancredi： Nothing. That was just my senior quote.

译文:
萨拉·唐克里迪： 我愿意做解决问题的途径之一,而不是问题本身。
迈克尔·斯科菲尔德:欲变世界,先变其身。什么?
萨拉·唐克里迪： 没什么,碰巧是我四年级时的座右铭。

点评:钱锺书在提到翻译时有"化境"说,其实就是一种对"间"关系的考虑:所谓"化",就是使某两种东西巧妙而完好地融合在一起,成为一体。"Be the change you want to see in the world"是《越狱》里一句俗语式的经典台词,蕴含很深的哲理,但汉语中没有与之相对应的话语,在对这句话的翻译中,译者给出的汉译字幕汉语韵味很浓:"欲变世界,先变其身",对照工整,意味深长,巧妙地融合了英语的和汉语的文化表达方式,两者都不显痕迹却又似乎朦胧可见。

④ **Lincoln Burrows**：You think I meant to knock up Lisa Rex? I was just being stupid. Hurt. Shouldn't have pushed her away, though.
Michel Scofield： You pushed everyone away.

译文:
林肯·巴罗斯： 你以为我喜欢?我当时是糊涂了,受到了伤害。不过不应该把地拒之门外。
迈克尔·斯科菲尔德:你把谁都拒之门外。

点评:阻断式翻译策略即是平常所说的省略翻译方法。采取这种翻译策略主要有两方面的原因,一是某处根本就不需要翻译出来,因为电影除了台词以外,还有即时画面可以补充受众所需要的信息;另外是因为某处的言语信息由于受文化差异的影响,不可译,或即使译出来反而会引起受众的疑惑或误会,所以就索性不译。

"You think I meant to knock up Lisa Rex?"中"knock up"是"使某人怀孕"的意思,而Lisa Rex可能是林肯在与Veronica之后又认识的一个女孩。译者没有译出"使Lisa Rex怀孕",因为中美文化的差异,这里若把林肯过去复杂的"恋爱史"译出来,只会让很多受众感到莫名其妙,所以阻断省略为宜。

【例16】
Gone with the Wind《乱世佳人》
① **Ashely**：Well, isn't it enough that you gathered every other man's heart today? You always had mine. You cut your teeth on it.

译文：

卫希礼：今天你取得那么多男人的心，还不够吗？我的心总是你的。

点评："You cut your teeth on it"与前面"you always had mine"意思完全相同，只是后者更加形象、生动，由于受字幕出现时间的限制，后面可以删掉。

② **Scarlett**：why don't you say it, you coward？You're afraid to marry me. You'd rather live with that silly little fool who can't open her mouth except to say "yes" "no", and raise a houseful of mealymouthed brats just like her！

译文：

斯嘉丽：你这个胆小鬼，不敢娶我。你宁可娶那个听话的傻瓜，然后生群傻瓜孩子。

点评：这句台词的场景是斯嘉丽在十二橡园对卫希礼表白，被拒绝后情绪愤怒，语气由温柔变得倔强、不服气，语速加快。激烈的争吵使画面转换很快，受众没有时间看太长的字幕，所以浓缩翻译为好

③ **Rhett**：If I tried drawing a draft, the Yankees would be on me like a duck on a junebug. So you see, my dear, you've based yourself to no purpose.

译文：

瑞德：我一动那笔钱，北佬就会闻着味儿追上来。亲爱的，你这次真得让自己白白蒙受屈辱了。

点评："be on me like a duck on a junebug"是个俚语，翻译过来受众也无法理解，反而增加了受众处理语境的负担，因此省略翻译为宜。

④ **Charles**：He refused to fight.

Asheley：Not quite that, Charles. He just refused to take advantage of you.

译文：

查尔斯：他不敢接受我的挑战。

卫希礼：并非如此，他不过不想占你的便宜。

点评：此对白的字面直译为，"查尔斯：他拒绝去打仗。卫希礼：不是那样，他只是不想利用你。"但是这样的译文与对白场景关联性较弱，会导致受众的不理解。这里的"fight"不是即将爆发的南北内战，而是查尔斯看不惯瑞德的高傲，要挫他傲气，向他挑战，要求决斗。因此，在考虑了实际需要后，改译为好。

⑤ **Scarlett**：I couldn't let you do anything like that, and anyway, it's done now.

Asheley：Yes, it's done now. You wouldn't let me do anything dishonorable yet you'd sell yourself in marriage to a man you didn't love.

译文 1：

斯嘉丽：我不会让你做那种事，无论如何，木已成舟。

卫希礼：是的，木已成舟。你不让我做不名誉的事情，自己却卖给不爱的婚姻。

译文 2：

斯嘉丽：我不会让你做这种事情的，不管怎么样，现在事情已经解决了。

卫希礼：是啊，解决了。你不让我做任何不名誉的事，却允许你把自己卖给一个不爱的人。

点评：两种翻译均可接受。而两个译本相比，译文 1 虽简练，但与电影情节发展不一致。译文 2 运用解释性翻译策略，更清楚明了。这里关键是对"it's done now"的理解，斯嘉丽嫁给不爱的人，已经是铁定的事实，这是一种感叹：无论如何，不管采取什么办法，庄园的 300 元税有了着落，庄园终于保住了。结合故事前后发展以及卫希礼说这句话时的心情，以译文 2 更恰当。

⑥ **Scarlett**：Oh, fiddle—dee—dee, Melannie, aren't things bad enough without you talking about dying？

译文：

斯嘉丽：废话，媚兰，事情都到这个地步了，你还说死呀死呀的。

点评：此句是意译，传递了说话者的意图，而且非常口语化，符合说话的场景。

⑦ **Ashely**：You can drop the moonlight and magnolia，Scartlett。

译文：

卫希礼：你能把月亮都说圆了，斯嘉丽。

点评：中国受众对"moonlight"和"magnolia"很陌生，暗含意图是卫希礼知道斯嘉丽在说谎，意译为"把月亮说圆"更加形象生动。

⑧ **Mammie**：Miss Scarlett! Don't spoil it, miss Scarlett.
Scarlett：Turn me loose, you fool, turn me loose! It's Asheley.

译文：

奶　妈：斯嘉丽小姐，别打扰他们！

郝思嘉：放开我，你这傻瓜，那是卫希礼。

点评："spoil it"直译为"破坏"，这里结合语境，解释性翻译为"别打扰她们"，更容易理解。

⑨ **Strew**：Ah, buddy, of course there's going to be a war.

译文：

思图：噢，哥们，当然会有战争。

⑩ **Scarlet**：Well, that's fine. But I warn you just in case you change your mind. I intend to lock my door.

译文：

斯嘉丽：好，那好。不过我先要告诉你，为了防止你变卦，我要给我的房门上锁。

点评:美国翻译理论家劳伦斯·韦努蒂提出了二分的翻译方法:归化和异化。归化和异化不仅体现在语言形式层面上,而且表现在对文化因素的处理上。归化法要求译者向目的语读者靠拢,采取目的语读者所习惯的表达方式,原文的文化特色也要符合译入语的文化规约;而异化法要求译者以源语文化为归宿,在风格和形式上应完全保留源语的特色。

实际上,归化、异化都是在不同情况下寻找两方关系的平衡点。这里翻译为"哥们"、"变卦",都具有浓厚的中国色彩,且更加口语化,拉近了受众与影片的距离。

⑪ **Scarllet**: I'm scared to death, and if you had the sense of a goat you'd be scared, too!

译文:

斯嘉丽:我吓得要死了。你就是木得像头驴,也该觉得害怕。

⑫ **Ellen**: Look at Scarlett, she's never even noticed Charles before, now just because he is your beau, she is after him like a hornet!

译文:

爱伦:看斯嘉丽,她以前从不多看查尔斯一眼,现在就因为他是你的男友,她就缠着他。

⑬ **Scarlett**: That man looking at us and smiling. A nasty dog.

译文:

斯嘉丽:那个笑着看我们的人,真是个丑八怪!

点评:形象生动的比喻具有浓厚的文化色彩,但中国受众对此很陌生,直译不易被受众理解,因此字幕翻译采取了省略或替换喻体的策略。

⑭ **India**: Can't stand that Scarlett. If you'd see the way she throws herself at Ashley.

译文:

英迪亚:我受不了那个斯嘉丽,你看她向卫希礼投怀送抱的样儿。

⑮ **Rhett**: I think it's hard winning a war with words, gentleman.

译文:

瑞德:各位,我认为纸上谈兵没有什么用。

⑯ **Rhett**: Don't flatter yourself; I am not a marrying man.

译文:

瑞德:别自我陶醉了,我可不是个结婚的人。

点评:上述翻译,提高了影片的感染力和亲切感,提供了最大的文化语境效果。

⑰ **Mammy**: You done had a baby, Miss Scarlett, and you ain't never goin' to be. No 18 and a half inches again. Never. And there ain't nothing to do about it.

译文：

奶妈：你生过孩子了,小姐,你永远也不能回到18寸半了！永—远！我—没—有—办—法！

点评：一部译制片的成功有多种因素,除了原剧本和演员的表演之外,剧本的翻译与配音演员的再表演起了重要的作用。此时,电影译文还要受到时间、演员口型、字幕字数等因素的严格限制。影响配音电影质量的最重要因素就是要对口型。所谓"口型",主要就是汉语配音的时间长度和原声完全一致,同时照顾到每句台词第一个音节和最后一个音节的开合。一般说来,口型的制约与尊重表达习惯并不矛盾,因为译者在考虑措词的同时就已想到口型问题了。万一出现不可调和的矛盾,一般采取放弃口型的吻合,尊重译文的表达习惯的原则。上述电影《乱世佳人》的一段对白中,老黑奴奶妈的话语中含有浓浓的黑人英语气息,根据剧情,译语受众可以了解到斯嘉丽刚刚生完孩子没多久,腰围也增加了,正急得让奶妈给量尺寸、想办法。画面中奶妈说这句话时语气坚定,且为自己的正确判断而洋洋得意。译者在处理时结合了画面中奶妈口型的开合程度,运用"—"这一符号来对口型,"永—远！我—没—有—办—法！",再结合配音演员栩栩如生的配音效果,巧妙处理了口型开合和意义传达的矛盾,把精彩的银幕形象栩栩如生地传达了出来。

【例17】

《大腕》Big Shot's Funeral

① 王小柱：谁,谁的葬礼？

　　尤　优：文艺界的人。

译文：

Louis Wang：All right. Whose funeral?

Yo Yo：　　Someone in the arts.

点评：《大腕》Big Shot's Funeral 讲述的是好莱坞大腕导演泰勒在心力交瘁、突然病倒之际,留下遗嘱让他的摄影师尤优为他办一个喜剧葬礼的故事。

依照泰勒的"遗愿",他的葬礼由尤优全权负责。尤优找来老同学王小柱(又名路易·王)共商此事。王小柱自称多次组织过大型活动,可一听是葬礼便觉得不可思议。在确定尤优没和他开玩笑后,他才直奔主题,问尤优是谁的葬礼。然而尤优并没有直截了当地告诉他是泰勒的葬礼,却只说是"文艺界的人"。显然,尤优的回答是为了引起王小柱的兴趣,故意设置悬念。他想传达的会话含义其实是说"想不想知道这个人在文艺界有多大的影响力？"那么,如何将这层弦外之音在译文中得以重现？此例中译者采用了直译的方法,准确地向目的语受众传递了源语对白中的会话含义。

② 尤优：这小狐狸是谁呀？

　　张总：这是泰勒先生的情人！

译文：

Yo Yo：　　Who's this?

Mr. Zhang：Tyler's lover!

点评：举办葬礼需要 300 多万元经费，于是王小柱找人掏钱，请来影视公司的张总谈条件。张总为让新签约的女演员一夜成名，要求在整个葬礼过程中，让她始终"傍"着泰勒的遗体。尤优一看那女子长得百般妖娆，就叫她"小狐狸"。从字面意思来看，把人说成狐狸，显然是不真实的。但这看似荒谬的话语在该字幕语境中恰恰产生了会话含义。尤优话语中暗含的信息是，泰勒葬礼上要这个妖媚女子干什么。通过分析可以看出，此处采用直译较妥，即译为"Who's this fox?"。这种处理不会引起英美受众的误解或费解，因为英语"fox"一词的词义与汉语中"狐狸"对应。另外，此处的直译恰如其分地再现了会话含义。

再来看看张总的回答。张总听尤优出言不逊，于是采取回击。他当然明白女演员不是泰勒的情人，而只是借此身份在葬礼上曝光罢了。由此产生的会话含义可以理解成"你敢说她是'小狐狸'？她可要在葬礼上扮演泰勒情人呢！"同理，直译为上策。

③ 尤优：你要是不怕那什么，就先住我这儿。不是，我不是这意思。我是说住宾馆还是贵，费钱。我也不是说你没钱，你有的是钱。这不是钱的事，那什么，我是说你这儿也没朋友。你要是不怕那什么，我要说什么来着？

露西：你可不可以过来抱抱我？

译文：

Yo Yo：You can sleep with me if you want. No, that's not what I mean. I mean, hotels aren't cheap. Not that you don't have money, because I'm sure you do. It's not the money, it's just... So if you don't care about, you know... If you're not afraid... What the hell am I talking about?

Lucy：Could you come here and hug me?

点评：由于英汉两种语言在思维方式、语言习惯和认知结构等方面存在差异，直译有时不能把会话含义准确贴切地表达出来。这时，可以采取补译，在直译的基础上适当增加一些词句，使原来的会话含义更加明显，从而让受众在有限的时间里更快速准确地领会会话含义。泰勒病危，拍片取消。露西（泰勒的私人助理）手头紧，不得不离开高档旅馆找别处住。一个大雨倾盆的夜晚，尤优帮露西把行李搬到他家，煮了碗热汤让她喝。上面对白是露西喝汤时尤优对她说的话。不难看出，尤优说话啰唆、条理不清。联系电影，此时这对男女主角的关系正在不断升温。由此判断，尤优其实是在说服露西住下来，但又觉得难以启齿，所以采取了这种迂回的言语策略。原文"你要是不怕那什么，就先住我这儿"如果直译成"If you're not afraid of that, you can stay here"，会让目的语受众摸不着头脑，因此需要适当增补词语。译者对原对白中的"那什么"进行补充，添加了"sleep with me"，使原来的会话含义清晰明了。但是，由于译文和原文在语义上存在一定的出入，建议译为"Stay if you don't care about sleeping with me"。

④ 王小柱：以后要再出这种事，我拧下你的脑袋！听见没有？

尤　优：你跟谁说话？你给我听着，葬礼的事我说了算！该给你的钱，一分也少不了你的！你要再多嘴，我让你的葬礼提前办了！

译文：

Louis Wang：This happens again, I'll rip your damn head off. Hear me?

Yo Yo: Who do you think you are talking to? Listen up! I am in charge here, not you! You'll get your money! But shoot your mouth off again, it'll be your funeral!

点评：为筹备巨额的葬礼经费，王小柱除了让影视公司掏钱外，还将葬礼广告进行拍卖。拍卖会上，尤优取消了一款盗版影碟机的广告发布资格，宣布无偿用于公益广告的发布。这事让王小柱尤为恼火。对白是会后王小柱和尤优之间发生的争执。其实王小柱说的只是气话，他当然明白自己绝不会拧下尤优的脑袋。译文在直译的基础上增加了"damn"一词，不但有效地再现了原对白的会话含义，而且充分地表现出王小柱当时恼怒的语气。

⑤ 尤　优：你就别脱裤子放屁了。
　 王小柱：你怎么现在跟美国人似的，这么务实？

译文：

Yo Yo:　　Cut the crap, all right?
Louis Wang: When did you become so pragmatic, like a goddamn American?

点评：电影字幕受到一定的时间和空间限制。从时间上看，电影中的语言和图像要力求同步配合。因此，字幕必须在和源语话语大致相同的时间内完成信息传递。从空间上看，字幕一般不超过两行。这些制约因素使得字幕必须具有高度浓缩性。翻译字幕时也应尽量做到言简意赅。直译有时尽管能符合这个要求，但却很有可能会造成理解障碍。补译虽能较充分地传达源语对白中的隐含意义，帮助目的语受众更好地理解对白，但是容易造成字幕过长，使受众来不及对译文进行信息处理。在这种情况下，套译便不失为一种两全其美的方法。具体来说，套译就是套用目的语中与源语相对应的表达法。

王小柱和露西初次见面，商谈举办葬礼之事。露西是美籍华裔，懂中文，也会讲。然而王小柱却故弄玄虚，请了翻译，一见面便是寒暄，寒暄过后是冗长的开场白，推销他们公司的广告词。露西觉得没必要翻译，可他依然不想放弃他的政策。这让一旁的尤优沉不住气了，于是他让王小柱"别脱裤子放屁了"。其实，尤优这样说，旨在传达这句话的寓意——"少说废话"。如果直译为"Stop taking off your pants and passing the wind"，英美受众很难理解这句话所要表达的会话含义；如果补译，就成了"Stop taking off your pants and passing the wind—don't talk nonsense"。显然，译文不论在内容上还是字数上都不符合字幕的要求。此例中，译者采用套译技巧，成功地解决了以上种种问题，用了"cut the crap"，既有效地再现了原文的会话含义，又保留了原文粗俗的风格，堪称佳译。

⑥ 王小柱：这位是中国电视制片界的大鳄，张总。张总在影视投资方面相当凶猛。胃口大！全国有一半以上古装剧集都是您投的吧？
　 张　总：嗯。

译文：

Louis Wang: Mr. Zhang is the Genghis Khan of Chinese TV. His investments are quite aggressive. A ferocious appetite! You produce half of all TV dramas, correct?

Mr. Zhang: Yeap.

点评:王小柱想找人对葬礼进行投资,就请来影视公司的张总。此对白是王小柱对张总的介绍词,把张总比作"大鳄"。显然,在此语境下,这个词所体现的会话含义应是指具备与大鳄相似特征的人。换句话说,王小柱的真正用意是夸张总资产雄厚,在电视制片界竞争力强。为在目的语字幕中体现这层会话含义,译者套用了"Genghis Khan"(成吉思汗)这个已被纳入英语中的人名。译者主要是出于以下两方面的考虑:一方面,作为世界历史上的一位杰出人物,成吉思汗对大多数英美受众来说并不陌生;另一方面,成吉思汗在位期间多次发动过侵略战争,征服地域西达黑海海滨,东到几乎整个东亚,作战具有野蛮残酷的特点。因此,把他作为"大鳄"的代名词,准确贴切。

⑦ 露西:这不是你的工作啊?
　　尤优:导演的话不听,你哪头的?

译文:

Lucy: What are you doing?

Yo Yo: Following orders. What are you doing?

点评:有时会遇到以下情况:直译容易造成理解障碍,补译会使字幕过长,套译也较难实现。在这种情况下,可考虑采用换译,即在充分考虑双方语言、文化的前提下,对译文作适当转换变通,以期再现原对白中的会话含义。

泰勒拍片时情绪低落,叫尤优通知收工。露西想让泰勒继续拍下去,于是拦住了尤优。对白中,露西的言外之意是让尤优别管闲事,因为合同上规定,尤优除了把泰勒在中国的工作拍下来外,不准干预其他事情。尤优非但没有回答露西的问题,反而质疑露西。如果直译成"You didn't follow his orders",既会造成理解困难,又会显得啰唆;补译和套译也较难操作。这时,就有必要对译文作灵活的变通,换个角度翻译。这样的译文保留了原文的会话含义,且表达简练,符合字幕的要求。具体来说,露西的言外之意实为"It's not your business","it"指通知收工这件事。尤优故意违反语言的关联性,意在表达的会话含义是"I know it's not my business. But anything wrong when I'm following orders?"

⑧ 尤优:为什么不用美国摄影师?
　　露西:如果你想得到这份工作,就不要问那么多为什么。

译文:

Yo Yo: Why not hire an American?

Lucy: Why not cut the 20 questions?

点评:此对白出现在片首。尤优前去应聘,露西让他现场演示装胶片。尤优一边装胶片,一边问露西是谁,叫什么名字,干什么的,然后又问她要拍什么。对于这些问题,露西都作了比较详尽的回答。于是尤优继续问露西为什么不用美国摄影师。对于这个问题,露西却避而不答,因为她不想透露"内部机密",也不想让尤优干预与他无关的事。为求字幕的高度浓缩,字幕翻译时往往省略次要信息,因此译者把露西话语中的从句部分省略不译。为再现原对白中的会话含义,译者对露西话语中的主句部分作了处理,把原文中的祈使句变为疑问句,与译文中尤优的话语针锋相对;把抽象的"那么多为什么"变为具体的"20 questions",形象生动地传递了源语对白的会话含义。

【例 18】

《魂断蓝桥》Waterloo Bridge

Announcer's Voice:At eleven-fifteen this morning, the Prime Minister, speaking to the nation from Number Ten Downing Street, announced that Great Britain is at war with Germany.

译文:

广播员:今天上午 11 点 15 分,首相在唐宁街 10 号向全国发表了讲话,宣布英国与德国处于交战状态。

点评:由于中外受众知识面及文化背景等方面存在着巨大的差异,电影翻译工作者应尽可能地帮助受众去理解那些与一个民族的历史、地域文化、宗教习俗等有着密切相关的语言现象。电影翻译中如果对某些特定文化意象不作任何修润处理,就事论事直译,会造成这一文化意象的缺损、文化涵义支离破碎。英国电影《魂断蓝桥》一开始,就有上述这样一段画外音。

应该指出,此例忠实地译出了原文的字面意义,但若对"唐宁街 10 号"这一隐含文化意象地名不作些补充说明的话,相信绝大多数中国普通受众会茫然不知其所云。其一,受众不知道这个"唐宁街 10 号"在什么地方;其二,他们更不知道广播员在这里特地提及这个地名有何特别的寓意。为了使电影译文能在有限的时间内到达广大受众,译者应对上述译文作恰如其分的增补修润:"今天上午 11 点 15 分,首相在唐宁街 10 号——英国首相府邸向全国发表了讲话,宣布英国与德国处于交战状态"。通过增补"英国首相府邸",受众会真正认识到"唐宁街 10 号"的政治内涵。

【例 19】

《呼啸山庄》Wuthering Heights

Isabella: It's a brother's duty, dear Edgar, to introduce his sister to some other type than fops and pale young poets.

Edgar: Oh, you want a dragon?

Isabella: Yes, I do. With a fiery mustache.

译文:

依莎贝拉:这是一个哥哥的义务,亲爱的埃得加,你总不能把自己的妹妹介绍给那些花花公子或弱不禁风的年轻诗人吧。

埃 得 加:哦,你该不是想嫁一个龙骑兵吧?

依莎贝拉:是的,还长着火红的大胡子。

点评:语言学家认为,即使世界上各族人看到同一客观现象,不同的民族语言会给它"刷上不同的颜色"。缘于此,文化意象的错位(nonequivalence of culture image)会具体表现为作为喻体的文化意象上的差异。换言之,在一种文化传统中一个具有正面寓意的美好文化意象,在另一种文化里却成了反面寓意的丑陋文化意象。如上述英国电影《呼啸山庄》对白中展示的那样。

在上述翻译中"dragon"是一个关键词。在英语文化中"dragon"作"魔鬼"解释。每当提及此词,西方人立刻会想到一个面目狰狞的魔鬼。由此不难看出"dragon"在西方语言文化中隐含贬义。而在中国文化中"龙"象征着"高贵、至高无上"等褒义,昔日中国人称皇帝为"真龙天子",因此与"龙"字相关的词语绝大多数具有崇敬之意。如中国人称自己为"龙的传人",祈盼着自己的子女将来有出息为"望子成龙"等。"dragon"在东西方语言中,其文化意象的寓意是截然相反的。简言之,它们的物象虽同,但寓意却完全相异。由此可见,用"龙骑兵"来硬译"dragon"一词显然不妥。因为当中国受众在观赏影片时忽然听到"龙骑兵"这一词语,他们肯定会立即联想到"他"可能是个"皇家骑兵"。但依莎贝拉的回答却又使受众对影片的阐释如坠云雾。受众不禁要问,这个堂堂正正的"皇家骑兵"怎么会"长着火红的大胡子"呢?在中国传统历史文化中,只有那些三头六臂的怪物才有一张长着可怕的绿眉毛、红胡子的嘴脸。如此生搬硬套不仅不能处理好东西方语言文化中意象错位这一棘手问题,同时也不能传神地译出这段对白的真实含义,反而给上下文语义的贯通设置了语言障碍。因此,上文中埃得加与依莎贝拉的对话不妨翻译如下:

埃 得 加:哦,你该不是想嫁给一个野蛮人吧?
依莎贝拉:是的,还长着火红的大胡子。

由于东西方文化的差异,电影翻译中许多英语词语若直接硬译会令广大中国受众无法接受与认同。此外,电影翻译文本受电影画面切换时间的限制,不能像翻译文学作品那样可以在一些晦涩难懂之处作些注释,所以对白译文一定要让受众一听、一看即能明了。在面对文化意象时,译者尤应慎重考虑"间"的关系。

【例 20】

《花木兰》*Mulan*

① Khan-ie baby, hey, we need a ride.

译文:

阿汗小亲亲,搭个便车吧。

② Urgent news from the general! What's the matter, you've never seen a 'black and white' before?

译文:

将军府有令!怎么,没见过特殊快递吗?

③ Pack your bags Cri—Kee, we're movin' out.

译文:

收拾行李,咱们走人。

④ So you'll get back to me on the job thing.

译文:

那你会考虑录用我吗?

点评:娱乐是电影的重要功能之一,电影的娱乐倾向也反映在字幕翻译上面,尤其是一些轻松的卡通片。迪士尼的动画片《花木兰》中,花木兰是个热情活泼的年轻女孩,她想尽办法让父母高兴,但结果却总让他们失望。当朝廷要从每户人家征集一名壮丁去抵御外敌时,花木兰女扮男装,代父从军。在守护神木须龙的帮助下,木兰在抵御胡人的侵略战争中起了关键的作用,但她在受伤之际暴露了女儿身,被驱逐出军队。后来木兰发现胡人军队准备袭击京城,便赶往京城,凭高超的武艺和过人的智慧打败了胡军首领,解救了皇帝,为自己为家族扬眉吐气,也赢得了将军翔的尊重。电影中有不少幽默的对话,而字幕翻译中通过在古代语境运用现代词汇所产生的反差使其对话颇具喜剧效果。

"小亲亲"、"搭个便车"、"特殊快递"、"行李"、"录用"等都是现代词汇。"Baby"可以翻译成"宝贝"、"心肝儿",但"小亲亲"听起来更亲昵而且滑稽。木须、木兰和李将军是生活在古代的人,古人说现代的话,这种不协调吸引了受众,差异越大,幽默效果越强。虽然影片故事基于中国的《花木兰》,但导演 Barry Cook 和 Tony Bancroft 加入了不少迪士尼元素,而这种迪士尼式的幽默使迪士尼电影独树一帜。《花木兰》影片级别为 G,即面向所有受众。如此翻译,使其既有童趣又有成人的幽默。

⑤ Dishonor on you. Dishonor on your cow.

译文:

你跟你的牛会很没面子。

⑥ Now let's see your war face.

译文:

快装狠给我看。

⑦ I'll get that arrow, pretty boy.

译文:

我去拿回来,小白脸。

⑧ The truth is we're both frauds.

译文:

其实我们都是冒牌货。

⑨ Yeah, the only girl who'd love him is his mother!

译文:

痴痴想念他的,是他老妈。

⑩ Head up … and strut, 1, 2, 3, break it down, 1, 2, 3, and work it beautiful, isn't it?

译文：

抬头，开步走。神气点，一、二、三。就这样，二、三、四。很帅吧？

⑪ And there's nothin' you girls can do about it.

译文：

你们这些娘娘腔绝摆不倒我。

点评：《花木兰》面对的是大众，通俗化就很必要，即应该适合群众的水平和需要，容易让群众理解和接受。"没面子"、"装狠"、"小白脸"、"冒牌货"、"很帅"、"老妈"、"娘娘腔"等这些口语词汇听起来朗朗上口，比译成"面上无光"等更贴近老百姓的生活。木须龙，所谓的守护神，实际上是先祠中被贬的一员，没有什么重要地位。为了在木兰面前装出一副守护神的模样，他总是吵吵嚷嚷地给出建议来显示他的重要性和权威性，但这些建议总是误导人，结合木须龙爱闹、爱说话的特点，以及兵丁的平民身份，使译文更具通俗色彩，翻译时需更具娱乐性。

⑫ Punch him; it's how men say hello.

译文：

扁他，男人都这样打招呼。

⑬ Whach'you mean loser?

译文：

你说我很衰？

⑭ How'bout I pop one of your antenna's off and throw it across the yard. Then who's a loser, me or you?

译文：

看我拔掉你的胡须扔到院子里，再看看谁比较衰？

⑮ Ahh, notes, in case I forget something?

译文：

小抄，我怕会临时出糗。

⑯ Those boys are no more fit to be soldiers than you are to be, Captain.

译文：

那些男生……跟你这校尉一样逊。

点评："衰"、"小抄"、"糗"、"逊"、"男生"等目前是台湾用的流行词汇，有着强烈的方言特色与搞笑功能。这些流行词汇以娱乐消遣为目的，以与大众情趣的趋近为追求，从而赢得大众的欢迎和喜爱，获得生存的土壤。

5　本章结语

德里达曾说过:"我们正在处理的翻译问题,不过是在处理哲学的通道问题(the problem of the passage to philosophy)"。伊格尔顿在 *After Theory* 中说:"解构主义颠覆西方传统的思维模式,是因为后者所依赖的'二项对立'不能成立,但与此同时,解构主义本身也已因其特有的虚无主义而走向式微。"那么,在"后理论"时代,学术探讨及翻译,究竟拿什么来做"理论"或指导?

实际上,"间"性理论的来源之一是现象学的还原:翻译中要尽量还原,即承认翻译的复杂性与多元性,要正视人在其中的作用。中世纪哲学家圣托马斯指出,"真理是智慧与事物的全适性"。在胡塞尔那里,"真理主要被理解为存在与它的显现方式的一致性或共属性"。因此,现象学的真理观自胡塞尔开始已经有了"突破",尽管海德格尔认为这是"以迂回的方式回到希腊人那里"。胡塞尔的"回到事物本身"、海德格尔的"让存在者以自身的存在方式显示出自身"都含有一种基本思路:让事物"站立"在人的面前,因为这样的站立在突出它们自身的同时,也就显现了"真理"。换言之,事物突出自身,这本身就是"真理"的表现或显现。这种思路有可能限制了传统的形而上学的某种独断论的趋势:因为事物一旦真正出场,人的思想就要依从这种事物,而不是相反地要使事物依从于人及其思维方式。但是,它的形而上特性依然如故:事物毕竟是在人的"注视"下、在人"看"的时候才显示出自身的,因而人既然是作为"主体"出现的,谁又能说她/他不是主宰着事物的呈现过程以及结果呢?从这一点来说,现象学只是一种理想化的哲学,因为它希望"看到"的正好是不能或无法看到的,或者说它竭力追求的正好是遮蔽性的。无怪乎梅洛—庞蒂会认为,真正的还原是不可能的。尽管如此,人类的追求还是永远需要的,因为理想与理想化的境界的出现,意味着人回到了某种艺术的或诗意的氛围之中:人本来就可能不去那么条分缕析地分析事物,而是应该更多地尊重事物的"原貌",而这样的"原貌"也只有在尊重事物的整体性意义上才可达到或得到保护。从这一点上说,现象学的思路还是可行的,至少是一种富有诗意的哲学思想。

同理,本章中整个提到的"间"的理论,也可能只是一种诗意的理想。实际上,对于电影翻译,不论是什么样的翻译理论,都很有必要以批判的态度对它们加以分析、应用,而不应毫不怀疑地予以全盘接受:翻译,尤其是电影翻译,是鲜活的翻译,是人的翻译,是关系的结晶,是变动的。这也是本章提到的"间"性理论的终极指向所反复提醒译者的。谨以此为电影翻译贡献绵薄的一纸添加。

各章翻译练习

第二章 新闻翻译

一、英译汉

1.

News of Apple Inc. co-founder Steve Jobs's death began to spread on Sina Weibo, China's popular Twitter-like microblogging service, almost immediately after it was confirmed on Apple's website.

Among the first to comment was Kai-Fu Lee, the former head of Google China. "Bon voyage, Master Jobs," Mr. Lee wrote on his verified Weibo account. "Your products changed the world and your thinking influenced a generation."

Thousands of Weibo users echoed Mr. Lee in mourning Mr. Jobs, littering the site with innumerable burning candle icons, while thousands more hopefully wondered whether the news was just another Chinese Internet rumor gone wild. "I really hope this is fake," wrote Weibo user Astroboy. "Jobs is gone," wrote another user going by the handle Buting Zheteng. "This is the first time a foreigner's death has been hard for me to take."

Others, however, seized on the Apple founder's death to register their disappointment with the company's latest offering: "No doubt he saw the iPhone 4S and died out of anger," quipped user MoKayan.

Still others urged Apple to push out a line of affordable iPhones and iPads so more people can have access to the products. "This is the best way to remember Steve Jobs," wrote Water Cube.

Apple products have soared in popularity among increasingly affluent Chinese consumers. Demand for white iPhones sparked a scuffle outside the Beijing Apple Store in Sanlitun earlier this year, resulting in a broken window and closing the store for several hours.

In the fiscal third quarter ended June 25, Apple said it sold $3.8 billion in products in greater China, which includes Hong Kong, a more than sixfold increase from a year earlier. Apple opened new stores in Hong Kong and in Shanghai last month.

(Selected from "Netizens Respond to Steve Jobs's Death" in 2011)

2.

The head of the European Financial Stability Facility, Klaus Regling, arrives in Beijing Friday as all eyes turn to China as it decides what role—if any—it will play in funding Europe's bailout plan.

Mr. Regling will meet with the head of the State Administration of Foreign Exchange, Yi Gang, and Vice Minister of Finance Zhu Guangyao, before flying onto other Asian countries.

European leaders secured a deal Thursday to reduce Greece's debt and expand the firepower of the euro zone's bailout vehicle, by four—or five—fold, suggesting it could provide guarantees for around 1 trillion, or about $1.4 trillion, of bonds issued by flailing EU member countries. The expansion could in part be funded by cash-rich emerging economies such as China.

With foreign exchange reserves in excess of $3.2 trillion, China has long been looked upon by struggling economies as a potential white knight. This time is no different with rumors swirling of a potentially large contribution from Beijing to the European rescue fund.

According to people at the International Monetary Fund, for at least a month China has expressed its willingness to help the Europeans, but only through the IMF and in conjunction with contributions from other Brazil, India and Russia, the major emerging economies that together with China make up the so-called

BRIC nations. But others in the BRIC group seem wary of putting in substantial amounts of money, and China is unlikely to act by itself.

It would also mark a major change in the way China allocates foreign exchange reserves. SAFE allocates the lion's share of its resources to low risk and low yield—investments. While the low return has long been a source of frustration, the reserve administrators are wary of the political fallout likely to result from the national reserves posting a significant loss.

China's $400 billion sovereign wealth fund, China Investment Corp., is fully invested and currently doesn't have the resources to make a significant contribution to Europe's bailout.

Still, Chinese leaders have hinted that they would be more interested helping Europe if they could count on a pay off elsewhere, such as being recognized as a "market economy", a status that would help its chances of winning anti-dumping or subsidy cases brought against it. But European leaders have thus far opposed such a quid-pro-quo.

Sentiment in China is divided over whether the country should take a role in helping bail out Europe.

China should ride to Europe's rescue,' said Peng Junming, a former official at the People's Bank of China who now serves as chief investment officer of Empire Capital Management LLP, an investment-management firm in Beijing. Mr. Peng sees it as a way to get a better return for the reserves.

In addition, Mr. Peng thinks that the Euro-debt crisis also offers Beijing an opportunity to further promote the global use of the yuan.

(Selected from "China in Focus After Europe Deal" in 2011)

二、汉译英
1.
2012年夏季奥运会将于星期五正式开幕,伦敦迎接大约1万名运动员、数十万名旅游者和全世界的电视观众。

伦敦奥运组织者已经解决了最后时刻出现的一系列问题,包括确保配备足够的安保人员,此前一个私人承包商表示在调集足够安保人手方面存在困难。

英国女王伊丽莎白二世将宣布伦敦奥运会开幕。到8月12日闭幕之前,奥运会将举办26个运动竞赛项目。

(选自2012年"伦敦为奥运做最后准备")

2.
美国总统奥巴马和中国国家主席习近平结束了两天的非正式会谈,讨论了网络安全、朝鲜核项目以及气候变化等问题。

美国国家安全顾问多尼伦说,这两位领导人一致认为,解决网络安全方面的分歧是发展两国关系的关键。多尼伦还说,这两位领导人还同意,朝鲜必须放弃核项目。

多尼伦和中国国务委员杨洁篪都分别在记者会上说,习近平对奥巴马说,在朝核问题上,北京和华盛顿的立场是一致的,双方都不接受朝鲜为核国家。

朝鲜严重依赖中国的援助和贸易。北京和平壤保持着密切关系。然而,朝鲜近几个月来发出对美国发动核打击等一系列好战言论,明显地给朝中关系降了温。

奥巴马和习近平也一致同意共同努力解决气候变化的问题。

美中领导人结束在加州的两天非正式会谈之后,多尼伦和杨洁篪都接受了记者的提问。

(选自2013年"美中峰会结束,同意新的合作")

3.
这是充满惊人剧变以及重大变革的一年,从金融风暴到几位公众名人的离世,2011年见证了全球的惊人变化。尽管外部环境存在诸多不利因素,但缓步增长的中国经济却依然是全世界的一大亮点。在这里,《二十一世纪英文报》汇总了包括美联社、时代周刊和新华社在内的诸多国际新闻机构的分析,为您呈现一份年度热点新闻列表。眼下,2011年即将接近尾声,我们寄望于新的一年中社会更加安定,国际经济秩序能够得以重建。
(1) 经济软着陆
　　今年,中国正式超越日本一举成为全球第二大经济体。新华社表示,在全球经济中,中国仍然是一个必要的亮点。尽管经济增长有所放缓,但仍然高出世界平均水平。在全球经济低迷而严峻的环境下,今年中国的经济增长率保持稳定并平稳下降。由中国人民大学发布的一份报告预测到,中国今年经济增长达到9.4个百分点,明年预计下滑至9.2个百分点。同时该报告也表示,尽管相关数据出现下滑,我国经济仍然跑赢其他主要经济体,并保持健康稳定的状态。这种经济降温的趋势彰显出中国正在努力寻求经济软着陆。现在中国正将重心从出口盈利转向扩大内需。同时中国也正尝试在抑制通货膨胀与稳定经济增长率之间寻求平衡点。今年,中国为其"十二五"规划起了个好头。这一规划旨在升级中国的发展模式以及经济结构。
(2) 高铁
　　2011年,中国发展高速列车的雄心壮志遭遇重创,最终放慢了脚步。中国最新的高速铁路系统自六月份投入使用以来遭遇了几次技术故障。7月23日,两列高速列车在浙江温州附近追尾,致使40人死亡,近200人受伤。事故原因仍在调查之中。事故惨剧的发生促使各方呼吁,全面检查高铁服务系统。撞车事故发生之后,铁道部部长盛光祖下令所有高速列车降速。一些预计于今年开工的铁路工程被延期。
(3) 神八与天宫一号
　　2011年,中国朝着打造永久性空间站的目标又迈近了一步。9月29日,中国成功发射了首个无人空间实验舱"天宫一号"。11月3日,也就是神州八号无人飞船发射升空的两天之后,"神八"与"天宫一号"空间实验舱成功对接。国家主席胡锦涛将此次成功对接形容成中国航天事业发展史上的一座里程碑,为人类探索外太空作出了卓越的贡献。同时胡锦涛主席也表示,尽管中国的航空事业有了很大进步,中国整体的科技水平,尤其是本土的创新能力还远远达不到世界领先水平。
(4) 建党90周年纪念
　　2011年,我们欢庆了中国共产党建党90周年的生日。7月1日,中国共产党总书记胡锦涛在庆祝中国共产党成立90周年大会上发表讲话。他总结了在过去90年中,中国人民在中国共产党的领导下所取得的成就。此次讲话的口号都围绕"人民"二字,一共提及了136次。这也强调了一切"把人民利益放在第一位"的原则思想。胡锦涛主席说道:"人民是真正的英雄,这一点我们永远不能忘记。"他呼吁所有党员要"保持与人民的血肉联系",并提醒道,脱离群众是我们党的最大危险。胡锦涛总书记在发言中还表示党将吸收更多年轻优秀成员。他强调人才是第一资源,是国家发展的战略资源。他说:"青年(党员)是我们党的未来和希望。"
(5) 南海争端
　　过去数月中,中国与几个邻国在南海领土问题上的争端不断激化。2011年7月,有关方面就《南海各方行为宣言》的实施准则达成共识,承诺将在海洋保护和科研、海上搜救以及打击海上跨国犯罪等方面进行合作。但11月时,美国与菲律宾签署了一项宣言,呼吁进行多方会谈,以此来解决南海领土争端。2011年,温家宝总理在多个场合反复重申,中国承诺采取和平方式来解决诸多争端问题。
(6) 日本大地震引发海啸
　　3月11日,日本东北部海域发生了里氏9.0级的大地震,进而引发大规模海啸,造成近1.6万人死亡。海啸除了造成巨大人员伤亡以及基础设施的毁坏,还引发一系列核泄漏事故。其中,福岛第一核电站发生了7级事故,三个核反应堆熔毁,数十万周边居民被疏散。据时任日本首相的菅直人称,"此次大地震是日本战后65年以来遭遇的最艰难的危机。"地震海啸带来的最直接后果是,日本东北部地区有约440万户居民断电,150万户断水。
(7) 欧债危机
　　今年,欧洲多国政府债台高筑,引发各方焦虑,进而引发一场全球危机。自2010年底起,各方对于欧洲经济稳定性表现出的担忧愈演愈烈。希腊、爱尔兰和葡萄牙无法再筹债款。该事件波及全球各地,所有大型股票交易所都遭遇股市重创。很多西方国家都在寻求来自中国的援助承诺,帮助重振欧洲经济,增强市场信心。一些人认为欧洲动荡的金融局势会影响到该地区对于中国出口产品的需求。而中国的经济专家则坚持认为中国不应该再盲目购买欧债。

(8) 阿拉伯国家动乱

2011年,一波接一波的游行示威以及抗议活动席卷了整个阿拉伯世界。突尼斯和埃及的国内政局发生了激烈动荡;利比亚爆发内战;巴林、叙利亚、也门、阿尔及利亚、伊拉克、约旦、科威特、摩洛哥以及阿曼等地爆发大规模抗议活动。从突尼斯的宰因·阿比丁·本·阿里,到埃及的胡斯尼·穆巴拉克,再到也门的阿里·阿卜杜拉·萨利赫,这些政治巨头一个又一个地在动荡中谢幕。利比亚前任最高领导人穆阿迈尔·卡扎菲被杀。同时,叙利亚总统巴沙尔·阿萨德仍然在国内的不满以及国外的压力中努力维护自己的政权。这些平民运动与先前的抗议活动有所不同,其中并未有宗教因素推波助澜。

(9) 金正日逝世

朝鲜最高领导人金正日于12月17日逝世。据朝鲜中央通讯社的一篇新闻报道称,69岁的金正日在进行高强度的视察时因身心劳累过度而突发心脏病在列车上逝世。12月19日中国就金正日逝世向朝鲜发去吊唁,称这位已故朝鲜领袖不断巩固和加深中朝传统友好关系。观察员认为,金正日的逝世不会引发朝鲜国内动乱。朝鲜中央通讯社表示,朝鲜全国上下、人民以及军队都将忠实于尊敬的金正恩的领导。

(10) 本·拉登被击毙,伊拉克战争宣告结束

12月18日,美国在入侵伊拉克,驱逐萨达姆·侯赛因的9年后,正式宣布伊拉克战争结束。在这场战争中,近4500名美军士兵牺牲、数以万计的伊拉克人民丧生。今年美军也结束了自越战以来最不得人心的远征。在美军撤军之前,奥萨马·本·拉登的死亡已经证明了美国反恐战争取得了胜利。5月,本·拉登被美国特种部队击毙。本·拉登一直被认为是美国9·11事件的幕后策划者,他的死亡也成为以美国为首的"反恐战役"的一个决定性时刻。

(选自"盘点2011年国内外焦点事件")

第三章 政论翻译

一、英译汉

1.

Her Majesty the queen has asked me to form a new government and I have accepted. Before I talk about that new government, let me say something about the one that has just passed. Compared with a decade ago, this country is more open at home and more compassionate abroad, and that is something we should all be grateful for.

On behalf of the whole country I would like to pay tribute to the outgoing prime minister, for his long record of dedicated public service.

In terms of the future, our country has a hung parliament where no party has an overall majority and we have some deep and pressing problems—a huge deficit, deep social problems and a political system in need of reform.

For those reasons, I aim to form a proper and full coalition between the Conservatives and the Liberal Democrats. I believe that is the right way to provide this country with the strong, the stable, the good and decent government that I think we need so badly.

Nick Clegg and I are both political leaders who want to put aside party differences and work hard for the common good and for the national interest. I believe that is the best way to get the strong government that we need, decisive government that we need today.

I came into politics because I love this country, I think its best days still lie ahead and I believe deeply in public service. And I think the service our country needs right now is to face up to our really big challenges, to confront our problems, to take difficult decisions, to lead people through those difficult decisions, so that together we can reach better times ahead.

One of the tasks that we clearly have is to rebuild trust in our political system. Yes, that is about cleaning up expenses; yes, that's about reforming parliament; and yes, it's about making sure people are in control and that the politicians are always their servants and never their masters.

But I believe it's also something else. It's about being honest about what government can achieve. Real change is not what government can do on its own. Real change is when everyone pulls together, comes together, works together, when we all exercise our responsibilities to ourselves, to our families, to our communities and to others.

And I want to help build a more responsible society here in Britain, one where we don't just ask "what are my entitlements?" but "what are my responsibilities?". One where we don't just ask "what am I just owed?" but more "what can I give?". And a guide for that society, that those who can, should, and those who can't, we will always help.

I want to make sure that my government always looks after the elderly, the frail, the poorest in our country. We must take everyone through with us on some of the difficult decisions that we have ahead.

Above all, it will be a government that will be built on some clear values — values of freedom, values of fairness, and values of responsibility.

I want us to build an economy that rewards work, I want us to build a society with stronger families and stronger communities, and I want a political system that people can trust and look up to once again.

This is going to be hard and difficult work. A coalition will throw up all sorts of challenges. But I believe together we can provide that strong and stable government that our country needs, based on those values — rebuilding family, rebuilding community, above all rebuilding responsibility in our country.

Those are the things that I care about, those are the things that this government will now start work on doing.

(The UK Prime Minister David Cameron's inauguration speech in May 2010)

2.

Our Constitution declares that from time to time, the President shall give to Congress information about the state of our union. For 220 years, our leaders have fulfilled this duty. They've done so during periods of prosperity and tranquility. And they've done so in the midst of war and depression; at moments of great strife and great struggle.

It's tempting to look back on these moments and assume that our progress was inevitable — that America was always destined to succeed. But when the Union was turned back at Bull Run, and the Allies first landed at Omaha Beach, victory was very much in doubt. When the market crashed on Black Tuesday, and civil rights marchers were beaten on Bloody Sunday, the future was anything but certain. These were the times that tested the courage of our convictions, and the strength of our union. And despite all our divisions and disagreements, our hesitations and our fears, America prevailed because we chose to move forward as one nation, as one people.

Again, we are tested. And again, we must answer history's call.

One year ago, I took office amid two wars, an economy rocked by a severe recession, a financial system on the verge of collapse, and a government deeply in debt. Experts from across the political spectrum warned that if we did not act, we might face a second depression. So we acted—immediately and aggressively. And one year later, the worst of the storm has passed.

But the devastation remains. One in ten Americans still cannot find work. Many businesses have shuttered. Home values have declined. Small towns and rural communities have been hit especially hard. And for those who'd already known poverty, life has become that much harder.

(Selected from "Remarks by the the American President Obama in State of the Union Address" in January 2010)

二、汉译英

1.

90年来,我们党团结带领人民在中国这片古老的土地上,书写了人类发展史上惊天地、泣鬼神的壮丽史诗,集中体现为完成和推进了三件大事。

第一件大事，我们党紧紧依靠人民完成了新民主主义革命，实现了民族独立、人民解放。经过北伐战争、土地革命战争、抗日战争、解放战争，党和人民进行28年浴血奋战，打败日本帝国主义侵略，推翻国民党反动统治，建立了中华人民共和国。新中国的成立，使人民成为国家、社会和自己命运的主人，实现了中国从几千年封建专制制度向人民民主制度的伟大跨越，实现了中国高度统一和各民族空前团结，彻底结束了旧中国半殖民地半封建社会的历史，彻底结束了旧中国一盘散沙的局面，彻底废除了列强强加给中国的不平等条约和帝国主义在中国的一切特权。中国人从此站立起来了，中华民族发展进步从此开启了新的历史纪元。

第二件大事，我们党紧紧依靠人民完成了社会主义革命，确立了社会主义基本制度。我们创造性地实现由新民主主义到社会主义的转变，使占世界人口四分之一的东方大国进入社会主义社会，实现了中国历史上最广泛最深刻的社会变革。我们建立起独立的比较完整的工业体系和国民经济体系，积累了在中国这样一个社会生产力水平十分落后的东方大国进行社会主义建设的重要经验。

第三件大事，我们党紧紧依靠人民进行了改革开放新的伟大革命，开创、坚持、发展了中国特色社会主义。党的十一届三中全会以来，我们总结我国社会主义建设经验，同时借鉴国际经验，以巨大的政治勇气、理论勇气、实践勇气实行改革开放，经过艰辛探索，形成了党在社会主义初级阶段的基本理论、基本路线、基本纲领、基本经验，建立和完善社会主义市场经济体制，坚持全方位对外开放，推动社会主义现代化建设取得举世瞩目的伟大成就。

这三件大事，从根本上改变了中国人民和中华民族的前途命运，不可逆转地结束了近代以后中国内忧外患、积贫积弱的悲惨命运，不可逆转地开启了中华民族不断发展壮大、走向伟大复兴的历史进军，使具有5000多年文明历史的中国面貌焕然一新，中华民族伟大复兴展现出前所未有的光明前景。

（选自2011年7月胡锦涛在庆祝中国共产党成立90周年大会上的讲话）

2.

当今世界正处在大发展大变革大调整时期，和平、发展、合作的理念更加深入人心。世界多极化、经济全球化深入发展，各国经济相互依存日益加深，新兴市场国家和发展中国家快速成长，区域经济合作方兴未艾，科技创新孕育新突破，国际经济秩序深刻变化。同时，我们也应该看到，国际金融危机发生两年多来，世界经济复苏步伐仍然缓慢，基础依然薄弱，还存在诸多不确定因素，危机的深层次影响仍未消除。国际和地区热点问题此起彼伏，南北发展不平衡问题更加突出，各种形式的保护主义重新抬头。人类生存和发展面临着气候变化、能源安全、粮食安全等一系列新的全球性挑战。

中国愿积极参与讨论和解决世界经济发展中的重大问题，同各国一道应对挑战。这里，我愿提出以下看法。

第一，加强全球经济治理，继续推进国际金融体系改革。国际金融危机不仅给世界经济和各国经济发展造成严重冲击，而且凸显了现行国际金融体系的缺陷，凸显了全球经济治理机制应对危机能力的不足。目前，新兴市场国家和发展中国家在世界经济中的分量不断增加，在全球治理中的作用日益显现。新的全球经济治理机制应该反映世界经济格局变化，遵循相互尊重、集体决策的原则，特别是应该增加新兴市场国家和发展中国家在机制中的代表性和发言权。我们应该支持和推动二十国集团在全球经济治理中发挥更大作用，推动世界经济全面复苏和增长。以金砖国家为代表的新兴市场国家合作机制为全球经济合作开创了新模式，是多边主义的重要实践。我们应该积极完善全球经济治理，推动建设公平、公正、包容、有序的国际货币金融体系，推动建立均衡、普惠、共赢的多边贸易体制，反对各种形式的保护主义，促进国际经济秩序朝着更加公正合理的方向发展。

第二，加快转变经济发展方式，合理调整经济结构布局。世界经济发展给各国既带来了机遇，也带来了挑战。我们应该深刻认识和紧跟世界发展潮流，主动适应国际经济环境变化，坚定不移转变经济发展方式，坚定不移调整经济结构，有效解决各种经济问题，在发展中促转变，在转变中谋发展。在推动转变经济发展方式、调整经济结构布局的过程中，各国应该相互借鉴、取长补短，共同为促进世界经济强劲、可持续、平衡增长作出不懈努力。

第三，充分发挥科技成果潜力，加快科技和经济融合。科技创新发展的广度和深度正迅速拓展，各国都在加快实施科技创新战略，加大研发投入，加快创新人才培养。中国也在积极致力于增强科技创新能力，推进创新型国家建设。我们应该推动各国加强科技创新领域合作，推动科技成果产业化，推动世界经济发展更多依靠科技创新驱动,破解世界经济发展中的诸多难题和制约因素,积极推动科技创新和提高人类福祉紧密结合,使科技创新成果更多惠及各国人民。

(选自 2011 年 6 月胡锦涛在圣彼得堡国际经济论坛开幕式演讲"共创互利共赢、共同发展的美好未来")

第四章　旅游翻译

一、英译汉

1.

The Maya civilization is a Mesoamerican civilization, noted for the only known fully developed written language of the pre-Columbian Americas, as well as its act, architecture, and mathematical and astronomical systems. Initially established during the Preclassic period, many of these reached their apogee of development during the Classic period, and continued throughout the Postclassic period until the arrival of the Spanish. At its peak, it was one of the most densely populated and culturally dynamic societies in the world.

The Maya civilization shares many features with other Mesoamerican civilization due to the high degree of interaction and cultural diffusion that characterized the region. Advances such as writing, epigraphy, and the calendar did not originate with the Maya; however, their civilization fully developed them. Maya influence can be detected as far as central Mexico, more than 1,000 kilometers from the Maya area. Many outside influence are found in Maya art and architecture, which are thought to result from trade and cultural exchange rather than direct external conquest. The Maya peoples never disappeared, neither at the time of the Classic period decline nor with the arrival of the Spanish conquistadores and the subsequent Spanish colonization of the Americas. Today, the Maya and their descendants from sizable populations throughout the Maya area and maintain a distinctive set of traditions and beliefs that are the result of the merger of pre-Columbian and post-Conquest ideologies (and structured by the almost total adoption of Roman Catholicism). Many different Mayan languages continue to be spoken as primary languages today; *the Rabinal Achi*, a play written in the Achi language, was declared a Masterpiece of the Oral and Intangible Heritage of Humanity by UNESCO in 2005.

(The Maya Civilization)

2.

Northern Ireland's beauty is intertwined with tragic history, rich culture and the renowned friendliness of its people.

The wild craggy mountains, splendid lakes and sweeping coastline make it an ideal playground for watersports enthusiasts, walkers, cyclists, hikers, rock climbers and sailors.

But there are lots of things to keep those after a dose of culture enthralled, too. From boisterous oyster festivals to authentic horse fairs, and from ancient castles to elegant country houses, this spectacular part of Ireland is packed with things to do.

(Northern Ireland)

3.

The Great Barrier Reef is a site of remarkable variety on the north-east coast of Australia. It contains the world's largest collection of coral reefs, with 400 types of coral, 1,500 species of fish and 4,000 types of mollusk. It also holds great scientific interest as the habitat of species such as the dugong and the large green turtle, which are threatened with extinction.

(The Great Barrier Reef)

4.

The Elysee Palace in France enjoys equal popularity in the world with the Buckingham Palace in the United Kingdom, the Kremlin in Russia as well as the White House in the U.S.A. it is the residence of the president of the French Republic and the symbol of the supreme authority of France.

The Elysee Palace, with an area of 11,000 square meters, is at the eastern end of the Champs Elysee in the bustling city of Paris proper and backed by a large and tranquil garden of more than twenty thousand square meters. Its main building, quite handsome and graceful, is a 2-story classical stone architecture of European style, flanked by two side buildings facing each other and with an extensive rectangular courtyard in the middle. There are altogether 369 halls and rooms of different size.

The Elysee Palace, built in 1718, has a long history of closing to 300 years to date. This house was at first a private residence of a count named d'Evreau, hence it was called Hotel d'Evreau. It had later gone through many vicissitudes and its owners had been changed for many times, but all the dwellers in it were distinguished personages and high officials. The house was renamed Bonaparte Mansion when it was owned by Louis XV and Louis XVI successively when they acted as emperors. Napoleon I signed his act of abdication here when he had suffered crushing defeat in the Battle of Waterloo in 1815. Napoleon III moved in the Mansion in 1848 when he was elected president, and the house became a Royal Palace when he proclaimed himself as emperor. The third hundred odd years since then, almost all the presidents of the French Republic every year in September on the French Castles Day.

（ELYSEE PALACE）

二、汉译英
1.
江油李白纪念馆位于江油市区风景秀丽的昌明河畔，是国家 AA 级景区，全国最大的仿唐建筑群落，中国百家名园之一。融观光旅游、学术研究、陈列收藏、旅游服务于一体，纪念馆以其独特的园林风光、丰富多彩的展品、充实的讲解指南以及应有的学术地位而享誉当地，是九寨沟游的重要项目。

（李白纪念馆简介）
2.
周庄位于苏沪之间稠密的水网之中，像一片荷叶，四面环水依靠着淀山湖，以她旖旎的水乡秀美，九百年的人文历史，古韵犹存的建筑格局，纯朴的民俗风情，冠绝江南，被吴冠中誉为"集中国水乡之美"。

周庄桥桥傍河，灯灯傍水，衬得夜色如诗如画。在灯光水色里，小船红灯摇曳，游客一边尽览波光流翠，一边船上橹声咿呀，昆曲缠绵，吴歌悠扬，情景交融，美不胜收，疑是人间仙境。

（周庄）
3.
古朴幽雅、自然、富有民族特点和地方特色的高原水乡丽江古城，风景宜人的万里长江第一湾，幽雅俊秀的玉泉公园，以及被喻为"云岭第一枝"、"环球第一树"的万朵山茶等景色，组成了一幅优美的自然画卷。旅游资源以"二山、一城、一湖、一江、一文化、一风情"为主要代表。

4.
三亚汇集了阳光、海水、沙滩、气候、森林、动物、温泉、岩洞、田园、风情 10 大风景资源和丰富的历史文化资源，是中国热带海滨风景旅游资源密集的地区。在南山佛教文化旅游区，有以生态和佛教文化为主题的雕塑精品；在天涯海角游览区，有伴着不息涛声的历史名人雕塑群；鹿回头山顶公园那栩栩如生的人物雕塑，在诉说"鹿回头"美丽的爱情故事；亚龙湾中心广场，一座荣获了国家建筑"鲁班奖"的现代园林广场及雕塑群，将把您带回久远的历史。一切的一切让您目不暇接。

（三亚）
5.
黄山与黄河、长江、长城齐名，成为中华民族的又一象征。它以"奇松、怪石、云海、温泉"四绝而闻名于世。她是中国十大风景名胜中唯一的山岳风景区，作为中国山之代表，黄山集中国名山之大成，自古就有"五岳归来不看山，黄山归来不看岳"的说法。黄山还兼有"天然动物园和天下植物园"之称。黄山正以它雄奇的容貌迎接着四海宾客。①

(黄山)

6.
    人们说,如果世界上真有仙境,那肯定就是九寨沟。这是一个佳景荟萃、神奇莫测的旷世胜地;是一个不见纤尘、自然纯净的"童话世界"。"黄山归来不看山,九寨沟归来不看水",水是九寨沟的精灵,湖、泉、瀑、滩连缀一体,飞动与静谧结合,刚烈与温柔相济,不愧为"中华水景之王"。

(九寨沟)

7.
    鼓浪屿原名"圆沙州",又名"圆州仔",明朝时改称"鼓浪屿"。它位于福建省厦门市西南,与厦门隔海相望,仅1000米之遥。因岛上有一中空巨石,波浪拍打,其声如鼓,故名"鼓浪屿"。鼓浪屿虽有街区闹市,却无车马之喧,这里空气清新,环境幽静,整个小岛,一年四季草木葱郁,鲜花竞放,故有"海上花园"之称。

(鼓浪屿)

8.
    长城是世界闻名的奇迹之一,它像一条巨龙盘踞在中国北方辽阔的土地上。它是中国古代劳动人民血汗的结晶,是中国古代文化的象征和中华民族的骄傲。山峦起伏,雄沉刚劲的北方山势,尽收眼底。

(长城)

9.
    张家界自然景观奇特,举世罕见。峰奇,奇在千姿百态,景色各异;山秀,秀在云遮雾锁,郁郁葱葱;谷幽,幽在幽静深奥,幽在秀丽沉静;洞神,神在妙趣横生,妙在各有瑰宝。

    难怪李白曾叹道:"功成拂衣去,归于武陵源。"有"大自然的迷宫"、"天然博物馆、地球纪念物"之誉。

(张家界)

10.
    杭州的精华无疑是在西湖,西湖之胜不在自然,而在人文,更在湖水浸润出的无数诗词歌赋、古今传奇。上千年的经营将西湖变成一座精致的园林,长堤漫步凭栏,随处皆可吟咏两句古诗。

(西湖)

第五章 广告翻译

一、英译汉

1.
    Home-made ice cream, sorbet or iced yoghurt is not only delicious but extremely easy to make in the modern electric machines that are now available.

    This MAGIMIX machine makes 1.5 pints of ice cream which is enough for a family or for a dinner party. It is very simple to use—just place the bowl in a 3/4 freezer for 10 hours (the bowl measures approx. 7 in diameter by 5.5 in height), prepare your ice mixture, place the lid which holds the electric motor and pour the mixture through the feeder inlet at the top. The machine will gently churn and freeze to give perfect soft ice cream in only 20 minutes. Enjoy it immediately or store it in your freezer for later use. The Teflon lined bowl is easy to clean and the machine comes fitted with a plug. Also supplied is a comprehensive set of instructions 35 delicious recipes and a full one year manufacturer's guarantee.

    The ice cream scoop, which has been designed in the USA, is of high quality and extremely sturdy. The body of the scoop is made from stainless steel; the handle is made from durable, hardwearing A. B. S. plastic. It will provide many years of use even on very solid ice cream.

("MAGIMIX Ice Cream Maker and Quality Ice Cream Scoop" ad.)

2.
    Braun Flex Control. It knows your face almost as well as you do. In fact, there isn't a curve or an angle

---

① 请读者思考汉译英第5段最后一句如何处理。

on your face that Braun Flex Control can't adjust to. What's the secret? The unique pivoting head. It automatically adjusts the twin foils to every contour of your face, ensuring continuous contact with your skin, to give you the best Braun shaver ever. Under your nose. Under your chin. Under your lip. There's an extendable long hair trimmer too, for precision cutting of mustache and side-burns. Like all Braun rechargeable shavers, Braun Flex Control recharges quickly for up to 14 days of cordless shaving. You'll also be impressed by the way it combines advanced technology with an attractive, functional design—you'll love the natural, comfortable way it sits in your hand.

Braun Flex Control—the first electric shaver with a pivoting head.

("Braun Flex Control: Nobody knows your face better" ad.)

3.

Odd, isn't it? Before some business-class travelers fly off to do battle in Europe, they surrender. They give in to the high-fare demands of our competitors.

They fly in the face of facts.

The fact that the lowest of our three business-class fares costs no more than an economy seat with most other airlines.

And the fact that our new airside lounge at Heathrow is a radical departure from the norm.

Lounge? "Sanctuary" might be a better word. It's a place to take stock, to plan your strategy, to keep in touch with base, by phone or fax.

It's peace, perfect peace.

At a perfect price!

("Peace: But not At Any Price" ad.)

4.

Swan Symbol of a Life-Long Romance

In swan lore, when two young swans pair, they swim to a secluded spot, touch forming a heart and become mated for life. Gliding dreamily across their imaginary pond, reflected light glitters in water droplets at wing tips represented by 14 tiny diamonds.

As a symbol of life-long romance, the Cross Swan Pin is a deeply moving gift conveying the essence of that foul-felt bond of love between two people. With genuine ruby eyes, 14K yellow gold combination pin-pendant comes beautifully gift-wrapped with the sentiments expressed by this piece on a small card tucked inside the velvet box.

("Pin" Ad.)

二、汉译英

1.

古有"和氏璧",今有"金猪玉璧"。"和氏璧",价值连城,玉中至尊;"金猪玉璧",价值无限,收藏极品。"金猪玉璧"是由中国印钞造币总公司发行的"金玉良缘"系列生肖藏品之首款藏品。它金相玉映,品质卓越,格调不凡,身价不菲。宜馈赠,永志良缘;宜珍藏,金吉玉瑞。"金猪玉璧"一相逢,便胜却人间无数。"金猪玉璧"是作为情缘礼品、亲情赠品和艺术藏品的理想选择。

("'金猪玉璧',和谐盛世的收藏极品"广告语)

2.

北京市豆制品三厂始建于20世纪50年代,历史悠久,所有产品系纯大豆做原料,精工细做,保持传统的制作技术及独特风味,至今可生产甜、辣、咸80余种品位俱全的产品。20世纪80年代市场转变,开始向包装化产品转变,北京市豆制品三厂曾研制出受市场欢迎的包装产品,获得市优及部优荣誉称号,目前畅销市内大中型商场,产品供不应求。90年代随着市场的不断发展,新一代的产品又走向市场。"渺渺"豆茶系列营养价值比同类产品更高,采用最新科学配方,精制而成。要想健康长寿,请食用"渺渺"豆茶。

("渺渺豆茶"广告语)

第六章 商务翻译

一、英译汉

1.

  Thanks to slumping markets, investment banks are shedding many of their highly paid traders. When markets recover, the banks might be tempted to replace them with rather cheaper talent. One alternative has been around for a while but has yet to catch on: autonomous trading agents computers programmed to act like the human version without such pesky costs as holidays, lunch breaks or bonuses. Program trading has, of course, been done before; some blamed the 1987 stock market crash on computers instructed with simple decision-making rules. But robots can be smarter than that.

  Dave Cliff, a researcher at Hewlett Packard Laboratories in Bristol, England, has been creating trading robots for seven years. In computer simulations he lets them evolve "genetically", and so allows them to adapt and fit models of real world financial markets. His experiments have suggested that a redesign of some markets could lead to greater efficiency. Last year, a research group at IBM showed that Mr. Cliff's artificial traders could consistently beat the human variety, in various kinds of market. Nearly all take the shape of an auction. One well-known type is the English auction, familiar to patrons of the salesrooms of Christies and Sothebys, where sellers keep mum on their offer price, and buyers increase their bids by stages until only one remains.

  At the other extreme is the Dutch auction, familiar to 17th century tulip-traders in the Netherlands as well as to bidders for American Treasury bonds. Here, buyers remain silent, and a seller reduces his price until it is accepted. Most markets for shares, commodities, foreign exchange and derivatives are a hybrid of these two types: buyers and sellers can announce their bid or offer prices at any time, and deals are constantly being closed, a so-called "continuous double auction".

  Mr. Cliff's novel idea was to apply his evolutionary computer programs to marketplaces themselves. Why not, he thought, try and see what types of auction would let traders converge most quickly towards an equilibrium price? The results were surprising. In his models, auctions that let buyers and sellers bid at any time like most of today's financial exchanges were less efficient than ones that required relatively more bids from either buyers or sellers. These "evolved auctions" also withstood big market shocks, such as crashes and panics, better than today's real world versions. Mr. Cliff's most recent results, which will be presented in Sydney, Australia, on December 10th, show that the best type of auction for any market depends crucially on even slight differences in the number of buyers and sellers.

  Bank of America has been investigating these new auctions, along with robotic traders, for possible use in electronic exchanges. The hope is that today's financial auctions and online marketplaces might work better by becoming more like their English and Dutch forebears. But what to call such multi-ethnic hybrids? Here's introducing the "Cliffhanger".

     (Selected from Computerised Trading Agents May Help Humans Build Better Markets)

2.

  "We are committed to a successful round. And it's going to take hard work." George Bush's comment this week on the Doha round of global trade talks sums up the official line in most capitals. Of course Doha must succeed, goes the mantra; yes, it will be a hard slog.

  The next few weeks will determine whether this mantra means anything. Trade ministers gather in Geneva on June 29th for a last-ditch attempt to agree on a "framework" for freeing trade in farm and industrial goods. Negotiators have been haggling over such a framework, which will define just how tariffs and subsidies are to be cut, for more than four years. They have set themselves—and missed-endless deadlines.

  So why expect a breakthrough now? The only reason for hope is that all sides may finally realize that they can procrastinate no more. Most trade talks drag on for years. The Doha round cannot, because Mr.

Bush's fast track negotiating authority, which prevents a trade deal being unpicked by Congress, expires in June 2007. To meet that deadline, an agreement must be reached by the end of the year; its broad outlines need to be in place before negotiators pack up for the summer (note that no one has suggested canceling any holidays).

The trouble is that the important parties are still miles apart. The path to a deal is no secret. The European Union must offer bigger cuts in farm tariffs; America must promise to slash subsidies more; and big emerging economies must reduce their industrial tariffs. No one has yet offered anything new, but there are rumors that America will offer bigger cuts in subsidies in Geneva next week.

Less noticed but equally worrying are chasms between other countries. Among emerging economies, for instance, there is a big row about how much special treatment to demand for farm tariffs. Countries such as India and Indonesia want lots of exceptions for their farm goods. Others, such as Thailand and Argentina, want far fewer.

In all, the latest draft agreement on farm trade has around 700 pairs of square brackets on language where there is still disagreement. Unresolved issues abound. Add in the World Cup and the lure of the beach in August, and you have to be starry-eyed to give the Doha round much of a chance.

(Selected from Doha's Last Stand —Critical Days for the Global Trade Talks)

3.

World food prices are pushing higher — the United Nations overall food index shows a 28.3% annual increase, with cereals up 44.1% — sparking concerns that a new food crisis may be emerging, just three years after the last one. Does this mean the world is running out of food?

The quick answer is that the world does seem to be running low on cheap food. This supply shortage stems from the failure of governments and donors over nearly three decades to fund the basic agricultural research, investments in rural infrastructure, and training for smallholder farmers necessary to push out the productivity frontier.

Until recently, world food crises have been relatively rare events—occurring about three times a century. The food crises of 2007—2008, although scary at the time, was relatively mild by comparison. Prices for wheat, rice and maize — the staple foods that provide well over half the world population's energy intake directly and a good deal more indirectly via livestock products—rose 96.7% between 2006 and 2008, not approaching the spikes in the mid-1970s when corrected for inflation. Yet here we are just a few years later, talking about food prices again.

Suddenly spikes in food prices have a political dimension. Nothing can bring angry people into the streets faster and more spontaneously than a rapid run-up in the costs of food staples in urban markets. That's why politicians in many developing countries are highly sensitive to the level and rate of change in food prices. A food-price crises focuses the minds of political leaders on a quick, short-term resolution. But this focus comes with a real cost to longer-run investments and policy initiatives, even if this cost is hardly noticed at the time.

Policy makers who forever live in the short run, putting out the bush fires from banking crises, food riots, or the palpable fear they are about to lose their jobs, do not focus on long-run needs. Because of this tendency, agricultural research and rural infrastructure is getting neglected in most countries. The price of that neglect is there for all to see. Between the mid-1980s and the mid-1990s public agricultural research expenditures did not expand at all in Sub-Saharan Africa, whereas they grew by 5% per year in Asia. The differential impact on agricultural productivity per worker was dramatic — increases in Africa between 1990—2002 and 2001—2003 of just 7%, whereas the increases in Asia was 36%.

We can do better. In the greater scheme of things, agricultural research is not that expensive. A group of experts convened by the Asia Society and the International Rice Research Institute calculated that the productivity of rice growing on a global basis could be raised by 8.5% over baseline trends through an annual investment of $120 million between 2010 and 2030— an investment that is about 0.0002% of global GDP. Similar opportunities exist for most of the world's important food crops. It is hard to imagine investments with higher payoffs.

(Selected from : *Failed Policies Lead to Food Shortages* written by C. Peter Timmer)

二、汉译英

1.
  国际收支是衡量一定时期内所有国内与国外居民之间的交易状况。使用"所有交易"可能会产生误导，因为有些交易可能是估算出来的。交易的记录采用复式记账法。就是说，每笔交易都必须记入贷方和借方。这样，贷方和借方总额等于一个国家的收支总额。

2.
  公司闲置资金最好该如何处理？最佳选择是购买有价证券，因为有价证券也是很有流动性的，当企业急需资金时可以很容易地将其变现。有价证券是指股票和债券，虽然股票有一定的风险，但是债券同样也有风险。没有风险就没有收益。公司进行有价证券投资的目的就是让闲置的资金产生收益，比如债券利息、股票红利。

第七章 科技翻译

一、英译汉

1.
  Until recently, scientists knew little about life in the deep sea, nor had they reason to believe that it was being threatened. Now, with the benefit of technology that allows for deeper exploration, researchers have uncovered a remarkable array of species inhabiting the ocean floor at the depths of more than 660 feet, or about 200 meters. At the same time, however, technology also enabled fishermen to reach far deeper than ever before, into areas where bottom trawls can destroy in minutes what has taken nature hundreds in some cases thousands of years to build.

  Many of the world's coral species, for example, are found at the depths of more than 200 meters. It is estimated that roughly half of the world's highest seamounts—areas that rise from the ocean floor and are particularly rich in marine life—are also found in the deep ocean.

  These deep ecosystems provide shelter, spawning and breeding areas for fishes and other creatures, as well as protection from strong currents and predators. Moreover, they are believed to harbor some of the most extensive reservoirs of life on earth, with estimates ranging from 500,000 to 100 million species inhabiting these largely unexplored and highly fragile ecosystems.

  Yet as we are beginning to recognize the tremendous diversity of life in these areas, along with the potential benefits newly found species may hold for human society in the form of potential food products and new medicines, they are at the risk of being lost forever. With enhanced ability both to identify where these species-rich areas are located and to trawl in deeper water than before, commercial fishing vessels are now beginning to reach down with nets the size of football fields, catching everything in their path while simultaneously crushing fragile corals and breaking up the delicate structure of reefs and seamounts that provide critical habitat to countless species of fish and other marine life that inhabit the deep ocean floor.

  Because deep sea trawling is a recent phenomenon, the damage that has been done is still limited. If steps are taken quickly to prevent this kind of destructive activity from occurring on the high seas, the benefits to both the marine environment and to future generations are incalculable. And they far outweigh the short-term costs to the fishing industry.

(Selected from *Selected Readings of the True Real Paper Questions of English Written Translation Grade Two*)

2.
Universal Design is an emerging approach which aims to develop a theoretical framework and practical means to a more user-friendly living environment. It aims to do this specifically by incorporating features accommodating the widest possible range of human needs. In doing this, it has a close relationship with Accessibility Design, yet it is important to differentiate between the two. Accessibility design necessarily focuses on the sometimes specialized needs of groups whose mobility has traditionally been limited. Universal Design takes that body of knowledge and seeks to extract from it, features which can become the norm, for the benefit not only of special groups but of everyone.

Universal Design incorporates accessibility issues but seeks a broader consensus as a means to broader application. In that sense, Universal Design needs to respect the average and to take account of related issues, such as cost effectiveness, space efficiency, flexibility and identity. At its most effective, Universal Design can be invisible. It is an inclusive approach which embodies the hope that the largest number of people can access the widest variety of places with the greatest degree of safety and convenience. It is important to all of us because we are all challenged at various times of our lives. We were all children. We will all become ill. If we are lucky, we will become old. By some definitions, a large proportion of society is in some way disabled; even if people prefer not to think of themselves, or to present themselves in that way. In many societies with an aging population, that proportion will rise, as the number of caregivers declines.

Many countries have legislated on behalf of the aged and people with disabilities and have produced design guidelines, particularly related to accessibility design over a number of decades. The contributors to this guidebook think that Universal Design is the next step.

(Selected from *Universal Design Guidebook For Residential Development in Hong Kong*)

3.
Coal ash, fertilizer and even seawater may provide nuclear fuel.

One of the factoids trotted out from time to time by proponents of nuclear power is that conventional coal-burning power stations release more radioactivity into the environment than nuclear stations do. The reason is that the ash left over when coal is burned contains radioactive elements, notably uranium and thorium.

Turn that logic on its head and it suggests that such ash is worth investigating as a source of nuclear fuel. And that is exactly what Sparton Resources, a firm based in Toronto, is doing. It has signed a deal with the China National Nuclear Corporation (CNNC), the authority that runs the country's nuclear-power stations, to recover uranium from coal ash at a site in Lincang, Yunnan Province.

Uranium is usually extracted from ore that contains 1,000 or more parts per million (ppm) of the element. The Lincang coal ash holds much less, about 300ppm. That said, it does not need to be mined—which brings costs down. Sparton says it can extract a kilogram of uranium for $77 or less. Uranium's spot price is now near $90 a kilo. That is not a huge margin, but it is a profit nonetheless.

To extract the uranium, Sparton adds sulphuric and hydrochloric acids to the ash, along with water, to make a slurry. With some sorts of ash, nitric acid is also used. The acids dissolve the uranium, and various other things, leaching them from the ash. The trick is to get the dissolved uranium out of the resulting solution.

Sparton's process uses a charcoal filter made from burned coconut husks to trap floating particles and eliminate organic compounds. The filtered solution is then passed through small beads of an ion-exchange resin. These selectively remove uranium ions while leaving the others behind—extracting about two thirds of the uranium in the ash, according to the company. The uranium is then dissolved from the beads using a solution of ammonium carbonate and precipitated as "yellow cake", a mixture of uranium oxides.

China is developing ash-mining for reasons of energy security more than economics, according to Wang Hongfang, a marketing manager at CNNC. The country wants to get uranium from "every possible channel", Mr Wang says. These include stripping it out of the tailings from gold and copper mines, and also from phosphoric acid produced during the manufacture of fertilizer. Nor is CNNC alone in this aspiration. NUKEM, a German-American company that enriches and sells nuclear fuel, hopes soon to begin "mining" fertilizer in Florida.

Some people are even turning to seawater as a source of uranium, in an eerie recapitulation of Fritz Haber's attempt to pay off Germany's first-world-war debts by extracting gold from the ocean. Though seawater contains only three parts per billion of uranium, mostly in the form of uranyl tricarbonate, the element can be sucked out of it by ion exchange.

Several organizations, including Japan's Atomic Energy Agency and the Bhabha Atomic Research Centre in India, are attempting to do so. Their methods include the use of strips of ion-exchanging plastic, braided with polystyrene to toughen them up. These are placed in wire cages and anchored in a current of seawater. After a month or two, the plastic is removed and soaked in acid to dissolve the uranyl tricarbonate. The solution is then treated to precipitate uranium oxide.

At the moment, this process costs more than ten times as much as conventional mining, but some countries might regard that as a small price to pay for security of supply. Perish the thought that the supply is for anything other than providing fuel for civilian nuclear-power stations.

(Selected from *Novel Sources of Uranium*)

二、汉译英

1.

移动电话正在成为 21 世纪一个主要的技术领域。在几年之内,移动电话将会发展成为多功能的通信工具,除了语音之外,还可以传输和接收视频信号、静止图像、数据和文本。个人通信的新纪元即将到来。

在一定程度上多亏了无线网络的发展,电话正在与个人电脑和电视融合起来。不久之后,配有高分辨率显示屏的轻巧手机便可以与卫星连接。人们可以随时随地通话,收发电子邮件或者参加视像电话会议。这种手机也许还会吸收电脑的许多主要功能。移动通信工具有望带来一些互联网所能提供的新服务,如股票交易、购物及预订戏票和飞机票。

电信革命已在全球范围内展开。不久之后,用一台装置就可以收到几乎任何形式的电子通信信号。最有可能的是一部三合一手机。在家里它可以用作无绳电话,在路上用作移动电话,在办公室里用作内部通话装置。有些专家甚至认为移动视像电话将超过电视,成为主要的视频信息来源。

(选自《英语二级笔译考试真题精选》)

2.

40 年前,黄河入海口曾经是鸟类的乐园。后来随着黄河三角洲地区河水水量的减少以及人为的开垦,这里的湿地面积减少了,来访鸟儿的数量也减少了。

近年来,黄河三角洲湿地生态系统明显改善。现在,每年都有近百万只鸟到这里越冬栖息,它们中有许多是世界上的珍稀种类。黄河三角洲湿地保护只是中国在保护湿地方面的一个成功例子。它反映中国在保护湿地方面取得了很大成效。

中国现已建立 353 个湿地自然保护区。湿地自然保护区的建立还保护了中国大江大河的源头、主要河流入海口,以及候鸟繁殖和越冬栖息地。

目前,湿地保护仍然是中国生态建设中的一个薄弱环节。中国政府将采取有力措施制止掠夺性开发湿地资源的行为,以保证湿地资源的可持续利用。

(选自《英语二级笔译考试真题精选》)

第八章 法律翻译

一、英译汉

1.
II. General Conditions of Liability
Chapter 2. Damage
Art. 2:101. Recoverable damage
Damage requires material or immaterial harm to a legally protected interest.
Art. 2:102. Protected interests
(1) The scope of protection of an interest depends on its nature; the higher its value, the precision of its definition and its obviousness, the more extensive is its protection.
(2) Life, bodily or mental integrity, human dignity and liberty enjoy the most extensive protection.
(3) Extensive protection is granted to property rights, including those in intangible property.
(4) Protection of pure economic interests or contractual relationships may be more limited in scope. In such cases, due regard must be had especially to the proximity between the actor and the endangered person, or to the fact that the actor is aware of the fact that he will cause damage even though his interests are necessarily valued lower than those of the victim.
(5) The scope of protection may also be affected by the nature of liability, so that an interest may receive more extensive protection against intentional harm than in other cases.
(6) In determining the scope of protection, the interests of the actor, especially in liberty of action and in exercising his rights, as well as public interests also have to be taken into consideration.
Art. 2:103. Legitimacy of damage
Losses relating to activities or sources which are regarded as illegitimate cannot be recovered.
Art. 2:104. Preventive expenses
Expenses incurred to prevent threatened damage amount to recoverable damage in so far as reasonably incurred.
Art. 2:105. Proof of damage
Damage must be proved according to normal procedural standards. The court may estimate the extent of damage where proof of the exact amount would be too difficult or too costly.

(Selected from *Principles of European Tort Law*)

2.
Increasingly, overseas manufacturers of pharmaceutical grade materials are supplying raw materials for incorporating into pharmaceutical products that will eventually be imported into the United States. These products face numerous legal and regulatory requirements before they can be lawfully sold in the United States, not the least of which is the US patent laws.

Many US pharmaceutical patents contain claims directed to a process of manufacturing pharmaceutical materials. While US process patents do not reach processes used outside the United States, once products manufactured according to a patented US process reach the US border, the provision of 35 U.S.C. § 271 (g) becomes applicable, which states:

> *Whoever without authority imports into the United States or offers to sell, sells, or uses within the United States a product which is made by a process patented in the United States shall be liable as an infringer, if the importation, offer to sell, sale, or use of the product occurs during the term of such process patent...* (35 U.S.C. § 271[g]) (*emphasis added.*)

It can be seen that § 271(g) prohibits importation of a "product which is made by a process patented in the United States". This article focuses on whether there is infringement when some of the steps of the patented process are performed outside the United States by one entity, while the remaining steps of the patented process are performed outside the United States by another entity, and then the resulting product is imported into the United States. In other words, when multiple entities collectively perform all of the steps in the patented process outside the United States but no single entity performs all of those steps outside the United States, does the resulting product constitute a "product which is made by a process patented in the United States" within the meaning of § 271(g)?

For processes where all the process steps are taken within the United States, it is well established that the only way to prove direct infringement, where some of the claimed steps are performed by one accused infringer and other claimed steps are performed by another accused infringer is through the doctrine of "divided infringement". BMC Resources, Inc. v. Paymentech, L. P., 498 F. 3d 1373 (Fed. Cir. 2007); MuniAuction, Inc. v. Thomson Corp., 532 F. 3d 1318 (Fed. Cir. 2008). Proof of infringement under the "divided infringement" doctrine requires the patent holder to prove the process utilized by one accused infringer was done under the "control or direction" of another accused infringer. Essentially, one of the accused infringers must "mastermind" the coordinated infringement of all the claimed process steps so that one actor can fairly be said to perform each patented process step. The other actor or actors behave essentially as contractor(s) for the mastermind. MuniAuction, 532 F. 3d at 1329. Under the "direction or control" standard, mere "arms-length cooperation" will not give rise to direct infringement by any party. BMC Resources, 498 F. 3d at 1381; MuniAuction, 532 F. 3d at 1329.

However, whether the doctrine of "divided infringement" is applicable to the use of patented process outside the United States has yet to be concluded. This doctrine was developed with reference to 35 U. S. C. § 271(a), which applies to the use of patented processes within the United States. It was not developed with reference to § 271(g), which applies to the use of patented processes outside the United States and the subsequent importation of the resulting product. This is necessarily so as § 271(g) is a fairly recent addition to U. S. patent law. But there is a reason to believe that the "divided infringement" defense under § 271(g) could be successful.

(Selected from *Some Issues Relating to Infringement of a Process Patent in the US*)

二、汉译英
1.
　　致：_____人民法院
　　原告：
　　地址：
　　法定代表人：
　　职务：
　　被告：
　　地址：
　　法定代表人：
　　职务：
　　诉讼请求：
　　1. 请求法院判决被告向原告支付已发出货物_____元人民币的价款以及_____人民币的利息,总计_____元人民币；
　　2. 判决被告承担诉讼费用。
　　事实和理由：
　　被告系原告在中国_____地区各种产品的分销商之一。自_____至_____,原告向其发送了价值总计_____人民币的各种产品(见证据一)。上诉每笔交易均由被告正式签署和接受(见证据二)。尽管原告多次催讨货款,被告仍未能清偿到期债务。
　　原告认为,因原告与被告之间交易引起的债务应由中国法律管辖。被告在收到上述货物之后未能按时付清货款,由此给原告造成了巨大的经济损失(见证据三)。因此,按照中国的相关法律法规,被告必须承担因不付款所致的相应民事责任。

基于以上理由,根据中华人民共和国民法通则第106条和第112条、民事诉讼法第108条以及其他相关可适用法律法规,原告特此向贵院提起本案诉讼。

原告(签名或盖章):
日期:
附件:
一、原告营业执照复印件;
二、法定代表人资格复印件;
三、授权委托书复印件;
四、证据一:历次交易发货单;
五、证据二:历次交易收据;
六、证据三:损失明细。

(《民事起诉书》)

2.
第一章 总 则
第一条 为促进和规范境外投资,根据《国务院对确需保留的行政审批项目设定行政许可的决定》,制定本办法。
第二条 本办法所称境外投资,是指在我国依法设立的企业(以下简称企业)通过新设、并购等方式在境外设立非金融企业或取得非金融企业的所有权、控制权、经营管理权等权益的行为。
第三条 企业开展境外投资应当认真了解并遵守境内外相关法律法规、规章和政策,遵循"互利共赢"原则。
第四条 商务部负责对境外投资实施管理和监督,省、自治区、直辖市、计划单列市及新疆生产建设兵团商务主管部门(以下简称省级商务主管部门)负责对本行政区域内境外投资实施管理和监督。
第二章 核 准
第五条 商务部和省级商务主管部门对企业境外投资实行核准。商务部建立"境外投资管理系统"(以下简称"系统")。对予以核准的企业,颁发《企业境外投资证书》(以下简称《证书》,样式见附件一)。《证书》由商务部统一印制,实行统一编码管理。
第六条 企业开展以下情形境外投资应当按本办法第十二条的规定提交申请材料,并按本办法第十三条的规定报商务部核准:
(一)在与我国未建交国家的境外投资;
(二)特定国家或地区的境外投资(具体名单由商务部会同外交部等有关部门确定);
(三)中方投资额1亿美元及以上的境外投资;
(四)涉及多国(地区)利益的境外投资;
(五)设立境外特殊目的公司。
第七条 地方企业开展以下情形的境外投资应当按照本办法第十二条要求提交申请材料,并按第十四条的规定报省级商务主管部门核准:
(一)中方投资额1000万美元及以上、1亿美元以下的境外投资;
(二)能源、矿产类境外投资;
(三)需在国内招商的境外投资。
第八条 企业开展本办法第六条、第七条规定情形以外的境外投资,须提交《境外投资申请表》(以下简称申请表,样式见附件二),并按第十六条规定办理核准。
第九条 企业境外投资有以下情形之一的,商务部和省级商务主管部门不予核准:
(一)危害我国国家主权、安全和社会公共利益,或违反我国法律法规;
(二)损害我与有关国家(地区)关系;
(三)可能违反我国对外缔结的国际条约;

(四) 涉及我国禁止出口的技术和货物。

境外投资经济技术可行性由企业自行负责。

第十条 商务部核准第六条规定的境外投资应当征求我驻外使(领)馆(经商处室)意见。涉及中央企业的,由商务部征求意见;涉及地方企业的,由省级商务主管部门征求意见。

省级商务主管部门核准第七条第二款规定的境外投资应当征求驻外使(领)馆(经商处室)意见;其他情形的境外投资核准,省级商务主管部门可视情征求驻外使(领)馆(经商处室)意见。

(选自中华人民共和国商务部令 2009 年第 5 号《境外投资管理办法》)

第九章 散文翻译

一、英译汉

1.

　　One windy spring day, I observed young people having fun using the wind to fly their kites. Multicolored creations of varying shapes and sizes filled the skies like beautiful birds darting and dancing. As the strong winds gusted against the kites, a string kept them in check.

　　Instead of blowing away with the wind, they arose against it to achieve great heights. They shook and pulled, but the restraining string and the cumbersome tail kept them in tow, facing upward and against the wind. As the kites struggled and trembled against the string, they seemed to say, "Let me go! Let me go! I want to be free!" They soared beautifully even as they fought the restriction of the string. Finally, one of the kites succeeded in breaking loose. "Free at last," it seemed to say. "Free to fly with the wind."

　　Yet freedom from restraint simply put it at the mercy of an unsympathetic breeze. It fluttered ungracefully to the ground and landed in a tangled mass of weeds and string against a dead bush. "Free at last" free to lie powerless in the dirt, to be blown helplessly along the ground, and to lodge lifeless against the first obstruction.

　　How much like kites we sometimes are. The Heaven gives us adversity and restrictions, rules to follow from which we can grow and gain strength. Restraint is a necessary counterpart to the winds of opposition. Some of us tug at the rules so hard that we never soar to reach the heights we might have obtained. We keep part of the commandment and never rise high enough to get our tails off the ground.

　　Let us each rise to the great heights, recognizing that some of the restraints that we may chafe under are actually the steadying force that helps us ascend and achieve.

(Selected from Nameless: *Free to Soar*)

2.

　　I am the gentle wind; I am the clouds, the slow, drifting clouds; I am the water, the silent water; I am the mountains, the boundless mountains… If you so want, I will be the gentle wind that will wrap around your lonely spirit! If you so desire, I will be the slow, drifting clouds that will unquestioningly be your support! If you so wish, I will be that silent water, without a murmur, protecting you by your side. If you so will, I will love you unrelentingly, just like those boundless, unbroken mountain ranges and valleys! But, I regret I am not the wind and not able to take care of you. I hate that I am not the clouds and not able to bring you warmth; I pity myself that I am not the water and not able to be so pure; I am angry that I am not the mountains and not able to have my love will be as immovable as I would like. I can only be myself this time, my mortal, earthly self, my only self, the only self that I can ever hope to be. I thirst for love but I do not understand her deep mystery. I strive for transcendence but I would rather be silent and nameless. I want to be mature but I would rather remain innocent. I would like that she loves me, but I do not know even if I truly love her! Endless searching, thirsting, striving, pursuing. Where are my goals? Where is my future? In this mundane world, I am one lonely speck; in this universe I am a powerless particle of dust. My love, though beautiful, is nothing great in itself. And so, I ask only to live as well as I can. In truth, there is no need to live one's life basking in glory, rising above men—so long as one's life has some value, has some security... Fearless and capricious, love will cause me great pain. Youth, transient and inconstant, will bring me loneliness. Work, busy and mindless, will make me lost. I am just searching for and waiting for some of that which shines, that which is radiant in life...

(Selected from Nameless: *I Am the Gentle wind*)

3.

Three passions, simple but overwhelmingly strong, have governed my life: the longing for love, the search for knowledge, and unbearable pity for the suffering of mankind. These passions, like great winds, have blown me hither and thither, in a wayward course, over a deep ocean of anguish, reaching to the very verge of despair.

I have sought love, first, because it brings ecstasy—ecstasy so great that I would often have sacrificed all the rest of life for a few hours of this joy. I have sought it, next, because it relieves loneliness—that terrible loneliness in which one shivering consciousness looks over the rim of the world, into the cold unfathomable lifeless abyss. I have sought it, finally, because in the union of love I have seen, in a mystic miniature, the prefiguring vision of the heaven that saints and poets have imagined. This is what I sought, and though it might seem too good for human life, this is what—at last—I have found.

With equal passion I have sought knowledge. I have wished to understand the hearts of men. I have wished to know why the stars shine. And I have tried to apprehend the Pythagorean power by which number holds sway above the flux. A little of this, but not much I have achieved.

Love and knowledge, so far as they were possible, led upward toward the heavens. But always pity brought me back to earth. Echoes of cries of pain reverberate in my heart. Children in famine, victims tortured by oppressors, helpless old people a hated burden to their sons, and the whole world of loneliness, poverty, and pain make a mockery of what human life should be. I long to alleviate the evil, but I cannot, and I too suffer.

This has been my life. I have found it worth living, and would gladly live it again if the chance were offered me.

(Selected from Bertrand Russell: *What I Have Lived for*)

二、汉译英

1.

这几天心里颇不宁静。今晚在院子里坐着乘凉,忽然想起日日走过的荷塘,在这满月的光里,总该另有一番样子吧。月亮渐渐地升高了,墙外马路上孩子们的欢笑,已经听不见了;妻在屋里拍着闰儿,迷迷糊糊地哼着眠歌。我悄悄地披了大衫,带上门出去。

沿着荷塘,是一条曲折的小煤屑路。这是一条幽僻的路;白天也少人走,夜晚更加寂寞。荷塘四面,长着许多树,蓊蓊郁郁的。路的一旁,是些杨柳,和一些不知道名字的树。没有月光的晚上,这路上阴森森的,有些怕人。今晚却很好,虽然月光也还是淡淡的。

路上只我一个人,背着手踱着。这一片天地好像是我的;我也像超出了平常的自己,到了另一世界里。我爱热闹,也爱冷静;爱群居,也爱独处。像今晚上,一个人在这苍茫的月下,什么都可以想,什么都可以不想,便觉是个自由的人。白天里一定要做的事,一定要说的话,现在都可不理。这是独处的妙处,我且受用这无边的荷香月色好了。

(选自朱自清:《荷塘月色》)

2.

我在花园里种满了芬芳的玫瑰花,远远望去,像一片燃烧的晚霞。我想等朋友来做客的时候,让他们携带些玫瑰回家。我相信朋友捧着火红的玫瑰渐渐走远的背影,一定能点燃易感的情怀。

有一天,一位非常要好的女友来探望我,我知道她平素最喜欢花花草草了,临别时我说,采一束玫瑰点缀你的闺房,保证十里飘香。

女友轻轻跨进花园,东闻闻,西嗅嗅,神采飞扬,就是不肯采摘。我说没关系,多的是,我又不是花店的老板,不会靠玫瑰赚钱的。说完我就举起剪刀准备献美。女友急忙拦住,高声叫着不可不可。

这么美丽的玫瑰剪下来,让人心疼。她抓紧我的袖子叮咛:千万不能剪啊,玫瑰是泥土的微笑,谁忍心杀戮美得醉人的微笑?

(选自栖云:《泥土的微笑》)

3.
  日照,我的家乡,其历史可以追溯到汉代。这是一座新兴的海滨城市,也是一座历史悠久的城市。日照博物馆里,一排排的展柜中,若干汉墓出土文物业已面世。日照,意为"日出先照",是一座充满活力的中型城市。黎明时分,目不转睛的游客眺望海上日出,兴致勃勃;此时,渔船穿梭来往,海鸥竞翔。如果您想品尝生猛海鲜,在市区可如愿以偿。

  日照国家森林公园,坐落在市区北部15公里处。约百万株林木挤挤拥拥,毗邻海滩。盛夏时节,浓荫之下,小憩片刻,心旷神怡。这儿海风阵阵,鸟儿啁啾,游人恍惚置身仙境一般。四座浴场,一线排列,点缀海滨。外地泳客,邀游其中,多么引人入胜!

  日照景色不但风姿绰约,而且生机勃勃。您最好亲自光临,游览一番。我的家乡定然不会令您失望。如果您想眺望蔚蓝的天空,请不要迟疑了,动身吧!如果您想享受一尘不染的空气,不要犹豫了,起程吧!日照,我真诚地爱着你,我心飞翔,飞翔,飞翔!

(选自岳守国:《日照:我可爱的家乡》)

第十章 小说翻译

一、英译汉

1.
  Both doors and lattices were open; and yet, as is usually the case in a coal district, a fine, red fire illumined the chimney; the comfort which the eye derives from it, renders the extra heat endurable. But the house of Wuthering Heights is so large, that the inmates have plenty of space for withdrawing out of its influence; and, accordingly, what inmates there were had stationed themselves not far from one of the windows. I could both see them and hear them talk before I entered, and looked and listened in consequence, being moved thereto by a mingled sense of curiosity and envy that grew as I lingered.

  "Con-trary!" said a voice, as sweet as a silver bell — "That for the third time, you dunce! I'm not going to tell you, again — Recollect, or I pull your hair!"

  "Contrary, then," answered another, in deep but softened tones. "And now, kiss me, for minding so well."

  "No, read it over first correctly, without a single mistake."

  The male speaker began to read — he was a young man, respectably dressed, and seated at a table, having a book before him. His handsome features glowed with pleasure, and his eyes kept impatiently wandering from the page to a small white hand over his shoulder, which recalled him by a smart slap on the cheek, whenever its owner detected such signs of inattention.

  Its owner stood behind; her light shining ringlets blending, at intervals, with his brown locks, as she bent to superintend his studies; and her face — it was lucky he could not see her face, or he would never have been so steady — I could, and I bit my lip, in spite, at having thrown away the chance I might have had, of doing something besides staring at its smiting beauty.

  The task was done, not free from further blunders, but the pupil claimed a reward, and received at least five kisses, which, however, he generously returned. Then, they came to the door, and from their conversation, I judged they were about to issue out and have a walk on the moors. I supposed I should be condemned in Hareton Earnshaw's heart, if not by his mouth, to the lowest pit in the infernal regions if I showed my unfortunate person in his neighborhood then, and feeling very mean and malignant, I skulked round to seek refuge in the kitchen.

(Selected from Emily Brontë: *Wuthering Heights*)

2.

　　William appeared at half past twelve. He was a very active lad, fair-haired, freckled, with a touch of the Dane or Norwegian about him.

　　"Can I have my dinner, mother?" he cried, rushing in with his cap on. "'Cause it begins at half past one, the man says so."

　　"You can have your dinner as soon as it's done," replied the mother.

　　"Isn't it done?" he cried, his blue eyes staring at her in indignation. "Then I'm goin' be out it."

　　"You'll do nothing of the sort. It will be done in five minutes. It is only half past twelve."

　　"They'll be beginnin'," the boy half cried, half shouted.

　　"You won't die if they do," said the mother. "Besides, it's only half past twelve, so you've a full hour."

　　The lad began hastily to lay the table, and directly the three sat down. They were eating batter-pudding and jam, when the boy jumped off his chair and stood perfectly stiff. Some distance away could be heard the first small braying of a merry-go-round, and the tooting of a horn. His face quivered as he looked at his mother.

　　"I told you!" he said, running to the dresser for his cap.

　　"Take your pudding in your hand—and it's only five past one, so you were wrong—you haven't got your twopence," cried the mother in a breath.

　　The boy came back, bitterly disappointed, for his twopence, then went off without a word.

　　"I want to go, I want to go," said Annie, beginning to cry.

　　"Well, and you shall go, whining, wizzening little stick!" said the mother. And later in the afternoon she trudged up the hill under the tall hedge with her child. The hay was gathered from the fields, and cattle were turned on to the eddish. It was warm, peaceful.

　　Mrs. Morel did not like the wakes. There were two sets of horses, one going by steam, one pulled round by a pony; three organs were grinding, and there came odd cracks of pistol-shots, fearful screeching of the cocoanut man's rattle, shouts of the Aunt Sally man, screeches from the peep-show lady. The mother perceived her son gazing enraptured outside the Lion Wallace booth, at the pictures of this famous lion that had killed a negro and maimed for life two white men. She left him alone, and went to get Annie a spin of toffee. Presently the lad stood in front of her, wildly excited.

　　"You never said you was coming—isn't the' a lot of things?—that lion's killed three men—I've spent my tuppence—an' look here."

　　He pulled from his pocket two egg-cups, with pink moss-roses on them.

　　"I got these from that stall where y'ave ter get them marbles in them holes. An' I got these two in two goes—'aepenny a go—they've got moss-roses on, look here. I wanted these."

　　She knew he wanted them for her.

　　"H'm!" she said, pleased. "They ARE pretty!"

　　"Shall you carry 'em, 'cause I'm frightened o' breakin' 'em?"

　　He was tipful of excitement now she had come, led her about the ground, showed her everything. Then, at the peep-show, she explained the pictures, in a sort of story, to which he listened as if spellbound. He would not leave her. All the time he stuck close to her, bristling with a small boy's pride of her. For no other woman looked such a lady as she did, in her little black bonnet and her cloak. She smiled when she saw women she knew. When she was tired she said to her son:

　　"Well, are you coming now, or later?"

　　"Are you goin' a'ready?" he cried, his face full of reproach.

　　"Already? It is past four, I know."

　　"What are you goin' a'ready for?" he lamented.

"You needn't come if you don't want," she said.

And she went slowly away with her little girl, whilst her son stood watching her, cut to the heart to let her go, and yet unable to leave the wakes. As she crossed the open ground in front of the Moon and Stars she heard men shouting, and smelled the beer, and hurried a little, thinking her husband was probably in the bar.

(Selected from D. Lawrence: *Sons and Lovers*)

二、汉译英

1.

大家吐口气，放了心。顾尔谦忽然聪明地说："假如学校款子没有汇，那就糟透了。"四人不耐烦地口气说他过虑，可是意识里都给他这话唤起了响应，彼此举理由，倒不是驳斥顾尔谦，而是安慰自己。顾尔谦忙想收回那句话，仿佛给人拉住的蛇尾巴要缩进洞，道："我也知道这事不可能，我说一声罢了。"鸿渐道："我想这问题容易解决，我们先去一个人。吉安有钱，就打电报叫大家去；吉安没有钱，也省得五个人全去扑个空，白费了许多车钱。"

辛楣道："是呀！咱们分工，等行李的等行李，领钱的领钱，行动灵活点，别大家拼在一起老等，这钱是汇给我的，我带了行李先上吉安，鸿渐陪我走，多个帮手。"

孙小姐温柔而坚决："我也跟赵先生走，我行李也来了。"

李梅亭尖利地给辛楣一个 X 光的透视道："好，只剩我和顾先生，可是我们的钱充公了，你们分多少钱给我们？"

顾尔谦向李梅亭抱歉地笑道："我行李全到了，我想跟他们去，在这儿住下去没有意义。"

李梅亭脸上升火道："撇下我一个，好！我无所谓。什么'同舟共济'！事到临头，还不是各人替自己打算？说实话，你们到吉安领了钱，干脆一个子儿不给我得，难不倒我李梅亭。我箱里的药要是在内地卖千把块钱，很容易的事，你们瞧我讨饭也讨到上海。"

辛楣诧异说："咦！李先生，你怎么误会到这个地步！"

顾尔谦抚慰地说："梅亭先生，我决不先走，陪你等行李。"

辛楣道："究竟怎么办？我一个人先去，好不好？李先生，你总不疑心我会吞灭公款——要不要我留下行李作押！"说完加以一笑，减低语意的严重，可是这笑生硬倔强宛如干浆糊粘上去的。

李梅亭摇手连连道："笑话！笑话！我也绝不是以'不人之心'推测人的——"

鸿渐自言自语道："还说不是"——"我觉得方先生的提议不切实际——方先生，抱歉抱歉，我说话一向直率的。譬如赵先生，你一个人到吉安领了钱，还是向前进呢？向后转呢？你一个人作不了主，还要大家就地打听消息共同决定的——"鸿渐接嘴道："所以我们四个人先去呀。服从大多数的决定，我们不是大多数么？"李梅亭说不出话，赵顾两人忙劝开了，说："大家患难之交，一致行动。"

(选自钱钟书：《围城》)

2.

话说宝玉来至院外，就有跟贾政的几个小厮上来拦腰抱住，都说："今儿亏我们，老爷才喜欢，老太太打发人出来问了几遍，都亏我们回说喜欢，不然，若老太太叫你进去，就不得展才了。人人都说，你才那些诗比世人的都强。今儿得了这样的彩头，该赏我们了，"宝玉笑道："每人一吊钱。"众人道："谁没见那一吊钱！把这荷包赏了罢。"说着，一个上来解荷包，那一个就解扇囊，不容分说，将宝玉所佩之物尽行解去。又道："好生送上去罢。"一个抱了起来，几个围绕，送至贾母二门前。那时贾母已命人看了几次。众奶娘丫鬟跟上来，见过贾母，知不曾难为着他，心中自是欢喜。

少时袭人倒了茶来，见身边佩物一件无存，因笑道："带的东西又是那起没脸的东西们解了去了。"林黛玉听说，走来瞧瞧，果然一件无存，因向宝玉道："我给的那个荷包也给他们了？你明儿再想我的东西，可不能够了！"说毕，赌气回房，将前日宝玉所烦他作的那个香袋儿——才做了一半——赌气拿过来就铰。宝玉见他生气，便知不妥，忙赶过来，早剪破了。宝玉已见过这香囊，虽尚未完，却十分精巧，费了许多工夫。今见无故剪了，却也可气。因忙把衣领解了，从里面红袄襟上将黛玉所给的那荷包解了下来，递与黛玉道："你瞧瞧，这是什么！我那一回把你的东西给人了？"林黛玉见他如此珍重，带在里面，可知是怕人拿去之意，因此又自悔莽撞，未见皂白，就剪了香袋。因此又愧又气，低头一言不发。宝玉道："你也不用剪，我知道你是懒得给我东西。我连这荷包奉还，何如？"说着，掷向他怀中便走。黛玉见如此，越发气起来，声咽气堵，又汪汪的滚下泪来，拿起荷包来又剪。宝玉见他如此，忙回身抢住，笑道："好妹妹，饶了他罢！"黛玉将剪子一摔，拭泪说道："你不用同我好一阵歹一阵的，要恼，就撂开手。这当了什么。"说着，赌气上床，面向里倒下拭泪。禁不住宝玉上来"妹妹长妹妹短"赔不是。

前面贾母一片声找宝玉。众奶娘丫鬟们忙回说："在林姑娘房里呢。"贾母听说道："好，好，好！让他姊妹们一处顽顽罢。才他老子拘了他这半天。让他开心一会子罢。只别叫他们拌嘴，不许扭了他。"众人答应着。黛玉被宝玉缠不过，只得起来道："你的意思不叫我安生，我就离了你。"说着往外就走。宝玉笑道："你到那里，我跟到那里。"一面仍拿起荷包来带上，黛玉伸手抢道："你说不要了，这会子又带上，我也替你怪臊的！"说着，"嗤"的一声又笑了。宝玉道："好妹妹，明儿另替我作个香袋儿罢。"黛玉道："那也只瞧我高兴罢了。"一面说，一面二人出房，到王夫人上房中去了，可巧宝钗亦在那里。

（选自曹雪芹：《红楼梦》）

第十一章 诗歌翻译

一、英译汉

1.

A Red, Red Rose

By Robert Burns

O my Luve is like a red, red rose
That's newly sprung in June;
O my Luve is like the melody
That's sweetly played in tune.

As fair art thou, my bonnie lass,
So deep in luve am I;
And I will luve thee still, my dear,
Till a' the seas gang dry.

Till a' the seas gang dry, my dear,
And the rocks melt wi' the sun;
O I will luve thee still, my dear,
While the sands o' life shall run.

And fare thee weel, my only Luve!
And fare thee weel a while!
And I will come again, my Luve,
Tho' it were ten thousand miles.

2.

The Daffodils

By William Wordsworth

I wander'd lonely as a cloud
That floats on high o'er vales and hills,
When all at once I saw a crowd,
A host, of golden daffodils;
Beside the lake, beneath the trees,
Fluttering and dancing in the breeze.

Continuous as the stars that shine

And twinkle on the Milky way,
They stretch'd in never-ending line
Along the margin of a bay:
Ten thousand saw I at a glance,
Tossing their heads in sprightly dance.

The waves beside them danced, but they
Out-did the sparkling waves in glee:
A poet could not but be gay
In such a jocund company!
I gaze—and gazed—but little thought
What wealth the show to me had brought:
For oft, when on my couch I lie
In vacant or in pensive mood,
They flash upon that inward eye
Which is the bliss of solitude;
And then my heart with pleasure fills,
And dances with the daffodils.

3.

Sudden Light

By Dante Gabriel Rossetti

I have been here before,
But when or how I cannot tell:
I know the grass beyond the door,
The sweet keen smell,
The sighing sound, the lights around the shore.
You have been mine before—
How long ago I may not know:
But just when at that swallow's soar
Your neck turned so,
Some veil did fall, I knew it all of yore.
Has this bee thus before?
And shall not thus time's eddying flight
Still with our lives our love restore
In death's despite,
And day and night yield one delight once more?

4.

Elegy Written in a Country Churchyard

By Thomas Gray

The curfew tolls the knell of parting day,
The lowing herd wind slowly o'er the lea,
The plowman homeward plods his weary way,
And leaves the world to darkness and to me.

Now fades the glimmering landscape on the sight,
And all the air a solemn stillness holds,
Save where the beetle wheels his droning flight,

And drowsy tinklings lull the distant folds;

Save that from yonder ivy-mantled tower,
The moping owl does to the moon complain
Of such as, wandering near her secret bower,
Molest her ancient solitary reign.

Beneath those rugged elms, that yew-tree's shade,
Where heaves the turf in many a mouldering heap,
Each in his narrow cell for ever laid,
The rude Forefathers of the hamlet sleep.

The breezy call of incense-breathing morn,
The swallow twittering from the straw-built shed,
The cock's shrill clarion, or the echoing horn,
No more shall rouse them from their lowly bed.

For them no more the blazing hearth shall burn,
Or busy housewife ply her evening care;
No children run to lisp their sire's return,
Or climb his knees the envied kiss to share,

Oft did the harvest to their sickle yield,
Their furrow oft the stubborn glebe has broke;
How jocund did they drive their team afield!
How bow'd the woods beneath their sturdy stroke!

Let not Ambition mock their useful toil,
Their homely joys, and destiny obscure;
Nor Grandeur hear with a disdainful smile
The short and simple annals of the Poor.

The boast of heraldry, the pomp of power,
And all that beauty, all that wealth e'er gave,
Awaits alike th' inevitable hour:—
The paths of glory lead but to the grave.

二、汉译英

1.

静夜思
李白
床前明月光,疑是地上霜。
举头望明月,低头思故乡。

2.

无题
李商隐
相见时难别亦难,东风无力百花残。
春蚕到死丝方尽,蜡炬成灰泪始干。
晓镜但愁云鬓改,夜吟应觉月光寒。
蓬山此去无多路,青鸟殷勤为探看。

3.
西江月
辛弃疾

醉里且贪欢笑,
要愁哪得工夫。
近来始觉古人书,
信着全无是处。
昨夜松边醉倒,
问松"我醉何如"
只疑松动要来扶,
以手推松曰"去"!

4.
木兰花慢
辛弃疾

中秋饮酒,将旦,客谓前人诗词有赋待月,
无送月者,因用《天问》体赋。

可怜今夕月,
向何处,去悠悠?
是别有人间,
那边才见,光影东头?
是天外,空汗漫,
但长风浩浩送中秋?
飞镜无根谁系?
嫦娥不嫁谁留?

谓经海底问无由,
恍惚使人愁。
怕万里长鲸,
纵横触破,玉殿琼楼。
虾蟆故堪浴水,
问云何玉兔解沉浮?
若道都齐无恙,
云何渐渐如钩?

第十二章 戏剧翻译

一、英译汉

DUKE　　Have mercy on Antonio, Shylock. Do not be so bitter.

SHYLOCK　　I've promised to take my pound of flesh. If you do not let me have it, that will be a sign of weakness and no one will trust your laws any more. The greatness of Venice will soon be lost. Antonio is my enemy, and I hate him.

BASSANIO　　Do all men kill the things they do not love?

ANTONIO　　It is useless trying to argue with Shylock. Don't wait any longer. Pass judgement on me and give Shylock what he wants.

BASSANIO　　I'll pay you six thousand ducats for the three thousand ducats that Antonio borrowed.

SHYLOCK　　If you offered me six times what you have just offered, I would still take my pound of flesh. Give me my pound of flesh!

DUKE　　Let us be calm, gentlemen. Shylock, how can you hope for mercy yourself when you show none?

SHYLOCK I have done nothing wrong and I fear no judgement. I desire my pound of flesh.

As the Duke is wondering what to do, Nerissa, dressed like a lawyer's clerk, arrives with a letter from the famous lawyer whom Portia has visited. While the Duke is talking to Nerissa, Shylock gets ready to cut his pound of flesh from Antonio.

Then the letter is read out for all in the court to hear. "I am very ill. When your letter reached me, I had with me a learned young doctor from Rome. I told him about the quarrel between Shylock and Antonio. We studied many law books and he knows what I would say. I ask you to let him stand in my place and give judgement. He is young, but I never knew so young a body with so wise a head."

After the letter has been read out to the court, Portia, in lawyer's clothes, enters the room and takes her seat as judge.

DUKE	Greetings, learned judge! I do not envy you your job. This is a most troublesome case.
PORTIA	Greetings! Please be seated. Are you Antonio, and is this your agreement with Shylock?
ANTONIO	It is.
PORTIA	Then Shylock must be merciful. He must have mercy on Antonio.
SHYLOCK	Why must I have mercy on him? Tell me that!
PORTIA	Mercy brings good. Mercy falls like the gentle rain from the sky upon the earth. It blesses those who give it, and those who receive it. We should learn to show mercy to others. Do you still ask for this pound of flesh?
SHYLOCK	I ask for what is mine by law!
BASSANIO	I offer ten times the money that Antonio has borrowed. Please change the law a little so that we may save Antonio.
PORTIA	Use your head a little, sir! We cannot change a law. If one law is changed, then people will later want to change other laws.
SHYLOCK	Oh, wise young judge!
PORTIA	Let me see this agreement, this promise of Antonio to you.
SHYLOCK	Here it is.
PORTIA	I see. According to the law, Shylock may have a pound of flesh to be cut off by him nearest to Antonio's heart. Be merciful! Let me destroy this paper. —No? Then, Antonio, be ready. And Shylock, take your knife and prepare to do the deed.
SHYLOCK	Oh, learned judge! Oh, wise young man!
PORTIA	Have you brought anything to weigh the flesh?
SHYLOCK	Yes. I have everything ready here.
PORTIA	Do you have a doctor, Shylock, to stop Antonio's blood?
SHYLOCK	There was no write in the agreement.
BASSANIO	That fox!
PORTIA	Do you wish to say anything, Antonio?
ANTONIO	Only a little. Goodbye Bassanio. Don't be sad for me. Tell your wife about me and how much I loved you. If Shylock cuts deep enough, I'll pay him back with all my heart.
BASSANIO	Let me take you in my arms and say goodbye. I love you more than my own life, more than my wife, and more than all the world. (*He cries.*)
PORTIA	Your wife would not be pleased to hear you say that.
SHYLOCK	We are wasting time.
PORTIA	Take your pound of flesh! I declare the court allows it and the law gives it to you.

Shylock advances towards Antonio and prepares to use his knife.

PORTIA	Wait! There is something else. Antonio has promised to give you a pound of his flesh. But he has not promised to give you any of his blood. If you let one drop of his blood fall, you

	will lose all your land and all your money.
SHYLOCK	Is that the law?
PORTIA	That is the law. You wanted justice, so you shall get justice, more than you wanted.
SHYLOCK	I will take the money. Give me three more than Antonio borrowed from me.
BASSANIO	Here it is. (*He cries out, full of joy.*)
PORTIA	Wait! Shylock would not take the money earlier. All he wanted was right to be done. That is all he can have now. You must cut off one pound of flesh, no more, no less. And not one drop of blood must fall.

Shylock turns and starts to leave the court.

PORTIA	Wait, Shylock. The law of Venice says that if anyone tries to kill or murder any citizen of Venice, everything that he owns shall be taken away from him. One half of his money and his goods shall be given to the city of Venice and the other half shall be given to the person he has tried to kill. His life shall be at the mercy of the Duke. Therefore, go down on your knees and beg the Duke for mercy.
SHYLOCK	Good, sir. I beg for mercy and beg your pardon.
DUKE	I shall not have you killed. But as your punishment, half of your money is now Antonio's. You must give the other half to the city of Venice.
SHYLOCK	Take my life too! My money and goods are as dear to me as life itself. They are my only comfort. When you take those away from me, you also take my life.
ANTONIO	I shall be happy to give up my part of Shylock's money. Shylock must promise to leave the money upon his death to his daughter and her husband.
SHYLOCK	I promise. Let me go home now. I am not well.

(Selected from William Shakespeare: *The Merchant of Venice*)

二、汉译英

刘麻子	说说吧,十两银子行不行?你说干脆的!我忙,没工夫专伺候你!
康 六	刘爷!十五岁的大姑娘,就值十两银子吗?
刘麻子	卖到窑子去,也许多拿一两八钱的,可是你又不肯!
康 六	那是我的亲女儿!我能够……
刘麻子	有女儿,你可养活不起,这怪谁呢?
康 六	那不是因为乡下种地的都没法子混了吗?一家大小要是一天能吃上一顿粥,我要还想卖女儿,我就不是人!
刘麻子	那是你们乡下的事,我管不着。我受你之托,教你不吃亏,又教你女儿有个吃饱饭的地方,这还不好吗?
康 六	到底给谁呢?
刘麻子	我一说,你必定从心眼里乐意!一位在宫里当差的!
康 六	宫里当差的谁要个乡下丫头呢?
刘麻子	那不是你女儿的命好吗?
康 六	谁呢?
刘麻子	庞总管!你也听说过庞总管吧?伺候着太后,红的不得了,连家里打醋的瓶子都是玛瑙作的!
康 六	刘大爷,把女儿给太监做老婆,我怎么对得起人呢?
刘麻子	卖女儿,无论怎么卖,也对不起女儿!你糊涂!你看,姑娘一过门,吃的是珍馐美味,穿的是绫罗绸缎,这不是造化吗?怎样?摇头不算点头算,来个干脆的!
康 六	自古以来,哪有……他就给十两银子?
刘麻子	找遍了你们全村儿,找得出十两银子找不出?在乡下,五斤白面就换个孩子,你不是不

	知道!
康　六	我,唉!我得跟姑娘商量一下!
刘麻子	告诉你,过了这个村可没有这个店,耽误了事别怨我!快去快来!
康　六	唉!我一会儿就回来!
刘麻子	我在这儿等着你!
康　六	(慢慢地走出去)
刘麻子	(凑到松二爷、常四爷这边来)乡下人真难办事,永远没个痛痛快快!
松二爷	这号生意又不小吧?
刘麻子	也甜不到哪儿去,弄好了,赚个元宝!
常四爷	乡下是怎么了?会弄得这么卖儿卖女的!
刘麻子	谁知道!要不怎么说,就是一条狗也得托生在北京城里嘛!
常四爷	刘爷,您可真有个狠劲儿,给拉拢这路事!
刘麻子	我要不分心,他们还许找不到买主呢!(忙岔话)松二爷(掏出个小时表来),您看这个!

(选自老舍:《茶馆》)

第十三章　典籍翻译

1.

　　常摐有疾,老子往问焉,曰:"先生疾甚矣,无遗教可以语诸弟子者乎?"常摐曰:"子虽不问,吾将语子。"常摐曰:"过故乡而下车,子知之乎?"老子曰:"过故乡而下车,非谓其不忘故耶?"常摐曰:"嘻,是已。"

　　常摐曰:"过乔木而趋,子知之乎?"老子曰:"过乔木而趋,非谓敬老耶?"常摐曰:"嘻,是已。"

　　张其口而示老子曰:"吾舌存乎?"老子曰:"然。""吾齿存乎?"老子曰:"亡。"常摐曰:"子知之乎?"老子曰:"夫舌之存也,岂非以其柔耶?齿之亡也,岂非以其刚耶?"常摐曰:"嘻,是已。天下之事已尽矣,无以复语子哉!"

(选自刘向:《说苑·舌存齿亡》)

2.

　　十年春,齐师伐我,公将战。曹刿请见。其乡人曰:"肉食者谋之,又何间焉?"刿曰:"肉食者鄙,未能远谋。"乃入见。问:"何以战?"公曰:"衣食所安,弗敢专也,必以分人。"对曰:"小惠未徧,民弗从也。"公曰:"牺牲玉帛,弗敢加也,必以信。"对曰:"小信未孚,神弗福也。"公曰:"小大之狱,虽不能察,必以情。"对曰:"忠之属也。可以一战。战则请从。"

　　公与之乘。战于长勺。公将鼓之。刿曰:"未可。"齐人三鼓。刿曰:"可矣。"齐师败绩。公将驰之。刿曰:"未可。"下视其辙,登轼而望之,曰:"可矣。"遂逐齐师。

　　既克,公问其故。对曰:"夫战,勇气也。一鼓作气,再而衰,三而竭。彼竭我盈,故克之,夫大国,难测也,惧有伏焉。吾视其辙乱,望其旗靡,故逐之。"

(选自《左传·曹刿论战》)

3.

　　杭有卖果者,善藏柑,涉寒暑不溃。出之烨然,玉质而金色。置于市,贾十倍,人争鬻之。

　　予贸得其一,剖之,如有烟扑口鼻,视其中,干若败絮。予怪而问之曰:"若所市于人者,将以实笾豆、奉祭祀、供宾客乎?将炫外以惑愚瞽也?甚矣哉,为欺也!"

　　卖者笑曰:"吾业是有年矣,吾赖是以食吾躯。吾售之,人取之,未尝有言,而独不足子所乎?世之为欺者不寡矣,而独我也乎?吾子未之思也。今夫佩虎符、坐皋比者,洸洸乎干城之具也,果能授孙吴之略耶?峨大冠、拖长绅者,昂昂乎庙堂之器也,果能建伊、皋之业耶?盗起而不知御,民困而不知救,吏奸而不知禁,法斁而不知理,坐糜廪粟而不知耻。观其坐高堂、骑大马、醉醇醴而饫肥鲜者,孰不巍巍乎可畏、赫赫乎可象也?又何往而不金玉其外、败絮其中也哉?今子是之不察,而以察吾柑!"

　　予默然无以应。退而思其言,类东方生滑稽之流。岂其愤世疾邪者耶?而托于柑以讽耶?

(选自刘基:《卖柑者言》)

4.

　　孔子年十七,鲁大夫孟厘子病且死,诫其嗣懿子曰:"孔丘,圣人之后,灭于宋。其祖弗父何始有宋而嗣让厉公。及正考父佐戴、武、宣公,三命兹益恭,故鼎铭云:'一命而偻,再命而伛,三命而俯,循墙而走,亦莫敢余侮。饘于是,粥于是,以糊余口。'其恭如是。吾闻圣人之后,虽不当世,必有达者。今孔丘年少好礼,其达者欤?吾即没,若必师之。"及釐子卒,懿子与鲁人南宫敬叔往学礼焉。是岁,季武子卒,平子代立。

孔子贫且贱。及长,尝为季氏史,料量平;尝为司职吏而畜蕃息。由是为司空。已而去鲁,斥乎齐,逐乎宋、卫,困于陈蔡之闲,于是反鲁。孔子长九尺有六寸,人皆谓之"长人"而异之。鲁复善待,由是反鲁。

鲁南宫敬叔言鲁君曰:"请与孔子适周。"鲁君与之一乘车,两马,一竖子俱,适周问礼盖见老子云。辞去,而老子送之曰:"吾闻富贵者送人以财,仁人者送人以言。吾不能富贵,窃仁人之号,送子以言,曰:'聪明深察而近于死者,好议人者也。博辩广大危其身者,发人之恶者也。为人子者毋以有己,为人臣者毋以有己。'"

孔子自周反于鲁,弟子稍益进焉。

(选自司马迁:《史记·孔子世家》)

第十四章　影视翻译

一、英译汉

1. 电影片名翻译

(1) The Portrait of a Lady

(2) The Legend of 1900

(3) The Far Side of the World

(4) The Bridges of Madison County

(5) Sleepless in Seattle

(6) Shakespeare in Love

(7) Scent of a Woman

(8) Pretty Woman

(9) Possession

(10) Meet Joe Black

(11) Legends of the Fall

(12) Love Actually

(13) Mrs. Doubtfire

(14) Going on 30

2. 电影字幕翻译

(1)

Mozart: I know your music well. You know, I actually composed some variations on a melody of yours.

Salieli: Really? I'm flattered.

King: And now he has returned the compliment. Herr Salieri composed this little march of welcome for you.

Mozart: Really? Thank you, sir.

King: There it is. Down to business. Young man, we're going to commission an opera from you. What do you say?

Mozart: Your Majesty!

King: Did we vote in the end for German or Italian?

Salieli: I don't think it was really decided, your Majesty.

Mozart: German! Please let it be German!

King: Why so?

Mozart: Because I've already found the most wonderful libretto. The language is not finally the point so long as the subject is full of proper German virtues.

Salieli:	Excuse me, Majesty, but what do you think these could be? As a foreigner, I'd love to learn.	
King:	Tell him, Mozart, name us a German virtue.	
Mozart:	Love, sir!	
Salieli:	Love! Of course, in Italy, we know nothing about love.	
Mozart:	No, I don't think you do. I mean, watching Italian opera, all those male sopranos screeching, fat couples rolling their eyes about. That's not love. It's rubbish! Majesty, you choose the language. It will be my task to set it to the finest music ever offered a monarch.	
King:	Well, there it is. Let it be German.	

(Selected from *Amadeus*, 1984)

(2)

Keating:	Why do I stand up here? Anybody?
Student:	To feel taller.
Keating:	No! Thank you for playing, Mr. Dalton. I stand upon my desk to remind myself that we must constantly look at things in a different way. You see, the world looks very different from up here. You don't believe me? Come see for yourselves. Come on, come on! Just when you think you know something you have to look at it in another way. Even though it may seem silly or wrong, you must try! Now, when you read, don't just consider what the author thinks, consider what you think. Boys, you must strive to find your own voice, because the longer you wait to begin, the less likely you are to find it at all. Thoreau said, "Most men lead lives of quiet desperation." Don't be resigned to that, break out! Don't just walk off the edge like lemmings, look around you. There! There you go, Mr. Priske. Thank you! Dare to strike out and find new ground. Now, in addition to your essays, I would like you to compose a poem of your own, an original work. That's right! You have to deliver it aloud in front of the class on Monday. Bon chance, gentlemen. Mr. Anderson? Don't think that I don't know that this assignment scares the hell out of you, you mole.

(Selected from *Dead Poets Society*, 1989)

(3)

Forrest:	What's the matter, Mama?
Mrs. Gump:	I'm dying, Forrest. Come on in, sit down over here.
Forrest:	Why are you dying, Mama?
Mrs. Gump:	It's my time. It's just my time. Oh, now, don't you be afraid, sweetheart. Death is just a part of life. Something we're all destined to do. I didn't know it, but I was destined to be your mama. I did the best I could.
Forrest:	You did good.
Mrs. Gump:	Well, I happen to believe you make your own destiny. You have to do the best with what God gave you.
Forrest:	What's my destiny, Mama?
Mrs. Gump:	You're going to figure out for yourself. Life is a box of chocolates, Forrest. You never know what you're going to get.

(Selected from *Forrest Gump*, 1994)

(4)

Frida:	Senor Rivera? Diego!
Diego:	Who are you? What do you want?
Frida:	I have something important to discuss with you.

Diego: I'm working.
Frida: I'll wait.
Diego: I don't have time to chat with schoolgirls.
Frida: I'm not a schoolgirl, panzon.
Diego: Okay. Come on up here.
Frida: No. You come down.
Diego: What?
Frida: Look, I didn't come here for fun or to flirt. I've done some paintings which I want you to look over professionally, and I need an absolutely straightforward opinion.
Diego: You were that girl in the auditorium.
Frida: Yes, I was, but that has nothing to do with now. I just want your serious opinion.
Diego: What—what do you care about my opinion? If you're a real painter, you'll paint because you can't live without painting. You'll paint till you die, okay?
Frida: I have to work to earn a living, so I don't have time to fool around just for vanity. If I'm not good enough, I have to do something else to help my parents.
Diego: Leave the best one here. Go home and paint another one. If this one's any good, I'll come and look at that one on my day off.

(Selected from *Frida*, 2002)

(5)

Lawyer: Mrs. Kramer, would you tell the court how long you've been married?
Mrs. Kramer: Eight years.
Lawyer: And would you describe those years as happy?
Mrs. Kramer: The first two, yes. But after that it became increasingly difficult.
Lawyer: Mrs. Kramer, did you hold a job before you were married?
Mrs. Kramer: Yes, I did. When I first got out of Smith I worked in the Art Department of *Mademoiselle* magazine for several years.
Lawyer: Did you continue to work after you were married?
Mrs. Kramer: No, I did not.
Lawyer: Did you wish to?
Mrs. Kramer: Yes. But every time I talked to Ted, to my ex-husband about it, he wouldn't listen. He refused to discuss it in any serious way. I remember once he said that I probably couldn't get a job that would pay enough to hire a babysitter for Billy.
Lawyer: Tell me, are you employed at the present time?
Mrs. Kramer: Yes, I'm a sports wear designer here in New York.
Lawyer: And what is your present salary?
Mrs. Kramer: I make 31,000 a year.
Lawyer: Mrs. Kramer, do you love your child?
Mrs. Kramer: Yes, I do, very much.
Lawyer: And yet you chose to leave him.
Mrs. Kramer: Yes. During the last five years of our marriage, I was becoming more and more unhappy, more and more troubled. And I really needed somebody to help me. But when I turned to Ted, he just wasn't there for me. So we became more isolated from one another, more and more separate. He was very involved in his career. And because of his attitude towards my fears and his inability to deal with my feelings, I had come to have almost no self-esteem. I was scared and I was very unhappy. In my mind, I had no choice but to leave. At the time I left, I felt that there was something terribly

	wrong with me and that my son would be better off without me. And it was only after I got to California, after getting into therapy, that I realized, that I wasn't such a terrible person. And just because I needed some kind of creative or emotional outlet other than my child, that doesn't make me unfit of being a mother.
Lawyer:	(*To the judge*) I would like to submit in evidence a report by Mrs. Kramer's therapist, Dr. Eleanor Freedman. Mrs. Kramer, can you tell the court why you're asking for custody?
Mrs. Kramer:	Because he's my child, and because I love him. I know I left my son. I know that's a terrible thing to do. Believe me, I have to live with that every day of my life. But in order to leave him, I had to believe it was the only thing I could do and it was the best thing for him. I was incapable of functioning in that home. And I didn't know what the alternative was going to be, so I thought it was not best that I take him with me. However, I have worked very, very hard to become a whole human being. I don't think I should be punished for that. I don't think my little boy should be punished. Billy is only 7 years old. He needs me. I'm not saying that he doesn't need his father, but I really believe he needs me more. I was his mommy for five and a half years and Ted took over that role for 18 months. But I don't know how anybody can possibly believe that I have less of a stake in mothering my son. I am his mother. I am his mother.

(Selected from *Kramer vs. Kramer*, 2002)

(6)

Christopher:	Marisa, Caroline, I don't know which name to use.
Marisa:	Marisa.
Christopher:	I don't get it, what just happened?
Marisa:	What don't you get? I'm the maid.
Christopher:	What was all this, some kind of bet? A little game of what, get-the-guests?
Marisa:	No, look, I was trying on her clothes and you were there and you invited me out, and everything.
Christopher:	And you thought you had to lie to keep me interested?
Marisa:	Who's kidding who here? You think you would've taken a second look at me if you knew I was the maid?
Christopher:	Well?
Marisa:	Come on, with respect for your bighearted politics, I don't think so, Mr. Assemblyman.
Christopher:	How did you know? You didn't give me a chance. You stand on your soapbox judging everyone, so sure that they're judging you.
Marisa:	And you think they're not? Come on, half the time I'm a stereotype they're making fun of. The other half of the time, I'm just invisible. You know what, maybe that's the point. The first time you saw me, I was cleaning your bathroom floor, only you didn't see me.
Christopher:	What was I supposed to do, introducing myself while I'm taking a leak? You can't nail me for that. I just want the truth, Marisa.
Marisa:	All right, you want the truth? There was a part of me that wanted to see what it felt like to have someone like you look at me the way you did, just once. And I'm sorry. Truly. If I could rewind the past week, I would.
Christopher:	Was any of it real?

Marisa: Yeah, it was real. It was so real that it made me wonder how I was ever gonna give you up. But I had to give you up. That was the plan. And then, last night, I couldn't.

(Selected from *Maid in Manhattan*, 2002)

(7)

Bill: Hello. Is anyone here?
Joe: Quiet down.
Bill: Where are you?
Joe: I'm here.
Bill: What is this, a joke, right? Some kind of elaborate practical joke? At my 40th reunion, we delivered a casket to the class president's hotel room and ...
Joe: Quiet. Where are you going, Bill?
Bill: I, uh ...
Joe: The great Bill Parrish at a loss of words? The man from whose lips fall "rapture" and "passion" and "obsession"? All those admonitions about "being deliriously happy, that there is no sense living your life without". All the sparks and energy you give off, the rosy advice you dispense in round, pear-shaped tones.
Bill: What the hell is this? Who are you?
Joe: Just think of millenniums multiplied by eons compounded by time without end. I've been around that long. But it's only recently that your affairs here have piqued my interest. Call it boredom. The natural curiosity of me, the most lasting and significant element in existence, has come to see you.
Bill: About what?
Joe: I want to have a look a round before I take you.
Bill: Take me where?
Joe: It requires competence, wisdom and experience. All those things they say about you in testimonials. And you are the one.
Bill: The one to do what?
Joe: Show me around. Be my guide. And in return, you'll get ...
Bill: I'll get what?
Joe: Time, minutes, days, weeks. Let's not get encumbered by detail. What matters is that I stay interested? Yes.
Bill: Yes what?
Joe: "Yes" is the answer to your question.
Bill: What question?
Joe: Oh, come on, Bill, the question you've been asking yourself with increased regularity, at odd moments, panting through the extra game of handball, when you sat up in bed last night and hit the floor in the office this morning. The question that is in the back of your throat choking the blood to your brain, ringing in your ears over and over as you put it to yourself.
Bill: The question.
Joe: Yes, Bill, the question.
Bill: Am I going to die?
Joe: Yes.
Bill: Am I dreaming this? Are you a dream?
Joe: I'm not a dream.
Bill: You're coming to take me? What is that? And who the hell are you? You are?
Joe: Yes? Whom am I?

Bill: Death. You're Death?
Joe: Yes.
Bill: Death.
Joe: That's me.
Bill: You're not Death, you're just a kid in a suit.
Joe: The suit came with the body I took, let me ask your opinion, "Do I blend in?"
Bill: You want me to be your guide?
Joe: You fill the bill, Bill.
Bill: I do?
Joe: Mmm.
Bill: Will you be staying long?
Joe: We should hope quite a while.
Bill: And then? It's over.
Joe: Then lead the way, Bill.

(Selected from *Meet Joe Black*, 1998)

二、汉译英
1. 电影片名翻译
(1)《霸王别姬》
(2)《大话西游之月光宝盒》
(3)《花样年华》
(4)《鹿鼎记》
(5)《心动》
(6)《滚滚红尘》
(7)《水浒传》
(8)《非诚勿扰》
(9)《东邪西毒》
(10)《活着》

2. 电影字幕翻译
(1) 我代表党,代表人民,宣判你的死刑。 (选自《党的女儿》)
(2) 各位父老乡亲,想不到吧?我胡汉山又回来了!这如今还是我胡汉山的天下!过去谁拿了我什么,给我送回来;谁吃了我什么,给我吐出来! (选自《闪闪的红星》)
(3) 同志们,为了新中国,前进! (选自《董存瑞》)
(4) 要送,要送,不管花多大代价,一定要送! (选自《上甘岭》)
(5) 为了胜利,向我开炮! (选自《英雄儿女》)
(6) 哪部分的? (选自《奇袭白虎团》)
(7) 站着进来,躺着出去! (选自《保密局的枪声》)
(8) (a) —天王盖地虎,
    (b) —宝塔镇河妖。

(选自《林海雪原》)
(9) (a) 高,实在是高!
    (b) 就是挖地三尺,也要把八路军给我找出来!

(选自《地道战》)
(10) (a) 打仗我不行,打牌你不行,长江防线就全靠你们几位仁兄啦!
     (b) 中国人民站起来了!

(选自《开国大典》)

(11)（a）我们今天大踏步地后退，就是为了明天大踏步地前进！
　　（b）看在党国的份上，拉兄弟一把吧。

（选自《南征北战》）

(12)（a）付钱？老子在城里吃馆子都不要钱，别说吃你几个烂西瓜。
　　（b）别看今天闹得欢，小心日后拉清单！

（选自《小兵张嘎》）

(13)（a）头可断，血可流，共产党员的意志你永远打倒不了！
　　（b）人生自古谁无死，一个人的生命能够和无产阶级永葆青春的事业拥抱在一起，我感到无上的光荣。

（选自《烈火中永生》）

(14) 你要想找一帅哥就别来了，你要想找一钱包就别见了。硕士学历以上的免谈，上海女人免谈，女企业家免谈（小商小贩除外），省得咱们互相都会失望。刘德华和阿汤哥那种财貌双全的郎君是不会来征你的婚的，当然我也没有做"诺丁山"的梦。您要真是一仙女我也接不住，没期待您长得跟画报封面一样看一眼就魂飞魄散。外表时尚、内心保守、身心都健康的一般人就行，要是多少还有点儿婉约那就更靠谱了。心眼儿别太多，岁数别太小，允许时有不切实际的想入非非，但三句话就能给轰回现实，还不气恼，顶多有点儿难为情地咧嘴一笑就该干吗干吗去了。我喜欢会叠衣服的女人，每次洗完烫平叠得都像刚从商店里买回来的一样。说得够具体了吧。

自我介绍一下：我，岁数已经不小了。日子小康，抽烟不喝酒。留学生身份出去的，在国外生活过十几年，没正经上过学，蹉跎中练就一身生存技能，现在学无所成、海外归来，实话实说应该定性为一只没有公司、没有股票、没有学位的"三无劣海龟"。性格OPEN，人品五五开，不算老实人，但天生胆小，杀人不犯法我也杀不了人，伤天害理了自己良心也备受摧残，命中注定想学坏当不了大坏蛋。总体而言，基本上还是属于对人类对社会有益无害的一类。

有意者，电联。非诚勿扰。

（选自《非诚勿扰》）

各章翻译练习参考答案

第二章 新闻翻译

一、英译汉

1.
苹果公司共同创始人史蒂夫·乔布斯去世，这个消息几乎是在得到苹果官网证实的同时，就开始在中国高人气的新浪微博上流传开来。

曾为谷歌中国（Google China）掌门人的李开复是最先评论此事的人之一。他在经过认证的微博账户中说："乔帮主一路走好，您的产品改变了世界，您的思想影响了一代人。"

成千上万名微博用户与李开复一起悼念乔布斯，新浪微博页面上满是点亮的小蜡烛图标，还有数千人满怀希望地怀疑这则消息是否只是又一次失控的中国互联网谣言。微博用户"阿童木"写道："我真希望这是假的。"名为"不停折腾"的微博用户写道："乔布斯走了，头一次因为一个外国人的离去而感到不好受。"

也有人抓住苹果创始人去世的机会表达自己对苹果公司最新产品的不满。微博用户"魔卡言"调侃说，"他肯定是看到 iPhone 4S 后被气死的。"

还有人敦促苹果推出一系列低价 iPhone 和 iPad，让更多的人能够用上苹果产品。水立方说："这是对史蒂夫·乔布斯最好的纪念。"

在越来越富有的中国消费者中，苹果产品的流行程度一直飙升。今年早些时候在北京三里屯苹果专卖店，曾对白色 iPhone 的需求引发混战，导致商店玻璃被打破，并停业几个小时。

在截至 6 月 25 日的第三财季，苹果宣布在包括香港的大中华区实现销售收入 38 亿美元，较上年同期增长 6 倍以上。苹果上个月在香港和上海新开了门店。

（选自 2011 年"中国网民悼念乔布斯"）

2.
欧洲金融稳定基金（European Financial Stability Facility）负责人雷格林将于周五抵达北京。此时所有人都注视着中国，看它决定在资助欧洲救援计划的过程中怎样发挥作用——如果决定参与资助的话。

雷格林将会晤国家外汇管理局局长易纲和财政部副部长朱光耀，然后飞往亚洲其他国家。

欧洲领导人周四达成一个方案，决定削减希腊的债务，并将前述欧元区救援基金的规模扩充四到五倍。他们暗示，这只基金可以为欧盟财政困难的成员国发行的债券提供约 1 万亿欧元（约合 1.4 万亿美元）的担保。可由中国等现金充裕的新兴经济体来为基金规模的扩大提供部分支持。

中国的外汇储备超过 3.2 万亿美元，困难经济体长期以来都指望中国能够成为拯救它们的白衣骑士。现在依然有传言说，北京将为欧洲的救援基金出资，数额可能很大。

据国际货币基金组织（International Monetary Fund，简称 IMF）人士说，中国表达帮助欧洲的意愿至少已经有了一个月时间，不过条件是经由 IMF 并与其他"金砖国家"（除中国以外还有巴西、印度和俄罗斯）联合出资。但其他金砖国家似乎不敢拿出大笔资金，而中国也不太可能单独行动。

如果出资，那么还将意味着中国分配外汇储备的方式出现重大改变。国家外汇管理局把手中大部分资源都投资于低风险、低收益的投资产品中。虽然这种低回报曾长期招致不满，但国家外汇储备出现巨亏可能带来的政治后果，却是外储管理者不愿意见到的。

中国 4000 亿美元的主权财富基金中国投资有限责任公司（简称中投）已经是满仓投资，目前没有资源来为欧洲的救援作出较大的贡献。

不过中国领导人曾经暗示，如果他们能在别的方面获得回报（比如说承认其"市场经济"地位），他们对援助欧洲的兴趣会更高。一旦市场经济地位获得承认，中国在遭遇反倾销或不公平补贴诉讼时获胜的机率会更高。但欧洲领导人迄今一直反对这样的交换条件。

在中国是否应当参与救助欧洲的问题上,中国民众的看法存在分歧。

曾在中国央行任职、现为北京君投资本管理中心首席投资长的彭俊明说,中国应当救援欧洲。他认为这是中国外汇储备获得更好回报的一个途径。

此外,彭俊明还认为,欧债危机也为中国提供了进一步促进人民币全球化的机会。

(选自2011年"中国是否救援欧洲引全球关注")

二、汉译英

1.

London is welcoming around 10,000 athletes, hundreds of thousands of visitors and a worldwide television audience for the formal opening of the Olympic Games this Friday in July 27, 2012.

Organizers have dealt with a series of last-minute problems, including scrambling to deploy enough security personnel, after a private contractor reported problems putting together a large enough force.

Britain's Queen Elizabeth will officially open the games. The competition in 26 sports runs until August 12.

(Selected from "London Prepares for Olympic Games Opening" in 2012)

2.

U.S. President Barack Obama and his Chinese counterpart, Xi Jinping, have completed a two-day informal summit that addressed issues including cybersecurity, North Korea and climate change.

National security adviser Tom Donilon told reporters the two leaders agreed that resolving cybersecurity differences would be "key to the future" of the bilateral relationship. Donilon also said the two leaders agreed that North Korea must abandon its nuclear weapons program.

Both Donilon and Chinese State Councilor Yang Jiechi said President Xi told Obama that Beijing and Washington were in agreement on the North Korean nuclear issue and that neither country will accept North Korea as a nuclear state.

North Korea depends heavily on China for aid and trade, and Beijing maintains close ties with Pyongyang. However, North Korea's recent bellicose rhetoric, including threats of nuclear strikes on the United States and other South Korean allies, has visibly cooled those ties in recent months.

Both presidents also agreed on a joint effort to combat climate change.

Both Donilon and Chinese State Councilor Yang spoke to reporters separately, as the leaders of the world's two largest economies ended the two-day summit in California.

(Selected from "US, Chinese Presidents Cap Summit with Vows of New Cooperation" in 2013)

3.

This has been a year of tremendous upheavals and remarkable changes. From economic turmoil to the death of several well-known public figures, 2011 has seen the world transformed dramatically. Despite the tough external environment, China's economy remains a bright spot in the world, with a slowed down pace of growth. Here at 21*st Century*, we've combined the analyses of international news agencies, like that of AP, *Time* magazine and Xinhua News Agency, to bring you a list of the year's top news items. Now, as 2011 draws to a close, we can only hope the new year will bring with it greater social stability and the restoration of a strong international economic order.

(1) Economic Soft Landing

This year, China officially overtook Japan as the world's second largest economy. Xinhua News Agency said that China remained a much-needed bright spot in the world economy. Economic growth is slowing a little, but it still stayed above the global average. Facing a tough and depressing world economic situation, China has maintained a steady but slowed-down growth rate this year. A report by Renmin University of China (RUC) forecast that China's economic growth this year would hit 9.4 percent before slipping to 9.2 percent next year. However, it said that even with that figure, the country still outperforms other major economies and stays in shape. The cooling trend reflects China's efforts to seek an economic soft-landing. The country now puts the emphasis on domestic consumption rather than export gains. It's also trying to strike a balance between curbing inflation and maintaining the economic growth rate. This year, China made a good, fresh start on the 12th Five-Year Plan (2011—2015). The plan aims at upgrading China's growth model and economic structure.

(2) High-Speed Train

China's bullet-train ambitions hit problems in 2011 and ultimately slowed down. The country's latest high-speed railway system suffered several technical breakdowns since it came into service in late June.

Later, on July 23, one bullet train rear-ended another in a collision near Wenzhou, Zhejiang Province, killing 40 people and injuring almost 200. The cause of the accident is still under investigation. The tragic accident prompted calls for thorough check-ups on all high-speed rail services. After the crash, Sheng Guangzu, Railway Minister, ordered a slowing down of the speed of all bullet trains. Several high-speed railway projects scheduled to open this year will be postponed.

(3) Shenzhou VIII and Tiangong-1

In 2011, China moved closer toward the goal of operating a permanent space station. On September 29, China launched its first space lab module Tiangong-1, which was unmanned. On November 3, unmanned spacecraft Shenzhou VIII successfully docked with the Tiangong-1 space lab module, after it was launched two days earlier. President Hu Jintao described it as a milestone in China's space program and a remarkable contribution to humanity's exploration of space. Despite progress made in the country's space program, President Hu also said that China's overall level of scientific technologies, especially indigenous innovation capabilities, lagged far behind world-leading standards.

(4) Party's 90th Anniversary

The year of 2011 celebrated the 90th anniversary of the founding of the Communist Party of China (CPC). On July 1, Party General Secretary Hu Jintao delivered a formal speech at a rally to mark the special occasion. He summarized the Chinese people's achievements of the past 90 years, under the leadership of the CPC. The catchphrase of the speech was the word "people", which was repeated 136 times. This highlighted the principle of "putting people first". "We will never forget that the people are the real heroes," he said. He urged all Party members to "maintain close ties with the people", and warned that alienation from the people posed the greatest risk to the Party. Hu also stated that more talented young members will be recruited into the Party. He stressed that talent is the most important resource and a strategic resource for a country's development. "They (young members) represent the future and hope of the Party," he said.

(5) South China Sea Disputes

Territorial disputes between China and some of its neighbors over the South China Sea have intensified in the past few months. In July 2011, relevant parties reached an agreement on the guidelines of implementation of the DOC (the Declaration on the Conduct of Parties in the South China Sea), vowing to cooperate in maritime protection, search and rescue, as well as transnational crime busting. But in November, the US and the Philippines signed a declaration calling for multilateral talks to resolve maritime territorial disputes. On several occasions in 2011, Chinese Premier Wen Jiabao re-affirmed China's commitment to peaceful resolutions of the various disputes.

(6) Japanese Earthquake and Tsunami

An earthquake measuring 9.0 on the Richter scale struck the northeast coast of Japan on March 11 and triggered a massive tsunami that led to the death of almost 16,000 people. In addition to this enormous loss of life and the destruction of infrastructure, the tsunami also caused a number of nuclear accidents. This included a level 7 meltdown at three reactors in the Fukushima No. 1 Nuclear Power Plant complex and saw the evacuation of hundreds of thousands of neighboring residents. According Naoto Kan, the Japanese Prime Minister at the time, "In the 65 years after the end of World War II, this is the toughest and the most difficult crisis for Japan." In the immediate aftermath, around 4.4 million households in northeastern Japan were left without electricity and 1.5 million without water.

(7) European Debt Crisis

This year saw anxiety over rising government debt in Europe escalate into a crisis of global proportions. From late 2010 onwards, concerns over Europe's economic stability had begun to intensify. Greece, Ireland and Portugal had difficulties refinancing their debts. This sent ripples around the world and all major stock exchanges exhibited significant losses. Many Western countries are seeking China's pledge to help stimulate the continent's economy and lift market confidence. Some contend that Europe's financial turmoil can threaten the demand for Chinese exports to the region. However, Chinese economic experts insist China should not blindly buy the euro debt.

(8) The Arab Unrest

2011 saw a wave of demonstrations and protests sweep across the Arab world. There have been drastic upheavals in Tunisia and Egypt, a civil war in Libya and protests in Bahrain, Syria, Yemen, Algeria, Iraq, Jordan, Kuwait, Morocco and Oman. The upheavals have seen the departure of political strongmen such as Tunisia's Zine El Abidine Ben Ali, Egypt's Hosni Mubarak and Yemen's Ali Abdullah Saleh. Muammar Gadhafi, the former leader of Libya, was killed. Meanwhile, Syrian President Bashar al-Assad is still struggling to remain in power amid domestic discontent and foreign pressure. These grassroots movements have differed from previous protests in that religion has not been a driving force.

(9) Death of Kim Jong-il

Kim Jong-il, leader of the Democratic People's Republic of Korea (DPRK) passed away on December 17. According to a report by the DPRK's official KCNA news agency, the 69-year-old died of a heart attack on a train due to "great mental and physical strain" during a "high intensity field inspection". China on December 19 sent its condolences on the death of Kim, noting that the late DPRK leader had carried on and further developed the traditional friendship between China and the DPRK. Observers maintain that the death will not result in turbulence in the DPRK. The KCNA news agency said the country, people and military "should remain loyal to the guidance of respected Kim Jong-Un".

(10) Death of Osama bin Laden and the End of the Iraq War

On December 18, the US military officially ended its war in Iraq nearly nine years after the invasion that ousted Saddam Hussein. In a conflict that has seen almost 4,500 US soldiers and tens of thousands of Iraqis lose their lives, this year has thus seen the end of the most unpopular US military venture since Vietnam. Prior to the withdrawal of troops, US anti-terrorist efforts had already sustained a victory following the death of Osama bin Laden. In May, bin Laden, was killed by a US special forces. Believed to have ordered the attacks on the US on September 11, 2001, bin Laden's death came as a defining moment in the American-led "war against terrorism".

(Selected from "Focus on China and the Globe" in 2011)

第三章 政论翻译

一、英译汉

1.

女王陛下邀请我组建新一届政府,我接受了这一邀请。在谈论新政府之前,我先说一些上一届政府的事情。与十年前相比,我们英国在国内更加开放,对外更富有同情心,我们应该为此感到高兴。

我代表整个国家,对长期致力于公共服务的前首相表示赞扬和感谢。

谈到未来,我们国家现在有一个任何党派都不占绝对议席优势的议会,我们还面临着一些深刻而迫切的问题:巨额的赤字、深层次的社会问题和需要改革的政治体制。

因此,我的目的是联合保守党和自由民主党,建立一个同心协力的联盟。我相信,这是我们能形成一个强大、稳定、良好和受尊敬的政府的正确途径,而且我们太需要这样了。

尼克克莱格和我都想成为撇开各自党派利益,为公众利益和国家利益而努力奉献的政党领袖。我相信,这是我们能够得到我们今天需要的强政励治的新一届政府的最好途径。

我之所以从政是因为我热爱这个国家。我认为最好的时代近在眼前并且我深信公共服务。我认为服务我们的国家,此刻需要面对真正的挑战,直面困难,作出艰难的决定,并带领国民克服这些困难,这样我们才能共同迈向美好的明天。

很明显,我们的任务之一就是重建对我们政治体系的信任。是的,这就要求我们精简开支、改革议会、保证对国民的妥善管理并确保政治家始终是人民的公仆而非主人。

但是我相信还有其他方面。就是要诚实地表现政府可能达到的业绩。真正的变革不是仅靠政府之力就能完成的。真正的变革需要所有人齐心协力、众志成城,需要我们每个人各守本分,为自己,为家庭,为社会,也为其他人。

我希望帮助不列颠建立一个更有责任心的社会。一个不是仅仅问"我们的权利是什么"而是"我们的责任是什么"的社会。我们不应该问"我应该得到什么"而是问"我能给这个社会贡献什么"。为了实现这些责任,不管是那些能够做到、应该做到和那些不能做到的人,我们会始终愿意去帮助。

我希望确保我的政府总能照顾关心我们国家的老弱病残和最贫穷的人。我们必须让大家每个人与我们一起走过我们即将面对的困难。

最重要的是,我们将组建一个具有清晰价值观的政府。这些价值观就是自由、公平和责任。

我希望,我们会组建一个多劳多得的经济体制、一个有更强的家庭和社会责任心的社会、一个重新让民众可以期待和信任的政治体制。

这将是一个艰巨的工作。联合政府将会面临各种挑战。但是,我坚信,基于这样的价值观——重建家庭,重建社会,尤其是重建我们的责任感,我们能够共同创建一个我们国家需要的强大而稳定的政府。

这些就是我关心的事情,这些事情也正是我们这一届政府眼下要着手处理的。

(英国首相卡梅伦2010年5月就职演讲)

2.

我国宪法要求美国总统必须定期向国会报告国家状况。在过去二百二十年里,我国领导人履行了这一职责。他们不仅在经济繁荣和国家安定的时期发表讲话,也在战争期间、经济衰退和有冲突时发表国情咨文。

回顾这些历史时刻是非常有吸引力的,并可认为我们国家的进步是不可避免的,美国注定会获得成功。但在当美国股市持续了10年的牛市崩溃、二战期间盟军登陆奥马哈海滩之时,我们是否能够获得胜利还充满质疑。当华尔街股市在黑色星期二崩盘和追求民权的游行者在"血腥星期天"遭到殴打的时候,美国是不确定的。这是考验我们勇气与政府实力的时刻。尽管我们之间存在分歧以及有些犹豫和担心,美国最终获得了胜利,因为我们选择团结在一起,作为一个国家、一个民族向前进。

我们再次受到挑战,必须再次回答历史的疑问。

一年之前,我在两场战争之中成为美国总统。当时美国正受到经济衰退造成的冲击,金融系统已到崩溃边缘,政府负债累累。所有政治领域的专家发出警告,认为如果我们不采取行动,美国将出现历史上第二次经济衰退。所以我们迅速、积极地作出反应,并在一年以后,度过了最严重的经济风暴。

但金融风暴造成的损失仍然存在。十分之一的美国人找不到工作,大批公司破产,房价下跌,小城镇和农村社区损失尤其惨重。对穷苦百姓而言,生活变得更为艰难。

(选自美国总统奥巴马2010年1月国情咨询演说)

二、汉译英

1.

Over the past 90 years, our Party has united with and led the Chinese people in writing a grand epic in the history of human development on this ancient land of China, evidenced in three earthshaking events.

The first is that our Party, firmly relying on the people, completed the new-democratic revolution, winning national independence and liberation of the people. The Party and the people fought through the Northern Expedition, the Agrarian Revolutionary War, the War of Resistance Against Japanese Aggression and the War of Liberation in 28 years, during which they defeated Japanese imperialist aggressors, overthrew the Kuomintang reactionary rule and established the People's Republic of China. With the founding of New China, the Chinese people became masters of their country and society and determined their own destiny. China achieved a great transition from a feudal autocracy that was several thousand years old to a people's democracy. Great unity and unprecedented solidarity of all ethnic groups were realized in China. The history of old China being a semi-colonial and semi-feudal society which was like a heap of loose sand was brought to an end once and for all. The unequal treaties imposed on China by imperialist powers and all the privileges they had in China were abolished. The Chinese people stood up, and the Chinese nation entered a new era of development and progress.

The second is that, firmly relying on the people, our Party completed the socialist revolution and established the basic socialist system. We creatively achieved the transition from new democracy to socialism, therefore creating a socialist society for a quarter of the world's population in this large country in the East, and brought about the most extensive and profound social changes in Chinese history. We established industrial and economic systems that were independent and fairly complete, and we gained important experience of building socialism in China, a country with backward productive forces.

The third is that, firmly relying on the people, our Party carried out a great new revolution of reform and opening up, creating, upholding, and developing socialism with Chinese characteristics. Since the Third Plenary Session of the Eleventh CPC Central Committee, we have reviewed China's practices of building socialism and drawn on the experience of other countries. We have embarked on the path of reform and opening up with tremendous political and theoretical courage and courage in practice. Going through an arduous process of trial and error, we have formed the Party's basic theory, line and platform and gained basic experience in the primary stage of socialism, established a socialist market economy and constantly improved it, made China fully open, and made world-renowned progress in the socialist modernization drive.

These three major events reshaped the future and destiny of the Chinese people and the Chinese nation. They irreversibly ended the misery endured by China in modern times when it suffered from both domestic turmoil and foreign invasion and was poor and weak. They also irreversibly started the Chinese nation's historic march for development, growth, and great rejuvenation. They gave China, a civilization of over 5,000 years, a completely new look and created unimagined prospects for the great rejuvenation of the Chinese nation.

(Selected from Hu Jintao's speech on the celebration of the CPC's 90th anniversary)

2.

Our world is experiencing major development transformation and adjustment. There is a stronger call for peace, development and cooperation among the people. The trend towards a multi-polar world and economic globalization is gaining momentum. Economies around the world are becoming increasingly interdependent. Emerging markets and developing countries are growing rapidly, and regional economic cooperation is making robust progress. Science and technology is on the eve of new breakthroughs, and the global economic order is undergoing profound changes. Even with all these positive developments, however, we should not lose sight of the potential risks. More than two years after the international financial crisis, the world economic recovery remains slow and fragile. The underlying impacts of the crisis are still with us, and the outlook of the world economy is uncertain. In addition, international and regional hotspot issues keep flaring up, uneven development between the North and the South is more acute, and protectionism of various forms is resurfacing. There are a range of new global challenges such as climate change, energy security and food security that threaten the very survival and development of mankind.

China will take an active part in discussing and resolving major issues in the world economic development, and work with all other countries to meet the various challenges. To this end, I wish to make the following observations.

First, we need to enhance global economic governance and press ahead with the reform of the international financial system. The international financial crisis has taken its toll on individual economies and the world economy as a whole. The crisis has highlighted the deficiencies of the existing international financial system and the inadequacy of the global economic governance mechanism in dealing with crises. Today, emerging markets and developing countries are taking a growing share in the global economy and playing a bigger role in global governance. The global economic governance mechanism should adapt to the new changes in the world economic landscape and observe the principle of mutual respect and collective decision-making. It is of special importance to increase the representation and voice of emerging markets and developing countries in the new mechanism. We need to support and promote a greater role of the G20 in global economic governance in order to bring about full recovery and growth of the world economy. Cooperation mechanisms of emerging markets, notably the BRICS, represent a new model of global economic cooperation and a prime example of multilateralism. We need to improve global economic governance, build a fair, just, inclusive and well-managed international monetary and financial system and a balanced multilateral trading regime that benefits all, oppose all forms of protectionism, and work towards an international economic order that is more just and reasonable.

Second, we need to accelerate transformation of the economic development pattern and make appropriate adjustment to economic structure. World economic development has brought both opportunities and challenges. We need to fully grasp and follow the development trend of the world and adapt ourselves to the changing international economic environment. We should make unremitting efforts to transform economic development pattern and adjust economic structure so as to resolve various economic problems and achieve development and transformation all at once. In this process of transformation and adjustment, countries should learn from each other and work together for the strong, sustainable and balanced growth of the world economy.

Third, we need to harness advances in science and technology and quicken the steps to make them a key driver of our economies. As scientific and technological innovation widens and deepens at a rapid pace, countries around the world are losing no time in implementing their science and innovation strategies, channeling more resources to research and development, and training more innovation-minded personnel. China, too, is working vigorously to build innovation capability and become an innovation-oriented country. We should encourage cooperation in innovation between countries and promote the application of scientific and technological achievements. We should make innovation a key driver of world economic development and part of the solution to various constraints and obstacles hampering economic growth. We should combine the effort to spur innovation with that to improve people's well-being so that the fruits of scientific and technological innovation will benefit more countries and peoples.

(Selected from the Speech made by Chinese President Hu Jintao——"Work Together for a Bright Future of Mutual Benefit and Common Development" at the St. Petersburg International Economic Forum 2011 in June 2011)

第四章 旅游翻译

一、英译汉

1.
玛雅文明即中美洲文明,以前哥伦布时期美洲大陆上众所周知的唯一高度发展的书面语言以及艺术、建筑、数学运算和天文历法等而著称。玛雅文明始于前古典期,其中大部分在古典期发展到了顶峰,并持续到后古典期,直至西班牙人登上美洲大陆。在顶峰阶段,玛雅文明是世界上人口最为稠密、文化最具有活力的社会之一。

玛雅文明与其他中美洲文明有着许多共同的特点,这是因为该地区这些文明之间互动程度和文化传播程度都很高。文字、铭文学、历法等的进步并非源自玛雅族,但是该民族的文明却促使他们全面发展。玛雅文化的这种影响甚至可以在远离玛雅地区1000公里以外的墨西哥中部得到验证。许多外部影响表现在玛雅艺术和玛雅建筑两个方面,被认为是贸易和文化交流的结果,而不是直接来自外部的征服。不论在古典期衰落的年代,还是在西班牙征服者到来时以及随后的西班牙人对美洲的殖民期间,玛雅文化从未消失过。

今天,玛雅民族及后裔在整个玛雅地区形成了人口颇多的若干群体,并保持了各具特色的种种传统和信仰。这些都是前哥伦布时期和西班牙征服美洲大陆后的时代的意识形态相互融合的结果(同时也是因人民几乎全部信奉天主教而形成的)。今天仍有许多玛雅语言被作为当地的主要语言。例如,《拉维纳尔的武士》(或《鼓舞》),用阿奇语写成的一部玛雅剧,在 2005 年被联合国教科文组织宣布为人类口头和非物质遗产代表作。

(玛雅文明)

2.
  北爱尔兰的魅力在于其悲惨的历史、丰富的文化和那里友好的人民。
  北爱尔兰崎岖的山脉,壮观的湖泊和广阔的海岸线都让那里成为喜欢水上运动、散步、骑车、徒步旅行、攀岩和航海人士的理想游乐场所。
  除此之外,那里还有众多文化盛事,从热闹的牡蛎节到正宗的马交易会,从古老的城堡到典雅的乡村别墅,这片引人入胜的土地让你拥有众多可选择的活动。

(北爱尔兰)

3.
  大堡礁位于澳大利亚东北海岸,这里物种多样。这里有世界上最大的珊瑚礁群,共 400 种珊瑚,1500 种鱼类和 4000 种软体动物生活在这里。大堡礁还是一处得天独厚的进行科学研究的场所,因为这里栖息着多种濒临灭绝的动物,比如儒艮和巨型绿甲海龟。

(大堡礁)

4.
  法国的爱丽舍宫和美国的白宫、英国的白金汉宫以及俄罗斯的克里姆林宫一样闻名于世。它是法兰西共和国的总统府,也是法国最高权力的象征。
  爱丽舍宫位于巴黎香榭丽舍大街的东端,占地 1.1 万平方米,地处喧闹的市中心,背倚一个 2 万多平方米的恬静大花园。它的主楼是一座两层高的欧洲古典式石建筑,典雅庄重。两翼各有一座两层高的石建筑,相峙而立,中间是一个宽敞的矩形庭院。宫内共有 369 间大小不等的厅室。
  爱丽舍宫兴建于 1718 年,迄今已有近 300 年的历史。此处原是一位名叫戴夫罗的伯爵的私人住宅,所以当时称为戴夫罗庄园。后来历经沧桑,几易其主,但长期都为达官贵人所享用。路易十五和路易十六称帝期间都先后入住过,并将其改名为波旁大厦。1815 年拿破仑一世滑铁卢战役大败之后曾在此签降书退位。拿破仑三世在 1848 年当选总统后也曾迁居于此,他称帝后,此处即称为皇家宫殿。法兰西第三共和国于 1873 年颁布法令,正式指定爱丽舍宫为法国总统府。此后的百余年里,历届法兰西共和国的总统几乎都在此工作和生活。自 1989 年起,每逢 9 月份法国古堡节这一天,爱丽舍宫便向公众开放。

(爱丽舍宫)

二、汉译英
1.
  The Li Bai Museum, located by the scenic Changming River in Jiangyou City, ranks among the national AA-grade scenic spots and the country's 100 famous gardens, constituting the biggest Tang-style courtyard architecture of its kind in China. Integrating sightseeing, academic research, exhibition and collection, and tourist service, the museum is noted for its unique garden landscape, rich variety of exhibits, informative guide, and supposed academic status. It is a highlight of the Jiuzhaigou tour.

(A Short Description of the Li Bai Museum)

2.
  Zhouzhuang lies in the dense network of rivers and lakes between Shanghai and Suzhou. Like a lotus leaf surrounded by water and near the Dianshan Lake in Kunshan. It is described by famous artist Wu Guanzhong as "featuring the integration of all beauty of Chinese water towns": serene charm, a 900-year history, time-honored architectural patterns, and simple folk customs.
  In Zhouzhuang, all bridges span the canals or brooks, and lanterns are hung along the banks, which

makes a poetic and picturesque water town at night. Tourists may fully enjoy night scenes in the boats or on the banks while listening to Kunqu Opera and folk song.

(Zhouzhaung)

3.

As the water town on the plateau, the Old Town of Lijiang (World Heritage Site) is a city of ancient elegance with natural, ethnic and local features. The picturesque First Bend of the Yangtze River, the tranquil and tasteful Jade Spring Park, Number One Camellia in northwest Yunnan, and countless camellias known as the world's Number One fire-red flowers growing in the snow-capped Yunling Mountain combine to present a gorgeous painting of nature. Mainly representing the tourism resources of the city are the Jade Dragon Snow Mountain, the terraced Lao Jun Mountain, the Old Town, the plateau Lugu Lake, the Jinsha River, Naxi Dongba culture, and Mosuo ethnical customs.

(Lijiang)

4.

Sanya boasts China's tropical seashore area with the most plentiful tourism resources. It features a combination of rich historical and cultural resources and ten kinds of tourism resources, including sunshine, sea, beaches, climate, forests, animals, spa, caves, rural scenes, and local customs. In the South Mountain tourist area of Buddhist culture, there are exquisitely carved statues featuring ecosystems and Buddhism culture. In the tourist area known as the End of the Earth stands a group of sculptures of noted historical figures that accompany the eternal sounds of the sea waves. In the mountaintop park called the Turn-Round Deer Park can be seen the lifelike stone sculpture of a boy, a girl and a deer, which symbolizes the beautiful love story entitled the Turn-Round Deer. And what impress you in the central square of the Yalong Bay are sculpture groups and the modern garden-style square that is the winner of master carpenter "Lu Ban Prize", a national architectural prize. By the way, Lu Ban is the best-known carpenter in ancient China that dates back some 2,500 years. All these will bring you back to the ancient history, which offers so great a deal that you simply can't take in.

(Sanya)

5.

Enjoying equal fame with the Yellow River, the Yangtze River and the Great Wall, the Mt. Huangshan has become another symbol of China. It is celebrated in the country for odd-shaped pines, spectacular rocky peaks, seas of cloud and hot springs. It is ranked as the only mountain scenic spot among China's Ten Scenic Spots. Having all the wonders of mountain scenery, this most representative mountain is best described in the ancient saying: "One won't wish to see any other mountain after visiting the Five Sacred Mountains, whereas one won't wish to see any of the Five Sacred Mountains after returning from the Mt. Huangshan. In addition, the Mt. Huangshan is known as "a natural zoo and a world-famous botanical garden".

(Mt. Huangshan is welcoming domestic and international tourists with its imposing and unique scenes)①

(the Mt. Huangshan)

6.

It is said that there would be no fairyland in the world except the Jiuzhaigou Valley. The valley consists of nine villages, hence the name. It offers a stunning blend of enchanting scenes, known as a unique wonderful resort. It is also likened to a pure fairy-tale world. "As one will lose interest in other mountains

---

① 原句"黄山正以它雄奇的容貌迎接着四海宾客"在汉语中似乎合乎表达习惯,起码有比没有好。而根据英语的表达习惯(如话语模式),该句译成英语并无此必要。因而特将英译文放在括号中。希望初学者逐步了解目标语英语的谋篇布局、语用习惯等。这也是旅游汉译英的特色之一。

after his visit to the Mt. Huangshan, one will lose interest in other water after his return from the Jiuzhaigou Village." Water is the spirit of the Jiuzhaigou Valley, the scenery of which links up lakes, springs, waterfalls and shoals. Scenes of both dynamic and tranquil nature have ranked the valley as the best water landscape in China.

(the Jiuzhaigou Valley)

7.
　　Gulangyu Island, originally known as a "round sandy islet", did not obtain its present name until the Ming Dynasty. At that time the island had a huge hollow rock, which sounded like the beating of a drum when it was lapped by sea waves. Hence the name "Drum Wave Islet".
　　Gulangyu lies only 1,000 meter southwest of the coast of Xiamen City, Fujian Province. It is laid out like a city with no tourist vehicles allowable. With fresh air, quiet surroundings and all kinds of trees and flowers in four seasons, it is known as the "garden on the sea".

(Gulangyu Island)

8.
　　The Great Wall is one of the World Wonders. Just like a gigantic curling dragon, straddling the vast northern part of China, it rises and falls, twists and turns along the ridges of the Yanshan and Yinshan mountains.. It commands the whole rolling mountain ranges, which are lost in the horizon. The 6,700-kilometer-long Great Wall represents the fruit of labor and the crystallization of wisdom of ancient Chinese people. It also symbolizes the ancient Chinese culture and the pride of Chinese nation.

(the Great Wall)

9.
　　Located in Wulingyuan, Zhangjiajie Mountain boasts unusual scenic attractions characteristic of peaks, mountains, valleys, and caves. Its spectacular peaks lie in a rich variety of shapes and formations. Its mountains are mysterious as they are enveloped in the cloud. Its deep valleys are tranquil and secluded. And its divine caves are various with treasures.

(Zhangjiajie Mountain)

10.
　　No doubt, the essence of Hangzhou is in West Lake (World Heritage Site). Aside from her natural beauty, the lake owes much to her time-honored culture and history. An untold number of poetry and prose, legends and romances throughout the ages all stem from the lake. About a thousand years' work on the West Lake has turned it into a highly refined garden. Any element of the garden—a waterside promenade or pavilion railings for ancient ladies' rest—could be a source of poetic inspiration.

(the West Lake)

第五章　广告翻译

一、英译汉
1.
　　自制的冰淇淋、果汁冰糕、冰化酸奶不仅味道可口，而且用已上市的现代电机设备制作起来也非常方便。
　　MAGIMIX冰淇淋机每次可制1.5品脱冰淇淋，足够一家人或一次晚宴使用，其操作非常简单，只需将盒(直径大约为7英寸，高为5.5英寸)放置3/4冷冻器内10小时，调制好冰淇淋混合液，移开与电机相联结的盖子，把混合液通过顶端的添料口加入。机器开始缓缓转动，在短短20分钟内冷冻成特别酥软的冰淇淋。赶紧享它的美味或将其储存起来以备后用。特氟纶衬砌的盒易清洗。整机安装有电插头，同时配有35种美味冰淇淋配方的整套说明。厂家提供一年的保质期。
　　由美国设计的冰淇淋勺质量超群，结实耐用。勺身由不锈钢制成；勺柄由耐用耐磨的A.B.S.塑料制成,即使用来挖非常坚硬的冰淇淋,也能使用多年。

("MAGIMIX冰淇淋机和优质冰淇淋勺"广告语)

2.

博朗活动式剃须刀。它对您的脸部的了解不亚于您本人。事实上,您脸上的每一个弧度没有博朗活动式剃须刀适应不了的。秘密何在?一独特的轴头。它可自动调节双叶使之适合于您的面部轮廓,确保与您的皮肤进行不间断的接触,给您以最佳的剃须服务。鼻下、鄂下、唇下无一遗漏。

此外,还有一伸缩式胡须修剪器,可准确无误地剪去长须和短腮胡子。

像所有博朗牌电动剃须刀一样,博朗活动式剃须刀充电快,一次充电后可连续使用14天。它那把先进技术与富有魅力、功能齐全的设计完美地结合起来的方式也同样会给您留下印象。您一定会对握在您手中的剃须刀爱不释手,因为它使用起来是那么自然,那么舒适。

博朗牌活动式剃须刀——第一把带有轴头的电动剃须刀。

("博朗活动式剃须刀:没有人比它更了解您的脸部"广告语)

3.

有点怪,不是么?有些商务舱的乘客在飞往欧洲进行商战之前就先投降了:他们在我们的竞争对手的高额机票前退却了。

他们公开反抗这种不合理的事情。

事实是:我们三种公务舱机票中最低的价格也不比大多数其他航空公司的一张经济舱的票价贵。

事实还是:我们在希思罗机场的候机大厅与普通候机厅比起来是一个更为新潮的离港之地。

与其说是候机厅,还不如说是"圣殿"更确切。此乃运筹帷幄之地,制定战略计划之所。可与总部通电话或传真保持联系。

这是一片宁静,尽善尽美的宁静。

而价格也无懈可击!

("宁静:但无需付出任何代价"广告语)

4.

天鹅,浪漫一生的象征

有关天鹅的传说说道,当两只天鹅恋爱时,它们会游到一个鲜为人知的地方,互相接触以培养感情,最后皆为终身伴侣。它们如痴如幻般滑过梦想中的池塘,翅尖挂着的水珠在光的折射下熠熠生辉,这些翅尖用14颗小钻石点饰而成。

作为浪漫一生的象征,十字形天鹅胸针是一件动人的礼物,它传递着那种种关爱的心灵感应的精髓。眼睛为纯正的红宝石,鹅身是用14K黄金打制的一对组合胸针。这对组合胸针别在一张小卡片上,放在包装精美的天鹅绒礼盒中,表达着一片深情。

("胸针"广告语)

二、汉译英

1.

In ancient China, our forefathers already crafted "he shi bi", a precious emerald, and today, we are proud to present Gold Pig and Crystal Emerald. The former was invaluable and second to none, while the latter is superb treasure for collection. Gold Pig and Crystal Emerald, issued by China Banknote Printing and Minting Corporation (CBPMC), is its first of Gold-Emerald-Match series. With excellent quality and exceptional style, it can be both a present suggesting good luck and a treasure indicating auspiciousness. Gold Pig and Crystal Emerald, distinctive and priceless, a perfect match of gold with emerald. Gold Pig and Crystal Emerald, an ideal present for lovers and families as well as ideal treasure for collection.

("Gold Pig and Crystal Emerald——Superb Treasure for Collection in an Age of Harmony and Prosperity" ad.)

2.

Beijing No. 3 Soybean Factory was established in the 1950s. It uses choice soy-beans as its material and adopts traditional technique in its production, turning out over 80 kinds of soybean food with sweet, spicy, and salty flavour. To follow the trend of the market, it introduced conveniently packed soybean food in the 1980s. All its products are well received and some have won awards for their good quality. The factory further developed many new products in the 1990s, the latest of which is the highly nutritious and refined Miaomiao Bean Tea, which adopts the latest scientific formua. Drink Miaomiao Bean Tea and keep you healthy!

("Miaomiao Bean Tea" ad.)

第六章　商务翻译

一、英译汉

1.
　　由于市场不景气，投资银行辞退了许多高薪交易员。等到市场恢复，银行也许会用薪资更低廉的人才来取代他们。现在他们又多了一个选择：电子交易员——经过编程可以像人一样工作，但却不需要休假、午餐休息或者奖金等烦人的支出的电脑。这种电子交易员已经面世一段时间了，但尚未流行起来。以前当然也出现过程序交易；有人就把1987年的股市崩盘归罪于那些只按照简单决策规则指令工作的电脑。不过机器人会聪明得多。

　　戴夫·克里夫是英国布里斯托惠普实验室的研究员，7年来他一直致力于创造交易机器人。在计算机仿真试验中，他使这些机器人"按照遗传方式"不断发展，以使它们调整并且适应真实金融市场的各种模式。他的实验意味着对某些市场进行重新设计可能会大幅度提高效率。去年，IBM的一个研究小组证明克利夫的人造交易员可以在各种市场上击败真人交易员。几乎所有这些实验都是以拍卖的形式进行的。其中一种著名的拍卖形式就是英式拍卖，克里斯蒂和索斯比拍卖行的顾客对此都很熟悉，卖家不报出他们的竞拍价，而买家则不断抬高竞拍价铬，直到只有一位买家出价为止。

　　另外一种形式是荷兰式拍卖，它是17世纪荷兰的郁金香商人以及美国国库券竞标人所熟悉的一种拍卖形式。这一回，买家不报价，由卖家不断降价，直到有人接受这个价格为止。大部分股票市场、商品市场、外汇市场和衍生产品市场则采用这两种类型的混合模式；买卖双方可以随时宣布他们的竞价或者报价，交易也随时完成，即所谓"连续双向拍卖"。

　　克利夫的新思路就是把他研制的可以不断升级的电脑程序应用于市场。他想，为什么不试试看哪种拍卖形式能最快地让交易员达成一个均衡价格呢？其研究结果令人吃惊。在他的模式中，现今大多数金融交易中采用的让买卖双方随时竞价的拍卖方式比起那些买卖双方提出更多竞价的模式效率要低。这些"进化的拍卖方式"还承受住了大的市场震荡，比如崩盘和恐慌，要比真人拍卖表现出色。克利夫将于12月10日在澳大利亚悉尼演示他的最新研究成果，这些成果对于市场来说，最好的拍卖形式取决于表明买卖双方人数的轻微差异。

　　美洲银行已经开始研究这些新型拍卖形式以及机器人交易员，看看是否可能在电子交易中使用。今天的金融拍卖和网上市场如果能更多地模仿它们的英国和荷兰前辈生意也许就会更好。但这种多种类混合体该叫什么呢？下面介绍"克利夫模式"？

(选自《电子交易员可以帮助人类建立更好的市场》)

2.
　　"我们致力于谈判的成功，这就需要努力工作。"这周，乔治·布什在多哈回合关于全球贸易讨论上的评论总结概括了大多数政府的官方工作路线。当然，多哈回合一定要成功；然而，这也是非常艰难的。

　　接下来的几个星期将决定这首凯歌是否意味着什么。6月29日，贸易部长们齐聚日内瓦，对工农业产品自由贸易框架协议达成一致作最后的努力。谈判代表们就这样一个框架相互进行讨价还价。这个框架规定在四年多时间里，如何削减贸易关税和补贴。他们设置——并错过——永无止境的最后期限。

　　所以为什么都期待一个突破呢？希望存在的唯一理由就是所有各方最终都或许意识到他们谁也不能再耽搁了。绝大多数贸易谈判要拖延数年。多哈回合不能这样，因为阻止了国会进行贸易交易的布什快速谈判当局将在2007年6月份届满。为了应付这个期限，今年年底必须达成一项共识。共识的一些大致轮廓要在谈判代表们休假之前完成到位（要注意的是：没有人建议取消任何假期）。

问题是重要谈判团体之间仍然存在巨大的分歧。达成协议的途径不是秘密。欧盟需要更多地削减农业关税；美国要承诺更多地减少补贴；新兴工业化大国要削减他们的工业关税。然而到现在还没有哪个国家提出新的东西，但是有消息称美国将会在下周的日内瓦会议上对其补贴作出更大的削减。

不大被注意但同样令人担心的是其他国家之间的巨大分歧。在新兴经济体中，例如，在农业关税要求多少最惠国待遇上存在严重的分歧。像印度和印度尼西亚要求对他们的许多农产品执行例外政策。其他的，像泰国和阿根廷，要求的相当少。

总之，关于农业贸易的最后草案协议上还有大约 700 个方括号，这些方括号里的句子的表述还没有达成一致。未解决的争议非常多。在有世界杯和诱人的海滩的八月里，如果你对多哈回合还抱有希望，你就是在幻想。

（选自《多哈的最后立场——全球贸易谈判的关键时刻》）

3.

世界粮食价格正在推高——联合国食品综合指数显示年均上涨 28.3％，其中谷类上涨 44.1％——引发人们担心可能会出现又一轮粮食危机，尽管距离上一场危机只不过三个年头。那么，粮价上涨，是不是意味着全世界的粮食快要吃完了呢？

现成的回答是，全世界的廉价粮食确实在减少。造成这种供应短缺的原因是，过去近三十年来，各国政府和各类资助机构未能大力资助鼓励农业基础研究，对农村基础设施投资不足，对小农提高农业生产率所需要的培训也不够重视。

直到最近几年，世界粮食危机一个世纪之内发生了三次，相对而言并不频繁。2007—2008 年间的粮食危机当时虽说很吓人，但比较起来也不算多么严重。小麦、大米和玉米向世界一半以上的人口直接提供了口粮，并向更多的人通过肉食品间接地提供了食物。这三种粮食的价格在 2006—2008 年间上涨了 96.7％，扣除通货膨胀因素后并没有达到 20 世纪 70 年代中期的最高点。然而，仅仅几年之后，我们又在谈论粮食价格了。

粮价突然上涨往往具有政治意义。没有什么能比城市市场上主要粮食的成本的快速上涨更快地把愤怒的人群带到大街上。这就是许多发展中国家的政治家对粮价的波动幅度和上涨速度十分敏感的原因。粮食危机致使政界领导人专注于迅速、短期的解决办法。但是这种专注会让比较长期的投资和政策的出台付出真正的代价，即使现在很难注意到这种代价。

政策制定者的任职期限有限，所以永远生活在短线思维中，忙于补救源自银行危机的火山，因食物短缺而起的骚乱，显而易见，还得压抑自家可能会失去官职的担忧。因此，他们并不专注于人口的长期需求。由于大多数国家的政策制定者都有这种倾向，因此都忽视了农业科研和农村基础设施的建设。这种忽视的代价有目共睹。上世纪八十年代中期至九十年代中期，公共农业研究开支在撒哈拉沙漠以南的非洲地球都没有增加，而亚洲每年增长了 5％。这种差异对于每个劳动者平均生产率的影响引人注目——1990 年至 2002 年期间，非洲的生产率仅增长 7％，而亚洲增长了 36％。

我们可以做得更好。总的来看，农业科研的费用并没有多么高。亚洲协会和国际水稻研究所组织一些专家研讨过，他们测算出，如果在 2010 年至 2030 年年间每年投资 1.2 亿美元，那么稻谷生产率可在目前的基数上提高 8.5％，而这笔投资只占全球 GDP 的 0.0002％。多数作物种类都有类似的机会。很难想象还有比这更划算的投资吗。

（选自彼得·蒂墨：《农业政策不力，世界粮食短缺》）

二、汉译英

1.

The balance of payments is a measurement of all transactions between domestic and foreign residents over a specified period of time. The use of the words "all transactions" can be somewhat misleading, since some transactions may be estimated. The recording of transactions is done by double-entry bookkeeping. That is, each transaction is recorded as both a credit and debit. Thus, total credits and debits will be identical for a country's balance of payments in the aggregate.

2.

What is the best way to deal with the idle cash? The best choice is buying marketable securities because marketable securities are also liquid. When the business is in an urgent need of cash, marketable securities can be easily sold for cash. Marketable securities mean stocks and bonds. Though stocks are somewhat risky, however, bonds also have some risk. There wouldn't be any gain without risks. The purpose of investing in marketable securities is to profit from the cash lying idle by means of earning interest or dividends.

第七章　科技翻译

一、英译汉

1.

前不久,科学家们对深海生物还知之甚少。他们也不相信海洋生物正在受到威胁。现在,随着现代深海探测技术的发展,研究人员发现660多英尺即大概200米深的海底生活着大量种类繁多的海底生物。同时,技术的发展也使渔民可以到达更深的地方进行海底拖网捕捞。这种捕捞会在几分钟内毁灭掉大自然几百年甚至上千年才能形成的一切。

例如,世界上的很多珊瑚物种是在200多米的海底发现的。据估计,在最高的海底山中,几乎一半是在深海海底,这些海底隆起的地方,海洋生物特别丰富。

这些深海生态系统为鱼类以及其他生物提供生存、产卵以及繁殖的场所,也保护它们免受强流以及猎食者的袭击。此外,它们还蕴藏着世界上最丰富的生命宝库。据估计,有50万到1亿的生物物种栖息在这些没有开发且极其脆弱的生态系统中。

然而,正当我们开始认识到这些地区丰富多样的生命以及它们对人类社会的潜在好处时,如新食品以及新药物,这些地区却面临着永远消失的危机。随着人们鉴别丰富生物地区能力的增强以及深海拖网捕鱼技术的提高,现代商业渔船开始向海里撒入足球场大的拖网,把所行之处的所有的鱼一网打尽,同时也极大地破坏了脆弱的珊瑚以及礁石和海底山。而它们却是海底无数鱼类和其他海洋生物赖以生存的场所。

由于深海拖网捕捞是最近才出现的,所以它造成的损害目前还是有限的。如果我们可以尽快采取措施来禁止这种公海破坏性活动,它为海洋环境以及我们的子孙后代带来的好处是无法估量的。这些好处远远超过渔业的短期成本。

(选自《英语二级笔译考试真题精选》)

2.

通用设计作为一个崭新的设计手段,渐渐出现于当代设计潮流中。它将设计理论构架与实践相结合,使设计元素能尽可能地满足广泛人士的不同需求,以创造出一个方便用户使用的生活环境。为达到此目的,通用设计与畅达设计有紧密的联系,然而二者却有本质上的区别。畅达设计着重顾及传统概念上身体活动受到限制的人士的特殊需求,而通用设计取畅达设计概念之精华,并使可普遍使用的元素成为设计的标准,不仅让有特殊需要的人士,而且让每一个人都可受益。

通用设计包含了畅达设计,但它亦寻求更广泛意义上的一致性,以在更广范围内得以应用。因此,通用设计需要尊重一般需求的人,并考虑与其相关的问题,如成本效益、空间效用、灵活性和同一性。最有效的通用设计可以是无形的。它是一种无歧视的设计途径并体现了一种希望,即让尽可能多的人士能以最安全和最方便的途径,到达不同类型的地方。这对我们每一个人都很重要,因为我们在人生的不同阶段都会面临不同的挑战。我们都曾是小孩。我们都会生病。若幸运的话,我们都会有终老的一天。根据有关定义,社会上大部分人士都有各种程度的障碍,即使他们不愿视自己为残障人士,或不愿如残障人士般生活。在很多人口老化的社会,由于护理人士数目相应减少,此类残障人士的比例将会增加。

数十年来,许多国家代表长者和残障人士立法,并制定了畅达设计指南。本书认为,通用设计将会成为未来路向。

(选自《香港住宅通用设计指南》)

3.

煤灰、化肥甚至海水都可以提供核燃料。

核电支持者时不时抛出一些支持核电的传言,其中之一就是传统的燃煤发电厂释放到自然环境的辐射比核电站更多。理由是煤灰烧过后的煤灰中含有放射性元素,尤其是铀和钍。

转换一下其中的思路,它表明,煤灰是一个值得研究的核燃料来源。这也恰恰是多伦多斯帕顿资源公司正在研究的。这家公司与掌管整个中国核电站的中国核工业集团公司(CNNC)达成了协议,在云南省临沧的一个地方回收煤灰中的铀。

铀通常是从铀含量在百万分之一千(1000ppm)以上的铀矿中提炼出来的。临沧煤灰的铀含量比这少得多,约为300ppm。不过这些煤灰并不需要采掘,这会令成本降低。斯帕顿说,从中提炼出一千克铀的成本不高于77美元,而铀的现货价格目前接近每公斤90美元。虽然相差不远,但这也是一笔利润。

要提炼铀,斯帕顿先要往煤灰中加入硫酸和盐酸,用水稀释,使之变成浆状。对于某些种类的煤灰,还需要加入硝酸。这些酸会把铀以及其他物质溶解,使它们与煤灰分离。关键则在于要把铀从上述溶液中提取出来。

斯帕顿的工序用的是一个由烧过的椰壳制成的木炭过滤器,它会俘获悬浮的微粒,除去有机化合物。然后,经过过滤的溶液会通过离子交换树脂里的小珠子。这些小颗粒会选择性地吸附铀离子,而不吸附其他物质——据公司透露,运用这个方法,煤灰中的铀可以萃取出其中的2/3。接下来,小珠子里头的铀离子会被碳酸铵溶液溶解,然后沉淀,析出"黄饼",即各种铀氧化物的混合物。

据CNNC市场经理王红芳(音译)介绍,中国发展采铀业更多是从能源安全的角度出发,而非为了谋求经济利益。国家希望从"每个可能的渠道"获得铀。其中包括从金矿和铜矿的矿尾中提取铀,以及利用化肥制造过程中产生的副产物硫酸。不仅CNNC有这个愿望,德美合资的生产及销售核燃料公司NUKEM也希望尽快可以在佛罗里达"开采"化肥。

有的人甚至把目光投向铀的另一个来源——海水。这想法是弗里茨·哈伯(德国化学家——译者注)从海洋里提取金子以偿还德国一战债务的可怕企图的重演。虽然铀在海洋中的含量只有十亿分之三,但其中大部分都以三碳酸铀的形式存在,使得铀元素可以通过离子交换吸出。

包括日本原子能委员会和印度的巴巴原子能研究中心在内的一些机构都尝试着采取此类做法。他们使用的方法包括使用以坚固的聚苯乙烯材料编制成的带状离子交换塑料。这些塑料被放入金属笼中,在海水中固定起来。一两个月后,塑料会被拿走,并浸在酸性物质之中使其中的三碳酸铀溶解。得出的溶液会通过处理来析出铀氧化物。

目前来说,这个工艺的成本是传统的开采铀矿的10倍,不过一些国家可能会把它看做是为安全供应而付出的小小代价。但愿他们只是为民用核电站提供核燃料。

(选自《铀的新来源》)

二、汉译英

1.

The cell phone is becoming one of the major technologies of the 21st century. Within a few years, it will become a multi-functional communicator capable of transmitting and receiving not only sound, but also video, still images, data and text. A new era of personal communication is on the way.

Thanks in part to the growth of wireless networks, the telephone is converging with the personal computer and the television. Soon light-weight phones outfitted with high-resolution screens will be connected to satellites. People can talk, send and receive e-mail, or take part in video conferences anytime, anywhere. These phones might also absorb many of the key functions of computers. Mobile devices are expected to be ideal for some of the new services that are available via the Internet, such as trading stocks, shopping and booking theater and airline tickets.

The telecommunication revolution is developing around the globe. It will soon be possible to receive almost all forms of electronic communication through a single device. A three-in-one phone is most likely. It can serve as a cordless at home, a cell phone on the road and an intercom at work. Some experts even suggest that cell videophones could overtake television as the major source of visual information.

(Selected from *Selected Readings of the True Real Paper Questions of English Written Translation Grade Two*)

2.

Forty years ago, the area around the Yellow River estuary was a heaven for birds. With the lessening volume of river water and land reclamation in the delta area, however, wetland coverage here has been greatly reduced, so has the number of birds visited the area.

In recent years, the ecological system of the Yellow River Delta wetland has significantly improved. Every year nearly 1 million birds escape the winter and stay here, among which many are rare species in the world. Conservation of the Yellow River Delta wetland is only one successful example of China's wetland protection effort. It indicates that great strides have been made in this field.

Up to now, China has built 353 wetland natural preservation zones. The establishment of these zones has also protected headstreams of China's big rivers, estuaries of main rivers and migratory birds' breeding places and winter-escape habitats.

At present, wetland protection still remains to be a weak link in China's overall ecological improvement. The Chinese government will take effective measures to stop activities of predatory exploitation of wetland resources to guarantee their sustainable utilization.

(Selected from *Selected Readings of the True Real Paper Questions of English Written Translation Grade Two*)

第八章　法律翻译

一、英译汉

1.
　　第二篇　责任原则
　　第二章　损害
　　第二条:101.可受偿损失
　　该损失必须对合法保护的利益造成物质上或非物质上的损害。
　　第二条:102.受保护的利益
　　(1)某一利益受保护的范围取决于该利益的性质;其价值越高,定义越精确,利益越明显,对该利益的保护范围越广泛。
　　(2)生命,人身或精神上的完整性,人格尊严和人身自由享受最广泛的保护。
　　(3)财产权,包括无形资产享受广泛的保护。
　　(4)对纯经济损失和合同利益的保护范围相对受限。在此情况下,应适当考虑行为人与受害方的接近程度,或考虑到行为人明知其行为将造成损失的事实(尽管其利益的价值被认为低于受害方的利益)。
　　(5)利益保护范围也受责任性质的影响,因此对利益造成的故意损害的保护应比其他情况下的保护更广泛。
　　(6)决定利益保护范围时,应考虑行为人的利益,尤其该行为人行动与行使权利的自由,以及公共利益。
　　第二条:103.损害的合法性
　　与非法行为及非法资源相关的损失不能得到赔偿。
　　第二条:104.预防措施的费用
　　为避免紧急威胁造成的费用在合理的范围内可以得到赔偿。
　　第二条:105.举证责任
　　损害的证明必须依据通常的程序标准进行举证。在无法举证损害的确切数额或举证费用过高时,法院有权判定损害数额。

（选自《欧洲侵权法基本原权》）

2.

越来越多的，外国医药的制造商提供用于制药的原材料，这些药品最终将出口到美国。这些药品在美国进行合法销售前，将面对众多的法律和监管要求，其中就有美国专利法。

许多美国药品专利都含有针对保护制药方法的条款。尽管美国的制药方法专利并不延伸至美国境外的制药方法，但是根据美国专利方法制造的产品到达美国边境，美国法典第35编271条(g)款的规定即可适用，其规定为：

"任何人未经授权而擅自进口*根据*美国专利方法制造出的产品或在美国境内擅自许诺销售、出售或使用该产品，或对该产品的进口、许诺销售、出售或使用是在有效期内，其将被追究侵权责任……"美国法典第35编271条(g)款(额外强调)。

由此可以看出，271条(g)款禁止进口"根据美国专利方法制造出的产品"。本文的重点在于，当专利方法的一些步骤由一个实体在美国境外实施，而专利方法的其余步骤由另一实体在美国境外实施，然后将生产出的产品进口到美国时，是否存在侵权行为。换句话说，当多个实体在美国境外共同实施了专利方法的全部步骤，但并没有某一单个实体在美国境外实施全部步骤时，其产品是否构成271条(g)款所指的"根据美国专利的方法制造出的产品"？

对于那些全部都在美国境内运用的方法，当一个被告实施了某些权利要求保护的步骤，而另外的被告实施了其他的权利要求的步骤时，众所周知，证明直接侵权的唯一方式就是通过"分别侵权"原则。BMC Resources, Inc. 诉 Paymentech, L.P. 498 F. 3d 1373（联邦巡回上诉法院 2007）；MuniAuction, Inc. 诉 Thomson Corp., 532 F. 3d 1318(联邦巡回上诉法院 2008)。满足"分别侵权"原则的需要专利持有人证明受控于或在另一被告的"指使"下侵权。本质上，被告之一必须"策划"了整个侵权行为。因此，该策划人就可以合理地被认定是实施了专利方法步骤的每一个步骤。而其他行为人仅仅是协助了策划人的行为。MuniAuction, 532 F. 3d at 1329。根据此原则，仅"在公平交易原则下的合作"将不足以产生任何一方的直接侵权。BMC Resources, 498 F. 3d at 1381；MuniAuction, 532 F. 3d at 1329。

然而，就分别侵权原则是否适用于美国境外实施，目前尚无定论，此原则是由美国境内使用方法专利的美国法典第35编第271条(a)款所发展而来的，而并非由美国境外使用专利方法及对其产品的进口的第271条(g)款所发展而来的。这是必然的，虽然第271条(g)款最近才加入美国专利法，但我们有理由相信，在第271条(g)款内，"分别侵权"辩护有可能会成功。

（选自《有关美国专利保护的程序被侵权之争议》）

二、汉译英

1.

    To: _____ People's Court
    Plaintiff:
    Domicile:
    Legal Representative:
    Position:
    Defendant:
    Domicile:
    Legal Representative:
    Position:
    CLAIMS:

1. To order the Defendant to pay to the Plaintiff the due amount of RMB _____ for the dispatched products, plus the interests of RMB _____ thereon, in the aggregate of RMB _____;

2. To order the court fees to be borne by the Defendant.

FACTS AND REASONS:

The Defendant was one of the distributors of the Plaintiff for various kinds of products in the territory of _____, China. From _____ to _____, the Plaintiff dispatched various kinds of products in the aggregate values of RMB _____. (see Exhibit I).

Each of the said transactions was duly signed and received by the Defendant (see Exhibit II). Though the Plaintiff has repeatedly demanded payment, the Defendant fails to liquidate the outstanding debts in due time.

It is the Plaintiff's position that the indebtedness arising out of the transactions between the Plaintiff and the Defendant shall be under the jurisdiction of the China's laws. The Defendant's refusal to satisfy the agreed amounts after receipt of the above-mentioned products resulted in tremendous economic losses on the side of the Plaintiff (see Exhibit III). Therefore, pursuant to the relevant PRC laws and regulations, the Defendant shall assume the civil liabilities accordingly for such nonpayment.

By reason of the forgoing, in accordance with Articles 106 and 112 as set forth in the PRC General Principles of the Civil Law, Article 108 as set forth in the PRC Civil Procedural Law and other applicable laws and regulations, the Plaintiff hereby files this case with the Court for your adjudication.

Plaintiff(Signature or seal):

Date:

ATTACHMENTS:

1. One copy of the Plaintiff's business license;
2. One copy of the original Certificate of the Legal Representative;
3. One copy of the original Power of Attorney;
4. Exhibit I: Invoices for each transaction;
5. Exhibit II: Receipts for each transaction; and
6. Exhibit III: List of Losses.

(Selected from *Format of Complaint*)

2.

Chapter I General Provisions

Article 1 These Measures have been formulated in accordance with the Decision of the State Council on the Establishment of Administrative Licensing for Necessarily Retained Administrative Approval Items for the purpose of promoting and regulating overseas investments.

Article 2 The term "overseas investments" as used in these Measures means activities whereby enterprises lawfully established in China (hereinafter referred to as "enterprises") establish non-financial enterprises or acquire the ownership, control rights, operating rights and other rights and interests in a non-financial enterprise established outside the territory of China by means of establishment, merger, acquisition, etc.

Article 3 In engaging in overseas investment activities, enterprises shall understand and conscientiously abide by relevant domestic and foreign laws, regulations and policies, and shall observe the principle of mutual benefit.

Article 4 The Ministry of Commerce is responsible for the administration and supervision of overseas investments. The competent commerce authorities of provinces, autonomous regions, municipalities directly under the Central Government and the Xinjiang Production and Construction Corps (hereinafter referred to as the competent provincial commerce authorities) are responsible for the administration and supervision of overseas investments within their own administrative regions.

Chapter II Examination and Approval

Article 5 Overseas investments made by enterprises shall be examined and approved by the Ministry of Commerce and the competent provincial commerce authorities. The Ministry of Commerce shall establish an

"Administrative System for Overseas Investments" (hereinafter referred to as the System) and issue Certificates of Overseas Investment by an Enterprise (hereinafter referred to as Certificates, see the format in Appendix 1). Certificates shall be printed and coded in a uniform manner by the Ministry of Commerce.

Article 6 For any of the following types of investment, enterprises shall submit the application materials specified in Article 12 of these Measures to the Ministry of Commerce for examination and approval as required by Article 13 of these Measures:

1. Overseas investments made in a country without diplomatic relations with China;
2. Overseas investments made in a particular country or region (the specific list shall be determined by the Ministry of Commerce in conjunction with the Ministry of Foreign Affairs and other relevant departments);
3. Overseas investments in which the Chinese contribution is 100 million dollars or above;
4. Overseas investments involving the interests of more than one country or region; and
5. The establishment of overseas special purpose companies.

Article 7 For any of the following types of investment, local enterprises shall submit the application materials specified in Article 12 of these Measures to the competent provincial commerce authority for examination and approval as required by Article 14 of these Measures:

1. Overseas investments in which the Chinese contribution is between 10 million dollars and 100 million dollars;
2. Overseas investments in the energy and mining sectors; and
3. Overseas investments in which there is a need for domestic investors.

Article 8 In conducting overseas investments other than those specified in Articles 6 and 7, enterprises shall submit an Overseas Investment Application Form (hereinafter referred to as the Application Form, see the format in Appendix 2) and go through the examination and approval procedures in accordance with Article 16 of these Measures.

Article 9 In any of the following circumstances, the overseas investment proposed by the relevant enterprise shall not be approved by the Ministry of Commerce or competent provincial commerce authority:

1. Where the investment damages China's sovereign, security or public interests or violates Chinese laws and regulations;
2. Where the investment harms relations between China and the relevant country or region;
3. Where the investment may violate an international treaty concluded by China; or
4. Where the investment involves technology or goods prohibited from being exported.

Enterprises shall be responsible for the economic and technological feasibility of their overseas investments.

Article 10 When examining and approving the overseas investments specified in Article 6, the Ministry of Commerce shall solicit the opinions of the economic or trade offices of Chinese embassies and consulates. Where an enterprise managed by the Central Government is involved, opinions shall be solicited by the Ministry of Commerce; and where a local enterprise is involved, opinions shall be solicited by the competent provincial commerce authority.

When examining and approving the overseas investments specified in Clause 2 of Article 7, the competent provincial commerce authority shall solicit the opinions of the economic or trade offices of Chinese embassies and consulates. When examining and approving other types of overseas investment, the competent provincial commerce authority may solicit the opinions of the economic or trade offices of Chinese embassies and consulates according to the actual situation.

(Selected from Decree No. 5 of the Ministry of Commerce of the People's Republic of China in 2009—Administrative Measures for Overseas Investments)

第九章 散文翻译

一、英译汉

1.
　　在一个有风的春日,我看到一群年轻人正在迎风放风筝玩乐,各种颜色、各种形状和大小的风筝就好像美丽的鸟儿在空中飞舞。当强风把风筝吹起,牵引线就能够控制它们。

　　风筝迎风飘向更高的地方,而不是随风而去。它们摇摆着、拉扯着,但牵引线以及笨重的尾巴使它们处于控制之中,并且迎风而上。它们挣扎着、抖动着想要挣脱线的束缚,仿佛在说:"放开我!放开我!我想要自由!"即使与牵引线抗争着,它们依然在美丽地飞翔。终于,一只风筝成功挣脱了。"终于自由了,"它好像在说,"终于可以随风自由飞翔了!"

　　然而,脱离束缚的自由使它完全处于无情的微风的摆布下。它毫无风度地向地面坠去,落在一堆乱草之中,线缠绕在一棵死灌木上。"终于自由"使它自由到无力地躺在尘土中,无助地任风沿着地面将其吹走,碰到第一个障碍物便毫无生命地滞留在那里了。

　　有时我们真像风筝啊!上苍赋予我们困境和约束,赋予我们成长和增强实力所要遵从的规则。约束是逆风的必要匹配物。我们中有些人如此强硬地抵制规则,以至从来无法飞到本来能够达到的高度。我们只遵从部分戒律,因此永远不会飞得足够高以使尾巴远离地面。

　　让我们每个人都飞到高处吧,并且认识到这一点:有些可能会令我们生气的约束,实际上是帮助我们攀升和实现愿望的平衡力。

(选自佚名:《自由飞翔》)

2.
　　我是风,轻轻的风;我是云,缓缓的云;我是水,静静的水;我是山,连绵的山……如果你愿意,我愿做那轻轻的风,抚慰着你寂寞的心灵!如果你愿意,我就是那缓缓的云,从容地让你依偎!如果你愿意,我来做你身边静静的水,默默地将你守护!如果你愿,我将会不懈地爱你,就像那连绵不断的山川!我悔我不是风,因为我不够体贴;我恨我不是云,因为我不够温柔;我怨我不是水,因为我不够清澈;我怒我不是山,因为我的爱不够坚定……我只能做回自己,平凡的自己、唯一的自己、寻求中的自己。我渴望爱情但是却不懂她的深奥,我向往不平凡但是却甘愿默默无名。我追求成熟但是我宁愿单纯。我但愿她能喜欢我,但是我又不知道我是否喜欢她!寻求、渴望、向往、追求,哪里是我的目标和未来?俗世间我是孤独的一颗粒,宇宙间我是无为的尘埃,我的爱虽然美好,但并不伟大,所以我只是想好好的活着。其实人生未必要过的轰轰烈烈,出人头地。只要过得有价值,活得很踏实…… 无畏的爱,会让我很痛苦;悸动的青春,会让我很寂寞;忙碌的工作,会让我容易迷茫。我只是在寻找,我亦是在等待生命中的璀璨光辉……

(选自佚名:《我是轻轻的风》)

3.
　　对爱情的渴望,对知识的追求,对人类苦难不可遏制的同情,是支配我一生的单纯而强烈的三种感情。这些感情如阵阵巨风,吹拂在我动荡不定的生涯中,有时甚至吹过深沉痛苦的海洋,直抵绝望的边缘。

　　我所以追求爱情,有三方面的原因。首先,爱情有时给我带来狂喜,这种狂喜竟如此有力,以致使我常常会为了体验儿小时爱的喜悦,而宁愿牺牲生命中其他一切。其次,爱情可以摆脱孤寂——身历那种可怕孤寂的人的战栗意识,有时会由世界的边缘,观察到冷酷无生命的无底深渊。最后,在爱的结合中,我看到了古今圣贤以及诗人们所梦想的天堂的缩影,这正是我所追寻的人生境界。虽然它对一般的人类生活也许太美好了,但这正是我透过爱情所最终发现的。

　　我曾以同样的感情追求知识,我渴望去了解人类。也渴望知道星星为什么会发光,同时我还想理解毕达哥拉斯的力量。

　　爱情与知识的可能领域,总是引领我到天堂,可对人类苦难的同情经常把我带回现实世界。那些痛苦的呼唤经常在我内心深处回响。饥饿中的孩子、被压迫被折磨者、给子女造成重担的孤苦无依的老人,以及全球性的孤独、贫穷和痛苦的存在,是对人类生活理想的无视和讽刺。我常常希望能尽自己的微薄之力去减轻这些不必要的痛苦,但我发现我完全失败了,因此我也感到很痛苦。

这就是我的一生,我发现人是值得活的。如果有谁再给我一次生活的机会,我将欣然接受这难得的赐予。

(选自伯特兰. 罗素:《我到底为了什么活着》)

二、汉译英

1.

I have felt quite upset recently. Tonight, when Iam sitting in the yard enjoying the cool, it occurs to me that the Lotus Pond, which I pass by every day, must assume quite a different look in such a moonlit night. A full moon is rising high in the sky; the laughter of children playing outside has died away; in the room, my wife is patting the son, Run-er, sleepily humming a cradle song. Shrugging on an overcoat, quietly, I make my way out, closing the door behind me.

Alongside the Lotus Pond runs a small cinder footpath. It is peaceful and secluded here, a place not frequented by pedestrians even in the daytime; now at night, it looks more solitary, in a lush, shady ambience of trees all around the pond. On the side where the path is, there are willows, interlaced with some others whose names I do not know. The foliage, which, in a moonless night, would loom somewhat frighteningly dark, looks very nice tonight, although the moonlight is not more than a thin, grayish veil.

I am on my own stroll, hands behind my back. This bit of the universe seems in my possession now; and I myself seem to have been uplifted from my ordinary self into another world, I like a serene and peaceful life, as much as a busy and active one; I like being in solitude, as much as in company. As it is tonight, basking in a misty moonshine all by myself, I feel I am a free man, free to think of anything, or of nothing. All that one is obliged to do or to say, in the daytime, can be very well cast aside now. That is the beauty of being alone. For the moment, just let me indulge in this profusion of moonlight and lotus fragrance.

(Selected from Zhu Ziqing: Moonlight over the Lotus Pond)

2.

All over my garden I planted nothing but fragrant roses. If looked at from afar—ablaze with color like sunset clouds. I would be very happy if any one of my visiting friends should desire to pick and take some for their homes. I trusted that any friend of mine carrying the roses would vanish into the distance, feeling that his emotion had been rekindled.

A close friend came for a visit the other day. I know her to be a lover of flowers and plants, and for that reason I told her at her departure that she should pick a bunch of roses to decorate her boudoir. I promised that the scent of the roses would be wafted far, far away.

That girl friend of mine, tiptoeing into the garden in high spirits, sniffed here and smelt there, but in the end she didn't pick a single rose. I said there were so many of them that she could pick as many as she'd like to; I told her that I was not a florist and didn't make a living out of them. While saying so I raised the scissors for the sacrifice of the flowers, but she vehemently stopped me, crying no, no, no.

To cut such beautiful roses would hurt one, she said. With her hands clutching at my sleeves, she told me that by no means should they be cut. Roses are the smiling face of the earth, and who could be so iron-hearted as to destroy a smile so exhilarating?

(Selected from Qi Yun: Smile of the Earth)

3.

Rizhao, my hometown, which can be traced back to the Han Dynasty, is a newly-rising coastal city, yet it's also one of long-standing cities. In Rizhao Museum, stacks of relics excavated in Han mausoleums are exhibited in rows of showcases. Rizhao, meaning "the Sun Shines", is a medium-sized city full of vitality. Wide-eyed tourists eye sunrise on the sea at twilight with delight, while fishing boats are shuttling and seagulls are darting about. If you desire to sample seafood alive and kicking, OK, no problem in the city proper.

15 kilometres to the north of the city there lies a National Forest Park, where approximately one million trees and shrubs grow densely, adjacent to the seashore. In high summer, it's agreeable to relax yourself under thick shades, in an atmosphere of maritime breeze and melodious twitters of birds. You seem to have found yourself in a wonderland. The four bathing beaches dotting about the coastline are great draws to outside swim-lovers.

Rizhao is not only charming but also lively. It's best you come to tour it by yourself. Definitely, my hometown won't fail you! If you love to look at the azure sea, don't hesitate to leave for my hometown. If you love to enjoy spotless air, don't hesitate to head for my hometown. Rizhao, I love you with all my heart and my heart will go on and on and on!

(Selected from Yue Shouguo: Rizhao ——My Lovely Hometown)

第十章 小说翻译

一、英译汉

1.
门窗都洞开着。然而,正如煤区常见的那样,一炉红红的旺火把壁炉照得通明,一眼望去使人产生一种舒适感,觉得也能忍受那过多的热量了。不过呼啸山庄的堂屋大得很,有的是空地方,可以躲开那热的威力。因此,这屋里的人就呆在离一个窗口不远的地方。我还没进门,就能看清他们,能听见他们在说话,于是便望着,听着,这是受了好奇心和嫉妒心驱使的缘故,我在那里流连的时候,这种交织的感觉还在滋长着。

"相——反!"一个银铃般动听的声音说道。"这是第3遍了,你这笨蛋!我不想再教你了。用心点,不然我就揪你的头发!"

"那好,相反,"另一个人以深沉而柔和的语调答道。"那就亲亲我吧,我学得这么用心。"

"不行,先给我准确地念一遍,不许有一个错。"

那说话的男子开始念了。他是个年轻人,穿得很体面,坐在一张桌子边,面前放着一本书。他那漂亮的面孔喜气洋洋的,一双眼睛总也不安分,一次次地从书页上溜到搭在他肩头的一只白白的小手上,小手的主人一发现这种不专心的迹象,就用这只手朝他脸上啪地打一下,让他收心。

小手的主人站在他背后。她俯身辅导他学习时,她那轻柔的鬈发,有时和他的棕色头发交错在一起。而她那张脸——幸亏男方瞧不见她那张脸,不然他决不会这么安稳——我却看得见。我咬着嘴唇,悔恨自己丢掉了一个机会,本来可能是有所作为的事情,现在却只能对着那令人倾倒的美貌干瞪眼。

课上完了,做学生的并没有根绝错误,但却要求奖励一下,获得了至少5个吻,而他又慷慨地回报了。接着,他们来到了门口,从他们的谈话中,我断定他们要出去,到荒野上散散步。我想,在这当口,要是哈雷德·恩肖看见我这个没福气的人出现在他面前,他即使嘴里不说,心里也要诅咒我下到地狱的最底层。我觉得自己太窝囊,有些气不过,便悄悄绕了个圈子,想到厨房里去躲一躲。

(选自艾米莉·勃朗特:《呼啸山庄》,孙致礼译)

2.
十二点半,威廉回来了。他是个活泼好动的孩子,金发,满脸雀斑,带有几分丹麦人或挪威人的气质。

"可以吃饭了吗,妈妈?"他帽子也不脱,就冲进屋里直嚷嚷"人家说,一点半集市就开始了。"

"饭一做好你就可以吃了。"母亲答道。

"还没做好吗?"他嚷道,一双蓝眼睛气冲冲地瞪着她,"那就要错过时间了。"

"误不了。再过五分钟就好了。这会儿才十二点半呢。"

"人家就要开场了。"男孩又哭又叫。

"他们开场就要你的命啦,"母亲说,"再说,这会儿才十二点半,你还有整整一个钟头呢。"

男孩急急忙忙摆好餐桌,母子三个人就马上坐了下来。他们正吃着果酱布丁,男孩一下子从椅子上跳了下来,怔怔地站在那儿,远处传来旋转木马开动的轻快的喇叭声和嘟嘟的号角声。他望着母亲,一张脸抽搐着。

"我早就跟你说了嘛!"说着他奔向碗柜去拿帽子。

"拿上你的布丁——这才一点过五分,是你搞错了——你还没拿你那两便士呢!"母亲连声喊着。

男孩极为失望地又转回头来,拿了两个便士,一声不吭地走了。

"我要去,我要去嘛。"安妮哭了起来。

"行了,你去好了,你这个哭哭啼啼的小傻瓜!"母亲说。午后,她带着女儿,沿着高高的树篱艰难地爬上了小山。田里的干草都堆了起来,牛群也转去了麦茬田上。天气暖洋洋的,四周一片宁静。

莫莱尔太太并不喜欢这假日集市。那儿有两套木马:一套靠蒸汽发动,一套由小马拉着转;三架手风琴在演奏,夹杂着手枪射击的零星噼啪声,卖椰子的小贩粗嘎而刺耳的叫卖声,投掷木人游戏的摊主的吆喝声,和摆西洋镜摊的女人的尖叫声。母亲看到自己的儿子正站在狮子华莱士的棚子外,欢天喜地地盯着那些关于那头著名狮子的图片,据说它曾经咬死过一个黑人和两个白人。她没去管他,自己去给安妮买了点奶糖。不一会儿,孩子异常兴奋地站到她跟前。

"你没说你要来的——这儿东西很多吧?——那头狮子咬死了三个人呢——我把我那两便士都花了——瞧。"

他从口袋里掏出两个盛煮蛋的小杯子,杯子上有粉红的蔷薇花图案。

"我在那个摊子上赢来的,只要你把玻璃弹子打进洞里就可以了。我玩了两次就得了这两个杯子——玩一次一便士。瞧,这杯子上有蔷薇花。我要的就是这种。"

她知道他是要来给她的。

"唔,"她高兴地说,"这杯子真漂亮。"

"你拿着好吗?我怕把它们打破了。"

母亲来了,他兴奋得不得了,领着她四处转悠,把东西一样样地指给她看。后来,在看西洋景时,她将图片的内容像讲故事一样讲给他听,他听得简直入了迷。他寸步不离地跟着。一路上他都紧挨着她,满怀着一个小男孩对母亲的自豪感。她戴着黑色的小圆软帽,披着斗篷,没有人比她更像一位贵妇人了。她向她认识的女人微笑着打着招呼。她累了,于是对她儿子说:

"好了,你这就回去呢,还是再待会儿?"

"你就要走了吗?"他满脸不高兴地叫。

"要走了,都四点多了。"

"你回去做什么呀?"他难过地说。

"你要是不想回去,就别回去。"她说。

于是她带着小女孩慢慢地走了,儿子站在那儿望着她远去,他很伤心,他既舍不得让她走,可又不愿离开集市。当她穿过星月酒馆门前的空地时,听到男人们的嚷嚷声,又闻到一股啤酒味儿,想着她丈夫可能就在里面,不由加快了脚步。

(选自 D. H. 劳伦斯:《儿子与情人》,李蓉译)

二、汉译英

1.

Everyone breathed a sign of relief and relaxed. Ku suddenly said brightly, "What a mess it'll be if the money from the school hasn't been sent."

The four of them all replied impatiently that he worried too much, but his remarks had called up an echo in their consciousness, and the reasons they gave one another weren't meant to refute Ku so much as to assure themselves. Ku immediately tried to retract his remarks, like a snake trying to draw its tail back into its hole after it has been pulled, and he said, "I know such a thing is impossible. I was just mentioning it."

Hung-chien said, "I think the problem could be easily solved. One of us should go there first. If Chian has the money, it'll save all five of us from going there for nothing and wasting a lot of money on bus fare."

"Good idea!" said Hsin-mei. "We can divide the work. Some of us can wait for the luggage while others can pick up the money. That'll liven things up a bit, and we won't all be stuck in one place waiting. The money was remitted to me. I'll take my luggage and go to Chian first. Hung-chien can come along to help me out."

Miss Sun said gently but firmly, "I'll go with Mr. Chao too. My luggage has also arrived."

Giving Hsin-mei a sharp x-ray glance, Li Mei-t'ing said, "All right. That leaves just me and Mr. Ku. But all our money has gone into the general funds. How much are you going to leave us?"

Ku smiled apologetically at Li and said, "My luggage is all here. I think I'll go with them. There's no point staying here any longer."

Li's face flushed with anger as he said, "So you're all going off and leaving me here alone. All right. I don't care. So much for the 'comradeship of the road'! When the going gets tough, isn't it every man for himself? To tell you the truth, once you get to Chian and pick up the money, if you don't give me a cent, it won't bother Li Mei-ting at all! If I were to sell the medicine in my trunk, I could easily get about a thousand dollars for it in the interior. Just see if I can't beg my way to Shanghai."

Hsin-mei said in surprise, "Why, Mr. Li, how could you arrive at such a gross misunderstanding?"

Ku said soothingly, "Mr. Mei-ting, I won't go. I'll wait for the luggage here with you."

Hsin-mei said, "Just what should we do, then? How about if I go first by myself? Mr. Li, you wouldn't suspect me of embezzling the general funds—you want me to leave my luggage behind as security?" He finished with a laugh to lighten the severity of his tone, but the smile was stiff and obstinate as though stuck on with dried paste.

"Nonsense! Nonsense!" repeated Li. "I'm certainly not judging others with a petty man's mind."

"The hell you aren't!" muttered Hung-chien.

"I just don't think Mr. Fang's suggestion is entirely practical—forgive me, Mr. Fang, but I always speak frankly. I mean, for example, Mr. Chao, after you get to Chian and pick up the money, will you go on ahead or turn around and go back? You can't decide that by yourself. We all have to learn the news on the spot and come to a common decision—"

"So," continued Hung-chien, "we four will go on first, following the majority's decision. Aren't we the majority?"

Li Mei-t'ing was without words. Chao and Ku hastily intervened, "As friends in adversity, we'll all stick together."

(Selected from Qian Zhongshu: *Fortress Besieged*, translated by Jeanne Kelly & Mao Guoquan)

2.

But as soon as he was in the courtyard outside, he was waylaid by a group of Jia Zheng's pages who laid hands on him and prevented him from going.

"You've done well today, haven't you, coming out top with all those poems? You have us to thank for that! Her Old Ladyship sent round several times asking about you, but because the Master was so pleased with you, we told her not to worry. If we hadn't done that, you wouldn't have had the chance to show off your poems! Everyone says they were better than all the others. What about sharing your good luck with us?"

Bao-yu laughed good-naturedly.

"All right. A string of cash each."

"Who wants a measly string of cash? Give us that little purse you're wearing!"

And without a "by your leave" they began to despoil him, beginning with the purse and his fan-case, of all his trinkets, until every one of the objects he carried about him had been taken from him.

"Now," they said, "we'll see you back in style!"

And closing round him, they marched him back to Grandmother Jia's apartment in triumphal procession.

Grandmother Jia had been waiting for him with some anxiety, and was naturally delighted to see him come in apparently none the worse for his experience.

Soon after, when he was back in his own room, Aroma came in to pour him some tea and noticed that all the little objects he usually carried about his waist had disappeared.

"Where have the things from your belt gone?" she said, "I suppose those worthless pages have taken them again."

Dai-yu overheard her and came up to inspect. Sure enough, not one of the things was there.

"So you've given away that little purse I gave you? Very well, then. You needn't expect me to give you anything in future, however much you want it!"

With these words she went off to her own room in a temper, and taking up a still unfinished perfume sachet which she was making for him at his own request, she began to cut it up with her embroidery scissors.

Bao-yu, observing that she was angry, had hurried after her—but it was too late. The sachet was already cut to pieces.

Although it had not been finished, Bao-yu could see that the embroidery was very fine, and it made him angry to think of the hours and hours of work so wantonly destroyed. Tearing open his collar he took out the little embroidered purse which bed all along been hanging round his neck and held it out for her to see.

"Look! What's that? When have I ever given anything of yours to someone else?"

Dai-yu knew that he must have treasured her gift to have worn it inside his clothing where there was no risk of its being taken from him. She regretted her over-hasty destruction of the sachet and hung her head in silence.

"You needn't have cut it up," said Bao-yu. "know it's only because you hate giving things away. Here, you can have this back too since you're so stingy!"

He tossed the purse into her lap and turned to go.

Dai-yu burst into tears of rage, and picking up the little purse, attacked that too with her scissors. Bao-yu hurried back and caught her by the wrist.

"Come, cuzzy dear!" he said with a laugh. "Have mercy on it!"

Dai-yu threw down the scissors and wiped her streaming eyes.

"You shouldn't blow hot and cold by turns. If you want to quarrel, let's quarrel properly and have nothing to do with each other!"

She got up on the kang in a great huff, and turning her back on him, sobbed into her handkerchief and affected to ignore his presence. But Bao-yu got up beside her, and with many soothing words and affectionate endearments humbly entreated her forgiveness.

Meanwhile in the front room Grandmother Jia was calling loudly for her beloved grandson.

"Master Bao is in the back with Miss Lin," they told her.

"Ah, good!" said the old lady. "Let us leave them alone together, then. It will be a nice relaxation for him after the strain of being so long with his father — as long as they don't argue."

"Yes, milady."

Finding herself unable to shake off Bao-yu's attentions, Dai-yu got up from the kang:

"I can see you are determined not to let me live in peace. I shall just have to go elsewhere."

And off she went.

"Wherever you go, I shall go with you," said Bao-yu, taking up the purse and beginning to fasten it on again.

But Dai-yu snatched it away from him.

"First you say you don't want it, and now you are trying to put it on again. You ought to be ashamed of yourself!"

Her anger dissolved in a little explosion of laughter.

"Dearest cuzzy!" said Bao-yu. "Won't you please make me another sachet?"

"That depends on whether I feel in the mood or not," said Dai-yu.

Chatting together they went out of the room and round to Lady Wang's apartment. Bao-chai was there already.

(Selected from Cao Xueqin：*The Story of the Stone*, translated by David Hawkes)

第十一章　诗歌翻译

一、英译汉

1.

一朵红红的玫瑰
罗伯特·彭斯

啊,我爱人像红红的玫瑰,
在六月里苞放;
啊,我爱人像一支乐曲,
乐声美妙、悠扬。

你那么美,漂亮的姑娘,
我爱你那么深切;
我会永远爱你,亲爱的,
一直到四海枯竭。

直到四海枯竭,亲爱的,
直到太阳把岩石消熔!
我会永远爱你,亲爱的,
只要生命无穷。

再见吧,我唯一的爱人,
再见吧,小别片刻!
我会回来的,我的爱人,
即使万里相隔!

(袁可嘉译)

2.

水仙
威廉·华兹华斯

独自漫游似浮云,
青山翠谷上飘荡;
一刹那瞥见一丛丛、
一簇簇水仙金黄;
树荫下,明湖边,
和风吹拂舞翩跹。

仿佛群星璀璨,
沿银河闪霎晶莹;
一湾碧波边缘,
绵延,望不尽;
只见万千无穷,
随风偃仰舞兴浓。

花边波光潋滟，
怎比得繁花似锦；
面对如此良伴，
诗人怎不欢欣！
凝视，凝视，流连不止；
殊不知引起悠悠情思；
兀自倚憩息，
岑寂，幽然冥想；
蓦地花影闪心扉，
独处方能神往；
衷心喜悦洋溢，
伴水仙、舞不息。

(孙梁译)

3.
闪光
但丁·迦百利·罗塞蒂

我曾在这里留停，
却忘了何时、何故留踪：
还记得门前草儿青青，
乱把微香吹送，
沿岸的灯火，叹息的涛声。
你曾长属于我——
只忘了是什么时候：
但随着燕子掠空飞过，
你惊起回头，
纱巾旁落！——往事翩然又回到心窝。
难道这一切就是如此？
难道时光的飞轮
不会让你我的爱与生活重新比翼，
穿越死亡之门，
引我们不分昼夜，再享欢乐无羁？

(辜正坤译)

4.
墓园挽歌
托马斯·格雷

白昼将残尽，晚钟促落晖。
黄犊鸣草原，逶迤缓缓归。
田夫荷锄走，赴家意沉昏。
玄冥盈天地，孤影立乾坤。

夕曛逐黯淡，晚景渐暝灭。
万化皆偃息，阴肃笼四野。
唯见虫旋舞，但闻语切切。
牧铃声思睡，催羊人圈歇。

薜荔摇青气，蒙络罩尖顶。

栖栖枝上枭,磔磔怨蟾光:
窥我私巢久,徘徊未离休。
古已长居此,何事扰清幽。

峥嵘耸青榆,蔼蔼立紫杉。
翳下多荒坟,隆冒蒿草间。
隘隘见方穴,寂寂长眠人。
欲问谁偃卧,野夫与村氓。

侵晓花香郁,翦翦风轻唤。
茅庐草堂下,家燕语呢喃。
司晨雄鸡啼,行猎号角鸣。
陋塌一已卧,万声莫能醒。

炉膛火烁烁,主妇忙夜活。
烧饭兼添火,此景已不复。
娇儿尚学语,哑哑迎父归。
爬膝争宠爱,斯景亦难追。

昔往镰刀利,行处皆披靡。
瘠土硗薄地,犁沟亦能理。
驱驾于南亩,耦耕欢时务。
千斤挥巨斧,群林纷鞠伏。

妄者莫嘲讽,劳碌终有功。
微贱无须叹,家乐可颂扬。
蓬户家史短,简略不足耀。
权贵或有闻,无为相讥诮。

炫炫之豪族,煌煌之王侯,
美貌所招徕,财货所添购,
最终皆难免,灰飞烟灭时。
荣华何足道,百年归丘垄。

(王佐良译)

二、汉译英
1.

A Tranquil Night
By Li Bai

Abed, I see a silver light,
I wonder if it's frost aground.
Looking up, I find the moon bright;
Bowing, in homesickness I'm drowned.

(许渊冲译)

2.

To One Unnamed

By Li Shangyin

It's difficult for us to meet and hard to part;
The eastwind is too weak to revive flowers dead.
Spring silkworm till its death spins silk from love-sick heart,
Red candles but when burned up have no tears to shed.
At dawn I'm grieved to think your mirrored hair turns grey;
At night you would feel cold while I croon by moonlight.
To the three fairy isles it is not a long way.
Would the blue birds oft fly to see you on the height!

（许渊冲译）

3.

To the Tune of Moon over the West River

By Xin Qiji

Getting drunk is meant to be for fun
I've no time for being glum
Our old sages tell us not to seek for pleasures
And curb indulgence to short measures
Now my faith in them is shaken
In fact I know they were mistaken
Last night I keeled over by a pine tree
I asked the tree most amicably
"Don't you think that fall was very artistic
Given the fact that I'm—paralytic?"
Methought the tree did move as if to help me up
I motioned it to stay and waved my empty cup
"get you gone!"

（David Pollard 译）

4.

To the Tune of Mulanhuaman

By Xin Qiji

Mid-autumn festival. We had been drinking overnight until the dawn was breaking. My friends said there had been poems to greet the rising moon, but none to see a setting one off. So I wrote this piece, in the form of Questioning Heaven.

You, the lovely Moon, where are you heading,
on this lonely journey of yours?
Is there another world,
to greet you rising in the East?
Out in the space, vast and void, only
that generous wind escorts you
to deliver the festivity?
You, rootless like a flying mirror,
who holds you up in the sky?
And who provides for the Goddess,
since she refuses to marry again?

>Why should you make your trip through the ocean?
>Without an answer, I am so worried.
>What if those gigantic whales knock you down,
>with all your delicate palaces,
>in their careless dives?
>The Toad is said to be a good swimmer,
>but what about the Jade Rabbit?
>And if everyone comes out safe and sound,
>why should you pine away so?

（朱纯深译）

第十二章　戏剧翻译

一、英译汉

公　　爵　宽恕安东尼奥吧，夏洛克，别这样怀恨在心。

夏 洛 克　我说过一定要拿走我应得的那一磅肉。要是您不准许我得到它，那将是一种软弱的表现，人们将不再信你们的法律了。威尼斯不久就会丧失它的伟大。安东尼奥是我的敌人，我恨他。

巴萨尼奥　难道所有的人都要铲除他们所不爱的东西吗？

安东尼奥　跟夏洛克讲理是没有用的。别再等待了。对我宣判吧，把夏洛克想要得到的东西给他。

巴萨尼奥　我将付给你六千块钱，用来归还安东尼奥借的那三千块钱。

夏 洛 克　即使你愿意我六倍于你刚才提出的钱数，我仍然要拿我应得的那一磅肉。把那一磅肉判给我！

公　　爵　先生们，请安静。夏洛克，如果你不宽恕别人，你自己怎能希望得到别人的宽恕呢？

夏 洛 克　我并没有做错事，我不怕审判。我要求给我应得的那一磅肉。

（正当公爵不知道应该怎么办的时候，尼莉莎扮成一个律师的书记员，带着鲍西娅刚拜访过的那位著名的律师的一封信，来到法庭。当公爵与尼莉莎谈话时，夏洛克准备好要从安东尼奥身上割下他应得的一磅肉。

这时，当庭宣读了律师的信。"我重病缠身。收到你的信时，我正同一位从罗马来的很有学问的年轻博士在一起。我把夏洛克与安东尼奥之间的争执对他讲了。我们研究了很多法典，因此他知道我想要说的话。我请您让他替我做出判决。他很年轻，但是，我还从来不知道有这么年轻又这么聪明的人。"

这封信当庭宣读之后，鲍西娅穿着律师的衣服进屋来了。她作为法官就座了。）

公　　爵　您好，博学的法官！我并不羡慕您的职业。这是一个最麻烦的案子。

鲍 西 娅　您好！请坐下。你叫安东尼奥吗？这是你与夏洛克签订的借约吗？

安东尼奥　是的。

鲍 西 娅　那么，夏洛克可得大发慈悲才是。他可得宽恕安东尼奥啊。

夏 洛 克　为什么我必得宽恕他呢？请告诉我这一点！

鲍 西 娅　慈悲带来益处。慈悲像甘露从天空中降到地面上，它不但赐福施予的人，而且赐福于受施的人。我们应该学会宽恕他人。你还要求得到这一磅肉吗？

夏 洛 克　我要求得到根据法律属于我的东西。

巴萨尼奥　我愿出十倍于安东尼奥的借款，请您把法律稍为变更一下，使我们能够救出安东尼奥的生命。

鲍 西 娅　请用你的脑袋想一想，先生。我们不能变更法律，要是变更了一条法律，那么人们还会要变更别的法律的。

夏 洛 克　噢，聪明年轻的法官啊！

鲍 西 娅　让我看一看借约，就是安东尼奥向你许下的诺言。

夏 洛 克　给您。

鲍 西 娅	我明白了。根据法律,夏洛克可以得到一磅肉,由他从最靠近安东尼奥心脏的部位割下来。慈悲一点吧!让我撕毁这张借约吧。不能撕?那么,安东尼奥,你做好准备;夏洛克,拿起你的刀子准备割肉吧。
夏 洛 克	噢,博学的法官!噢,聪明的年轻人!
鲍 西 娅	你带来了称肉的器具吗?
夏 洛 克	是的。我把一切都准备好了。
鲍 西 娅	夏洛克,你是否请了医生来给安东尼奥止血呢?
夏 洛 克	借约上可没有这一条。
巴萨尼奥	你这只狐狸!
鲍 西 娅	安东尼奥,你还想说什么吗?
安东尼奥	我只想说一点。巴萨尼奥,永别了。不要为我悲伤。把我的情况告诉你的妻子,对她说我多么爱你。要是夏洛克割得够深的话,我就要以整个心偿还他的债了。
巴萨尼奥	让我拥抱你一下,说声再见吧。我爱你胜过爱我自己的生命、自己的妻子和整个世界。(他哭了。)
鲍 西 娅	你的妻子听到你那么说是会不高兴的。
夏 洛 克	我们是在浪费时间。
鲍 西 娅	割走你要的那一磅肉吗!我宣布法庭许可你(这样做),法律(把它)判给你。

(夏洛克走向安东尼奥,准备动他的刀子。)

鲍 西 娅	且慢!事情还没完。安东尼奥许诺给你他身上的一磅肉。但是他并没有答应给你他身上的任何一滴血。要是你让他身上的血流下一滴,你将失去你所有的土地和财产。
夏 洛 克	法律上是这样说的吗?
鲍 西 娅	这就是法律。你要求公正,那么就让你得到公正吗,比你要求的还要多。
夏 洛 克	我愿意要钱。请给我加三倍还给我安东尼奥向我借的钱。
巴萨尼奥	钱在这儿。(他满怀喜悦地喊了出来。)
鲍 西 娅	别忙!夏洛克先前已经拒绝要钱了。他所要求的只是公正。这是他现在所能得到的一切。你必须割下整一磅肉,不准多也不准少。而且不准流一滴血。

(夏洛克转过身,要离开法庭。)

鲍 西 娅	等一等,夏洛克。威尼斯的法律规定任何企图杀害或谋害任何威尼斯公民的人,他所有的一切必须被没收。他的钱和财产的一半必须给威尼斯,另一半必须给他企图杀害的人。他的生命全凭公爵处置。因此你快快跪下请求公爵开恩吧。
夏 洛 克	仁慈的先生,我乞求你的饶恕和原谅。
公 爵	我将不处死你,但是作为对你的惩罚,你的财产的一半现在是安东尼奥的了。你必须把另一半交给威尼斯城。
夏 洛 克	把我的命也拿走吧!我的钱财对我就像生命一样宝贵。它们是我唯一的安慰。你们没收了我的财物,也就是要了我的命。
安东尼奥	我将高兴地放弃我应得的夏洛克财产的那一半。夏洛克必须答应在他死后把这笔财产留给他的女儿和女婿。
夏 洛 克	我答应。现在让我回家吧。我不舒服。

(选自威廉·莎士比亚:《威尼斯商人》,梁实秋译)

二、汉译英

Pock-mark Liu	Now, let's talk it over. Will ten taels of silver do? Be quick! I'm a busy man. I haven't got all day to wait on you!
Kang Liu	Master Liu! A fifteen-year-old girl only worth ten taels?
Pock-mark Liu	A brothel mig give you a few taels more, but you don't want that.

Kang Liu	My flesh and blood, how could I...?
Pock-mark Liu	But you can't feed her. Who's to blame?
Kang Liu	We peasants can't live any more. If we had a bowl of gruel each every day...and I still wanted to sell my daughter, then I'd be a beast!
Pock-mark Liu	That's your problem, not mine! You asked me to help you, so I'll see to it you're not cheated and your daughter fills her belly. What more do you want?
Kang Liu	Who's she being sold to?
Pock-mark Liu	This should please you. A palace official!
Kang Liu	What palace official wants a peasant girl?
Pock-mark Liu	That's why your daughter's a lucky girl!
Kang Liu	But who is he?
Pock-mark Liu	The Grand Eunuch Pang! Even you must have heard of him. A personal attendant of the Empress Dowager, her great favourite! Even the vinegar bottle in his house is made of agate!
Kang Liu	But Master Liu, please, how could I ever face my daughter again if I sold her to be the wife of a eunuch?
Pock-mark Liu	But you are selling her, aren't you? How can you face her any way? Don't be a fool! Think about it. Once she's married, she'll eat delicacies and wear brocades! I call that a lucky fate! Well, make up your mind, yes or no. Let's get it over with!
Kang Liu	But who's ever heard of such a thing...? Ten taels. Is that all he'll pay?
Pock-mark Liu	Where in your whole village can you scrape up ten taels? You know very well in the countryside a child can be bought for five catties of wheat flour.
Kang Liu	I, well, I'll have to talk it over with my daughter.
Pock-mark Liu	I'm telling you, you won't find another chance like this. If you lose it, don't blame me!
Kang Liu	Yes. I'll be back as soon as I can.
(*Exit Kang Liu, dragging his feet.*)	
Pock-mark Liu	(*Moving over to Song and Chang*) These country bumpkins are a nuisance. They're so slow making up their minds!
Song	Another big deal?
Pock-mark Liu	Not so big. If all goes well, I may get about twenty taels of silver.
Chang	What's going on in the countryside? Why are they selling their children like this?
Pock-mark Liu	Who knows? That's why people say, even a dog wants to be born in Beijing.
Chang	Master Liu, it takes nerve to have a hand in such a business!
Pock-mark Liu	But if I didn't bother, they might not find a buyer! (*Changing the subject abruptly*) Master Song (*Taking a small pocket-watch out of his pocket*), have a look at this!

(Selected from Lao She: *Teahouse*, translated by Ying Ruocheng)

第十三章 典籍翻译

1.

Chang Chuang was sick and Laotse went to see him. The latter said to Chang Chuang, "You are very ill. Have you not something to say to your disciple?" "Even if you don't ask me, I was going to tell you," replied Chang Chuang. "Do you know why one has to get down from one's carriage when coming to one's old village?" And Laotse replied, "Doesn't this custom mean that one should not forget one's origins?"

"Ah, yes," said Chang Chuang.

Then the sick man asked again, "Do you know why one should run when passing under a tall tree?"

"Doesn't this custom mean we should respect what is old?" "Ah, yes,"said Chang Chuang.

Then Chang Chuang opened his mouth wide and asked Laotse to look into it, and said, "Is my tongue still there?" "It is," replied Laotse. "Are my teeth still there?" asked the old man. "No," replied Laotse. "And do you know why?" asked Chang Chuang. "Does not the tongue last longer because it is soft? And is it not because the teeth are hard that they fall off earlier?" replied Laotse. "Ah, yes," said chang Chuang. "There you have learned all the principles concerning the world. I have nothing else to teach you."

(Selected from Liu Xiang: Shuo Yuan • How the Tongue Survived the Teeth, translated by Lin Yutang)

2.

In the tenth year of his reign, in spring, in the first moon, duke Chuang defeated the army of the Ch'i State at Ch'ang-cho.

The State of Ch'i had declared war against us, our duke was about to give battle, when a man named Kuei begged for an audience. Kuei's clansmen had said to him, "The authorities will decide upon the proper strategy; what place will there be in their counsels for you?" To which Kuei had replied, "They are but a poor lot, and have no idea whatever of deep-laid plans."

Accordingly, Kuei was admitted to see the duke, and at once enquired, saying, "On the strength of what is your Highness about to fight?" "I have never monopolized the comforts of food and raiment," replied the duke, "I have always shared with others." "That," said Kuei, "is a small favour, extending only to a few. The people will not rally round you on that account alone." "Then,"continued the duke, "in the sacrifices to the Gods I have trusted more to earnestness of heart than to costly displays." "That again," objected Kuei, "is an insufficient basis. The God will not bless your arms on that account alone." "And in all judicial investigations," added the duke, "though oft-times unable to ascertain the precise truth, I have always given my decision in accordance with the evidence before me." "Ha," cried Kuei; "so far you have done your duty to the people, and you may risk a battle on that. I myself pray to be allowed to accompany your highness." To this the duke acceded, and took Kuei with him in his own chariot.

The battle was fought at chang-cho; and on sighting the enemy our duke would have forthwith given orders to beat an attack, but Kuei said, "Not yet!" only when the enemy's drums had sounded thrice did Kuei shout out, "Now!"

Our victory was complete; and the duke would promptly have given orders to pursue, had not the Kuei again said, "Not yet!" The latter then alighted and examined the tracks of the enemy's chariot-wheels; after which he got up on the hand-rail in front, and following the flying foe with his eye, cried out, "Now!" Thereupon the order was given to pursue.

When the battle had been gained, our duke asked Kuei for an explanation of his tactics. "A battle," replied Kuei, "depends wholly upon the martial ardour of the combatants. At the first roll of the drum, that ardour is violently excited; with the second, it begins to flag; with the third, it is exhausted. Now, when the enemy's ardour was at this last stage, ours was at its highest pitch; therefore, we conquered them. Still, against a formidable foe, one should be prepared for anything. I feared an ambuscade; but I found that their wheel-tracks were in evident disorder. I then looked at their standards, and saw that these also were in confusion. Therefore I gave the word to pursue."

(Selected from Zhuo Zhuan: The Battle of Ch'ang-Cho, translated by Giles A. Herbert)

3.

A fruit vendor of Hangzhou was so skilled in storing oranges the whole year round that when he brought out his splendid wares, bright as gold and smooth as jade, people flocked to buy at ten times the market prices. I purchased one myself, but to my amazement when I opened it something like smoke puffed into my mouth and nostrils, and I found the inside as shrivelled as old cotton wadding.

"Are you selling these to be put in sacrificial vessels and offered to the spirits?" I demanded. "To be served to guests? Or just to impose on fools? This is a disgraceful swindle."

"I have earned my living in this way for years," the man replied with a smile. "And none of my customers has ever complained. Who are you, sir, to find fault? There are plenty of worse cheats in the world than me, I'd have you know! Those generals with tiger tallies seated tiger skins look like magnificent defenders of the state but have they mastered military strategy? Those ministers with imposing headgear and belts look like dignified officers of the court, but can they really administer the state? They neither prevent revolts nor relieve the sufferings of the people, neither check corrupt officials nor rectify violations of the law. Instead they sit around wasting government grain without any sense of shame. True, they stay in lofty mansions, ride on big horses, feast on wine and meat and appear splendid and awe-inspiring, yet their fine gold and jade exteriors hold nothing but old cotton wadding. Why don't you investigate them instead of finding fault with my oranges?"

I was silenced and had no answer. After leaving him, I thought over what he had said. He appeared to be a cynic like Dongfang Shuo, so disgusted with the abuses of our time that he used his oranges to ridicule men.

Notes: Dongfang Shuo: A famous jester in the second century BC.

(Selected from Liu Ji: *The Orange Vendor*)

4.

When Confucius was seventeen, Meng Hsi-tzu the minister of Lu fell ill and as he was dying he told his successor Yi-tzu, "Kung Chiu is descended from sages. One of his ancestors was killed in Sung. One of his ancestors, Fu-fu-ho, should have been the ruler of Sung but made over the state to his younger brother Duke Li. And Cheng Kao-fu, his great-grandson who served Duke Tai, Duke Wu and Duke Hsuan, behaved more modestly after each appointment. Thus this tripod inscription reads, 'At the first appointment I inclined my head, at the second I bowed, at the third I bent low. I hug the wall and no one dares insult me. Pap and gruel stay my hunger.' See how unassuming he was! I have heard that even if he does not hold office the descendant of sages is always a wise man. Kung Chiu is young, but he sets such store on the rites that I am sure he is a man of understanding. When I am gone, make him your teacher."

So after Meng His-tzu's death, Yi-tzu and Nankung Ching-shu, another native of Lu, studied the rites with Confucius. That same year Chi Wu-tzu died and Ping-tzu succeeded him.

Confucius was poor and humble. Growing up and working as keeper of the granaries for the Chi clan he measured the grain fairly; when he was keeper of the livestock the animals flourished; and so he was made minister of works. Subsequently he left Lu, was dismissed from Chi, driven out of Sung and Wei and ran into trouble between Chen and Tsai. Finally he returned to Lu.

Well over six feet, Confucius was called the Tall Man and everybody marveled at his height. He returned to the state of Lu as it had treated him well. Nankung Ching-shu asked the duke of Lu to let him accompany Confucius to Chou, and the duke gave them a carriage, a pair of horses and a page boy. They went to Chou to study rites and there met Lao Tzu.

When Confucius was leaving, Lao Tzu's parting words to him were, "I have heard that the rich and great offer farewell gifts of money while the good offer advice. I am neither rich nor great but, unworthy as I am, have been called good; so let me offer you a few words of advice." Then he said, "A shrewd observer, prone to criticize others, risks his own life. A learned man who exposes the faults of others endangers himself. A filial son must never thrust himself forward, and neither may a good subject."

On his return from Chou to Lu, Confucius began to gather more disciples.

(Selected from Sima Qian: *Records of the Grand Historian*, translated by Yang Hsien-yi and Gladys Yang)

第十四章 影视翻译

一、英译汉

1. 电影片名翻译

(1)《贵妇画像》/《淑女画像》/《淑女本色》
(2)《海上钢琴师》
(3)《怒海争峰》
(4)《廊桥遗梦》
(5)《西雅图夜未眠》/《西雅图未眠夜》
(6)《莎翁情史》/《恋爱中的莎士比亚》
(7)《女人香》/《闻香识女人》
(8)《漂亮女人》/《风月俏佳人》
(9)《情诗百载牵》
(10)《邂逅乔·布莱克》/《死神情缘》
(11)《燃情岁月》
(12)《真爱至上》
(13)《肥妈先生》
(14)《女孩梦三十》

2. 电影字幕翻译

(1)

  莫 扎 特：我对您的音乐很熟悉。您知道，我其实修改过你的一首作品。
  萨里埃利：真的吗？我受宠若惊。
  国　　王：他现在回报了你的赞美。萨里埃利写了这首欢迎你的进行曲。
  莫 扎 特：真的吗？谢谢您，先生。
  国　　王：就这样吧。现在来谈正事。年轻人，我们要你写一部歌剧，觉得如何？
  莫 扎 特：好啊，陛下！
  国　　王：但是我们最终还未定下是用德语还是意大利语？
  萨里埃利：是的，还未最后决定，陛下。
  莫 扎 特：德语！拜托用德语！
  国　　王：为什么？
  莫 扎 特：因为我已经找到最精彩的剧本。语言并不是重点，只要主题充满了高尚的德意志之美。
  萨里埃利：对不起，陛下，什么是"德意志之美"？身为外国人，我很想了解。
  国　　王：告诉他，莫扎特，给我们举一个"德意志之美"的例子。
  莫 扎 特："爱"，陛下！
  萨里埃利："爱"！当然，我们意大利人不懂得爱。
  莫 扎 特：是的，我认为你们意大利人不懂得爱。看意大利歌剧时，男高音扯着嗓子尖叫，肥硕的情侣转动着眼珠调情。那不是爱情。那是垃圾。陛下，您决定用什么语言，我负责配上献给君主的最优美的音乐。
  国　　王：好，就这样，就用德语吧。

(选自《莫扎特传》，1984)

(2)

  基丁：我为什么要站到这儿？谁知道？
  学生：感觉高一些呗。
  基丁：不！谢谢你的幽默，道顿。我站在讲台上是要提醒自己，我们必须时刻用不同的眼光来看待事物。从这里看世界大不相同。如果你们不信，可以自己来看看。来吧，来吧！一旦你觉得自己明白了什么，就必须换一个角度来看。即使这可能显得荒唐或者愚蠢，但必须试一下！看书的时候，不要只琢磨作者怎么看，要想想你自己怎么看。孩子们，你们必须努力寻找自己的声音，因为你越迟开始寻找,找到的可能性就越小。梭罗曾说:"大多数人都生活在平静的绝望中。"不要陷入这种境地。冲出来!别像老鼠逃跑似的。看看你的周围。对了!就这样,布里斯克,谢谢!对极了!敢于冲出来开拓新天地。好了,除了写篇作文之外,我要你们每人写一首诗,自己的诗,全新的创作。这就对了!下星期一上午的课,每个人都要在全班面前大声念自己的诗。祝各位好运。安德森先生,别以为我不知道这作业把你的魂儿都吓没了,胆小鬼。

(选自《死诗人诗社》/《春风化雨》,1989)

(3)
  阿 甘:你怎么了,妈妈?
  甘 太 太:我快死了,儿子。过来,坐在这儿。
  阿 甘:妈妈,你干嘛要死?
  甘 太 太:我的时辰到了,时辰到了。别怕,亲爱的,死只是生命的一部分。这是所有人的命运。我以前不知道,但我命中注定要做你妈妈,我尽了我的所能。
  阿 甘:妈妈,你做得很好。
  甘 太 太:我也相信你会主宰自己的命运。上帝赐给你的,你要尽量发挥。
  阿 甘:妈妈,我的命运是怎样的?
  甘 太 太:你要自己去寻找答案。人生就像一盒巧克力,阿甘,你永远不知道会尝到什么。

(选自《阿甘正传》,1994)

(4)
  弗里达:里维拉先生?迭戈!
  迭 戈:你是谁?你想干什么?
  弗里达:我有重要事情跟你谈。
  迭 戈:我在工作。
  弗里达:我等你。
  迭 戈:我没空和女生闲扯。
  弗里达:我不是女生,大肚腩。
  迭 戈:好吧,你上来吧。
  弗里达:不,你下来。
  迭 戈:什么事?
  弗里达:听着,我不是来找乐子或调情的。我画了些画,希望你能以专业眼光鉴别一下。我需要你毫无保留地发表意见。
  迭 戈:你就是礼堂里的那个女孩。
  弗里达:是我。不过我来这儿和那事儿没关系。我只想听听你中肯的意见。
  迭 戈:我的意见对你有什么意义呢?如果你是一个真正的画家,你就会画下去,因为没有绘画你就无法生存,你会一直画到临终那一天,明白吗?
  弗里达:我需要工作来养家糊口,所以我没精力为华而不实的事情浪费时间。如果我天资不够,为了赡养父母,我得及早改行。
  迭 戈:把最好的那张留下,回去再画一张。如果这张画不错,有空我会去看你另一张画。

(选自《弗里达》,2002)

(5)
  律 师:克莱默太太,请你告诉法庭你结婚几年了?
  克莱默太太:八年。
  律 师:这几年你是否快乐?
  克莱默太太:头两年很快乐,但之后就越来越艰难。
  律 师:克莱默太太,你结婚之前有工作吗?
  克莱默太太:有。从史密斯学院毕业后,我在《女士》杂志设计部门工作了好几年。
  律 师:结婚之后你继续工作吗?

克莱默太太：没有。
律　　师：你当时想工作吗？
克莱默太太：想。但每次我和泰德，同我的前夫商量，他都不听。他拒绝认真和我商量。我记得他曾说，我就算找到工作，薪水可能还不够付比利的保姆费。
律　　师：告诉我，你现在有工作吗？
克莱默太太：有。我现在是纽约一家运动服装的设计师。
律　　师：你现在的薪水是多少？
克莱默太太：年薪三万一千元。
律　　师：克莱默太太，你爱你的孩子吗？
克莱默太太：爱，非常爱。
律　　师：但你却选择离开他。
克莱默太太：不错。在过去的五年婚姻中，我变得越来越不开心，越来越困惑。我很需要有人帮我。但当我向泰德求助时，他就是不帮我，所以我们越来越疏远，越来越分离。他对事业非常投入。由于他对我的恐惧漠不关心，对我的感受无力面对，我几乎没有任何自信。我很害怕，很不快乐。在我心里，除了离开，别无选择。当我离开的时候，我觉得自己很糟糕。所以孩子没有我比较好。只有我到了加州经过心理治疗后，才发现自己没那么糟糕。除了孩子以外，我还需要创作上或情绪上的舒解，但这并不表示我是个不称职的母亲。
律　　师：(对法官)我要呈上一份证明，是克莱默太太的心理治疗师弗里德曼医生的报告。克莱默太太，请告诉法庭你为何要申请监护权？
克莱默太太：因为他是我的孩子，而且我爱他。我知道我离开了我儿子，我知道这样做很糟糕。相信我，我这一辈子都会因此而自责。但请相信，当时我别无选择，那样做对他最好，因为当时我觉得我在那个家一无是处。我不知道有什么其他办法，所以我想最好不要带他离开。但后来我非常努力成为一个健全的人。我不应该因此受到惩罚，我也不认为我的小孩应该受到惩罚。比利只有七岁，他需要我。我并不是说他不需要他的父亲。但我真的认为他更需要我。我当了他五年半的母亲，而泰德接替这个位子才十八个月。我不懂谁会认为我不如他有资格抚养我儿子。我是他的母亲，我是他的母亲。

（选自《克莱默夫妇》，2002）

(6)

克利斯多弗：玛莉莎，卡罗琳，我不知道该称呼你哪个名字。
玛　莉　莎：玛莉莎。
克利斯多弗：我不明白发生了什么。
玛　莉　莎：你不明白什么？我是个女佣。
克利斯多弗：这一切是怎么回事，是什么赌局吗？什么游戏？接客游戏？
玛　莉　莎：不是。我试穿她的衣服时，你正好在场。然后你邀我出去，一切就这样发生了。
克利斯多弗：你觉得你必须说谎才能吸引住我吗？
玛　莉　莎：究竟是谁跟谁开玩笑？如果知道我是女佣，你会再看我一眼吗？
克利斯多弗：嗯？
玛　莉　莎：算了吧，就依你那一套大度的政治理论，我才不会这样认为呢，议员先生。
克利斯多弗：你怎么知道？你又没有给我机会。你站在自己的立场上判断每个人，自以为是地认为他们也在论断你。
玛　莉　莎：你认为他们没有吗？很多情况下，要么我是他们取笑的对象，要么没人注意我。可能关键就在这里。你第一次见到我时，我在清扫你卫生间的地面，只不过你没看见我罢了。
克利斯多弗：你当时要我怎么做？难道要我一边小便一边跟你打招呼吗？你不能责备我这个。我只要知道真相，玛莉莎。
玛　莉　莎：好，你要知道真相，是吗？有时，我希望有一个像你这样的人，像你这样看着我，就只要一次。我希望体会一下是何种感受。我很抱歉，真的。如果我能让过去的一星期重来一遍的话，我愿意。
克利斯多弗：这件事当中有没有真实的成分？
玛 莉 莎：我很难放弃你，这是真的，很真实。但我必须放弃你，这是计划之中。但是昨晚，我实在无法放弃你。

（选自《曼哈顿女佣》，2002）

(7)
比尔：喂，有人在吗？
乔：安静。
比尔：你在哪里？
乔：我在这里。
比尔：这是开玩笑吗？精心设计的恶作剧吗？40周年的同学会上，我们把棺材送到班长下榻的饭店……
乔：安静。比尔，你要去哪里？
比尔：我要，呃……
乔：伟大的比尔·派瑞也许说不出话了？这个满嘴"狂喜"、"激情"和"迷恋"的人？所有那些告诫人们要"欢喜雀跃，否则人生缺乏意义"的话。你浑身上下散发着活力，你用圆润、洪亮的语气教人积极乐观。
比尔：这究竟是怎么回事？你是谁？
乔：千年恒久无界的时光，我已常存其中。只是最近你的行为引发我的好奇。是因为无聊吧，本能的好奇，蠢蠢欲动引我前来。我是人世间最永久、最意义深远的事物。
比尔：要做什么？
乔：带你走之前我要到处看看。
比尔：带我去哪里？
乔：它要求能力、智慧与经验。纵观各界对你的颂扬，你最合适。
比尔：合适做什么？
乔：带我参观，做我的向导，作为交换，你会得到……
比尔：得到什么？
乔：时间，几分钟，几天，几周……不必详加叙述。要紧的是我仍感兴趣。是的。
比尔：什么"是的"？
乔：是回答你的问题。
比尔：什么问题？
乔：比尔，得了！你知道最近你不断问自己的问题。打球激烈喘气时、昨晚上床时、今早在办公室摔倒时没说出口的疑问。令你反复思考萦绕耳际的声音，不断问自己的问题。
比尔：这个问题。
乔：对，比尔，那个问题。
比尔：我快死了吗？
乔：是的。
比尔：我在做梦吗？你是一场梦吗？
乔：我不是梦。
比尔：你来带我走？怎么回事？你究竟是谁？你是……
乔：什么？我是谁？
比尔：死神。你是死神？
乔：是的。
比尔：死神。
乔：就是我。
比尔：你不是死神。你只不过是个穿西装的年轻人。

乔：西装是附在我夺去的那个生命的躯体上的。你认为"和我相称吗"？
比尔：你要我当你的向导。
乔：你很合适，比尔。
比尔：是吗？
乔：对。
比尔：你要待很久吗？
乔：应该时间不短。
比尔：之后呢？生命结束吗？
乔：请带路吧，比尔。

(选自《邂逅乔·布莱克》，1998)

二、汉译英
1. 电影片名翻译
(1) Farewell，My Concubine
(2) A Chinese Odyssey
(3) In the Mood for Love
(4) Royal Tramp
(5) Temper of Heart
(6) Red Dust
(7) All Men Are Brothers: Blood of the Leopard
(8) If You Are the One
(9) Ashes of Time
(10) To Live

2. 电影字幕翻译
(1) I sentence you to death, in name of the Party and the people.

(Selected from *Daughter of the Party*)

(2) Everybody, could you image it? I, HU Hanshan, come back again! Now, it still is my domain. Whoever took something from me, return it to me, and occupy anything of mine, restitute it to me.

(Selected from *Red Sparkling Star*)

(3) Comrades, for new China, let's go!

(Selected from *Dong Cunrui*)

(4) Deliver, deliver, and deliver it in spite of any cost!   (Selected from *Mountain Shanggan*)

(5) For victory, shoot at me!   (Selected from *Heroic Sons and Daughters*)

(6) Which column are you in?   (Selected from *Legendary Voluntary Army*)

(7) Come in with stand, and get out with sleep!   (Selected from *Pops in the Secrecy Bureau*)

(8) —How are you?
　　—Fine, thank you. And you?
　　—I'm fine too.

(Selected from *Legend in Snowy Forest*)

(9) (a) Great! It' so great!
　　(b) For find out the 8th R—Army, even dig into three feet.

(Selected from *Tunnel Warfare*)

(10) (a) I don't specialize in war, and so do you in cards. The line of defense along the Yangtze River is up to you!
　　(b) Chinese stand up!

(Selected from *Grand Ceremony*)

(11) (a) Now we withdraw at a stride, just for advance with strides tomorrow!
    (b) Help me for the Party and Country's sake, please!

(Selected from *Civil War*)

(12) (a) Payment? I have never paid at restaurants in the town, let these stupid watermelons alone.
    (b) Don't be cocky today; just be careful of your dog-ass day!

(Selected from *Little Soldier Zhang Ga*)

(13) (a) Kill me, or slay me, but you never beat down a commy's will!
    (b) Whoever will die at some day? I'm so honored for my life with timelessly flourishing proletariat's career.

(Selected from *Perpetuity in Blood and Fire*)

(14) If you are looking for a handsome guy or a wallet, don't reply. If you hold a Masters' degree or higher, not possible; girls born in Shanghai, not possible; female entrepreneurs (except small business hawker), not possible; so that we don't waste each other's hope. The Andy Liu or Tom Cruise kinds, who are both wealthy and good-looking, would not make an announcement looking for you. Surely, I don't expect a Notting Hill story either. Even if you're indeed an angle, I won't be able to handle you; I don't expect that you look like that girl on the magazine cover, just one look crushing people's souls. An average person, with outside stylishness and inside conservativeness, with fit body and mind, will just do, even better if you're beautifully shy. You need not to play too many tricks or be too young. From time to time, you're allowed to have unrealistic dreams, but a few words is enough to get you back into reality without getting you angry—a little embarrassed grin at most, and then do what you ought to do. I like a woman who knows how to fold clothes in a way that whenever you finish washing, ironing and folding them; they will look just like when you bought them from stores. It cannot be more specific than this, can it?

Let me introduce myself for you. I'm a man whose age is no longer young, living a moderately well-off life, who doesn't drink but smoke. I went abroad as a student and spent more than a decade living abroad, but never attended a real education. In wasting time, I learned all sorts of ways to make a living. Now I returned with no achievement at all. To tell you the truth, I should be judged as a "Fake Turtle" without the three—no company, no stocks and no degree. My personality is open. My character is neither good nor bad. I'm not exactly an honest man, but I am without much courage since I was born. Even it is not illegal to kill, I wouldn't kill anyone. My conscience will be tortured by the guilt if I do anything cruel to others. I am meant not to be a villain, even if I try to be one. In general and basically, I'm still one of those who are beneficial and harmless to the mankind and our society.

Contact me by phone, if you're the one.

(Selected from *If You Are the One*)

参考文献

Baker, M. *In Other Words: A Coursebook on Translation*. London: Routledge /Beijing: Foreign Language Teaching and Research Press, 1992 /2000.

Bassnett, S. *Translation Studies* (Third Edition). Shanghai: Shanghai Foreign Language Education Press, 2004.

Bassnett, S. & A. Lefevere. *Constructing Cultures: Essays on Literary Translation*. Shanghai: Shanghai Foreign Language Education Press, 2001.

Bassnett, S. & A. Lefevere. *Translation, History and Culture*. Shanghai: Shanghai Foreign Language Education Press, 2004.

Beaugrande, R. de & W. Dressler. *Introduction to Text Linguistics*. London: Longman, 1981.

Bell, R. T. *Translation and Translating: Theory and Practice*. London: Longman/Beijing: Foreign Language Teaching and Research Press, 1991/2001.

Cai, Xinle. Towards a Philosophy of Translation, in 2nd Asian Translators' Forum, Seoul: Korean Society of Translators, 1998.

Catford, J. C. *A Linguistic Theory of Translation*. London: Oxford University Press, 1965.

Fan, Min. A Study of Translatological Dictionaries from the Perspective of Text Linguistics. *Across languages and Cultures*, 2009(1). 85—107.

Fan, Min. Cultural Issues in Chinese Idioms Translation. *Perspectives: Studies in Translatology*, 2007(4). 215—229.

Gentzler, E. *Contemporary Translation Theories*. London: Routledge, 1993.

Giles, A. H. *Gems of Chinese Literature*. Shanghai: Kelly and Walsh Ltd., 1923.

Gutt, E. A. *Translation and Relevance: Cognition and Context* [M]. London: Basil Blackwell Ltd., 1994.

Halliday, M. A. K., M. McIntosh & P. Strevens (eds.). *The Linguistic Sciences and Language Teaching*. London: Longman, 1964.

Halliday, M. A. K. *An Introduction to Functional Grammar*. London: Arnold/ Beijing: Foreign Language Teaching and Research Press, 1994/ 2000.

Hardy, T. *Tess of the d'Urbervilles*. New York: Bantam Books, 1992.

Hatim, B. & I. Mason. *Discourse and the Translator*. London: Longman/Shanghai: Shanghai Foreign Language Education Press, 1990/2001.

Hatim, B. & I. Mason. *The Translator as Communicator*. London: Routledge, 1997.

Hatim, B & J. Munday. *Translation An Advanced Resource Book*. London & New York: Routledge, 2004.

Holmes, J. S. Translation Theories, Translation Studies, and the Translator. J. S. Holmes. *Translated! Papers on Literary Translation and Translation Studies*. Amsterdam:Rodopi. 1988. 93—98.

Jakobson, R. Linguistics and Poetics. In T. A. Sebeok (ed.) *Style in Language*. MIT Press, 1960.

Katharina, R. *Translation Criticism: The Potentials & Limitations*. Manchester: St. Jerome Publishing Company, 2000.

Kelly, L. G. The True Interpreter: A History of Translation. *Theory and Practice in the West*. New York: St. Martin's Press, 1979.

Lado, R. *Linguistics Across Cultures*. ANN Arbor: The University of Michigan Press, 1957.

Martin, J. R. & D. Rose. *Working with the Discourse: Meaning Beyond the Clause*. Sydney/Hong Kong: Continuum Press, 2003.

Munday, J. *Introducing Translation Studies: Theories and Applications*. London & New York: Routledge, 2001.

Neubert, A. & G. M. Shreve. *Translation as Text*. Kent: The Kent University Press, 1992.

Newmark, P. *A Textbook of Translation*. New York & London: Prentice Hall, 1988.

Newmark, P. *Approaches to Translation*. Oxford: Pergamon, 1981.

Newmark, P. *About Translation*. Clevedon: Multilingual Matters, 1991.

Nida, E. A. Principles of Translation as Exampled by Bible Tanslating. In Dil. Anwar S. (ed). *Language Structure and Translation——Essays by Eugene A. Nida*. Stanford: Stanford University, 1975.

Nida, E. A. *Language and Culture: Contexts in Translating*. Shanghai: Shanghai Foreign Language Education Press, 2001.

Nida, E. A. & W. D. Reyburn. *Meaning Across Cultures*. Maryknoll & New York: Orbis, 1981.

Nord, C. *Translation as a Purposeful Activity: Functional Approaches Explained*. Manchester: St. Jerome Publishing, 1997.

Nord, C. *Translating as a Purposeful Activity* [M]. Shanghai: Shanghai Foreign Language Education Press, 2001.

Nord, C. *Text Analysis in Translation: Theory, Methodology, and Didactic Application of a Model for Translation-Oriented Text Analysis* (Second Edition). Beijing: Foreign Language Teaching and Research Press, 2006.

Reiss, K. *Möglichkeiten und Grenzen des Übersetzungskritik. Kategorien und Kriterien für eine sachgerechte Beurteilung von Übersetzungen*. Munich: Hueber, 1971.

Reiss, K. Texttypes, Translation Types and Translation Assessment (translated by Andrew Chesterman) [A]. In A. Chesterman (ed). *Readings in Translation Theory*. Finland: Oy Finn Lectura Ab, 1989.

Sager, J. C. Quality and Standards: The Evaluation of Translations [A]. In C. Picken (ed.), *The Translator's Handbook*. London: Aslib, 1983, pp. 121—128.

Simpmn, R. Translation Specifications. In C. Picken (ed.) *The Translator's Handbook*. London: Aslib, 1983, 129—139.

Snell, B. & P. Crampton. Types of Translations. *The Translator's Handbook*. C. Picken (ed.). London, Aslib. 1983, 109—120, Snell-Hornby, M. *Translation Studies: An Integrated Approach*. Amsterdam/Philadelphia: John Benjamins Publishing Company, 1988.

Shuttleworth, M. & M. Cowie. *Dictionary of Translation Studies*. Manchester: St. Jerome Publishing, 1997.

Toury, G. *In Search of a Theory of Translation*. Tel Aviv: The Porter Institute for Poetics and Semiotics, 1980.

Toury, G. *Descriptive Translation Studies and Beyond*. Shanghai: Shanghai Foreign Language Education Press, 1995.

Trosborg, A. Register, Genre and Text Type. A. Trosborg (ed). *Text Typology and Translation*. Amsterdam/Philadelphia: John Benjamins Publishing Company, 1997.

Trosborg, A. (ed.) *Text Typology and Translation*. Amsterdam/Philadelphia: John Benjamins Publishing Company, 1997.

Wilss, W. *The Science of Translation: Problems and Mehods*. Shanghai: Shanghai Foreign Language Education Press, 2001.

白靖宇. 文化与翻译. 北京:中国社会科学出版社,2010.

包通法. 论'简''达''雅'与科技翻译. 贵州工业大学学报,2003(1),69—73.

蔡新乐. 翻译的本体论研究:翻译研究的第三条道路、主体间性与人的元翻译构成. 上海:上海译文出版社,2005.

蔡新乐. 试论'化境'的反翻译倾向及'不隔'的理论意义. 外语与翻译,2000(1),22—29.
蔡新乐. 文学翻译理论需要人文主义的艺术哲学. 外语与外语教学,1999(11),43—46,57.
柴梅萍. 电影翻译中文化意象的重构、修润与转换. 苏州大学学报,2001(4),91—94.
陈福康. 中国译学理论史稿(修订本). 上海:上海外语教育出版社,2000.
陈 刚. 应用文体翻译:理论与实践. 杭州:浙江大学出版社,2008.
陈 刚. 旅游英汉互译教程. 上海:上海外语教育出版社,2009.
陈 刚. 旅游英语导译教程. 上海:上海外语教育出版社,2010.
陈 刚. 旅游翻译与涉外导游(原创版). 北京:中国对外翻译出版公司,2010.
陈 刚. 翻译学入门. 杭州:浙江大学出版社,2011.
陈 刚,滕超. 会展翻译研究与实践. 杭州:浙江大学出版社,2011.
陈良廷译,阿瑟·米勒著. 推销员之死. 上海:上海译文出版社,1989.
陈同仇,张锡嘏. 国际贸易. 北京:对外贸易教育出版社,1994.
杜金榜等. 中国法律法规英译的问题和解决. 中国翻译,2004(3),74—78.
范 敏. 目的论对《红楼梦》中谚语翻译的启示. 红楼梦学刊,2007(2),187—202.
范武邱. 科技翻译研究:困境和对策. 中国科技翻译,2007(1),49—52.
方梦之. 译学辞典. 上海:上海外语教育出版社,2004.
冯大同. 国际商法. 北京:对外贸易教育出版社,1994.
冯庆华. 文体翻译论. 上海:上海外语教育出版社,2002.
冯庆华. 红译艺坛:红楼梦翻译艺术研究. 上海:上海外语教育出版社,2006.
高等学校外语专业教学指导委员会英语组. 高等学校英语专业英语教学大纲. 北京:外语教学与研究出版社,2000.
高嘉正. 吃透原诗——古诗英译的首要之举. 上海科技翻译,1999(4),24—27.
辜正坤. 《中西诗歌翻译百年论集》序. 海岸著. 中西诗歌翻译百年论集. 上海:上海外语教育出版社,2007.
何固佳. 科技英语语言特点. 中国科技翻译,1998(4),8—11.
胡庚申. 翻译适应选择论. 武汉:湖北教育出版社,2004.
胡庚申. 从译文看译论——翻译适应选择论应用例析. 外语教学,2006(4),90—95.
胡庚申. 从术语看译论——翻译适应选择论概观. 上海翻译,2008(2),1—5.
胡庚申. 适应与选择:翻译过程新解[J]. 四川外语学院学报,2008(4),50—55.
胡壮麟,朱永生,张德禄. 系统功能语法概论. 长沙:湖南教育出版社,1989.
胡壮麟. 系统功能语言学活动近况. 余渭深等主编《语言的功能——系统、语用和认知》. 重庆:重庆大学出版社,1998.
胡壮麟,刘世生. 西方文体学辞典. 北京:清华大学出版社,2004.
黄国文. 《清明》一诗英译文的人际功能探讨. 外语教学,2002(3),34—38.
黄国文. 唐诗英译文中的引述现象分析. 外语学刊,2002(3),1—6+112.
黄国文,张美芳. 语篇语言学与翻译研究. 中国翻译,2002(3),5—9.
黄国文. 功能语言学分析对翻译研究的启示——《清明》英译文的经验功能分析. 外语与外语教学,2002(5),1—6,11.
黄国文. 对唐诗《寻隐者不遇》英译文的功能语篇分析. 解放军外国语学院学报,2002(5),67—70+115.
黄国文. 关于语篇与翻译. 外语与外语教学,2002(7),1—2.
黄国文. 从语篇功能的角度看《清明》的几种英译文. 钱军编《语言学:中国与世界同步》. 北京:外语教学与研究出版社,2003.
黄国文. 古诗英译文里的时态分析. 四川外语学院学报,2003(1),95—100.
黄国文. 从《天净沙·秋思》的英译文看"形式对等"的重要性. 中国翻译,2003(2),23—25.
黄国文. 翻译研究的功能语言学途径. 中国翻译,2004(5),17—21.
黄国文. 翻译研究的语言学探索. 上海:上海外语教育出版社,2006.
黄俊雄编译. 英译中国小小说选集. 上海:上海外语教育出版社,2008.

黄凯. 科技英语翻译技巧. 广州:华南工学院出版社,1987.
黄源深译,夏洛蒂·勃朗特著. 简·爱. 上海:译林出版社,2008.
黄忠廉. 变译理论. 北京:中国对外翻译出版公司,2002.
黄忠廉. 变译的性质及其宏观特征. 四川外语学院学报,2002(5),108—110.
黄忠廉. 变译的七种变通手段. 外语学刊,2002(1),93—96.
黄忠廉. 变译(翻译变体)论. 外语学刊,1999(3),80—83.
黄忠廉. 翻译变体研究. 北京:中国对外翻译出版公司,2000.
霍华译,老舍著. 茶馆. 北京:外文出版社,2001.
姜秋霞. 文学翻译与社会文化的相互作用关系研究. 北京:外语教学与研究出版社,2009.
金隄译,詹姆斯·乔伊斯著. 尤利西斯. 北京:人民文学出版社,1994.
鞠玉梅. 英汉古典诗格律对比研究. 西安外国语学院学报,2003(1),21—23.
老舍. 老舍论剧. 北京:中国戏剧出版社,1981.
黎孝先. 国际贸易实务. 北京:对外贸易教育出版社,1994.
李桂媛编著. 看电影学英语:英美经典电影对白赏析. 天津:天津科技翻译出版公司,2008.
李国庆. 翻译策略的选择与文化语境的对等. 外语学刊,2008(6),117—120.
李国庆. 体裁社会目的的实现与翻译策略的选择——从Halliday的功能语言观谈仿拟广告的翻译策略和广告套译法,2009(5),133—136.
李克兴. 法律翻译理论与实践. 北京:北京大学出版社,2007.
李欣. 倾听电影:66部英语电影对白精选. 上海:上海大学出版社,2006.
李新颜,王贵元. 科技英语的特点及翻译原则. 大众科技,2008(6),167—168.
李咏吟. 审美活动的主体性与主体间性. 厦门大学学报,2002(3),11—18.
李运兴. 语篇翻译引论. 北京:中国对外翻译出版公司,2001.
李运兴. 语篇翻译论纲. 北京:清华大学出版社,2010.
栗长江. 科技英语误译的原因分析与对策探讨. 公安大学学报(自然科学版),2002(2),71—77.
梁静璧. 电影字幕翻译的娱乐化倾向——迪士尼电影《花木兰》的个案研究. 北京教育学院学报,2006(1),19—23.
梁实秋. 威尼斯商人. 北京:中国广播电视出版社,2001.
廖七一. 当代西方翻译理论探索. 南京:译林出版社,2000.
林克难. 关联翻译理论简介. 中国翻译,1984(4),8—11.
林语堂. 论翻译[A]. 罗新璋编. 翻译论集. 北京:商务印书馆,1984.
林语堂译. 扬州瘦. 天津:天津百花文艺出版社,2002.
林语堂. 中英对照丛书. 天津:百花文艺出版社,2002.
刘红缨. 法律语言学. 北京:北京大学出版社,2003.
刘绩生译,鹫田清一著. 梅洛-庞蒂:认识论的割断. 石家庄:河北教育出版社,2001.
刘宓庆. 新编当代翻译理论. 北京:中国对外翻译出版公司,2005.
刘其中. 新闻翻译教程. 北京:中国人民大学出版社,2004.
刘若愚译,詹姆斯·乔伊斯著. 尤利西斯. 北京:燕山出版社,2004.
刘重德. 西方译论研究. 北京:中国对外翻译出版公司,1998.
龙千红.《花样年华》的英文字幕翻译策略研究——兼谈中国影片的对外译介. 西安外国语学院学报,2006(1),35—38.
卢敏主编. 英语二级笔译考试真题精选. 北京:外文出版社,2009.
罗卫华. 论法律英语的语言与文体特点. 大连海事大学学报,1996(3),103—106.
罗新璋. 翻译论集. 北京:商务印书馆,1984.
吕叔湘. 翻译工作的'杂学'. 翻译理论与翻译技巧论文集. 北京:中国对外翻译出版公司,1985.
陈嘉映、王庆节译,马丁·海德格尔. 存在与时间. 北京:生活·读书·新知三联书店,1999.
马祖毅,任荣珍. 汉籍外译史. 武汉:湖北教育出版社,2003.

孟瑾,冯斗. 古诗格式塔意象和意境的传递. 外语学刊,2005(4),91—94.
牟宗三. 中国哲学的特质(《牟宗三学术论著集·讲座系列》之一). 上海:上海古籍出版社,1997.
倪梁康. 现象学及其效应——胡塞尔与当代德国哲学. 北京:生活·读书·新知三联书店,1994.
倪梁康. 胡塞尔现象学概念通释. 北京:生活·读书·新知三联书店,1999.
宁一中. 米勒论文学翻译的理论. 外语与外语教学,1999(5),37—39.
钱钟书. 管锥编(第一册). 北京:中华书局,1986.
钱钟书. 论不隔. 钱钟书散文. 杭州:浙江文艺出版社,1997.
钱钟书. 七缀集. 北京:生活·读书·新知三联书店,2002.
尚 杰. 解构的文本——读书札记. 北京:中国社会科学出版社,1999.
邵志洪. 汉英对比翻译导论. 上海:华东理工大学出版社,2005.
余碧平. 现代性的意义及其局限. 上海:上海三联书店,2000.
司显柱,曾剑平. 语篇:功能 类型 翻译. 中国科技翻译,2007(1),8—11,24.
司显柱. 翻译语篇质量评估模式再研究——功能语言学路向. 中国翻译,2008(2),57—60.
孙法里译,托马斯·哈代著. 德伯家的苔丝. 南京:译林出版社,2002.
孙 翀. 交织在历史中的中西异质文化碰撞——自唐至明清之际基督教精神对中国文学的影响. 许志伟编. 基督教思想评论.上海:上海人民出版社,2009.
孙迎春. 文学翻译意境问题刍议. 山东外语教学,2000(3),33—38.
谭 兴,谈宏慧.《越狱》中文化词语的翻译策略. 电影评介,2008(6),68—69.
谭载喜. 翻译学. 武汉:湖北教育出版社,2000.
谭载喜. 语篇与翻译:论三大关系. 外语与外语教学,2002(7),3—10,60.
谭载喜. 西方翻译简史. 北京:商务印书馆,2004.
陶丹丹. 从会话含义理论看电影对白的字幕翻译——以《大腕》为个案研究. 宁波广播电视大学学报,2006(1),64—66,70.
王秉钦. 20世纪中国翻译思想史. 天津:南开大学出版社,2004.
王东风. 功能语言学与翻译研究. 广州:中山大学出版社,2006.
汪桂芬.《卧虎藏龙》字幕中"文化词语"的英译策略分析. 电影评介,2008(1),59—60.
王宏印. 中国传统译论经典诠释:从道安到傅雷. 武汉:湖北教育出版社,2003.
王 宁. 翻译学的理论化:跨学科的视角. 中国翻译,2006(6),6—10.
王 宁. 翻译研究的文化转向. 北京:清华大学出版社,2009.
王 荣. 从关联理论看字幕翻译策略——《乱世佳人》字幕翻译的个案分析. 北京第二外国语学院学报,2007(1),5—9.
王宗炎. 辨义为翻译之本. 杨自俭、刘学云编. 翻译新论(1983—1992). 武汉:湖北教育出版社,1994.
王佐良、巴恩斯译. 曹禺著. 雷雨. 北京:外文出版社,2001.
翁显良. 千面千腔——谈戏剧翻译. 翻译研究论文集(1949—1983). 北京:外语教学与研究出版社,1984.
吴春梅. 电影对白的语言特点及其翻译. 电影评介,2008(13),60—64,
夏喜玲. 科技英语翻译技法. 郑州:河南人民出版社,2007.
夏写时. 中国戏剧批评的产生和发展. 北京:中国戏剧出版社,1982.
萧 乾、文洁若译,詹姆斯·乔伊斯著. 尤利西斯. 南京:译林出版社,1994.
许 钧. 翻译释意理论辨——与塞莱斯科维奇教授谈翻译. 中国翻译,1998(1),9—13.
张宁译,雅克·德里达著. 书写与差异. 北京:生活·读书·新知三联书店,2001.
严俊人. 科技英语翻译方法.长沙:国防工业大学出版社,2000.
杨晓荣. 翻译批评导论. 北京:中国对外翻译出版公司,2005.
姚锦清. 翻译硕士专业学位(MTI)与专业笔译理念. 东方翻译,2010(4),8.
姚克译,阿瑟·米勒著. 推销员之死. 北京:中国对外翻译出版公司,2004.
英若诚译,老舍著. 茶馆. 北京:中国对外翻译出版公司,1999.
英若诚译,阿瑟·米勒著. 推销员之死. 北京:中国对外翻译出版公司,1999.

余富林. 商务英语翻译. 北京:中国商务出版社,2003.
于建平. 科技论文汉译英中若干问题分析. 中国翻译,2001(1),32—34.
赵贵山等. 商贸英语. 北京:原子能出版社,1997.
张法连. 法律文体翻译基本原则探究. 中国翻译,2009(5),72—76.
张法连. 法律英语翻译中的文化因素探析. 中国翻译,2009(6),48—51+93.
张法连. 法律英语翻译. 济南:山东大学出版社,2009.
张法连,张茜. 关于汉英法律翻译中的词汇问题. 中国成人教育,2009(20) 143—145.
张谷若译,托马斯·哈代著. 德伯家的苔丝. 北京:人民文学出版社,2003.
张国荣. 英语修辞格的解码和翻译. 西安外国语学院学报,2004(2),37—40.
张璟慧. 方式即意义——自《黑暗之心》到《现代启示录》改编的中国古典美学观照. 北京:人民文学出版社, 2008.
张美芳. 翻译研究的功能途径. 上海:上海外语教育出版社,2005.
郑月莉等. 商务英语翻译教程. 保定:河北大学出版社,2001.
中国文学出版社编. 中国文学(古代散文卷). 北京:外语教学与研究出版社,1998.
周领顺. 汉英语法差异在汉诗英译中的处理. 外语与外语教学,1999(3),37—40.
朱生豪译,威廉·莎士比亚著. 莎士比亚全集. 北京:人民文学出版社,1978.
朱永生,严世清. 系统功能语言学多维思考. 上海:上海外语教育出版社,2001.
朱志瑜. 类型与策略:功能主义的翻译类型学. 中国翻译,2004,5—11.
庄绎传. 英汉翻译教程. 北京:外语教学与研究出版社,1999.